BOTTOM LINE YEAR BOOK 2018

BY THE EDITORS OF
Bottom Line PERSONAL
BottomLineInc.com

Bottom Line Year Book 2018

10 9 8 7 6 5 4 3 2 1

ISBN 0-88723-775-4

Bottom Line Books® publishes the advice of expert authorities in many fields. These opinions may at times conflict as there are often different approaches to solving problems. The use of a book is not a substitute for legal, accounting, investment, health or any other professional services. Consult competent professionals for answers to your specific questions.

Offers, prices, rates, addresses, telephone numbers and websites listed in this book are accurate at the time of publication, but they are subject to frequent change.

Bottom Line Books® is a registered trademark of Bottom Line Inc.
3 Landmark Square, Suite 201, Stamford, CT 06901

BottomLineInc.com

Bottom Line Books® is an imprint of Bottom Line Inc., publisher of print periodicals, e-letters and books. We are dedicated to bringing you the best information from the most knowledgeable sources in the world. Our goal is to help you gain greater wealth, better health, more wisdom, extra time and increased happiness.

Printed in the United States of America

Contents

3 • CURES FOR COMMON CONDITIONS

4 • FITNESS & DIET FINDS

5 • NATURAL HEALTH NOW

6 • PRIVATE & PERSONAL

PART TWO: YOUR MONEY

7 • MONEY MATTERS

8 • INSURANCE INSIDER

9 • TAX AND ESTATE PLANNING TALK

10 • INVESTMENT INSIGHT

11 • SAVVY SHOPPING

PART THREE: YOUR FUTURE

12 • RICHER RETIREMENT

PART FOUR: YOUR LEISURE

13 • TRAVEL TIME

14 • FOCUS ON FUN

PART FIVE: YOUR LIFE

15 • AUTO ADVISER

16 • HAPPY HOME

17 • HOUSEHOLD HELP

18 • WISE WAYS

19 • BUSINESS BULLETIN

20 • SAFETY SOLUTIONS

Preface

We are happy to bring you our *Bottom Line Year Book 2018.* Here you will discover numerous helpful and practical ideas for yourself and for everyone in your family.

At Bottom Line Books, it is our mission to provide all of our readers with the best information to help them gain better health, greater wealth, more wisdom, extra time and increased happiness.

The *Year Book 2018* represents the very best and the most useful Bottom Line articles from the past year. Whether you are looking for ways to get the most from your money or how to land a great new job after age 50... boost your heart health naturally or choose the right hospital for you...get your adult children to call you more or deal with those difficult people in your life, you'll find it all in this book...and a whole lot more.

Over the past 37 years, we have built a network of thousands of expert sources.

When you consult the *2018 Year Book*, you are accessing a stellar group of authorities in fields that range from natural and conventional medicine...to shopping, investing, taxes and insurance...to cars, travel, security and self-improvement. Our advisers are affiliated with the premier universities, financial institutions, law firms and hospitals. These experts are truly among the most knowledgeable people in the country.

As a reader of a Bottom Line book, you can be assured that you are receiving reliable, well-researched and up-to-date information from a trusted source.

We are very confident that the *Bottom Line Year Book 2018* can help you and your family have a healthier, wealthier, wiser life. Enjoy!

The Editors, *Bottom Line Personal*
Stamford, CT

1

Health Hotline

5 Healthy Foods That Can Hurt You

What is your favorite superfood? Could it be kale? Quinoa or avocado? These and other superfoods *deserve* their superstar status. They are loaded with protein, fiber, healthy fats and other important nutrients. But it is possible to go overboard on even the healthiest of foods—and too much of a good thing can be a bad thing.

See if you're affected by any of these superfood risks…

AVOCADOS AND WEIGHT GAIN

Avocados are loaded with healthy mono- and polyunsaturated fats, which are linked to heart health and cholesterol management. And they're not just for guacamole anymore—avocados add delicious flavor to salads, sandwiches, omelets and tacos. Their creamy texture also provides a healthier alternative to mayo, cheese, sour cream and other high-fat spreads.

Risk: Avocados are shockingly high in calories. One medium-sized avocado delivers 320 calories and 30 g of fat.

The healthy fats make it worth the calories. One study published in *Journal of the American Heart Association* found that people who ate one avocado a day, in addition to other healthy foods, decreased their LDL (bad) cholesterol by 14 milligrams per deciliter (mg/dL).

Bottom line: Enjoy avocados, but limit yourself to one per day and include them in your calorie count.

JUICES AND DIABETES

Few things are more refreshing or more all-American than having a glass of juice with breakfast. Millions of people start their day with a glass of orange, grapefruit or other juice.

Torey Armul, MS, RD, spokesperson for Academy of Nutrition and Dietetics and a nutritionist in private practice in Lewis Center, Ohio. She is a board-certified specialist in sports dietetics. ToreyArmul.com

Risk: A Harvard study found that people who consumed one or more servings of fruit juice daily were up to 21% more likely to develop type 2 diabetes.

Studies also show that people who ingest liquid calories typically don't compensate by eating fewer calories, so they may be more likely to gain weight.

You can blame the lack of fiber. Fruit juices retain the sugary sweet fructose found naturally in whole fruits, but they don't have the fiber found in whole fruits. Fiber is a key component of satiety, or fullness, as well as a factor in weight control and digestive health.

An average-sized orange contains just over 60 calories. The calorie count nearly doubles when you swig an eight-ounce glass of orange juice. And with little fiber, juice is less filling, so you may consume more calories overall.

The same Harvard study found that people who ate at least two servings per week of whole fruit—notably blueberries, grapes and apples—had a 23% reduced risk for type 2 diabetes, compared with those who ate no fruit at all.

Bottom line: You should always try to stick to whole fruits when possible. But if you really love juice, look for one with no added sugar and limit yourself to only an occasional glass of six ounces or less.

KALE AND THYROID DISEASE

For the average person, the risk from this superstar green is remote. But some people—particularly those who engage in lengthy, juice-based diets and detoxes—consume extreme amounts of kale. I had a client who drank more than 64 ounces of "liquid kale" a day on a juice cleanse, and it was replacing other vital nutrients in her diet.

Risk: Kale contains *thiocyanate,* a chemical compound that, in large amounts, interferes with iodine metabolism. Insufficient iodine can cause a drop in thyroid hormones and lead to hypothyroidism. Kale is *goitrogenic,* meaning that it can affect thyroid hormones if consumed in excess. The body can develop an enlarged thyroid gland (a goiter) in an attempt to compensate for low thyroid levels.

Bottom line: A normal amount of kale should not cause thyroid problems. Extended juicing, on the other hand, could pose a problem, particularly for those who avoid foods high in iodine. It would be hard to overdo it on cooked kale, but limit juiced kale to less than 10 cups of raw kale per week.

QUINOA AND STOMACH UPSET

Quinoa is one of the rare plant foods considered a complete protein, containing all of the essential amino acids. One cup of quinoa has 8 grams (g) of protein, twice the amount found in rice or a baked potato. It's also a great source of fiber, with 5 g in a one-cup serving, and it is high in folate, manganese, magnesium and B vitamins.

But the outer layer of the quinoa seed contains *saponin,* a coating that acts as a natural insect repellent. One advantage of saponin is less need for chemical pesticides. The disadvantage of saponin is the potential for stomach upset and even damage to the lining of the small intestine.

Many quinoa brands are prewashed to remove the saponin, but it's a good idea to thoroughly rinse the seeds again prior to cooking.

In addition, try not to overdo it on quinoa. Rapid increases in fiber intake can cause digestive issues and discomfort, such as flatulence, bloating and diarrhea.

Bottom line: If you're not already consuming 21 g to 38 g of fiber a day (the recommended amount), increase your quinoa intake slowly. Give your body time to adjust by increasing fiber intake by 3 g to 5 g every few days.

Also important: Drink an extra glass or two of water while you're eating more fiber.

DID YOU KNOW THAT...

Americans Think They Eat Well

75% of Americans say they eat healthfully—even though they don't. That is the percentage that rated their diets good, very good or excellent.

But: More than 80% of Americans don't eat the recommended amount of fruits and vegetables.

Survey by NPR and Truven Health Analytics of 3,000 US adults, reported at NPR.org.

Fiber absorbs water in the gastrointestinal tract, so you'll need more fluid to keep things moving efficiently.

SALMON AND MERCURY

Dietitians often encourage their clients to eat more fish because it's a nutritional powerhouse. Fish boasts the rare combination of high protein and heart-healthy omega-3 fatty acids.

Risk: Virtually all fish contain some mercury, a neurotoxin that is particularly dangerous for developing brains. This explains why pregnant women and young children are advised to limit their seafood consumption. Adults who consume too much mercury can develop numbness, tremors, headaches and problems with balance or coordination.

Bottom line: Salmon, along with sardines, crab, shrimp and tilapia, is one of the lower-mercury seafoods. (The highest mercury sources include ahi tuna, king mackerel, swordfish and shark.) But mercury poisoning still is possible with excessive salmon intake. Adding salmon to your menu two or three times a week carries little risk and has big health benefits for the whole family. Even pregnant women and children now are encouraged to eat more seafood, with a weekly recommendation of eight to 12 ounces of lower-mercury seafood. However, even adults who are not pregnant should be cautioned against eating salmon much more than that.

TAKE NOTE...

Self-Test for Alcohol Tolerance

If you're interested in learning how your genes might affect the way your body metabolizes alcohol, there's a self-test I have developed based on genetic indicators found in one's earwax. It is not as accurate as genetic testing but will give you some basic information.

Moderate drinking (described in the main article) is considered good for the heart, but some people (such as many of those who become flushed while drinking) should never drink...and everyone's alcohol tolerance is highly individualized. How much alcohol (if any) is right for you?

The earwax test: Carefully swab some of your earwax and take a look. People with flaky, *dry,* gray earwax probably had ancestors from eastern Asia who rarely drank. Those with the wet type of earwax (it's a yellow/brownish color and is somewhat sticky) typically had African or European ancestors who drank alcoholic beverages routinely.

My advice: If you have dry earwax, the safest approach is for you to avoid alcohol altogether—your genetic profile does not prepare you to safely metabolize alcohol. Also, people in this group are likely to have inherited the gene that predisposes them to squamous cell esophageal cancer. For this reason, it's wise to forgo alcohol since it is an important risk factor for this type of cancer. If you have wet earwax, you are unlikely to have the same difficulty metabolizing alcohol.

Sharon Moalem, MD, PhD, a physician, scientist and inventor based in New York City.

How Your Genes Affect Your Diet

Sharon Moalem, MD, PhD, a physician, scientist and inventor based in New York City. He has served as an associate editor for the *Journal of Alzheimer's Disease* and has been awarded more than 25 patents for inventions in the fields of biotechnology and health. He is author of *The DNA Restart: Unlock Your Personal Genetic Code to Eat for Your Genes, Lose Weight and Reverse Aging.*

Have you ever wondered why a cup of coffee keeps you up at night, while your spouse downs cup after cup and sleeps like a baby? Or why a glass of wine with your supper makes you tipsy, while your friends can keep sipping for hours?

You could chalk it up to random variation, but it's actually not random at all. It's largely determined by your genes. Research has shown that specific genes and gene "variants" (or mutations) can affect how your body metabolizes nutrients and other substances such as caffeine and alcohol.

For certain medical conditions, it has long been established that there is a genetic link to how specific nutrients are metabolized. For example, if you're among those of western European ancestry who have different versions of the HFE gene, it can cause you to absorb two to three times more iron than those without this genetic profile. Hereditary hemochromatosis, commonly known as iron overload disease, can be life-threatening—and is diagnosed, in part, with genetic testing.

But recent research in the emerging field of nutrigenetics (the study of how individual genes affect nutrition) shows that there may be important genetic links to many more nutrients and substances than previously thought.

So far, scientists have identified hundreds of genes and gene variants that may affect how your body metabolizes different nutrients and substances.

The question is, can knowing this genetic information help people make smarter nutrition choices? Right now, the jury is still out, but some individuals find that testing helps them identify certain dietary tweaks that may improve their overall health. *Key nutrients and substances with genetic links…*

• **Folate.** Specific versions of the MTHFR gene slow the rate at which the body converts folate into a usable form of the vitamin. People who inherit this gene may be more likely to suffer a heart attack or stroke because of a folate deficiency.

Who might benefit from this test: If you have a personal or family history of heart attack, you may want to discuss this test and/or a blood test for folate deficiency with a nutritionist. If you test positive for the gene and/or a blood test identifies a folate deficiency, ask your doctor about taking a supplement with a methylated (active) form of folate.

• **Caffeine.** The body's ability to metabolize caffeine is controlled mostly by the CYP1A2 gene. People with a particular variant of this gene are "slow metabolizers"—they don't have the same ability to break down caffeine as other people. They might develop high blood pressure from drinking amounts of coffee or tea that wouldn't similarly affect a person without this gene.

Who might benefit from this test: If you have high blood pressure or become jittery when consuming caffeine, you may want to discuss this test with a nutritionist. If you test positive, you would likely benefit from reducing your intake of caffeinated beverages and foods.

• **Alcohol.** Research has found that moderate daily alcohol consumption—up to two alcoholic beverages for men…and up to one for women—can improve cardiovascular health.

But people who have the ALDH2*2 gene might want to disregard this finding. They don't have the same ability to detoxify an alcohol by-product (acetaldehyde), which increases their risk for a deadly esophageal cancer.

Who might benefit from this test: Anyone with Asian ancestry…risk factors for esophageal cancer (such as gastroesophageal reflux disease)…and those who notice their skin becoming red or flushed after drinking alcohol. If you test positive for this gene, avoid alcohol.

GETTING TESTED

Either a nutritionist or a health-care professional (such as a doctor) can order a test kit for nutritional genetic testing online. You provide a saliva sample, and the kit is returned for analysis. The test usually costs a few hundred dollars to check for a set of genes that may have nutritional links. The professional who ordered the test will likely charge you for a follow-up consultation to discuss the results. These fees are unlikely to be covered by insurance.

The Germ Hot Spots You've Never Thought About

Miryam Z. Wahrman, PhD, professor of biology at William Paterson University in Wayne, New Jersey, where she specializes in microbiology, hand hygiene and the interactions between bacteria and environmental surfaces. Dr. Wahrman also is author of *The Hand Book: Surviving in a Germ-Filled World.*

Whether it's Zika virus, Ebola or MERS (Middle East Respiratory Syndrome), there is a long list of infectious diseases that get our attention when they dominate the news. Even though these are frightening illnesses, this intense level of scrutiny of exotic diseases minimizes the real threat.

The microbes that pose the biggest threat—in terms of annual sickness rates and death—are the potentially fatal ones that we are exposed to every day, such as influenza and hospital-acquired infections known as superbugs.

Why it matters to me: My research on the transmission of infectious disease is fueled, in part, by personal tragedy. Following heart bypass surgery at a highly regarded American hospital, my mother died after contracting a type of virulent hospital-acquired bacterial infection. Hospital-acquired infections kill about 75,000 patients in the US each year. But hospitals aren't the only place where pathogens hang out.

Most people think that they have a good idea where these germs reside. Doorknobs, elevator buttons and handrails in public places are among the best-known hot spots. But hardly anyone thinks about the numerous other places that harbor pesky pathogens.

What you need to know…

HIDDEN GERMS

Effective handwashing removes the germs that can make you sick. But sometimes we fail to recognize hidden sources of microbial contamination, which so often do not get cleaned properly (or at all).

Many of the germs we encounter are not harmful, and a healthy immune system can often handle most of the rest. In fact, some exposure to germs helps *strengthen* the immune system. However, with the smart hygiene practices described below, you will greatly reduce the odds of putting yourself, your colleagues and your loved ones at risk for a variety of illnesses, ranging from the common cold to the flu and pneumonia. *Germ hot spots that will surprise you…*

• **Neckties.** Some physicians have stopped wearing ties in order to protect their patients. A study at a New York hospital found that nearly half of the ties tested were contaminated with *Staph, K. pneumoniae* and other disease-causing organisms.

I advise *all* men (not just doctors) to keep in mind that ties pick up and transmit germs, since they are rarely cleaned, dangle and sweep across surfaces, and are handled frequently. Men who are not working in health-care settings are less likely to pick up drug-resistant superbugs on their ties, but risks still abound, so clean your ties now and then.

My advice: Buy ties made from microfiber—these textiles tend to resist bacterial contamination more than silk, cotton or polyester. Some ties made of cotton, linen, polyester and/or microfiber can be hand-washed with detergent, air-dried and ironed, but silk and wool usually must be dry-cleaned, which isn't foolproof in killing germs.

Note to women: Handbags have been found to harbor deadly germs, but a sanitizing alcohol wipe can be used to clean straps and the exterior of bags. Vinyl may be easier to clean than cloth or other materials.

• **Cell phones.** Have you ever washed your smartphone? It is certainly not recommended to immerse any cell phone in water, but most people don't even wipe off the surface of their phones.

Important finding: A 2011 British study reported that 92% of cell phones had bacteria, with 16% carrying *E. coli,* bacteria typically found in feces.

My advice: Clean your phone every day by wiping it down with a microfiber cloth (the kind used to clean eyeglasses) that's been moistened with 70% ethyl or isopropyl alcohol (commonly found in drugstores). Or try other products, such as Wireless Wipes, that are made specifically for cell phones.

Another option: An ultraviolet (UV) cellphone sanitizer, such as PhoneSoap Charger or Cellblaster, which uses exposure to UV radiation to kill most bacteria. These products are available online for about $50 to $110.

• **Rings and other jewelry.** Whether you're wearing a plain band or a ring with elaborate settings, bacteria can thrive underneath it—an area that's usually missed by handwashing.

My advice: When possible, remove rings before washing your hands. You should also clean your jewelry, including wristwatches. To avoid water damage, swab the surfaces with 70% ethyl alcohol or use a UV sanitizer device (described earlier).

• **Paper money.** On average, paper currency stays in circulation for about six years. During that time, it comes in contact with wallets, purses, sweaty palms and filthy fingertips. When we tested dollar bills that we collected as change from New York food vendors, we found that about two-thirds were contaminated with different strains of bacteria...and two-thirds of those harbored *coliform* (fecal) bacteria.

If you use credit cards, you can largely avoid touching money, although sometimes you must hand your credit card to the cashier, which exposes it to someone else's germs. You also have to touch the scanner and stylus, which have been touched by many customers.

My advice: Try to cleanse your hands after handling money, especially before you eat or touch your eyes, nose or mouth. And do *not* lick your fingers when counting out bills. Coins aren't germ-free, but the metal alloys in the coins tend to inhibit bacterial growth.

• **Airports.** People who travel a lot encounter germs from other travelers. In airplanes, the tray tables, armrests and seat-back pockets can be teeming with pathogens. But there are other hot spots as well.

My advice: At the airport, for example, it's a good idea to put your cell phone, keys and other personal possessions in a Ziploc bag before putting them in a security bin, which has held innumerable shoes, phones...and who knows what.

• **Rental cars.** Even though most rental car agencies vacuum and quickly wipe down surfaces between rentals, studies show the steering wheel may harbor nasty bacteria. Who knows where the previous drivers' hands have been?

My advice: When you rent a car, consider wiping down the steering wheel and door handles with sanitizing alcohol wipes.

Don't Fall for These Blood Pressure Traps

Holly Kramer, MD, MPH, an associate professor in the department of public health sciences and the department of medicine, Division of Nephrology and Hypertension, at Loyola University Medical Center in Maywood, Illinois. She received the 2016 Garabed Eknoyan Award from the National Kidney Foundation.

When it comes to treating serious medical conditions, you would think that high blood pressure (hypertension) would be one of the nation's great success stories. Doctors test for it. Patients know the risks. And there are dozens of medications that treat it.

Yet the results are still disappointing. About one in every three American adults has hypertension...but only about half of them keep it under control.

Why are we still losing the battle against hypertension? Scientists now are discovering some of the traps that prevent people from adequately controlling their blood pressure. *What you need to know...*

TRAP #1: **Not treating soon enough.** Even though normal blood pressure is defined as below 120/80 mmHg, researchers continue to debate *optimal* blood pressure targets. In reality, most doctors don't consider treatment until readings reach 140/90 mmHg or above—the official definition of hypertension.

But recent research has shown us that is *too late.* The risks associated with hypertension—stroke, heart attack, kidney disease and vision loss, among others—start to increase at lower levels.

Important recent finding: When researchers compared target blood pressure readings in more than 9,350 adults with hypertension and other cardiovascular risk factors, the results were striking. Those who got intensive treatment to lower their systolic (top number) pressure to below 120 mmHg were 27% less likely to die from *any* cause over a three-year period than those whose target was below 140 mmHg. In the study, diastolic (bottom number) pressure was not measured because it tends to decline as people get older.

Starting treatment earlier than 140 mmHg to achieve a normal reading could save more than 100,000 American lives a year, the researchers estimated.

My advice: If your systolic blood pressure is 120 mmHg or above (or your diastolic pressure is 90 mmHg or above), tell your doctor that you *want* to be treated.

Note: If your systolic blood pressure is less than 150 mmHg, you may be able to avoid medication if you adopt healthier habits—not smoking…losing weight, if necessary…getting regular exercise…eating a well-balanced diet, etc.

If these steps have not lowered your blood pressure after six months, you may need medication. If systolic pressure is above 150 mmHg, medications may be needed *in addition* to lifestyle changes.

Caution: Intensive blood pressure treatment usually involves taking multiple blood pressure–lowering drugs, which increases risk for side effects, such as dizziness and light-headedness. Therefore, blood pressure should be checked frequently (see below) and regular tests should be given for potassium and electrolyte levels. Electrolytes and kidney function should be checked within one month of starting a diuretic or when a dose is increased. After that, levels should be checked every six to 12 months.

***TRAP #2:* Not testing at home.** Don't rely only on the blood pressure tests that you get at your doctor's office. They can be too intermittent—and too rushed—to give accurate readings. Your pressure is likely to be artificially high…or artificially low, since people who are seeing a doctor often abstain from some of the things (such as drinking coffee) that raise it.

My advice: Buy a digital blood pressure monitor, and use it at home. Omron upper-arm blood pressure monitors (available at pharmacies and online for about $40 and up) are about as accurate as office monitors. A *JAMA* study found that 72% of people who tested at home had good blood pressure control versus 57% of volunteers who were tested only by their doctors.

What to do: Every day, check your blood pressure in the morning before eating, exercising or taking medication…and again in the evening. (If your blood pressure is normal, test every few months.) Before testing, empty your bladder (a full bladder will cause higher readings). Then sit with both feet on the floor, and relax for five minutes. Rest your arm, raised to the level of your heart, on a table, and place the cuff on bare skin.

Do each reading twice: Measure your blood pressure once…wait a few minutes…then repeat—the second reading will be more accurate. Write down the readings, and share them with your doctor during your office visits.

***TRAP #3:* Taking the wrong drug.** About 70% of patients with hypertension require two or more drugs to achieve good control. Many will be given prescriptions for one of the newer drugs, such as an angiotensin-converting enzyme (ACE) inhibitor or an angiotensin receptor blocker (ARB). Some patients (such as those with heart failure) will need one of these drugs. Most people do not—at least not right away.

If you've recently been diagnosed with hypertension, consider a thiazide diuretic, such as *chlorthalidone*. It's an older drug that is available as a generic. It's inexpensive, and studies have shown that thiazide diuretics lower blood pressure as effectively as other drugs, with less risk for heart failure and stroke. Thiazide diuretics may be paired with an ARB or ACE inhibitor, since these drugs are synergistic (each drug increases the other's effectiveness).

The caveats: Even though diuretics generally are safe, you'll urinate more often (they're known as "water pills" for a reason). Thiazide diuretics might also lower potassium levels in some patients—if so, your doctor may advise you to take potassium supplements. And diuretics can raise urate levels, triggering gout in some people.

***TRAP #4:* Not timing your medication.** Most people take medications when it's convenient—or at a set time, such as with their morning coffee. But blood pressure medication should be *scheduled*.

It's natural for blood pressure to vary by about 30 points at different times of the day. It almost always rises in the morning, which is why strokes and heart attacks are more common in the early hours. One study found that patients who took at least one of their blood pressure medications at night were about one-third less likely to have a heart attack or stroke than those who took all of their pills in the morning.

My advice: With your doctor's OK, take at least one of your blood pressure medications (not a diuretic) at bedtime to help protect you from blood pressure increases in the morning. Diuretics should be taken in the morning so that frequent urination won't interrupt sleep.

Warfarin Warning

Warfarin risk is greater than previously believed among patients with dementia and certain other conditions.

Recent finding: One in 50 US veterans over age 75 who took the anticoagulant *warfarin* for atrial fibrillation (irregular heartbeat) developed severe bleeding inside the skull.

Newer anticoagulants are available, but they have risks of their own.

John Dodson, MD, assistant professor, department of medicine, and director of the Geriatric Cardiology Program at NYU Langone Medical Center, New York City.

How to Survive a Heart Attack: A Leading Cardiologist Shares His Secrets

Gregory S. Thomas, MD, MPH, medical director for the MemorialCare Heart & Vascular Institute at Long Beach Memorial Medical Center in California and clinical professor at the University of California, Irvine. He is author or coauthor of more than 100 scientific papers that have appeared in leading medical journals.

Every year, about 750,000 Americans have a heart attack. Even though advances in emergency care and cardiology have greatly improved one's odds of survival, roughly one of every six of these individuals dies.

What determines whether a heart attack sufferer lives or dies? Certainly, the person's age and overall health play an important role. But there's another factor that gets far less attention than it should.

Lifesaving strategy: When a person on the scene knows how to *recognize* that someone is having a heart attack and then *respond* to the emergency appropriately, it can have a profound effect on whether the victim lives or dies.

Sobering research: When a heart attack occurs, the average sufferer waits *two hours* or more before calling 911 and going to the hospital. This delay often occurs because victims can't believe that they are really having a heart attack...or they don't want to feel embarrassed at the hospital if it turns out that it's not a heart attack and they've "wasted" everyone's time.

But each minute of delay during a heart attack destroys more heart muscle, putting the victim at greater risk for disability and death.

RECOGNIZE AND RESPOND

My advice for quickly and accurately identifying heart attack symptoms...*

- **Chest discomfort.** Chest *pain* is widely believed to be the classic heart attack symptom, but severe chest *discomfort* usually is a more accurate way to describe it. Pain typically is sharp, but the sensation that usually occurs with a heart attack is not sharp but rather a severe pressure, squeezing or tightness—as if a massive weight had been placed on the chest.

Also: Many women report having *no* chest discomfort during any part of the heart attack.

How to respond: If a person is having severe chest discomfort, don't assume that it can't be a heart attack because he/she isn't complaining of chest *pain*. Call 911 immediately. It is important to tell the dispatcher that you believe the person is having a heart attack because saying this increases the likelihood that an ambulance specializing in heart care will be sent.

*There are some exceptions to the heart attack symptoms described in this article. If you have any question, play it safe and call 911.

• **Referred pain.** The nerves that supply the heart also serve many other areas of the body between the jaw and the navel—places that can produce *referred* pain during a heart attack.

Case history: A woman who had tooth pain while exercising was referred to me. Her exercise stress test showed that her tooth pain was referred pain. In actuality, the pain was due to *angina*, a sign that her arteries were significantly blocked, putting her at high risk for a heart attack. Other areas of referred pain during heart attack can include one or both arms or shoulders...the upper back or abdomen...the neck and lower part of the face, including the jaw.

• **Other common symptoms.** A heart attack can produce many other symptoms, including sudden shortness of breath...nausea and vomiting...a cold sweat, or feeling cold and clammy...fatigue...and/or light-headedness.

Important: All of these symptoms (except for feeling cold and clammy) tend to be more common in women than in men.

How to respond: If a man has chest discomfort and at least one other symptom...or if a woman has chest, back or jaw pain and at least one other symptom, it's *very* likely the individual is having a heart attack. Or if a person's discomfort or pain is particularly severe—even without another symptom—a heart attack is also likely. In either instance, call 911.

Another red flag: Sometimes, a victim has a feeling of "impending doom" and asks a loved one or friend to take him to the hospital. If someone says to you, "I think I should go to the hospital," call 911. Never drive a victim to the hospital—lifesaving treatments start when the paramedics show up. The only exception is if you are within a few minutes of emergency care.

KNOW WHO'S AT GREATEST RISK

Knowing one's risk for a heart attack also helps prevent delays in treatment.

While some heart attack victims don't have any of the risk factors described below, people generally are at increased risk due to smoking, age (generally, over age 50 for men and over age 60 for women) and being at least moderately overweight. Diabetes or a chronic inflammatory disease, such as rheumatoid arthritis or lupus, can cause heart disease 10 or 20 years earlier than the norm, increasing risk for heart attack.

Important: Diabetes damages nerves, so a diabetic having a heart attack is less likely to have nerve-generated chest discomfort or referred pain—and more likely to have sudden shortness of breath.

MORE LIFESAVING ACTIONS

In addition to calling 911, do the following to aid a heart attack victim...

• **Position the person correctly.** Contrary to popular opinion, the best position for a conscious heart attack victim is not lying down—this fills the heart with a bit more blood, straining it. The best position is *sitting up,* which puts the least amount of stress on the heart. An exception is if the person is light-headed, which might indicate low blood pressure. In that case, lay the person down and call 911 immediately.

• **Give aspirin.** Give the person *uncoated aspirin*—either four 81-mg baby aspirin or one full-strength aspirin (325 mg). The pills should be *chewed*—this releases clot-busting medicine within 15 minutes into the bloodstream versus up to 30 minutes or more when aspirin is swallowed whole. If someone is already taking a daily blood thinner, aspirin may not be needed. If the person has been prescribed *nitroglycerin,* it should be taken as directed.

• **Reassure.** A heart attack is frightening—and fear floods the body with adrenaline, speeding up and further stressing the heart. Reassure the person that help is on the way and that he will get through this.

If the victim is unconscious: If the individual doesn't appear to be breathing and you cannot feel a pulse or are unable to check for one, start CPR if you know how to do it. If you don't, simply press down on the victim's chest at least two inches deep (where the ribs meet at the base of the breastbone) and pump as fast as you can (100 times per minute). Like CPR, this technique pushes air into the lungs—the best action you can take until paramedics arrive.

The "Silent" Stroke Trigger: You Can Have This Condition and Not Even Know It...

Walid Saliba, MD, medical director of the Center for Atrial Fibrillation and director of the Electrophysiology Lab at Cleveland Clinic. His research has been published in many journals, including *Circulation: Arrhythmia and Electrophysiology* and *American Journal of Cardiovascular Drugs.*

When it comes to preventing stroke and heart-related disorders such as heart failure, it's *crucial* to identify and properly treat "Afib"—short for atrial fibrillation, the most common type of abnormal heart rhythm. Unfortunately, a significant number of the estimated 3 million Americans who have Afib don't even realize it.

Now: With new diagnostic and treatment approaches, one's chances are greater than ever that this potentially dangerous condition can be spotted and stopped—if you receive the right tests and medical care. *What you need to know...*

WHEN AFIB IS SILENT

If you have Afib, it's possible to experience a range of symptoms including a quivering or fluttering heartbeat...a racing and/or irregular heartbeat...dizziness...extreme fatigue...shortness of breath...and/or chest pain or pressure.

But Afib can also be "silent"—that is, symptoms are so subtle that they go unnoticed by the patient. Silent Afib is sometimes an incidental finding during a physical exam when the doctor detects an irregular heartbeat. It may also be suspected in patients with nonspecific symptoms such as fatigue or shortness of breath—especially in those with a family history of Afib or a condition such as high blood pressure or diabetes that increases risk for Afib. But whether the symptoms are noticeable or not to the patient, the risk for stroke and potentially heart failure remains just as high, so Afib needs to be diagnosed.

To check for Afib: The standard practice has been to perform an electrocardiogram (ECG) for a few minutes in the doctor's office to record the electrical activity driving the heart's contractions. But if Afib episodes are intermittent, the ECG may be normal.

When Afib is suspected based on symptoms such as dizziness and/or palpitations or racing heartbeat, but the ECG is normal, doctors have traditionally recommended monitoring for 24 to 48 hours. This involves wearing a small device that is clipped to a belt, kept in a pocket or hung around your neck and connected to electrodes attached to your chest. But this approach, too, can miss occasional Afib episodes.

What works better: Longer-term monitoring. Research published in *The New England Journal of Medicine* found that Afib was detected in five times more patients when they were monitored for 30 days instead of only 24 hours. Guidelines from the American Heart Association now recommend Afib monitoring for 30 days within six months after a person has suffered a stroke with no known cause.

New option: With a doctor's supervision, mobile ECG devices (about the size of a cell phone) can now be used periodically to record 30-second intervals of your heart rhythm. Ask your doctor for details.

GETTING THE RIGHT TREATMENT

Afib almost always requires treatment. Besides the danger of stroke, the condition tends to worsen if left alone—symptoms become

GOOD TO KNOW...

What to Do After a Ministroke

Take aspirin *immediately* after a ministroke to cut the risk for a fatal or disabling stroke over the next few weeks by up to 80%.

The symptoms of ministroke: Muscle weakness, especially on only one side, trouble speaking, numbness/tingling, confusion and/or balance problems. These symptoms may last for only a few minutes.

If you suspect a ministroke: Get to the ER, and take a regular-strength, 325-mg aspirin.

Peter Rothwell, MD, PhD, professor of clinical neurology and founder and head of Centre for the Prevention of Stroke and Dementia, University of Oxford, UK.

more troublesome, and normal rhythm is harder to restore.

There are numerous options depending on other risk factors, your treatment goals and your own preference. Treatment is chosen based on frequency and severity of symptoms and whether the patient already has heart disease. *Examples...*

• **Prevent stroke.** To keep clots from forming, many patients need blood-thinning medications (anticoagulants). The old standby, *warfarin* (Coumadin), is effective but requires regular blood tests and dietary restrictions.

In recent years, a new generation of easier-to-use anticoagulants has appeared, including *dabigatran* (Pradaxa), *rivaroxaban* (Xarelto) and *apixaban* (Eliquis). These newer drugs have no dietary restrictions and do not require routine blood tests. However, all anticoagulants carry the risk for bleeding, which is harder to stop with the newer drugs.

Some patients at otherwise low risk for stroke may need only low-dose aspirin (such as 81 mg daily).

• **Slow down a rapid heart rate.** This is usually done with a beta-blocker like *atenolol* (Tenormin) or a calcium channel blocker like *amlodipine* (Norvasc) or *diltiazem* (Cardizem).

• **Normalize heart rhythm.** Anti-arrhythmic drugs, such as *amiodarone* (Cordarone), *flecainide* (Tambocor) and *dofetilide* (Tikosyn), are available. However, these are powerful drugs, with potentially serious side effects (such as dizziness and uncontrollable shaking), that can worsen rhythm abnormalities and must be used cautiously.

• **Ablation.** Another option to normalize heart rhythm and reduce stroke risk is known as *ablation*. With this procedure, the doctor threads a series of catheters up a vein to the heart to destroy the tiny group of cells that generate electrical impulses that cause fibrillation.

The procedure may have to be repeated but may be a good alternative to lifelong drug treatment. Ablation used to be saved for patients who didn't respond to drugs, but it's being offered as first-line therapy nowadays for those who want to avoid lifelong medication.

New procedure: In 2015, the FDA approved a procedure that can sharply reduce Afib stroke risk—*left atrial appendage occlusion* places a plug in a tiny sac of the atrium where 90% of clots form.

Each of these procedures, which eliminates the need for long-term blood thinning, carries a small risk for serious complications, such as stroke, and is best performed in a hospital that has experience with the surgery and the resources and expertise to provide emergency backup if needed.

• **An anti-Afib lifestyle.** The best way to cut your odds of developing Afib is to modify risk factors. If you have high blood pressure or sleep apnea, get effective treatment. If you're obese, lose weight. Exercise regularly. If you have Afib, these steps will make your treatment work better—and reduce symptoms.

Red Flag for Stroke Risk

Middle-aged adults who experience an aura (a sensory disturbance, such as flashing lights and/or blind spots) before a migraine are twice as likely to have an ischemic stroke (caused by a blood clot) than migraineurs who don't have auras, according to a recent study. Migraines with auras not only affect blood vessels in the brain but may also affect vessels in the heart and neck, loosening existing clots that travel to the brain.

Souvik Sen, MD, MPH, chairman of neurology, University of South Carolina School of Medicine, Columbia.

TV Linked to Fatal Blood Clots

TV viewing raises risk for fatal blood clots. Those who watch TV for two-and-a-half to five hours a day are at 70% higher risk for pulmonary embolism (a blood clot from another part of the body that travels to the lungs) than people who watch TV for less than two-and-a-half hours. Those who watch more than five hours of TV daily have 250% higher risk.

Reason: Prolonged inactivity increases the chance of developing an embolism.

Study of 86,024 healthy people by researchers at Osaka University Graduate School of Medicine, Japan, published in *Circulation.*

Can Your Cell Phone Really Cause Cancer?

Devra Davis, PhD, MPH, president of Environmental Health Trust, a nonprofit scientific and policy think tank focusing on cell phone radiation. She is a former senior advisor to the assistant secretary for health in the Department of Health and Human Services and a former member of the National Toxicology Program's Board of Scientific Counselors. She is author of *Disconnect: The Truth About Cell Phone Radiation.* EHTrust.org

You may have heard that cell phones have been linked to cancer but wondered if that could really be true. A recent study offers strong evidence that this is the case—cell phones and other wireless devices emit a type of microwave radiation termed *radiofrequency radiation* (RFR) that can cause brain cancer and other cancers.

Here are the findings and what to do to minimize this risk to your health...

THE NEWEST EVIDENCE

The government's National Toxicology Program (NTP) conducts scientific studies on toxins to see how they might affect the health of Americans. More than 90 studies show that the radiation emitted by cell phones and other wireless devices can damage DNA, the first step on the road to cancer.

In May 2016, the NTP published preliminary results from a two-year animal study on the health effects of cell phone radiation—this was the largest study on animals and cell phone radiation ever published.

One out of every 12 of the animals studied were affected by the radiation. Some of those that were exposed to daily, frequent doses of cell phone radiation from birth developed *glioma,* a rare, aggressive type of brain cancer already linked to cell phone use in people. (Glial cells surround and support neurons.) Other animals had precancerous changes in glial cells. And some developed rare tumors of the nerves around and within the heart called *schwannomas.* In contrast, a control group of animals not exposed to wireless radiation had *no* gliomas, *no* precancerous changes in glial cells and *no* schwannomas.

There are two crucial takeaways from this recent study...

1. For decades, many scientists and governments have embraced the following scientific dogma—the only unsafe radiation is "thermal" radiation that heats tissue, such as an X-ray. "Nonthermal" RFR doesn't heat tissue and therefore is safe. The latest study—during which animals exposed to RFR were monitored to ensure that there was no heating of tissue—contradicts this dogma.

2. Epidemiological studies that analyze health data from hundreds or thousands of people have linked gliomas and schwannomas to long-term cell phone use—and this latest study found the same type of cancers in animals exposed to wireless radiation, strengthening the link.

EVEN MORE DANGERS

Gliomas and schwannomas aren't the only dangers. *Research links wireless-device use to a range of other cancers, diseases and health conditions...*

- **Meningioma.** A recent study published in *Oncology Reports* showed that heavy users of mobile and cordless phones had up to twice the risk for meningioma, cancer in the protective coverings that surround the brain.
- **Salivary gland (parotid) tumors.** Salivary glands are below the ear and in the jaw—exactly where many people hold cell phones during conversation. A study published in *American Journal of Epidemiology* showed a 58% higher risk for these (usually) noncancerous tumors among cell phone users.
- **Acoustic neuroma.** Studies show that heavy or longtime users of cell phones have nearly triple the risk of developing acoustic neuromas (also called vestibular schwannomas), noncancerous tumors on the nerve that connects the inner ear to the brain. Symptoms can include

gradual hearing loss and tinnitus in the affected ear, along with balance problems, headaches and facial numbness and tingling.

• **Breast cancer.** A study published in *Case Reports in Medicine* describes four young American women, ages 21 to 39, who had tucked their smartphones into their bras for up to 10 hours a day for several years. Each of them developed breast tumors directly under the antennas of their phones. None of the women had the cancer-causing BRAC1 or BRAC2 gene, a family history of cancer or any other known risk factors.

• **Male infertility and potency.** Several studies link close contact with wireless devices—wearing a cell phone on the hip or using a laptop computer on the lap—with fewer sperm, sluggish sperm, abnormally shaped sperm, sperm with damaged DNA and erectile dysfunction.

• **Sleeping problems.** Research shows that people who use cell phones and other wireless devices in the hours before bedtime have more trouble falling asleep and staying asleep. Both wireless radiation and the "blue light" from screens suppress *melatonin*, a sleep-inducing hormone.

HOW TO PROTECT YOURSELF

Every step you take to decrease radiation is protective because exposure to radiation is *cumulative*—the higher the exposure, the higher your risk for cancer and other serious health problems.

The devices you should be concerned about include cell phones, cordless phone handsets and bases, Wi-Fi routers, wireless computers, laptops, iPads and other tablets, smartwatches, wireless fitness bands, iPods that connect to the Internet, wireless speakers, cordless baby monitors, wireless game consoles and any other type of wireless device or equipment such as thermostats, security networks, sound systems and smart meters.

• **Keep it at a distance.** To decrease your exposure to wireless radiation, keep wireless devices as far away from you as possible. *Just a few inches can make a big difference...*

• Never put the phone next to your head. Instead, use the speakerphone function or a wired headset or an earpiece.

CANCER ALERT...

Hot-Drink Danger

Think twice before drinking piping hot coffee or tea. In a recent review of more than 1,000 studies, scientists found a link between drinking beverages that exceed 149°F and tissue damage that can lead to cancer of the esophagus.

Self-defense: Let your hot beverages cool some before drinking.

Dana Loomis, PhD, deputy section head, International Agency for Research on Cancer, Lyon, France.

• Never place a turned-on device in a pocket or jacket or tucked into clothing. Keep it in a carrier bag, such as a briefcase or purse. Never rest a wireless device on your body. This includes laptops and tablets—keep them off your lap.

• Never fall asleep with your cell phone or wireless tablet in the bed or under your pillow. Many people fall asleep streaming radiation into their bodies.

• Prefer texting to calling. And avoid using your cell phone when the signal is weak—radiation is higher.

• **Turn it off.** Putting your cell phone in "airplane" mode stops radiation. Also, look for the function key on your wireless device that turns off the Wi-Fi. Turn it off when the device isn't in use. There's also a function key to turn off Bluetooth transmissions. If you must use a Wi-Fi router at home, locate it as far away from your body as possible. And turn it off at night.

To stop a gaming console from emitting radiation, you need to turn it off and unplug it.

• **Don't use your cell phone in metal surroundings** such as a bus, train, airplane or elevator. Using the phone creates radiation "hot spots" that increase exposure.

Exception: It is OK to use a cell phone in a car if your phone is hooked into the car's Bluetooth system—this reduces radiation to the user.

• **Trade in the cordless phone.** Cordless phones and wireless routers that use a technology called DECT emit as much radiation as cell phones whether you are using them or not. At home, install telephones that get their signal by being plugged into a jack.

Forward your cell phone to your landline whenever you're home.

Lung Cancer Is on the Rise Among Nonsmokers… How to Protect Yourself

Timothy Burns, MD, PhD, assistant professor of medicine in the department of medicine, division of hematology/oncology, at the University of Pittsburgh Cancer Institute, where his laboratory focuses on discovering targeted therapies for lung cancer. His scientific papers on lung cancer have appeared in *Nature Genetics, Cancer Research, Oncogene* and many other medical journals.

People who have never smoked often assume that they'll never get lung cancer. But they *can*—and the prevalence of these cases is increasing at a troubling rate.

Update: Two important recent studies have found that the rates of lung cancer among so-called "never-smokers" (less than 100 cigarettes smoked in a lifetime) are mysteriously skyrocketing—in one study, from 9% to 20% of all such malignancies.

But it's not all bad news.

The recent discovery of genetic mutations called "oncogenes" that drive lung cancer in never-smokers has fueled the development of powerful medications that are often more effective and have fewer side effects than conventional chemotherapy. *Bonus:* These new drugs are taken orally rather than intravenously, as is more common with conventional chemotherapy.

TESTING FOR MUTATIONS

If you're one of the roughly 24,000 never-smokers diagnosed with lung cancer each year in the US, it's crucial for you (as well as current and former smokers) to be tested for a genetic mutation that might be driving your disease.

Shockingly, many of these patients are not tested despite the recommendations of national cancer organizations. This is due, in part, to the lack of awareness of many community oncologists in the US.

The most accurate test uses a tissue biopsy to screen for a handful of critical mutations that predict a more than 70% chance of responding to FDA-approved drugs. If the size and location of the tumor make a biopsy impossible, the oncologist should order a blood or urine test to check for mutations.

Important: If possible, get your genetic testing at one of the 47 medical institutions designated by the National Cancer Institute (NCI) as a "Comprehensive Cancer Center" (find one at Cancer.gov/research/nci-role/cancer-centers/find). You will have the most accurate testing at one of these centers and the most reliably up-to-date information on the latest cutting-edge medicine and clinical trials. A medical oncologist near you can administer the treatment. If you're not able to travel to an NCI-designated center, a tissue sample from a biopsy performed at your local medical facility can be sent to certain institutions (such as the Mayo Clinic and Johns Hopkins) that offer molecular testing.

KEY GENETIC MUTATIONS

If you have a genetic mutation, a targeted medication can be used to treat the lung cancer. (Patients who do not test positive for a mutation receive standard cancer care, including conventional chemotherapy and/or radiation.)

Genetic mutations may include…

- **Epidermal growth factor receptor (or EGFR).** This is the most common mutation in never-smokers with lung cancer, occurring in about 40% of these patients. Several FDA-approved drugs called EGFR-inhibitors can counter this mutation, including *gefitinib* (Iressa)…*erlotinib* (Tarceva)…and *afatinib* (Gilotrif). Additionally, *icotinib* (Conmana) is in clinical trials.
- **Anaplastic lymphoma kinase (or ALK).** About 5% to 8% of lung cancer patients (most of these never-smokers) have this genetic mutation. The FDA-approved drug is *crizotinib* (Xalkori) for ALK-positive patients who have never received lung cancer treatment.

TIME FOR A DIFFERENT DRUG

Even when a genetic mutation is identified, eventually a new mutation is generated and the tumor starts growing again—a phenomenon called *acquired resistance.* This typically occurs after about a year of treatment. Therefore, patients on these therapies undergo regular CT scans at two- to three-month intervals to make sure their disease is not growing.

Best approach: When your tumor develops acquired resistance, it's important to have another biopsy so that your doctor can determine which drug is right for you. Two months after starting a second-line drug, the patient will undergo a new CT scan to make sure it is shrinking the tumor.

Important: The patient should alert the physician if he/she is taking any over-the-counter supplements—some can have life-threatening interactions with the targeted therapies.

EARLY DETECTION

The cause of lung cancer in never-smokers is unknown, but it is believed that up to 50% of cases are due to exposure to radon, a naturally occurring radioactive gas, and/or secondhand smoke. A distant third is indoor air pollution, such as particles from wood-burning stoves and cooking fumes from stir-, deep- or pan-frying. *Main risks...*

- **Radon.** Get your home tested. If levels are high (4 pCi/L or above), hire a state-licensed "radon mitigation contractor" to reduce levels to 2 pCi/L or below by installing a pipe that vents the gas outdoors.
- **Secondhand smoke.** Avoid it whenever possible.
- **Indoor air pollution.** If you have a wood stove, get a high-efficiency particle arresting (HEPA) air filter...and if you fry food, be sure to vent the fumes—they may contain harmful carcinogens.

Important: If you are a never-smoker who has one or more of the symptoms of lung cancer—a persistent cough, chest pain, shortness of breath and/or sudden weight loss...or if you've had pneumonia that's persisted for months in spite of several rounds of antibiotics—ask your doctor to test for lung cancer.

Unfortunately, never-smoker lung cancer often has no (or only vague) symptoms that doctors may not immediately suspect as a malignancy. For this reason, it is usually diagnosed when the cancer has spread to the bone, brain, liver and/or other organs. At that point, the most that can be done is to *control* the disease, giving the patient as much as three to five or more extra years of life if the disease is treated. As new therapies continue to emerge, the goal is to make never-smoker lung cancer a chronic disease and to someday provide a cure.

New Melanoma Drug Boosts Survival

A new drug for advanced melanoma can boost long-term survival. *Pembrolizumab* (Keytruda)—one of the medications used to treat former president Jimmy Carter—helps the immune system fight cancer cells.

Recent finding: 40% of the patients given Keytruda were alive after three years, and 15% showed no sign of cancer. The drug is given intravenously every three weeks.

Among the more common side effects: Fatigue, itchiness, rash.

Caroline Robert, MD, PhD, chair of dermatology, Institut de Cancérologie Gustave Roussy, Villejuif, France, and lead author of a study of 655 patients, presented at the 2016 meeting of the American Society of Clinical Oncology.

TAKE NOTE...

Better Skin Checks

When checking your skin for changes (in the size, color and/or shape of moles or for any that bleed), don't forget to examine the bottoms of your feet.

Recent finding: In a study of more than 100 melanoma patients, the deadly skin cancer was found to often be more advanced when it developed on the soles of the feet, possibly because this area is not examined as often as skin exposed to the sun.

Also: Repeated skin damage due to walking was identified as a possible trigger for melanoma on the soles of the feet.

Ryuhei Okuyama, MD, professor of dermatology, Shinshu University School of Medicine, Matsumoto, Japan.

More Precise Brain Cancer Surgery

Stereotactic radiosurgery, which can precisely target radiation to a few small tumors, results in less damage to the patient's short-term memory and thinking skills than whole-brain radiation, a recent study of about 200 brain cancer patients concluded. The current method of radiation to the entire brain may be more appropriate for patients with large or more widespread tumors.

Paul Brown, MD, radiation oncologist, Mayo Clinic, Rochester, Minnesota.

Kidney Stones...Never Again! How to Avoid This Painful Condition

Fredric L. Coe, MD, a nephrologist and professor of medicine at The University of Chicago Pritzker School of Medicine. Dr. Coe has published more than 250 peer-reviewed medical journal research articles and an additional 200 reviews, chapters and books.

If you've ever endured the searing pain of a kidney stone—it's often described as worse than childbirth—then you probably felt like celebrating once the pain was gone and now consider yourself home free. But that's a mistake.

What most people don't realize: Once you've suffered a kidney stone, which can be as small as a grain of sand or as large as a golf ball, you have a chronic condition that must be managed over a lifetime to prevent a repeat performance.

Here's what you need to know to control this condition over the long haul—and prevent it in the first place if kidney stones run in your family...

A GROWING PROBLEM

Even if you've never had a kidney stone, that doesn't mean you're in the clear. About one in every 10 Americans will have a kidney stone during his/her lifetime.

Eye-opening recent finding: For unknown reasons, the prevalence of kidney stone disease has *doubled* in the past 15 years—more than three million Americans receive medical care for the condition each year.

BEST TREATMENT OPTIONS

Treatment for a kidney stone mainly depends on its size. If you develop a small stone (less than 4 mm—or about one-sixth of an inch), count yourself lucky. You may be able to simply drink lots of water (about three liters per day)...take an over-the-counter nonsteroidal anti-inflammatory drug, such as *ibuprofen* (Motrin)...and wait for it to pass on its own within a few days, though it sometimes takes a week or longer. A prescription medication, such as *tamsulosin* (Flomax), may also be used to help pass the stone.

Important: It's crucial that a urologist monitor the patient (for example, with an abdominal X-ray or ultrasound), since the stone may cause an obstruction that damages the kidney—even if the pain has subsided.

A larger stone (4 mm or more) usually needs more extensive medical intervention. While doctors once relied on external sound waves (*shock wave lithotripsy)*, which was only moderately successful at breaking apart a kidney stone in the body, there's now a more effective method. An ultra-thin lighted tube (*ureteroscope*) can be threaded into the urethra, into the bladder, then up to the ureter. A laser at the tip of the scope pulverizes the stone, turning it into dust that is urinated out.

When a kidney stone exceeds 2 cm (or about three-quarters of an inch), surgery is usually required. With *percutaneous nephrolithotomy*, the surgeon creates a small incision in your back to remove the stone.

KNOW YOUR STONE

To avoid a recurrence, the key is to know the composition of your kidney stone. *Main types of stones...*

- **Calcium oxalate.** These small, black or dark brown stones account for about 80% of all kidney stones.

• **Calcium phosphate.** These stones, which are usually tan to beige, form when urine is more alkaline.

• **Uric acid.** These red or orange stones form when urine is too acidic due to heredity, obesity or kidney disease.

• **Cystine.** These lemon yellow stones are associated with the hereditary disorder *cystinuria*, which causes high urine concentrations of the amino acid cystine.

• **Struvite.** These brownish-white stones are produced when bacteria get introduced into the urinary tract—due, for example, to the use of a urinary catheter.

PREVENTION SECRETS

To prevent a kidney stone recurrence, your goal is to stop the stone-forming process by changing the composition of your urine.

Here's how to do that...

***STEP 1:* Get your kidney stone analyzed.** If you pass a stone at home, save it so that your doctor can have its composition analyzed. Urine analysis shows what stone-causing compounds are in your urine so that you can take appropriate preventive steps.

What to do: Strain your urine through gauze in a funnel and then put the stone into a small plastic bag.

Important: It's best to have *all* stones analyzed, since your kidneys can produce stones of varying crystals at different times in your life, which may require a change in treatment. Anyone who has ever suffered a kidney stone should also see a doctor at least once a year for urine analysis.

***STEP 2:* Provide two 24-hour urine samples after the stone has passed.** This requires catching and saving all your urine for 24 hours after you've resumed your normal diet and lifestyle habits. Getting *two* samples provides a more accurate view than a single sample.

***STEP 3:* Raise your urine volume.** The more dilute your urine becomes, the less likely that stones will form. The goal is to produce about 2.5 liters daily in urine volume. This will require drinking three liters or more of fluid daily (spaced out during waking hours). People who sweat a lot due to heat or physical activity may need to drink four to six liters of water per day.

TAKE NOTE...

Kidney Stone Basics

When a stone forms in the kidney, it typically moves through the urinary tract to exit the body in urine. At various points along that journey, the stone may become lodged, leading to extreme pain (usually in one's side or back near the bottom of the rib cage, though it may spread to the lower abdomen and groin).

Important: Kidney stones may also cause blood in the urine, an inability to pass urine, nausea and vomiting and/or fever and chills. Get to an emergency room if you suffer from any of these symptoms—they may signal an infection that requires immediate medical care.

Note: High water intake can sometimes be harmful for people with heart, kidney or liver disease...the elderly...and people taking certain medications (such as diuretics). Consult your physician for advice on how much water you should drink.

***STEP 4:* Change your diet.** This should start immediately when you have a kidney stone and continue for a lifetime. *A kidney stone prevention diet is...**

• **Low sodium and high calcium.** If your daily sodium intake is below 1,500 mg, you can eat 1,000 mg to 1,200 mg of calcium daily (mainly from dairy foods and leafy green vegetables, except for spinach), and urine calcium losses will be as low as possible. Why do you need calcium? High calcium intake will reduce oxalate absorption—oxalate is a component of most kidney stones.

Helpful: After following a low-sodium/high-calcium diet for about one month, repeat the 24-hour urine test to see if additional dietary restrictions are required.

Important: If urine oxalate remains high (over 30 mg per day) despite a high calcium intake, then you need to go low oxalate. To reduce your risk for calcium oxalate stones, avoid high-oxalate foods (such as spinach, rhubarb, beets, cocoa, raspberries and soy products).

*If you have chronic kidney disease, your dietary and treatment needs may differ—consult your doctor.

Note: Even though many of these foods are healthful, there are safer substitutes—for example, instead of spinach, you can try arugula or kale. For a full list of high-oxalate foods and good substitutes, go to KidneyStones.UChicago.edu/how-to-eat-a-low-oxalate-diet.

• **High potassium.** When food sources of potassium—all fruits and most vegetables—are consumed, they are converted to bicarbonate. This process reduces the risk for calcium and uric acid stones. *Recommended daily potassium intake:* 4,700 mg.

• **Low protein and refined sugar.** These foods can promote uric acid stones. Ideally, intake of refined sugar should be less than 10% of total caloric intake, and protein intake should be about 0.8 g to 1 g of protein per 2.2 pounds of body weight.

STEP 5: **Ask your physician about medication.** A variety of medications can help prevent a kidney stone recurrence. These include potassium citrate tablets for people who have had uric acid stones or calcium stones...thiazide diuretics, which help prevent calcium stones...and antibiotics for struvite stones that are triggered by, say, a urinary tract infection.

For more on kidney stones, go to the website KidneyStones.UChicago.edu.

Attention Men: This Bone Danger Can Kill You

Harris H. McIlwain, MD, founder of McIlwain Medical Group in Tampa and former chair of the Florida Osteoporosis Board. He is board-certified in rheumatology, internal medicine and geriatric medicine. He is the pain expert for Dr. Oz's ShareCare.com website and is a coauthor of *Reversing Osteopenia*.

If you're a man, here's something important you probably don't know—about 25% of men will have an osteoporosis-related bone fracture in their lifetimes, and a man's risk of dying in the year following a hip fracture is twice as high as a woman's.

Women try to protect themselves against osteoporosis because rapid bone loss is a hallmark of menopause. Men eventually will lose as much bone strength as women, but it happens more slowly and later in life—and the consequences of ignoring it can be terrible. *Here's what men need to know to protect their bones...*

MALE BONE LOSS

Bone is always breaking down and building up. This process, known as *remodeling,* depends on things such as exercise, vitamin D and calcium intake, hormone levels and other factors. Osteoporosis (or osteopenia, an earlier stage of bone loss) occurs when more bone is lost than gained.

Women can lose 20% or more of their total bone mass within just five years of menopause. Men are somewhat protected but only at first. They have more bone mass to begin with... are more likely to have been physically active, which builds bone...and don't have the same midlife estrogen changes that deplete bone. But men may lose bone when testosterone levels are low. Men tend to have their first bone fractures about 10 years later than women.

By the time men have reached their 70s, their osteoporosis risk is the same as women's. In severe cases, the bones can become almost paper thin. This can lead to fragility fractures—bone breaks that are caused by seemingly minor mishaps such as stepping off a curb in an unusual way or merely bumping into a doorframe.

RISK FACTORS

With a few exceptions (see below), men don't need to be tested for osteoporosis until about age 65. Before that age, they should assume that they'll eventually lose bone and start taking steps to prevent it.

The DEXA (dual-energy X-ray absorptiometry) test, which measures bone density at the hip and spine (and sometimes in the wrist), usually costs between $100 and $200 and often is covered by insurance. It assigns a T-score, a measure of your bone density. A negative reading (for example, a score of –1) indicates some bone loss. A score of –2.5 means that you have possible early osteoporosis. Anything lower indicates serious bone loss.

Most at risk: Older men who are underweight are up to 20 times more likely to get osteoporosis than heavier men. Smoking greatly increases bone loss. So does low testosterone, lung disease and a poor diet. Some drugs used to treat prostate cancer and other diseases (including some lung diseases) cause bone loss as a side effect.

Men with any of these risk factors should get tested earlier—say, at about age 50. So should men who have suffered fragility fractures. The fractures usually occur in the hips or spine, although wrist and shoulder fractures also are common. (Broken fingers and toes aren't considered fragility fractures.)

WHAT WILL SAVE YOUR BONES?

Men with early osteoporosis (or a high risk of getting it) can improve their diet, take calcium and vitamin D supplements, and get more exercise. Such men probably won't need medication right away—or ever. *Steps to take...*

• **Plenty of exercise.** Forty minutes a day is ideal. It's the best way for middle-aged men to build bone mass and for older men who already have osteoporosis to slow the rate of bone loss. Research has shown that people who exercise will have fewer hip or spine fractures than those who are sedentary.

• **Weight-bearing exercises**—walking, lifting weights, playing tennis, etc.—are the most effective at slowing bone loss.

My advice: Take frequent walks. Many people enjoy walking more than other forms of exercise, and it's foolproof. It does not matter whether you walk slow or fast—simply standing up and working against gravity stimulates bone growth in the hips and spine.

• **More calcium.** You cannot build strong bones without calcium. Unfortunately, most Americans don't get enough. The problem is compounded in older adults, who absorb dietary calcium less efficiently. Men and women need a daily calcium intake of 1,000 milligrams (mg) up to age 50 and 1,200 mg thereafter.

Important: The guidelines include the calcium that you get from foods and supplements. There's no reason to take a high-dose calcium supplement if you also get plenty of calcium from dairy, fortified juices or high-calcium foods such as sardines with bones. For most people, a 500-mg calcium supplement is enough—take more if you tend to avoid calcium-rich foods. Your body absorbs calcium more efficiently when it is taken in smaller amounts (500 mg or less) several times a day. Taking 50 mg to 100 mg of magnesium a day also helps with absorption.

• **Add vitamin D.** You can't absorb calcium without enough vitamin D in your system, and older adults' bodies are not very efficient at using sun exposure to create the needed form of vitamin D.

My advice: I recommend taking 1,000 units of vitamin D-2 daily. Check with your doctor to see how often you should get your blood levels tested to make sure that you're getting enough.

• **Go easy on drinking colas.** Research has shown that people who consume a lot of cola (but not other carbonated beverages) tend to have lower hip-bone densities. It could be that the phosphoric acid in colas reduces calcium absorption or that people who drink a lot of soft drinks tend not to consume calcium-rich foods in general and need to be aware of this. I agree with the National Osteoporosis Foundation recommendation to have no more than five cola soft drinks a week.

• **If you smoke, do everything you can to quit.** Smoking interferes with the hormones that you need for bone strength...decreases blood supply to bones...and slows the production of bone-forming cells. By the age of 80, smokers are about 71% more likely to have bone fractures than nonsmokers.

MEDICATIONS

Men with more advanced disease may need medication. Some of the same drugs used to treat osteoporosis in women also work in men. Bisphosphonates such as Fosamax and Actonel slow the rate of bone loss. The most common side effects include heartburn or an upset stomach. Using bisphosphonates for more than five years has been linked to two rare but serious side effects—thighbone fracture and osteonecrosis (bone death) of the jaw. Prolia, a different type of drug, helps prevent fracture and requires an injection every six months. Discuss this drug with your physician because it too has osteonecrosis of the jaw and thighbone fractures as possible side effects of long-term use. For men with low testosterone, hormone replacement will help increase bone mass and reduce the risk for fractures. Testosterone replacement should be done only under the guidance of a physician because too much testosterone has been linked to stroke and heart attack.

When to Delay Hip Surgery

If you are considering hip replacement, you may want to put it off for a few months if you have just received a steroid shot in your hip.

Recent study: Infection rates jumped 40% in hip replacement patients who received a steroid injection in the three months prior to surgery...but those who received an injection earlier showed no increased risk.

Steroids may weaken the immune system, which could account for the higher infection rate. Although rare, an infection in the hip joint could require additional surgery, intravenous antibiotics and a prolonged recovery.

William Schairer, MD, orthopedic surgeon, Hospital for Special Surgery, New York City.

Antidepressant Alert

Antidepressants raise risk for dental implant failure. A recent study looked at 74 patients who received dental implants. The odds of implant failure were about four times higher among antidepressant users than among those who weren't taking antidepressants.

Takeaway: A patient needs to weigh the risks and benefits of each (and possible alternatives) with his/her psychiatrist and dentist.

Latifa Bairam, BDS, a clinical assistant professor of restorative dentistry at University at Buffalo School of Dental Medicine, New York.

Do You Ever Feel Dizzy? Here's What It Might Mean...

Jack J. Wazen, MD, an otolaryngologist and otological/neurotological surgeon at the Silverstein Institute in Sarasota, Florida, where he is the director of research for the nonprofit Ear Research Foundation. He is one of the nation's leading experts on hearing and balance disorders and is coauthor of *Dizzy: What You Need to Know About Managing and Treating Balance Disorders.*

Have you ever felt dizzy and light-headed? Chances are the answer is yes. About 50% of adults experience dizziness at some time in their lives.

Feeling dizzy isn't just uncomfortable. It can be dangerous—for example, if you fall or lose control of your car while driving.

There are many different causes of dizziness or vertigo (the feeling that you or the world around you is spinning), so it can be tricky to figure out what's triggering your symptoms.

Here are the five most common causes—and important clues to determine which one is affecting you. Many causes of dizziness aren't serious, but some are, so it's always a good idea to get checked by your doctor.

- **Benign paroxysmal positional vertigo (BPPV).** Millions of tiny crystals, or otoliths, are attached to hair cells in the inner ear. They bend the hairs when you change position, which tells the brain that you've moved. When you have BPPV, the crystals break free and float into a part of the ear where they're not supposed to be.

Result: A bout of vertigo that usually lasts 60 seconds or less.

Important clues: Suspect BPPV when the attacks occur only after you've moved your head...there's a delay of three to five seconds between the head movement and the vertigo...and the severity decreases when you have multiple episodes over a period of minutes or hours.

What to do: Ask your doctor to recommend a therapist who can show you how to do the Epley maneuver. Named after its originator, it consists of five steps that can eliminate symptoms in about 80% of patients. Other maneuvers practiced by therapists also can work.

The Epley maneuver includes reclining on a bed or table and then, in very particular ways, tipping your head to both sides, rolling over on your side and then sitting up, which causes the crystals to return to their usual location. Videos are available on YouTube.com.

• **Ménière's disease.** No one knows what causes Ménière's disease, although it's been linked to autoimmune diseases, viral infections, head injuries and other conditions. It causes intense dizziness, nausea and vertigo when a buildup of *endolymph fluid* in the inner ear causes pressure changes that interfere with balance.

The episodes come and go. Some people have attacks every few days. Others go weeks or months between attacks. Some people are lucky and have just a single attack—but this is rare.

Important clue: Hearing loss in one ear that mainly affects lower frequencies (such as difficulty hearing a man's voice). This is the opposite of normal, age-related hearing loss, which usually affects high frequencies first.

What to do: Reducing fluid in the inner ear is the cornerstone of treatment. Some patients can achieve this just by consuming less sodium. The FDA advises limiting sodium to no more than 2,300 milligrams (about one teaspoon daily of table salt). But most patients also will need to take a diuretic (sometimes referred to as a "water pill") that helps your body get rid of unneeded salt and water through urine. These include *acetazolamide* (such as the brand Diamox) or *hydrochlorothiazide* (such as the brand HydroDIURIL).

It's helpful to give up caffeine. Caffeine reduces blood circulation in the inner ear. Also, cut back on alcohol and sugar—these can increase dizziness in some people. Reducing stress can help, too. We don't know why, but stress can trigger attacks.

• **Acoustic neuroma.** This is a benign tumor that grows at the base of the brain and can affect a variety of nerves including the auditory nerve. About 3,000 Americans are diagnosed with one of these tumors every year. The symptoms include dizziness, a loss of balance and nausea.

The tumors aren't cancerous, but they can cause serious impairments and even death if they grow large enough. They typically grow about 2 mm (about one-eighth of an inch) a year.

Important clue: Slight hearing loss (usually in one ear), along with the other symptoms mentioned above. Some patients also experience tinnitus, ringing or buzzing sounds in the affected ear.

What to do: Because the tumors are slow-growing, your doctor might decide just to track your progress with periodic MRIs, especially if your symptoms are minor. But there's always a risk that a tumor will cause permanent hearing loss, along with damage to the facial nerve or other structures in the brain. If your doctor is concerned that an acoustic neuroma is dangerous, he/she will probably recommend either surgery or radiation to remove or shrink it.

• **Orthostatic hypotension.** Almost all of us have experienced the occasional dizziness that occurs when we stand up too quickly. For some people, these episodes happen often—this is particularly true for the elderly...those taking blood pressure medication...and people with certain conditions (including heart disease or Parkinson's disease).

What happens: When you stand up, blood is pulled downward and away from your brain. It takes about a minute for your body to adjust to the change in position by increasing the strength of your heartbeat and tightening your blood vessels. In the meantime, a lack of circulation and oxygen to your brain can make you feel dizzy.

Important clue: Suspect orthostatic hypotension when you experience dizziness or light-headedness only when you're changing position—usually when you go from a seated or lying position to standing.

What to do: See your doctor. Orthostatic hypotension, while itself relatively harmless, can be caused by cardiovascular or nervous system disorders that are serious and require treatment. If you are on blood pressure medication, the dosage may need to be adjusted.

Whatever the cause of orthostatic hypotension, it helps if you change positions slowly to give your body time to adjust. *Example:* To get out of bed, swing your legs off the bed and sit up...but don't stand up yet. Wait a minute for your blood pressure to stabilize. Then stand up slowly.

• **Dehydration.** You might not think that skimping on fluids could cause your head to spin, but it's not uncommon.

What happens: When you do not drink enough water, your blood volume falls. Reduced blood volume can reduce the amount of blood that circulates through the brain. The result can be dizziness or even fainting spells. Older adults are particularly at risk because the sense of thirst declines with age.

Important clues: People who live in hot climates or take diuretics (the "water pills" often used to treat high blood pressure) are particularly prone to dehydration.

What to do: Drink plenty of water throughout the day—and sip even when you aren't feeling particularly thirsty. Eight glasses a day is a good amount to shoot for. If you're taking a diuretic, ask your doctor whether switching drugs or changing doses might be helpful.

Ch-ch-chilly? Hidden Reasons Why You're Always Cold

Michael Aziz, MD, a board-certified internist and attending physician at Lenox Hill Hospital and founder and director of Midtown Integrative Medicine, both in New York City. Dr. Aziz is also author of *The Perfect 10 Diet.*

You find yourself reaching for a sweater when everyone else is comfortable in short sleeves. Your hands and feet often feel like ice. What's going on? Could something be wrong with you?

It could be perfectly normal. Some people are naturally more prone to feeling chilled—especially women. Ironically, it stems from the way women's bodies keep internal organs warm, which protects the uterus and future generations. In women, insulating body fat is concentrated around their core—leaving toes and fingers in the cold. Plus, when women are exposed to cold, their blood vessels contract more dramatically than men's, which sends more blood to protect inner organs—but leaves their hands and feet colder.

Result: While a woman's core body temperature tends to be slightly warmer than a man's (97.8°F versus 97.4°F), her *hands* register about three degrees colder—87.2°F versus 90°F. But it isn't just women who are feeling the chill. Men do, too. *Here's why...*

MEDICAL CONDITIONS THAT CAN LEAVE YOU COLD

The following two medical conditions often go undiagnosed. *They affect both genders, although they're more common in women...*

• **Underactive thyroid.** A telltale symptom of hypothyroidism—when the thyroid gland does not produce sufficient thyroid hormone—is feeling constantly cold. Other symptoms can be weight gain, constipation and fatigue. Your doctor can diagnose a low-thyroid condition with a simple blood test. Once your thyroid levels have been normalized, usually by taking daily thyroid hormone medication, your tolerance to cold should improve.

• **Raynaud's disease.** Cold fingers and toes are also symptoms of Raynaud's disease. It's a usually benign condition in which the small blood vessels in the extremities overreact to cold, as well as stress. This causes fingers and toes to feel cold to the touch and, in many cases, to change color—from white to blue or red and back to normal again.

While Raynaud's has no cure, lifestyle modifications can help—such as keeping hands and feet warm by wearing mittens (they keep fingers warmer than gloves) and socks...or keeping hand and foot warmers in your boots or pockets.

MORE COLD CULPRITS...

COLD CULPRIT #1: **You're too thin.** Muscle generates heat, and fat acts as insulation. But if you're underweight—with a body mass index (BMI) under 18.5—you may lack sufficient body fat or muscle to maintain a normal core body temperature.

My advice: If your low body weight is the result of extreme dieting, a nutritionist can help you adopt healthier dietary strategies. Also, certain medications, including bronchodilators for asthma and the antidepressant *bupropion* (Wellbutrin), can cause weight loss. If you've shed pounds without trying, see your primary care physician to rule out a possible serious medical condition, such as an overactive thyroid, diabetes or cancer.

COLD CULPRIT #2: **You're on a low-carb diet.** Diets that severely restrict carbohydrates, such as Atkins and Paleo, are popular for their ability to promote quick weight loss. But one of their downsides is that they can make you feel as cold as a caveman. One reason is that carb-restricted diets are very high in protein and fat, which require more energy to be digested, so after a meal your body directs more blood toward your stomach and intestines. Over the long term, a high-protein diet can also inhibit the conversion of thyroid hormone to its active form, which results in feeling cold...or eventually a full-blown underactive thyroid.

My advice: Rather than omit or limit an entire category of food, stick to a balanced 40/40/20 diet—40% of your calories from carbohydrates...40% from (healthy) fats... and 20% from protein. Aim for three meals and one or two snacks per day, depending on your activity level. Your body needs high-quality whole grains, such as brown rice and quinoa, as well as other complex carbohydrates, such as sweet potatoes and squash, for energy and essential vitamins and other nutrients.

A sample day might include a veggie omelet and two slices of rye toast for breakfast... grilled salmon and a mixed greens salad for lunch...chicken with vegetables and brown rice for dinner...and a few chocolate-covered strawberries for dessert.

Also: Don't skip meals. Being hungry causes the body to conserve energy, producing less heat as a result.

COLD CULPRIT #3: **You don't get enough sleep.** Lack of sleep disturbs the physiological mechanisms of the brain, especially the hypothalamus, which controls body temperature.

My advice: Aim to get seven to eight hours of sleep a night. Do not keep your bedroom too warm—the National Sleep Foundation puts the optimal room temperature for sleep at around 65°F.

If you have trouble falling asleep, give meditation a try. A *JAMA Internal Medicine* study found that meditating five to 20 minutes a day can help you fall asleep more quickly than using basic sleep-hygiene techniques such as establishing a bedtime routine.

COLD CULPRIT #4: **You're dehydrated.** Your body is 60% water, and if you are dehydrated, it can affect circulation, making you feel colder.

My advice: Be sure to drink plenty of fluids—and drink even more than usual if you are physically active. Water is best, but contrary to common beliefs, tea and coffee can count—your body still holds onto some of these fluids despite their mild diuretic effect.

Best self-check: If your urine is very yellow and concentrated, you are not drinking enough water and other fluids.

COLD CULPRIT #5: **You're a vegetarian.** Vegetarians are sometimes deficient in iron. Why? Red meat has plenty of iron and it's easily absorbed, while vegetarian sources, such as beans and greens, have less iron and it's in a less available form. Low iron intake can lead to iron-deficiency anemia—and feeling cold is a common symptom. Vegans, who eat only plant-based foods, may also be low in vitamin B-12, found primarily in animal products, including meat, fish, poultry, eggs and dairy. A B-12 deficiency can lead to "pernicious anemia," which can cause you to feel cold as well.

GOOD TO KNOW...

Is a Drink Warming?

Alcohol, in moderation, will dilate blood vessels, making you feel warmer quickly. But here's the rub—the effect is fleeting because your body temperature will drop as heat escapes through those dilated blood vessels.

Note: Antacids and proton pump inhibitors, commonly used to treat acid reflux, also can inhibit iron and B-12 absorption. And people who have Crohn's disease and celiac disease are at risk for anemia.

My advice: If you're a vegetarian or vegan, have your doctor run a simple blood test for iron deficiency. *Warning:* Only take an iron supplement if it's prescribed, as too much iron can be dangerous.

Vegans also need a supplementary source of B-12, since it's found only in animal foods. But so do many omnivores and lacto-ovo vegetarians.

Here's why: Between 10% and 30% of older adults have gastritis, which interferes with the absorption of B-12 from food—but they can absorb B-12 from supplements and fortified foods. That's why the Institute of Medicine recommends that adults older than age 50 get much of their vitamin B-12 from vitamin supplements or fortified foods.

Tip: If you rely on antacids or proton pump inhibitors, or have a condition such as Crohn's or celiac, get your B-12 levels tested.

Headaches and Hypothyroidism

In hypothyroidism, the body does not produce enough thyroid hormone. This can lead to mood swings, weight gain, fatigue and other symptoms.

Recent finding: People with a history of headache had 21% greater risk for hypothyroidism than people without a headache history...and people with migraines had 41% greater risk.

If you have headaches: Talk to your doctor about being screened for hypothyroidism.

Vincent Martin, MD, professor of medicine and codirector of the Headache and Facial Pain Center, Gardner Neuroscience Institute, University of Cincinnati, and coauthor of a study of 8,400 people, published in *Headache: The Journal of Head and Face Pain*.

Better Sleep Apnea Treatment Alternative

A customized oral appliance that moves the jawbone slightly forward throughout sleep helps keep the airway open and may work better for some adults who cannot tolerate a continuous positive airway pressure (CPAP) mask and machine.

Recent finding: Nearly 100 adults with mild-to-moderate sleep apnea who wore this type of mouth guard nightly showed improvement in sleep apnea and snoring.

If you've been diagnosed with sleep apnea: Ask your doctor whether an oral appliance would be appropriate. If so, a dentist can custom-fit one. Most devices cost about $2,000 and may be covered by insurance.

Karl Franklin, MD, senior lecturer, Umea University, Sweden.

It May Not Be Alzheimer's After All: What Can Mimic Dementia

Marc E. Agronin, MD, vice president for behavioral health and clinical research at Miami Jewish Health and an adult and geriatric psychiatrist and affiliate associate professor of psychiatry and neurology at the University of Miami Miller School of Medicine. Dr. Agronin is also author of *How We Age*. His website is MarcAgronin.com.

People joke about having the occasional "senior moment," but the humor partly deflects an unsettling concern: What if this memory lapse—forgetting an appointment, calling someone by the wrong name, losing your car in the parking lot, etc.—marks the beginning of an incurable mental decline? *Not so fast.*

Some middle-aged adults (defined roughly as ages 40 to 65) do develop early-onset Alzheimer's or other forms of dementia, but it's rare. Their flagging memories are much more likely to have simpler—and very treatable—explanations. If you have memory or other cognitive changes, it's critically important to seek early diagnosis and treatment before more serious problems ensue...or the changes become irreversible.

FORGETFULNESS HAPPENS

The fear of mental decline makes sense for older adults. While the prevalence of Alzheimer's disease and other types of dementia is nearly 10% at age 65, it jumps to up to half of those age 85 and older.

However, many patients in their 50s and 60s are convinced that the mildest mental slips mean that the worst is just around the corner. This is usually not the case.

Once you reach your mid-40s, your brain processes information more slowly. Memories are more transient than they used to be. Forgetting facts or incorrectly recalling details becomes more common. *These are normal changes.*

If you've noticed that you're more distracted or forgetful than usual, ask your doctor to perform a general checkup to rule out any obvious medical issues, such as a vitamin B-12 deficiency or a thyroid problem. If nothing is uncovered, it's still possible that something other than dementia is causing your cognitive symptoms. *Possible suspects...*

- **Medications.** If you're taking codeine or another opioid medication for pain, you expect to be a little fuzzy. But some of the drugs that affect memory aren't the ones that most people are aware of—or think to discuss with their doctors.

Examples: Cholesterol-lowering statins. A small percentage of people who take these drugs describe mental fuzziness as a side effect. The *benzodiazepine* class of sedatives/antianxiety drugs (such as Valium, Xanax, Halcion, etc.) can also cause cognitive problems and frequently affect memory. The mental effects are amplified when you take multiple drugs—say, one of these medications for sleep and another for daytime anxiety.

Do not overlook the possibility that some over-the-counter drugs (decongestants and antihistamines are common offenders) can also cause mental fuzziness.

Dr. Agronin's advice: Pay attention (and tell your doctor) if your cognitive symptoms seem to get worse after starting a new medication. You might need to change drugs or take a lower dose.

- **Mental health.** When you meet people at a party, do you remember their names? Or are you so nervous about making a good impression that their names don't register?

Anxiety and stress cause distraction, and it's impossible to form memories when you're not paying attention. Some people become so worried about memory problems that every slip causes them to freeze up and quit paying attention to what's happening around them. It becomes a self-fulfilling prophecy.

Depression is also linked to cognitive lapses, especially since it interferes with concentration...interest in activities...and sleep—all essential factors for good memory.

Dr. Agronin's advice: If you notice that your memory has good days and bad ones—and some days when it's horrible—it's reasonable to suspect that the problem is benign and you might just be going through an emotionally difficult time.

Talk to your doctor about what may be bothering you emotionally. If there's a problem with stress, anxiety or depression, get a referral to a mental health provider for a more thorough evaluation to assess your mood, thinking and behavior.

Important: Your doctor or a mental health professional should also talk to you about potential alcohol or recreational drug abuse, which can have a significant impact on cognition.

All of these conditions can be treated with medication, therapy and/or a variety of lifestyle changes, such as getting more exercise and practicing relaxation techniques.

- **Obstructive sleep apnea.** It's a common sleep disorder, particularly among those who are overweight. A blocked airway during sleep impedes the flow of oxygen to the brain. This can occur dozens or even hundreds of times a night. Diminished nighttime oxygen can impair memory and concentration. Patients with sleep apnea also have a higher risk for stroke and heart disease.

Warning signs: Gasping, snorting or loud snoring during sleep…a dry mouth in the morning…morning headaches…and/or difficulty staying alert during the day.

The good news is that obstructive sleep apnea can be overcome almost completely with the use of a continuous positive airway pressure (CPAP) machine, a small bedside device that delivers mild air pressure through a hose to help keep the airways open. These machines can be noisy, and the mask or nose piece that connects to the air hose can be somewhat uncomfortable—but CPAP does work. And it's definitely preferable to a lifetime of brain fog.

- **Adult ADD.** People associate attention deficit disorder (ADD) with children, but it also affects 2% to 4% of adults—and most are never diagnosed. It's a lifelong neurobiological disease that makes it difficult to focus or pay attention.

People with ADD are easily distracted… may have a history of work problems…and often don't follow through on tasks at home. It's easy to confuse these symptoms with cognitive impairments.

ADD is usually diagnosed by taking a history from the patient and family members. If the patient then responds to medication such as *methylphenidate* (Ritalin), he/she is considered to have ADD.

Worried About Dementia? Memory Loss Isn't Always the First Sign

James E. Galvin, MD, MPH, professor and associate dean for clinical research at the Charles E. Schmidt College of Medicine and professor in the Christine E. Lynn College of Nursing, both at Florida Atlantic University (FAU) in Boca Raton, Florida. He also has developed a number of dementia-screening tools, including the "Lewy Body Composite Risk Score" and the "Quick Dementia Rating System." You can find these tests by searching at FAU.edu.

Chances are you notice every little blip in your memory if you're over age 40. That's because most people who are middle-aged or beyond fear that any indication of memory loss is a red flag for Alzheimer's disease.

What you may not realize: While memory loss does occur with Alzheimer's disease, there are other symptoms that often get overlooked by patients and their doctors. These symptoms can also be the key to identifying other causes of dementia that are less well-known than Alzheimer's disease.

Important: Dementia-like symptoms are sometimes due to medical conditions, including depression…traumatic brain injury…diabetes…tumors…thyroid disease…vitamin B-12 deficiency…and kidney disease. Certain medications can also be to blame—including drugs that block the neurotransmitter *acetylcholine*, such as those for overactive bladder, allergies, anxiety and depression.

If you or a loved one is showing any of the symptoms described in this article, consult your primary care provider. He/she can perform simple memory tests or refer you to a specialist, such as a neurologist, psychiatrist, neuropsychologist or geriatrician, for a more comprehensive evaluation, which may include an imaging test of the brain, such as an MRI or a CT scan.

To learn more about the complex interplay between memory and dementia, we spoke with Dr. James E. Galvin, a renowned authority on dementia.

4 MAIN CAUSES OF DEMENTIA

Of all the possible causes of dementia, the majority of cases are due to one of the following disorders—and many people have a combination of two or more disorders…

- **Alzheimer's disease.** It's true that memory (problems with learning new things and recalling past information) is significantly affected by this disease. But memory problems aren't the only warning signs.

Non-memory symptoms include: Changes in mood (including the onset of depression, anxiety or paranoia)…behavior (such as withdrawing from hobbies and social activities)… language ability (such as difficulty finding the right word)…and problem-solving skills and concentration (such as finding it hard to keep track of monthly bills).

When Alzheimer's typically strikes: It primarily hits people in their mid-60s to mid-80s. Early-onset Alzheimer's disease can appear in one's 40s or 50s.

- **Lewy body dementias.** Lewy body dementia and a related form of dementia that accompanies Parkinson's are caused by clumps (called Lewy bodies) of a protein that forms in cells throughout the brain. With Lewy body dementia, the protein clumps start in the cerebral cortex, which can lead to memory loss.

Non-memory symptoms that may occur with Lewy body dementia: Visual hallucinations...perceptual difficulties (for example, bumping into doors)...frequent staring spells... and/or sleep disruptions that cause one to act out dreams.

When dementia accompanies Parkinson's, disease similar cognitive symptoms develop a year or more after the onset of the movement changes that characterize Parkinson's, including slow movement, muscle rigidity and tremors. The movement problems occur when abnormal protein clumps form in the brain stem and later spread to other brain regions.

When Lewy body dementia and Parkinson's disease with dementia usually strike: In one's 60s to late 70s, but early-onset Parkinson's with dementia can occur under age 50.

- **Vascular dementia.** In people with vascular dementia, brain cells become damaged by "mini" strokes that are often so small that they may go unnoticed. Memory problems may occur but sometimes *after* the other symptoms described below.

Non-memory symptoms could include: Changes in one's ability to plan, organize and make decisions (such as those required for daily activities)...and mood (such as depression and lack of motivation).

When vascular dementia strikes: Risk is highest after age 65, but it can occur at any age.

- **Frontotemporal dementia (FTD).** This degenerative disorder mainly affects brain cells in two parts of the brain—the frontal lobe (responsible for behavior and emotions) and temporal lobe (involved in language and memory skills).

Memory problems are more prominent at a later stage than with Alzheimer's disease. Language is frequently affected, either with difficulty producing words or in understanding the meaning of words.

Non-memory symptoms that may occur: Changes in personality (a shy person becoming boisterous, for example) and/or trouble with problem solving and other executive functions (such as the ability to handle everyday situations, including driving a car and shopping for groceries) develop when the frontal lobe is mainly affected.

When FTD strikes: Typically in one's 50s or 60s.

ALZHEIMER'S ALERT...

Apathy and Alzheimer's

Apathy could be an early sign of Alzheimer's. Families should watch their older loved ones for emotional apathy and other behavioral changes, such as suspicion or paranoia...greater-than-usual agitation or aggression...and loss of socially appropriate behavior. If new and sustained, these behaviors may be signs of mild behavioral impairment, an early indicator of Alzheimer's disease and other dementias.

Zahinoor Ismail, MD, FRCPC, a neuropsychiatrist and assistant professor of psychiatry and neurology at Hotchkiss Brain Institute, University of Calgary, Canada.

Early Alzheimer's Sign?

Difficulty identifying certain smells, such as lemon or smoke, could signal Alzheimer's disease 10 years before the onset of memory loss, according to a recent study of older adults.

Why: Alzheimer's can cause brain circuits to lose memory of certain smells.

Self-defense: If you or a loved one has difficulty identifying familiar smells, talk to your doctor about screening for Alzheimer's disease.

Mark Albers, MD, PhD, assistant professor of neurology, Harvard Medical School, Boston.

TREATMENT OPTIONS

Regardless of the cause of dementia, an early diagnosis helps...

• **For Alzheimer's disease,** medications are available to help slow the progression, and doctors may use the same medications to help treat the symptoms of other causes of dementia.

• **For vascular dementia,** you can work with a doctor to control risk factors, such as high blood pressure or high cholesterol. For Lewy body dementia and frontotemporal dementia, there are no treatments for the diseases themselves, but research is ongoing to change that.

There is also accumulating evidence that certain lifestyle factors may decrease risk of developing dementia and slow symptoms of disease. These include daily exercise (aerobic, resistance training, flexibility)...mental stimulation (games, lectures)...social engagement... and a healthful diet (fruits, vegetables, whole grains, lean meats).

Rosacea/Alzheimer's Link

People with the common skin disorder rosacea are at higher risk for Alzheimer's disease. Rosacea patients are 25% more likely, on average, to develop Alzheimer's disease than people without rosacea. The increased risk is greatest among women, who had a 28% greater risk. It is not known whether rosacea actually causes Alzheimer's, but the presence of rosacea in elderly people may aid in early detection and treatment.

Alexander Egeberg, MD, PhD, associate professor of dermato-allergology, Herlev and Gentofte Hospital, University of Copenhagen, Denmark, and leader of a 15-year study of 82,439 rosacea patients, published in *Annals of Neurology.*

Calcium Caution

Calcium supplements may increase dementia risk.

Recent finding: Women over age 70 with a history of stroke who regularly took calcium supplements had nearly seven times higher risk for dementia than other stroke survivors.

If you had a stroke, ask your physician whether the risk from calcium supplements outweighs the benefit.

Silke Kern, MD, PhD, a neuropsychiatric researcher at Sahlgrenska Academy, University of Gothenburg, Sweden, and coauthor of a study of 700 women, published in *Neurology.*

Heartburn Drug Danger

Regular use of a proton-pump inhibitor (PPI), such as *omeprazole* (Prilosec) or *esomeprazole* (Nexium), increased risk for dementia by up to 44% in a recent seven-year study of adults age 75 and older. Further research is needed on long-term use of PPIs and the possible effects on cognition in the elderly.

If you take a PPI: Follow your doctor's guidance.

Britta Haenisch, PhD, group leader, German Center for Neurodegenerative Diseases, Bonn, Germany.

TAKE NOTE...

New Hope for Parkinson's?

In a recent finding, low-dose *nilotinib* (Tasigna), a drug currently approved for treating leukemia, increased dopamine and reduced toxic proteins in Parkinson's patients. The drug also caused improvements in cognition/motor function.

Journal of Parkinson's Disease.

2

Medical Manager

6 Common Medical Tests Most People Don't Need

You expect your doctor to order tests during routine checkups and to investigate unexplained symptoms. But do you *need* all of those tests? Maybe not.

The American College of Physicians and other groups have joined a project called Choosing Wisely that uses evidence-based medicine to identify tests, treatments and medical screenings that most people do not need. *Common offenders...*

CT SCANS FOR HEADACHES

If you start getting migraines or pounding headaches, you'll want to know why. So will your doctor.

Result: About one in eight patients who sees a doctor for headaches or migraines winds up getting scans.

Yet CT scans find abnormalities in only 1% to 3% of cases—and many of those abnormalities will be harmless or have nothing to do with the headaches. The scans are highly unlikely to change your diagnosis or affect your treatment options. But doctors order them anyway.

The tests create their own problems. Excess radiation is one concern. So is the likelihood that a scan will reveal "incidentalomas," a somewhat tongue-in-cheek name for unimportant abnormalities that can lead to additional (and unnecessary) tests.

Bottom line: CT scans are rarely needed because doctors can readily diagnose headaches just by talking with patients and taking detailed medical histories.

Tanveer P. Mir, MD, chair of the Board of Regents of the American College of Physicians and medical director of palliative care and ethics at Florida Hospital, Orlando. She is board-certified in internal medicine, geriatrics and hospice and palliative medicine and formerly served as associate chief of geriatrics and palliative medicine at North Shore-Long Island Jewish Medical Center, New York.

Who might need it: You might need a scan if your headaches are accompanied by neurological symptoms (such as a seizure or fit, change in speech or alertness or loss of coordination) or if you suffered from an accident that involved a sharp blow to the head.

PREOPERATIVE CHEST X-RAY

If you've ever had an operation, you almost certainly had one or more chest X-rays. Many hospitals require them to "clear" patients for surgery. They have become a part of the presurgical routine even though a study published in *JAMA* found that only 2% of the X-rays provided useful information for the surgeon/anesthesiologist. Most patients don't need them.

Bottom line: If you're generally healthy, tell your doctor you don't want the X-ray.

Who might need it: Patients who have been diagnosed with heart or lung disease or who are having surgery on the heart, lungs or other parts of the chest should get the X-ray. So should those who are older than 70 and haven't had a chest X-ray within the last six months (the likelihood of an abnormal X-ray is higher in these people).

HEART DISEASE STRESS TEST

If you're between the ages of 40 and 60, there's a chance that you've had (or been advised to have) an exercise stress test to determine your risk for heart disease and heart attack. A 2010 study that looked at nearly 1,200 people in this age group found that nearly one out of 10 had been given a stress test.

Unless you're having symptoms of heart disease—such as chest pain and shortness of breath—a stress test will probably be useless. The cost is considerable—you can expect to spend $200 to $300. Stress tests tend to produce unclear results. This can lead to additional tests, including coronary angiography—an expensive test that exposes you to as much radiation as 600 to 800 chest X-rays.

Bottom line: You're better off reducing your particular risks—giving up smoking, controlling hypertension and lowering cholesterol—than getting a stress test.

Who might need it: Agree to an exercise stress test only if you're having symptoms of heart disease or your doctor suspects that you already have heart disease.

> **GOOD TO KNOW...**
>
> ### Physicians on Probation
>
> Thousands of practicing physicians in the US are on probation for offenses ranging from unprofessional treatment of patients to drug addiction and sexual misconduct. Doctors' disciplinary records are kept in a database called the National Practitioner Data Bank, which is not open to the public. Patients must ask state medical boards for data.
>
> *Consumer Reports*, ConsumerReports.org.

IMAGING FOR BACK PAIN

There's a good chance that your doctor will order an MRI or a CT scan if you complain of sudden back pain. Yet 80% to 90% of patients will improve within four to six weeks. You might need an imaging test when symptoms are severe or don't improve, but there's no reason to rush it—or to expose yourself to unnecessary radiation from a CT scan.

Bottom line: Don't agree to a test that's unlikely to change your diagnosis or treatment options. Since most back-pain patients will recover with physical therapy, over-the-counter painkillers and other "conservative measures," imaging tests usually are unnecessary.

Who might need it: A scan typically is warranted if your doctor suspects a compression fracture from osteoporosis...you have burning pain down a leg that doesn't improve...or you're also having numbness, muscle weakness, a loss of bowel/bladder control or other neurological symptoms.

PELVIC EXAM

Some gynecologists and primary-care physicians believe that a pelvic exam is a good way to detect ovarian cancer or problems with the ovaries, uterus, vulva or other pelvic structures. It's usually combined with a Pap test to screen for cervical cancer.

A study published in *JAMA* concluded that routine pelvic exams are unlikely to detect ovarian cancer. Nor are they likely to help women with uterine fibroids or cysts.

Bottom line: The routine pelvic exam is a low-yield test that should be discontinued, particularly because it makes women anxious.

Important: Do not eliminate regular Pap smears—you can get them without having a pelvic exam. Women 30 years old and older should have a Pap smear—along with testing for the human papillomavirus (HPV), which is done at the same time—every five years. For those with a family history of cervical cancer or other risk factors, the Pap test should be repeated every three years.

PSA TEST

For a long time, men were routinely advised to have this blood test, which measures prostate-specific antigen (PSA) and screens for prostate cancer. However, the test can't differentiate harmless cancers (the majority) from aggressive ones. Studies have shown that men who test positive are only marginally less likely to die from prostate cancer than those who were never tested...and they're more likely to have biopsies, surgeries and other treatments that will make no difference in their long-term health, that pose serious risks of their own and that cause unnecessary anguish.

The US Preventive Services Task Force (or USPSTF), an independent group of national experts that makes evidence-based recommendations about medical tests, recommends that men ages 55 to 69 discuss the harms and benefits of PSA screening with their doctors in order to make the best decisions for themselves based on their values and preferences. But for men age 70 and older, the USPSTF believes the risks of routine testing outweigh the benefits. The USPSTF does not address PSA screening in men under age 55, but the American Cancer Society advises that men at average risk for prostate cancer discuss screening with their doctors beginning at age 50 and that men at high risk consider screening at age 45.

Bottom line: Men should discuss the pros and cons of PSA testing with their doctors.

Who might need it: Those with a family history of prostate cancer—particularly a cancer that affected a close relative, such as a sibling or parent—may want to get tested.

What Your Genes Say About Your Health

Mary Freivogel, president of the National Society of Genetic Counselors, Chicago, Illinois.

More and more research is zeroing in on genetic components that can play a role in a variety of health problems. Genetic testing is available for conditions ranging from certain heart disorders to Alzheimer's disease—and is increasingly being used for common cancers.

Underutilized resource: Genetic counseling can help patients (and their families) understand the potential benefits—and complex issues—that may arise with genetic testing.

Examples: Someone with colon cancer may have a gene mutation that could increase cancer risks for his/her close relatives. Testing can show whether this is the case—and family members might (or might not) want to know about it. Or a woman who discovers early in life that she has a particular type of hereditary colon cancer will know that she's at increased risk for uterine and ovarian cancer. She might get more frequent screenings or decide to have her ovaries/uterus removed.

Family members who get tested and learn they have a heightened cancer risk might become more committed to taking precautions—for example, getting earlier screenings.

Smart approach: Seeing a genetic counselor before committing to testing can help you sort out the pros and cons. To find a genetic counselor in your area, consult FindaGenetic Counselor.com.

Get *Faster* Test Results

Charles B. Inlander, a consumer advocate and health-care consultant based in Fogelsville, Pennsylvania. He was founding president of the nonprofit People's Medical Society, a consumer advocacy organization credited with key improvements in the quality of US health care.

Sometimes, *waiting* for your medical test results can cause more anxiety than the actual findings. That's particularly true if you or your doctor suspects that you might have a problem. The longer you have to wait, the more worried you become. But it doesn't have to be that way. *Here are the smart steps you can take to get your test results as soon as possible...*

• **Get immediate results.** Immediate results may sound like a very high order, but they are possible. The key is to work closely with your doctor. It probably sounds obvious, but the first step is to let your doctor know that you want to get results as soon as possible—either good or bad news. This increases the chance that your doctor will pass results on quickly to you and that he/she will recommend a lab or center that is known for providing quick results.

Don't assume that you have to wait...and wait. For imaging tests, such as mammograms and other scans, many imaging centers will give you the radiologist-reviewed results on the spot. Ask your doctor to recommend such imaging centers in your area. Or call several centers near you and ask what their policies are on giving patients immediate results. Other centers will let you know if everything is OK but tell you to contact your doctor if there is a problem. In that case, you should *immediately* call your physician to discuss the results.

My story: When an MRI of my brain found I had a tumor a while back, the results were sent to my physician while I was at the imaging center, and we talked on the phone while I was still there about the next steps.

• **Find out when results will be available.** Of course, not all test results are immediately available. Blood work and other types of tests, such as tissue analysis of a biopsy, can often take several days or even weeks to be analyzed by a pathologist or other medical professional. And quite often your doctor will need to review the results and even discuss them with the pathologist and/or other physicians to make an accurate interpretation of the results. But you can still help move things along by calling your doctor's office as soon as you have completed the test. Let the office know what test you had...where it was done...when it was done...and the best way to reach you as soon as the doctor has the results. Again, let the doctor's office know that you want the results as soon as possible.

Note: If you have a condition, such as cancer, that may require frequent tests and/or biopsies that tend to take a long time for results, be sure to ask your doctor at your follow-up appointments if any future tests are likely or needed and if you should have them sooner rather than later.

• **Go online.** Most major hospitals and large medical practices, along with laboratories and imaging centers that are owned or affiliated with them, now make test results available to the patient online at the same time they become available to the doctor. *Important:* The onus is on you to sign up or register for this service. Ask the doctors, hospitals, labs and imaging centers that you use if they offer such online services and how you can enroll.

Helpful: After you have a test but before you get the results, schedule an appointment with your doctor to go over the results.

Note: Some doctors prefer to do this over the phone, which is fine. But be sure to speak directly with the doctor, especially if the results are worrisome.

What to Do When an Imaging Test Finds an Unexpected Abnormality

Stella K. Kang, MD, MS, an assistant professor of radiology and population health at NYU Langone Medical Center in New York City. She is author or coauthor of more than two dozen scientific papers that have been published in the *Journal of the American College of Radiology, Clinical Oncology* and other leading medical journals.

You're having abdominal pain and visit your primary care physician. As part of the workup, your doctor orders a CT scan of your abdomen and pelvis to rule out possible causes, such as an infection. The results arrive two days later, and there's nothing obviously wrong with your bowels. *But...*

In the report accompanying the scan, the radiologist noted an *incidental finding* (IF)—a spot on your kidney that was "too small to characterize."

Is it a harmless cyst…or a tumor that might grow and spread if left untreated? Should your doctor ignore it for now…or order more tests, possibly opening a medical Pandora's box that could perhaps entail a biopsy and raise radiation exposure? More and more patients and doctors are facing such questions.

Incidental findings—when a physician investigating a specific problem finds *another* possible problem (known in doctor-speak as an "incidentaloma")—are on the rise, in part because scanning technology is more precise than ever before.

Eye-opening statistics: On average, about 40% of all scans reveal an incidental finding. For two common imaging tests—CT of the abdomen and pelvis…and CT of the thorax (below the neck and above the abdomen)—IFs are now detected 61% and 55% of the time, respectively. *Basic types of IFs…*

• **High risk.** This type could cause real harm, even death, if it's not discovered and dealt with. *Example:* A large cancerous kidney tumor.

• **Intermediate risk.** This type has some potential to cause future harm, with a need for medication or other treatment. *Example:* A kidney stone that is asymptomatic.

• **Low risk.** This type has a greater than 99% chance of never causing harm. *Example:* A benign kidney cyst, which does not interfere with kidney function.

Why it gets tricky: Even though the discovery of an abnormality can sometimes be lifesaving (when an asymptomatic malignancy is found, for example), there are few medical standards for reporting and managing IFs—often leading to unnecessary testing and treatment of low- and intermediate-risk IFs.

BEST STRATEGIES

Here are ways to increase the likelihood that IFs are responded to safely and effectively—but unnecessary follow-up is avoided…

• **If your doctor orders any type of imaging test (X-ray, CT, PET or MRI scan, for example), ask about the likelihood of an IF.** You should know *before* the test whether or not it's likely to uncover an IF—so you're less apt to be surprised and frightened if an IF is found.

Helpful: Before the test, ask your doctor to give you a quick overview of high-, intermediate- and low-risk IFs commonly produced by the test.

To ensure that you are made aware of any IFs from an imaging test, ask to receive a copy of the radiologist's report so that you can discuss it with your doctor.

• **Partner with your primary care doctor.** With its array of specialists and subspecialists, medical care is increasingly fractured—making it more likely that specialist-ordered testing will follow the discovery of any IF, including those that are intermediate- and low-risk.

Best: Even if a specialist ordered the test, talk over the results with your primary care physician. He/she is likely to have a sense of your overall health and preferences regarding medical interventions such as testing.

• **If there's an IF, get an *accurate* description of the risk.** Sometimes a doctor will talk in vague terms about the risk from an IF—for example, "It's probably not going to hurt you." But that's not enough information to effectively partner with your doctor in deciding if more testing is appropriate.

Best: Ask for a statistical estimation of risk. Is the likelihood of harm (such as cancer that could metastasize or an enlarged blood vessel that could rupture) from the IF one out of 10? One out of 1,000? If the numerical level of risk is hard to understand, ask the doctor to explain it another way.

• **Ask if the American College of Radiology (ACR) recommends further imaging for this type of IF.** The ACR, the professional organization for radiologists, has guidelines for further investigation of some of the most common IFs, such as thyroid nodules, ovarian nodules and IFs discovered during abdominal CTs.

Best: Ask your physician if there are ACR guidelines for your IF and if he is following them.*

• **Ask your doctor to consult with the radiologist.** When certain IFs don't fall under ACR guidelines, radiologists don't always agree about their significance or management. One radiologist might recommend further testing. Another might say no additional testing is necessary. A third might not make a recommendation, letting the primary care physician decide what to do next.

Best: If your test has an IF with unclear implications for management, your doctor might schedule a joint consultation with the radiologist so the three of you can talk through your options—a strategy that is effective but underutilized.

• **Get a second opinion.** When a lesion is indeterminate (unclear in importance), consider asking your doctor to have another radiologist take a look at the result.

Best: Ask your doctor to recommend a consultation with a subspecialist—for instance, if the IF is on the kidney, talk to a radiologist who is expert in examining the kidney.

WHEN FOLLOW-UP IS NEEDED

Some IFs require follow-up testing and medical care. *Discuss follow-up options with your doctor for...*

• **Lung nodules—**a risk factor for lung cancer—found during a CT of the thorax.

• **Coronary artery calcification—**a risk factor for a heart attack—detected during a CT of the chest or a CT of the abdomen and pelvis.

• **A solid lesion on an ovary,** which could be a tumor, revealed by an abdominal and pelvic CT.

• **Enlarged lymph nodes,** which may be related to infection or malignancy, found during a pelvic MRI.

• **Enlarged aorta (aneurysm) found by an abdominal CT.** If this major blood vessel is enlarged, you could be at increased risk for it to break open and cause severe bleeding that could be fatal.

*To view the American College of Radiology's guidelines on incidental findings, go to Nucradshare.com/images/Misc/ACR%20Incidental%20Findings%20Guidelines.pdf.

Just Diagnosed with Cancer? Steps to Manage This Difficult Time

Mark J. Fesler, MD, an assistant professor of hematology and medical oncology at Saint Louis University Cancer Center and director of the Blood and Marrow Transplant Program at SSM Health Saint Louis University Hospital.

Getting a diagnosis of cancer is one of the scariest, most stressful situations a person can experience. Reeling from the distressing news and overcome with emotion, virtually all new cancer patients find it hard to know exactly what actions should be taken next.

What works best: Following certain steps the *first week* after a cancer diagnosis greatly reduces stress and sets the course for a treatment plan that involves good decision-making, stronger support systems and perhaps even an improved chance of recovery. The steps below can be adapted to each patient's personal situation, but they will help bring order to what can otherwise be a chaotic and tremendously challenging time...

• **Don't keep your cancer a secret.** Many patients keep their diagnosis to themselves at first. They may be in denial, don't have all the facts yet and/or don't want to worry loved ones. But it's much better to reach out to key family members and close friends *right away.*

Meet with close family members and friends individually or in a group to share your diagnosis and let them know that you would appreciate their support. You can give them more information at a later time. You could also call your friends and family members to give them the news, but don't communicate this information via text or social media.

The love and moral support as well as practical help with meals and rides that they can give will lessen your burden and anxiety much more than you realize.

• **See an oncologist within the first week after diagnosis.** There's a tremendous amount of anxiety during the time between the cancer diagnosis and the initial visit with an oncologist. I have observed that patients who see their oncologists right away tend to be less anxious.

Oncologists should make it a point to see newly diagnosed patients quickly, certainly within a week of diagnosis and sometimes even sooner. You should try to see at least one oncologist who specializes in your specific cancer subtype, for example, a gynecologic oncologist—if not on the first appointment, then during a second opinion (see below).

At the appointment, you'll get detailed information about the stage of your cancer...where it's located in your body...what kind of prognosis to expect...what treatment is most appropriate...and how it will affect your life. Having this knowledge often helps to ease anxiety.

To prepare for your appointment...

Write down a list of questions. You no doubt will have questions for the oncologist based on the initial conversation with your doctor. Be sure to write them down so that you don't forget them during the stress of your appointment.

In preparation for your appointment, you may also want to research your condition online, but restrict your browsing to well-respected sites, such as Cancer.gov (National Cancer Institute)...Cancer.org (American Cancer Society)...and Cancer.net (American Society of Clinical Oncology).

Important: Be cautious about drawing conclusions from information on the web. Data on cancer can be complicated, and treatments can change over a short period of time. And prognoses and other stats are usually based on medians or averages. Use the information you glean from the web to add to your list of questions for the oncologist.

Bring one to three people with you to the first oncologist visit. Patients are often so emotionally overwhelmed by the diagnosis that their brains do not process all the important information that's given to them during the appointment. Loved ones and/or friends can help listen, take notes and ask questions. They may also be able to tell the doctor about symptoms they've noticed that the patient isn't even aware of. I advise bringing as many as three loved ones or close friends because they can help the patient in different ways and will ask different questions. With your doctor's permission, you could also record the appointment (a recorder app on your smartphone is easy to use).

• **Consider a second opinion.** Ideally, you should get a second opinion before treatment begins, and it should be from a doctor not affiliated with the first. You should not feel uncomfortable telling your doctor about your plans for a second opinion—in the case of cancer, it's a very common practice and is even required by some insurance providers. Your doctor may facilitate the process of getting a second opinion with an unaffiliated doctor.

Having information you already received corroborated by a second opinion can be reassuring. And if the second opinion conflicts with the first, it's better to know that sooner than later. Insurance will usually cover the cost of a second opinion, but check with your insurance company or your insurance case manager, if you have one.

• **Address your stress.** After a cancer diagnosis, you may suffer from anxiety and/or lack of sleep. To take care of yourself, cut back on nonessential tasks so that you can focus on activities that will help relieve stress, such as getting more exercise and eating well. Talk to your doctor about the best exercise and diet for your specific situation.

Be sure to tell your doctor about any anxiety or depression you're feeling. He/she may refer you to a mental health provider, such as a therapist, psychologist or psychiatrist, and/or may prescribe a short-term medication, such as *alprazolam* (Xanax), to relieve anxiety and help you get some rest.

Also: Support groups can be beneficial. A good resource is Cancer.net (click on "Coping with Cancer," then on "Finding Support and Information" and finally on "Support Groups"). But some patients feel that support groups make them overly consumed by their diagnosis and choose not to join one. That's

OK—the patient should decide the form of support that is best for him.

• **Learn about clinical trials.** Even though most people assume that clinical trials enroll only patients who are in very advanced stages of their illnesses, that's not true. There are clinical trials designed for different types and stages of cancer, but they may have very specific requirements. That's why you should ask your doctor early on about clinical trials that may be right for your case.

• **Ask about support services.** Keeping up with all the details of your illness can be overwhelming. A social worker can help with health insurance, financial aid, etc., free of charge. The medical center where your doctor practices may have social workers on staff or be able to refer you to one.

Doctor's Gender May Matter

Among more than one million patients age 65 and older who were treated for sepsis, pneumonia or other conditions, those with female internists were 4% less likely to die prematurely and 5% less likely to be readmitted to the hospital within 30 days than those with male doctors.

Possible reason: Previous studies have suggested that women internists may be more likely to have better communication with patients and to follow established recommendations for care.

Ashish Jha, MD, MPH, professor of health policy, Harvard T.H. Chan School of Public Health, Boston.

Don't Forget to Discuss This with Your Doctor...

Older adults tend not to discuss memory problems with doctors, and doctors often don't raise the subject. Only 25% of adults age 45 or older with memory problems talked about their problems with health-care professionals during routine checkups—and the likelihood of discussing memory concerns declined with advancing age.

Likely reason: Denial and avoidance on the part of both patient and doctor.

Self-defense: Bring up any memory concerns at your annual physical. Memory issues often are not the start of dementia but result from a different, highly treatable cause, such as depression. And memory trouble that is linked to dementia needs to be caught early for treatment to be effective.

Analysis of government data from 2011 on more than 10,000 people by researchers at On Target Health Data, West Suffield, Connecticut, published in *Preventing Chronic Disease.*

Watch Out for Your Doctor's Smartphone: Infection and "Distracted Doctoring" Are Dangers

Peter J. Papadakos, MD, director of critical care medicine at the University of Rochester Medical Center and professor of anesthesiology, neurology, surgery and neurosurgery at the University of Rochester, both located in Rochester, New York. Dr. Papadakos was one of the first experts to identify the potential for distraction from smartphones and to popularize the recent term "distracted doctoring."

If you're like most people, you *love* your smartphone, tablet or laptop. Doctors, nurses and other medical personnel are no different. But when they use these devices in the workplace, does that help or hurt your medical care?

It's true that smartphones, tablets and laptops allow doctors to quickly look up the newest drug information and case studies. Many hospitals and doctors' offices have invested large amounts of money in smartphones, tablets and other computer devices to make staff more efficient and prevent medical errors. And it's great to be able to reach your physician in an emergency during off-hours, since doctors will sometimes share their cell-phone numbers and/or e-mail addresses with patients who require extra attention.

But there can also be dangerous downsides for the patient when medical staff has constant access to this type of technology.

To find out what patients can do to protect themselves, we spoke to Peter J. Papadakos, MD, director of critical care medicine at the University of Rochester Medical Center and an expert on the impact of technology on medical care.

TAKE NOTE...

Deaths Due to Medical Error

Medical error is the third-leading cause of death in the US. More than 250,000 people die each year due to medical errors. Only heart disease and cancer cause more deaths annually.

Analysis of studies of medical death rate data from 2000 through 2008 by researchers at The Johns Hopkins University School of Medicine, Baltimore, published in *BMJ*.

A NEW DANGER

Nearly 90% of all physicians currently use smartphones or tablets while at work. *The most significant potential dangers to patients include...*

- **Bacterial contamination.** Although there are many nonsterile surfaces in a health-care setting, cell phones are of particular concern because they are typically handled so often. When the cell phones of orthopedic surgeons in the operating room were tested, a whopping 83% of the phones had infection-causing bacteria on them, according to a study that was published in *The Journal of Bone & Joint Surgery*.

Self-defense: When admitted to a hospital, ask what the guidelines are for disinfecting electronic devices, particularly any that are brought into and handled in an operating room. Some hospitals now have ultraviolet (UV) sterilizing devices that are 99.9% effective at decontaminating objects in 10 seconds.

If your doctor is holding a cell phone or other personal device, ask him/her if the device was cleaned before attending to you and make sure the doctor washes his hands as well.

Also: When visiting someone in the hospital, don't pull out your cell phone to show photos in an effort to cheer up the patient. Better yet, leave your cell phone at home or in the car. If you are a patient or visitor in the hospital and feel you need your phone, clean it regularly with sanitizing wipes (such as Wireless Wipes) or a UV sterilizing device for cell phones.

- **Interruptions to workflow and distractions.** Researchers at Oregon State University and the Oregon Health & Science University tested the impact of distractions on residents performing a simulated gallbladder surgery. When the surgeons were interrupted by a cell-phone ring, the sound of a dropped metal tray clanging or other distraction, 44% made serious errors that could have led to a fatality, including damage to organs and arteries. Only one surgeon made a mistake when there were no interruptions.

Self-defense: To protect yourself from such forms of "distracted doctoring," ask your hospital whether it has a policy on the safe use of electronic devices throughout the hospital, and ask for a copy if it does. If electronic devices are allowed in the operating room, share your concerns with your surgical team.

At the University of Rochester Medical Center, we have a "Code of eConduct" to minimize the distractions caused by devices including smartphones and tablets. Guidelines include that devices must be in "silent" mode (no ringing or vibrating) when in a patient's room... work-issued devices should not be used for personal use...and all personal business must be conducted only in break rooms and out of view of patients.

- **Addiction.** Just like everyone else, many doctors and other health-care professionals do not even realize how addicted they are to their smartphones and social media.

In a survey of more than 400 perfusionists (technicians who operate heart-lung bypass machines during heart surgery), more than half admitted that they had used a cell phone during heart bypass procedures to access their e-mail, surf the Internet and use social networking sites.

While 78% of the technicians said that cell phones could potentially pose a safety risk to patients, when asked about speaking on the phone and texting, only 42% and 52% of them said that these, respectively, were always unsafe practices. Paradoxically, while 93% reported that they were not distracted by using their phones, 34% said that they had witnessed other perfusionists being distracted by their phones or texting during procedures.

In order to make health-care professionals more aware of a possible addiction to technology, my colleagues and I at the University of Rochester modified a widely used screening survey for alcoholism to help gauge people's addiction to their phones, texting and/or social media.

• **iPatient.** When doctors are fixated on the computerized record of a patient, what I call an "iPatient," they miss important information such as speech patterns and body language.

Self-defense: Politely ask your doctor to put the device away for a few minutes and listen to you.

Beware These Dental Treatments

Fred Quarnstrom, DDS, a dentist with Beacon Hill Dental Associates in Seattle and coauthor of *Open Wider: Your Wallet, Not Your Mouth—Everything You Need to Know When You Visit the Dentist.* OpenWider.org

Dentists sometimes recommend treatments that might not be needed. Large dental chains often require their dentists to meet a specific quota...today's new dentists graduate from dental school with huge debt...and dental practices must purchase expensive equipment, all of which create pressure to maximize income. *Be cautious if your dentist suggests...*

• **Deep cleaning.** Also called "scaling," this typically costs $700 or more, often is not well-covered by dental insurance and is appropriate only for patients who have major periodontal problems—that is, problems with their gums or the bones that support their teeth.

Response: If your dentist recommends deep cleaning and you do not have a history of gum problems, ask to see your periodontal chart. If the number five or higher is listed for some of your teeth, you likely have experienced losses to the tissue and bone around those teeth and deep cleaning might be warranted. If not, seek a second opinion.

• **Drilling and filling a cavity identified only by laser.** "Laser decay finders" have their place in dentistry, but if your dentist can't see decay on your X-ray, there is no reason to treat the cavity, at least for now.

Response: If your dentist says you have a cavity that requires treatment, ask to see this cavity on your X-ray. There should be an obvious dark spot, likely triangular in shape. If you don't see this, get a second opinion.

• **Extensive procedures during your first visit.** It's a red flag if you have never needed extensive dental work in the past...you go to a new dentist for just a cleaning or what seems to you like a relatively small problem...and your new dentist says you require extensive work.

Response: Get a second opinion.

The Trouble with Online Symptom Checkers

Ateev Mehrotra, MD, MPH, associate professor of health-care policy and medicine, Harvard Medical School, and hospitalist, Beth Israel Deaconess Medical Center, both in Boston. He was lead investigator of "Comparison of Physician and Computer Diagnostic Accuracy," a study published in *JAMA Internal Medicine.*

Computers are amazing. They can beat world-class chess champions. But they can't yet replace your doctor. Case in point—online symptom checkers.

The checkers, free at sites such as WebMD, Mayo Clinic and the American Academy of Pediatrics and through free smartphone apps such as AskMD and iTriage, are powered by pretty sophisticated medical algorithms.

If you are like millions of other people, you may have turned to one of these to figure out what's triggering a chronic cough or repeated headaches, a rash, insomnia or unexplained weight gain or loss.

These programs are easy to use—you just plug in one or more symptoms, the program asks you a few questions and then it suggests what condition or conditions you might have. The checkers make recommendations, too, such as what to do to feel better and whether to see your doctor—or head immediately to the ER. While symptom checkers may not explicitly promise to give you a diagnosis, it's become increasingly common for people to turn to them to try to figure out what's causing their symptoms.

A smarter approach: Don't rely on these programs to help you figure out what's wrong with you. While they may have some educational value, the latest research finds that they are not only unlikely to give you the most probable cause of your symptoms but also prone to putting people in a panic and sending them for urgent medical care when it is not needed. They do have a place, however—if you know the smart way to use them.

DIAGNOSTIC ROBOTS VS. DOCTORS

In the first study to compare the diagnostic accuracy of these online tools with the accuracy of live MDs, researchers at Harvard Medical School asked 234 doctors trained in internal medicine, family practice or pediatrics to evaluate 45 "clinical vignettes"—symptoms and medical histories of hypothetical patients—and give the most likely diagnosis plus two additional possibilities for each patient. The conditions ranged from common to uncommon, from minor to life-threatening—for example, canker sores to pulmonary embolism (a very dangerous blood clot in the lung).

Results: The white coats won by a mile. Computerized symptom checkers identified the most likely correct diagnosis only 34% of the time...doctors, 72% of the time. Counting all three suggested diagnoses, checkers included a correct diagnosis only 51% of the time—but docs included a correct diagnosis 84% of the time. (In case you were wondering, no particular symptom checker was better than the others.)

More findings from the study...

- **For the mildest diseases,** the automated symptom checkers did a little better, nailing 40% of the cases on the first try. But docs nailed 65%.
- **For the most common diseases,** checkers got 39% versus 70% for doctors.
- **For acute illnesses**—the kind that really need immediate attention—checkers guessed right only 24% of the time...doctors, 79%. That's a huge difference and could make a big impact on a patient's life.
- **For the rarest diseases,** checkers got it right only 28% of the time versus 76% for doctors.

THE ART OF DIAGNOSIS

It's not that doctors have reached diagnostic perfection, either. While they beat the technology tested in the Harvard study, they still failed to give the right diagnosis from three options in about 15% of the cases, which is consistent with previous estimates of human misdiagnoses.

A goal of the study was to see whether computers could help doctors get better at diagnosis. One way to improve is for the programs to build in data from epidemiology—real-time information about the frequency of illness in the community. After all, if you see your doctor with digestive ills and he/she knows that there's a GI infection going around town, that may help target the diagnosis. Ideally, as the checkers improve, they'll help doctors improve their diagnostic skills—and help the public, too.

In the meantime, patients should exercise extreme caution in using these programs. They can play a role if they help you educate yourself about *possible* causes of your symptoms—and that prompts a discussion with your doctor. That is, use them to educate yourself so that you can ask smart questions. But for a real diagnosis, there's no substitute for a real doctor.

Better Telephone Therapy

Adults living in rural areas often have trouble getting to therapists for mental health treatment.

Recent study: Adults over age 60 with generalized anxiety disorder who received at least nine sessions of cognitive behavioral therapy (CBT) by telephone reported that their symptoms were reduced more than those who got only traditional talk therapy on the phone. CBT focuses on symptom recognition, coping strategies, relaxation and problem-solving.

For more information on CBT by phone: Go to PsychCentral.com or APA.org.

Gretchen A. Brenes, PhD, professor of psychiatry and behavioral medicine, Wake Forest School of Medicine, Winston-Salem, North Carolina.

How Your Doctor's Free Lunch Affects Treatment

Rebecca Shannonhouse, editor, *Bottom Line Health*, 3 Landmark Square, Stamford, Connecticut. BottomLineInc.com

By now, you've likely heard about pharmaceutical companies that try to earn a little goodwill (and perhaps coax a doctor to prescribe a costly brand-name drug over a cheaper generic) by giving him/her freebies, such as a free lunch. Doctors who accept such gifts insist that their medical decisions aren't influenced by company freebies.

Now: Recent research tells a different story. A study recently published in *JAMA Internal Medicine* found that doctors who are given a single free meal were 52% to 70% more likely to prescribe brand-name drugs for hypertension...more than twice as likely to prescribe a brand-name antidepressant...and 18% more likely to prescribe a brand-name statin.

Sometimes a brand-name drug makes sense. Maybe a generic isn't available...or you've tried a generic in the past without success. But you have to wonder why doctors who have taken drug-company payouts are so much more likely to prescribe a lot of these drugs. What can you do?

Check your doctor's history: Drug companies are required by law to disclose physician payments. Search for your doctor's name at Projects.Propublica.org/docdollars.

If you see that your doctor regularly receives money from drug companies (for speaking engagements, meals and/or travel expenses, for example), you may want to discuss this practice with him. Listen carefully to your doctor's response...if there's an air of defensiveness in the reply, you should probably keep a close eye on what you're prescribed—and perhaps even look for a new doctor.

When Drugs Are Too Pricey

Charles B. Inlander, a consumer advocate and healthcare consultant based in Fogelsville, Pennsylvania. He was founding president of the nonprofit People's Medical Society, a consumer advocacy organization credited with key improvements in the quality of US health care, and is author or coauthor of more than 20 consumer-health books.

I recently heard from a woman whose ophthalmologist prescribed a drug for her to clear up an eye infection. When the pharmacist told her that the 10-day supply cost $400 and her drug plan did not cover it, she decided not to fill the prescription. Fortunately, she then called her doctor, who prescribed another drug. It cost her $10 out-of-pocket and worked fine.

This woman's experience just goes to show that even if you have prescription drug insurance through a Medicare Part D plan, a Medicare Advantage plan or a plan provided by your employer or purchased on your own, the out-of-pocket costs for many drugs can be *overwhelming*. On top of that, insurance companies that provide these plans are notorious for changing the terms of coverage even while your plan is in effect—removing a drug from their list of covered medications, for example. But there are ways that you can protect yourself. *Here's how to get the drugs you need at a price you can afford…*

• **Keep up to date.** If you have prescription drug insurance, check the insurer's list of covered drugs (it's called the formulary) at least once every three months. This helps you stay ahead of the game if a notification from the insurer (see below) is ill-timed based on your schedule for refilling a prescription. Find out if the medications you take are still covered and if there are any changes in co-pays for those drugs. It's easy to access the list via your plan's website, but it's smart to call, since websites are often outdated.

If your doctor prescribes a new drug: Call your plan before filling the prescription to see if the drug is on the formulary. If the drug is not covered, ask your doctor if he/she can prescribe an acceptable alternative drug, such as a generic that is on your formulary.

• **Get help from your doctor.** If a drug you are taking is removed from the formulary while you are covered by the plan, the insurer must notify you in writing about the change. You and your doctor have three possible ways to respond. First, your doctor may prescribe another drug that's already on the formulary. Second, your doctor may put you on "step therapy"—that is, a similar drug on the formulary is tried, but you can return to the original drug if the alternative medication does not work. Or third, your doctor can file an exception with the insurer, explaining that only the prescribed drug can effectively treat your condition. If the exception is granted (the answer usually comes within a few days), the plan will continue to cover the drug.

• **Look for free money.** Some of the newer "wonder" drugs are mind-bogglingly expensive. For example, the hepatitis C drug Sovaldi can cost $80,000 or more for a 12-week course of treatment. Even if your insurance covers it, co-payments and deductibles could easily reach $5,000 or more. But there is help. Most pharmaceutical companies have patient-assistance programs for many of their costlier drugs. In most cases, the drugs are provided at no charge or low cost to people who don't have drug coverage and meet the program's qualifications—typically based on income levels and/or liquid assets. Most pharmaceutical companies also offer assistance to people who have drug coverage but are unable to afford the co-payments and deductibles.

My advice: To check out patient-assistance programs for any drug, go to RxAssist.org or Medicare.gov/pharmaceutical-assistance-program. This step could save you hundreds or even thousands of dollars!

Expired Meds OK?

An FDA review of 122 different drugs found that 88% were still effective a year past their dates of expiration. In general, prescription tablet and capsule medications are good for one year from the date that they are dispensed from the pharmacy…over-the-counter drugs for a year after you open them. However, these medications may have some potency after that. Powders that are mixed with water to make a liquid solution just before being given to the patient are normally good only for 14 to 21 days. Drugs that require refrigeration are also less likely to remain viable past their expiration dates. You may be able to safely take some drugs that are just past their expiration date, such as *acetaminophen* (Tylenol), but never use any critical medicine, such as insulin, that has expired.

Amy Tiemeier, PharmD, associate professor of pharmacy practice, St. Louis College of Pharmacy.

BETTER WAY…

Don't Distract the Nurse!

Don't talk to the nurse when he/she is preparing your medications while you are in the hospital. Each interruption raises the risk for a medication error by 12%.

Sally Rafie, PharmD, hospital pharmacist at UC San Diego Health System, quoted in *Reader's Digest*.

Deadly Drug Combo

Many doctors are not aware that the following common drug combination can be deadly. Opioids, such as Percocet and OxyContin, and benzodiazepines, such as Valium and Xanax, often are prescribed together for pain and spasms. But combining the two medicines can cause slow, shallow breathing, which can lead to oxygen deprivation, causing organ failure, brain injury and death.

Lewis S. Nelson, MD, a professor in the Ronald O. Perelman Department of Emergency Medicine, NYU Langone Medical Center, New York City.

Antibiotics and Delirium

More than 50 of the most commonly prescribed antibiotics, which include *sulfonamides* (such as Bactrim) and *fluoroquinolones* (such as Cipro), were linked to temporary mental confusion (delirium) in a review of nearly 400 patients (hospitalized and outpatient).

Self-defense: If you're taking an antibiotic and experience symptoms of delirium, such as disorientation, agitation or social withdrawal, a loved one should talk to your doctor about your medication.

Shamik Bhattacharyya, MD, instructor in neurology, Harvard Medical School, Boston.

How to Choose the Right Hospital for You

Steven Z. Kussin, MD, gastroenterologist and founder of the Shared Decision Center of Central New York. He has taught at Albert Einstein College of Medicine and Columbia College of Physicians and Surgeons, both in New York City. He is author of *Doctor, Your Patient Will See You Now: Gaining the Upper Hand in Your Medical Care.* He appears on WKTV in Utica, New York, as The Medical Advocate.

Sooner or later, nearly everyone winds up in a hospital. It might be for testing...an ER visit...or treatment for serious illness.

If you get hit by a bus, the best hospital is the closest one. Fortunately, most health problems aren't that pressing. It makes sense to choose a hospital with the best record for treating patients with your particular condition.

How can you tell which hospital? It may not be easy. You cannot trust the billboards that appear in metropolitan areas. (Hospitals and other health-care facilities spend billions on advertising every year.) Recommendations from friends and family members generally are based on limited anecdotes and are not authoritative. Even your doctor might not have the best advice. *Here's how to find the right hospital for you...*

DIFFERENCES MATTER

People spend more time shopping for flat-screen TVs than choosing hospitals. They just assume that all hospitals provide more-or-less equal care.

They don't. One study found that heart attack patients who went to higher-quality hospitals had a 1% increase in survival. That is significant in itself, and for patients who need procedures for particular conditions such as some cancers or abdominal aortic aneurysms, the differences are starker. There might be a three- or four-fold difference in survival and complication rates between great and so-so hospitals.

CHOOSE THE BEST

Everyone wants to use a hospital that's close to home. Your local hospital may be superb, but you can't count on it.

To find the best hospital, investigate the following...

- **Web-based lookups.** There are many resources to choose from including...
  - Medicare's Hospital Compare (Medicare.gov/hospitalcompare)
  - Why Not the Best (WNTB.org)
  - The Leapfrog Group (LeapfrogGroup.org).

These and other sites use publically available information to rate hospitals on various measures of performance—death rates from serious conditions (such as heart failure and pneumonia)...frequency of hospital-acquired infections...patient satisfaction...etc.

TAKE NOTE...

Best Hospital in the US

The best hospital in the US is Mayo Clinic, according to *US News & World Report*. The Rochester, Minnesota, clinic earned an overall top ranking plus first place for eight of 16 specialty areas. Second was the Cleveland Clinic, followed by Massachusetts General Hospital in Boston...Johns Hopkins Hospital in Baltimore...and UCLA Medical Center, Los Angeles. Nearly 5,000 US medical centers were compared in 16 specialties and nine conditions and procedures. Evaluators looked at patient survival rates and infection rates...quality of nursing staff...and patient satisfaction.

To see the full list: Go to Health.USNews.com/best-hospitals.

US News & World Report study, "Best Hospitals 2016–17."

On these websites, you plug in your zip code to find hospitals in your area. You then can check to see how well (or poorly) each hospital manages patients with various conditions.

These web-based services are useful even when they don't discuss your particular condition. Some hospitals cultivate a *culture of excellence*. If they rate highly in one area, they're more likely to do well in others.

• **Hospitals farther away.** When patients are given a choice, they almost always choose the hospital that's closest to home. It might be the best hospital in your area—but a better one might be just a little farther away.

Surgical death rates tend to be higher at small, local hospitals than at regional medical centers. Hospitals that treat large numbers of select patients do better than those that treat fewer. If you're seriously ill and need a risky procedure, you should be willing to drive the extra miles to get the best possible care.

In one interesting study, patients were given a hypothetical scenario. They were asked to imagine that they had pancreatic cancer and needed surgery...and they could choose among different hospitals. All of the patients preferred having surgery locally if the risk of dying was the same as at a regional hospital. But when they were told that the risk of dying was twice as high at a local hospital, 45% *still* chose to stay close to home!

Do not use a second-rate hospital just because you are reluctant to travel. For routine procedures, it probably does not matter—the risks will be negligible wherever you go. But for serious illnesses or higher-risk procedures, a large, regional medical center probably will be the safer choice.

• **Number of patients.** Suppose that you need a back operation or a bypass procedure. Do you want to go to a hospital that does a handful of procedures a year? Or should you choose one that packs them in by the hundreds?

An analysis by *US News & World Report* found that the risk for death for patients with congestive heart failure and chronic obstructive pulmonary disease was 20% higher at facilities that saw the fewest patients.

My advice: Choose a hospital that treats a lot of patients with your particular condition—ask a hospital administrator or patient-care supervisor how many of your procedures are done each year. If you can't get this information, ask the surgeon how many he/she does. One study found that endocrine surgeons who did 100 or more operations a year accounted for 5% of total complications, while those who did three or fewer a year accounted for 32%.

• **Doctor qualifications.** Your doctor's experience is just as important as your hospital's. As mentioned above, doctors who see a lot of patients with similar conditions tend to have better track records. Those who work at top medical centers usually are better than those at smaller facilities—but not always.

ProPublica (a nonprofit investigative news service) looked at data from more than 2.3 million Medicare patients. The analysis revealed that a small number of surgeons accounted for about 25% of all surgical complications. Some had complication rates that were two or three times the national average, and some of them worked at the nation's most prestigious medical centers.

It's difficult to assess a doctor's competence. One thing you can do is ask other doctors, including your own, about a particular doctor's expertise. In addition, you can check out his/her education on the Web. It might sound snobbish, but other things being equal, I'd prefer to see a doctor who went to a great college, medical school and training program rather than lower-tier institutions.

You also can ask a prospective surgeon about his/her success and failure rate and rates of complications. Some surgeons won't discuss these matters. The good ones probably will be proud to do so.

Helpful resource: Healthgrades.com allows you to enter medical conditions and procedures into a search window and then provides the doctors who treat them and their Healthgrades rratings.

• **Patient satisfaction.** Patient satisfaction is not a perfect proxy for quality, but you might glean some useful information. Check the patient satisfaction measures on hospital-comparison websites.

How long did it take for nurses to answer calls? Were the doctors warm or brusque? Was the food delicious or dreadful? These might seem like minor considerations, but research has shown that patient satisfaction and good health care often go together.

Hospital Stay? Remember, You're the Customer!

Charles B. Inlander, a consumer advocate and health-care consultant based in Fogelsville, Pennsylvania. He was founding president of the nonprofit People's Medical Society, a consumer advocacy organization credited with key improvements in the quality of US health care, and is author or coauthor of more than 20 consumer-health books.

For most of us, a hospital stay feels like being in custody. We're awakened at all hours to have our temperature taken. We're carted off for a test and wait for more than an hour before it's given. Our doctor, who was supposed to be there at 9 am, doesn't show up until 3 pm. Being in the hospital can definitely make you feel like a second-class citizen. But it doesn't have to be that way. In fact, you can take charge of much of your hospital stay and command the respect you deserve by remembering that you're the customer and that hospital personnel (including doctors) are working for you. *What to do...*

• **Make signs.** Today's hospitals are bigger and busier than ever. This means that you may not see the same nurses, aides or even in-house doctors on each day of your stay. As a result, the staff barely gets to know you. And unless they scrupulously review your complete record (which rarely happens), they may not know that you have only one kidney, are allergic to certain medications or that you are hard of hearing. So before you go to the hospital, make bold-lettered signs that you or a family member can tape above your hospital bed saying, for example: "ALLERGIC TO PENICILLIN" or "Hard of hearing—SPEAK UP."

• **Use the phone.** When I was in the hospital some time ago, the nurses were not responding when I pushed the "call button." Finally, I picked up the bedside telephone, dialed the hospital operator and asked to be connected to my unit's nurse station. Someone picked up right away, and I told her that I needed help. From that point on, I had a quick response whenever I pushed the button.

Insider tip: Use the bedside phone to call for what you need. If you have an unanswered question about your care, call your personal doctor at his/her office. Or if you have a question about a medication that you are being given, call the hospital pharmacy. You'll usually get quick answers from a knowledgeable pharmacist.

• **Bring your own creature comforts.** Hospitals are notoriously noisy places. For most of us, it's hard to sleep with all the endless clatter and chatter. So bring your own earplugs, noise-reducing headphones or a portable DVD player and headset to help block out disturbing noises.

Another comfort: Bring a favorite pillow and/or cozy quilt.

Also: You can bring your own regularly used medications with you, including vitamins. This could save you a bundle if you have a high-deductible insurance policy, since the same hospital drugs are usually *much* more costly. For example, the hospital may charge $3 for an over-the-counter baby aspirin that you could buy retail for 3 cents! You may have to sign a waiver absolving the hospital of any liability, but if you can bring the pill yourself, do it.

Insider tip: If you bring your own medications or supplements, just be sure to check with your doctor to make sure that taking them while hospitalized is OK.

• **Don't be afraid to say "NO!"** If someone comes to give you a new drug or take you to a test that you weren't informed about, just say "NO." This puts you in the driver's seat, forcing the hospital to send a doctor or nurse to explain to you who ordered the drug or test and why. If you're satisfied, you can say "yes," but either way, you're in control!

Recover *Much Faster* from Abdominal Surgery

Jeffrey Campsen, MD, surgical director of kidney and pancreas transplantation at University of Utah Health Care in Salt Lake City.

Each year, millions of Americans get abdominal surgery. If you are one of them, you want to get back on your feet as quickly as possible. But many things that patients—and hospitals—do actually *slow down* recovery and can even lead to uncomfortable, sometimes dangerous complications.

Exciting new trend: Many hospitals now employ "enhanced recovery after surgery" (ERAS) protocols for pre-op eating and drinking, pain management and post-op exercise.

Results: Recovery time drops by more than one-third—that means you go home a few days earlier—and complication rates drop, too.

Whether your surgery is to repair a hernia, remove a gallbladder, treat colorectal cancer or have a hysterectomy...whether it's traditional "open" surgery or minimally invasive laparoscopy...these steps can help you recover faster—and better.

BEFORE ELECTIVE SURGERY...

• **Get walking.** Cardiovascular exercise will boost lung capacity and function, which helps you better handle anesthesia. Walk, or do any other aerobic activity that you enjoy, three or four times weekly in the weeks prior to scheduled surgery.

• **Lose weight, if you need to.** The more tissue and fat an incision must cut through, the longer healing and recovery will take.

• **If you have a heart condition,** see your cardiologist, who may need to adjust medications that interfere with surgery. Let your anesthesiologist know about your heart condition, too.

WHILE RECOVERING...

• **Get walking as soon as possible.** Aim for three or four daily walks. Movement allows the lungs to expand, reducing the likelihood of developing pneumonia, a post-surgery risk. It also gets blood moving in the extremities, decreasing the risk for blood clots, a potentially life-threatening complication.

It's also important to protect your abdominal wound for at least the first four to six weeks after surgery to avoid getting a hernia. To do that, when you put stress on your core muscles, such as when you cough or laugh, push a pillow against your abdominal wall over your incision. This will help protect the incision.

• **If you are taking narcotic painkillers, start cutting back.** Your hospital may use nonopioid pain relievers and/or an epidural—

GOOD TO KNOW...

Heart Attack Help

If you have heart attack symptoms, don't use a car to get to the hospital. Call 911 for an ambulance because it will have equipment that can restart your heart if it stops—cardiac arrest is rare but is fatal without prompt treatment. And many dispatchers receiving 911 calls about heart attack symptoms send paramedics who are trained to give patients electrocardiograms (ECGs). The ECG results are then sent to the emergency department of the hospital to help speed treatment on arrival.

Harvard Health Letter, Health.Harvard.edu.

a numbing injection—to help protect bowel function. But you may still be given narcotic medications such as *codeine* or *acetaminophen/oxycodone* (Percocet).

Risk: These drugs slow intestinal functioning, leading to constipation, which is quite troubling after abdominal surgery and can delay recovery time.

What to do: With your doctor's approval, cut the amount of narcotics you take *by half daily until you are off them completely.*

• **Drink liquids—including coffee.** Start drinking water and other liquids as soon as you're allowed so that you can get off IV fluids quickly.

If you drink coffee, you can start that up as well—to ward off caffeine withdrawal symptoms such as headaches.

Important: Be sure that you drink plenty of water to avoid dehydration, which can cause constipation.

Warning: Avoid carbonated drinks at least for the first week—they can cause gas and stomach discomfort.

• **Chew gum.** After abdominal surgery, the digestive system becomes sluggish and can stop working for a few days. It can be uncomfortable and can prolong your hospital stay. In a study published in *Archives of Surgery*, abdominal surgery patients who chewed gum for five to 45 minutes three times a day after surgery had a bowel movement one day sooner.

Why: Chewing gum tricks the body into thinking it is eating, causing the digestive system to start working again.

• **Rock in a rocking chair.** Sitting opens the lungs better than lying flat. But if you can spend part of your sitting time rocking in a rocking chair, the extra activity is beneficial. However, it's best to get up and walk.

• **Before you leave the hospital, discuss with your surgeon what to expect during recovery at home,** what your incision should look like as it heals and how to communicate if you have questions/concerns. Ask if you can send a photo (a "selfie") of your incision if it is red, hot to the touch or has abnormal damage. You may need to use a secure patient portal.

Call your doctor right away if you: Have a fever above 101.5°F, vomit, feel dizzy or think you might pass out.

• **If you do get constipated,** before doing anything on your own, such as taking an enema, talk to your doctor about the best approach so that you don't injure your incision.

GETTING BETTER AT HOME

You'll be able to leave the hospital when you can walk, drink liquids, be off intravenous medications and fluids, and show signs that your digestive system and bowels are moving again. Keep walking every day, and start to eat easy-to-digest, bland foods—for instance, clear liquids, saltine crackers and Jello. If you do all right with those, move on to clear soups, such as broths...and then move on to more solid foods. *Tips...*

• **Don't lift more than 10 pounds.** For at least the first four weeks, straining your core abdominals risks causing a hernia or rupture of sutures. Walking and light exercise are usually fine, but if you feel pressure in the surgical area from any activity, stop. Listen to your body.

• **Go to your two-week post-op visit.** Your surgeon will examine your incision area and, based on how well it is healing, will review what activities you can and can't do.

• **Take the "stomp" test.** Once they're not taking narcotics and can walk around, most patients assume they have the all clear to drive. But a sudden stop could cause you to brake hard. To make sure you're ready to drive, try the "stomp" test.

What to do: Stomp on the ground with the foot you use for the brake. You're unlikely to injure your incision, but go easy. Try a gentle stomp first, and if that doesn't hurt try a harder one. If doing this hurts, the abdominal wall has not healed enough. It usually takes a few weeks before you'll be able to drive.

Shower Sooner After Knee Replacement?

Knee-replacement patients can shower as soon as two days after surgery if their doctors agree. The usual recommendation is to wait 10 days to two weeks after surgery before showering. But researchers found no difference in bacterial cultures of skin next to incisions in patients who waited and those who were allowed to shower 48 hours after surgery.

Study by researchers at Loyola University Chicago Stritch School of Medicine, published in *Journal of Arthroplasty.*

A Furry Visitor to the Hospital

New guidelines adopted by some hospitals allow visits from dogs in special circumstances, such as during a lengthy stay or a final visit with a terminal patient. Many hospitals also use specially trained therapy dogs to help ease patient anxiety. Check with your hospital to find out if it has a program.

Note: Wash your hands or use an alcohol-based hand sanitizer before and after petting any dog.

David Weber, MD, MPH, professor of epidemiology, The University of North Carolina at Chapel Hill.

Is Your Medical Record Wrong?

Charles B. Inlander, a consumer advocate and health-care consultant based in Fogelsville, Pennsylvania. He was founding president of the nonprofit People's Medical Society, a consumer advocacy organization credited with key improvements in the quality of US health care, and is author or coauthor of more than 20 consumer-health books.

You have probably heard plenty about medical errors that happen when the wrong drug is prescribed or a surgeon operates on the wrong body part.

But there's another type of medical error that needs much more attention than it's getting: Errors in your medical records. More than just an administrative snafu, this type of mistake can have serious consequences—it can lead to inappropriate treatment, higher insurance premiums or even difficulty finding a doctor. And with electronic medical records that travel across computer networks in a matter of seconds, a wrong entry in your record can spread widely and be accessed by insurers, other doctors and hospitals before you even know it. *To protect yourself from such mishaps, follow these steps...*

- **Get your records.** Under both state and federal laws, you have the right to receive a copy of your medical records. Most major hospitals, medical practices and insurance networks no longer keep paper records, opting instead for electronic record keeping. And those records are usually made available to you online.

Beware: Not all doctors and hospitals share the same electronic record systems, so you may need to access several different online sources. Ask the doctors and hospitals you have used for access information. If you don't have Internet access, you can ask for paper copies of your medical records—a verbal request usually suffices, but you may need to put it in writing. You may also be asked to pay

BETTER WAY...

Ask Your Doctor to Double-Check Vital Signs

Hospital patients with abnormal vital signs within 24 hours of being discharged had a higher risk for death and/or readmission within 30 days, according to a recent study of almost 33,000 adults.

What to do: Before leaving the hospital, ask your doctor to make sure your temperature, blood pressure, pulse, respiratory rate and oxygen level have been stable for 24 hours.

Oanh Kieu Nguyen, MD, assistant professor of medicine, The University of Texas Southwestern Medical Center, Dallas.

copying fees. To avoid getting overwhelmed by massive records—for example, after a lengthy hospital stay—ask for copies of reports from tests on an ongoing basis and/or request a discharge summary from the hospital.

• **Review your records carefully.** Look for gross errors such as a wrong diagnosis…medications you haven't been prescribed…and/or medical procedures you have never undergone. Also look for anything that contradicts what you may have been told during an office visit. For example, your doctor may have said that your blood pressure is under control, yet the reading listed in your record may indicate that it's not. You'd want to ask your doctor about this—you may need a different medication or change in the dose.

Also: Be sure that your records have your correct contact information and that your name and insurance information, including policy number, are accurate. Such errors could mean the difference between an insurance payment and a denial.

• **Correct errors.** Under federal law, you have the right to correct any error in your medical record. Do it in writing—by either crossing out the wrong information on a copy of the page where the error appears and writing in the correction…or by writing a more detailed explanation. Once the correction is received at the location where the record originated, the provider has 60 days to act on your request. This deadline may be extended by 30 days if the provider gives an explanation for the delay in writing. Technically, the correction is considered an "amendment" to your record—this may mean that the old, wrong information remains with the correction added. Even if your correction is denied, you can submit a letter of disagreement that must be put into your record.

Important: Double-check your record online to ensure that the correction was made, and keep a copy of the correction for yourself to take to medical appointments in case the error lingers in another provider's system.

Rx for Big Hospital Bills

Charles B. Inlander, a consumer advocate and health-care consultant based in Fogelsville, Pennsylvania. He was founding president of the nonprofit People's Medical Society, a consumer advocacy organization credited with key improvements in the quality of US health care, and is author or coauthor of more than 20 consumer-health books.

Recently, a friend received a hospital bill for $80,542.49 for shoulder surgery that required a one-night stay. And that didn't include the doctor bills.

Why are hospital bills so high? Because patients are not being billed just for their stays, they also are paying a share of the hospital's staggering overhead including expensive medical equipment and professionals on hand at all times.

What to do…

• **If you have private health insurance** (or Medicare), your insurer has negotiated a lower rate and you probably will pay "only" your deductible and co-payment.

• **If you do not have health insurance**—or your insurance doesn't cover the procedure—be sure to negotiate! Contact the hospital's billing administrator, and tell him/her that you can pay only the amount that Medicare would pay (Medicare.gov).

The hospital probably will not agree to the Medicare price but might make a counter offer. If not, ask the physician who performed the procedure to contact the hospital billing department on your behalf. (Professional patient advocates can negotiate for you, but they typically charge 25% to 35% of the amount that they get medical bills reduced.)

• **When possible, shop around before you receive treatment**—the price differences can be huge. For example, a 2013 *JAMA Internal Medicine* study found that the prices charged for hip-replacement surgery at top-ranked hospitals ranged from about $12,500 to $105,000. That is a potential 88% savings simply for placing a few phone calls.

3 Cures for Common Conditions

"Best of the Best" Natural Cures

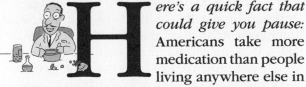

Here's *a quick fact that could give you pause:* Americans take more medication than people living anywhere else in the world. Put another way, Americans make up only about 5% of the world's population but consume more than 50% of prescription drugs.

A sad irony: People in parts of the world (including the US) with the highest expenditures on conventional medicine—a treatment category dominated by prescription drugs—actually live *shorter, less healthy lives* than those in other cultures. How could that be?

Drug reactions and side effects are just part of the problem. The bigger issue is that drugs *suppress* symptoms but are unlikely to reverse whatever it is that's making you sick.

My advice: Whenever possible, try natural remedies *before* pharmaceuticals. Natural therapies are more likely to target the "root" causes of illness, increasing the likelihood of a cure. These therapies also have fewer (or no) side effects.

Finding the "best of the best": As a medical doctor who has spent more than 44 years studying the full range of holistic modalities—from supplements to herbs and folk remedies—and treated more than 30,000 patients who have failed to respond to conventional medicine, I have identified the most effective natural therapies for the following common health problems...*

*Consult your doctor before trying any of these remedies if you take medication or have a chronic medical condition.

C. Norman Shealy, MD, PhD, founding president of the American Holistic Medical Association, editor of the *Journal of Comprehensive Integrative Medicine* and a leading expert in the use of holistic and integrative medicine. He is author of *The Healing Remedies Sourcebook.* NormShealy.com

HEADACHES

About 90% of patients who see a doctor for headaches suffer from tension-type headaches. Despite the name, they're not always related to tension or stress. They are commonly triggered by certain fumes or other sinus irritants.

Nonsteroidal anti-inflammatory drugs, or NSAIDs, such as *ibuprofen* (Motrin), are often used for tension headaches, but they can cause side effects, including nausea and diarrhea. *What I prefer...*

- **Coriander seeds.** Coriander, an anti-inflammatory herb, has been used for headache pain for thousands of years. Inhaling the steam will improve sinus drainage and soothe irritated tissues.

What to do: Put about one teaspoon of the seeds in a small bowl...cover with boiling water...drape a towel over your head and the bowl...and carefully inhale the steam for about 15 minutes.

INSOMNIA

Medications for insomnia—such as *zolpidem* (Ambien) and *eszopiclone* (Lunesta)—can cause many troubling side effects such as confusion, lack of coordination and sleepwalking. They also can make you feel like you have a hangover the next morning. *The following natural remedy is very effective for insomnia—without the side effects...*

- **Lavender.** It's a "calming" herb that's among the best natural treatments for sleepless nights. Many people swear by chamomile tea, but I've found that lavender is even more effective.

What to do: Sip a cup of lavender tea at bedtime...or inhale the aroma from a drop of lavender oil placed on a cotton ball under your nose. To use on your skin (for example, on your temples or pulse points on your wrists), add a drop or two of lavender oil to a tablespoon of almond or olive oil to dilute it.

A study at Wesleyan University found that people exposed to the scent of lavender reported more deep sleep and felt better in the morning than those who did not inhale the scent. Lavender can also help you fall asleep more quickly.

RESTLESS LEGS

This neurological disorder causes an irresistible urge to move the legs when you lie down at night—and the drugs that are often prescribed, such as benzodiazepines and muscle relaxants, aren't very effective and can cause drowsiness, confusion and dizziness. *What helps...*

- **Magnesium lotion.** Most Americans don't get enough magnesium, a mineral that reduces overexcitability of the central nervous system. You can take oral supplements, but the absorption is much faster when magnesium is applied to the skin. Apply it to your legs/feet before bedtime.

SHINGLES

This viral infection can cause recurring outbreaks of blisters and rashes—and, in some cases, excruciating pain. Antivirals and other medications can shorten the duration of outbreaks but are unlikely to completely eliminate the discomfort. *The following can be used along with medication to provide more effective relief...*

- **Vitamins A, C and E.** Research has shown that each of these nutrients can reduce pain and the severity of shingles rashes. Combining these vitamins is about four times more effective than taking them individually.

My advice: At the first sign of a shingles outbreak (typically marked by numbness, tingling or itching on the face or abdomen), take 1,000 mg of vitamin C daily...25,000 international units (IU) of beta-carotene (which is converted to vitamin A in the body)*...and 400 IU of vitamin E (the tocopherol form). Keep taking them until your symptoms are gone, typically for several weeks.

TOOTHACHE

Few things are more painful than a toothache—and it always seems to erupt on weekends or late at night, when you can't get to a dentist. *What to try until you can see a dentist...*

- **Cinnamon oil.** Dip a cotton ball in the oil and apply it to the painful area. The oil often curbs pain almost instantly. It's also an antimi-

*Smokers and heavy drinkers should not take beta-carotene supplements—they may increase cancer and heart disease risk in these people.

crobial that kills oral bacteria and can reduce inflammation and swelling.

If cinnamon oil doesn't help after five to 10 minutes, add crushed garlic. Like cinnamon, it's a natural antibiotic with analgesic properties. If it doesn't hurt too much, you can chew a whole clove, using the tooth (or teeth) that is aching. Or you can crush a clove and apply the pulp to the area that's hurting.

Stop a Migraine *Before* It Happens

Mark W. Green, MD, a professor of neurology, anesthesiology and rehabilitation medicine at Icahn School of Medicine at Mount Sinai in New York City, where he directs Headache and Pain Medicine and is the vice chair of Neurology for Professional Development and Alumni Relations. He is coauthor of *Managing Your Headaches* and several medical textbooks.

There are more than 37 million Americans who suffer from migraines, but the odds aren't in their favor when it comes to drug treatment.

Sobering statistics: Preventive drugs work for only about half of the people who have these awful headaches—and even when the medication does help, migraine frequency is reduced by only about 50%.

The drugs that stop migraines once they've started—mainly prescription triptans (such as *sumatriptan*, *rizatriptan* and *almotriptan*) ... as well as OTC nonsteroidal anti-inflammatory drugs, such as *ibuprofen* (Motrin), and Excedrin Migraine, which contains *acetaminophen*, aspirin and caffeine—are not always effective. They work best when they're taken soon after the pain begins. Some of the drugs also cause side effects, such as fatigue or gastrointestinal bleeding. And taking them too often can lead to *more*—and more severe—headaches, known as overuse headaches or "rebound" headaches. So preventive drugs may be needed to avoid overuse of these medications.

A COMPLEX PROBLEM

Why are migraines so hard to manage? Experts once believed that migraines were mainly caused by the dilation (widening) of blood vessels in the brain. That's why drugs usually prescribed for other conditions, such as *propranolol*, a blood pressure drug, have been used to reverse these changes.

But we now believe that migraines have more to do with overstimulation of the *trigeminal* nerve in the face and head—this can cause blood vessels in the brain to expand and become inflamed. Treatments that affect this nerve (see below) are often very effective.

Important: Everyone who suffers from migraines should pay attention to possible triggers that precipitate attacks. Some people react to strong scents. Others are vulnerable to specific foods (such as bacon, ripened cheeses or alcohol)...food additives such as monosodium glutamate (or MSG)...emotional stress...bright lights, etc. Avoiding triggers can be an effective way to prevent some attacks.

BEST NONDRUG OPTIONS

Preventing a migraine is always better than trying to treat one that's already taken hold. Unfortunately, not all doctors are aware of the more recent effective migraine-prevention approaches. *Among the best...*

- **Cefaly.** In March 2014, the FDA approved the first device for migraine prevention. Cefaly is known as an external trigeminal nerve stimulation unit. It electrically stimulates branches of the trigeminal nerve, which transmits sensations to the face and head.

How it works: The prescription-only device, which blocks pain signals, includes a battery-powered headband with a reusable, self-adhering electrode. Patients position the headband around the forehead, just above the eyes. It may cause a slight tingling, but no pain. It's used for 20 minutes once a day. Anyone who has an implanted device in the head, a pacemaker or an implanted defibrillator should not use Cefaly.

Scientific evidence: One study found that more than half of migraine patients who used Cefaly were satisfied and intended to keep using it. The unit costs about $350 and is usually not covered by insurance. The device manufacturer offers a 60-day guarantee, so people can get their money back if it doesn't seem to help.

• **Biofeedback.** Emotional stress is one of the most common migraine triggers. A biofeedback machine allows people to monitor skin temperature, muscle tension, brain waves and other physical stress responses that affect blood flow in the brain. The idea is that once people feel how they react to stress—with tightened forehead muscles, for example—they can modify their reactions with things like deep breathing, muscle relaxation, etc.

Scientific evidence: There's strong research showing that biofeedback can reduce both the frequency and severity of migraines by 45% to 60%—but only for patients who are willing to *practice*.

Biofeedback can work about as well as many drugs, but it takes most people a few months before they're good at it. It can also be costly because you have to work with an instructor at first. To find a certified biofeedback practitioner, go to the website of the Biofeedback Certification International Alliance, BCIA.org. Insurance often won't cover it.

• **Supplements.** Some people do well when they combine one or more of these supplements with the previous approaches...*

• Riboflavin, a B vitamin, may improve oxygen metabolism in cells. In one study, migraine frequency was reduced by 50% in patients who took riboflavin (400 mg daily).

• Feverfew is an herbal headache remedy. Some research shows that 50 mg to 125 mg daily can help prevent and ease migraines, while other studies suggest that it's no more effective than a placebo. For some people, it might be a helpful addition to more mainstream treatments.

• Magnesium (500 mg daily) can help reduce the frequency of migraines in people with low levels of the mineral.

BOTOX

Known for smoothing facial wrinkles, these injections were FDA-approved for chronic migraines in 2010. Botox is a good treatment option for patients who have 15 or more days of headaches each month.

We still do not know how Botox works to prevent headaches. It probably deactivates pain receptors in the scalp and blocks the transmission of nerve signals between the scalp and the brain.

How it's done: The drug is injected in multiple locations on the head and neck—and the injections are repeated every three months. It sounds terrible, but the injections are only mildly painful. The procedure takes about 15 minutes, and it's usually covered by insurance if drugs or other treatments haven't worked. Botox treatments are given by headache specialists. Side effects may include swallowing problems, blurred vision and speech difficulties.

Important: I advise patients to commit to at least three treatments. If Botox relieves your pain, you and your doctor can decide how frequently you need additional treatments. If you haven't noticed relief after three treatments, Botox is unlikely to be a good choice for you.

*Check with your doctor before taking these supplements, since they can interact with certain medications and/or cause side effects such as diarrhea.

What's Really Causing That Annoying Cough? It May Surprise You

Jonathan P. Parsons, MD, MSc, FCCP, professor of internal medicine at The Ohio State University College of Medicine and director of the Multidisciplinary Cough Clinic and the OSU Asthma Center at The Ohio State University Wexner Medical Center, all in Columbus.

The occasional cough is nothing more than your body's normal lung maintenance—a quick spasm that expels mucus or other irritants from the airways.

On the other hand, a cough that *sounds unusual* or is unpredictable (for example, there's no identifiable trigger or the cough occurs at different times of day)...severe...or long-lasting suggests that *something* else is going on—but what?

Surprising finding: A recent study published in *Annals of Family Medicine* found that a cough from a cold or the flu sticks around longer—for about 18 days, on average—than the one-week threshold that most people consider normal.*

But a cough's duration is not the only clue to its cause. While it's not surprising that infections such as pneumonia or whooping cough would lead to coughing, there are other conditions that most people wouldn't expect. *For example...*

- **Asthma.** People with asthma assume that they'll have moments of wheezing or breathlessness. But for some patients, a persistent cough is the *only* symptom.

What to watch out for: A wheezy-sounding cough that is usually worse at night. Frequent wheezing and/or coughing means that inflamed airways have narrowed, and it's a hallmark of poorly controlled asthma. Your doctor might recommend spirometry (a simple test that measures your lung capacity) or other lung tests to assess how well—or how poorly—you're doing.

My advice: If you have a wheezy cough but have never been diagnosed with asthma, see your doctor. If you know that you have asthma and find that you're using a "rescue" inhaler—a fast-acting bronchodilator that quickly relieves coughing and other symptoms—more than twice a week, see your doctor. You probably need to work harder to reduce flare-ups. This may include adjusting medication, avoiding pollen and air pollution, reducing stress and other measures.

- **Gastroesophageal reflux disease (or GERD).** Most GERD patients suffer from both heartburn *and* coughs, but about one-third experience *only* a cough or unexplained sore throats. A GERD-related cough occurs when a surge of stomach acid reaches the voice box (the larynx). The irritation and inflammation that result from the acid can lead to a persistent, raspy cough.

What to watch out for: The cough sounds "barky" rather than wheezy. It gets worse when you lie down...after heavy meals...and/or when you consume certain trigger foods or drinks, such as spicy dishes, alcohol, chocolate, onions or citrus. You might also notice that your voice is more hoarse than it used to be.

My advice: To get relief, take an over-the-counter (OTC) acid-suppressing drug such as *omeprazole* (Prilosec) or *ranitidine* (Zantac). Such a drug is unlikely to cause side effects and often is effective—although it might require long-term use (eight to 12 weeks) before your symptoms improve, so you should be monitored by a doctor.

Also important: Medication usually doesn't work unless you also make lifestyle changes. For example, don't eat large meals late at night. In fact, you should avoid food altogether for at least three hours before going to bed. Propping up your upper body with pillows also can prevent stomach acid from going upstream while you sleep.

- **Postnasal drip.** When there's a persistent drip of mucus from the sinuses, you're going to periodically cough. Typically, allergies are to blame. People with hay fever often have congestion and postnasal drip. The mucus can irritate the throat as well as the larynx and cause a nagging cough.

What to watch out for: A seasonal cough. If you mainly cough during the spring, summer and/or fall, an allergy-related cough is likely. This cough could sound barky and will probably get worse at night due to mucous drainage. It might be accompanied by other

*Be sure to see your doctor if a cough lasts for more than three to four weeks.

EASY TO DO...

Faster Cold Recovery

Are sneezing, congestion and other cold symptoms making you miserable?

Recent finding: Adults who used zinc lozenges reduced the cold's duration—to about four days instead of the average seven.

Best: 80 mg a day. Avoid lozenges that have citric acid (it binds to zinc and keeps it from working properly). If you take blood pressure drugs, antibiotics or other medications, check with your doctor before trying zinc.

Harri Hemilä, MD, PhD, research fellow, University of Helsinki, Finland.

allergy symptoms such as a tickling in the throat, itchy eyes, sneezing, etc.

My advice: Reduce drainage by taking a daily OTC nonsedating antihistamine such as *loratadine* (Claritin) or *cetirizine* (Zyrtec).

Nasal steroid sprays are another effective alternative. They start working within hours, although it may take several days—or even weeks—to get the full benefit. Some brands (such as Flonase) are available in OTC versions.

• **ACE inhibitor drugs.** Patients who take these blood pressure–lowering drugs—such as *lisinopril* (Zestril), *captopril* (Capoten) and *enalapril* (Vasotec)—are told that they may experience occasional dizziness. They aren't always warned, however, about the nasty cough that can result in up to 20% of patients taking them.

What to watch out for: A throat tickle followed by a nagging, dry cough that begins anywhere from a few weeks to a year after starting the medication.

My advice: You can keep taking the drug if the cough is not bothering you (and you're successfully managing your blood pressure). Switching to a different ACE inhibitor may help if you have a mild cough. Patients with severe coughs from ACE inhibitors are often advised to switch to a different drug class altogether—usually an angiotensin-receptor blocker (ARB) such as *losartan* (Cozaar) or *valsartan* (Diovan). They work like ACE inhibitors but without the cough.

WHEN A COUGH IS COPD OR CANCER...

A chronic cough (persistent or episodic) may be the first symptom of two of the most serious lung conditions—lung cancer and chronic obstructive pulmonary disease (COPD), a lung disease that includes emphysema and chronic bronchitis. Both diseases are more common in people who smoke, once smoked or have had significant secondhand smoke exposure than in nonsmokers.

Important: Even though people who have never smoked are less likely than smokers to get COPD or lung cancer, it can still happen. Don't take chances. Anyone who has a cough for more than three to four weeks should see a doctor. And call your doctor anytime you cough up blood.

The Allergy-Fighting Diet

Leo Galland, MD, director of the Foundation for Integrated Medicine in New York City. He has held faculty positions at Rockefeller University, Albert Einstein College of Medicine and State University of New York, Stony Brook. He is coauthor of *The Allergy Solution: Unlock the Surprising, Hidden Truth About Why You Are Sick and How to Get Well.* DrGalland.com

---

The right diet can help relieve your allergies whether you're allergic to pollen, dust, mold, certain foods or other allergens. And it can relieve symptoms that you might not even know come from allergies—including fatigue, weight gain and depression. The key is to use foods to improve your immune response. *Here's how...*

BOOST YOUR T-REGS

Immune cells known as regulatory T-cells, or *T-regs,* limit inflammation and dampen the allergic response. The cells don't function properly in people with allergies, which can lead to a host of allergic symptoms.

If you know you're allergic to something, avoidance is an obvious solution. But many people don't know what they're allergic to—or even if they are allergic. You can use dietary changes to increase T-regs and dampen any allergic response.

STEP 1: THREE-DAY POWER WASH

I advise my patients to completely give up the foods that commonly aggravate allergies. These include dairy (including yogurt), wheat, seafood, eggs, soy, nuts, peanuts, yeast (found in bread, alcohol, vinegar, commercial fruit juice and commercial soups and sauces) and nightshade vegetables (such as tomatoes, bell peppers, potatoes and eggplant).

This is not meant to be a permanent diet. You have to give up these foods for three days (unless you discover that you're allergic to a particular food, in which case you'll give it up altogether). Taking a break from likely offenders resets the immune system—it clears your

BETTER WAY...

Sore Throat Gargle

Mix two teaspoons of apple cider vinegar in eight ounces of warm water. Take a mouthful, gargle and spit it out, then swallow a mouthful. Repeat until there's no more. Do this once an hour until your sore throat is better.

Joan Wilen and Lydia Wilen, writers and researchers who have spent decades collecting household tips and "cures from the cupboard." They are authors of *Bottom Line's Treasury of Home Remedies & Natural Cures*. BottomLineInc.com

body of potential allergens and lets you start with a clean slate.

For three days, you'll consume only the soup and the smoothie (see below) that I developed for blunting the immune response (you will also drink oolong tea). Have the smoothie for breakfast and a midafternoon snack. The soup is lunch and dinner. Eat until you are satisfied but not too full. Have your doctor look at the recipes to make sure that they are appropriate for you.

• **Immune balance smoothie.** In a blender, combine one cup of strawberries, one medium avocado, one cup of chopped arugula, one-half head of chopped romaine lettuce, two tablespoons of ground chia seeds and one cup of brewed green tea. If desired, add one medium banana.

Blend until smooth. The smoothie will become thicker and creamier if you refrigerate it after blending.

If you happen to be allergic to any of the ingredients, just leave it out.

• **Immune balance soup.** This is one of the Galland family's favorite recipes.

Sauté three cups of sliced carrots in three tablespoons of extra-virgin olive oil for 10 minutes. Add one cup of chopped parsley, two cups of chopped scallions (green parts only), 12 ounces of chopped broccoli, three ounces of chopped baby kale, one teaspoon of turmeric powder and one-quarter teaspoon of ground black pepper. Add salt to taste. Cook and stir for one minute. Add 12 cups of water, and bring to a boil. Cover and simmer for 20 minutes.

Add one tablespoon of shredded daikon radish just before serving.

• **Organic oolong tea.** I emphasize this tea for a specific reason. It's very high in *catechins,* which are flavonoids that inhibit allergic reactions—they're even stronger than the compounds in green tea. One study found that a majority of patients with allergic eczema who didn't respond to medications had significant improvements after drinking oolong tea for one to two weeks. Drink four cups daily (no more) during the Power Wash and a cup or two daily after that.

STEP 2: REINTRODUCTION

After three days, continue to consume the homemade smoothie and soup and organic oolong tea as you gradually reintroduce foods from your regular diet—a new food or food group each day. Start with foods that are less likely to provoke allergic reactions such as rice or free-range poultry, and gradually move toward the more allergenic foods such as nuts, seafood, eggs and dairy products, one group at a time. Keep notes about what you're eating and symptoms (if any) that you experience—including symptoms you don't typically associate with allergies (see below). This will help you determine whether particular foods—or ingredients in packaged foods—are triggering symptoms.

I've found that patients who give up problem foods for at least six months can sometimes eat them again, in small amounts, without having symptoms return. This doesn't apply to things such as sodas, candies or other junk foods, including commercially prepared pastries. These foods always contribute to allergies (including common dust and pollen allergies) by increasing inflammation and should be avoided.

Important: Consult your doctor prior to reintroducing foods, especially if you suffer from anaphylaxis or asthma or if you previously have experienced an adverse reaction to any of the foods.

TAKE NOTE...

Hidden Allergy Symptoms

Here are allergy symptoms that aren't typically associated with allergies...

- Anxiety
- Bloating
- Brain fog
- Constipation or diarrhea
- Depression
- Fatigue
- Headaches
- Insomnia
- Joint pain
- Muscle aches
- Stomachaches
- Weight gain

STEP 3: IMMUNE BALANCE

No matter what you're allergic to, make an effort to eat healthier foods that fortify T-regs. *Most important...*

• **Natural folate.** Many foods are fortified with folic acid, an important (but synthetic) B vitamin. Natural sources of folate are better for T-reg function. *Examples:* Leafy vegetables, legumes, peas, asparagus, cauliflower and brussels sprouts.

• **More flavonoids.** I believe that many of the inflammatory disorders that plague Americans, including allergies and asthma, are due in part to flavonoid deficiencies. Flavonoids, an important family of plant compounds, have anti-inflammatory and antioxidant effects. A Tufts University study found that animals given a flavonoid-enhanced diet had an increase in T-regs and a decrease in Immunoglobulin E (IgE) antibodies—molecules involved in the allergic response.

The flavonoids in tea are particularly helpful. But you'll get healthy amounts from many different plant foods, including onions, blueberries, sweet potatoes, apples and bell peppers.

• **Lots of strawberries.** Strawberries are the richest food source of *fisetin,* a type of flavonoid that helps preserve T-regs. Fisetin blunts the allergic response and has been shown in laboratory studies to help prevent allergic asthma.

Important: Organic strawberries, fresh or frozen, have more vitamin C and other antioxidants than conventionally grown berries.

• **Put parsley on your plate.** It's more than just a garnish. It is high in *apigenin,* a flavonoid that decreases the activity of allergy-inducing lymphocytes and reduces levels of IgE. The carotenoids in parsley (it has more than carrots) also are helpful.

• **Eat seafood twice a week (as long as you're not allergic).** A lack of omega-3 fatty acids can cause or aggravate allergy symptoms. People with allergies actually need more of these fats because their cells don't metabolize them efficiently.

• **Broaden your palate.** While tea, parsley and strawberries are among the allergy-fighting stars, all plant foods can help balance the immune system and reduce symptoms. I am a big fan of legumes (such as black beans, garbanzo beans and lentils), along with carrots, sweet bell peppers, spinach and brussels sprouts. Most of your diet should consist of these and other healthful plant foods.

Skin Patch May Help Fight Peanut Allergy

Nearly half of the participants who wore a patch that delivered small amounts of peanut protein to their bodies for one year were able to consume at least 10 times more peanut protein at the end of the year than they were able to tolerate at the beginning of the study.

Study of 74 children and young adults led by researchers at US National Institute of Allergy and Infectious Diseases, Bethesda, Maryland, published in *Journal of Allergy and Clinical Immunology.*

5 Mistakes to Avoid If You Have Asthma

Gailen D. Marshall, MD, PhD, the R. Faser Triplett Sr. MD Chair of Allergy and Immunology at The University of Mississippi Medical Center in Jackson. His major research interests include factors affecting asthma risk and the effectiveness of integrative approaches to clinical care for asthma and other immune-based diseases. Dr. Marshall is in his third term as editor in chief of the *Annals of Allergy, Asthma & Immunology.*

Whether it's the wintertime pleasure of sitting next to a crackling log in the fireplace...or the summertime thrill of cooling off in a swimming pool, many of our most treasured seasonal pastimes can mean big trouble for some people.

Hidden threat: If you or a family member is among the 24 million Americans coping with asthma, such seemingly harmless activities could be a mistake.

Asthma, which inflames and narrows the airways, is serious business. Half of all adults with asthma have poorly controlled or even *uncontrolled* asthma, meaning they are at increased risk for sudden worsening of symptoms, which can lead to complications—such as persistent breathing difficulties and even death.

That's why it is imperative for asthma sufferers to avoid common missteps that may prevent them from properly controlling their condition. *Among the biggest mistakes...*

MISTAKE #1: **Not seeing the right doctor.** Too many asthma patients—and even some doctors—fail to recognize the crossover component between asthma and allergies. For about one-third of adult asthma patients, acute episodes and poor control can be triggered by allergies to common substances such as mold, dust, pollen and animal dander. When the immune system of an asthma patient mistakes these substances for a foreign intruder, allergy antibodies (known as IgE) are produced and make their way to the lungs, often leading to an asthma attack.

An internist or a family doctor can manage asthma cases that flare up only occasionally. But for people with severe and persistent asthma (marked by repeated episodes of coughing, wheezing and/or difficulty breathing that take multiple medications to control), the best doctor is often an allergist, who can perform testing to determine whether a patient's asthma triggers are allergy-based.

My advice: Consider seeing an allergist if you have persistent asthma symptoms (described above) that limit everyday activities or you've ever had a life-threatening asthma attack. If an allergist is not available in your area, ask your doctor for a referral to a pulmonologist (a lung function specialist).

MISTAKE #2: **Not getting treated for allergies.** To pinpoint allergies that may be contributing to their asthma, patients should undergo allergy testing as soon as possible after an asthma diagnosis.

Unfortunately, some asthma patients who learn they indeed have allergies don't get allergy shots, a form of immunotherapy that can reduce sensitivity to these triggers. Until this step is taken, repeated bouts of severe asthma symptoms are likely.

A relatively new treatment, sublingual immunotherapy (in which an allergen in tablet form is taken under the tongue) may be an option for certain allergy sufferers. If you're interested, talk to your doctor.

MISTAKE #3: **Missing some less obvious triggers.** Asthma triggers include anything—whether a true allergen or other irritant—that can aggravate symptoms. While most people already know about many of their own asthma triggers, such as strenuous exercise, rapidly breathing in cold air, certain medications, including nonsteroidal anti-inflammatory drugs like aspirin, *ibuprofen* or *naproxen*, or even strong emotions, many other triggers fly under the radar. What are some of these less obvious irritants?

• **Household plants.** Asthma attacks can be precipitated by mold spores that are often found in the soil of many household plants.

My advice: Mold-sensitive patients should minimize indoor plants and keep them out of rooms in which they spend a lot of time, such as the bedroom. If you want to have some plants in your home, you may want to try English ivy, a peace lily or a rubber plant. These plants have been found in research to reduce airborne toxins, including mold spores.

Note: Keep English ivy, peace lily and the Indian rubber plant out of the reach of pets and children—these plants can be toxic if consumed.

• **Wood smoke.** Most people realize that cigarette and cigar smoke are irritants, but wood smoke is often overlooked, even though it too can trigger an asthma flare-up.

My advice: If you have asthma, avoid exposure to wood smoke from fireplaces, grills and open fires to avoid worsening symptoms.

• **Chlorine.** A dip in the pool can be invigorating and even help build lung function, but it can also take your breath away if the water is highly chlorinated. While not a true allergy, chlorine sensitivities can trigger chest tightness, coughing and wheezing.

My advice: If you have asthma, limit your exposure to freshly chlorinated pools—especially hyper-chlorinated public pools—and be sure to shower thoroughly afterward. If possible, swim in a saltwater pool.

Also, if chlorinated pools make your symptoms worse, be careful about using household cleaning products that contain bleach—only use these products in areas that are well-ventilated.

• **Candles and air fresheners.** Pleasant aromas from scented candles and air fresheners can irritate nasal passages and contribute to an asthma attack.

My advice: To prevent a possible allergic reaction, it's best to avoid scented candles and air fresheners.

MISTAKE #4: **Not getting a flu shot.** Getting an annual flu shot is especially important for asthmatics, who are at increased risk for dangerous flu complications, such as pneumonia. It's best to get the flu shot in October, but it's still helpful to get it up until March. Pneumonia vaccines, which can be given anytime during the year, are also recommended for people with asthma.

MISTAKE #5: **Not recognizing flare-up symptoms.** It's crucial that people with asthma watch for subtle warning signs—such as increasing shortness of breath while exercising or restless sleep—that indicate their asthma may be veering out of control.

Rule of thumb: Asthma is considered poorly controlled if wheezing or other symptoms occur more than twice a week or if you awaken more than twice a month with asthma symptoms. Other red flags include needing to use "rescue" inhalers, such as *albuterol* more than twice a week...requiring oral *corticosteroids* to treat severe attacks...and/or changing activity patterns (such as avoiding stairs, etc.).

Vitamin D and Asthma

Vitamin D supplements can reduce asthma attacks.

Recent study: Patients who took vitamin D supplements every day had an average of 37% fewer asthma attacks that required oral corticosteroids. Vitamin D also cut the likelihood of emergency department visits/hospitalizations by 50%.

Important: Vitamin D should not be used as a substitute for regular asthma medications.

Editor's note: The RDA for vitamin D is 600 international units (IU). If you are age 70 or older, 800 IU.

Christopher Griffiths, PhD, deputy director for research at Centre for Primary Care and Public Health, Blizard Institute, Barts, and The London School of Medicine and Dentistry.

Survive an Asthma Attack with No Inhaler

Richard Firshein, DO, director and founder of The Firshein Center for Integrative Medicine in New York City. He is an innovator and leading authority in preventive and nutritional medicine. A certified medical acupuncturist, he is board-certified in family medicine and has served as a professor of family medicine at New York College of Osteopathic Medicine. He is author of *The Vitamin Prescription (for Life)* and *Reversing Asthma.*

A rescue inhaler can be your best friend if you're gasping from a serious asthma attack. But what do you do if you don't have it?

First question: Emergency or not? People can die from severe asthma attacks. This won't happen if you get to an emergency room fast enough—but you have to make a quick decision about the severity of your symptoms. *What to look for:* Feelings of panic…shortness of breath…a cough that won't quit…inability to speak…sudden exhaustion…or soreness/tightness around the ribs. If you have a peak-flow meter, use it. A reading that's 25% (or more) lower than usual means that you're in trouble. Get to an ER or call an ambulance.

STOP THE ATTACK

If my patients are not in immediate danger, I advise them to do all of the following…

• **Take an oral medication.** Oral *prednisone* or *theophylline* will quickly improve breathing. Certain over-the-counter medications—including antihistamines, cough medicines and *guaifenesin* (an expectorant)—can help out in a pinch.

Also helpful: Vitamin C (1,000 mg during an attack) reduces inflammation and is a mild antihistamine…magnesium (500 mg) opens airways…and quercetin (about 1,500 mg) has antihistamine and anti-inflammatory effects.

• **Change locations.** Do it as soon as you notice that your breathing is labored. Attacks often are triggered by irritants in your immediate environment such as traffic fumes, pet hair, pollen, etc. Going a short distance away can make a surprising difference.

• **Grab a cup of coffee or caffeinated tea.** The body metabolizes caffeine into *theophylline,* the same compound in some asthma medications—and the caffeine itself relaxes airways.

• **Relax.** During an attack, your body increases production of *adrenaline* and *cortisol.* You need these hormones to reduce inflammation and improve breathing…but anxiety depletes them. Breathing exercises will help keep the airways open. Inhale deeply through your nose for about four seconds, then exhale through your nose for a count of six. Keep breathing like this until you're feeling better.

Another relaxation tool is visual imagery. In your mind, see your lungs opening up. Or picture yourself in nature or another restful place. Fill the picture with as much detail as possible.

• **Press the "lung points."** You can use acupressure to stimulate the points that control breathing. One is the LU5 point at the outer part of the elbow crease when your elbows are bent. Another is the LU1 point, which is located at the intersection of your chest and your shoulder. If you get into trouble, press each of these points one at a time for one to three minutes, starting with light pressure and gradually increasing it.

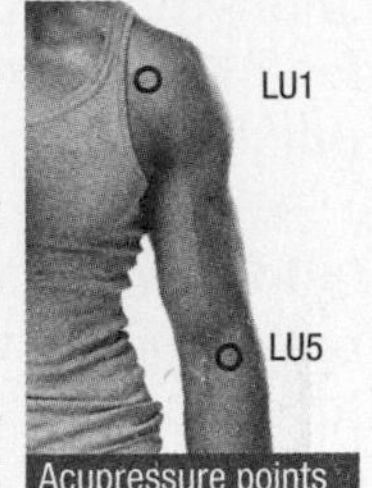

Acupressure points

• **Take a long shower or bath.** It will help you relax, and the steam will loosen mucus and make it easier to breathe.

---

5 Little Habits That Can Do Big Damage to Your Teeth

Marvin A. Fier, DDS, FASDA, Diplomate of the American Board of Aesthetic Dentistry. He teaches continuing-education courses to practicing dentists and has a private practice, Cosmetic & Family Dentistry, in Pomona, New York, providing care for residents of the NY Tri-State area and beyond. SmileRockland.com

Are you an ice-chomper or perhaps a nail-biter? These and four other "mouth habits" mean that you should start saving for dental work—you're going to need it.

Brushing and flossing (and dentist visits) won't save your teeth if you engage in mouth-mangling habits. Forget the obvious things such as smoking or chewing on pencils. *Habits that seem innocuous actually can cause significant (and expensive) damage…*

NAIL-BITING

There's a scientific name for nail-biting—*onychophagia.* It's among the most common nervous habits and is listed in the Diagnostic and Statistical Manual of Mental Disorder, fifth edition (DSM-5, the official manual of mental disorders) because some people do it compulsively—in some cases, for hours a day.

Fingernails are harder than you might think, especially if you use nail polish. Constant nibbling can fracture tooth enamel. It damages the cuticle and soft tissue surrounding the nail and exposes your mouth to hand bacteria. It forces your jaw into a protruding position that puts painful pressure on the joint.

My advice: You have to be aware of a habit before you can stop it. An awful-tasting nail polish or cream (such as neem oil, Control-It! or Mavala Stop) will remind you of what you're doing. People are more likely to bite their nails when they're stressed, so it's helpful to substitute healthier (and more soothing) activities—deep breathing, going for walks, etc. Or chew sugarless gum to dispel nervous energy and keep your mouth busy. Also, keep your nails short—they're harder to bite.

HARD BRUSHING

As a dentist, I always encourage people to brush their teeth. Done correctly, it's among the best ways to protect your teeth as well as your gums. But many people think that a soft touch won't get the job done. They apply way too much force or use a brush that's hard enough to clean bathroom grout.

Hard brushing abrades tooth enamel along with gums. It does even more damage to the tooth roots, which are softer than enamel. When I see patients with notches or abrasions in the roots, I know that they're brushing too hard. *Hint:* Tooth sensitivity to cold temperatures or sweets can be caused by root damage due to brushing too hard.

My advice: Never buy a hard toothbrush. Those that are labeled "medium" still are too hard. Use only a soft brush. And even with a soft brush, don't bear down when you're brushing—use the lightest touch you can muster. Think "massage," not "scrub."

Helpful: Hold the brush (manual or electric) with your fingertips instead of clenching it in your fist. This makes it almost impossible to apply too much pressure.

CHEWING ICE CUBES

Ice is harder than hard candy. According to the Mohs Scale of Mineral Hardness, it has a hardness of 1.5. That makes it a little harder than talc but not quite as hard as gypsum. No one would think to chew rocks, but that's exactly what you're doing when you munch the ice cubes in your drinks. It can cause microscopic cracks in tooth enamel, which increase the risk for decay and fracturing teeth

My advice: If you can't stop yourself from chomping ice from your drinks, quit putting it in drinks. Stick to chilled beverages without ice. Or use a straw to reduce temptation. *Another option:* Use ice chips. They're smaller than cubes and less likely to crack your teeth.

ALL-DAY GRAZING

Snacking isn't bad if your taste runs to nuts, fruits and vegetables. But many people who snack crave sweets. The average American consumes about 20 teaspoons of added sugar a day.

Bacteria in the mouth love sugar. They convert it to acids that damage the teeth as well as the gums.

People who eat a lot of sugary snacks have a much higher risk for cavities and periodontal disease (loss of gum and bone), the leading cause of tooth loss in adults.

My advice: Limit your snacking. Eat larger (nutritionally balanced) meals so that you feel full longer.

When you do snack, keep it healthy. Avoid the usual culprits—sweetened soft drinks... candy bars...hard candies, etc.

Also helpful: If you can't brush after snacks, at least swish your mouth with water. It will remove some of the sugar and bacterial acids.

USING TEETH AS TOOLS

This should be obvious, but many people don't hesitate to use their teeth for all sorts of odd jobs—opening bags, snipping plastic tags off clothes, tearing open clamshell packages and even opening bottles.

EASY TO DO...

Remedy for Garlic Breath

Eating an apple or lettuce or mint leaves decreased the chemical compounds that cause garlic breath by 50% or more compared with drinking water.

Study conducted by researchers at The Ohio State University, published in *Journal of Food Science*.

I see a lot of patients who have chipped or fractured their teeth because they didn't take the time to look for a pair of scissors or dig through the toolbox for pliers.

My advice: Don't use your teeth as tools. You might think you're saving time by nibbling off a price tag, but the eventual damage and repair will take longer than looking for the right tool—and will cost a lot more.

THE DANGERS OF GRINDING AND CLENCHING YOUR TEETH

Australian researchers made a surprising discovery when they compared human skulls to those of other animals. Using sophisticated engineering software, they found that the human jaw actually generates more biting force than the jaws of great apes. When you use all of your jaw muscles to bite down, you're generating a force as great as 55 pounds.

That's what allows us to chew hard foods. The downside is that it's more than enough to fracture the teeth and even damage the jaw joints. Some of the worst damage I see in my practice comes from bruxism, clenching or grinding the teeth during sleep or times of high stress. It can cause visible wear and flattening of the tooth surfaces.

People who grind their teeth while sleeping, known as nocturnal grinders, can protect themselves by wearing a customized mouth guard. The daytime grinders are a bigger challenge because they don't even know they're doing it (and would be unlikely to wear mouth guards while they're awake).

My advice: Start with relaxation exercises. Grinding/clenching almost always increases during times of stress, anger or even deep concentration. People who manage their stress with activities such as yoga, meditation or regular workouts will naturally grind less.

Helpful: The next time you're feeling very stressed, pay attention to your shoulders. You'll probably notice that they're tight and hunched upward toward your neck. It's impossible to relax when the shoulders are tensed. Make a conscious effort to relax your shoulders and let them "drop." You'll feel less tension the moment you do this.

Dental Cleanings Lower Pneumonia Risk

In a study of the records of more than 26,000 people, those who never saw a dentist were 86% more likely to get bacterial pneumonia than those who had dental checkups twice a year. Regular dental cleanings reduce levels of bacteria that cause the lung infection.

Michelle E. Doll, MD, MPH, assistant professor and associate hospital epidemiologist in the department of internal medicine, division of infectious diseases, Virginia Commonwealth University School of Medicine, Richmond.

Delicious Dry-Eye Remedy

Pterostilbene (PS), a compound in blueberries, has been found to fight the oxidative damage linked to dry eye.

Details: When PS was added to corneal epithelial cells in the lab, oxidative damage was significantly reduced, curbing the inflammation that leads to dry eye.

Tip: Eat one-half cup of fresh or frozen blueberries daily.

De-Quan Li, MD, PhD, associate professor of ophthalmology, Baylor College of Medicine, Houston.

Salt Spray for Nosebleeds

People who have *hemorrhagic telangiectasia* (HHT) have as many as two nosebleeds a day.

Recent study: Individuals with HHT who sprayed a saline solution into their noses twice daily for 12 weeks got as much relief from nosebleeds as those who used the medicines *bevacizumab*, *estriol* or *tranexamic acid*.

Nosebleeds in HHT are not very different from common nosebleeds, so saline spray might help those as well.

Kevin J. Whitehead, MD, associate professor of internal medicine at University of Utah School of Medicine, Salt Lake City, and leader of a study of 121 people with HHT, published in *JAMA*.

Link to Hearing Loss

When women ages 48 to 73 used over-the-counter pain relievers such as *ibuprofen* (Motrin) or *acetaminophen* (Tylenol) two or more days a week for more than six years, they were 16% more likely to suffer hearing loss than those who took aspirin or no pain reliever. The exact reason for this link is unknown. Further research is needed to determine whether men could be similarly affected by pain relievers.

Brian M. Lin, MD, resident in otolaryngology, Brigham and Women's Hospital, Boston.

Lawn Mower Warning

Lawn mowers, leaf blowers and loud music can cause temporary hearing loss that lasts up to several hours and may even lead to permanent hearing loss.

Recent research: When volunteers wore earplugs during a four-hour 100-decibel concert, only 8% had temporary hearing loss, compared with 42% who didn't wear earplugs. And 12% of those who wore earplugs reported developing chronic *tinnitus* (ringing in the ears) compared with 40% of those who didn't wear them.

Wilko Grolman, MD, PhD, professor of otolaryngology, University Medical Center Utrecht, the Netherlands.

Best Way to Wash a Rash

Don't apply soap on a rash—the soap can make the rash worse, especially some types of eczema and rashes in the groin and underarm areas. Instead, wash other body areas and let the diluted soapy water runoff cleanse the rash. Use warm, not hot, water. Hot water can make an itchy rash itch more.

Neal Schultz, MD, dermatologist in private practice in New York City.

Better Splinter Removal

A splinter that appears to be deeply embedded, should be removed with tweezers to avoid infection.

Here's how: Gently wash the area with soap and water and dry. Use rubbing alcohol to sterilize the tip of tweezers and then use them to grab onto the splinter. (If the splinter is under the skin, use a sterilized needle to bring it to the surface.) Use a magnifying glass if the splinter is very small. Pull gently, then wash again with soap and water after the splinter is out. Apply petroleum jelly and a bandage, which should stay on for at least 24 hours. If you are unable to remove the splinter (or if it's in or near the eye), see your doctor.

Robert Sidbury, MD, MPH, chief of dermatology, Seattle Children's Hospital.

Beat Body Odors Naturally

Jamison Starbuck, ND, naturopathic physician in family practice and producer of *Dr. Starbuck's Health Tips for Kids*, a weekly program on Montana Public Radio, MTPR.org, both in Missoula. She is also a past president of the American Association of Naturopathic Physicians and a contributing editor to *The Alternative Advisor: The Complete Guide to Natural Therapies and Alternative Treatments.* DrJamisonStarbuck.com

"Stinky feet" can be cute in a toddler, but for most of us, smelly body parts are something we'd rather avoid. Whether it's feet, armpits, ears, breath or genitals, certain body parts are especially vulnerable to odor. Deodorant can help temporarily but isn't a cure. Body odor can develop for several reasons—poor hygiene, poor diet, inadequate hydration, disease and the use of certain medications, such as antibiotics. Fungi and bacteria can live on the skin and in body parts, too, causing musty, funky odors. Infections of all sorts—such as strep throat or an ear or a vaginal infection—will cause a putrid odor around the affected body part. Liver disease can result in a dusty, mousy body odor.

If you don't like how you smell...

• **Consider what you eat.** A diet high in animal fat and protein—such as cheese, milk, meat and eggs—will create more body odor than a diet high in fruits and vegetables. This odor comes mainly from the by-products of fat and protein digestion.

What helps: Reduce your animal food intake by half and double your fruit and vegetable intake. Do this for 10 days. If your diet was the culprit, you'll start smelling better!

• **Avoid garlic and onions.** These foods release sulfur-smelling compounds through the lungs and skin.

If you can't make yourself give them up, try this: Rather than having garlic or onions raw, cook them. This helps reduce the sulfuric compounds that lead to body odor. The spice cumin can also make you smell bad. If it does, avoid it.

• **Drink water as your primary beverage.** Coffee creates the infamous "coffee breath," and sugary beverages (and sweets in general) increase your risk for fungus, the organism primarily responsible for jock itch, vaginitis and stinky feet.

What helps: Drink half your body weight in ounces of water daily. In addition, certain herbal teas gently support liver health, reducing body odor caused by medication or high-fat foods. My favorite is a combination of the liver-healthy herbs dandelion root, burdock root, yellow dock root and milk thistle.* You may be able to find all of these herbs in a premixed tea, or you can buy small amounts of each and combine them in equal parts yourself.

*Avoid these herbs if you have a ragweed allergy. Check first with your doctor if you have a chronic condition or take medication, since these herbs could interact.

What to do: Use two teaspoons of dried herb mix per 10 ounces of water. Simmer or steep for five minutes, and drink 24 ounces a day. It may take 10 or more days to notice significant changes in body odor with this tea.

• **Do a vinegar spritz.** While it won't cure the problem—smells are most often generated from the inside out—vinegar can kill fungi and bacteria on the skin, thus reducing odor caused by these organisms. Use a 50/50 white vinegar/water solution and spray it over your feet, armpits and genitalia. Towel off after a minute or two (the vinegar smell will quickly dissipate).

Important: If your body odor persists and/or is noticed by others—and does not improve with these suggestions—see your doctor. Very strong body odor can be a sign of serious disease such as infection, cancer or organ failure.

Heartburn Remedies You've Never Heard Of—They're Safer Than Drugs

Jacob Teitelbaum, MD, board-certified internist and nationally recognized expert in the fields of chronic fatigue syndrome, fibromyalgia, sleep and pain. Based in Kailua-Kona, Hawaii, Dr. Teitelbaum is author of numerous books, including *The Fatigue and Fibromyalgia Solution, Pain-Free 1-2-3* and *Real Cause, Real Cure*. He also developed the free smartphone app *Cures A-Z* and is founder of Practitioners Alliance Network (PAN), which brings health-care practitioners together for improved patient care. Vitality101.com

If you have heartburn, you may be taking an acid-suppressing drug called a proton pump inhibitor (PPI). About 20 million of us are. PPIs include *esomeprazole* (Nexium), *dexlansoprazole* (Dexilant), *rabeprazole* (Aciphex), *lansoprazole* (Prevacid) and *omeprazole* (Prilosec).

As you may have read, long-term use of PPIs has been linked to serious health problems. *Here, more on the dangers—and what's safer and effective...*

THE DANGERS

Yes, stomach acid may cause heartburn. But stomach acid also is a necessary component of everyday digestion and health. PPIs block the natural production of stomach acid—often with disastrous results. *PPIs have been linked to...*

• **Chronic kidney disease.** Chronic kidney disease (CKD) causes high blood pressure, increasing risk for heart attack and stroke, and can lead to a need for dialysis or a kidney transplant. In people using PPIs long-term, the risk of developing CKD is 50% higher.

• **Bone loss and fractures.** Because PPIs cut the absorption of bone-building calcium and magnesium, they decrease bone density. In one study, using PPIs for less than one year increased the risk for hip fractures by 26% and spinal fractures by 58%.

• **Heart attacks.** Researchers at Stanford University found that people taking PPIs long-term had 16% higher risk for heart attack...and double the risk of dying from heart disease.

• **Cancer.** Long-term use of PPIs can raise the risk for stomach and esophageal cancers, according to Australian researchers in an issue of *Expert Opinion on Drug Safety*.

PPIs also have been linked to dementia, pneumonia, gastrointestinal infection and deficiency of magnesium and/or B-12.

To add insult to injury, a recent study from University of California, San Francisco, published in *JAMA Internal Medicine*, found that up to 70% of PPI prescriptions are "inappropriate." That's because PPIs frequently are prescribed for any digestive complaint, rather than for FDA-approved medical conditions such as *gastroesophageal reflux disease* (GERD)—the medical term for heartburn, erosive esophagitis (inflammation of the esophagus) and stomach or duodenal ulcers. "Inappropriate" also means that the drugs—which are FDA-approved for only short-term use of a few weeks—often are used long-term.

SAFER REMEDIES

Your body produces stomach acid for a reason—to digest your food. Turning off that stomach acid with PPIs can decrease the pain from heartburn. But it doesn't treat the poor digestion that is *causing* your heartburn. To put it another way...your real problem isn't excess stomach acid—it's indigestion. Below are my recommendations to banish indigestion—you can try any of these remedies or even all of them at the same time if you wish. Continue to take a PPI drug at first while following these recommendations. You also may want to avoid foods that trigger heartburn, including citrus fruits, tomatoes, garlic, onions and chili.

Important: If problems persist after two months, see your doctor.

• **For quick heartburn relief, try bicarbonate of soda (baking soda).** One-half teaspoon of alkaline bicarbonate of soda (baking soda) in four ounces of water can quickly neutralize stomach acid and relieve the pain. Over-the-counter antacids with alkalinizing minerals (calcium combined with magnesium, such as Rolaids) also work—as little as one-quarter tablet can squelch the pain of heartburn. But there is some evidence that long-term use of calcium is associated with increased risk for heart attacks in women.

• **Take digestive enzymes.** One of the primary reasons for indigestion in the US is lack of enzymes in food, which have been removed during processing. I recommend the enzyme-containing supplement Complete GEST from Enzymatic Therapy. Take two capsules with every meal to digest food properly.

Caution: Some people find that digestive enzymes irritate the stomach. If this happens, start with GS-Similase—it's the gentler of the two products. If it causes irritation, don't use it. Instead, use the DGL licorice and mastic gum remedies (see below) until your stomach feels better, usually in a month or two—and then start taking digestive enzymes. The enzymes are used long-term to support healthy digestion.

• **While eating, sip warm liquid rather than cold.** Cold drinks slow and even can stop digestion. Drink warm liquids during meals to aid digestion.

• **Avoid coffee, carbonated beverages, alcohol and aspirin.** All of them can hurt your stomach. Once your stomach has healed, and indigestion and heartburn are a dim memory, you can use them again in limited amounts. (You'll know you're using too much if indigestion and heartburn return.)

- **Take DGL licorice.** This herb helps resolve the symptoms of heartburn and underlying indigestion. In fact, research shows it's as effective as the H2 blocker *cimetidine* (Tagamet)—but unlike Tagamet, which has been linked to some of the problems caused by PPIs, DGL licorice is good for you. I recommend Advanced DGL by EuroPharma, which doesn't have the licorice taste. Take one capsule twice a day—after one to two months, it can be used as needed.

Caution: You must use the DGL form of licorice. Other forms can cause high blood pressure.

- **Take mastic gum.** This gum (resin) from an evergreen tree is a wonderful remedy for heartburn and indigestion. Take mastic gum in supplement form. I recommend one or two 500-mg capsules twice a day for two months, then as needed.

"ADDICTED" TO PPIs?

After reading about the downsides of proton pump inhibitors (PPIs), you may want to stop taking them—immediately. But you may not be able to!

Researchers in Denmark gave *esomeprazole* (Nexium) for two months to 120 people without heartburn. Within two weeks of stopping the drug, 44% of the study participants developed heartburn. In 22%, those symptoms continued for the next four weeks.

Why did healthy people stopping the drug develop heartburn? Because of the phenomenon that the researchers call *rebound acid hyper-secretion*. It's natural for the stomach to produce stomach acid. If you foil that function and then allow it to resume, it returns with a vengeance, generating huge amounts of stomach acid that cause heartburn.

Best: Use the heartburn remedies from the main article for two months, and then—under your doctor's guidance—start "tapering" your PPI, cutting the dose in half every week (or at the rate your doctor suggests). When you're at the lowest possible dose, switch to Tagamet, which decreases stomach acid without totally turning it off. The Tagamet can be stopped after one month.

Foot-tastic! Natural Remedies for Your Feet

Johanna Youner, DPM, podiatrist and podiatric surgeon. She is founder of Healthy Feet NY, a private practice in New York City. She also is a certified laser specialist for tattoo removal and a member of The American Society for Laser Medicine and Surgery. HealthyFeetNY.net and ParkAvenueLaserTreatment.com

Most of us—75% of Americans—will have foot problems at least sometime in our lives. Think about the stresses that your feet endure. They're subjected to significant impact pressure just from walking—and a lot more from running. They're squeezed into tight shoes and stuffed into hot socks.

But you can treat many foot problems at home—without potent drugs or high-priced medical care.

Natural remedies that work...

ARNICA FOR INJURIES

This homeopathic remedy has become the go-to treatment for athletes—including members of the US Men's National Soccer Team—who need to reduce their post-injury swelling, inflammation and bruises.

Arnica pellets (taken internally), ointments, creams and gels contain *thymol derivatives*, compounds that reduce inflammation. A study published in a rheumatology journal found that homeopathic arnica relieved pain as well as *ibuprofen*—without the side effects that often occur with traditional over-the-counter painkillers.

How to use it: Quickly apply arnica gel, ointment or cream (or put five sublingual arnica pellets under your tongue) after you've banged or twisted your foot or ankle. It works best when it's applied or taken within 10 minutes after an injury. Repeat the treatment three times a day until the pain is gone.

For homeopathic products, I recommend Boiron, a leading manufacturer of these remedies. They're available at pharmacies and supermarkets.

CASTOR OIL FOR ARTHRITIC AND CHRONIC PAIN

Many doctors advise their patients to apply moist heat for arthritic conditions and other chronic pain. Heat dilates blood vessels, stimulates blood flow and increases the supply of oxygen and nutrients...and it accelerates the removal of fluids that cause swelling.

Castor oil is even better because it's an anti-inflammatory and an antioxidant that is readily absorbed by the skin. It contains the unsaturated omega-3 fatty acid *ricinoleic acid*, which quickly reduces inflammation and pain. Buy hexane-free castor oil (it will say so on the label). Hexane is a petrochemical that may be hazardous.

How to use it: For foot or ankle pain, soak a piece of flannel (flannels are sold online for this purpose) in castor oil...wrap it around the foot...then wrap a warm towel around that... and leave it in place for about one hour. It will reduce the inflammation and swelling. (You also can use a heating pad or hot-water bottle to heat the towel.)

Caution: Castor oil stains! Take a shower after you remove the wrapping...and keep the oil away from your good towels. You can store the flannel in the refrigerator in a plastic bag or container for about one month.

EPSOM SALT FOR CELLULITIS

Cellulitis is a common skin infection that often affects the feet, particularly in patients with athlete's foot, fluid retention in the legs (from poor circulation) and/or diabetes. You might notice redness, swelling or warmth in the early stages.

Epsom salt is an osmotic agent. It pulls material (fluids, pus and even splinters) toward the surface of the skin. When your foot is swollen, an Epsom salt soak will reduce swelling right away—it's almost magical. I use it for many nonemergency foot conditions, including cellulitis, painful warts and infected nails.

How to use it: For a foot bath, add one-half cup of Epsom salt to a basin of warm water.

TEA TREE OIL FOR INFECTIONS AND FUNGUS

Tea tree oil is extracted from the leaves of an Australian tea tree. It has been used for centuries to treat skin infections. Research has shown that it is an effective treatment for athlete's foot as well as nail fungus (*onychomycosis*).

How to use it: Apply the oil twice a day to new skin infections or toenail infections (don't apply to broken skin). Fungal infections that have gone on for a month or more probably will require a medicated over-the-counter cream such as Tinactin or Lotrimin.

COCONUT OIL TO MOISTURIZE

Feet do not have oil glands. Without this natural lubrication, the skin is naturally dry. Too much dryness can cause itching, peeling or even deep cracks that can be painful and sometimes get infected.

Coconut oil is an excellent moisturizer for the feet—one that also has antibacterial and antifungal properties. It is solid at room temperature and is available in jars at supermarkets and pharmacies.

How to use it: Apply it to your feet several times a day. Because it's readily absorbed, it won't look (or feel) greasy.

MUSTARD, PICKLE JUICE OR VINEGAR FOR FOOT CRAMPS

It sounds like an old wives' tale, but each of these traditional remedies really can help when you have foot or ankle cramps. In a study published on the website of the American College of Sports Medicine, researchers used electricity to induce toe cramps in young athletes who

QUICK CURE...

Soak Those Smelly Feet in This...

Soak stinky feet in strongly brewed, cooled black tea for 30 minutes daily for seven to 10 days... then once a week for maintenance. The tannic acid in the tea dries out the sweat glands responsible for foot odor in many people.

Jane E. Andersen, DPM, doctor of podiatric medicine, Chapel Hill, North Carolina, and spokesperson for the American Podiatric Medical Association, quoted in *The Wall Street Journal.*

had just finished a workout. The athletes then drank 2.5 ounces of pickle juice or water—or nothing at all. The pickle juice stopped the cramps about 37% faster than water and 45% faster than drinking nothing.

Researchers speculate that a substance in pickle juice—possibly the vinegar—somehow short-circuits muscle-cramp reflexes. Apple cider vinegar has a similar effect, as does prepared yellow mustard (which contains vinegar).

How to use them: Keep any (or all) of them on hand if your feet are prone to cramps. When you feel a cramp coming on, add pickle juice, vinegar and/or mustard to your food.

Important: For most people, dehydration is the main cause of muscle cramps. You must hydrate after exercise. In addition to the vinegar or pickle juice, drink a few glasses of water, juice or a sports beverage.

DRUG-FREE CURES FOR PLANTAR FASCIITIS

Plantar fasciitis affects about 10% of the US population and is one of the most common causes of heel pain. A thick band of tissue (the plantar fascia) runs across the bottom of the foot. It connects the heel bone to the toes and creates the arch. Small tears in the tissue can cause burning/stabbing pain, particularly in the morning.

- **Apply ice.** Hold an ice pack over the painful area for 15 to 20 minutes, three or four times a day.
- **Replace your shoe insoles.** The Powerstep brand of insoles supports and cushions the plantar fascia and helps it heal more quickly. You can buy insoles at pharmacies, sporting-goods stores and online for $15 to $60. In many cases, they work as well as prescription products (which can cost as much as $550).
- **Use a tennis ball or rolling pin** to gently roll along the bottom of your foot (while sitting).
- **Replace worn-out athletic shoes.** They stop cushioning your feet after about 500 miles of use.

DASH Away from Gout

The DASH diet (Dietary Approaches to Stop Hypertension)—developed to lower blood pressure—can reduce uric acid levels enough to prevent gout flare-ups. The diet is rich in whole grains, fruits, vegetables and low-fat dairy...and low in salt, red meat, sweets and saturated fats. It sometimes can work as well as antigout medication.

Stephen P. Juraschek, MD, PhD, research and clinical fellow, The Johns Hopkins University School of Medicine, Baltimore.

Zika Warning: Ineffective Repellents

Joseph Conlon, technical adviser for the American Mosquito Control Association, a not-for-profit scientific organization of public health officials, mosquito-control professionals, university researchers, chemical engineers and others. He has 40 years of experience in mosquito control, including 20 as an entomologist for the US Navy. Mosquito.org

If you're thinking about going someplace warm, you may be wondering about protecting yourself from the Zika virus.

Beware: Many mosquito-repellent products actually provide little or no protection. These fraudulent products leave consumers just as vulnerable as ever to the Zika virus. Zika can cause fevers, rashes and joint pain...as well as serious birth defects when pregnant women are infected. Zika also has been linked to Guillain-Barré syndrome, which can lead to muscle weakness, temporary paralysis and even death.

Mosquitoes are spreading Zika in South America and Central America as well as in south Florida and Texas. Additional parts of the US could be affected in future years.

Products that have not been scientifically proven to provide significant protection against mosquitoes include ultrasonic mosquito repellers and mosquito-repelling wristbands. Many "natural" or "organic" bug sprays

EASY TO DO...

Better Way to Kill Ticks

To kill ticks on clothing, put the clothes in the dryer on high heat for six minutes—then wash if the clothes are dirty. Why? Ticks love water. In a recent study, 94% survived cold-water washes and 50% survived hot-water washes. Once the clothes were wet, it took 70 minutes to kill the ticks in dryers on low heat...50 minutes in dryers on high heat.

Study by researchers at Centers for Disease Control and Prevention, Fort Collins, Colorado, University of Vermont College of Medicine, Burlington, University of Massachusetts, Boston, and Vermont Agency of Agriculture, Barre, published in *Ticks and Tick-borne Diseases*.

are ineffective as well. The makers of sprays featuring garlic or oil of clove are technically correct when they claim that these ingredients repel mosquitoes...what they don't mention is that their products repel mosquitoes for only very short periods—some last just 20 minutes—and/or work only when used in extremely high concentrations.

What to do: Use a mosquito-control product that has an "EPA Registration Number" printed on its label. Mosquito repellents that have these numbers have been scientifically shown to be both effective and safe when used as directed.

An effective mosquito-repellent almost certainly will feature one of the following active ingredients...

- **DEET.** Choose a product that has a 25% to 35% DEET concentration.
- **Picaridin.** This odorless synthetic product is based on a compound found in black pepper plants. It is as effective as DEET and typically feels lighter and less greasy on the skin. Choose a product that has a 15% to 19% picaridin concentration.
- **Oil of lemon-eucalyptus.** This is the only natural ingredient that has been proven effective against mosquitoes (ticks, too). Choose a product that has an oil of lemon-eucalyptus concentration of around 40%.

It's 3 am and You're Awake! How to Get Back to Sleep

Michael Breus, PhD, a sleep specialist with a private practice in Los Angeles. Dr. Breus is also author of *The Power of When: Discover Your Chronotype—and the Best Time to Eat Lunch, Ask for a Raise, Have Sex, Write a Novel, Take Your Meds, and More.* TheSleepDoctor.com

In the world of sleep disorders, having difficulty *staying* asleep is just as troubling as having difficulty *falling* asleep.

Both sleep problems rob us of the consistent, high-quality rest that helps protect against high blood pressure, obesity, diabetes, stroke and depression.

Plenty of people who have nighttime awakenings turn to a prescription sleep aid, such as *zolpidem* (Ambien). But these pills are only a temporary fix and can cause prolonged drowsiness the next day or, in rare cases, sleepwalking or sleep-eating within hours of taking them.

A better option: Cognitive behavioral therapy for insomnia, known as CBT-I, is now recommended as a first-line treatment for chronic sleep problems.* With CBT-I, you work with a specially trained therapist (typically for six to eight sessions) to identify, challenge and change the patterns of thinking that keep you awake at night. A 2015 study found CBT-I, which is typically covered by health insurance, to be more helpful than *diazepam* (Valium), commonly used as a sleep aid, in treating insomnia.

But if you are not quite ready to commit to a course of CBT-I—or even if you do try it—there are some simple but effective strategies you can use at home to help you stay asleep and get the deep rest you need.

The best approaches to help avoid nighttime awakenings...

- **Get more omega-3 fatty acids.** While the research is still preliminary, a recent study published in *Sleep Medicine* found that the

*To find a CBT-I therapist, consult the Society of Behavioral Sleep Medicine, BehavioralSleep.org. You can also try the free CBT-i Coach app, available at iTunes or Google Play.

more omega-3–rich fatty fish adults ate, the better their sleep quality.

My advice: Eat fatty fish...and to ensure adequate levels of omega-3s, consider taking a fish oil supplement (one to two 1,000-mg capsules daily).**

• **Avoid "blue light" at night.** Exposure to blue light—the kind that's emitted by smartphones, computers, tablets and LED TVs—disrupts sleep patterns by blocking the release of the sleep hormone melatonin. Even if you do fall asleep fairly easily, blue light exposure may come back to haunt you in the form of a middle-of-the-night wake-up.

If you can't force yourself to power down your electronics within two hours of bedtime, try positioning handheld devices farther away from your eyes than usual.

In addition, consider various apps that filter blue light on your smartphone or tablet. Some operating systems are automatically programmed with this feature—newer Apple devices offer *Night Shift*, for example. Using your device's geolocation and clock, the colors of your display are automatically shifted to the warmer end of the spectrum (which is less disruptive to sleep) around sundown. Free apps for Android devices include *Night Shift: Blue Light Filter* and *Twilight*.

• **Use special lightbulbs.** If you wake up in the middle of the night and make a trip to the bathroom, the glare of the bathroom light tells your brain "It's morning!"

What helps: Use low-blue lightbulbs in your bathroom and bedroom that don't block the release of melatonin. A variety are available from Lighting Science (LSGC.com). Or look online for night-lights designed to emit low levels of blue light.

IF YOU DO WAKE UP

Even if you follow the steps described above, you may still have occasional nighttime awakenings with trouble falling back asleep (meaning you are awake for at least 25 minutes).

Experiment with the following strategies to see what works best for you...

**Consult your doctor if you take medication.

• **Resist the urge to check e-mail or do anything else on your phone.** Even short exposures to blue light are enough to suppress melatonin. Mentally stimulating activities, such as loud TV, are also best avoided. (However, a TV at low volume with the setting adjusted to dim the screen can be a great distractor for an active mind at night.)

My advice: Choose a relaxing activity like reading, listening to soothing music or knitting. If you read, use a book light or a bedside-table lamp that has one of the special bulbs mentioned earlier.

• **Don't look at the clock.** If you do, you'll start doing the mental math of how many hours you have left until you need to wake up. This will cause anxiety that will spike your levels of cortisol and adrenaline, sleep-disrupting hormones that make you feel wide awake!

My advice: Turn your clock around, and try counting backward from 300 by threes to distract yourself and promote drowsiness.

Also helpful: Try the "4-7-8 method"—inhale for four seconds...hold your breath for seven...and exhale slowly for eight. Breathe in this manner for up to 15 to 20 minutes or until you fall asleep. Inhaling and holding in air increases oxygen in the body, which means your body doesn't have to expend as much energy. The slow exhale helps you unwind and mimics the slow breathing that takes place during sleep, which will help you fall asleep.

• **Turn on some pink noise.** The well-known "white noise"—used to mask conversations and potentially startling sounds—is comprised of all frequencies detectable by the human ear. Pink noise, on the other hand, has a lower, softer frequency. Pink noise is generally considered more relaxing and has a steady sound like gentle rain.

Sleep experts believe that our brains respond better to the lower spectrum of pink noise than to the fuller spectrum of white noise. The result is a more peaceful and sleep-conducive feeling.

My advice: Search for a free app that contains pink noise, and listen to it with earphones on your smartphone, laptop or tablet if you wake up in the middle of the night. Just be sure to glance only briefly at the screen when turning on the device, and turn off the screen light while listening. You can set the pink noise to play for a set amount of time, such as 30 minutes. As an alternative, you can purchase a pink-noise generator online.

Midday Energy Lull? Try This...

When I start to feel sluggish after lunch, instead of taking a nap, I shut my office door, turn off the lights, stretch out on the floor—*Black's Law Dictionary* makes a surprisingly effective pillow—and focus only on my breathing for 20 minutes. When other thoughts come rushing in, I acknowledge them, set them aside and focus on my breathing once again. In the past, I had been somewhat skeptical of the value of meditation, but *The Relaxation Response*, a book by Harvard Medical School researcher Herbert Benson, MD, convinced me that there is actual science behind this. I am amazed at how well it works—after I meditate, I feel reenergized for the rest of the day.

Steven J. Weisman, Esq., senior lecturer in the department of law, tax and financial planning at Bentley University, Waltham, Massachusetts. He is founder of the scam-information website Scamicide.com.

Quick Memory Booster

Need to remember to make a phone call or take your medication? A whiff of rosemary oil could help.

Recent study: 150 people over age 65 performed memory tasks either in a rosemary-scented room or in a room without scent. The aroma of rosemary significantly improved both mood and prospective memory (the ability to remember planned events and tasks).

Explanation: The herb offers compounds that boost the area of the brain involved in memory.

Mark Moss, PhD, head of psychology, Northumbria University, Newcastle upon Tyne, UK.

To Make Your Brain Younger...

Older adults who did regular moderate-to-intense exercise such as running or swimming laps had the memory and other cognitive skills of someone a decade younger than those who were sedentary or did light exercise such as gardening, a recent study of 900 older adults found.

Possible explanation: Exercise helps boost blood flow to the brain and enhances brain cell connections. Exercise also lowers risk for high blood pressure, elevated cholesterol and diabetes—all of which can impair cognitive function.

Clinton Wright, MD, scientific director at the Evelyn F. McKnight Brain Institute, University of Miami.

BETTER WAY...

Trick to Get Out of a Funk

In several studies, participants who wrote about what was bothering them for 20 minutes a day, three days in a row, felt happier and less anxious...and had lower blood pressure and improved immune function for months.

James W. Pennebaker, PhD, Regents Centennial Professor of Liberal Arts at University of Texas at Austin.

Fitness & Diet Finds

11 Surprising Ways to Shed Pounds: No Willpower Needed!

If you store boxes of breakfast cereal in the wrong spot in your kitchen, you could end up 20 pounds heavier. If you set serving dishes in the wrong spot at mealtimes, you could consume 20% more calories than you otherwise would have. If you get seated at the wrong table in a restaurant, the odds that you will order a dessert could leap by 73%.

People tend to think that avoiding overeating is mainly a matter of willpower. But willpower alone is never enough. Almost all of us have moments when willpower wavers...and moments when we eat irresponsibly because we are not paying enough attention to eat properly.

The good news is that there are clever, surprising things you can do to avoid overeating without relying on superhuman willpower and vigilance...

FOOD STORAGE TRICKS

- **Segregate snack food.** Each time you open a cupboard that contains empty-calorie snack food, there's a reasonable chance that you will indulge—even if you originally opened the cupboard to retrieve something else.

To avoid this, it's best to just not buy unhealthy snack food. But if that's not in the cards, store all unhealthy snacks, such as potato chips and cookies, in a single cupboard rather than spread them throughout the kitchen as is common. (The typical US kitchen has five cupboards—and snack food is stored in the majority of them.) Do not store anything but snacks in your snack cupboard so that you never accidentally stumble upon temptation.

Brian Wansink, PhD, director of the Food and Brand Lab at Cornell University, Ithaca, New York. In 2007, the White House named him the US Department of Agriculture executive director in charge of Dietary Guidelines for 2010. He is author of *Slim by Design: Mindless Eating Solutions for Everyday Life.* SlimbyDesign.com

Healthy snacks such as fruit or whole-grain rice cakes can remain elsewhere in the kitchen—there is nothing wrong with stumbling upon these.

Next step: To reduce snacking even further, store unhealthy snacks in a cupboard located in a room that you enter less often than your kitchen, such as the basement or the laundry room.

- **Store snacks in single-serving portions.** When snack foods leave the kitchen, they rarely come back. Carry a family-size bag of chips to the living room, for example, and if you're like most people, there's a good chance that you will eat the entire thing...and even if you don't, you likely will eat more than you meant to.

One solution is to buy snacks pre-packaged in single-serving portions—but these tend to cost much more per ounce than larger sizes. Instead, buy economy-size bags, but immediately repackage these snacks into single-serving-size plastic bags or other small containers as soon as the snacks enter the house.

- **In the refrigerator, store healthy snacks in clear containers and unhealthy ones in opaque ones.** Remove fruit from the crisper drawer, and store it in clear plastic bags or storage containers at eye level in your fridge. Meanwhile, wrap unhealthy snacks in tin foil or put them in opaque food containers. The snacks that people are most likely to eat are not the ones they think taste best...they are the ones that they happen to see first.

- **Store cereal boxes out of view.** It probably comes as no surprise that people are especially likely to eat foods that are "on display" on countertops or exposed shelves in their homes. But what is surprising is that this seems to matter most not with candy but with breakfast cereal.

People who keep candy on display in their homes are, on average, three pounds heavier than people who do not...people who have cookies or crackers on display are about eight pounds heavier...while people who have cereal boxes out where they can be seen are in excess of 20 pounds heavier.

The most likely explanation is that people realize that snacking on candy and cookies is bad for them, so they often manage to stop themselves from grabbing these sugary treats...but breakfast cereal has the aura of healthfulness—even though it usually is quite sugary and fattening—so people who have it out on display are less likely to stop themselves from indulging.

MEALS

- **Leave serving dishes and pots on the kitchen counter or stove while you eat.** People who fill their plates at least six feet from the table tend to eat around 20% fewer calories at mealtime than people who bring serving dishes or pots to the table. The reason—having additional food within easy reach greatly increases the odds that people will help themselves to seconds or thirds.

Men are particularly likely to do this. They tend to eat faster than their wives and children, so they finish meals first—then take extra helpings even when they are not very hungry because they get bored sitting around doing nothing.

- **Eat off slightly undersized plates, and use undersized serving spoons.** You might have heard that people eat less when they eat off small plates—small plates make modest amounts of food look more substantial. It turns out that this can be taken too far. If you try to eat dinner off a very small plate, it only increases the odds that you will go back for more. The ideal dinner plate size is around nine inches in diameter—smaller than the typical 10-to-12-inch dinner plate but not so small as to encourage the taking of seconds.

Also: Using serving spoons of modest size reduces consumption, too...as does replacing serving tongs with serving spoons. (Do use tongs to serve salad. Taking large servings of salad makes people less likely to fill up on more fattening foods.) An undersized ice-cream scoop is an especially worthwhile investment—people tend to pay attention to the number of scoops of ice cream they take, not the total amount of ice cream they eat.

But do not try to eat with undersized utensils. It turns out that doesn't make people eat less—it just annoys them.

• **Put on slow music, and turn down the lights.** These things tend to calm people down—and people who feel calm at mealtimes tend to eat more slowly and eat less.

DINING OUT TRICKS

It's easy to overindulge when you eat out. These strategies will help...

• **Ask to be seated at a well-lit table...**by a window...at a table that is higher-than-normal table height...or in a bustling part of the dining room. When people feel on display in restaurants, they tend to order healthier meals, such as fish or salad. When they are seated in booths or dark, private corners, they are more likely to order fattening things such as ribs and desserts.

Example: People seated at the table farthest from a restaurant's front door are 73% more likely to order a dessert than people seated near the entrance.

• **Ask to be seated at least three tables away from the bar.** When people eat dinner at a restaurant's bar—or within two tables of its bar—they order three-and-a-half more alcoholic drinks per party of four. This applies only at dinner, however—people do not drink significantly more when they eat lunch near a restaurant's bar.

• **Adopt trim people's habits at buffets.** Trim people and heavy people tend to exhibit significantly divergent behavior when they dine at buffets—generally without even realizing they are doing so. Thin buffet diners choose tables far from the food (when given a choice of table)...they choose seats that face away from the food...they use smaller plates if multiple plate sizes are available...they use chopsticks (if this is an option)...and they scout out the entire buffet before taking any food. Heavy people tend to do exactly the opposite of each of these things. Act trim, and it will help you be trim!

• **Be aware of your waiter's weight.** If your waiter is overweight, you're more likely to overindulge. In a study of 497 people at 60 full-service restaurants, diners ordered more food—especially dessert—and more alcohol when the waiter had weight to lose than when the waiter was thin. This was true regardless of how much the diners themselves weighed. It's likely that the presence of a heavy person made the diners feel as if they had "permission" to indulge.

You can't control who your waiter is, but just recognizing the effect that a heavy waiter could have on your ordering can help you resist temptation. It's also helpful when eating out to have a "predetermination strategy," such as deciding in advance what you'll order (you usually can view menus online). Or you can have "rules" in place such as only one glass of wine with dinner.

Beware: "Big" Is the New Normal

Donald Cutlip, MD, Harvard Medical School, reported by Rebecca Shannonhouse, editor, *Bottom Line Health*.

Most Americans have obviously gotten heavier over the years. What is shocking is *how much* heavier. A few decades ago, the typical man weighed 181 pounds...now he's 196, according to a recent report from the CDC. For women, the average weight has gone from about 153 to 166.

The dangers of this alarming trend are not new—we all know that being overweight or obese is a risk factor for diabetes, heart disease, stroke and other serious conditions.

So why are so many people still tipping the scales? Part of the problem is how we see ourselves. Now that more than two-thirds of American adults are overweight or obese, "big" has become the new normal. We've simply stopped *noticing*.

To make matters even worse, the main tool for assessing obesity—a weight-to-height ratio known as the body mass index (BMI)—doesn't distinguish *patterns* of obesity. For example, visceral (abdominal) obesity—often evident from the size of one's belly—is the pattern that's linked to the greatest health risks.

For that reason, a waist-to-hip measurement can also be useful for people who suspect that they may be gaining too much weight, says Donald Cutlip, MD, of Harvard Medical School. All you need is a tape measure.

What to do: Measure your hips...measure your waist just above your belly button...and divide the waist number by the hip number. For women, a good reading is 0.8 or below... men should be 0.9 or under.

Important: Being underweight (a BMI below 18.5) or suffering unexplained weight loss can be harmful, too.

EASY TO DO...

3 Ways to Fight Off Hunger Pangs

To fight hunger pains without eating...

- **Smell peppermint every few hours.** In one study, participants who inhaled peppermint oil scent every two hours reported reduced hunger.
- **Drink water.** Hunger pangs sometimes really are a feeling of thirst. Drink one cup of water before eating anything. Or try flavored green or herbal teas.
- **Exercise.** One study found that men had reduced appetite after 60 minutes of cardio exercise—although other studies did not confirm this or find the same effect in women. It still can be worthwhile to try taking a walk or doing lunges or sit-ups to find out if this works for you.

Holly Klamer, MS, registered dietitian, Denver, writing at CalorieSecrets.net.

No More Stomach Rumbles! What to Eat When You're Hungry All the Time

Sharon Palmer, RDN, a Duarte, California–based registered dietitian nutritionist and the author of *The Plant-Powered Diet* and *Plant-Powered for Life*. Palmer is also the editor of the *Environmental Nutrition* newsletter and nutrition editor for *Today's Dietitian*. SharonPalmer.com

Nobody likes a growling stomach—it's embarrassing *and* makes you much more likely to gorge on less-than-stellar foods when you do eat.

What's new: Researchers are now discovering simple ways to harness the hunger-fighting effects of some healthy foods you've probably never considered to ease your growling stomach. *What you need to know...*

"WHY AM I SO HUNGRY?"

Hunger is normal—it's your body's way of helping you maintain a balance between the amount of calories being consumed and burned. But some people feel hungry even when they haven't missed a meal...and may feel ravenous *most of the time.** *Among the possible causes...*

- **Prolonged stress, anxiety and depression.** These strong emotions can trigger the release of appetite-fueling hormones, such as *cortisol*.
- **Lack of sleep.** A recent study shows that too little sleep kick-starts the body's *endocannabinoid system*—the same physiological response that causes the "munchies" in marijuana users.
- **Untreated diabetes.** It impairs the body's ability to properly use glucose as a source of energy, which leads to increased hunger.
- **Certain drugs.** A handful of medications cause hunger as a side effect.

Among the worst offenders: Antihistamines...antidepressants—especially tricyclic antidepressants such as *amitriptyline* (Elavil)...antiseizure drugs, such as *valproic acid*... diabetes drugs, such as sulfonylureas including *glipizide* (Glucotrol)...and corticosteroids (such as cortisone).

HUNGER-FIGHTING NUTRIENTS

When fighting excessive hunger that is not due to a medical condition or drug side effect, the best approach is to make smart food choices. Recent research shows that the trick is to focus on foods that are rich in fiber and protein—both are powerful hunger-fighting nutrients.

Fiber-rich foods tend to be chewy, and the longer it takes to chew a food, the more time

*If you experience excessive hunger, consult your doctor to rule out an underlying medical condition or medication side effect.

there is for the hormones that signal fullness (satiety) to reach your brain. Fiber also stays in the stomach for a long time, so you feel full-er...longer. Protein is also known to increase satiety.

TOP 5 HUNGER FIGHTERS

With these guidelines in mind, here are five great hunger-busting foods...

• **Wheat berries.** These nutty, chewy kernels of wheat are easy to add to your daily diet and offer generous amounts of both protein (6 g per quarter cup, uncooked) and fiber (6 g). They're better than, say, whole wheat pasta because they have a lot more fiber and protein.

My advice: For a hot morning meal, cook and enjoy wheat berries as you would oatmeal...or toss them in salads.

If you're gluten-free: Try quinoa or sorghum.

• **Almonds.** Nuts combine protein, healthy fat and fiber into one small package. For example, one ounce of almonds (about 23 nuts) delivers 6 g of protein and 3.5 g of fiber. Other high-protein nuts include peanuts and pistachios.

My advice: Snack on one ounce of high-protein nuts daily. If you enjoy baking, substitute one-fourth to one-third of the white flour you use with almond flour to give your baked goods more staying power.

BETTER WAYS...

To Avoid Holiday Weight Gain...

Weight gained from Thanksgiving until around New Year's takes *five months* to lose.

During the holiday season: Except for salad and vegetables, keep all other serving dishes off the table when eating. Place them on a counter. That way you have to leave the table to get seconds—and so are less likely to do so.

To limit the temptation of leftovers: Keep them out of sight by freezing them or wrapping them in aluminum foil.

Brian Wansink, PhD, director, Cornell Food and Brand Lab, Ithaca, New York, and author of *Slim by Design* and coauthor of a study of holiday weight gain, published in *The New England Journal of Medicine*.

• **Apples.** Even though apples are not a great source of protein (one medium-sized apple has about 0.5 g), this fruit contains a type of soluble fiber called pectin, which may help prevent the blood sugar spikes that can lead to increased fat storage and more sugar cravings.

My advice: Enjoy fresh apples. One medium apple contains 4 g of fiber.

Other fiber-rich fruits: Figs and prunes (8 g and 6 g, respectively, in one-half cup)...pears (6 g)...and oranges (4 g).

• **Lentils.** These plant-based gems are concentrated sources of vitamins, minerals and slow-digesting carbs for sustained energy. One-half cup of cooked lentils delivers about 8 g each of protein and fiber.

My advice: Sprinkle cooked lentils into salads and scrambled eggs.

• **Collard greens.** OK, so you might not think of collard greens as your go-to rescue food. But one cup of the cooked dark, leafy greens offers 7 g of fiber and 5 g of protein. Cooked spinach and mustard greens offer similar amounts.

My advice: Chop and sauté collard greens in olive oil, garlic, lemon and herbs to coax out their rich flavor. In a salad, dress any of these greens with a vinaigrette made with walnut, flaxseed or soybean oil—all three contain *alpha-linolenic acid*, which, according to a 2015 Japanese study, delays the release of the hunger hormone *ghrelin*.

Eating in "Moderation"? How It Can Cause Weight Gain

Michelle vanDellen, PhD, assistant professor, behavioral and brain sciences at the University of Georgia, Athens, and lead author of the study "How Do People Define Moderation?" published in *Appetite*.

"Eat in moderation." It's a clarion call for healthy eating and touted as an effective way to lose weight.

The idea: Depriving yourself of foods that you love is old-fashioned advice. It's better to eat what you like, including your favorite high-calorie foods—but not too much.

Here's a secret: It's a trap. And it may be making you fat, according to a new paper published in the peer-reviewed journal *Appetite*.

WHAT IS "MODERATION"?

On the fast-food chain Chick-fil-A's bags for takeout food, there was this statement...

"Moderation Is Key: All foods can fit within a healthy diet if consumed in moderation. With appropriate portion sizes and physical activity, you can enjoy treats like our Frosted Lemonade."

Moderation is one of many myths that Big Food uses to rationalize their calorie, fat and sugar bombs. (That Frosted Lemonade from Chick-fil-A contains 63 g of sugar, the equivalent of 16 teaspoons.) But according to recent research, food companies that proselytize moderation are not the core of the problem. The real problem is *you*.

Most people have no idea what moderation in eating really means—and find it easy to twist the idea unconsciously to excuse overeating. To learn more, we spoke with psychologist Michelle vanDellen, PhD, an assistant professor in the behavioral and brain sciences program at the University of Georgia.

THE REAL-LIFE TEST

A series of telling studies examined how people think about moderation, especially when it comes to foods that they know they should limit such as cookies, fruit-shaped gummy snacks, soda, pizza and fast food. *The findings below held true for both men and women...and normal-weight and overweight people...*

- **Most people define "eating moderately" as eating a bigger amount than they think they should eat.** For example, in one study, subjects were presented with a big plate with 24 cookies and asked how many a person should eat—and how many would constitute eating in moderation. On average, they said a person "should" eat about two cookies, but that "moderation" was a little more than three cookies.

- **The more you like a food, the bigger a "moderate" portion will be for you.** In another study, subjects were shown a picture of gummy snacks. The more a person *liked* gummy snacks, the researchers found, the bigger the "moderate" portion tended to be.

- **The more often you eat a particular kind of food, the more frequent you'll consider moderation to be.** In a third study, the researchers asked subjects how often over two weeks they ate 12 different high-calorie foods, including pizza and soda. No matter how often people ate a particular food, they consistently defined "moderate" frequency as *more* frequent than what they themselves did! Thus, if you eat ice cream twice a week, you might define moderate as four times a week.

These malleable definitions are likely contributing to the obesity epidemic—by encouraging overeating. The crucial moment occurs when you've eaten a portion of a food that you know isn't really good to eat a lot of. That's when you must decide if eating more would be going overboard.

To gain control over overeating, explains Dr. vanDellen, you need to *recognize* that you *have a conflict at that moment*—you would really like to eat another piece of pie, but you know you shouldn't. If you delude yourself that you're eating "moderately," you'll never feel that conflict—and you'll just keep eating.

MASTERING MODERATION

While there are many contributors to our obesity epidemic, including sugar and other low-fiber refined carbs, there's strong evidence

EASY TO DO...

How to Change a Bad Habit

Procrastinate! Postpone the negative behavior until tomorrow.

Example: If you're on a diet and want ice cream, tell yourself, I can have it tomorrow. Do that for a few days...and you will find it easier to resist entirely.

Zdravko Cvijetic, founder of the website ZerotoSkill.com, which focuses on mastering habits, and author of the e-book *The Ultimate Productivity Cheat Sheet*.

that the increasing size of portions is a major culprit. That's not to say you should *radically* cut down on how much you eat—this almost always backfires.

Ironically, however, paying attention to the *actual* amounts of foods that you eat may be the best way to truly eat in moderation. To illustrate this, let's go back to that Frosted Lemonade mentioned earlier. It's a 16-ounce, 330-calorie cup of lemonade blended with ice cream.

If you think of it as ice cream, and know your serving sizes, you would realize that a serving size for ice cream is one-half cup—four ounces. For juice, a serving size is six ounces.

So instead of drinking the entire 16 ounces, let's say you enjoy six ounces—three-quarters of a cup. You'll get about 125 calories and 24 g of sugar. It's still a high-sugar treat, but a more manageable one...and perhaps it's even "moderate."

The Breakfast Myth

Emily Dhurandhar, PhD, assistant professor of nutritional sciences at Texas Tech University, reported by Karen Larson, editor, *Bottom Line Personal.*

The saying "Breakfast is the most important meal of the day" has been traced back almost exactly 100 years to a 1917 article in *Good Health* magazine. Ever since then, we've heard that skipping breakfast increases our odds of developing heart problems...and leads to weight gain by encouraging us to eat more later in the day. But recent research has called breakfast's importance into question.

A 16-week study published in *The American Journal of Clinical Nutrition* examined the effect of skipping breakfast on weight loss in 283 participants and found...nothing. "Not eating breakfast had no discernible effect on participants' weight loss," says Emily Dhurandhar, PhD, assistant professor of nutritional sciences at Texas Tech University and lead author of the study.

Other recent studies have failed to find evidence that skipping breakfast harms the heart.

So why has the notion of breakfast's importance endured for nearly a century? One reason is breakfast cereal manufacturers. In fact, *Good Health* magazine was edited by John Harvey Kellogg, MD, coinventor of corn flakes. And there were earlier studies that indeed found that people who skipped breakfast were more likely to be overweight and have heart problems. But people who ignore a century of hectoring about the importance of breakfast would probably tend to be people who also ignore advice about, say, exercising and avoiding junk food.

None of this means that eating breakfast is a bad idea or that there might not be other problems caused by not eating breakfast. But putting on weight and getting heart disease aren't among them.

Better Lunch Choices

Cutting calories? Order lunch (or make it) at least one hour before eating.

Recent findings: People who ordered lunch (including a beverage) in advance made more healthful choices and ate about 10% fewer calories than those who ordered just before eating.

Why: When you are not hungry, it's easier to make wise choices—the same reason that experts suggest not grocery shopping on an empty stomach.

Eric VanEpps, PhD, postdoctoral research fellow at the Center for Health Incentives and Behavioral Economics at the Leonard Davis Institute, University of Pennsylvania, Philadelphia.

Worst Meal for Your Health

The worst meal for your health is The Whole Hog Burger with 2,850 calories. Sold by Uno Pizzeria & Grill, the burger contains five meats—beef, sausage, bacon, prosciutto and pepperoni—plus four cheeses. It is served with fries and onion rings, but those calories are not included in the count. The burger contains 62 grams of saturated fat and nearly 9,800 milligrams of sodium.

Other foods that are rated especially bad for health: Dave & Buster's Short Rib and Cheesy Mac Stack, a 1,910-calorie beef sandwich topped with macaroni and cheese that comes with a side of tater tots...and Buffalo Wild Wings Dessert Nachos, a 2,100-calorie fried flour tortilla with ice cream, cheesecake bites, and chocolate and caramel sauce.

Lindsay Moyer, MS, RDN, senior nutritionist, Center for Science in the Public Interest, Washington, DC, and coauthor of the group's Xtreme Eating 2016 list, quoted at WebMD.com.

High Fat Cheese May Be OK!

High-fat cheese may be as good for you as the low-fat type, when eaten in moderation. In a 12-week study, people who ate three ounces a day of cheese with 25% to 32% fat content had the same blood-chemistry picture—including cholesterol and triglyceride levels—as people who ate three ounces a day of cheese with 13% to 16% fat. And there were no significant differences in body weight change between the groups.

Study of 139 people by researchers at University of Copenhagen, Denmark, published in *The American Journal of Clinical Nutrition.*

Danger of the Paleo Diet

Joseph Feuerstein, MD, assistant professor of clinical medicine at Columbia University, New York City, and director of integrative medicine at Stamford Hospital, Connecticut. He is author of *Dr. Joe's Man Diet: Lose 15-20 Pounds, Drop Bad Cholesterol 20% and Watch Your Blood Sugar Free-Fall in 12 Weeks.* DrFeuerstein.com

Recent research has cast doubt on the trendy Paleo diet, an eating plan that encourages consumption of meat and discourages consumption of grains and other processed foods.

The Paleo diet has become popular in part because it makes some intuitive sense. Humans were hunter-gatherers long before the advent of farming, so it is not unreasonable to speculate that our bodies might be well-suited to subsist on the meats, vegetables and nuts that our Paleolithic hunter-gatherer ancestors ate for all of those millennia.

Proponents of the Paleo diet argue that modern humans are prone to packing on excess pounds in part because we now eat processed foods and farm products such as grains that our early ancestors did not eat.

But while the Paleo diet is a compelling theory, there has never been much research to back it up. And now a study has cast doubt on whether the Paleo diet even was healthy for people who lived during Paleolithic times. When researchers at St. Luke's Mid America Heart Institute in Kansas City conducted CT scans on 137 ancient mummies from four different parts of the globe, they discovered that more than one-third of them showed signs of heart disease (though it is worth noting that Paleolithic people probably smoked most or all of their meat over fires, a preparation technique that likely exacerbates heart disease dangers).

Meanwhile, a long-term study conducted in China by researchers from Cornell, Oxford and the Chinese Academy of Preventive Medicine found a strong correlation between the consumption of meat (as well as dairy products) and coronary heart disease, casting further doubt on the healthfulness of meat-heavy diets.

Advice: Exercise caution in trying the Paleo diet (or any other meat-heavy diet) if you have a history of heart disease and/or if heart problems run in your family. But this diet might be a reasonable option if your doctor confirms that your heart is in good shape and if you choose grains high in soluble fiber, such as oats or flax, which have been shown to help lower blood pressure and stroke risk.

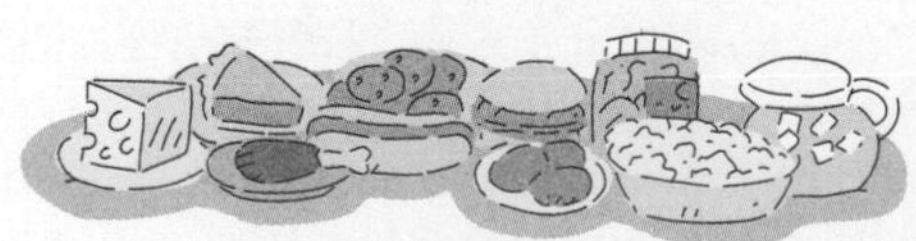

Chocolate and Dieting

Avoid chocolate candy when trying to lose weight. Stop eating it *completely*—trying to consume only a little typically leads to eating much more than you planned.

Alternative if you want to consume healthful cocoa: Plain, low-fat yogurt mixed with two tablespoons of unsweetened cocoa powder...a drink made with skim milk and unsweetened cocoa powder.

Stephen Gullo, PhD, author of *The Thin Commandments Diet.*

Best Produce to Keep Weight Down

The best produce to eat for weight management is apples, berries, pears, leafy greens and cruciferous vegetables, such as cauliflower and brussels sprouts—these are high in fiber and have a lower glycemic index than other produce. Avoid starchy vegetables such as potatoes and corn.

Study of the eating habits of 130,000 people led by researchers at Harvard T.H. Chan School of Public Health, Boston, published in *PLOS Medicine.*

Beware of "Bulletproof Coffee"

"Bulletproof coffee"—which is blended with butter and an oil similar to coconut oil—is being promoted for weight loss and overall health.

But: The recommended two-cup serving contains far more than the usual daily recommendation of saturated fat, and a recent study found that the drink significantly raises LDL (bad) cholesterol.

Bottom line: There is no evidence whatsoever that the drink has any health benefits.

University of California, Berkeley Wellness Letter, BerkeleyWellness.com.

Diet Soda Linked to Weight Gain

People who drank one or more cans of diet soda every day for nine years added 3.2 inches to their waistlines versus only 0.8 inches for people who did not drink diet soda. People who drank diet soda only occasionally expanded their waists by 1.8 inches.

Study of 749 people over age 65 by researchers at University of Texas Health Science Center at San Antonio, published in *Journal of the American Geriatrics Society.*

Easy Weight-Loss Trick

Drinking water—at the right time (and in the right amount)—really can help shed pounds, recent research has discovered. Obese adults who drank two 8-ounce glasses of tap or bottled water 30 minutes before each meal lost an average of nearly three pounds more over a 12-week period than study participants who didn't drink water...but simply imagined that their stomachs were full before each meal.

Helen M. Parretti, PhD, clinical lecturer, University of Birmingham, UK.

Lose the Clutter, Lose the Weight

Reduce clutter to make weight loss easier. People who live with extreme clutter are 76% more likely to struggle with weight issues than those who keep their homes orderly. Clutter causes stress that can lead to overeating and makes it harder to make healthy food choices.

Self-defense: Clear kitchen counters and tables regularly, and throw out anything that makes you feel stressed or guilty, such as expired, never-used spices.

Peter Walsh, professional organizer, Los Angeles, and author of *Lose the Clutter, Lose the Weight*, quoted in RedbookMag.com.

One-Hour Drive = Five Pounds

Adults who spend one hour per day driving are five pounds heavier and have waistlines that are more than one-half inch larger than those who drive less than 15 minutes a day, according to a recent study of 2,800 adults.

Why: Long commutes add to the harmful effects of sitting for hours at work.

What to do: Whenever possible, walk or bike instead of driving...and get at least 30 minutes of moderate-intensity exercise five days a week.

Takemi Sugiyama, PhD, professor at the Institute for Health & Ageing, Australian Catholic University in Melbourne.

Stress May Reverse a Healthful Diet

In recent research, women who ate a healthful unsaturated-fat meal and had a highly stressful day had identical levels of inflammatory markers as women who ate a saturated-fat meal of biscuits and gravy but reported no stress.

Self-defense: Take steps to manage stress—for example, do yoga or meditation, exercise regularly and get enough sleep.

Janice Kiecolt-Glaser, PhD, director, Institute for Behavioral Medicine Research, The Ohio State University, Columbus.

A Better Way to Weight Train: You Don't Have to Heave Heavy Weights

Brad Schoenfeld, PhD, a certified strength and conditioning specialist and an assistant professor in exercise science at Lehman College in New York City, where he directs the Human Performance Lab. Dr. Schoenfeld is also the assistant editor in chief of the National Strength and Conditioning Association's *Strength and Conditioning Journal*, and author of *Science and Development of Muscle Hypertrophy*.

To get the biggest bang from your exercise regimen, strength training is a must. It not only builds muscle and bone but also helps manage your weight and control chronic health problems such as diabetes and heart disease.

But not everyone relishes the idea of heaving heavy weights. And the practice can be risky for people with arthritis, osteoporosis and other conditions.

Good news: Researchers have now discovered that people who repeatedly lift *light* weights get nearly the same benefits as those who do heavy-weight workouts.

Why this matters: Whether you're using hand weights or exercise machines, the lighter-weight approach can make strength training safer and more enjoyable.

Men and women who lift light weights instead of heavy ones are also less likely to experience joint, tendon or ligament injury. Plus, the workouts are easier for older adults...those with arthritis or other health problems...and those who are new to weight lifting.

TAKE NOTE...

Caffeine May Improve a Workout

Men who were given 16 to 24 ounces of coffee before a workout did 11.6% more bench presses and 19.1% more leg presses, compared with men who did not drink coffee.

Federal University of Espirito Santo, Vitória, Brazil.

THE NEW THINKING

According to traditional thinking, you need to lift heavy weights to build your muscles. In practice, this meant identifying your *one-repetition maximum*—the heaviest weight that you could lift just one time. Then you'd design a workout that required lifting 65% or more of that weight eight to 12 times.

This approach is still favored by many elite athletes because lifting at the edge of your ability targets *fast-twitch muscle fibers*, the ones that grow quickly and create an admirable physique. But studies now show that *slow-twitch fibers*, the ones that are stimulated to a greater extent by light lifting, can also develop and grow.

Important finding: In a recent meta-analysis published in the journal *Sports Medicine*, people who lifted lighter weights for six weeks achieved the same muscle growth—although not quite as much strength—as those who lifted heavy weights.

Heavy lifting is still the preferred approach for people who need to develop their strength to the utmost—top athletes, construction workers, movers, etc. But those who simply want to look better and improve their *functional capacity*—the ability to carry groceries, work in the yard, play recreational sports, etc.—will do just as well with lighter loads.

Bonus: Building muscle mass also helps control blood sugar.

LESS WEIGHT, MORE REPS

Muscle growth occurs *only* when muscles are exhausted—when you simply can't move the weight one more time. So to get comparable benefits to a traditional heavy-weight workout requiring eight to 12 repetitions, you'll need to do 20 to 25 reps with lighter weights. Your weight workouts will take a little longer, but your muscles will be just as tired when you're done.

A LIGHT-WEIGHT PLAN

Lighter-weight workouts are easier on the joints than those done with heavy weights, and the results are still relatively fast—you'll likely notice an increase in strength/muscle size within a few weeks. *To start...*

- **Choose your weights wisely.** Instead of calculating percentages—a heavy-weight lifter, as described earlier, may aim to lift at least 65% of his/her one-repetition maximum—keep it simple. Forget the percentages, and let repetitions guide your starting weights. For example, do each exercise 20 to 25 times. If you can't complete that many, you're starting too heavy. Conversely, if you can easily do 20 to 25 reps, the weight's too light.*

Important: You're not doing yourself any good if you can easily lift a weight 25 times. You need to strain. On a one-to-10 scale of effort, the last few reps should rate nine-and-a-half or 10.

- **Do multiple sets.** You'll progress more quickly when you do three sets of each exercise—for example, bicep curls. Complete 20 to 25 repetitions...rest for two minutes...do them again...rest...and repeat one more time. If you don't have the time—or the desire—to do three sets, opt for a single-set approach. You'll still notice increases in strength and muscle size, but your gains won't be as great as with a multi-set approach.

- **Work out at least twice a week.** You want to work each muscle group—arms, legs, chest, midsection, etc.—at least twice a week. Three or four times weekly will give even faster results.

Important: Don't work the same muscles two days in a row. Growth occurs during the recovery phase...and injuries are more likely when you stress already-tired muscles.

If you work out every day: Alternate muscle groups—for example, do leg and back exercises on Monday...arm and chest exercises on Tuesday...then more leg and back work on Wednesday, etc.

EXERCISES FOR REAL LIFE

The strength-training exercises below will give you more confidence and power when doing your daily activities—follow the advice above for choosing your weights, repetitions, exercise frequency, etc....

*Hand weights are available in neoprene, iron and vinyl at many retail stores and online. I recommend holding various weights in a store to choose the one that feels best.

• **Bicep curls.** Exercising this upper-arm muscle will make carrying groceries a little easier.

What to do: Hold a hand weight in each hand. While keeping your elbows near your sides and your shoulders back, curl the weight toward your shoulder, then lower it back down.

• **One-arm triceps extensions.** This exercise will strengthen your triceps (muscles on the backs of the upper arms), which help balance the biceps—and give your arms a toned appearance. It will help when moving furniture or shoveling snow.

What to do: While sitting, hold a hand weight over your head, with your arm straight up and your elbow close to your head. Bend your elbow and lower the weight just behind your neck, then raise it back up. Repeat with the other arm.

• **Lunges.** This versatile exercise targets the buttocks and thighs, along with the arms, making climbing stairs easier.

What to do: With a weight in each hand, stand with your feet about shoulder-width apart. Take a long step forward with your right foot. As your foot lands, bend the knee until the thigh is nearly parallel to the floor. Pull your right leg back to the starting position, then lunge with the left foot.

GOOD TO KNOW...

15 Minutes to Better Health

People who worked out for only 15 minutes a day—half the widely recommended amount—had 22% lower risk for death (from heart disease, stroke, cancer and other causes) versus those who were sedentary, in an analysis of nearly 123,000 adults age 60 and older. Getting additional exercise lowered death risk even more—28% for those who worked out for 30 minutes...35%, for one hour or more.

Note: Exercise needs to be moderate-to-vigorous intensity, such as brisk walking or fast biking.

David Hupin, MD, physician, department of clinical and exercise physiology, University Hospital of Saint-Étienne, France.

You Can Work Out Like an Olympic Athlete

Timothy Miller, MD, director of the endurance medicine program, which specializes in treating endurance athletes, and associate professor of clinical orthopaedics at The Ohio State University Wexner Medical Center in Columbus. Dr. Miller is also a volunteer team physician for the US Olympic Track and Field Team.

Watching Olympic athletes perform their incredible feats can be awe-inspiring...and humbling. But don't despair.

Even if you're not an Olympic athlete, you can still perform at your highest potential by adding highly effective Olympic training routines to your own workout.

Helpful: You can add all—or just a few—of the exercises below to your current fitness routine to increase your endurance, gain strength and boost bone density...*

FARTLEK WORKOUT

Which Olympic athletes do this? Cyclists and distance runners.

Good for: Anyone who wants to add speed and endurance to a walking, running or cycling routine.

What is it? Short bursts of high-intensity movement—a few seconds to a minute—that take place within a longer aerobic routine. Many people refer to this workout method as Fartlek (which means "speed play" in Swedish), but it is also known as interval training.

How can I do this? Do a 30-minute walk or jog in your neighborhood. Begin with a 10-minute warm-up of a slower-paced run or walk (use a stopwatch to keep track of your time). Once you're warmed up, sprint (or walk fast) between two mailboxes (or telephone poles or any other regularly spaced marker)... then return to your regular pace for the distance of three mailboxes. Sprint or walk fast again, continuing the same interval pattern for 10 minutes. Afterward, return to your regular pace for 10 minutes. Then cool down for a few minutes with a slower run or walk.

*If you have a chronic medical condition or a recent injury, or are at increased risk of falling, consult your doctor before trying these exercises.

For a 30-minute cycling routine, pedal slowly for a 10-minute warm-up. Then do 30-second sprints pedaling as fast as you can followed by one minute of slow pedaling for a total of 10 minutes. Then cycle for 10 minutes at a comfortable pace and end with a cooldown.

ECCENTRIC EXERCISES

Which Olympic athletes do this? Power lifters and gymnasts.

Good for: Anyone who wants to strengthen his/her calves, Achilles tendons and biceps.

What is it? These exercises, which are the most efficient way to build strength, focus on working the muscle when it lengthens. In this phase, you consciously slow the descent of a weight (or gravity). This means that you use resistance twice—once while lifting the weight and once while lowering it.

How can I do this? Biceps curls and heel drops.

Biceps curl. To begin, choose a light hand weight (about three to five pounds)...or use small soup cans. Stand with your feet shoulder-width apart, elbows at your sides and forearms at 90-degree angles from your body, with your palms and weights facing up. Hold your left arm steady. Lift your right arm toward your shoulder for a count of two to three seconds, keeping your elbow at your side.

Lower the weight slowly and with control for a count of three to four seconds, keeping your muscles contracted. This is the eccentric phase of the exercise. Alternate arms for a total of 12 to 15 repetitions on each arm. Perform the whole set two to three times. When you can perform 10 reps easily, increase the weight.

Heel drop. Stand with the balls of your feet on the edge of a stair. Drop your heels as low as you can in a slow, controlled motion, taking about three to four seconds to completely lower them. Then push your heels back up for a count of two to three seconds. Repeat 12 to 15 times. Do two to three sets.

PLYOMETRIC TRAINING

Which Olympic athletes do this? High jumpers, gymnasts, sprinters and basketball players.

Good for: Anyone who wants to build leg strength.

BETTER WAY...

Racket Sports May Be Best for Health

Racket sports were associated with the greatest reduction in death from any cause (47%) and death from cardiovascular causes (56%). The next best reductions came from swimming—28% from any cause and 41% from cardiovascular causes. Aerobics was associated with a 27% reduced risk for death from any cause and 36% from cardiovascular factors. The study did not prove cause and effect but did indicate that participants' risk for death dropped more when they exercised more often.

Nine-year study by European and Australian researchers of 80,306 people, published in *British Journal of Sports Medicine.*

What is it? Also known as "jump training," these exercises require your muscles to exert maximum force in short intervals.

How can I do this? Box jumps. Most gyms have jump boxes of varying heights (six inches, 18 inches, etc.), or you can buy one at a sporting-goods store or online. Pick a height you can jump onto so that both feet land squarely on the box.

Stand with feet slightly wider than shoulder-width apart, knees bent. Using your arms to help generate power, jump on the box landing softly on two feet, knees flexed. Keep your hands in front of you for balance. Then jump back down to the starting position. Repeat 10 times for a total of three sets.

Reboot Your Workout!

Robert Hopper, PhD, an exercise physiologist and author of *Stick with Exercise for a Lifetime*, reported by Rebecca Shannonhouse, editor, *Bottom Line Health.*

Lately, my workouts have started to feel...well, like work. I still go to the gym, but not as often as I used to—or need to.

Does this sound familiar? Sooner or later, motivation vanishes from our exercise routines. But the "routine"—which inevitably leads to boredom—is actually part of the problem.

To get back on track, I reached out to Robert Hopper, PhD, an exercise physiologist and author of *Stick with Exercise for a Lifetime. His advice...*

• **Pick an activity that you really enjoy.** Sounds obvious—but how many of us head straight for the treadmill or the same piece of equipment every time we go to the gym? Instead, think of a sport you really love to do. It might be biking, skiing, golf or racquetball. Think of it as *your* activity, and do it whenever you can.

• **Choose your workouts strategically.** This means opting for activities that support your favorite form of physical activity.

Example: If you are a skier, biking and lower-body weight training will help keep you in shape to hit the slopes.

• **Pay yourself.** A bit too extreme? It actually works for a lot of people.

Helpful: Try one of the motivational smartphone apps—such as Pact, which allows you to team up with friends so you can all get paid for working out...or StickK, which donates your contribution to a favorite charity when you meet your fitness goals—or to one you despise when you don't.

I'm excited to try these new approaches, so if you'll excuse me...I'm off to the gym!

Hate to Exercise? Get a Dog

Dog owners were 34% more likely to meet the recommended minimum of 150 minutes of moderate exercise a week—and 69% more likely to be physically active—than people who don't own dogs, recent research has found.

Good idea: If you have a dog, work out with your pet. K9FitClub has lots of different classes in cities across the US. Go to K9FitClub.com.

Mathew J. Reeves, PhD, professor of epidemiology and biostatistics, Michigan State University, East Lansing.

Get Healthy the Italian Way

In Italy, the *passeggiata* is a short, sociable walk taken after meals. A recent study found that taking a 15-minute walk after each meal improves blood sugar levels for 24 hours. That helps lower the risk for diabetes.

Study by researchers at George Washington University School of Public Health and Health Services, published in *Diabetes Care*.

Walking and Weight Loss

A friend recently complained, "I thought I'd lose weight by walking for 30 to 60 minutes every day, but it's been six weeks and I've gained a couple of pounds! What's going on?"

What I told her: Walking itself is not usually enough for weight loss. Exercise can increase appetite, so many people eat more after a workout. It's also important to keep moving throughout the day. Studies show that people who exercise and are sedentary the rest of the day can end up burning few calories overall. To lose weight, cut calories in addition to walking—talk to your doctor about the best diet for you.

Eric Ravussin, PhD, associate executive director for clinical science, Pennington Biomedical Research Center, Baton Rouge, Louisiana.

Avoid Strenuous Exercise When You're Upset

People who are angry or upset and work out to help themselves handle the emotions triple their risk of having a heart attack within an hour. Both exercise and emotional stress put a strain on the heart, and the combination creates an even greater strain.

Self-defense: If you find that it helps to work out when you are stressed or upset, be careful not to go beyond your normal routine—the intensity of exercise at times of emotional upset raises cardiovascular risk.

Study led by researchers at Population Health Research Institute, McMaster University, Hamilton, Ontario, published in *Circulation*.

Headaches While Working Out...

Alan M. Rapoport, MD, clinical professor of neurology, David Geffen School of Medicine at UCLA, and immediate past president of the International Headache Society. IHS-headache.org

About 10% of healthy adults develop mild-to-moderate headaches during or after a workout, a condition known as "primary exercise headache." The headache usually comes on suddenly and can be on one or both sides of the head. It is not caused by another disorder, and researchers believe that changes in blood flow to the brain can trigger the headache.

Fortunately, you can take steps to avoid this problem. Since sustained exertion can cause this type of head pain, ease into exercise by warming up for five minutes. Start with a slow pace and increase speed every minute until you are at your treadmill exercise pace. And don't skip the five-minute cool-down walk at the end of your session.

Also, stay hydrated by drinking water before, during and after exercising. *Naproxen* (Aleve) or a similar pain reliever, taken about an hour before your workout, may prevent an exercise-related headache.

Primary exercise headaches usually last from five minutes to two days. They typically go away within three to six months as the body adapts to a regular exercise program. To help your body adjust, take several weeks to increase your speed and incline on the treadmill.

If these tips don't seem to help, or if headaches are severe and/or are accompanied by other symptoms, such as weakness, numbness, and/or visual or memory problems, tell your doctor. You may need to have a neurological evaluation.

Fitness Trackers Might Not Help You Lose Weight

Mitesh Patel, MD, assistant professor of medicine and health-care management at Perelman School of Medicine and The Wharton School at University of Pennsylvania, Philadelphia. Dr. Patel is also director of the Penn Medicine Nudge Unit, which steers providers as well as patients toward better health-care decisions. Healthcare Innovation.upenn.edu

A study published in *JAMA* found that dieters who wore fitness trackers for 24 months lost significantly less weight than dieters who did not—7.7 pounds versus 13 pounds, on average. Fitness trackers are wearable digital devices that measure fitness data such as the number of steps taken each day and calories burned. Their makers often boast that these devices promote weight loss, something this study calls into question.

But other research suggests that while these devices alone often are not effective, they can be paired with "engagement strategies" to promote weight loss and fitness, such as using them in a social way.

Example: The tracker's data could be shared with friends or family members for peer support...or a group of friends could wear fitness trackers and compete to see who can walk the farthest each week.

It also is worth noting that the recent study gave fitness trackers to people who already were participating in diet and exercise programs. In doing so, it might have accidentally undermined the healthy habits these people previously had established by asking them to change something that was already working.

What to do: Before purchasing a fitness tracker, use a smartphone fitness tracker app, a popular one is *Health Mate* by Withings. These apps are not quite as accurate as full-fledged fitness trackers, but they are a good way for smartphone owners to confirm that they will use a tracker before investing money in one. One of the reasons that trackers sometimes are ineffective is that many people discontinue use within a few months.

As noted above, if you purchase a tracker, share your tracker results with friends or, better yet, enlist those friends into a fitness-tracker competition.

Also, set reasonable fitness goals for yourself. Use your smartphone app or fitness tracker to determine your current daily activity level, and then set a personal daily target that is perhaps 1,000 to 2,000 steps above this. Increase this target slowly over time.

Sneakers That Strengthen Legs

"Barefoot sneakers" strengthen legs and feet more effectively than regular sneakers. These minimalist shoes have stretchy-fabric uppers, zero heel-to-toe drop and a three-millimeter outer sole—with no midsole cushioning or arch support. Runners who used them for six months had 7% larger leg muscles and 9% larger foot muscles—while those who used regular sneakers had no muscle increase.

Study of 38 runners led by researchers at Hong Kong Polytechnic University, Hung Hom, Kowloon, published in *Clinical Biomechanics*.

Simple Ways to Improve Balance

See how long you can stand on one foot with your eyes closed, and work on improving your time. *Rise up on your toes 10 times* with your eyes open and then 10 more times with them closed. *Balance yourself on one foot* for 10 to 15 seconds, then switch legs. Repeat 10 times, then do it again with your eyes closed. *Walk in a straight line*, placing the heel of one foot in front of the toes of the other foot.

Caution: When performing these exercises, stand near a wall or some other support.

University of California, Berkeley Wellness Letter, BerkeleyWellness.com.

Cool Exercise Treat

Having a slushy drink before a hot-weather workout may improve performance, recent research has found.

Details: Runners were given about two cups of either a frozen or room-temperature drink 45 minutes before a 10K event in 82°F weather.

Results: Those who drank the slushy ran an average of 15 seconds faster.

Possible reason: The ice increased body heat storage capacity, which allowed runners to improve running time by avoiding overheating. Eating an ice pop may have a similar effect.

Jason Kai Wei Lee, PhD, head, human performance laboratory, DSO National Laboratories, Singapore.

5

Natural Health Now

7-Step Heart Healthy Regimen from a Top Cardiologist

When it comes to your heart health, most cardiologists provide general recommendations—get regular exercise, consume a balanced diet and don't smoke. But wouldn't it be beneficial to know *exactly* what a physician who specializes in heart disease does to keep his/her own heart healthy?

To find out, we asked Joel K. Kahn, MD, a leading cardiologist, what he does to ensure that his heart stays strong. Here are his personal heart-health secrets, which he recommends—whether you want to prevent heart disease or already have it…

SECRET #1: **Drink room-temperature water.** You may not expect an MD who was trained in mainstream Western medicine to practice principles of the ancient Indian wellness philosophy of Ayurveda. But many of these lifestyle habits do carry important health benefits.

For example, according to Ayurvedic medicine, room-temperature water spiked with lemon or lime is good for digestive and cardiovascular health. Because the esophagus is located close to the heart, swigging ice water can cause changes in the heart's normal rhythm in some people.

What I do: If I don't have time to prepare a glass of lemon water, I always drink a big glass of room-temperature water before I get out of bed. *Here's why:* We all get dehydrated during the night. Drinking water pumps up the liquid volume of blood, which reduces the risk for blood clots.

Joel K. Kahn, MD, a clinical professor of medicine at Wayne State University School of Medicine in Detroit and founder of the Kahn Center for Cardiac Longevity in Bloomfield Hills, Michigan. He is also an associate professor at Oakland University William Beaumont School of Medicine in Rochester, Michigan, and author of *The Whole Heart Solution*. DrJoelKahn.com

I also drink a lot of liquids throughout the day. How much do you need? Divide your weight in half. That's the number of ounces you should drink. A person who weighs, say, 150 pounds, should drink at least 75 ounces (about nine cups) of fluids, including water, every day.

***SECRET #2:* Make time for prayer and reflection.** There's a strong link between stress and cardiovascular disease. A landmark study found that heart patients who had high levels of stress—along with depression, which is often fueled by stress—were nearly 50% more likely to have a heart attack or die than those with more emotional balance.

What I do: I like meditation and prayer—my routine includes counting my blessings before I get out of bed in the morning and saying a few prayers. I also appreciate the simple miracles of sunrises, hugs and special friends and family.

Other stress reducers: Listening to music and taking long walks.

***SECRET #3:* Do *fast* workouts.** Exercise is crucial to keeping your heart strong, but it's sometimes hard to fit this into a busy schedule. I exercise before breakfast (see below) and eat within 30 minutes after finishing my workout.

What I do: My usual morning workout (six days a week) includes 20 minutes of cardio—on a treadmill, recumbent bike or rowing machine—followed by about 10 minutes of weight lifting.

When I don't have time for a half-hour session, I may do just 12 minutes of *high-intensity interval training* (HIIT). This typically includes a two-minute warm-up of fast walking on the treadmill, followed by eight minutes of intervals—running all-out for 30 seconds, followed by 30 seconds of walking. I follow this with a two-minute cooldown of slow walking.

HIIT increases cardiorespiratory fitness, builds muscle and reduces inflammation and insulin resistance (which promotes diabetes). *Important:* HIIT is strenuous, so check with your doctor before trying it.

***SECRET #4:* Have a healthy breakfast.** Millions of Americans skip this important meal. That's a problem because skipping meals has been linked to obesity, high blood pressure, insulin resistance and elevated cholesterol.

Specifically, men who skipped breakfast were found to be 27% more likely to develop coronary heart disease than those who ate a healthy breakfast, according to a study in the journal *Circulation.*

What I do: To save time, I get my breakfast ready the night before. I fill a glass container with oatmeal and almond milk and let it soak in the refrigerator overnight. In the morning, all of the liquid is absorbed, and it's soft and ready to eat. I stir it well and top with a few tablespoons of chopped dried figs, unsweetened coconut flakes or sliced berries. *For variety:* I have a "super smoothie" with antioxidant-rich ingredients, such as kale, spinach; frozen blueberries, flax, etc., and organic soy or almond milk.

***SECRET #5:* Use heart-healthy supplements.** Dietary supplements aren't the best way to *treat* cardiovascular disease (although they can help in some cases). Supplements are better for preventing heart problems. *Note:* Check with your doctor before taking any of those listed here—they can interact with some medications. *What I take (follow dosage instructions on the label)...*

- **Magnesium glycinate,** which is easily absorbed. People who get enough magnesium (millions of Americans are deficient) are less likely to have a heart attack or stroke than

TAKE NOTE...

Here's to a Lower Heart Attack Risk!

Beer may be good for women's hearts. Women who drank one or two beers per week had *30% lower risk for heart attack* over three decades than those who drank beer several times per week/daily or never drank beer.

Possible reason: One or two beers per week may reduce triglycerides, blood fats that can raise heart attack risk.

Study of about 1,500 women over more than 30 years by researchers at Sahlgrenska Academy, University of Gothenburg, Sweden, published in *Scandinavian Journal of Primary Health Care.*

those who don't get adequate amounts of the mineral.

• **Vitamin D.** The evidence isn't yet definitive but suggests that vitamin D may improve heart health.

• **Coenzyme Q10 (CoQ10).** It is a vitamin-like substance that lowers blood pressure and can improve symptoms of heart failure.

SECRET #6: **Eat a plant-based diet.** It's been linked to a reduced risk for diabetes and certain types of cancer as well as heart disease.

What I do: I've been a vegetarian for nearly 40 years. I eat foods with a variety of colors, such as berries and peppers. For me, a huge salad can be a meal! I also enjoy a handful of raw nuts every day.

SECRET #7: **Get enough sleep.** People who sleep at least seven hours a night are 43% less likely to have a fatal heart attack than those who get by on six hours or less.

What I do: I usually get up at 6 am, so I make sure that I'm in bed by 11 pm. I also *plan* a good night's sleep. For example, I stop drinking caffeinated beverages at least 10 hours before bedtime (this means that I have nothing with caffeine after 1 pm)...and usually stop eating three hours before bed—active digestion makes it harder to fall asleep and increases nighttime awakenings.

Another trick: I have a sleep-promoting bulb in the reading lamp on my nightstand. Typical lightbulbs emit high levels of *short-wavelength blue light,* which suppresses the brain's production of the sleep-inducing hormone melatonin. You can buy bulbs (such as the Good Night LED or the GE Align PM) that emit small amounts of blue light.

Juice Up Your Heart!

Drinking a 2.4-ounce glass of beet juice daily reduced systolic (or top number) blood pressure by five to 10 points in a small, week-long study of older patients with a common form of heart failure that affects the pumping ability of the left ventricle. A 24% boost in aerobic endurance was also reported. Beet juice tastes sweet and is packed with *inorganic nitrate,* a nutrient that has been shown to improve vascular health and oxygen metabolism.

Dalane Kitzman, MD, professor of cardiology, Wake Forest Baptist Medical Center, Winston-Salem, North Carolina.

Nuts Lower Heart Disease Risk and More!

Just a few nuts a day may lower disease risk. In a review of studies, people who ate nuts had a 29% lower risk for coronary heart disease...21% reduced risk for cardiovascular disease...and 15% lower risk for cancer. Nut eaters also had a 52% lower risk for respiratory disease...39% lower risk for diabetes...and 75% reduced risk for infectious disease. Most risk reduction for all diseases occurred in people who ate just one ounce of nuts per day—about two dozen almonds or 15 pecan halves.

Review of data from 20 prospective studies led by researchers at Imperial College London, UK, and Harvard T.H. Chan School of Public Health, Boston, published in *BMC Medicine.*

Fish Oil Helps After Heart Attack

Adults who took high doses (4 g per day) of fish oil supplements for six months after a heart attack had better heart function and less scarring of heart muscle than those who didn't take fish oil, according to a recent study of 360 heart attack survivors.

Possible reason: Omega-3 fatty acids in fish oil reduce inflammation that harms the heart.

Important: Check with your doctor before taking fish oil—it can interact with blood thinners and certain other medications.

Raymond Kwong, MD, MPH, director, cardiac magnetic resonance imaging, Brigham and Women's Hospital, Boston.

Powerful Vitamin D

Vitamin D may improve cardiac function in heart failure patients.

Recent study: Patients with the chronic condition who took 4,000 international units (IU) of vitamin D daily for one year showed a 38% improvement in the heart's pumping ability. This may mean that for some heart disease patients, vitamin D supplementation could lessen the need for an implantable defibrillator.

Klaus Witte, MD, associate professor and consultant cardiologist at Leeds Institute of Cardiovascular and Metabolic Medicine, University of Leeds, UK.

Hit the Sauna to Reduce Cardiovascular Risk

Saunas are associated with lower death risk. Men in Finland who used a dry sauna two to three times a week over the long term (nearly 21 years) for at least 11 minutes each time had a 22% lower risk of dying from a sudden cardiovascular event than men who used a sauna only once a week. Men who used saunas four to seven times a week had a 63% lower risk of dying from a cardiovascular event. *Why:* Sauna use increases the heart rate to a level similar to that when doing low-to-moderate exercise and helps to lower blood pressure.

Study of 2,315 men by researchers at University of Eastern Finland, Kuopio.

The Dangerous Truth About Calcium

Susan Levin, MS, RD, director of nutrition education for the Physicians Committee for Responsible Medicine, a Washington, DC–based nonprofit group dedicated to promoting preventive medicine, better nutrition and higher standards in research.

The calcium supplements that millions of Americans take for bone health may cause serious damage to the heart. That's the conclusion of the latest study examining the long-term risks of these supplements.

The research, published in *Journal of the American Heart Association,* found that people who supplement with calcium are more likely to develop arterial calcification than those who get their calcium from foods. Calcium that accumulates in the arteries can impair circulation and increase the risk for heart disease.

Yet an estimated 43% of Americans continue to supplement with calcium.

WHAT YOUR BONES REALLY NEED

It is a fact that Americans don't get enough calcium. Only 42% meet the estimated average daily requirement of 1,000 milligrams (mg) to 1,200 mg (the exact amount depends on age and gender). It's a serious problem because both women and men need calcium—along with exercise, vitamin D and other nutrients—to prevent bone weakness and osteoporosis, a leading cause of disability and fracture-related deaths.

But supplements aren't the answer for many people. They may slightly increase bone density, but they do little to reduce your risk for bone fractures. In a recent analysis of studies published in *BMJ*, researchers concluded that "evidence that calcium supplements prevent fractures is weak and inconsistent."

The calcium that you get from food is different. It enters the body slowly and in small amounts. That's very different from the calcium rush that you get from supplements. Also, food delivers a "package" that includes calcium along with dozens of other minerals and nutrients, including vitamins, proteins, fiber, amino acids and, in the case of plant foods, phytonutrients. It seems likely that our bodies benefit from nutritional complexity. You don't get this from single-ingredient supplements.

CALCIUM IN THE WRONG PLACES

In the *Journal of the American Heart Association* study, researchers analyzed medical tests that were done on more than 2,700 people who participated in a large heart disease study. They were looking for *coronary artery calcium*, a heart disease risk factor.

Your calcium score (as measured by a heart CT scan) should be zero. But as people age, levels of calcium-based plaque tend to accumulate in the aorta and other arteries. These levels increase more in people who take calcium supplements.

The study found that people who supplemented with calcium were 22% more likely to have increased coronary calcium scores over a 10-year period than those who didn't supplement. It wasn't the amount of calcium that mattered most—it was the type. People who did not take supplements but who got a lot of calcium from foods (more than 1,400 mg daily) were 27% less likely than those who consumed the least amount of calcium from foods to have calcium scores that indicated an elevated heart risk.

Calcium deposits affect more than just the heart. A high calcium score also has been linked to increased risk for cancer including cancers of the prostate, lung, colon, breast, skin, blood, uterus and ovaries. It also has been linked to lung disease and chronic kidney disease. *Example:* A study published in Journal of the *American College of Cardiology: Cardiovascular Imaging* found that people with high coronary calcium scores were 70% more likely to develop kidney disease than those who had low scores.

Caveat: None of the calcium/heart disease studies prove conclusively that supplements increase risks. The only way to know for sure would be to conduct a randomized, double-blind clinical trial in which some participants would take supplements and others wouldn't and then track their health over time. This type of study will probably never be done. The evidence linking calcium supplements and heart disease has become so persuasive that it would be unethical to give supplements to people who don't need them.

WHEN CALCIUM MAKES SENSE

We know that many Americans don't get enough calcium in their diets and that some of these people will never try to get more in their diets. Can supplements take up the slack? Perhaps—but this makes sense only for people who absolutely need to supplement. Are you one of these people? *Here's how to know...*

- **Get a workup first.** Calcium supplements should be treated as cautiously as prescription drugs. If you're worried about osteoporosis, talk to your doctor. Have your blood-calcium levels tested. If you're deficient, you might be advised to use supplements. Your doctor also should advise you on how to get more calcium in your diet and when to decide if you need supplements.

- **Focus on food.** Some people—particularly those who have already been diagnosed with osteoporosis or who are at high risk for it—might be advised to supplement despite the possible increase in heart risks. But most people can get more than enough calcium from foods if they make a conscious effort.

Examples: One cup of low-fat yogurt has 415 mg of calcium...one cup of skim milk, 316 mg...one cup of boiled collard greens, 266 mg...one cup of white beans, 161 mg...and one cup of soy milk, 93 mg.

- **Consider *all* of the calcium in your diet.** The heart risks from supplemental calcium may be proportional to the dose. You don't want to take any more than you need to. Suppose that you're trying to get 1,200 mg of calcium in total each day. You're already getting some calcium from foods. Keep that in mind before choosing a calcium dose. Why take a high-dose supplement if you need only an extra 200 mg a day?

My advice: Work with a nutritionist to help you find out how much calcium you actually consume in an average day. Or use the Internet—the USDA has a good calcium-content list at NDB.NAL.USDA.gov and click on "Food Search."

If you supplement, keep the doses low—your body can't absorb more than 500 mg at a time. Calcium carbonate has the highest amount of calcium (40% calcium) compared with calcium citrate (21% calcium). But citrate may be better tolerated by those with low stomach acids, which is common among people age 50 and older.

- **Get vitamin D and magnesium, too.** These help with absorption of calcium. Milk and many breakfast cereals are D-fortified. You also can

GOOD TO KNOW...

Eggs Slash Stroke Risk

Eating up to one egg each day cut stroke risk by 12%—without increasing risk for heart disease—a recent study of more than 300,000 adults has found.

Theory: Eggs are rich in antioxidants (shown to reduce inflammation) and protein—both of which help lower blood pressure, an important risk factor for stroke.

Important: The new Dietary Guidelines for Americans eliminates restrictions on dietary cholesterol and notes that eggs are an inexpensive source of important nutrients.

Dominik D. Alexander, PhD, MSPH, principal epidemiologist, EpidStat Institute, Ann Arbor, Michigan.

get vitamin D from sunshine—between five and 30 minutes (depending on your skin type and age) twice a week is probably enough. Or your doctor may advise you to take a vitamin D supplement. There are different types of vitamin D (vitamin D-2, vitamin D-3). It doesn't matter which type you take—research has shown both types to be effective.

Magnesium helps with calcium absorption, too, but you don't need a magnesium supplement. You just need adequate magnesium in your diet. Magnesium is readily available in whole grains, nuts, seeds, beans and leafy greens.

• **Don't forget to exercise.** Physical activity slows the rate of bone loss in men and women with osteoporosis, and it's among the best ways to strengthen bones before they get weak. Weight-bearing exercises (such as walking, jogging and weight-lifting) are more efficient for strengthening bones than other types of workouts (such as biking or swimming).

Recommended: 30 to 40 minutes of walking or other weight-bearing exercises most days of the week.

4 Hidden Causes of Diabetes: New Thinking Upends Conventional Wisdom

George L. King, MD, a professor of medicine at Harvard Medical School. He is also research director, head of the vascular cell biology research section and chief scientific officer of Harvard's Joslin Diabetes Center, the world's largest diabetes research center and clinic, and author, with Royce Flippin, of *The Diabetes Reset.*

High blood sugar (glucose) is an obvious sign of diabetes. It's worrisome because elevated blood glucose can, over time, lead to serious diabetes-related complications, such as stroke, heart disease and eye damage.

We have long known how diabetes develops: Cells gradually become less responsive (or "resistant") to the glucose-regulating hormone *insulin*...the ability of the pancreas to produce insulin flags...and glucose readings creep upward.

However, it has not been clear, until recently, *why* people become insulin-resistant in the first place—and what they can do to stop it. Now that's changing.

NEW THINKING

The conventional wisdom is that carbohydrates—particularly those foods that are high in "simple" carbs, such as soft drinks, white bread and desserts—are a main driver of insulin resistance and diabetes. *But other factors, some of which are largely hidden, are also important to note...*

RISK FACTOR #1: **Ectopic fat.** It's clear that being overweight increases risk for diabetes. But we're learning that a specific type of fat that accumulates in the liver and muscles is especially harmful. This ectopic fat impairs the ability of insulin to metabolize glucose and can lead to insulin resistance. Certain people—including some who are not overweight—have a genetic tendency to develop ectopic fat.

RISK FACTOR #2: **Inflammation**. Persistent, low-grade inflammation—caused by air pollution, obesity, a poor diet, gum disease, etc.—causes cells to produce inflammatory molecules that increase insulin resistance.

***RISK FACTOR #3:* Mitochondrial dysfunction.** Mitochondria, the "batteries" that fuel the body's cells, naturally produce free radicals and other by-products. The harmful molecules are kept in check by endogenous (produced by the body) and dietary antioxidants. A shortage of either type of antioxidant can cause mitochondria to work less efficiently, resulting in less insulin production—and more insulin resistance.

***RISK FACTOR #4:* Psychological stress.** A Dutch study found that people who had suffered at least one major stressful event (such as the death of a loved one or serious financial troubles, etc.) within the past five years were 1.2 times more likely to have diabetes.

Why is stress linked to diabetes? Stressed people are more likely to be overweight, eat poor diets and avoid exercise. Also, stress raises levels of *cortisol*, a hormone that increases insulin resistance and can cause the liver to manufacture excess glucose.

WHAT CAN YOU DO?

Fortunately, the factors described earlier can be managed—and sometimes reversed—with diet, exercise and other changes. *Here's how...*

- **Double the fiber, halve the fat.** The Joslin Diabetes Center recommends an eating plan that's low in fat (15% of total calories) and high in high-fiber veggies, fruits and grains.

- **Forget what you've heard about carbs being bad.** Processed carbs (sugar, high-fructose corn syrup, etc.) are obviously a problem. But healthy complex carbohydrates (such as whole grains, veggies and legumes) are absorbed slowly...do not cause blood sugar spikes...and many are high in inflammation-fighting antioxidants. *Best:* An eating plan with a lot of complex carbohydrates—70% of total calories.

We've found that people who follow this diet for eight weeks show significant drops in insulin resistance...have improved blood glucose levels—and lose about 3% of their weight...and have a decrease in abdominal and overall body fat.

- **Be aware of hidden fat.** Excess body fat is one of the main causes of insulin resistance and diabetes—even when the fat isn't readily visible. People with a fatty liver, for example, are five times more likely to develop diabetes. Fat that accumulates in muscle cells might be completely invisible, but it increases inflammation levels and disrupts the action of insulin.

Fat that is visible—on the hips, buttocks and particularly around the waist—is especially troublesome. Most belly fat is *visceral fat*, which secretes higher levels of inflammatory chemicals than other types of fat. It also increases levels of "hidden" muscle fat. One large study found that obese men (with a BMI of 30 or higher) were seven times more likely to get diabetes than those with a BMI below 25. For obese women, the risk was 12 times higher than that for normal-weight women.

- **Boost *natural* antioxidants.** Millions of Americans supplement their diets with large doses of vitamin C, vitamin E and other antioxidants. But research has shown that these supplements are unlikely to improve insulin resistance/diabetes—and may be harmful because they can inhibit the action of the body's natural antioxidants.

What helps: Broccoli, blueberries, green tea and other plant foods that are high in *phase 2 antioxidants*—beneficial plant compounds that activate a protein called *Nrf2*, which triggers genes that produce antioxidant molecules. People who eat a lot of plant foods have less inflammation, less mitochondrial dysfunction and less insulin resistance.

- **Get off your duff!** Exercise is great for weight loss, but that's not the only reason to do it. People who are sedentary tend to accumulate more fat deposits in muscle cells. These fats inhibit insulin's ability to transport glucose into muscle cells, and insulin-resistant muscle cells are now thought to be a leading cause of diabetes.

It doesn't take hard-core exercise to get the benefits. If you walk three miles a day (about 6,000 steps)—all at once or in five- or 10-minute increments—you'll reduce your diabetes risk by more than 25%.

• **De-stress.** Take up an enjoyable hobby... go for leisurely walks...spend time with loved ones...and try stress-reducing habits such as yoga or meditation. For severe stress (or depression), consider seeing a professional. Any form of stress relief will help manage diabetes—and reduce your risk of getting it.

Diabetes/Psoriasis Link

If you have psoriasis, you are at increased risk for diabetes and vice versa.

Recent finding: People with the chronic skin condition are 53% more likely to have type 2 diabetes than other people.

Probable connections: Both diseases involve inflammation and have dietary and lifestyle factors in common.

To decrease risk for both: Keep your weight and blood sugar under control. If you have psoriasis, ask your physician to screen you for diabetes.

Ann Sophie Lønnberg, MD, a psoriasis researcher at Gentofte Hospital, University of Copenhagen, Hellerup, Denmark.

Cooking Oil vs. Diabetes

While many cooking oils, such as olive and canola oils, have long been associated with heart-health benefits, recent research shows that dietary oils rich in *linoleic acid* (such as grape seed oil) have special properties that help fight diabetes. Higher blood levels of linoleic acid were linked to lower insulin resistance, a main driver of diabetes. Previous studies showed that as little as one-and-a-half teaspoons of linoleic acid–rich oil daily increased lean body mass and decreased abdominal fat.

Martha Belury, PhD, professor of human nutrition, The Ohio State University, Columbus.

Get the Very Best Cancer Care—Complementary Therapies That Work

Barrie R. Cassileth, PhD, former Laurance S. Rockefeller chair and chief of the integrative medicine department at Memorial Sloan Kettering Cancer Center in New York City. She is also a founding member of the Advisory Council to the National Institutes of Health Office of Alternative Medicine, founding president of the Society of Integrative Oncology and author of *Survivorship: Living Well During and After Cancer.*

A cancer diagnosis is always fraught with fear and anxiety—not to mention nagging questions about the best possible treatments.

Bridging the gap: While surgery, chemotherapy and radiation have long been the mainstay treatments for cancer, major cancer centers throughout the US now offer a variety of additional "complementary" therapies that help patients cope with a wide range of cancer-related problems.

Latest development: Recent studies continue to be added to the growing body of evidence supporting the use of such nondrug and nonsurgical therapies, which are used along with conventional cancer treatment.

LOOK FOR PROVEN BENEFITS

Only a small number of complementary therapies have been thoroughly tested using randomized, placebo-controlled clinical trials—the gold standard of scientific research. Some of these approaches have now been *proven* to work.

Common cancer symptoms that can be relieved with complementary approaches—some services may be covered by insurance, so check with your health insurer...

• **Less nausea.** Nausea and/or vomiting are among the most common symptoms cancer patients have—and among the most feared. Antinausea medications help, but they're not a perfect solution. That's why they're sometimes used in tandem with acupuncture, a complementary therapy that has been shown to be particularly effective.

Scientific evidence: When acupuncture was tested in a group of breast cancer patients being treated with a form of chemotherapy that's notorious for causing nausea, those who were given acupuncture for five days had one-third fewer episodes of nausea than those who were treated only with medications that were used for nausea, such as *lorazepam* and *diphenhydramine*. *Self-acupressure*, in which patients merely press on certain points, such as the PC6 point on the wrist (without using needles), can also help.

To find the PC6 point: Turn your hand so your palm is facing up and locate the area, which is between the tendons three finger widths from the base of the wrist. Massage the area for four to five seconds...or longer, as needed.

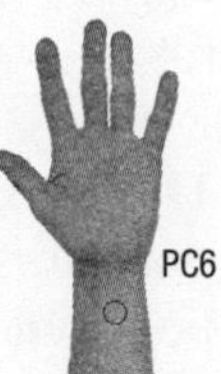

• **Pain relief.** Both gentle massage and acupuncture can reduce the pain that's caused by cancer (such as bone cancer) and cancer treatments (such as radiation)—and sometimes allow patients to take lower doses of medication, which can help reduce troubling side effects, including constipation.

Scientific evidence: A study that looked at nearly 1,300 cancer patients found that massage improved their pain scores by 40%...and the improvements lasted for hours and sometimes days after the massage.

Imaging studies show that acupuncture also helps by deactivating brain areas that are involved in pain perception. In one study, patients with chronic cancer pain were treated with either *auricular acupuncture* (needles placed in the ear) or with sham treatments. After two months, patients in the acupuncture group reported reductions in pain intensity of 36% versus 2% in the placebo group.

• **Less fatigue.** Only about 10% of cancer patients are physically active during treatment. But the vast majority can safely exercise before, during and after treatments...and exercise is among the best ways to reduce treatment-related fatigue.

Scientific evidence: When researchers at the University of Connecticut analyzed 44 studies focusing on patients who had cancer-related fatigue, they found that those who exercised had more energy than those who were sedentary.

Any form of exercise seems to help. Yoga that focuses on gentle postures and breathing is good because it's easy on the body and has been shown to reduce anxiety and other stress-related symptoms.

Bonus: Cancer patients who exercise tend to live longer than those who don't stay active. A study of more than 900 breast cancer patients found that those who engaged in brisk walking for two and a half hours a week—the same level of exercise that's recommended for the general population—were 67% less likely to die during the nine-year study period than those who were sedentary.

• **Fewer hot flashes.** Both men and women who have hormone-dependent cancers (such as breast and prostate cancers) often experience hot flashes when they're given hormone-based treatments. Once again, acupuncture seems to help.

Scientific evidence: One study found that nearly 90% of patients with breast or prostate cancers who were given acupuncture had a reduction in hot flashes of nearly 50% that lasted at least three months.

HOW TO STAY SAFE

Virtually all oncologists and respected cancer centers in the US now support the use of complementary therapies, such as acupuncture and massage, to help cancer patients cope with nausea, pain, anxiety and other symptoms. These and other complementary therapies are used in addition to conventional treatments.

To find an evidence-based complementary oncology program: Look for a comprehensive cancer center at the National Cancer Institute's site, Cancer.gov/research/nci-role/cancer-centers/find.

Very important: When seeking complementary care, it's vital that the practitioner (including massage therapists, acupuncturists, etc.) be properly trained to work with cancer patients. Getting therapy at a comprehensive cancer center helps ensure that.

Also crucial: Cancer patients should always talk to their doctors before taking any supplements (herbs, vitamins, etc.). They can sometimes interfere with chemotherapy and other cancer treatments. For more on specific supplements, go to Memorial Sloan Kettering's website, MSKCC.org/aboutherbs.

Foods That Increase Lung Cancer Risk

High-glycemic diets may increase lung cancer risk by 49% and perhaps even more in people who have never smoked. High-glycemic foods, such as sweets, white bread and white potatoes, trigger increased insulin levels in the blood. Increased insulin might increase certain growth factors associated with cancer.

Stephanie Claire Melkonian, PhD, an epidemiologist and postdoctoral research fellow in the department of epidemiology, The University of Texas MD Anderson Cancer Center, Houston.

Secrets to Managing COPD—Few Doctors Talk About These Crucial Steps

Dawn Fielding, RCP, AE-C, a licensed respiratory therapist and certified COPD and Asthma Educator based in West Haven, Utah. She is executive director of the Chronic Lung Alliance, a nonprofit organization involved in education and research related to chronic lung disease. She is also author of *The COPD Solution.*

If you are living with chronic obstructive pulmonary disease (COPD), the simple act of breathing can feel like you're pushing a boulder uphill.

What you may not know: Because your ability to breathe is affected by everything in your life—including your thoughts and emotions—few disorders have as strong a *mind-body connection* as COPD.

While most doctors talk to their patients with COPD about inhalers, oxygen therapy and sometimes even surgery, the additional approaches described here will help ensure the best possible results for those who have this disorder.

THE COPD SPIRAL

With COPD (which includes chronic bronchitis and/or emphysema), air can't flow easily into and out of the lungs because of a blockage in the airways, typically caused by excess mucus, inflammation or dysfunctional lung tissue.

Being unable to breathe is a primal terror. The constant worry and anxiety that accompany this fear push the body into a stress reaction that makes breathing even more difficult, triggering more fear and stress. The key is to break the spiral and create a steadier breathing environment.

In addition to proper breathing techniques that should be practiced regularly—such as pursed breathing (as though you're whistling) and belly breathing, which strengthens muscles that assist with breathing—try these simple steps...

SECRET #1: **Change your thoughts.** When you have a negative thought—such as I can't do this anymore because of my COPD—your brain registers the emotion behind it and reacts by signaling the body to produce stress

INTERESTING FINDING...

Garlic Reduces Lung Cancer Risk 50%!

Eating raw garlic may cut lung cancer risk. According to a recent Chinese study, people who ate raw garlic (serving size was not reported but probably was one to two cloves) at least twice a week were 50% less likely to develop lung cancer than people who ate no garlic. The cancer-fighting benefit comes mainly from garlic's organo-sulfur compounds. Earlier research has shown that the benefit is reduced if the garlic is cooked.

Lina Mu, MD, PhD, associate professor of epidemiology and environmental health, School of Public Health, The State University of New York, Buffalo, and coauthor of the study.

hormones and to speed up your respiration rate and blood pressure.

This is helpful in an emergency...say, if you fear an oncoming car and your body reacts to avoid a collision. But in the absence of an actual threat, the response can be physically harmful by lowering your body's natural defenses and sapping your energy levels.

What helps: Positive statements reduce anxiety, help you cope and tell your brain that it's OK to relax.

What to do: When you find yourself becoming stressed, stop! Break that cycle of anxiety by repeating a phrase, such as those below, to set your brain on a positive track...

"*No more negativity*...I'll just focus on what I can do."

"*One day at a time*. I got through yesterday. I'll get through today."

Positive thinking and deep breathing lower blood pressure, slow heart rate and make more oxygen available for breathing.

SECRET #2: **Watch what you eat.** Food choices are a surprisingly important factor in controlling COPD symptoms.

Here's why: Breathing is a process that involves the exchange of carbon dioxide (CO_2) and oxygen in the blood.

A person with COPD has a less efficient oxygen-CO_2 exchange process. Anything that increases the amount of CO_2 in blood (whether it's stress or a certain type of food, such as soda or sugary food products) revs up your breathing rate—which worsens COPD.

What to do...

- **Cut back on foods that increase levels of CO_2 in the blood.** The worst offenders are carbonated beverages (even fizzy water)...and anything made with refined sugar or white flour (everything from cakes and cookies to certain breads and pastas).

- **Avoid caffeinated beverages,** including coffee, tea and colas. Caffeine "wakes up" your nervous system, causing your body to work faster, accelerating your breathing rate. Whenever possible, replace soda and other caffeinated beverages with water. Why water? It helps thin mucous secretions and transports nutrients throughout our bodies. For variety, choose flavored waters (such as those infused with lemon or mint).

SECRET #3: **Do the right exercises.** For people with COPD, breathing alone is so physically taxing that it's crucial to also improve physical stamina.

In a recent study of people with COPD in *Respiratory Medicine*, researchers compared the benefits of specific types of exercise. All the study participants did cardiovascular exercise (such as walking and biking) twice a week for three months, but one group added more strength training (including weight training for the upper and lower body) than the other group.

Result: People who did the most *strength training* had much stronger muscles throughout the body, which resulted in more efficient breathing.

In addition to doing upper-body exercises, such as bicep curls, try the following three times a week...

- **Leg lifts.** This exercise targets large muscle groups that allow us to move about freely.

What to do: While sitting in a chair, straighten one leg and lift, foot flexed, as high as you can while keeping your back straight. Hold that position for a count of five, then lower your leg. Repeat five times with each leg. Don't worry if you cannot hold your leg up for very long—your strength will improve over time.

Also: Aerobic exercise is crucial—try to get at least 2,000 steps a day (use a pedometer or fitness tracker) while going about your daily activities, including getting the mail, going shopping, etc. Try to exercise when your energy levels are high...and check with your doctor about the best time to take your medications when exercising.

MAKE PEACE WITH COPD...

People with COPD can experience a wide range of troubling emotions, including denial, guilt, anger and depression. If you believe that you need help coping, consider joining a support group.

The American Lung Association (ALA) sponsors Better Breathers Clubs across the US. These groups are led by a trained facilitator and offer educational presentations as well as emotional support.

To find a local group, call the ALA at 800-LUNGUSA...or look online at Lung.org (under "Support & Community," click on "Better Breathers Club").

Liver Disease Is Rampant: Natural Ways to Fight It

Rich Snyder, DO, a nephrologist, osteopathic physician and clinical professor at Philadelphia College of Osteopathic Medicine. He maintains a part-time nephrology practice at Lehigh Valley Nephrology Associates in Easton, Pennsylvania, and is author of *What You Must Know About Liver Disease: A Practical Guide to Using Conventional and Complementary Treatments.*

Alarming fact—about 30 million Americans have some form of liver disease. That's one-tenth of the population. Yet it's normal for people to go undiagnosed for years or even decades.

Unless liver disease is detected and treated early, it can cause severe inflammation that can lead to scarring (cirrhosis), organ failure and/or cancer—and it even may require a transplant. It is a leading cause of death in the US.

Important: I advise patients who have risk factors for liver disease to get their livers checked—the inexpensive group of blood tests can be done during routine checkups. Risk factors include obesity, metabolic syndrome (see below), hepatitis and a history of alcohol or drug abuse.

If you have liver disease, medications may be required, but herbs and supplements can help reduce inflammation, improve liver function and slow ongoing damage. Always speak with your doctor before taking any natural supplements.

I usually advise patients to start with just one remedy at a time. After six to eight weeks, we reassess to see if there's improvement and if an additional supplement is required. Any of the herbs below can be started first, but milk thistle and turmeric are among the more common options.

MILK THISTLE

Milk thistle has been used for thousands of years for liver health. It's among the most studied herbs for treating hepatitis and other liver diseases.

Milk thistle (a member of the plant family that includes daisies and sunflowers) contains a flavonoid called *silymarin.* It's an antioxidant that reduces inflammation, blocks the movement of toxins into liver cells and increases the output of enzymes that prevent toxin-related damage.

Research suggests that milk thistle can improve liver function and improve survival in patients with chronic hepatitis and/or cirrhosis. One study found that it reduced the viral load (the amount of viral particles in the blood) in hepatitis C patients who hadn't responded to drug treatments.

Typical dosage: If you have risk factors for liver disease or if you've been diagnosed with liver disease, talk to your doctor about taking 100 mg twice a day, to start—your doctor might recommend a higher dose (between 200 mg and 600 mg) if lab tests aren't improving. Milk thistle is unlikely to cause side effects, although it should be avoided if you're allergic to ragweed or one of its relatives, such as sunflower seeds or chamomile.

TURMERIC

The active ingredient in this spice, *curcumin,* is an exceptionally potent antioxidant that has been shown to reduce jaundice (the dark urine and/or yellowing of the skin or eyes that often occurs in liver patients).

There's also some evidence that it reduces liver scarring. A study published in *Gut* found that turmeric helped prevent a hepatitis-causing virus from moving from one cell to another.

Typical dosage: Between 500 mg and 1,500 mg of a turmeric supplement daily, divided into two or three doses. (Exact dose will depend on your weight, symptoms and other factors.)

Caution: Turmeric has blood-thinning properties, so it may not be best if you are on a blood thinner such as *warfarin* or if your liver disease is advanced and clotting of the blood is a problem.

N-ACETYLCYSTEINE (NAC)

Doctors who specialize in natural health recommend this supplement for liver patients. It reduces inflammation and increases intracellular levels of *glutathione*, the "master antioxidant" that is mainly produced and stored in the liver and that is depleted by liver disease.

Doctors give it to improve the viability of transplanted livers. It also is used in patients with liver damage caused by acetaminophen overdose (acetaminophen rapidly depletes glutathione).

Typical dosage: 600 mg, twice daily.

GLUTATHIONE

You don't *have* to take this supplement if you already are using NAC (which is converted to glutathione in the body), but I often advise my patients to take glutathione because it helps rebuild body tissues, including liver cells.

Glutathione is particularly helpful if you regularly use acetaminophen for treating arthritis or another painful condition because acetaminophen, as mentioned before, can deplete glutathione levels. Oral glutathione usually needs to be taken with *cysteine*, which helps glutathione get into the cells.

Follow dosing directions on the label.

COFFEE

Coffee isn't a cure for liver disease, but there's good evidence that it reduces liver inflammation and may reduce liver-related health risks, including cirrhosis and cancer.

One study found that hepatitis B patients who drank more than four cups of coffee a week were only about half as likely to develop hepatocellular carcinoma (a form of liver cancer) as those who did not drink coffee.

Another study—one that looked at 430,000 people—found that people who drank an extra two cups of coffee a day could potentially reduce their risk for cirrhosis by 44%.

WEIGHT LOSS IS CRUCIAL FOR YOUR LIVER

Non-alcoholic fatty liver disease (NAFLD) is the leading type of liver disease in the US. It affects up to 25% of all adults and is linked to obesity and metabolic syndrome (a constellation of problems that includes high blood pressure, high blood sugar and elevated triglycerides, along with obesity).

A liver is considered "fat" if more than 5% to 10% of its weight comes from fatty tissue. This serious disease can lead to severe inflammation, cirrhosis or liver failure.

You *have* to lose weight if you've been diagnosed with NAFLD. Studies have shown that it may be possible to eliminate the condition altogether by losing as little as 10% of your total weight.

Also helpful: Alpha lipoic acid. It's a well-researched supplement that can decrease insulin resistance and improve metabolic syndrome. I advise patients with NAFLD to take 200 mg daily, increasing the dose by 100 mg weekly until they reach a maximum dose of 400 mg to 600 mg.

If you have diabetes or are at risk for diabetes, you may need to check your blood glucose levels because alpha lipoic acid has the potential to decrease glucose levels in some individuals.

The Natural Pain Cures You Need to Try

Heather Tick, MD, who holds the Gunn-Loke Endowed Professorship for Integrative Pain Medicine at the University of Washington in Seattle and is a clinical associate professor in both the departments of family medicine, and anesthesiology and pain medicine. She is author of *Holistic Pain Relief.*

If you are among the estimated 25% of adults in the US who live with moderate-to-severe chronic pain, from conditions such as arthritis, headaches and fibromyalgia, you may be so desperate for relief that you decide to try a powerful opioid—and take your chances with side effects.

It's widely known that people can become dependent on (or addicted to) these drugs—including older standbys such as morphine and codeine…as well as newer heavy hitters such as *hydrocodone* (Vicodin, Norco) and *oxycodone* (OxyContin, Percocet). Yet many doctors are still too quick to prescribe them.

Sadly, these drugs don't stop the root cause of the pain—they simply block the intensity of pain signals that a patient feels. While opioids can be appropriate for acute conditions (including broken bones and postsurgical pain), they rarely are the best choice for chronic pain.

What's more, a recent study published in *JAMA: The Journal of the American Medical Association* found that long-acting opioids, such as OxyContin or *fentanyl* (Duragesic), increase one's risk for death by 65%—due to heart attack and other cardiovascular events.

So what's the best solution for chronic pain? *We spoke with Heather Tick, MD, an expert in pain medicine, for answers...*

THE PAIN MEDICINE PARADOX

It's an unfortunate paradox that pain medicine can actually worsen pain. In fact, researchers are now finding that patients who are weaned off opioids, using such nondrug therapies as physical therapy and relaxation exercises instead, actually can experience less pain than they did while on opioids, and they have a greater sense of well-being and function better.

Here's what happens: It's relatively easy to develop a tolerance to an opioid, which requires increasingly higher doses for the drug to work. Even when properly prescribed, chronic high doses of these medications can trigger a condition called *hyperalgesia*, which results in new pain sensitivity either in the primary area of pain or in a new area. For example, a patient who takes an opioid for low-back pain may begin to develop neck pain and headaches.

The good news: Nonopioid therapies that stimulate the *parasympathetic* nervous system—the branch of the nervous system that helps us feel calm and relaxed—can be highly effective for pain relief.

Chronic pain patients tend to live in the sympathetic nervous system's "fight or flight" mode, which intensifies pain by secreting inflammation-promoting hormones. That's why it's crucial to fire up the parasympathetic system, which tells the body to secrete *acetylcholine* instead, a neurotransmitter that counteracts inflammation.

There's strong evidence supporting the effectiveness of meditation for fighting pain. It induces the relaxation response—literally altering your body's chemistry. Meditation also lowers stress hormone levels, decreases muscle tension and builds pain tolerance. *Other ways to trigger the parasympathetic system's pain-fighting mechanism...**

- **Autogenic training.** Autogenic training (AT) is a relaxation technique based on a set of affirmations (self-directed statements) that are designed to reverse the physical effects of stress. You can buy AT recordings online, in which a person with a soothing voice says the affirmations...or you can repeat them to yourself or make your own recording, using a script like the one below.

What to do: Sit or lie in a comfortable, quiet room. Repeat each of the following statements three times, then dwell on each statement for about 30 seconds afterward. Try to truly feel each sensation in the script. Do this daily.

I am completely calm.
My arms feel heavy and warm.
My legs feel heavy and warm.
My heartbeat is calm and regular.
My abdomen is warm and comfortable.
My forehead is pleasantly cool.
My shoulders are heavy and warm.

- **Ujjayi breathing.** Stress causes us to breathe shallowly from the chest instead of deeply from the belly. This leaves stale air trapped in the bottom of the lungs and hinders delivery of healing oxygen to muscles. Any deep-breathing technique can stimulate the parasympathetic system, but Ujjayi (pronounced oo-ja-EE) breathing is particularly effective.

What to do: To get the hang of this technique, inhale deeply through your nose and exhale through your open mouth, gently constricting the muscles at the back of your throat and making a *HAAAH* sound, as if you were trying to fog up a mirror. Then try to make the same sound on the inhale.

*Consult your doctor before trying these methods or the supplement described here—especially if you take blood thinners or have a chronic medical condition such as hypertension.

Oncc you've achieved the correct sound, close your mouth and breathe in and out through your nose, making the *HAAAH* sound on both the inhale and exhale. Spend equal time (at a pace that's comfortable for you) inhaling and exhaling several times a day. When you first start this technique, try to do it for six minutes at a time. You can work up to 15 to 20 minutes at a time.

Important: If you have a favorite deep-breathing technique of your own, feel free to use that—just be sure that you keep the flow of air constant, and you don't hold your breath for longer than a beat. Otherwise, you will stimulate the sympathetic nervous system, triggering the pain response.

ANOTHER NONDRUG SOLUTION

In addition to the approaches that are described above, the following supplement can help ease pain by reducing inflammation…

- **Turmeric.** This mildly bitter-tasting spice is a powerful analgesic that provides impressive anti-inflammatory powers. A 2014 study suggested it may be as effective as *ibuprofen* in reducing the pain of knee osteoarthritis.

Capsules are one option to try. But if you like the taste, try making "Golden Milk." *What to do:* Combine one-quarter cup of turmeric with one-half cup of water in a pot, and blend to create a thick paste. Heat gently, adding a pinch of ground black pepper and drizzling in water as needed to maintain a thick but stirrable consistency.

Refrigerate the mixture in a glass container, and add one heaping teaspoon to an eight-ounce glass of warm water mixed with a little almond milk every day. You can add some honey to cut the bitterness. Or use warm broth instead of water and a dash of ginger and/or garlic for a tasty soup.

BETTER WAY…

Meditation Beats Morphine

Mindfulness meditation, a practice that focuses on awareness and acceptance of daily thoughts and feelings, activates areas of the brain that reduce pain intensity, recent research finds.

Details: Adults who meditated for 20 minutes a day for four days before being touched with a hot probe reported feeling up to 44% less pain than those who did not meditate—which was twice the benefit provided by opioid drugs such as morphine.

Fadel Zeidan, PhD, assistant professor of neurobiology and anatomy, Wake Forest School of Medicine, Winston-Salem, North Carolina.

Better Exercises for Lower-Back Pain

A program known as *motor-control exercise* has patients doing simple tasks with their muscles that control and support the spine while being guided by a therapist or other expert. The tasks gradually become harder and include things that patients do during work or recreation that involve lifting, pushing and rotating the body. Among people ages 22 to 55 with lower-back pain, those who did supervised motor-control exercise showed greater improvement after three to 12 months and had less disability than those who did other types of exercise. Most physical therapists can guide you through these exercises.

Analysis of data from 29 clinical trials of more than 2,400 people by researchers at The George Institute for Global Health, Sydney, Australia, published in *Cochrane Library.*

Easy Way to Reduce Back Pain

If you sit a lot, stand up every hour, put your hands on your hips, bend backward as far as feels comfortable and hold for three seconds. Repeat five times. This helps extend the spine and relieve stiffness.

Anthony Delitto, PhD, professor of physical therapy and dean of the School of Health and Rehabilitation Sciences at University of Pittsburgh.

Beat Knee Pain *Without* Surgery—This Is Just as Effective and Safer

Mitchell Yass, DPT, a St. Augustine, Florida–based physical therapist and creator of the Yass Method for treating chronic pain. Yass is also author of *The Pain Cure Rx: The Yass Method for Diagnosing* and *Resolving Chronic Pain* and the PBS special *The Pain Prescription*. MitchellYass.com

Do you wince when you walk, kneel, squat or climb stairs? If so, you are definitely not alone. Nearly 20% of all cases of chronic pain are associated with the knee, and it's severe enough to limit the sufferer's mobility and affect quality of life.

Knee surgery, including knee replacement, is a widely used option, but it's rarely the best choice...and should *never* be the first choice. Knee pain is often caused by weak and/or imbalanced muscles, which surgery or other invasive treatments do *not* address.

A much better option: For most people with knee pain, exercise is at least as effective as surgery—with none of the risks, according to research. *What you need to know...*

MUSCLE PAIN

When you see a doctor because of nagging knee pain, you'll probably be advised to have an X-ray or MRI to look for arthritis, torn cartilage or other *structural* problems that can cause joint pain. But the tests, more often than not, point doctors in the wrong direction.

Eye-opening research: A study of nearly 1,000 patients with arthritis-related knee pain found that 63% had a damaged *meniscus* (cartilage that cushions and stabilizes the knee). But the same study also found that 60% of patients *without* pain had the same type of damage.

Most patients—and many doctors—fail to realize that there's a poor correlation between structural problems and knee pain. That's why I often advise clients not to have imaging tests—or consider surgery—until they've first tried my program of targeted exercise. In my experience, about 90% of knee patients have a muscle imbalance or weakness that causes all or most of their symptoms.

Here is a 30- to 60-minute workout that helps specific types of knee pain. Do the exercises on the side that is painful until the pain subsides—once the pain is gone, do the exercises on both sides. Stop if the exercise hurts.

A resistance band, ankle weight or machine in the gym can be used for resistance, which is key for strengthening muscles.* Start at a level where you feel you are working hard but not in pain, and gradually increase resistance.

The exercises can be performed by anyone, including those who have had knee surgery, but check first with your doctor. The quad stretch should be done daily. For each of the other exercises below, do three sets of 10 repetitions (resting 45 to 60 seconds between sets) and repeat the workouts three times a week (with a day between workouts).

WEAK HAMSTRINGS

The thigh muscles (quadriceps) tend to be a lot stronger than the opposing muscles (the hamstrings) on the backs of the legs. Why? It's because virtually all of our daily movements—including walking and climbing stairs—are "forward."

The problem: Weak hamstrings (they are mainly responsible for knee bending) cannot effectively counteract the force of much stronger quadriceps, causing a muscle imbalance. *Result:* The quadriceps shorten and pull up on the kneecap, causing excessive pressure and pain. The majority of people with knee pain will improve when they *strengthen* the hamstrings and *stretch* the quads.

EXERCISE #1: **Hamstring curls.** While sitting in a chair, tie the ends of a resistance band to a doorknob and slip it around the ankle...or try the seated leg curl machine at the gym.

What to do: Begin with the exercising leg pointing straight out, then bend the knee until it reaches 90 degrees. Return to the starting position.

*To increase muscle strength, add resistance (with heavier weights or a stronger exercise band) when the exercises become easy.

EXERCISE #2: **Hip extensions**. This exercise works the *gluteus maximus* muscles in the buttocks.

What to do: While standing, place a resistance band behind one knee. Then attach the ends to a fixed point—such as a doorknob. While standing (you can rest your hand on top of a chair or table for extra support), bring the knee about 10 degrees behind the hip, then return to the starting position.

EXERCISE #3: **Quad stretches.** Tight quadriceps pull the kneecap toward the top of the joint and prevent it from moving smoothly. Tight quads can cause both knee *and* back pain.

What to do: Stand near a wall (or a dresser, bookcase or other solid support), and use one hand for balance. Reach back with your other hand, and grip the ankle.

Pull the heel upward toward the buttock. The knee should be a few inches behind the hip. Keep pulling until you feel a stretch in the front of the thigh. Hold the stretch for 20 to 30 seconds, and do the stretch twice. Pull gently! If it hurts, you've pulled too far (or too quickly).

QUAD STRAIN

Another common cause of knee pain is quad strain. What are the telltale signs? You might notice a "pulling" sensation at the top of the knee or in the thigh when you walk or climb stairs. A weak quadricep can cause the kneecap to shift out of place. *Try this...*

EXERCISE #1: **Knee extensions.** They strengthen the quadriceps and help the kneecap stay in a "neutral" position.

What to do: In a seated position, strap on an ankle weight or tie a resistance band around the front of the ankle and attach the other end to the chair leg. Keep the other foot on the floor. Begin with the knee bent to a 90-degree angle, then straighten it. Return to the starting position.

Important: Make sure that the thigh of the leg being exercised stays on the seat. Raising it will make the exercise less effective.

EXERCISE #2: **Dorsiflexion.** This works the tibialis anterior, a muscle in the front of the shin. Strengthening the muscle can help keep the calf muscle lengthened and allow the knee joint to function properly to prevent knee pain.

What to do: Sit on the floor with one leg extended. Slip an exercise band over the top of the foot and tie the ends to a sturdy table leg. Start with the ankle angled about 30 degrees forward, then pull the foot toward the upper body until it is 10 degrees past perpendicular. Return to the starting position.

Vitamin C and Cataract Risk

Vitamin C may reduce cataract risk. But the vitamin is most protective when it comes from food—not supplements.

Recent finding: Study participants with a higher dietary intake of vitamin C had one-third lower risk for cataracts than people who consumed the least vitamin C. Those who took vitamin C supplements showed no significant risk reduction.

Christopher Hammond, MD, Frost Chair of Ophthalmology at King's College London, UK, and leader of a study of 2,054 twins, published in *Ophthalmology*.

The Groundbreaking Alzheimer's Prevention Diet

Richard S. Isaacson, MD, director of the Alzheimer's Prevention Clinic, Weill Cornell Memory Disorders Program at Weill Cornell Medicine and NewYork-Presbyterian, where he is an associate professor of neurology and director of the neurology residency training program, New York City. He is coauthor of *The Alzheimer's Prevention & Treatment Diet: Using Nutrition to Combat the Effects of Alzheimer's Disease.*

As head of the renowned Alzheimer's Prevention Clinic at Weill Cornell Medicine and NewYork-Presbyterian, Richard S.

TAKE NOTE...

Exercise for MS

Yoga or water exercise can dramatically reduce common multiple sclerosis (MS) symptoms like fatigue, depression and *paresthesia* (pins and needles tingling), a recent study of women with MS found. Those who did these forms of exercise for at least 30 minutes three times a week had a 35-fold lower risk of developing moderate-to-severe depression, as well as less fatigue and paresthesia, than those who did no exercise.

Serge Brand, PhD, professor of affective, stress and sleep disorders, University of Basel, Switzerland.

Isaacson, MD, is on top of the latest research on Alzheimer's disease. Groundbreaking studies show that proper diet can make a real difference not only in slowing the progression of the disease but also in preventing it.

Here, Dr. Isaacson explains how we can change our eating habits to fight Alzheimer's. His recommendations are not specifically designed for weight loss, but most overweight people who follow this eating plan will lose weight—important because obesity more than triples the risk for Alzheimer's.

FEWER CALORIES

The Okinawa Centenarian Study (an ongoing study of centenarians in the Japanese prefecture of Okinawa) found that these long-lived people typically consume fewer calories (up to 1,900 calories a day) than the average American (up to 2,600 calories).

Lowering calorie intake appears to reduce *beta-amyloid*, particles of protein that form brain plaques—the hallmark of Alzheimer's disease. A 2012 study at the Mayo Clinic found that people who overate had twice the risk for memory loss...and those who consumed more than 2,142 calories a day were more likely to have cognitive impairment.

I generally advise my patients to try to have fewer than 2,100 calories a day. I can't give an exact number because calorie requirements depend on body type, activity level, etc. Many of my patients tend to consume less than 1,800 calories a day, which may be even more protective.

Bonus: Calorie restriction also lowers insulin, body fat, inflammation and blood pressure, all of which can reduce the risk for cognitive impairment. It even improves *neurogenesis*, the formation of new brain cells.

LESS CARBS, MORE KETONES

Glucose from the breakdown of carbohydrates is the fuel that keeps the body running. But you don't need a lot of carbs. Ketones, another source of fuel, are healthier for the brain.

When you restrict carbohydrates, the body manufactures ketones from stored fat. On occasion, a "ketogenic diet" is recommended for some patients with Alzheimer's disease because ketones produce fewer wastes and put less stress on damaged brain cells. There's some evidence that this diet improves mild cognitive impairment symptoms (and theoretically may slow further damage).

We previously found in our clinic that patients consumed an average of 278 grams of carbohydrates daily before their first visits. We recommend reducing that slowly over the nine weeks of the diet plan to 100 to 120 grams of carbohydrates daily. (One sweet potato has about 23 grams.) The USDA SuperTracker website (SuperTracker.USDA.gov) gives carbohydrate amounts and other nutritional information for specific foods. Eat healthful carbohydrates such as beans and whole grains in moderation. Unlike refined carbs, they are high in fiber and can help to reduce insulin resistance and improve blood sugar control—which reduces risk for Alzheimer's.

FASTING

Some trendy diets recommend extreme fasts. With the Alzheimer's prevention diet, you will fast—but mainly when you wouldn't be eating anyway, during sleep!

Several times a week, you'll go without food (particularly carbohydrates) for more than 12 hours. After 12 hours, the body starts making ketones. This type of fast, known as time-restricted eating, reduces inflammation, improves metabolic efficiency and improves insulin levels, insulin sensitivity and brain health.

How to do it: Eat an early supper—say, at about 5 pm. You won't eat again until after 5 am the next day. Your eventual goal will be to fast for 12 to 14 hours five nights a week.

MORE PROTEIN

The Institute of Medicine recommends getting 10% to 35% of calories from protein—go for the higher end. On a 2,000-calorie diet, that's about 175 grams. (Five ounces of cooked salmon has about 36 grams of protein.)

The amino acids in protein are important for memory and other brain functions. Protein-rich foods often are high in B vitamins, including folic acid and vitamins B-6 and B-12. The Bs are critical because they reduce homocysteine, an amino acid linked to poor brain performance and an increased Alzheimer's risk.

Which protein: Chicken, fish, nuts, legumes and eggs all are good choices. I recommend limiting red meat to one weekly serving because of potential associated health risks, including an increased risk for certain cancers...and because too much saturated fat (see below) can be a problem.

Helpful: Aim for four to eight eggs a week. They're high in selenium, lutein, zeaxanthin and other brain-healthy antioxidants.

LIMIT SATURATED FAT

A large study found that people who eat a lot of foods high in saturated fat—rich desserts, red meat, fast food, etc.—may be up to 2.4 times more likely to develop Alzheimer's disease.

Saturated fat limits the body's ability to "clear" beta-amyloid deposits from the brain. It also raises cholesterol and increases the risk for cardiovascular diseases—and what's bad for the heart also is bad for the brain.

Consuming some saturated fat is healthful—it's only in excess that it causes problems. The American Heart Association advises limiting it to about 5% to 6% of total calories. I recommend a little more—up to 10% of your daily calories. On a 2,000-calorie diet, the upper limit would be about 20 grams. (One ounce of cheese can have as much as eight grams.)

FISH, TURMERIC AND COCOA

Studies have shown that a few specific foods can fight Alzheimer's...

- **Fish.** A UCLA study found that adults who regularly ate foods high in omega-3 fatty acids (the healthful fats in fish) had a lower risk for mental decline. Other research has shown that low blood levels of DHA (a type of omega-3) are linked to smaller brain volume and lower scores on cognitive tests.

My advice: Eat one serving of fatty fish (such as wild salmon, mackerel and sardines) at least twice a week.

- **Turmeric.** In India, where individuals use the spice turmeric frequently, the risk for Alzheimer's is lower than in the US. This doesn't prove that turmeric is responsible (genetic factors, for example, also could be involved), but other evidence suggests that it is protective. Turmeric contains the compound curcumin, which provides potent antioxidant and anti-inflammatory effects.

My advice: Use the spice in recipes—don't depend on supplements—because curcumin is fat-soluble and absorption is enhanced by the fat in foods.

- **Cocoa.** The flavanols in cocoa improve memory and other cognitive functions. They also have been linked to reduced blood pressure and improved insulin resistance.

My advice: Buy chocolate bars or cocoa powder that lists purified cocoa flavanols on the label.

Probiotics and Alzheimer's

When 52 patients with Alzheimer's disease took a probiotic supplement that contained four billion units of *Lactobacillus* and *Bifidobacterium,* they showed improvement in memory and other cognitive test scores after 12 weeks.

Theory: These probiotics may decrease inflammation in the brain.

If a loved one has Alzheimer's disease: Talk to his/her doctor about a probiotic supplement.

Mahmoud Salami, PhD, professor of neurophysiology, Kashan University of Medical Sciences and Health Services, Iran.

Best Nondrug Approaches for Parkinson's Disease

Michael S. Okun, MD, professor and chair of the department of neurology and codirector of the Center for Movement Disorders and Neurorestoration at the University of Florida College of Medicine in Gainesville. He is also the medical director at the National Parkinson Foundation and has written more than 400 medical journal articles. Dr. Okun's latest book is *10 Breakthrough Therapies for Parkinson's Disease.*

The telltale tremors, muscle stiffness and other movement problems that plague people with Parkinson's disease make even the mundane activities of daily living—such as brushing teeth, cooking and dressing—more difficult.

What's new: Even though medication—such as *levodopa* (L-dopa) and newer drugs including *pramipexole* and *selegiline*—have long been the main treatment to control Parkinson's symptoms, researchers are discovering more and more nondrug therapies that can help.

Among the best nondrug approaches (each can be used with Parkinson's medication)...

EXERCISE

For people with Parkinson's, exercise is like a drug. It raises *neurotrophic factors*, proteins that promote the growth and health of neurons. Research consistently shows that exercise can improve motor symptoms (such as walking speed and stability) and quality of life.

For the best results: Exercise 30 to 60 minutes every single day. Aim to work hard enough to break a sweat, but back off if you get too fatigued—especially the following day (this indicates the body is not recovering properly). Parkinson's symptoms can worsen with over-exercise. *Smart exercise habits...*

- **For better gait speed**—Choose a lower-intensity exercise, such as walking on a treadmill (but hold on to the balance bars), rather than high-intensity exercise (such as running), which has a higher risk for falls and other injuries.

A recent study showed that a walking group of Parkinson's patients performed better than a group of patients who ran. *Important safety tip:* Parkinson's patients should exercise with a partner and take precautions to prevent falls—for example, minimizing distractions, such as ringing cell phones.

- **For aerobic exercise**—Use a recumbent bicycle or rowing machine and other exercises that don't rely on balance.
- **For strength and flexibility**—Do stretching and progressive resistance training.

Excellent resource: To get a wide variety of exercises, including aerobic workouts, standing and sitting stretches, strengthening moves, balance exercises and fall-prevention tips, the National Parkinson Foundation's *Fitness Counts* book is available for free at Parkinson.org/pd-library/books/fitness-counts.

- **For balance**—Researchers are now discovering that yoga postures, tai chi (with its slow, controlled movements) and certain types of dancing (such as the tango, which involves rhythmic forward-and-backward steps) are excellent ways to improve balance.

COFFEE AND TEA

Could drinking coffee or tea help with Parkinson's? According to research, it *can*—when consumed in the correct amounts.

Here's why: Caffeine blocks certain receptors in the brain that regulate the neurotransmitter *dopamine*, which becomes depleted and leads to the impaired motor coordination that characterizes Parkinson's. In carefully controlled studies, Parkinson's patients who ingested low doses of caffeine—about 100 mg twice daily—had improved motor symptoms, such as tremors and stiffness, compared with people who had no caffeine or higher doses of caffeine.

My advice: Have 100 mg of caffeine (about the amount in one six-ounce cup of home-brewed coffee or two cups of black or green tea) twice a day—once in the morning and once in the mid-afternoon. *Note:* Even decaffeinated coffee has about 10 mg to 25 mg of caffeine per cup.

SUPPLEMENTS

Researchers have studied various supplements for years to identify ones that could help manage Parkinson's symptoms and/or boost

GOOD TO KNOW...

See the *Right* Doctor for Parkinson's

For anyone with Parkinson's, it's crucial to see a neurologist and, if possible, one who has advanced training in both Parkinson's disease and movement disorders.

Important recent finding: A large study showed that patients treated by a neurologist had a lower risk for hip fracture and were less likely to be placed in a nursing facility. They were also 22% less likely to die during the four-year study.

Neurologists are best equipped to treat the ever-changing symptoms of Parkinson's. For optimal care, see the neurologist every four to six months. The National Parkinson Foundation's Helpline, 800-4PD-INFO (473-4636) can assist you in finding expert care.

the effects of levodopa, but large studies have failed to prove that these supplements provide such benefits.

However, because Parkinson's is a complex disease that can cause about 20 different motor and nonmotor symptoms that evolve over time, the existing research may not apply to everyone. *Some people with Parkinson's may benefit from...*

- **Coenzyme Q10 (CoQ10).** This supplement promotes the health of the body's *mitochondria* ("energy generators" in the cells), which are believed to play a role in Parkinson's. In a large study, people with Parkinson's who took 1,200 mg per day showed some improvement in symptoms over a 16-month study period. However, follow-up studies found no beneficial effects.
- **Riboflavin and alpha-lipoic acid** are among the other supplements that are continuing to be studied.

Important: If you wish to try these or other supplements, be sure to consult your doctor to ensure that there are no possible interactions with your other medications.

MARIJUANA

A few small studies have concluded that marijuana can improve some neurological symptoms, but larger studies are needed to show benefits for Parkinson's patients, especially for symptoms such as depression and anxiety.

However: Marijuana is challenging for several reasons—first, it is illegal in most states. If you do live in a state that allows medical marijuana use, it has possible side effects—for example, it can impair balance and driving...it is difficult to know the exact dosage, even if it's purchased from a dispensary...and with marijuana edibles (such as cookies and candies), the effects may take longer to appear, and you may accidentally ingest too much.

If you want to try marijuana: Work closely with your doctor to help you avoid such pitfalls.

Can Marijuana Help You? Science Proves It Works for These Conditions

David Bearman, MD, vice president of quality assurance and credentials for the American Academy of Cannabinoid Medicine. Dr. Bearman has almost 50 years of experience working as a professional in substance- and drug-abuse programs, including as a medical officer in the US Public Health Service. He is author of *Drugs Are Not the Devil's Tools: How Discrimination and Greed Created a Dysfunctional Drug Policy and How It Can Be Fixed*. He is in private practice in Goleta, California, specializing in pain management. DavidBearmanMD.com

Almost every state in the US has legalized the medicinal use of marijuana in at least some form. And in early 2017, there was a remarkable development that should lead to greater acceptance of medical marijuana nationally. On January 12, the Health and Medicine division of the National Academies of Sciences, Engineering, and Medicine issued a report on the therapeutic use of *cannabis* (the term preferred by experts). To write their report, doctors from the Harvard T.H. Chan School of Public Health, Johns Hopkins University, Duke University Medical Center and other leading medical institutions reviewed and summarized the findings of more than 10,000 scientific studies on cannabis.

The studies show that cannabis has "therapeutic effects" on a variety of health conditions, including chronic pain, sleep disorders, anxiety, post-traumatic stress disorder, depression, chemotherapy-induced nausea and vomiting, epilepsy, the muscle spasms of multiple sclerosis, brain injury, Tourette's syndrome and other conditions.

Bottom line: Medical cannabis is a science-supported, effective therapy for symptomatic relief in a wide range of health problems.

Here's what you need to know about the medical benefits of cannabis and—if you decide to try it—how to take advantage of those benefits...

HOW CANNABIS WORKS

Researchers at St. Louis University School of Medicine in Missouri discovered that brain cells (neurons) have receptor sites for cannabinoids, the active compounds in cannabis. (There are more than 100 *cannabinoids* in cannabis, along with hundreds of other compounds.) In fact, they found that there are more receptors for cannabinoids than there are receptors for any other type of neurotransmitter—the chemicals that relay messages between neurons, activating functions in the brain and the rest of the body.

Scientists also soon found receptors for cannabinoids in the immune system, the peripheral nervous system (outside the brain and spinal cord) and the gut, spleen, liver, heart, kidneys, bones, blood vessels, endocrine glands and reproductive organs.

In subsequent years, they found that the body itself generates cannabinoid-like compounds called *endocannabinoids*.

Finally, they discovered an entire (and previously undetected) "endocannabinoid system" that regulates many mind-body functions, including memory, mood, aspects of digestion and energy balance. Scientists have concluded that the endocannabinoid system helps regulate a very large number of mental and physical functions.

Medical cannabis works by triggering the endocannabinoid system, which is why its effects are so wide-ranging. What's more, the endocannabinoid system employs a unique type of transmission called *retrograde inhibition,* which slows excessive activity in the body. With medical cannabis, there can be less pain, fewer muscle spasms, fewer seizures, less exaggerated tremors and less digestive upset.

NEW DISCOVERIES

The National Academies of Sciences report highlights many of the conditions helped by medical cannabis. *Here is a sampling of the most recent research supporting some of the conclusions...*

- **Chronic pain, including diabetic peripheral neuropathy and others.** Many studies have shown that medical cannabis works for chronic pain. *Example:* Many people with diabetes suffer from chronic nerve pain in the feet and hands—symptoms include burning, electric shocklike tingling and dismaying numbness. Publishing their results in *Journal of Pain*, researchers from University of California, San Diego, found that medical cannabis could control nerve pain in people with diabetes.

- **Parkinson's disease.** Use of medical cannabis led to improvement in well-being and quality of life for people with Parkinson's disease, according to a study published in *Journal of Psychopharmacology.*

- **Epilepsy.** A study that was published in *Lancet Neurology* by researchers at major medical schools across the US found that medical cannabis reduced the frequency of seizures in patients with "severe, intractable...treatment-resistant epilepsy."

- **Inflammatory bowel disease (Crohn's).** Israeli researchers at Meir Medical Center, publishing a study in *Clinical Gastroenterology and Hepatology*, found remarkable improvements in 21 Crohn's patients who hadn't responded to conventional medical treatment—five had "complete remission"...10 of the 11 had an average decrease in symptoms of 69%...and three were able to stop taking steroid drugs to control the disease. Many had improved appetite and slept better.

- **Multiple sclerosis.** A study published in *Journal of Neurology, Neurosurgery & Psychia-*

try found that cannabis extracts were twice as effective as a placebo in relieving muscle stiffness and pain in people with multiple sclerosis.

USING MEDICAL CANNABIS

In some states where medical cannabis has been legalized, getting a doctor's prescription for use of the medicine might be more or less automatic, just as it is with other sorts of medicines—you might spend a few minutes in the exam room and then be out the door with your prescription. But that is *not necessarily a good thing.*

You need to know how medical cannabis will work for your problem. You need to know the best dose for symptom control—one that controls your symptoms without a level of mental impairment that is uncomfortable or makes you dysfunctional. Starting with a low dose and slowly increasing the dose is the best approach—an approach that needs monitoring by your doctor and you.

Finding the best strain of cannabis to use for your health problem can be a matter of trial and error. Different cannabinoids have different effects. THC (*tetrahydrocannabinol*) is "psychoactive"—it creates euphoria (and is the reason that so many people use cannabis recreationally). *Cannabidiol* (CBD) is not psychoactive—it partially blocks some of the euphoria caused by THC. You and your doctor need to pick a strain and a dose that work best for you.

There also is the *route of administration*, which includes both vaping and smoking. Vaping requires the use of a vaporizer, which minimizes respiratory irritability—the plant matter is vaporized into gas rather than burned into smoke. This method is ideal for rapid relief in conditions such as severe, exacerbated chronic pain, migraines, nausea and vomiting, and asthma.

Another option is taking capsules of a cannabis extract such as Dronabinol. This is absorbed more slowly into the bloodstream and can provide three to six hours of therapeutic effect. For example, a dose that delivers five milligrams of THC works for patients who have trouble sleeping because of anxiety—it can provide three to six hours of good sleep if taken one hour before bedtime. There also are topical treatments. For example, topical tincture of cannabis can relieve muscle spasm or arthritic pain in the fingers and wrist.

To find a well-informed doctor, I recommend contacting the American Academy of Cannabinoid Medicine and asking for the name of a doctor near you who is a member of the academy (805-961-9988, info.aacm@gmail.com). Another organization that can help you find a doctor is Leafly (Leafly.com/doctors).

MORE ON SAFETY

As a physician who has worked with thousands of patients using medical marijuana, I can say that it is very safe—and not addictive.

In fact, cannabis produces fewer addictive symptoms than alcohol, nicotine and narcotic painkilling drugs. There is less risk for "dependency" than with any prescription pain or antianxiety medication. Little or no "tolerance" develops (tolerance is when you have to use more and more to achieve the same effect). There are few withdrawal symptoms, if any. All in all, cannabis is about as "addictive" as coffee.

There are some possible side effects, however. The main one is coughing, which you can avoid by using a vaporizer or a noninhaled form. Another possible downside is dysphoria (feeling out of touch with reality, dissatisfied with life) or, on the other hand, excessive euphoria, which despite what you might expect can be an unpleasant side effect. Dysphoria or excessive euphoria are most likely when a new user takes a dose of THC that is too high. On the other hand, in patients with cancer or AIDS, a little euphoria to relieve anxiety and depression might be just what the patient needs—again, all of these possibilities can (and should) be worked out in your discussions with your doctor.

Don't be afraid of medical cannabis. There are a great many people whom it has and can help.

New Dangers for Supplement Users—Beware These Interactions

Mark A. Moyad, MD, MPH, the Jenkins/Pokempner director of complementary and alternative medicine at the University of Michigan Medical Center, department of urology, in Ann Arbor. He is the primary author of more than 150 medical journal articles and author, with Janet Lee, of *The Supplement Handbook*.

By now, you know that the supplements you pop to stay healthy may turn harmful if you also take certain prescription and/or over-the-counter medications.

What you may not realize: Scientists are *still* uncovering what the interactions are—and just how dangerous they can be. *What you need to know to stay safe...*

THE LATEST FINDINGS

When researchers at the University of Minnesota recently looked at data from more than 23 million scientific studies, they identified *thousands* of potential drug–supplement interactions—including some that have only recently been recognized.*

The danger zone: Some supplements *increase* drug levels by slowing their breakdown in the body. Some accelerate drug metabolism/breakdown and reduce the desired effects. *Other interactions are additive:* Drugs and supplements can act on similar pathways in the body and increase the overall effects—and the risk for side effects.

PARTICULARLY RISKY

In the meta-analysis mentioned above, researchers discovered that echinacea, a popular herbal remedy for colds and other infections, reduced the activity of *exemestane* (Aromasin), a drug used for breast cancer. In fact, echinacea interferes with a number of chemotherapy drugs, including *cyclophosphamide* and *fluorouracil. Other drug–supplement interactions...*

- **Iodine.** Most Americans get enough iodine from salt, seafood, whole grains and other foods. But some people take supplements because they believe that extra iodine will improve thyroid health. The truth is, the supplement only helps if there's a true iodine deficiency.

Serious interaction: *Levothyroxine* (Synthroid and Levoxyl), a synthetic form of thyroid hormone that treats low thyroid (hypothyroidism). High doses of supplemental iodine—300 micrograms (mcg) or more—can interfere with thyroid function. When this happens, a dose of levothyroxine that was previously effective can suddenly stop working.

My advice: Do not take supplemental iodine unless you have been shown (via urine or blood tests) to be deficient, and your doctor OKs it. Supplements often contain 500 mcg to 1,000 mcg of iodine—far more than the recommended daily allowance of 150 mcg.

Helpful: Be cautious when taking any supplement that's dosed in micrograms. Anything that's measured in *millionths* of a gram requires careful minimal dosing.

- **Fish oil.** It has a number of proven benefits—lowering very high triglycerides (500 mg/dL and above)...improving pain from rheumatoid arthritis...slowing the progression of lupus...and even easing mild-to-moderate depression.

Serious interactions: All blood thinners—including not only the popular prescription blood thinner *warfarin* and newer blood thinners, such as Eliquis and Xarelto, but also over-the-counter drugs with blood-thinning effects, including nonsteroidal anti-inflammatory drugs (NSAIDs) such as aspirin and *ibuprofen* (Motrin).

Fish oil has a blood-thinning effect because it inhibits the ability of platelets to stick together and form clots. This can be beneficial since blood clots in the arteries are the main cause of heart attacks. But combining fish oil with other blood thinners can cause excess bleeding during surgery or dental pro-

*To search for drug–supplement interactions, go to the National Library of Medicine's website NLM.nih.gov/medlineplus/druginfo...or the fee-based Natural Medicines Comprehensive Database, NaturalDatabase.com.

cedures...or from wounds or internal injuries (such as ulcers).

My advice: Ask your doctor if you can take fish oil along with your usual blood thinner. The blood-thinning effects of fish oil are *dose-dependent*—you're less likely to have problems at typical doses of, say, 2,000 mg or less daily.

Don't make this mistake: If you're taking fish oil for high cholesterol, stop. A lot of my patients have been told that it lowers LDL "bad" cholesterol. Not true. At doses of 1,000 mg or more, it can actually *raise* LDL five to 10 points or more.

- **GABA (gamma-aminobutyric acid).** It's a neurotransmitter that's present in the brain and other parts of the body. In supplement form, it has a calming effect and is thought to lower cortisol, the body's main stress hormone.

Serious interactions: Sedative drugs, including opioids (such as codeine) and antianxiety medications, such as *lorazepam* (Ativan) or *alprazolam* (Xanax). Taking these drugs with GABA can cause excessive sedation.

My advice: Never combine sedatives—whether they're "natural" or pharmaceutical—without checking with your doctor.

- **St. John's wort**. This herbal supplement has been shown to be as effective as prescription antidepressants in treating mild-to-moderate depression—and with fewer side effects. However, when combined with SSRI (selective serotonin reuptake inhibitor) antidepressants, such as *escitalopram* (Lexapro) or *paroxetine* (Paxil), or other types of antidepressants, the supplement can cause *medication-induced serotonin syndrome*. This dangerous "overdose" of serotonin, a neurotransmitter that affects mood, can cause swings in blood pressure and heart rate, along with such symptoms as heavy sweating, diarrhea and extreme agitation. But that's not all.

Serious interactions: An increasing body of evidence shows that St. John's wort can interact with many other prescription drugs, including warfarin, *digoxin* and other heart medications, antiseizure drugs, certain cancer drugs and birth control pills. You *must* let your doctor know if you're taking St. John's wort.

- **L-arginine.** L-arginine increases blood levels of nitric oxide, a naturally occurring molecule that dilates blood vessels and can reduce blood pressure by 20 points or more. Some men take it for erectile dysfunction (ED).

Serious interactions: L-arginine can interact with *all* prescription blood pressure medications, causing blood pressure to drop to dangerously low levels, resulting in dizziness, blurred vision or even a loss of consciousness. The supplement can also cause dangerous drops in blood pressure in men taking ED medication.

My advice: Always check with your doctor before taking a blood pressure drug or ED medication with L-arginine.

Easy Cooking Tricks for Much Healthier Foods

Lisa R. Young, PhD, RD, a nutritionist in private practice and an adjunct professor in the department of nutrition and food studies at New York University in New York City. She is author of *The Portion Teller Plan: The No-Diet Reality Guide to Eating, Cheating, and Losing Weight Permanently.*

Loading up your grocery cart with fruits and vegetables is a great start to a healthful diet. But even if you hit the produce section on a regular basis, chances are you're not getting the same level of nutrients in your fruits and vegetables that earlier generations did.

Modern agricultural methods have stripped soil of important nutrients, so produce that is eaten today may be less healthful than it used to be.*

Troubling findings: A study published in the *Journal of the American College of Nutrition* found "reliable declines" in the amount of key vitamins and minerals in 43 fruits and vegetables compared with nutrient levels of those foods in 1950.

Other research has found that the levels of calcium in 12 fresh veggies dropped, on average, by 27%...iron by 37%...and vitamin C by

*Organic fruits and vegetables may have more nutrients than those that are conventionally grown.

30% over a 22-year period. Such changes in nutrient values can have a hidden danger by contributing to nutrition deficiencies, which are more common than one might imagine finding in the US.

For these reasons, it's crucial for you to do everything you can to squeeze *all* of the available nutrition from your foods. Besides stocking up on fruits and veggies, studies have shown that how you store, prepare and cook foods—and even how you combine them—can make a difference. *Six tricks that will help you get the greatest nutrition from your foods...*

• **Make steaming your first choice.** Vegetables are good for you no matter how they're prepared. But to get the most nutrients, steaming is the best choice.

Scientific evidence: Steamed broccoli retained virtually all the tested antioxidants in a study published in the *Journal of the Science of Food and Agriculture*, while microwaved broccoli lost 74% to 97% of these disease-fighting nutrients—possibly because microwaves can generate higher temperatures than other cooking methods.

Boiling is also problematic. The liquid—combined with the high heat and lengthy cooking time—strips out significant levels of important nutrients. *Example:* Broccoli that's been boiled loses large amounts of glucosinolate, a compound that's been linked to cancer prevention. *Helpful:* The liquid does retain nutrients, so consider using it in a soup.

A caveat: If you simply don't have time to steam your veggies and, as a result, risk not eating them, microwaving can be an acceptable option—if you add only a teaspoon or so of water and cook for the shortest time possible to retain nutrients.

Even though microwaving has been found to remove certain nutrients, it can be one of the best ways to preserve vitamin C and other water-soluble nutrients because the cooking times tend to be shorter. Other methods, such as sautéing and roasting, retain nutrients if you don't cook vegetables at high temperatures or for too long.

• **Cooked beats fresh.** Fresh, minimally processed foods should usually be your first choice—but not with tomatoes. Cooked tomatoes or canned tomato sauce or paste (best in a BPA-free can or glass jar) provides more lycopene than fresh tomatoes. Lycopene is a well-studied antioxidant that's been linked to reduced risk for prostate and other cancers, along with reduced risk for stroke.

Scientific evidence: A study in *The American Journal of Clinical Nutrition* found that the lycopene in tomato paste has 2.5 times the *bioavailability* of the lycopene in fresh tomatoes.

Why: The heat used during processing breaks down cell walls and releases more of the compound. Also, the oils that are added to processed tomatoes make it easier for the body to absorb lycopene.

• **Cook first, chop later.** Many people chop their veggies first, then add them to dishes before they go on the stove or into the oven.

Smart idea: Chop most veggies *after* you've done the cooking. *Here's why:* Vitamin C and other nutrients oxidize when they're exposed to air for an extended period of time. An oxidized vitamin loses some of its bioactivity. In addition, chopped or diced vegetables have a greater surface area than whole ones, which allows more nutrients to leach into cooking liquids. *Exception:* Onions and garlic *should* be chopped first (see below).

Scientific evidence: A recent study found that carrots, chopped prior to cooking, had 25% less *falcarinol*, a natural anticancer compound, than cooked whole carrots.

• **Try lemon (or lime) to boost iron levels.** Iron deficiency is among the most common nutrition deficiencies in the US, particularly among women of childbearing age. Meats are high in iron, but women with heavy periods might need more. Low iron can also be a problem for vegetarians/vegans. That's because the *non-heme* iron in plant foods isn't as readily absorbed as the *heme* iron in meats.

Helpful: Add a little vitamin C–rich lemon or lime juice to recipes. Vitamin C can boost the absorption of non-heme iron by four-fold.

• **Add a spoonful of fat.** A garden-fresh salad or a plate of steamed broccoli is undoubtedly healthy. But for an even greater nutrient boost, add a teaspoon of olive oil.

You need fat to absorb vitamin E, beta-carotene, vitamin A and other fat-soluble nutrients/antioxidants. The average meal contains more than enough fat to get the job done, but simpler, fat-free meals won't provide that extra boost.

My advice: Add a little bit of olive oil to dishes...or dress up fat-free dishes with ingredients that contain healthy fats, such as nuts, olives, feta cheese or a hard-boiled egg.

• **Chop garlic, and let it sit.** Many people love the robust flavor of whole garlic cloves that are roasted to buttery smoothness. But you'll get more health benefits from garlic that's been chopped.

Garlic (as well as onions) contains *alliin* and other sulfur-containing compounds that are locked within cell walls. The cells rupture when these foods are minced or chopped (or well-chewed), which releases enzymes that transform alliin into *allicin*, a compound with cardiovascular and anticancer benefits.

Good rule of thumb: Chopping and letting garlic or onions sit for about 10 minutes will allow the enzyme to make the healthful conversion. Heating garlic or onions before the completion of the enzymatic reaction will reduce the health benefits.

The Truth About Yogurt

Leslie Bonci, RD, CSSD, MPH, owner of the Pittsburgh-based nutrition consulting company Active Eating Advice by Leslie. The former director of sports nutrition for the University of Pittsburgh Medical Center, Bonci is author of numerous books, including *The Active Calorie Diet* and the *American Dietetic Association Guide to Better Digestion*.

Yogurt has long been a favorite of Europeans, but this creamy treat is now a staple in more American households than ever before.

Trap to watch out for: With yogurt's increasing popularity in the US, consumers must now be alert for trumped-up claims about the food's healthfulness.

It's true that researchers are uncovering more and more reasons to consume yogurt. For example, a study recently presented at a meeting of the American Heart Association found that women who consumed five or more servings of yogurt weekly lowered their risk of developing high blood pressure by 20% compared with those who ate one serving of yogurt per month. But anyone who has shopped for yogurt recently knows that the dairy aisle is chock-full of options ranging from Greek yogurt and "yogurt-style" drinks like kefir to coconut and soy yogurts—and even "desserty" yogurts with candy toppings. So how do you know what to believe about all these products? *Beware of these misconceptions...*

MISCONCEPTION #1: **Greek yogurt is always healthier than regular yogurt.** Yogurt is produced by the bacterial fermentation of milk (usually cow's milk). Greek yogurt takes it a step further by straining out whey (the watery part of milk) and lactose (milk sugar) so that the result is a thick, creamy texture not unlike sour cream. For the same amount of calories, most Greek yogurt has about twice the protein of regular yogurt...and less carbohydrates, sugar and sodium. Greek yogurt, however, has more saturated fat than regular yogurt. (For more on saturated fat, see the next page.) With regular yogurt, you also get more bone-strengthening calcium, which is partially lost from Greek yogurt when the whey is strained out.

Important: Although Greek yogurt's processing leaves it with less sugar to start with, some products still add in generous amounts of sugary flavoring. For example, plain, unsweetened Greek yogurt typically contains about 6 g of sugar per eight-ounce serving—thanks to the remaining naturally occurring lactose sugar. When you see a Greek yogurt with 20 g or 25 g of sugar per serving, that means extra sugar has been added, typically in the form of honey or fruit purée.

Best bet: Buy *plain* yogurt (Greek or regular), and mix in fresh fruit—you'll get an extra serving of produce without all the sugar of a purée. If you like crunch, sprinkle in some seeds (sunflower work well) or nuts (like pistachios). Check labels for sneaky sugar aliases like "evaporated cane juice," date or coconut sugar and high-fructose corn syrup (HFCS).

MISCONCEPTION #2: **Low-fat yogurt is a better choice than full fat.** A 2015 *American Journal of Clinical Nutrition* study made headlines when researchers found that people who ate the most high-fat dairy products had *lower* rates of type 2 diabetes.

As it turns out, it's not the *amount* of fat we consume but the *type* that's important. Full-fat yogurt is high not only in saturated fat but also in *conjugated linoleic acid*, which may have a protective effect against type 2 diabetes. Also, the full-fat yogurt's rich, thick mouthfeel sends a message to the brain that says, "I'm satisfied. I don't need to keep eating." Once in the stomach, the fat takes time to digest and, as a result, you feel full longer.

So feel free to include a daily serving of full-fat yogurt, but balance it by cutting back on other forms of saturated fat, such as fried foods, meat, eggs and/or butter.

MISCONCEPTION #3: **Yogurt offers the most probiotics of all dairy.** Probiotics are "friendly" bacteria that can enhance digestion, relieve constipation and bloating and even improve immune functioning.

While yogurt usually contains a few strains of probiotics, kefir, which is similar to yogurt but drinkable and more tart, offers far more. In fact, some kefir products contain 10 to 12 strains of probiotics! Don't ditch your yogurt entirely, but go ahead and switch things up with some kefir. Try it in a smoothie, swirled in oatmeal or in hummus recipes.

MISCONCEPTION #4: **People who have lactose intolerance should avoid yogurt.** The good bacteria in both Greek and traditional yogurt actually *predigest* some of the lactose in dairy products, lessening the odds of troubling symptoms such as gas, bloating and diarrhea. (Greek yogurt is especially low in lactose due to the straining process.)

In fact, research suggests that these bacteria are so potent that the enhanced lactose digestion may last for weeks following regular consumption. However, the bacteria must be alive, so be sure to select products with the words "live and active cultures" on the label.

Helpful: Start by eating only a couple of tablespoons and look for gastrointestinal symptoms. If there are none, slowly increase your intake over a period of days.

If you still cannot tolerate dairy, there are non-milk-based yogurts, such as soy and coconut. But be aware that they don't have nearly as much protein as Greek yogurt and can be high in sugar (natural and/or added).

Coconut yogurt, with about 4 g of saturated fat per one-half cup, contains fats called *medium-chain triglycerides*—research suggests that the body may prefer to use these fats for energy versus storing them as fat.

MISCONCEPTION #5: **Yogurt isn't just a breakfast food.** With the right mix-ins, yogurt is a delicious treat any time of day.

Ideas: Make a higher-protein version of Rondelé cheese by emptying a large container of unflavored Greek yogurt into a strainer lined with a coffee filter and set over a bowl. Let it drain, refrigerate overnight, mix peppercorns and chives into the resulting yogurt "cheese" and use it as a spread for crackers...or as a higher-protein cream cheese substitute.

Plain (regular) yogurt has a runnier consistency—use it to lighten up mac and cheese, mashed potatoes or a stroganoff recipe (just cut back a bit on the milk, butter and cream).

For an indulgent-feeling, lower-calorie dessert, top one-half cup of full-fat vanilla Greek yogurt with one-quarter cup of chopped strawberries and a drizzle of chocolate balsamic vinegar. At just 130 calories and 11 g of sugar, this is a refreshing treat with an intense, not-too-sweet flavor.

GOOD TO KNOW...

Chocolate for the Heart

Chocolate may help reduce your heart disease risk. In a recent study, people who ate a one-ounce serving of chocolate each week had a 17% lower rate of atrial fibrillation compared with people who ate one ounce or less a month. Researchers said that dark chocolate—with its higher cocoa content—is best.

Elizabeth Mostofsky, ScD, MPH, a postdoctoral fellow at Beth Israel Deaconess Medical Center, Boston, and lead author of a study of more than 55,000 adults.

6

Private & Personal

What Really Happens During Sex Therapy?

A*dmit it:* You are a little curious. When you hear the phrase "sex therapy," you wonder *who* actually goes and *why*. What do people do in sex therapy? And could it help me?

It's not as mysterious as it sounds. The point of sex therapy is to help partners or spouses—and sometimes singles not in committed relationships—regain an active and satisfying sex life. Sex therapy can be done individually, but it is more successful when done as a couple.

An under-recognized problem: More people could benefit from this specialized therapy than actually seek it—sexual problems, including low libido, premature ejaculation and erectile dysfunction, are more prevalent in the US than the incidence of anxiety and depression *combined*.

When a couple's sex life is going kaput, forgoing this very valuable tool may endanger one's relationship. Couples—both heterosexual and homosexual—often underestimate the importance of a mutually pleasing sex life to their overall bond.

Important finding: A study cited in the *Journal of Marital & Family Therapy* reports that contented partners attribute only between 15% and 20% of their happiness to a pleasing sex life, while unhappy mates ascribe 50% to 70% of their distress to sexual problems.

In addition, one of the major causes of divorce in the first five years of marriage (whether it's a first marriage or a second marriage) is sexual problems or dysfunction.

Barry McCarthy, PhD, a professor of psychology at American University in Washington, DC, a Diplomate in clinical psychology and a certified sex and couples therapist who has practiced for 42 years. In 2016, he received the Masters and Johnson award for lifetime contributions to the field of sex therapy. The author of 14 books, including *Sex Made Simple* and *Rekindling Desire*, he has presented more than 400 professional workshops in the US and internationally.

Here's what sex therapy is all about and how it may help you...

THE BIGGEST BEDROOM PROBLEM

Back in the 1970s, the biggest issues centered on arousal and orgasm. Now the major problem is desire—or lack thereof.

Perhaps surprisingly, healthy long-marrieds tend to be more sexually satisfied than others, even though they might not have sex as often as they used to. The most vulnerable time for couples to stop being sexual—defined as having sex fewer than 10 times a year—is within the first few years of marriage, after heady romance fades and day-to-day drudgery sets in. Many spouses have trouble transitioning to a more humdrum existence where they view each other as life partners and intimate friends but begin to de-eroticize the other person.

Danger points: It's during stress points such as childbirth or long-term infertility treatment when major sex problems, such as lack of desire, tend to spike. Other reasons people go to sex therapy include unwanted sexual fetishes, painful sex (resulting from a chronic medical condition, for example, such as arthritis) and/or poor body image (due to being overweight, for example, or a disfiguring operation). Sex therapy can also facilitate recovery for victims of sexual abuse and assault.

NO NUDITY REQUIRED!

Nudity or sexual touching isn't part of office-based therapy sessions. In the office, talk therapy is front and center, helping couples identify the anxiety, inhibitions and/or unrealistic expectations that interfere with their sexual pleasure.

A sex therapist will assure patients that they won't be pressured, and explain that he/she needs to understand each partner's psychological, relational and sexual strengths and vulnerabilities.

Homework: After each weekly or biweekly session—which, for most couples, continues for three months to a year—sex therapists assign partners homework. These exercises typically include talking, touching and setting up erotic scenarios.

Examples: A woman might practice her ability to veto touch she doesn't like and express her pleasure in touch she enjoys. A man might be given an exercise that involves the wax and wane of his erection.

About half of sex therapy takes place in the couple's home. If a couple has difficulty with an exercise at home, they can take a break and reestablish comfort and trust by holding each other and remaining calm before trying the exercise again.

OVERCOMING BARRIERS

Some people avoid seeking sex therapy because they're afraid of exposing themselves, whether physically or emotionally. Others, unfortunately, fall victim to a common public misconception that sex therapists don't work with mainstream, traditional couples. But most couples are traditional in the sense that they value their couplehood and maintain a traditional agreement about not having sexual relationships with others.

Shaking off shame: Many partners silently worry that their mate wouldn't love or respect them if they knew their deepest sexual secrets—unusual turn-ons, colorful histories, long-ago rape or abuse or a sexually transmitted disease. But confronting these issues in sex therapy typically reveals acceptance, not intolerance. Partners learn that their secrets no longer control them.

TAKE NOTE...

Light Therapy and Libido

Bright-light therapy may boost a man's libido...

Preliminary study: Men undergoing treatment for low sexual interest sat in front of a light box (similar to those used for seasonal affective disorder) for 30 minutes each morning. After two weeks, their sexual satisfaction scores—a measure of frequency and satisfaction with their performance—were more than *three times higher* than at the beginning of the study.

Likely reason: Using the light box increased testosterone levels by about 70%.

Andrea Fagiolini, MD, professor of psychiatry and chair of mental health at University of Siena School of Medicine, Siena, Italy, and leader of a study presented at the recent European College of Neuropharmacology conference.

THE BEST SEX THERAPISTS

Finding a qualified sex therapist isn't always an easy task. Most marital therapists are not trained to deal with sexual issues directly. In traditional couples therapy, sex problems are almost always considered to be a symptom of relationship problems, so sexual attitudes, behaviors and feelings are not directly addressed. Also, most states don't have licensing requirements for sex therapists.

The nonprofit American Association of Sexuality Educators, Counselors and Therapists (AASECT), AASECT.org/referral-directory, offers an easy-to-use online tool to help locate certified sex therapists in most parts of the US. Unfortunately, most health insurers don't reimburse for sex therapy.

To find the right therapist, look for a practitioner who...

- **Has a degree in mental health,** such as a doctorate of psychology (PhD) or a master's in social work (MSW).
- **Is certified by the AASECT to practice sex therapy.**
- **Has at least three years of experience working with couples**—including significant experience dealing directly with sexual issues.

It's worth the effort to find a therapist whom both partners like and respect. Talk to several therapists on the phone or e-mail a few to get a feel for who might be a good fit.

Vasectomy Concern

A patient who was considering vasectomy worried that his sex life would suffer...

My answer to him: After a vasectomy, the partners no longer have to worry about a surprise pregnancy, so in many instances, a couple's sex life *improves*—sometimes dramatically.

The vasectomy is a 15-minute outpatient surgery that severs the tubes that bring sperm to seminal fluid. The testicles still produce sperm, but it cannot get into the semen. The volume of ejaculation is reduced by less than 10%, which for most men is not noticeable.

Testosterone production is not affected by vasectomy, so sex drive is not impacted. The procedure does not cause nerve damage or impact erections or sensation. It is an extremely safe and effective form of birth control.

Sheldon Marks, MD, urologist and microsurgical specialist in private practice in Tucson.

Heart Health and Sex

Sex link to heart health differs for men and women. In a study of more than 2,200 people age 57 and older, men who had sex at least once a week had almost twice the cardiovascular risk of men who were sexually inactive. Women who reported the most satisfying sex had lower risk for high blood pressure and other cardiovascular conditions than other women.

Why: Women may benefit from hormones produced during orgasm, while men might subject themselves to undue stress through exertion or medication for erectile dysfunction.

Takeaway: Older men who are sexually active should be sure to monitor their cardiovascular health.

Hui Liu, PhD, associate professor of sociology, Michigan State University, East Lansing.

Caffeine and Conception

Caffeine consumption prior to conception can increase risk for miscarriage. Miscarriage risk increases when either the woman or the man consumes more than two caffeinated drinks a day (one drink of coffee is eight ounces) in the weeks leading up to conception. To be on the safe side, both people may want to limit caffeine when the woman is trying to become pregnant. And women should talk with their doctors about taking a daily multivitamin before conception and through early pregnancy—this also reduces miscarriage risk.

Analysis of data on 344 pregnancies, 28% of which ended in miscarriage, by researchers at US National Institute of Child Health and Human Development, Bethesda, Maryland, published in *Fertility and Sterility.*

Aspirin May Help Conception

Daily low-dose aspirin may aid conception in women who have previously lost a pregnancy and have high levels of C-reactive protein (CRP)—a substance in the blood that indicates system-wide inflammation. Among women with high CRP, daily aspirin use led to a 59% live-birth rate, compared with a 44% rate for women taking a placebo.

Study by researchers at National Institute of Child Health and Human Development, Rockville, Maryland, published in *The Journal of Clinical Endocrinology & Metabolism.*

Early Menopause Risk

Early menopause may raise depression risk. Women who reached menopause before age 40 had a higher likelihood of depression in later life than women who reached menopause later. The average age of menopause in the US is 51.

Analysis of studies of 68,000 women by researchers from the National and Kapodistrian University of Athens, Greece, published in *JAMA Psychiatry.*

Hot Flash Tip

Exercise may reduce hot flashes. Researchers found that women who exercised reported 60% fewer hot flashes than women who did not work out. And women who exercised and who had hot flashes perspired less...had a much better ability to regulate their body heat...and had less intense hot flashes.

Study by researchers at Liverpool John Moores University, Liverpool, UK, and published in *The Journal of Physiology.*

Better Hot Flash Defense

Menopausal women who received up to 20 acupuncture treatments reported 36.7% fewer hot flashes after six months, according to a recent study. Hot flashes and night sweats increased by 6% in the women who did not get acupuncture.

Theory: Acupuncture stimulates the production of endorphins, "feel-good" chemicals that help stabilize body temperature.

To locate an acupuncturist: Check the website of the National Certification Commission for Acupuncture and Oriental Medicine, NCCAOM.org.

Nancy Avis, PhD, professor of social sciences and health policy, Wake Forest School of Medicine, Winston-Salem, North Carolina.

Nonsurgical Fibroid Removal

Painful uterine fibroids can be removed without surgery—and the procedure also can improve a woman's sex life. The nonsurgical option *uterine fibroid embolization* eliminates fibroids by blocking their blood supply. The 90-minute treatment is very safe and has been shown to improve sexual desire, arousal and satisfaction by eliminating excessive menstrual bleeding as well as the pain and pressure of fibroids. The procedure is not used as often as it could be because not enough physicians are familiar with it. The risks are infection (less than 1%) and possibly pushing a woman into menopause (1% to 5% depending on age).

Robert Vogelzang, MD, Albert Nemcek Education Professor of Radiology, Northwestern University Feinberg School of Medicine, Chicago.

Avoid Ovary Removal

The removal of normal ovaries does more harm than good in women who are not at high risk for ovarian or breast cancer. The procedure, called *prophylactic oophorectomy,* is commonly done during hysterectomy to reduce the risk for cancer.

But: Ovary removal increases the risk for colorectal cancer by 30%, possibly because oophorectomy decreases a woman's levels of estrogen and androgens. Oophorectomy also raises the risk for cardiovascular disease and osteoporosis and can result in impaired sexual health.

Josefin Segelman, MD, PhD, senior consultant colorectal surgeon, department of molecular medicine and surgery, Karolinska Institute, Stockholm, Sweden.

Onions in Oncology

A natural compound extracted from onions, *onionin A* (ONA), inhibits the growth of epithelial ovarian cancer and enhances the effects of anticancer drugs—without harming healthy cells. The finding may lead to an ONA supplement.

Kumamoto University.

Restore Your Pelvic Floor! Get Help for Incontinence and More

Lesli Lo, DPT, a women's health physical therapist (WHPT) at Northwestern Medical Group and an instructor of obstetrics and gynecology at Northwestern University Feinberg School of Medicine, both in Chicago.

If you're a woman who urinates when you laugh or cough, or sometimes feels overcome by a sudden, nearly uncontrollable urge to urinate—that is, if you have *urinary incontinence*—you've undoubtedly heard of Kegel exercises…and maybe even tried them. The do-anywhere pelvic exercises are often recommended for this condition—and a wide variety of other pelvic problems, including fecal (bowel) incontinence and pelvic organ prolapse, in which the bladder or uterus bulges into the vagina.

But doing Kegels may be making your problem *worse.* Eventually, Kegels can be part of the solution, but you need to take these steps *first.*

A PELVIC FLOOR PRIMER

The pelvic floor is a network of muscles, ligaments and tissue that acts like a sling to support a woman's pelvic organs—the uterus, vagina, bladder/urethra and rectum. You control your bowel and bladder by contracting and relaxing these muscles and tissues. About 25% of women ages 40 to 59 will suffer pelvic floor dysfunction (PFD) in their lifetime. Risk factors for PFD include menopause, age, obesity, repeated heavy lifting and traumatic injury—as may happen during childbirth, for example, or from a hip or back injury. Over time, the likelihood of a pelvic floor disorder increases.

MYTHS ABOUT KEGELS

Women with PFD often think their internal muscles are too weak and perform Kegels to strengthen them. That's often true, but it isn't the biggest problem. For 99% of my patients, those muscles are *too tight*, so they often get stuck in a contracted position, unable to control the flow of urine or to fully relax and contract in a pleasurable way during intercourse. Kegels can worsen the situation by strengthening already too-tight muscles. What these patients really need is to relax these muscles.

The first step: Bring up your symptoms with your internist, ob/gyn, urogynecologist or urologist, who can rule out issues that are not musculoskeletal. If physical therapy is the next best course of treatment, he/she can refer you to a *women's health physical therapist* (WHPT). WHPTs treat not just the pelvic floor but the body as a whole. Three to six months of weekly manual therapy sessions, combined with homework, usually ease symptoms of urinary incontinence, painful intercourse and/or pelvic pain.

A WHPT will perform an internal exam to assess your areas of strength and weakness and design a plan to retrain your muscles. To find a WHPT in your area, go to WomensHealthAPTA.org for a locator from the American Physical Therapy Association. Insurance typically covers these services.

TONING THE RIGHT WAY

A crucial component of treatment is manual therapy—a WHPT uses her hands to gently massage, stretch and release spasms and trigger points within the deep and soft tissues of the vagina. This helps reduce tightness and tension and can even break up scar tissue that's further restricting tissues, allowing the pelvic floor muscles to fully relax and contract. Though it can feel uncomfortable initially, any pain quickly recedes as the muscles and tissues relax.

Manual therapy is a prime opportunity to assess how you do Kegels. During such therapy, I will insert one finger into the vagina and then ask my patient to perform a Kegel by imagining that she is stopping the flow of urine midstream. (Once a woman learns how to do this correctly, she can do it herself.) Two out of three women do this incorrectly, tightening their pelvic floor muscles *but not releasing them all the way back down*—or not tightening their pelvic floor at all. The goal is to fully relax these muscles. *What helps...*

• **Reverse Kegels.** In a conventional Kegel, you tighten your pelvic floor muscles, hold the contraction for 10 seconds, then fully relax back down. In a reverse Kegel, you begin by relaxing the muscles as you do when you've just sat down on the toilet with a full bladder and are able to urinate. You should feel your anus relax as well. Hold for 10 seconds while you continue to breathe. Then return to normal for 10 seconds. Repeat the reverse Kegel 10 times, two to three times daily.

• **Biofeedback.** This pain-free, nonsurgical technique allows patients to see their pelvic muscles at rest and while contracted—and improves their ability to retrain the pelvic floor. A sensor or small weight is inserted into the vagina, while a nearby computer provides visual feedback.

• **Home biofeedback.** The apps *Elvie* ($199, Apple and Android, Elvie.com) and *PeriCoach* ($249, Apple and Android, PeriCoach.com) use intravaginal devices to assess the strength and endurance of vaginal contractions, and then send data to your smartphone via Bluetooth. If you've already had a professional pelvic assessment and know how to do Kegels the right way, these products can be helpful.

A LIFESTYLE SOLUTION

Shallow breathing also contributes to pelvic floor disorders.

Why: The diaphragm, a sheet of muscle that separates the chest cavity from the abdomen, gets stuck in a contracted position—causing pelvic muscles to contract, too.

Solution: Learn diaphragmatic breathing. Lying down, pretend your belly is a balloon and fill it with air, keeping your chest still. Now exhale, deflating the balloon. Do this once an hour for five breaths...and for five minutes before bed. In two to three weeks, you should notice a change in the way you breathe.

GOOD TO KNOW...

Kegels for Men

Men have a pelvic floor, too. It supports the prostate, bladder and rectum. Age, a hip or back injury or surgical inguinal hernia repair can weaken pelvic floor muscles. This can lead to urinary incontinence, an inability to maintain an erection without pain, and pelvic pain and tightness. Like women, many men can benefit from pelvic floor muscle relaxation, manual therapy and reverse Kegels. Ask your internist or urologist for a referral to a pelvic floor physical therapist—especially if you're scheduled for prostate surgery.

Lesli Lo, DPT, Northwestern Medical Group, Chicago.

Urine Leaks? PT Can Help!

Physical therapy can help stop embarrassing urine leaks...

Recent study: Women with osteoporosis or low bone density who reported more stress incontinence (urine leaks when coughing, laughing or exercising) than women with strong bones had 12 weeks of physical therapy (PT) focusing on pelvic-floor muscles.

Result: The PT group had 75% fewer episodes of urinary leaking than those who did not get PT. The benefit lasted for about one year.

Meena M. Sran, PT, PhD, physiotherapist, BC Women's Hospital & Health Centre, Vancouver, British Columbia, Canada.

Cranberry Juice May Prevent UTIs

Urinary tract infections might be *prevented* with cranberry juice.

Recent finding: Over a 24-week period, drinking an eight-ounce glass of a cranberry beverage once a day cut UTI incidence in women who had had two or more UTIs within the past year by approximately 40%.

Always best: Avoid the sugary versions of cranberry and other fruit drinks.

Tomas L. Griebling, MD, MPH, distinguished professor of urology, University of Kansas School of Medicine, Kansas City.

Stubborn UTIs May Signal Bladder Cancer

In a recent study of more than 13,000 adults with a bladder malignancy, the cancer diagnosis took longer for those with UTIs—possibly because UTI symptoms, such as blood in the urine and frequent urination, also occur with bladder cancer. People with UTIs that don't improve after a single course of antibiotics should consult a urologist, who may recommend cystoscopy to examine the bladder.

Kyle Richards, MD, assistant professor of urology, University of Wisconsin School of Medicine and Public Health, Madison.

Melatonin Magic?

Melatonin, a hormone that regulates sleep, reduced both the size and the number of breast tumors in lab research. Researchers speculate that a lack of melatonin, common in sleep-deprived individuals, could increase cancer risks.

Genes & Cancer.

This Diet May Lower Breast Cancer Risk 68%!

Women who followed a Mediterranean diet had 68% lower risk for breast cancer than women who did not follow the diet—but whether the diet actually can prevent the disease is not yet clear. The number of people who developed breast cancer during the study was too small to make definitive comparisons. More research is necessary to clarify any possible link.

In the meantime: Many physicians recommend the Mediterranean diet—which is low in animal fats and rich in fruits, vegetables and olive oil—for its proven heart benefits.

Susan Love, MD, chief visionary officer at Dr. Susan Love Research Foundation, Encino, California, clinical professor of surgery, UCLA's David Geffen School of Medicine, Los Angeles, and author of *Dr. Susan Love's Breast Book.*

GOOD TO KNOW...

3-Step Plan Reduces Risk for Breast Cancer

Women can lower their risk for breast cancer by one-third by maintaining a healthy body weight... getting at least 30 minutes of moderate-intensity exercise daily...and avoiding alcohol or limiting it to no more than one drink per day, recent research finds.

Alice Bender, MS, RDN, head of nutrition programs, American Institute for Cancer Research, Washington, DC.

Better Mammograms

Digital breast tomosynthesis (DBT), which is also known as 3-D mammography, increased cancer detection and resulted in fewer false-positives than two-dimensional mammography, the traditional approach, in nearly 24,000 women recently studied over a four-year period. DBT provides radiologists with a clearer view of overlapping layers of breast tissue. The test has a bit more radiation than a conventional mammogram and may be covered by health insurance.

Emily Conant, MD, chief of breast imaging, Hospital of the University of Pennsylvania, Philadelphia.

Mammograms Predict Heart Disease, Too

In a recent finding, digital mammography was about 70% accurate in predicting the presence of calcium in coronary arteries, an early sign of heart disease. Researchers report that mammograms were often more accurate in predicting heart disease than standard predictors, such as high blood pressure and elevated cholesterol. If your mammogram shows calcifications in the breast arteries, be sure to follow up with your primary care doctor.

Harvey Hecht, MD, professor of medicine and cardiology, Icahn School of Medicine at Mount Sinai, New York City.

Better Breast Cancer Drug

Survivors of breast cancer who were on the estrogen-suppressing medication *letrozole* (Femara) for a decade lowered their risk for recurrence risk by 34%, according to a recent study of nearly 2,000 postmenopausal women.

Bonus: This medication has fewer side effects, such as blood clots and increased risk for stroke, than older hormone suppressants, such as *tamoxifen,* which are typically taken for five years.

Paul Goss, MBBCh, PhD, director of breast cancer research, Massachusetts General Hospital Cancer Center, Boston.

New Method Improves Radiation Therapy

Many radiation treatments given for cancer last for about two minutes, but because chest movement while breathing can increase the risk for damage to surrounding tissue, the therapies are often given over several shorter sessions.

Recent research: Women with breast cancer were successfully trained to safely hold their breath for a few minutes, which allowed them to receive their daily dose of radiation in a single breath-hold. This resulted in more accurate targeting of the tumor and spared more healthy tissue.

Mike Parkes, DPhil, senior lecturer in applied physiology, University of Birmingham, UK.

New Ways to Protect Your Prostate: Simple Steps to Avoid Toxins

Geo Espinosa, ND, a naturopathic doctor and expert in prostate cancer and men's health. He is founder and director of the Integrative and Functional Urology Center at New York University's Langone Medical Center in New York City. Dr. Espinosa is author of *THRIVE Don't Only Survive! Dr. Geo's Guide to Living Your Best Life Before & After Prostate Cancer.*

Drinking a tall glass of water several times each day sounds like one of the best things you can do for your health. But that may not be true for everyone.

Surprising recent finding: In an important study published in April 2016, researchers found that men who drank well water that contained relatively high levels of naturally occurring arsenic had a 10% higher risk of developing prostate cancer. It's a troubling statistic. And arsenic is just one of many prostate-harming toxins lurking in our environment.

Good news: Scientific evidence now shows that men can build their body's defenses against the effects of these disease-causing toxins.

WORST HABITS FOR MEN

We've all heard it over and over again—eat right and stop smoking. *But men should be especially attentive to the following advice...*

- **Diet.** Two studies that were published in 2016 showed just how crucial food choices are for prostate health.

Study I: Drinking sugary beverages (including not only sodas and sweetened iced tea but also fruit juices) was linked to a three times greater risk for prostate cancer...and eating processed lunch foods (such as pizza and hamburgers) doubled prostate cancer risk.

Study II: Among men who had already been diagnosed with prostate cancer, those who ate lots of saturated fats (found in fatty red meats, cheese and butter) were more likely to have the most aggressive form of the disease...but men who ate diets that emphasized fish and nuts—high in polyunsaturated fats—had less aggressive prostate cancer.

Bottom line on diet: Eat a diet that is rich in fruits, vegetables, nuts, fish, legumes and whole grains...and limit saturated fats, processed foods and sugary beverages.

- **Smoking.** Cigarette smoke is filled with toxins including *cadmium*, an inhalable metal that has been linked to prostate cancer. A study published in April 2016 showed that the more you smoke—and the longer you smoke—the greater your risk of developing prostate cancer.

Good news: Stopping smoking reduces prostate cancer risk almost immediately.

HERBS AND SUPPLEMENTS

Prostate health is all about detoxifying the body, protecting cells from damage—and reducing the inflammation that can promote the growth of cancers.

Several supplements have one or more of these anticancer effects—get a doctor's advice on which of the following would be most appropriate for you...*

- **Boswellia** reduces levels of lipoxygenase (LOX), an inflammatory marker associated with prostate cancer. *Typical dosage:* 200 mg to 400 mg a day.
- **Curcumin** helps control *nuclear factor kappa-B* (NF-kB), which is a chemical pathway to inflammation in the body. *Typical dosage:* 2,000 mg to 4,000 mg per day, in divided doses (morning, noon and night).
- **Modified citrus pectin (MCP)** may inhibit cancer growth and help remove heavy-metal toxins from the body. Pectins are typically found in the peel and pulp of citrus fruits (such as oranges, lemons and grapefruits). MCP is a form of pectin that is easily absorbed into the body. *Typical dosage:* 1,000 mg to 5,000 mg, two or three times a day.
- **Selenium** is a precursor to *glutathione*, a master antioxidant. *Typical dosage:* 200 micrograms (mcg) a day of selenized yeast (other

*Consult a physician who is knowledgeable about supplements before using any of those listed here—especially if you take any medication or have a chronic medical condition. To find such a doctor near you, consult The American Association of Naturopathic Physicians, Naturopathic.org.

TAKE NOTE...

Beware of Chemicals...

Toxins are almost ubiquitous in our modern lives. For example, most plastics contain two problematic chemicals—*bisphenol A* (BPA) and *phthalates*. These chemicals act like estrogen in the body and may cause or promote the growth of prostate cancer. While it's impossible to eliminate all contact with plastics, you can reduce your exposure. *Be sure to check your plastic bottles.* All recyclable plastic bottles have a code at the bottom—a number inside a triangle. To reduce your exposure to BPA and phthalates, look for plastics with the number 1, 2, 4 or 5. The worst numbers are 3, 6 and 7—bottles with any of these numbers may contain these and other harmful chemicals.

Also: Most food cans contain BPA. If you opt for canned food, look for "BPA-free" products.

Geo Espinosa, ND, founder and director of the Integrative and Functional Urology Center, New York University's Langone Medical Center, New York City.

forms of selenium have been linked to increased prostate cancer risk).

MORE WAYS TO DETOXIFY

The strategies below also can enhance your body's natural mechanisms to release toxins...*

- **Sweat it out.** Perspiration is one of the most effective ways for your body to shed toxins.

What to do: Exercise a minimum of three hours per week at an intensity that makes you break a sweat. The type of exercise doesn't matter—sweat is the key ingredient. *Also:* If possible, spend 15 minutes a few times a week in a dry-heat sauna.

- **Dry brush.** Another way to detoxify is to dry brush your skin.

What to do: Before you shower, use a dry towel, natural-bristle brush or loofah to gently brush from your hands and feet inward, toward your heart. This promotes the flow of lymphatic fluid, which drains toxins from the body. Brush for a total of three minutes.

- **Try hydrotherapy.** After brushing, shower as usual, but end with a hot water/cold water session of hydrotherapy. This process dilates and constricts blood vessels, promoting better circulation.

What to do: Turn on the hottest water you can tolerate without causing pain or scalding your skin, and let it pour over you for three minutes. Then turn on the cold water—as cold as you can tolerate—for 30 seconds. Repeat this for a total of three hot/cold cycles, ending with cold water.

*Check first with your doctor if you have conditions that impair circulation, such as diabetes or heart disease, before using a sauna or hydrotherapy.

Nuts Lower Prostate Cancer Deaths

Men with prostate cancer were 34% less likely to die if they ate a one-ounce serving of tree nuts (such as almonds, Brazil nuts, cashews, hazelnuts, macadamias, pecans, pine nuts, pistachios and walnuts) five or more times per week, according to a 26-year study of nearly 50,000 men.

Possible reason: Tree nuts are rich in unsaturated fat and nutrients that may lower inflammation.

However: Nut consumption did not reduce risk of developing prostate cancer.

Ying Bao, MD, ScD, assistant professor of medicine, Harvard Medical School, Boston.

No Link Between Vasectomy and Prostate Cancer

Vasectomy does not increase prostate cancer risk as is commonly believed. A recent, very thorough study by epidemiologists from the American Cancer Society found no link between vasectomy—an effective and inexpensive form of long-term birth control—and prostate cancer.

Sheldon Marks, MD, urologist and microsurgical specialist in private practice in Tucson, Arizona. The study of vasectomy and prostate cancer reviewed data on almost 364,000 men and was published in *Journal of Clinical Oncology.*

MRIs Reduce Prostate Biopsies

Giving men suspected of having prostate cancer an MRI can reduce unnecessary biopsies by 27%. Compared with a surgical biopsy, which relies on random tissue samples, an MRI covers the entire gland, making it easier to spot a cancer, determine its size and density, and assess how aggressive the malignancy appears. If findings are suspicious, a surgical biopsy will then be needed.

Hashim Ahmed, PhD, professor and chair of urology, division of surgery, Imperial College, London.

Prostate Cancer Update

Prostate cancer patients with malignancies that haven't spread and who are monitored, but do not receive treatment, have a nearly identical risk for death over the next decade as those who choose surgery and/or radiation, according to a recent study of more than 1,600 men. Surgery and/or radiation (with possible side effects such as incontinence and/or loss of sexual function) lowered the risk of the cancer spreading but did not result in lower risk for death over this 10-year period.

Note: Men with more advanced or aggressive forms of prostate cancer may need prompt treatment.

Jenny Donovan, PhD, professor of social medicine, University of Bristol, UK.

Depression Risk for Prostate Cancer Patients

Hormone therapy for prostate cancer can increase risk for depression. And the risk seems to rise the longer *androgen deprivation therapy* (ADT) is used—a 12% increase with six months or less of ADT...26% increase with seven to 11 months...and a 37% increase with 12 months or more. For most men with high-risk disease, the benefits outweigh the risks.

Paul L. Nguyen, MD, director of prostate brachytherapy at Dana-Farber Cancer Institute and associate professor of radiation oncology at Harvard Medical School, both in Boston.

Help for a Bent Penis...

Sheldon Marks, MD, urologist and microsurgical specialist with a private practice in Tucson, Arizona.

Peyronie's disease is a condition in which scar tissue forms in the penis and causes curvature and sometimes pain during an erection. The condition is usually seen in middle-aged men but can occur at any age.

The exact cause of Peyronie's is not known, but an injury to the penis can cause scar tissue to form. The condition has also been linked to autoimmune disorders, such as scleroderma and lupus. The immune system may attack cells in the penis, which leads to inflammation and scarring.

The curvature is usually upward or to one side. In many cases, the curvature is mild and does not progress, but it can become quite severe and painful.

If you think you have Peyronie's, see a urologist as soon as possible. You may need treatment to keep Peyronie's from worsening. Treatment may include oral, topical or injected medication, such as Xiaflex, to soften the scar tissue and reduce pain and curvature.

Other therapies to break up scar tissue include high-intensity focused ultrasound or *iontophoresis* (a painless, low-level electrical application of medication to the area). Mechanical and vacuum devices used to stretch the penis can also help reduce curvature.

If these measures don't produce results, a urologist may recommend surgery to remove scar tissue and replace it with a skin graft. Some men may require a penile implant.

Hide Those "Man Boobs"

If you want to hide oversized male breasts, try these tricks...

Wear a compression shirt...camouflage the area with small- or medium-scale patterns that have little color contrast, such as gray-and-black plaids or small blue checks on a darker blue background...avoid white and other light colors, which make your chest look bigger...wear layers or thicker clothing...be sure that shirts fit properly, even if that means having them tailored...wear suits, especially ones with vertical pinstripes, for an overall slimming look.

Joseph Rosenfeld, personal-style strategist, San Jose, California, quoted at MensHealth.com.

What Your Poop Says About Your Health

Anil Minocha, MD, professor of medicine at Louisiana State University Health Sciences Center and chief of gastroenterology at the Overton Brooks VA Medical Center, both in Shreveport. He is author of *Seven-X Plan for Digestive Health.*

This may be a personal question...but do you ever look at your poop? *Why we ask:* The color, shape and/or smell of your stools can offer telling clues about your health that are more important than you may realize.

CHECK IT OUT

There's no need to obsess about your stools, but you should take a look at least every week (or more often if you feel unwell or think something may be wrong). It's a good idea to know what's normal for you so that you can report anything out of the ordinary to your doctor.

As far as bowel movements go, "normal" encompasses a wide range—healthy stools can be beige to dark brown...texture can range from firm to a little bit loose...and the average frequency is once or twice a day, but some people only go three times a week.

Most abnormalities last a few days and resolve (perhaps you've eaten something you don't usually eat, or maybe you have a virus). But do take note of anything unusual that lasts for a week or more or recurs. *What to watch for...*

• **Bright or dark red blood.** Bright red blood on toilet paper typically originates from the anus or the lower part of the intestine—it could be coming from a hemorrhoid or a slight tear in the anal tissue that comes from straining during a bowel movement.

Take note: If this happens once or twice, there's less cause to worry, but let your doctor know. If there's a lot of blood or you regularly bleed, even intermittently, make an appointment with your doctor right away, or go to the ER. Bleeding polyps in the colon can produce red blood in the stool, as can diverticula, abnormal pouches that form in the intestine. Your doctor will probably advise a colonoscopy (and possibly an upper GI endoscopy) to investigate.

• **Black poop.** Stools that are black and sticky-looking (or tarry) could indicate that there's blood in your bowel movements—possibly from an ulcer...a tear in the esophagus...an abnormal blood vessel in the colon...or colon cancer.

Important: Call your doctor right away. He/she will probably order tests (such as a colonoscopy and/or endoscopy) to see where the blood is originating and recommend a treatment plan.

Exception: Some foods and supplements—black licorice, dark berries, iron supplements and medications such as Pepto-Bismol and Kaopectate—can make stools black. But check in with your doctor if you have any questions at all.

Note: If you've eaten lots of leafy green vegetables, your poop might turn *green*.

• **Pale or white stools.** Bile, produced in the liver, is what gives stools their brown color. When poop is pale, the liver isn't releasing enough bile and may be diseased. Gallstones, which block the flow of bile into the intestines, are another cause of light-colored stools. Pancreatic cancer can produce pale stools, too.

Take note: Make an appointment with your doctor to get this checked out. Tests could include an abdominal ultrasound, CT scan or MRI.

• **Pencil-thin shape.** It was once thought that pencil-thin stools were a warning signal for colorectal cancer. Now doctors believe that the size/shape of stools is largely affected by what you eat. People who eat a lot of meat tend to produce smaller stools than vegetarians who tend to get more fiber.

Take note: If you have a *sudden* and *consistent* change in stool thickness, it's best to mention this to your doctor. By itself, it's not likely to be caused by cancer, but it should be checked out.

• **Foul odor.** Stools are a combination of dead and live bacteria, cells from the lining of the intestine, fiber and other undigested food...and all of this produces odor.

The intensity of the smell depends on what you've eaten. High-sulfur foods, such as garlic, broccoli or meats, tend to cause stinky stools. So does sorbitol, an artificial sweetener that's added to some medications and processed foods. Also, the bacteria in the large intestine vary from person to person with some varieties causing more odor than others. Antibiotics often cause foul-smelling stools because they temporarily disrupt bacterial balance.

Take note: See a doctor if the odor is much stronger than usual or if the smell is accompanied by other digestive symptoms, such as diarrhea, cramps, a persistent increase/decrease in bowel movements, etc.

Possible causes: Celiac disease, in which your body is unable to tolerate gluten, a protein in wheat, rye and barley...an intestinal parasite (such as Giardia)...or a bacterial or viral infection in the intestine.

New Treatment for Severe Constipation

Electroacupuncture is acupuncture combined with electrical stimulation. After eight weeks of treatment—three to five sessions a week—31% of people who previously had no more than two bowel movements per week reported having three additional ones each week. The improvement continued during a 12-week follow-up period. Most licensed acupuncturists are trained in electroacupuncture.

Jia (Marie) Liu, MD, PhD, China Academy of Chinese Medical Sciences, Beijing, and leader of the electroacupuncture research published in *Annals of Internal Medicine.*

Frequent Constipation Linked to Kidney Disease

In a recent study, people who had constipation had an average 13% higher risk of developing kidney disease and 9% higher risk for kidney failure than people who were not constipated. Kidney function declined faster in people with more severe constipation.

Possible reason: Constipation may indicate changes in the mix of microorganisms in the gut, and those changes may lead to kidney disease. Further research is needed.

Study of the medical records of 3.5 million US military veterans by researchers at University of Tennessee Health Science Center, Memphis, and Memphis VA Medical Center, published in *Journal of the American Society of Nephrology.*

EASY TO DO...

Natural Relief for Constipation

Eating three dried figs a day can relieve chronic constipation, according to a recent eight-week clinical trial.

Asian Journal of Clinical Nutrition.

Surprising Cause of Chronic Constipation

Chronic constipation might be a viral disease, according to Yale researchers. In people infected with the herpes simplex virus, the infection can spread from the genitals and damage nerves in the colon, inhibiting normal digestion.

Cell Host & Microbe.

Colon Cancer on the Rise in Younger Adults: Screening May Be Needed *Before* Age 50

George J. Chang, MD, professor in the department of surgical oncology, chief of the Section of Colon and Rectal Surgery and director of the Clinical Operations, Minimally Invasive and New Technologies in Oncologic Surgery Program at The University of Texas MD Anderson Cancer Center in Houston.

Most people do not get a colonoscopy until they are 50 years old. That's the age at which the American Cancer Society and other groups advise patients with average risk to have their first screening for colorectal cancer.

The unloved procedure is the best way to detect and prevent these often lethal cancers, which are second only to lung cancer as the leading cause of cancer deaths in the US. But people who wait until their 50th birthday to get this test might be making a big mistake. *Here's why...*

THE RISKS START EARLY

For reasons that aren't entirely clear, the incidence of colorectal cancers has risen in patients younger than the traditional screening age. Based on the current trend, the number is expected to grow—sharply in some cases—in the coming years.

Should young adults get a first colonoscopy in their 20s, 30s or 40s? For now, doctors will make this decision case-by-case. But the projected increase in cancer cases has led some experts to suggest that earlier screening—along with a more watchful eye for cancer symptoms—could be the most effective way to protect a group of patients that was previously thought to be low risk.

WHAT WE KNOW SO FAR

Overall, about 90% of colon cancers will be diagnosed in people who are age 50 or older—but the age of these patients is trending downward.

When researchers from MD Anderson Cancer Center looked at data from more than 393,000 patients who had been diagnosed with colorectal cancers, they found that the increasing risk for younger adults is expected to continue—specifically, within the next 14 years, about one in four rectal cancers and one in 10 colon cancers will be diagnosed in adults under age 50. In people over age 50, incidence of these cancers is declining.

WHY THE DIFFERENCE?

Even though it's still unclear why colon cancer is increasing in younger adults, possible causes include...

- **Obesity.** It's become more common for people to be overweight or obese at younger ages. People who are obese or overweight have higher risk for colorectal cancer than those of normal weight.
- **Poor diets.** A Western-style diet—high in processed foods, fast food and saturated fat, and low in fiber-rich plant foods—has been linked to higher cancer rates. People born prior to the 1970s tend to have a lower lifetime exposure to processed foods.
- **Lack of physical activity.** People who engage in routine exercise are less likely to get colorectal cancer. Exercise also increases survival in those who have already been diagnosed and treated for these cancers. Younger people seem to be less active than previous generations.

WHAT SHOULD YOU DO?

The standard guidelines (first colonoscopy at age 50...repeat every 10 years) apply only to people with an "average" risk of developing colorectal cancer. Others (such as those with a parent, sibling or child with colorectal cancer or symptoms including blood in the stool) might be advised by their doctors to have earlier/more frequent tests. *My advice...*

• **Understand your risks.** I don't recommend an across-the-board increase in routine colonoscopies. It's an expensive test with potential complications such as bleeding, perforation of the bowel or a reaction to the sedative used. We have to balance risks and benefits.

Who might need an earlier test: Patients with a strong family history of colorectal cancer (or a family history of precancerous polyps) should ask their doctors if they should be tested before age 50. If a family member was diagnosed at age 50, for example, then screening should begin 10 years earlier—at age 40. Other possible risk factors, such as obesity and/or a lack of exercise, could also warrant earlier testing in some cases.

Note: Highly sensitive fecal DNA tests may be able to identify patients who need colonoscopy before age 50, and virtual colonoscopy (which is noninvasive) is used sometimes for this purpose.

Important: If an older adult has had polyps removed, he/she should tell his children so that they can discuss earlier and/or more frequent colonoscopies with their doctors.

• **Do not ignore early symptoms.** Young people tend to disregard "minor" bowel problems, such as rectal bleeding (they often blame it on hemorrhoids)...an increase/decrease in bowel movements...or unexplained changes in the consistency of stool. Don't assume that your age means you cannot get colorectal cancer—take any bowel symptom seriously.

Example: If you've noticed rectal bleeding, ask your doctor if you should have an anal exam to rule out hemorrhoids or other causes.

Anemia is another common finding that can indicate colorectal cancer. It is most often identified during routine blood work or testing for symptoms such as fatigue.

If your doctor isn't convinced that your symptoms aren't caused by cancer, you should consider colonoscopy.

• **Eat the right foods.** The foods that make up a healthy diet—fruits, vegetables, whole grains, fatty fish, etc.—can also protect against colorectal cancers. Avoid (or limit) processed meats...charred meats (the "char" contains carcinogenic compounds)...sugary soft drinks... and fast food.

It's particularly important to get more fiber. According to the American Institute for Cancer Research, every 10 g of fiber that you consume daily can reduce the risk for colorectal cancer by 10%. Women age 51 and older need at least 21 g of fiber each day, and men in this age group require at least 30 g daily. There are lots of great sources of fiber—leafy greens, fruits, vegetables, beans, popcorn and wheat germ.

• **Be smart about exercise.** People who exercise are about 40% less likely to get colon cancer than those who are sedentary. Exercise affects insulin regulation, immune activity, inflammation and other factors that influence your risk for colorectal cancer. It also increases motility, the movement of food through the intestine. Increased motility reduces the time that potential carcinogens can affect the intestinal wall.

How much exercise? Any is better than none, although 30 to 60 minutes of moderate-intensity daily exercise—swimming, biking, fast walking, etc.—is ideal.

TAKE NOTE...

Better Colonoscopy Prep

It could be time to drop the "no eating" rule the day before having a colonoscopy, according to a recent study.

Details: Participants who were allowed to eat a small amount of low-fiber food (such as mac and cheese, yogurt and ice cream) were less hungry and their bowels were better prepared for the procedure than those restricted to the traditional clear-liquid diet.

Why: Low-fiber foods liquefy and don't stay in the bowel...and eating stimulates bowel movements, which help to clear the colon before colonoscopy.

Jason Samarasena, MD, assistant clinical professor of medicine, University of California, Irvine.

Coffee Cuts Colorectal Cancer Risk

Coffee cuts colorectal cancer risk by more than 50%.

Recent finding: The more coffee you drink, the more you cut your risk—from a 22% decrease for drinking between one and less than two servings a day to at least a 41% decrease for between two and two-and-a-half servings and 54% for more than two-and-a-half servings daily. Both caffeinated and decaffeinated coffees have the protective effect.

Stephen Gruber, MD, PhD, MPH, director of University of Southern California Norris Comprehensive Cancer Center, Los Angeles.

Be on the Lookout for Colon Cancer Symptoms

About 10% of colorectal cancer cases are diagnosed before age 50 (when screening usually begins). Younger patients also tend to have more advanced disease, perhaps because they're diagnosed only after the cancer causes obvious symptoms.

Takeaway: At any age, consult a doctor if you have symptoms of colorectal cancer, such as frequent pencil-thin stools...persistent diarrhea and/or constipation...or blood in the stool. If you have a family history or other risk factors, ask your doctor if you should be screened before age 50.

Samantha Hendren, MD, MPH, associate professor of surgery, University of Michigan, Ann Arbor.

Supplements That Reduce Colon Cancer Risk

A 23% reduction in colorectal cancer risk is linked to regular use of *glucosamine* and *chondroitin* supplements. These supplements are thought to have anti-inflammatory properties, and this could explain why users of glucosamine and chondroitin may have a lower risk for colorectal cancer.

Elizabeth D. Kantor, PhD, MPH, an assistant attending epidemiologist at Memorial Sloan Kettering Cancer Center, New York City, and coleader of a study of colorectal cancer at Harvard T.H. Chan School of Public Health, Boston, published in *International Journal of Cancer.*

Best Time for Rectal Cancer Surgery

The best time for rectal cancer surgery is exactly eight weeks after completion of a combined course of chemotherapy and radiation therapy. Patients with stage two or stage three localized rectal cancer who had surgery exactly 56 days after chemoradiotheraphy had the best chance of tumor removal and the best survival rates. Delaying beyond 56 days was associated with significantly higher long-term mortality.

Study of 11,760 rectal-cancer patients by researchers at Duke University, Durham, North Carolina, published in *Journal of the American College of Surgeons.*

Are You Wearing the Wrong Underwear? Don't Make These Common Mistakes

Richard Bennett, MD, an associate professor of urology at Michigan State University in East Lansing and Oakland University William Beaumont School of Medicine in Rochester. He is also the director of urologic robotic surgery at McLaren Oakland Hospital and a staff urologist at William Beaumont Hospital and Huron Valley-Sinai Hospital.

Unless you're the type of person who shares lots of personal information, you probably don't discuss your underwear with your doctor. Perhaps you should.

Whether you're a man or a woman, there are certain types of underwear that may be better for you than others. *What you need to know about underwear—but may have been too shy to ask...*

PANTIES VS. THONGS

Once favored mainly by the young and daring, the G-string has become the go-to underwear for women of all ages who want to avoid panty lines.

Unlike panties, thongs press tightly against the genitals/anal area. Some experts speculate that this could cause irritation and skin damage—and that the back-and-forth movement of the "string" could spread the bacteria that cause vaginal or urinary tract infections and/or irritate hemorrhoids.

Over the years, I've heard anecdotes about a few thong-wearing patients who got infections. It makes intuitive sense that anything that transfers bacteria from one area to another could cause infection. But I'm not aware of any studies that have proved it.

My take: Wear a thong if it feels comfortable and you like the look. Women have been wearing thongs for a long time. If they were causing an increase in infections, we would have seen it by now.

BREATHABLE OR NOT?

"Pretty" panties and thongs are often made from rayon, nylon or other nonbreathable fabrics. These fabrics trap heat and moisture and can lead to *maceration* (skin damage) as well as infection.

Scientific evidence: Research published in the *European Journal of Obstetrics & Gynecology and Reproductive Biology* found that synthetic underwear was one of the factors associated with yeast infections. Synthetic "shapewear" such as Spanx, which limits air circulation, could cause similar problems.

My take: For all-day wear, cotton or other breathable fabrics are healthier than synthetics. It's fine to wear lacy/sexy underwear under a cocktail dress or when you're planning a romantic evening, but consider these fabrics "for recreational purposes only." After a few hours, change into cotton.

Another choice: Synthetic thongs/panties with cotton liners. You'll get the look you want without sacrificing breathability.

BOXERS OR BRIEFS?

Many fertility experts still recommend boxers for men who are trying to become fathers. Their thinking is that tight briefs increase testicle temperature and could decrease both the quantity and quality of sperm.

The testicles need to be about two degrees cooler than the rest of the body for optimal sperm production. Tight underwear holds the testicles close to the body. This could potentially heat things up just enough to cause a decrease in fertility—but the effect is probably minimal.

What recent research shows: Some older studies did find that briefs impaired sperm quality/production, but more recent evidence indicates that it makes little difference. Even when the testicles "overheat," the effects on sperm production are temporary.

My take: Your choice of underwear is less important than other fertility risk factors, such as smoking, getting too much saturated fat in your diet, substance abuse, etc.

Exception: For men who have been tested and diagnosed with sperm-related issues, boxers are probably a safer choice than briefs. If you prefer briefs, however, you can still give the testicles a break by wearing boxers or no underwear when you go to bed at night.

ANTIBACTERIAL UNDERWEAR

Undies impregnated with bacteria-killing *triclosan* or *nanosilver* (small silver particles with antimicrobial properties) are relatively new to the men's and women's underwear market. Manufacturers claim that killing bacteria reduces odors.

Does antibacterial underwear work? Maybe. The same products are often made with moisture-wicking fabrics, which might have more to do with reducing odors than the chemicals.

My take: You'll do just as well by wearing breathable underwear and changing it regularly (see next page). I worry that the chemicals could migrate and increase yeast infections by changing the vagina's bacterial balance.

GOING COMMANDO

Do you *need* to wear underwear? Not for health reasons. In fact, going bare gives the genital and anal areas a chance to air out. If you live in a hot, humid climate, it can be good for the skin. It can also help those who are overweight or obese—that's because yeast can proliferate in thigh creases, under the belly or in other sweaty areas.

Forgoing underwear could cause chafing when delicate skin rubs against pant seams, but this is not a problem for everyone. For women, going underwear-free could allow traces of natural discharge to end up on clothing, but this is an issue only if it bothers you.

My take: If you enjoy the feeling, go for it!

CHANGE THEM DAILY—OR NOT?

It makes sense to change out of damp or dirty underwear. But, in general, how often should underwear be changed?

My take: There's no health reason to change clean underwear more often than once a day.

However, if your underwear becomes damp from urine—even a few drops—swap them as soon as possible for a fresh pair. Odor is an obvious problem, but dampness increases the risk for yeast infections on the skin—which can affect men as well as women.

EXTRA PROTECTION...

If you "leak" now and then, you may benefit from disposable or washable *incontinence briefs* (available in several styles and all sizes) that look like regular underwear and aren't visible under clothing.

Alternative: Both men and women can wear thin disposable pads (such as Butterfly Men's Body Liners or Depend Shields for Men...or, for women, Poise Liners or Equate Thin Liners) that slip inside regular underwear and wick moisture away from the skin.

Shocking Treatment to Halt Bad Habits

The wristband Pavlok ($179 at Pavlok.com) encourages you to break bad habits by delivering a noticeable, but safe, electric shock of varying intensity, loud beeps, vibrations and other means. The device pairs with your phone. You can have the device give you a jolt if you oversleep, or tap the screen to shock yourself if you eat a donut. Online user feedback for Pavlok has been enthusiastic, although there is no scientific evidence supporting the long-term success of this device.

The New York Times, NYTimes.com.

Beat a Hangover with Beets

Drinking alcohol is dehydrating. Beet juice provides potassium, which helps to rehydrate the body and delivers energizing carbohydrates.

Best recipe: Juice together one beet, two stalks of celery and three handfuls of spinach, then stir in the juice of half a lemon. If you have it, add one teaspoon of spirulina or other protein powder.

Redbook, RedbookMag.com.

GREAT IDEA...

Better Way to Drink Less

To trick your brain into thinking you have had enough to drink, use a smaller wineglass.

Recent research: Restaurant customers ordered 9% more wine when it was served in large 12-ounce glasses than when it was served in standard 10-ounce or small 8-ounce glasses, even though the amount of wine in each glass was the same.

Explanation: Larger glasses may give people the impression that they are drinking less wine.

Theresa Marteau, PhD, director, behaviour and health research unit, University of Cambridge, UK.

Money Matters

How Big of an Emergency Fund Do You Need?

Most financial advisers would agree that consumers need to retain some readily available cash in a very safe account in case they face an unforeseen expense ranging from big health-care costs to the loss of a job. *But how much cash is enough?*

Too little could force you to draw on credit card or home-equity loans or liquidate long-term investments, and yet 28% of US adults have no cash savings at all, according to a recent Bankrate survey. And 46% do not have the equivalent of three months of expenses. Of course, there also are drawbacks to having money stashed in safe savings-type accounts—including the fact that it does not appreciate very much.

I have helped hundreds of clients—those still in the workforce and those who have retired—to create the right-size emergency funds for their situations. *Here is a five-step plan to help determine how large your emergency fund should be...*

WORKING OR RETIRED

***STEP 1:* Make sure you have suitable health, auto and property insurance coverage.** This is crucial because without such coverage, even a minor incident that involves going to the emergency room, fixing your car or repairing your roof could put a big dent in your finances. Talk with your insurance agent about the right coverage for you, taking into account annual premiums and deductibles. If you stop working before age 65, you will need to arrange for health insurance until you qualify for basic Medicare. Even then, you need to consider additional Medicare coverage and/or

Note: Prices, rates and offers throughout this chapter and book are subject to change.

Jim Holtzman, CFP, an adviser at Legend Financial Advisors, a fee-only financial advisory with $273 million under management, Pittsburgh. Legend-Financial.com supplemental private insurance for potentially costly items such as prescription drugs and dental work.

STEP 2: **Decide what is likely to be your most severe financial emergency that is not covered by insurance.** For individuals still in the workforce, that's likely to be a job loss, since you might have no income for many months until you find a new job. Also, your health insurance premiums could be much higher if you need to extend your workplace coverage through the COBRA program. Retirees don't have to worry about a disruption in wages, but despite that, many of them need a *larger* cash reserve than working people do, depending on how much income they draw down regularly from their retirement portfolios. That's because a retiree's costliest potential emergency might be a bear market that forces the sale of investments at the worst possible time, when investment values have plunged.

YOU ARE STILL WORKING

STEP 3: **Figure out what your monthly budget would be if your employment income stopped.** If you depend on wages and lose that source of income, you'll want to temporarily reduce your spending to basic living expenses. How much will that be? To find out, first create a list of all your normal expenses. Then cross off nonessential spending. This includes items such as vacations, gifts and restaurant meals...funding your retirement savings...and credit card and other debt payments above their minimum required levels.

Cutting out these expenses typically reduces average monthly expenses by 30% or more. What's left are bills that can't be skipped without negative consequences, including mortgage and utility payments, insurance premiums and discretionary expenses that you consider very important, such as helping support an aging parent.

STEP 4: **Decide on the size of your emergency fund.** Think in terms of how many months of current income you might need to cover basic living expenses. Use the following guidelines as a starting point to determine the number of months of income you are likely to need.

Three months: This is the smallest emergency fund most people should have. It's only for individuals with secure jobs and excellent insurance coverage, including short-term disability insurance that kicks in within 90 days of disability.

Six to nine months: This is the amount of emergency reserves many of my clients feel comfortable with. That's because most people who lose a job usually are able to find a new one within this period.

12 months: This longer time frame is for my clients who are self-employed or in high-risk industries where layoffs are common. I also recommend this larger emergency fund during recessions when layoffs are more common and the average length of unemployment is longer.

More than 12 months: Keeping more than one year's worth of basic living expenses in cash generally is not a good idea, because most people are likely to find a job within a year—even if you don't, you have that whole year to find ways to fund additional jobless months, such as obtaining a home-equity line of credit or downsizing your home.

STEP 5: **Fine-tune the time frame up or down depending upon your personal circumstances.** *Questions to ask yourself...*

How secure is my job, and how easy would it be to find a new one? According to the US Bureau of Labor Statistics, about half of the management-level professionals who lose their jobs find new jobs in about four months—but that varies by industry and position. The less certainty you feel, the greater the amount of emergency savings you'll want.

Do I have any supplemental income? Dependable income outside of your wages would allow you to cut down on the size of your emergency fund. For a limited time, so would any guaranteed severance or buyout package you have in place at your job and any unemployment benefits you can expect.

How many people depend on my paycheck for support? Two-income families often need less in emergency savings. I typically use the percentage that the higher-earning spouse contributes to monthly expenses to determine how much cash is needed.

Example: I had a client whose spouse had a steady job providing 30% of the family's basic monthly expenses versus 70% covered by my client's income. The monthly expenses came to about $8,000 a month, and the husband figured it would take him about four months to find work if he lost his job. Since 70% of $8,000 multiplied by four months comes to $22,400, that's the size his emergency fund should be. That amount also would be enough if the other, lower-earning spouse were to become unemployed.

YOU ARE RETIRED

Most retirees depend on at least some income from their investment portfolios to meet their monthly expenses, and that income often comes from periodically selling assets. If this describes you, you should have an emergency fund big enough that you aren't forced to sell investments during the course of a severe market downturn. *What to do...*

Follow Step 3 above to figure out your emergency monthly budget. Then make sure you have enough in cash to cover 18 months of basic living expenses—that is the average length of a bear market.

Example: I had a retired client who required a minimum of $4,000 a month for expenses. A pension from a former job provided her with $2,500 a month, but she had to draw down the additional $1,500 from her investment portfolio. She needed an emergency fund of $27,000 ($1,500 x 18 months).

Note: If you receive additional money each month from part-time work or from your family or children, it will reduce the amount of cash you need to put aside.

Even if retirees can meet their monthly emergency budget entirely through guaranteed income such as pensions, annuities and Social Security, I typically recommend that they keep the equivalent of six to 12 months' worth of expenses in cash. For those retirees, the biggest financial emergency is likely to be out-of-pocket medical costs.

Example: Typically, Medicare fully covers basic services for the first 20 days of a skilled-nursing facility after a major hospitalization. But what if you take longer to recover? If you don't have supplemental insurance, you typically pay $164.50 per day in coinsurance from day 21 to day 100 (totaling up to $13,160) and the full cost beyond day 100. Take such costs into account.

GOOD TO KNOW...

3 Emergency-Fund Calculators

Here are websites, worksheets and calculators that can help you determine the right size for your emergency fund...

To determine monthly expenses, go to Calcxml.com/do/bud03. It includes interactive worksheets.

For typical out-of-pocket medical costs during a health emergency depending on which Medicare coverage you have, go to Medicare.gov/your-medicare-costs.

To estimate how much in unemployment benefits you might receive, depending on the state in which you work, go to Unemployment-Benefits.org.

Banks Charge You for Doing Nothing

Ken Tumin, cofounder of DepositAccounts.com, an independent website that tracks bank and credit union rates and news.

Does it seem like your bank charges fees for everything these days? It might be worse than you think—some banks charge their customers a fee for doing nothing. If you fail to initiate any transactions in your checking, savings or money-market account for periods ranging from a few months to a year, you might get hit with an "inactivity" or "dormant account" fee of $5 to $15 every month until you do.

Continued inaction could mean that your bank freezes your account. If you then, say, start writing checks from a frozen account, those checks will bounce, potentially triggering multiple bounced-check fees. Or your bank might close your inactive account, resulting not only in bounced checks but also in a loss of any interest that you thought the account was earning.

Account holders might learn of this only after it has occurred—and then only if they log into their accounts and check their online statements carefully. Many financial institutions no longer automatically supply printed statements.

EXAMPLES

Essential Checking accounts at SunTrust in Florida face a $15 per month fee after 12 months of inactivity. Community Bank in New York and Pennsylvania imposes a $15 per month inactivity fee after 12 months for checking accounts and after 36 months for savings accounts. Commerce Bank, which has locations across the Midwest, imposes a $3 per month fee starting after just 60 days of inactivity for its checking accounts. Citadel Credit Union in Pennsylvania imposes a $15 per month fee when "Free Checking" accounts are inactive for 90 days.

WHAT TO DO

Ask your bank or credit union whether any of your accounts could face inactivity fees and how to avoid them. *Consider the following steps...*

• **Set up an automatic, online recurring transfer** of a small amount of money into or out of the account each month or quarter.

• **Use an institution that does not charge inactivity fees.** *Examples*: Capital One Bank 360 Checking and various Ally Bank accounts.

The Banks Customers Complain About

The banks that consumers complain about most are Regions Financial, 16.6 complaints per billion dollars in deposits...Citizens Financial, 16.2...SunTrust, 14...Fifth Third, 12.5... PNC Financial, 11.8...Huntington, 11.8...Comerica, 10.6...US Bancorp, 9.9...Bank of America, 9.6...and BB&T, 9.

The statistics are for complaints associated with bank accounts or services ranging from disagreements over fees to unhappiness about treatment by bank employees.

Data from the Consumer Financial Protection Bureau and S&P Global Market Intelligence, analyzed by and reported in *USA Today.*

Hackers Target Bank Accounts Through Your Phone

Steven J. Weisman, Esq., senior lecturer in the department of law, tax and financial planning at Bentley University, Waltham, Massachusetts. He is founder of the scam-information website Scamicide.com.

Cyberthieves might use your smartphone to steal money from your bank account. In this scam, the thieves sneakily get you to download malware onto your phone, possibly by sending you a link to a free app for a card game or risqué content. The malware, known by names such as *Acecard* and *GM Bot*, has been around for years but has been adapted to specifically target banking apps on smartphones. Using the malware, thieves record credentials, such as your user name and password, when you log into your bank account. With that information, they can initiate electronic transfers from your account to other accounts they control.

You can't necessarily rely on typical bank security measures, such as the use of a verification code that the banks send you by text, because some forms of the malware can capture that code, too. And most smartphone owners don't use anti-malware software on their phones.

Federal law says you can get all of your money back if you notify your bank within 60 days after the fraudulent transaction appears on your bank statement. However, you also typically are required to show that you weren't lax about safeguarding your information.

Self-defense: Don't click on a link in a text message if you do not recognize the sender.

Download apps only from reliable sources such as financial apps on your bank's website or other apps at Play.Google.com or iTunes.Apple.com. Also, install security software, and make sure it automatically updates.

Recommended: For smartphones and tablets with Android operating systems, *Malwarebytes Anti-Malware* (Malwarebytes.org)...for iPhones and iPads, *Avast SecureLine* (Avast.com). Both are free.

Theft by Bank Tellers Is Spreading

Adam Levin, JD, consumer advocate, founder of the cyber-security company CyberScout, Scottsdale, Arizona, and former director of the New Jersey Division of Consumer Affairs. He is author of *Swiped: How to Protect Yourself in a World Full of Scammers, Phishers, and Identity Thieves.* CyberScout.com

A Chase Bank teller in White Plains, New York, took part in an ID-theft ring that stole more than $850,000 from hundreds of accounts. A Capital One teller in Maryland passed customer account information to a partner who used phony checks to withdraw money from seven accounts. A Bank of Maine teller pilfered nearly $100,000 from one customer's account.

Theft involving bank tellers—by removing money from customer accounts or by selling customer information to ID thieves—has become surprisingly common. In Manhattan alone, prosecutors bring cases against tellers at least once a month. But it can happen anywhere.

What to do: Sign up to get e-mail or text alerts from your bank every time a transaction occurs in your account. Notify the bank if you see any transactions you don't recognize. If alerts are not offered by your bank, log into your account often to scan for transactions. Or better yet, shift your account to a bank that does offer transaction alerts.

Also monitor your credit reports for new accounts that you did not open. Bank-teller ID theft does not always lead to fraudulent withdrawals—it might instead lead to fraudulent accounts being opened in your name. A criminal might open credit cards in your name and not pay the bills, for example.

By law, you are entitled to one free copy of your credit report from each of the three credit-reporting agencies each year through AnnualCreditReport.com. Space out your requests so you receive one every four months. If you want to keep a closer eye on your credit, sign up for a credit-monitoring service that monitors your credit reports for suspicious activity, often for around $20 per month...or purchase additional copies of your reports from the credit-reporting agencies Equifax, Experian and TransUnion.

BETTER WAYS...

How to Track Multiple Rewards Cards

Carry only the cards you use regularly or ones on which you are trying to meet minimum spending requirements to get a reward. *Put sticky notes on cards that give bonuses* for specific categories, such as gas or restaurants. *Enable auto-pay* with your bank so that you never miss a payment. *Link reward cards to AwardWallet,* which tracks award information in one place. *Use alerts on your smartphone* or electronic calendar to track time-sensitive perks, such as a once-a-year free night's hotel stay.

CreditCards.com

The Worst Credit Card Contracts

Matt Schulz, senior industry analyst at CreditCards.com, which conducted a study on the complexity of more than 2,000 credit card agreements that included a poll of 1,000 US consumers.

To understand the agreements that you must sign to get a Visa card or MasterCard from Synovus Bank, you probably need an advanced degree. And the contract for a MasterCard from KeyBank runs 30 pages and 15,037 words—about as long as the Shakespeare play *The Comedy of Errors.* Despite efforts by consumer watchdogs and government regulators to crack down on the complexity of credit card contracts, more than half of US consumers find them too difficult to understand.

Here's how to select cards with relatively consumer-friendly contracts...

RATING THE CARD ISSUERS

The HSBC Platinum Rewards contract is the easiest to read, requiring just an eighth-grade reading level to understand. Other issuers that score well include, in order of declining readability, Navy Federal Credit Union...Citi...Synchrony Bank...USAA...Chase...Discover...and Capital One. Navy Federal Credit Union and Synchrony Bank also are among the issuers that keep their agreements relatively brief.

Large issuers that have especially unreadable agreements include Barclays, TD Bank and Bank of America. Those with especially long agreements include Fifth Third Bank, Citizens Bank and PNC Bank. (You can find rankings of various measures of card agreement complexity at CreditCards.com/credit-card-news/unreadable-card-agreements-study.php.)

CHECKING DETAILS

When reviewing any card's contract, search for the words below to help you determine whether it might be worth choosing a different card or trying to opt out of some provisions. You can find an issuer's contracts at ConsumerFinance.gov/credit-cards/agreements.

- **"Security interest."** If this phrase appears, the paragraph might grant the issuer the right to take assets from other accounts that you have with that financial institution to pay your credit card bill.
- **"Arbitration."** Many issuers require cardholders to use an arbitration process, not the courts, to resolve disputes. This process tends to be stacked in the issuer's favor. Major issuers that do not require arbitration include Bank of America, Capital One and Chase.
- **"Affiliates."** This section might grant the issuer the right to sell your account information, including your spending history, to various third-party organizations that will use it for marketing purposes.

Credit Cards Trick You into Paying More

Benjamin Keys, PhD, assistant professor at the Wharton School of the University of Pennsylvania, Philadelphia. His research focuses on mortgage and credit card markets. Real-Estate.Wharton.upenn.edu

Do you ever pay just the minimum required amount on a credit card balance even if you could afford to pay more? You're not alone. New research shows that 20% of credit card users who can afford to pay significantly more than the monthly required minimum—typically 2% to 3% of the balance—do not pay more than that or pay only a little more, which tremendously increases the amount of interest they end up paying over time.

Why do people pay less than they could? One reason is that the minimum payment often is featured by the credit card company as the most prominent number on the bill, so many consumers fixate on it—which is exactly what the card companies hope they will do.

Even worse: Decades ago, the typical required monthly minimum was closer to 5%, but credit card issuers found that it was more profitable to reduce that amount because the longer a consumer takes to pay off an outstanding balance, the more interest the consumer ends up paying.

To avoid this trap: Ignore the minimum payment amount suggested by the card company, and instead calculate a personal monthly minimum payment based on how long you want to take to pay off your debt and what you can reasonably afford.

Helpful: Search online for "Bankrate Credit Card Payoff Calculator."

Late-Payment Fees Are Rising

The federal government allowed late-payment fees for credit cards to go higher as of January 1, 2017—and American Express promptly raised its fee $1, to $38 for customers who are late on more than one payment in a six-month period. That is the highest level allowed by the Consumer Financial Protection Bureau (CFPB). Bank of America also charges a maximum of $38. Several other card issuers—including Citigroup and Discover—still charge a maximum of $37, and Capital One and JPMorgan Chase charge a maximum of $35. But the fees can change—check with your card issuer.

Self-defense: If you incur a late fee for the first time, ask the card issuer to remove it—about 90% of people are successful.

The Wall Street Journal, WSJ.com.

The Truth About Credit Card Customer Service

Information based on interviews with former and current customer service representatives, reported at CreditCards.com.

Customer service representatives are often given bonuses for getting callers off the phone quickly, usually in three minutes or less—and may be punished if they let customers stay on for too long. *Other truths...*

• **Reps are required to push additional services,** such as credit monitoring and balance transfers, and are rewarded for doing so and penalized if they do not.

• **Reps typically cannot evaluate requests for interest rate changes**—they can only put your information into a computer that says what interest rate you can get.

• **But they can waive late charges, over-limit fees, finance charges and some other costs**—and often will do so for callers who ask politely. A few banks allow reps to waive annual fees for certain specific cards—again, callers must ask nicely.

Caution: Reps make notes on callers who are rude or use profanity, and the information displays automatically each time the person calls. And threatening legal action is not effective—but threatening to go on social media may get you to a higher-level rep.

Signs of a Good Credit-Repair Company

Realistic advertising that does not make grand promises to restore your credit immediately and make it better than ever... *a physical place of business* rather than an Internet-only presence...*a contract you understand* that clearly lays out the company's commitments and your rights...*a detailed plan* showing what the company will do, including helping you settle debts if you simply cannot pay them...*willingness to contact actual creditors,* not simply the credit bureaus—this takes more time but can be much more effective...*no up-front charges*—federal law prohibits credit-repair firms from taking money until services are performed.

Caution: Do not rely on websites that review credit-repair firms. The sites get commissions or fees from the companies they review, so you cannot count on the objectivity of their ratings.

CreditCards.com

EASY TO DO...

Raise Your Credit Score with One Call

Nearly eight out of 10 US credit cardholders who asked for a higher credit limit were approved. And if you increase the amount of available credit but don't add to any balance you carry, you'll reduce your credit-utilization rate, which can raise your credit score.

Bankrate.com

Avoid Big Credit-Repair Mistakes

John Ulzheimer, president of The Ulzheimer Group, an Atlanta-based firm offering credit-related consulting services. He previously worked for Equifax Credit Information Services and Fair Isaac credit-scoring system. JohnUlzheimer.com

Having out-of-date or inaccurate information removed from your credit report could boost your credit score, making it less expensive for you to borrow money, obtain certain types of insurance and more. Changing how you use credit could help you, too. But sometimes when people try to improve their credit profiles, they take the wrong path—and make things worse. *Three of today's biggest credit-repair mistakes...*

MISTAKE: **Assuming that your credit card balances don't matter as long as you don't miss payments.** Although carrying a revolving balance—that is, not paying off your credit cards each month—will not reduce your credit score, it still is a black mark on your credit *report.* That's because research shows that people who carry revolving balances are several times more likely to default on new loans than are people who pay off their balances in full each month. Fannie Mae, the government-run mortgage giant, has included this factor in its automated underwriting system, so it could determine whether you qualify for a mortgage loan. Various lenders and scoring systems are likely to follow suit and begin considering whether you carry credit card balances as well.

What to do: If you expect to apply for a loan within a year, make every effort to pay off your credit card bills every month—even if you have cards that offer low interest rates and/or your credit score is good.

MISTAKE: **Closing unneeded credit card accounts.** People often assume that having lots of credit cards is bad for their credit score. In fact, having credit available that you are not using boosts your score—it shows that you can exercise self-control.

What to do: Leave credit card accounts open even if you do not need them. If you are worried that rarely used cards will be vulnerable to identity theft, stop carrying unneeded cards in your wallet and set up account alerts with issuers that offer them so that you learn of activity in these accounts quickly via e-mail or text. (Consider using these cards every few months to avoid having issuers close your accounts.)

MISTAKE: **Trying to have paid-off loans removed from a credit report.** Many people assume that old, paid-off car loans, student loans and refinanced mortgages make it look like they borrow too much. But if they contact credit bureaus to have these removed from their reports, there's a good chance they'll hurt their credit scores. That's because potential lenders actually like to see that you have successfully paid off loans in the past.

What to do: Leave paid-off debts on your credit reports.

States Stealing Little-Used Accounts

Tamara K. Salmon, associate general counsel of the Investment Company Institute, Washington, DC. She previously served as assistant director of the Florida Division of Securities. ICI.org

If you fail to contact the companies that manage your financial accounts every few years, the money in those accounts could be taken from you—by your state.

"Unclaimed property" laws require that financial institutions, including mutual funds, banks and insurers, forfeit "forgotten" accounts to state governments. These laws were enacted so that governments could safeguard overlooked assets until their rightful owners stepped forward to reclaim them—but the states soon realized that most of these assets were never reclaimed.

Previously, accounts were unlikely to be deemed unclaimed unless a financial institution could not reach the account holder for at least seven years after mail sent to the account holder was returned as undeliverable. Now these laws can claim accounts that were never forgotten at all. Accounts might be snatched up in as little as three years simply because the account holder has not called the financial institution or logged into a password-protected online account even if mail is not being returned. Contact your state's Department of the Treasury to learn more about unclaimed property laws where you live.

Account holders can reclaim these assets—if they realize they have gone missing—but they still lose out on the dividends and capital gains their money did not earn while it was in state coffers. States' liquidation of their investments can generate taxes and penalties, too.

What to do: Phone every financial institution where you have an account at least once every three years. Take this opportunity to discuss your accounts, or simply tell a representative, "I'm just calling to verify my contact information and get it on record that I have been in contact." Logging into a password-protected account...and/or completing and returning a proxy ballot at least once every three years should prevent unclaimed property problems, too. Interacting with a financial company's automated phone system typically will not.

Use MissingMoney.com to search every state in which you have ever lived to see if you have had assets snapped up. Check Delaware, Maryland and Massachusetts, too—occasionally assets are sent to the state in which the financial institution is based rather than the one where the account holder lives, and many financial companies are based in these three states.

Beware Fake Websites

Robert Siciliano, security analyst and CEO at the firm IDTheftSecurity.com, Boston. He has more than 30 years of experience in cyber and real-world security and is author of *99 Things You Wish You Knew Before...Your Identity Was Stolen.* RobertSiciliano.com

Until recently, if you made a typo and left out the "c" when typing "Netflix.com" into a web browser, the website you landed on might have told you to update your software to watch videos.

Sites like these with addresses that are only slightly different from those of trustworthy sites often are a scam sometimes referred to as "typosquatting." Victims reach these bogus sites when they accidentally type incorrect addresses...or when they click a link in an e-mail or at a website that contains the dangerous address, not noticing the minor alteration.

These bogus sites then might ask you to enter financial information, such as a credit card number, setting the stage for cyberthieves to misuse that information. Or they might ask you to update some software on your computer or download some other file, which actually contains spyware or malware. Or they might trick you into overpaying for products or services that are much less expensive on the site that you meant to go to.

Victims often lower their guard and comply, believing that they are on trustworthy sites.

Example: If you use a search engine to locate your state's Department of Motor Vehicles (DMV) site, similarly named fake sites likely will appear high in the listings as well. These sites might then ask you to pay for information or services that are provided for free by the real DMV. The fake sites typically end with .com or .org. Websites with the domain name .gov are much more likely to be a real DMV site.

What to do: Double-check that you have typed web addresses properly before hitting Enter. If you often make typos, create bookmarks in your web browser for sites that you visit often. Download and install a free web browser add-on such as McAfee SiteAdvisor (SiteAdvisor.com/download)* for Windows or Web of Trust (MyWOT.com) for Windows or Mac that will help protect you against fake sites, malware and scams.

*Disclosure: McAfee is among Siciliano's clients.

Phony Facebook Offers

Fake Facebook offers are designed to steal users' information and identities. A website may have millions of likes and great product photos but still can be phony. If a post claims that you will get something free in return for liking, sharing or clicking, it probably is a scam. Some of these scams are designed to download malware or a virus onto your device that allows criminals to track your online activities. Some scams direct victims to a legitimate-looking site that requires Facebook log-in to redeem an offer—but this leads immediately to identity theft.

Self-defense: If a Facebook page has zero negative reviews or comments, avoid it. If you cannot find a phone number or address for a company, it probably is a scam. Never click on a link in a Facebook post from a source you do not recognize. Research unknown sites before going to them. Run antivirus programs on all your devices frequently.

Clark.com, website run by consumer advocate Clark Howard.

Top 3 Phone Scams

The *Google business listing scam* tells small businesses that they are at risk of being removed from the top page of Google search results unless they pay a fee. *Loan scams* lure victims with lower rates or threaten victims with arrest for supposedly having past-due loans. *Free vacation scams* involve high-pressure tactics to get credit card information supposedly needed for taxes or fees.

Self-defense: Hang up immediately on robocalls—scams usually start that way, with live scammers picking up if you respond. Never give credit card or personal information over the phone to anyone you do not know. If a caller seems to be from a bank or company you know, hang up and call the firm at a number you find on your own—scammers have ways to make their telephone numbers seem as though they are coming from legitimate businesses.

USA Today, USAToday.com.

You Can Escape Password Overload

Paul Wagenseil, senior editor specializing in technology security for *Tom's Guide*, which reviews new computer technology products and software, New York City. TomsGuide.com

What sort of password person are you? Are your passwords all easy-to-remember variations of the same basic theme, so you don't forget them? Or do you have many different passwords that you can't remember, so you list them in a notebook or perhaps on sticky notes plastered around your computer?

Neither way of managing your passwords is good enough if you care about online safety.

If you want to be safe from potentially disastrous ID theft or hacking, you need a better way to manage your passwords—a solution that makes it simple for you to use your passwords but very difficult for cyberthieves to guess them, steal them or trick you into disclosing them.

A good solution: Password manager software. This type of secure, easy-to-use software allows you to automatically fill in your log-in "credentials" (typically a user name and password) at any site so that you don't have to remember them or look them up each time you visit the site.

HOW THEY WORK

There currently are more than one dozen password-manager products to choose from. With each, you download the software from the password manager's website to your computer and/or your mobile device such as a smartphone or tablet.

The software allows you to create the digital equivalent of a bank vault with your information heavily encrypted and stored in the cloud and/or on your hard drive. During the set-up process, the software automatically gathers all user names and passwords that you already have saved on your device and stores them in your vault...and, with some of the password managers, removes the information from your hard drive. It also captures and stores any additional user names, passwords and other personal information that you enter on various websites from then on.

You can set the password manager to always automatically activate itself...or you can activate it when you need it by clicking on a toolbar icon on your computer or an app on your smartphone and entering a single master password that you have previously created. Then, when you visit a password-protected website that you have logged into previously, the password manager automatically fills in your log-in information. It also can store and fill in other personal information such as your credit card numbers, mailing address and e-mail address, which is a more secure way to store that information than saving it on shopping sites, where it may be vulnerable to being stolen.

ARE THEY SAFE?

All communications between your device and the password manager—and the information stored by the password manager—are heavily encrypted using standards that the US military uses for some of its information encryption.

In addition, password managers evaluate all of your passwords to see how vulnerable each might be to hackers. Then they suggest more complex substitutes for passwords that are not safe enough and, with some password managers, for passwords used on too many sites. Because you no longer have to worry about remembering any of your passwords or typing them in, you can use complex ones that are extremely difficult to crack such as Sk$ltyF>z%OyQ4h^ijI.

Using a single master password to protect all of your other passwords may sound unwise because if someone gets hold of the master password, you're completely vulnerable. However, for most people, it is easier to create, memorize and protect a single, complex password that you never write down or tell anyone about than it is to remember and keep track of numerous weak ones.

For a guide on how to create a strong password, go to TomsGuide.com, click the magnifying glass in the top-right corner and search for "Create Secure Passwords."

Of course, a password manager can't protect information that you have stored with Google, Yahoo, Home Depot, your bank, your credit card issuer or any other company if a hacker is able to break into the company's user databases.

BEST PASSWORD MANAGERS

Password managers work with almost any computer, laptop, smartphone or tablet, and they support both the Windows and Mac operating systems on computers and the Android and Apple operating systems on mobile devices.

The three password managers below are among the best. The first two have a feature that allows you to automatically change weak or overused passwords on multiple sites to newly generated ones with the press of a button. Not every site allows third-party programs to do this, but even so, it can save a lot of time and help make your accounts more secure.

Best for people looking for a free version: *LastPass* is the most popular password

SAFETY ALERT...

Your Wireless Mouse Can Be Hacked

Hackers up to 700 feet away can send data packets on the frequency that your mouse uses—triggering keystrokes that let them take over your computer.

Self-defense: Install a firmware or software patch if available—Logitech and Microsoft have issued them...upgrade to newer equipment...switch your PC to an account that requires a password before making any significant changes...and install and constantly update security software.

Bastille Networks, security research firm.

manager, with more than 7 million users in more than 100 countries. Although the premium version costs only $12 per year, most people will find the free version to be adequate. That's because *LastPass* recently began allowing users to open a single account and use the free version on all devices. LastPass.com

Best for people who want a very user-friendly program: *Dashlane* has more than 3 million users and offers the most intuitive interface and easiest-to-use software of all the password managers.

Downside: Its premium version is more expensive than most competitors at $40 annually. The premium version enables you to sync passwords across multiple devices and also gives you priority access to customer service. Dashlane.com

Best for people who don't want to deal with remembering a password at all: *True Key,* offered by the technology giant Intel, lets you use facial recognition instead of a master password. It uses your webcam or smartphone camera to scan your face.

Cost for premium version: $20 per year, which lets you save up to 10,000 passwords... the free version lets you save only 15. TrueKey.com

---

Selling Your Home Without an Agent? Don't Make These Mistakes

Robert Irwin, author of more than 35 books on real estate including *Tips & Traps for Negotiating Real Estate.* Based in Los Angeles, he has been a real estate broker and investor for more than 25 years.

Selling a home on your own without a real estate agent can seem like a major money saver. Real estate agents typically claim a 6% commission—that's $21,000 on a $350,000 home, enough to pay for your move or even buy a new car. But selling a home without an agent won't save you money if you make mistakes that undermine the sale price—a real possibility for novices trying to navigate the confusing world of real estate transactions.

So what is the verdict on going it alone?

"For Sale by Owner" (FSBO for short) is a reasonable option if you are willing to invest time in learning about the local real estate market and process...the home is in a hot real estate market where buyers abound...and at least several other similar homes have sold in the neighborhood in the past month or so, making it easier to determine an appropriate asking price. *But be careful to avoid these common mistakes...*

MISTAKE: **Pricing at the high end of the market.** Most FSBO sellers are aware that the asking price should be based on asking prices of similar homes on the market in the same general neighborhood (or homes that have recently sold)—data that is available on real estate websites.

Unfortunately, sellers often set asking prices near the top end of this range for two flawed reasons...

First, many sellers believe that their homes are better than the other homes in their neighborhood. They have made improvements and design choices that they like, so for them, their homes truly are better—but shoppers likely have different priorities and preferences.

Second, sellers sometimes will assume that there's no harm in setting a high price initially and lowering it later if they don't get any bites. In reality, their high initial asking price will keep many potential buyers from even considering the property. And once a house has been on the market for more than 30 days, buyers and their agents tend to consider it "stale" and assume that either the home has major problems or that the seller is not very serious about selling. Once a listing goes stale, sellers must drop their asking prices way below those of similar homes to attract buyers.

Better: Set your asking price slightly below the average asking price for homes similar to yours in your neighborhood. Aiming a little low is better than aiming a little high because the low price might attract multiple would-be buyers you can play off one another.

MISTAKE: **Scaring away buyer's agents.** Most buyers work with agents—and those agents dislike deals involving FSBO sellers. FSBO transactions will take more of their time and are more likely to fall through because FSBO sellers tend not to understand all the ins and outs of the real estate transaction process and sometimes are not fully committed to selling. An even bigger concern for agents—some FSBO sellers do not understand that the buyer's agent traditionally expects a 3% commission (half the total commission), which would shrink your savings from going it alone.

Better: Include the phrase "buyer's agents protected" when you list your home online or in newspapers...and in any other printed marketing materials. This reassures buyer's agents that they will get their 3% commission if they work with you.

This also might help address another challenge. Selling a house entails providing buyers with disclosures about many things, including lead, asbestos and any defects in the property, as well as filling out a binding sales contract and arranging for escrow and title insurance for the buyer. Those can be very difficult tasks for a novice to handle. That may not be a problem in parts of the country—mostly on the East Coast—where real estate transactions typically include a real estate attorney.

But in many parts of the country, especially the West Coast, a real estate agent usually handles these tasks. So if you go it alone, you might end up relying on the buyer's agent to handle them, although that may require paying a little more than the standard 3% commission.

MISTAKE: **Selling before you are emotionally prepared to do so.** For the best chance to be successful, FSBO sellers must see their homes not as special places where they raised families and lived lives, but as assets like any other. Those who cannot view their properties objectively often fail to see and fix flaws that could scare off potential buyers...and/or they become offended and react in counterproductive ways when potential buyers or their agents point out problems with the home or make counteroffers.

MISTAKE: **Failing to "depersonalize" the property.** Most sellers know that they need to clean and declutter the home before listing it for sale, but some don't realize that they also should put away distinctive personal touches. The goal is for potential buyers to imagine themselves living their lives in this home. Anything that reminds them that this currently is someone else's home will only stand in the way.

Better: Before your home is listed, strive to make it a blank canvas on which potential buyers can project their own lives and decorating ideas. Pack away your family photos...quirky art and furniture...and/or religious items. Repaint dark walls in lighter, neutral colors such as white or light tan, which are universally inoffensive. Visit some homes in your area that are being offered by experienced agents, and then strive to present your home in a similar way. Better yet, pay a professional "home stager" $100 to $300 for a walk-and-talk consultation...or more to take charge of presenting the home in a way that will appeal to buyers. Search for an experienced home stager in your area on the websites of the Real Estate Staging Association (RealEstateStagingAssociation.com)...or the International Association of Home Staging Professionals (IAHSP.com).

MISTAKE: **Using DIY photos in online listings.** It is a false savings—these photos play a major role in convincing buyers which homes are worth seeing in person. When photos are not up to par, it makes the home itself seem not up to par.

Better: Hire a professional photographer with plenty of experience in real estate photos. A professional understands which elements of your home to highlight...and which to hide. One place to find these pros is at RealEstatePhotographers.org. Expect to pay anywhere from a few hundred dollars to $1,000, depending on what part of the country you're in and the size of your home. If listings for similar homes in your area include video tours, 3-D images or other visual materials, your listing should feature these, too.

MISTAKE: **Insisting that potential buyers view your home on your schedule.** Buyers who need to close on a home quickly are among the very best buyers to attract. They are unlikely to play hardball on price or to change their minds and back out of a deal. But these hurried buyers also tend to be unwilling to wait to see a home, and FSBO sellers who won't accommodate their tight schedules usually lose out on these very promising opportunities.

Better: Keep your house in ready-to-be-shown condition at all times when it is on the market. Be prepared to give potential buyers and their agents access at a moment's notice.

The 9 Things That Turn Off Home Buyers: Fix Them Fast!

Will Johnson, a real estate agent who is founder and leader of the Sell and Stage Team, which is part of the RE/MAX Elite real estate agency in Hendersonville, Tennessee. It also provides home-staging services.

As a home seller, you can't always guess the things about your home that might turn off potential buyers—but you really should try. In many cases, you could add thousands of dollars to the selling price by resolving potential problems—without spending much—before putting your home on the market. *Here are common "home buyer hates" that can be remedied for a very reasonable cost—in some cases for free...*

• **Popcorn ceilings.** These rough-surfaced ceilings, also known as stucco or acoustic ceilings, were popular from the 1950s through the 1970s, but now they make homes look old and outdated.

What to do: Instead of scraping off popcorn ceiling finishes, which is time-consuming and potentially expensive—or even dangerous if asbestos or lead was used—you can have a new layer of ceiling-grade gypsum board installed onto the popcorn ceiling. (Ceiling-grade gypsum board is lighter than regular gypsum board.) This costs about $2 to $2.50 per square foot installed and eliminates concerns about lead and asbestos. It lowers your ceiling height by about one-half inch—not enough to be concerned about.

• **Insufficient storage.** Small closets and cupboards are a major turnoff for home shoppers and a difficult problem to correct, but the effect can be minimized.

What to do: Remove at least half of the things you currently have stored in cramped closets and cupboards. Small storage areas seem roomier when they are half empty.

Example: Create enough room between garments hanging in a closet so that you can run your hand between them and barely brush the fabric on each side. Store excess items in a rental storage unit...or in matching, stackable plastic bins in the garage or basement (available in home centers for as little as $10 to $20 apiece).

• **Messy laundry rooms, garages, basements.** Most home sellers know that they should clean and declutter before their homes are shown. But some don't realize that cleaning for buyers is different from cleaning for houseguests. Unlike guests, buyers look everywhere and make judgments accordingly. If any part of the home is messy, cluttered or dirty, the whole home will seem less appealing.

What to do: If there is a pile of laundry in the laundry room when your real estate agent calls to arrange a quick showing, toss the laundry into the washer or dryer before heading out. If the washer and dryer are full, toss it in your car and take it with you.

If your garage or basement is cluttered, pack the clutter into matching, stackable plastic storage bins or rent a storage locker and stash the clutter there.

If your cupboards or closets are cluttered, buy matching baskets or bins and stow the mess in these inside the cupboards or closets—attractive small baskets or bins can be found for less than $10. They make storage spaces seem organized even when they aren't.

• **Insufficient light.** Dark, shadowy areas can create a sense of foreboding and ill ease. Shadows can make a room or hallway appear dirty, too.

What to do: Open all window blinds, curtains and shades and turn on all lights before showings. If there still are dim areas or dark corners, increase bulb wattage and/or add lamps. Reasonably attractive freestanding lamps are available at stores such as Target, Home Depot and Lowe's for less than $100 apiece—and you can take these with you when you move. Confirm that every bulb in the house is working before showings. Burned-out bulbs don't just make the house darker, they send a message that the home is flawed.

• **Dark or boldly colored paint on interior walls.** Even though distinctive or dark wall colors have become trendy, they turn off many buyers. Any brash colors inevitably are not the ones many potential buyers would have picked, making it hard for them to imagine themselves living in your home. Your colors also might not work with buyers' furniture... and dark walls can make rooms feel smaller and less inviting.

What to do: Apply a coat of primer/sealer over dark or boldly colored paint and then repaint in a neutral color such as beige or off-white. Primer/sealer is especially important—you even might need more than one coat of primer and perhaps two coats of paint, too. There's no need to buy expensive primer or paint, however. A primer that costs about $15 per gallon and a paint that costs $25 per gallon or less should do. If you don't want to do the job yourself, professional painters might charge $400 to $800 or so for an average 10-foot-by-12-foot room, not including the cost of the paint. Four to eight gallons of primer and two to four gallons of paint should do.

• **Wallpaper.** Many types of wallpaper have been falling out of fashion and can make a home seem out of date. There are exceptions —interior designers sometimes hang stylish new wallpaper prints in bathrooms and dining rooms, for example...or a period-correct wallpaper might be appropriate for a historic home. But as a rule of thumb, wallpaper will be a turnoff to most buyers.

What to do: Unless your wallpaper was selected by an interior designer within the past decade—or was selected to match the home's history—strip it away and paint the walls instead. If you don't want to remove the wallpaper yourself—it can be tricky—expect to pay a professional around $1 per square foot for paper removal.

• **Dated or dingy bathrooms.** It's no secret that an unappealing bathroom can greatly detract from a property's appeal. What many sellers do not realize is that they can downplay this problem without renovating the bathroom.

What to do: Buy a set of big, fluffy, bright white towels. Do not use them—just hang them on bathroom towel racks before showings. Roll some smaller white hand towels and stack these rolls in the bathroom, too. Also hang a new, bright-white shower curtain. These items make the whole bathroom feel cleaner, fresher and more welcoming, all for less than $100—and you can bring your new towels and shower curtain with you when you move.

It also can be helpful to bleach stained grout...repaint peeling trim...replace failing caulk...and update dated faucets (see below).

• **Gold faucets and fixtures and crystal faucet handles.** These glitzy fixtures have gone out of style and now make kitchens and bathrooms seem dated.

What to do: Replace these with brushed-nickel faucets—it is a classic, timeless finish. You can find very nice-looking kitchen faucets at home centers for $100 to $200...and bathroom faucets for $50 to $100. Professional installation typically costs $100 to $200 per faucet, though this can vary.

• **Pets in the house.** It creates problems when dogs or cats are in a house when it is shown. Some buyers do not like (or are allergic to) animals...and some animals do not like strangers in their homes.

What to do: If your home is going to be shown many times during a short period, board the pet with a kennel, pet day-care service or a friend. Alternately, you could take the pet with you when you go out...or arrange for a neighbor or local pet walker/pet boarder to pick up the pet when necessary.

WHEN TO UNCONVERT A ROOM

That bedroom you turned into a workshop or den—or that garage you turned into a bedroom—might suit your needs, but it probably doesn't suit the needs of most potential home buyers. Converted rooms often feel out of place, and unless they were converted by a skilled remodeler, they may feel unprofessionally done.

What to do: The prudent option usually is to convert these rooms back to their original purposes before putting the home on the market. The cost of this varies dramatically depending on what needs to be done.

Exception: If you converted a garage into living space, don't undo this if the finished space was (or appears to be) professionally done—the value of this added living space might outweigh the value of the garage for some buyers, particularly when the cost of converting the space back into a garage is taken into account.

Financial Risks of Renting Out Your Home

Stephen Fishman, JD, who writes about legal and tax issues at Nolo.com, publisher of do-it-yourself legal guides. Based in Alameda, California, he is author of *Every Landlord's Tax Deduction Guide*. FishmanLawandTaxFiles.com

If you'd like to bring in some extra money by renting out your home—as a growing number of people are doing, thanks to websites such as Airbnb—you may take comfort in the protections that home-rental websites offer.

Example: Airbnb offers $1 million in insurance coverage against liability claims in case a guest sues you over an injury and up to $1 million for property damage caused by guests.

But beware: *There still are potential financial consequences if you take in paying guests...*

• **Taxes.** The IRS lets you rent out your home only up to 14 days a year without having to pay tax on the income.

Self-defense: Ask your accountant whether you owe any state and city taxes on the income in addition to federal tax. If you rent your home for more than 14 days per year, you can deduct certain related expenses from your rental income, such as fees you pay to Airbnb, as well as mortgage interest and real estate taxes for the rental portion of your home. But your expense deduction cannot exceed your rental income for the year.

• **Penalties for illegal subletting or renting.** Many municipalities have restrictions on short-term rentals.

Self-defense: Check with the local housing authority. Also, make sure you are not violating the terms of your lease if you yourself are a renter...or the rules of your condo association, homeowners association or other relevant body.

• **Items not covered by the Airbnb property damage "guarantee."** It's called a guarantee because Airbnb itself, not an insurance company, provides coverage and establishes its own rules. For instance, damage to any fine art or antiques you own isn't covered by Airbnb. Neither are losses due to guests stealing items.

Self-defense: Add a "security deposit" to your listing. Guests are charged if Airbnb later determines that a guest is responsible for damages not covered by the Airbnb guarantee. Airbnb allows the host to set the security deposit from $95 to $5,100. Browse other local listings to help choose an amount that's right for your home.

Landlord Alert

Questions landlords are not allowed to ask under the Fair Housing Act—*Where were you born?...What is your sexual orientation?...Do you have any disabilities?* This last question may be well-intentioned if the building has access difficulties, but it is up to you to decide if that matters.

Landlords also cannot ask about age, race, children, marital status or church attendance—these have no relevance to a rental application. (There are different requirements for senior housing.)

WiseBread.com

Get Cash Back for College

Mark Kantrowitz, publisher and vice president of strategy for Cappex.com, which helps match students with colleges and scholarships. He also serves on the editorial board of *Journal of Student Financial Aid.*

Paying for your purchases with certain credit cards could earn you money for a child's college education. It even might help pay down student loans after graduation. *Here's how…*

• **Fidelity Rewards Visa Signature card.** This no-fee credit card gives you 2% cash back on all purchases, and you can have Fidelity automatically shift the money to a 529 college savings plan, which includes various mutual fund investments that you can choose plus tax-free investment growth and possible tax deductions in some states.

Those 2% rewards can add up.

Example: If you spend $25,000 a year with the credit card for 20 years and the investments you select for your 529 plan earn a 7% annual return, that's nearly $22,000 for college.

Grandparents also can take advantage of the Fidelity card for college savings, but there's a twist. If you want to save on behalf of a grandchild, it's best to call the number on the back of the card and ask to always have your rewards pushed directly into the Fidelity 529 account previously opened by the parents. (Grandparents can open 529 accounts, but grandparent-controlled 529 accounts receive less favorable treatment from college financial-aid offices than parent-controlled accounts.) For details, put "Visa Signature" in the Fidelity.com search box.

• **Register your credit cards and store loyalty cards with Upromise.** This free program offered by student-loan issuer Sallie Mae enables students and their family members to earn cash for college by spending at any of the thousands of participating merchants and restaurants. *You can…*

• Earn up to 10% back on online purchases made from hundreds of merchants. To do this, simply navigate to the online merchant's website through a link on the Upromise site. *Examples*: Earn 3% cash back at Amazon.com…5% back at WalMart.com.

• Earn 2.5% cash back on meals at more than 10,000 participating restaurants. Simply pay using a credit card that has been registered on the Upromise website.

• Qualify for cash back on certain purchases at many supermarket and pharmacy chains. Earning this money takes a bit more effort—you not only have to register your store loyalty cards with Upromise, you have to activate the offers that interest you online before shopping.

Cash earned through Upromise is automatically deposited into a college savings plan, such as a 529 or Sallie Mae "Upromise GoalSaver Account."

Alternatively, this money can be automatically transferred to a loan issuer to pay down a college loan…or you can request it in the form of a check.

You also can sign up for the Upromise MasterCard. It offers 1% cash back on most purchases and as much as 5% back on purchases made at Upromise partners—on top of the rewards program described above. For more details, go to UPromise.com.

Colleges Where Tuition Is Free

Alice Lloyd College in Kentucky serves 108 area counties. All full-time students must work at least 10 hours per week on campus. Room and board, fees and books cost $9,600/yr. *Barclay College* in Kansas is Bible-centered and offers mainly religious degrees. Room and board and other costs are $13,220/yr. *Berea College* in Kentucky admits only students with financial need. All must work 10 to 15 hours a week on campus while taking a full course load. Room and board and other costs are $10,142/yr. *College of the Ozarks* in Missouri requires 15 hours of work a week on campus plus two 40-hour workweeks annually when classes are not in session. Room and board and other costs are $7,530/yr. *Curtis Institute of Music* in Philadelphia is for top-quality musicians who participate in more than 200 concerts annually around the world. Room and board and other costs are $21,627/yr.

Kiplinger.com

DID YOU KNOW...

Small FAFSA Errors Cost Big Money

Families that make minor mistakes on the Free Application for Federal Student Aid (FAFSA) can lose out on thousands of dollars in college assistance or create delays in getting student aid. *Misspelling a name* or misreporting a birth date can delay an application. *Adding an extra zero* when entering income information can lead to a demand for backup documentation. *Use of an incorrect Social Security number* requires doing a whole new form. *Failure to track the many different school and state deadlines* can lead to loss of eligibility. *Entering assets that do not have to be disclosed,* such as retirement accounts, can reduce aid packages. *Failure to respond quickly to requests for additional information* can lead to loss of all aid.

Experts on FAFSA, reported at MarketWatch.com.

Paying Off a Student Loan? Avoid These Costly Mistakes

Mark Kantrowitz, publisher and vice president of strategy for Cappex.com, which helps match students with colleges and scholarships.

The cost of college has skyrocketed in recent decades, and so has the burden of student loans. More than 40 million Americans now owe a total of $1.3 *trillion* in student-loan debt. Repaying those loans is especially challenging when borrowers make loan-repayment mistakes—some that even the government is duping them into!

***MISTAKE:* Assuming the Department of Education's new RePAYE program is the best plan for you.** RePAYE (Revised Pay As You Earn) allows borrowers who have modest incomes to repay certain government-subsidized student loans at slower-than-normal rates. That can sound very appealing to cash-strapped grads. But the government actually offers four different "income-driven repayment plans," and for most borrowers RePAYE is not the best. It does not cap monthly payments, so while required payments can be appealingly low for recent grads earning entry-level wages, the payments might skyrocket in future years. RePAYE also gives some borrowers an unwelcome wedding present—a spouse's earnings must be included in income calculations, which can trigger a sudden spike in repayment requirements. (A cynic might even argue that the government is pushing RePAYE not because it saves borrowers money, but because it will net the government more money.)

Better: The older income-driven repayment plan known as Pay-As-You-Earn repayment (PAYE) is always the best option if you are eligible. Unlike RePAYE, PAYE caps monthly payment requirements and lets borrowers exclude spousal income if separate tax returns are filed. Under certain circumstances, PAYE forgives debt sooner than RePAYE, too. Consider RePAYE—and Income-Based Repayment (IBR), a third program—only if you do not qualify for PAYE.

Choosing between RePAYE and IBR is less clear-cut—IBR requires borrowers to devote a higher percentage of their discretionary income to loan repayment...but like PAYE, it caps required payments and provides a way around the marriage penalty. (The fourth income-based repayment plan—Income-Contingent Repayment—is never the best option.)

If your total student-loan debt is less than your annual income, skip income-based repayment—these programs won't benefit you unless you work in the public sector. (Full-time public sector employees typically should sign up for IBR even if they have substantial incomes, because special rules might allow them to have any remaining debt completely wiped away in as little as 10 years.)

MISTAKE: **Consolidating student loans into a single larger loan just to make repayment a little easier or interest rates a little lower.** Private lenders make student-loan consolidation and refinancing sound appealing, advertising that it will lower interest rates and monthly payments and simplify borrowers' lives. (The federal government has a Direct Consolidation Loan program as well.)

But for most borrowers, consolidation has more downside than upside. It means borrowers cannot pay off their highest-rate loans first. And replacing federally subsidized student loans with a private consolidation loan often costs borrowers advantageous loan terms.

Example: Federal student loans often let borrowers defer repayment if they enroll in graduate school...reduce repayments if they have modest incomes...or stop making payments entirely if they become permanently disabled. Private loans generally are far less flexible.

It is almost never a good idea to refinance federally subsidized student loans, particularly if they are fixed-rate loans. It could be worth consolidating and refinancing private student loans if this leads to significantly lower interest rates. In that case, wait at least two to three years after graduation to refinance—recent grads' credit scores usually are too low to qualify for attractive private loan rates.

In contrast, it might make sense to refinance a Parent PLUS loan with a private lender if the interest rate savings are significant—at least two percentage points is a good rule of thumb. Parent PLUS loans lack many consumer protections provided by federal student loans, so the downside of refinancing is limited.

MISTAKE: **Skipping auto-debit.** Many borrowers are hesitant to have their student-loan payments automatically withdrawn from their bank accounts each month because they fear that it gives the lender too much control over their money. But you can cancel auto-debit to regain control at any time. And meanwhile, not only is auto-debit a great way to avoid late or missed payments, but many lenders will lower student-loan interest rates by 0.25 to 0.5 percentage points if you use auto-debit.

MISTAKE: **Paying off the smallest loans first rather than highest interest rate loans.** There's a loan-repayment technique called the "snowball strategy" that advocates paying off the lowest-balance student loans first. The idea is that paying off these small loans in full as quickly as possible will give borrowers a sense of accomplishment that will help them pay off their larger loans sooner.

Better: If you can afford to make more than the minimum payments on your loans, target your loans with the highest interest rates first, not your smallest loans. The faster you pay off high-rate loans, the less you will pay overall.

Example: Say you have a $10,000 student loan with a 4.5% interest rate and $100 minimum monthly payment...a $50,000 loan with a 7.9% rate and a $200 minimum monthly payment...and you can afford to make $200 in additional payments each month. If you used that extra money to pay off the small, low-rate loan rather than the large, high-rate one, you would end up making more than $4,300 in unnecessary interest payments.

MISTAKE: **Failing to tell lenders how extra payments should be applied.** Making payments greater than the minimum required amount is a great way to reduce the overall cost of this debt. But when borrowers try to do this, their lenders often do not apply the extra money in the manner that is most beneficial to these borrowers.

Examples: If the borrower has two loans with the lender, his/her excess payment might be applied to the loan that has a lower interest rate. Or if the borrower sends in an extra check, that payment might be treated as an early payment of the following month's required payment rather than as an additional payment. In that case, the lender might not charge the borrower for the following month's required payment, and as a result, the balance of the loan would not be paid off any quicker.

Better: Include a cover letter with any extra payment (or payment in excess of the minimum required amount) clearly stating, "This is an extra payment to be applied to [a particular loan number] to reduce the principal balance of that loan." If you make an extra payment electronically through a lender's website, there typically is a way to identify specifically how the money should be applied, such as clicking on a particular loan number. If it isn't obvious, call the lender and ask how to proceed.

MISTAKE: **Paying off student loans at the expense of employer-matched contributions to retirement plans.** In general, it is better to pay down student loans than to invest your money. The one big exception is if your employer offers matching on certain retirement plan contributions. It's like getting free money.

Better: Contribute the full amount matched by your employer before making any college loan payments above the minimum.

COSIGNING MISTAKES PARENTS MAKE

MISTAKE: **Agreeing to cosign a student loan if you intend to refinance your mortgage (or take out any other loan).** Lenders will treat the student loan as if it were your own debt. That might inflate your debt-to-income ratio enough that you will not qualify for better interest rates until the student loan is paid off.

MISTAKE: **Letting cosigned loans languish when students do not keep up the payments.** Those late or missed payments will devastate the parent cosigner's credit scores.

MISTAKE: **Making payments for the student if your goal is to be released as a cosigner.** Many student loans offer cosigners a path toward being removed from the loan—if the student proves he can make the payments himself. But if the cosigner makes even one loan payment on the student's behalf, the lender will take it as a sign that the student was unable to make that payment himself and deny the cosigner's release request.

Better: Give the money to the student, and let the student make the payment.

Get Paid to Move After College

Some states and municipalities are offering college graduates cash to help pay back student loans if the graduates move there. In *Kansas*, graduates can get tax breaks and up to $15,000 in student-loan repayments in 77 counties through the Rural Opportunity Zones program. In *Niagara Falls, New York*, $3,492 a year is available for two years to a small number of graduates. *Chattanooga, Tennessee*, plans to offer up to $11,250 to young computer-software developers who move there—$10,000 of the money is to be used to help buy a home and the rest for relocation expenses. *Detroit* has a similar program, offering $20,000 for a down payment or $3,500 for two years toward rental costs.

Check local chambers of commerce and government agencies to find out about programs elsewhere.

Fortune.com

8

Insurance Insider

Wow! Health Insurance Pays for This...

My friend just received a 40% discount on a fitness watch. And after a dental procedure, he paid nothing for acupuncture to help ease the pain. His wife recently saved more than $800 on hearing aids. The surprising thing is that all these savings were benefits of their health insurance plan. Such benefits vary from state-to-state and plan-to-plan, but there are some widely used services and programs that your health plan may cover.

Important: The onus is on you to find out about these programs (see below) and enroll in them. *What you should check out...*

- **Weight-loss programs, grief counseling and more.** Are you having a hard time shedding those extra pounds? Chances are your health plan will pay all or most of the cost of a weight-loss and/or nutritional counseling program (often affiliated with a hospital and led by certified nutritionists). Your plan may also cover 10 or more sessions of grief counseling or even life coaching (which helps individuals cope with stressful work or life situations) as long as you see a licensed therapist (such as a psychiatrist, psychologist or social worker). Additionally, most health plans provide disease/condition-management programs ranging from diabetes control to pain management. These plans often assign nurses, counselors and others to work directly with you to effectively deal with your condition.

You may need a doctor's prescription or order to enroll in some of these programs—check with your insurer for details.

Note: Rates, prices and offers throughout this chapter and book are subject to change.

Charles B. Inlander, a consumer advocate and health-care consultant based in Fogelsville, Pennsylvania. He was founding president of the nonprofit People's Medical Society, a consumer advocacy organization credited with key improvements in the quality of US health care, and is author or coauthor of more than 20 consumer-health books.

Here's how: If you are enrolled in traditional Medicare, check with your Medicare supplemental carrier for services. If you are in a Medicare Advantage Plan, check your plan website or call for details. If your insurance plan is through your employer or a health exchange, contact the insurer.

• **Healthy living.** Don't want to pay hefty gym membership fees? You could be in luck! Most of the larger health insurance carriers offer healthy-living programs.

Examples: Blue Cross Blue Shield 365... Cigna Healthy Rewards...and Humana Go365 offer a wide range of incentives to keep you active and healthy. Most pay all or part of gym membership fees for you and your family through programs such as Silver Sneakers. You may also be eligible for 10% to 50% off personal-training sessions.

Other programs offer you reward points for participating in fitness activities, such as Zumba classes, swimming programs, etc. You can then "cash in" the points for rewards ranging from cameras to walking shoes. Other programs pay for smoking-cessation classes.

• **Save hundreds on these special services.** Chances are your health insurer has partnered with companies offering health-related products and services at steep discounts. For example, recent offerings by some plans include a more than $800 discount on Lasik eye-correction surgery...up to 70% off teeth whitening...partial payment for massage therapy for pain management...and much more.

Beware: Discount programs change regularly, adding new or discontinuing little-used services. So check regularly with your carrier to find out what's being offered.

TAKE NOTE...

Handy Health-Cost Finder

At FairHealthConsumer.org, enter your zip code to get estimates for common medical and dental procedures, including the out-of-pocket costs for people who don't have insurance. Free apps are available for Android and Apple devices.

Beware, You Might *Not* Be Covered

Charles B. Inlander, a consumer advocate and health-care consultant based in Fogelsville, Pennsylvania. He was founding president of the nonprofit People's Medical Society, a consumer advocacy organization credited with key improvements in the quality of US health care, and is author or coauthor of more than 20 consumer-health books.

Joe, a friend of mine, recently had chest pain and went to a nearby emergency room to get checked out. He was there for about 12 hours, and fortunately, nothing serious was found. About a month later, however, Joe was shocked when he received a bill from the ER doctor for $350. When he called the hospital to inquire, he was told that all their ER doctors are contracted and not part of the network. Joe then called his insurer and was told that his health plan paid the doctor the network rate but that the doctor could charge patients for the difference. Rather than fight back (see below), Joe reluctantly paid the bill.

Surprise medical bills, like Joe's above, have become increasingly common because insurers are limiting their networks and hospitals are using more contracted services—in order to save money. A 2015 *Consumer Reports* survey found that about one-third of all privately insured patients received a surprise medical bill (when their insurers paid less than what they expected) in the previous two years. And there are only five states (New York, Illinois, Florida, Connecticut and California) that have laws prohibiting or limiting such bills. But even without laws that protect you, there are ways to reduce your chances of getting a surprise medical bill. *Here's how...*

• **Know your providers.** Most private health insurance plans, including Medicare Advantage plans, have a limited network of doctors, hospitals and other providers (such as physical therapists) that you must use to receive maximum coverage. Some insurers provide a reduced level of coverage if you use a provider outside the plan's network, while others offer no coverage for out-of-network providers—unless it is an emergency or you get prior authorization from the insurer.

Self-defense: Ask any doctor or hospital you might use or are referred to if your insurance is accepted. If you are expecting to be hospitalized for elective surgery, such as a knee or hip replacement, you have a right to ask the facility (start with the billing office) if all the personnel involved with your care and treatment are in network. They must provide you with the answer.

Important: Surprise bills most often come from anesthesiologists, radiologists, ER doctors, pathologists and neurosurgeons—doctors you generally don't select (or sometimes even meet) when hospitalized. Be sure to ask *in advance* about those specialties, in particular, at the hospital you will be using.

- **Negotiate!** Even with careful prechecking, a surprise bill may still arrive.

Self-defense: If you receive a surprise bill, don't be afraid to challenge it. A good first step is to ask the provider to check the bill for accuracy. If the provider says the amount you owe is correct, you can try to negotiate a lower rate on the bill. Call your insurer's customer-service department and ask for help. If you still suspect a potential error, your insurer can also order an audit. It never hurts to ask your primary care physician or the doctor who managed your care to intervene on your behalf, too. You may also want to file a complaint about the bill (for misbilling, for example, or for failing to inform you in advance of a service you never agreed to) with your state's insurance department. Even in states without laws protecting you, the state insurance department may help resolve the issue. If the bill is $1,000 or more, consider using a lawyer to help negotiate with the provider. Even with the attorney's fee, you may come out ahead!

Win Your Health Insurance Denial

Charles B. Inlander, a consumer advocate and health-care consultant based in Fogelsville, Pennsylvania. He was founding president of the nonprofit People's Medical Society, a consumer advocacy organization credited with key improvements in the quality of US health care, and is author or coauthor of more than 20 consumer-health books.

Until just a few years ago, if your health insurer denied a claim, it was complicated and frustrating to fight the decision. But thanks to the federal law known as the Affordable Care Act (ACA), it has now become *much* easier to win an appeal. The law requires that any time an insurer denies an insurance claim or payment for a medical service, it must do so in writing and spell out the appeals process. It also requires that even if you lose the appeal, you can still appeal that decision to a noninsurance company–affiliated third party (such as a state insurance department). Since passage of the law in 2010, appeals have increased, and a greater number of them (up to 60%) are now won. Still, it's not a slam dunk that you will prevail if you appeal an insurance claim denial. *To increase your odds of winning...*

- **Know what's covered.** Your health insurance is like money in the bank that's set aside for your medical care. But surprisingly most people do not know what is and is not owed to them (or "covered") by their insurance plans, including private employer-provided insurance, Medicare, Medicare Advantage or Medigap plans. Later, these same people are surprised when they receive an unexpected bill. For example, you might assume that a routine tetanus shot would always be covered by Medicare. Not so. In fact, Medicare will cover a tetanus shot only if it's deemed medically necessary (for example, you've stepped on a rusty nail).

My advice: If you don't read your health insurance policy, then call your insurer to confirm coverage (or coverage limits) before you receive any medical procedure.

• **Be on the lookout for errors.** Several years ago, I received an $8,000 bill when my insurer said that a second night's hospital stay wasn't covered. As it turned out, the insurer mixed up my claim file with my wife's, and the error was corrected. This just goes to show that many claims are denied because of administrative errors.

Other times the doctor or hospital may have used the wrong code when submitting the claim. If you are turned down, call your insurer and ask for the code that was submitted. Then call your doctor or hospital to see if that is the correct code for the service that was provided. Your provider can resubmit the claim and include a letter of explanation that describes what you had done.

Helpful: Ask your doctor's office or hospital billing office for copies of everything your doctor or hospital has submitted to the insurer in case you need to file an appeal.

• **Be smart when going out of network.** If your insurer requires you to use certain in-network doctors or facilities and you get a service outside of this network, you will likely be charged for all or part of the cost. However, you can win that denial if you can show that the service was necessitated by an emergency or your insurer's network could not meet your medical need. I once helped a family find an out-of-network surgeon who was one of only two doctors in the US who performed a pediatric brain procedure needed by their son. The claim was initially denied, but they submitted an immediate appeal with supporting documentation about the doctor's skill and the child's needs. The claim—almost $500,000—was approved!

My advice: Get out-of-network services preauthorized. Gather all the supporting evidence you can to back up your request and/or enlist all the medical experts you can find to support you.

Avoid These 5 Big Medicare Enrollment Mistakes

Philip Moeller, author of *Get What's Yours for Medicare.* He is a research fellow at Sloan Center on Aging & Work at Boston College and writes a column at PBS.org called "Ask Phil, the Medicare Maven." GetWhatsYours.org

Medicare beneficiaries frequently make expensive mistakes during the annual year-end "open enrollment" period during which they are allowed to make adjustments for the following year of coverage. *Five common mistakes...*

MISTAKE: **Missing Medicare's odd deadline.** The Medicare enrollment deadline is not, as you might assume, December 31, and it is not the same as the Obamacare deadline of December 15. Instead, the Medicare enrollment deadline is *December 7.* You must make any changes you want between the start of enrollment on October 15 and December 7. If you miss the early December deadline, you might not be allowed to alter your coverage for another year unless you experience any of a number of "life events," such as marriage or relocation.

MISTAKE: **Assuming that the options that were best for you in the past are still best for you for the coming year.** Medicare beneficiaries often stick with the same selections for many years simply because re-evaluating their earlier selections would be time-consuming and confusing. But if your health-care needs have changed, those earlier selections might no longer be good options—the expensive prescription drugs you now require might be better covered by a different Part D prescription drug plan, for example.

In fact, your current Medicare selections might no longer be good options even if your medical needs have *not* changed—your Part D plan or Medicare Advantage (private Medicare-approved coverage) plan might have changed. Many Part D plans recently have reduced or eliminated their coverage of certain drugs due to sudden spikes in the prices of those drugs, for example...and many Medicare Advantage plans have been making substantial changes to their provider networks, meaning that your health-care providers might no longer be in-network.

What to do: Ideally, you would use Medicare's online "Plan Finder" tool to reanalyze your Medicare options each year (to do that, go to Medicare.gov, then click the green "Find Health & Drug Plans" tab). *But if you don't do that this year, at least...*

- Read the Plan Annual Notice of Change (ANOC) sent to you by your current Medicare Part D plan and/or Medicare Advantage plan each September. This notice will lay out any changes made to the plan from the prior year in relatively easy-to-understand language. Look for changes that will affect you, such as a drug you take being dropped from coverage or made available only in certain situations...or increases to premiums, deductibles and/or co-pays.
- Call your health-care providers, and ask them to confirm that they will still be "in network" for your Medicare Advantage plan (or for original Medicare) in 2018.

MISTAKE: **Assuming that you can easily make changes with Medigap plans during open enrollment.** Open enrollment is a great opportunity to change Medicare Advantage plans and/or Part D plans, but that isn't true with Medigap plans—and that limitation means that it sometimes isn't wise to make other Medicare coverage changes, either.

A Medigap plan is supplemental insurance that covers certain out-of-pocket costs not covered by original Medicare.

Example: Medicare Part B, which covers medical services such as doctor visits and surgeries, typically pays 80% of incurred costs, leaving patients to pay 20% out of pocket. A Medigap plan could cover much or all of that remaining 20% in exchange for your paying a monthly premium. (Medigap plans are not used with Medicare Advantage plans.)

But many Medicare recipients do not realize that the companies that sell Medigap coverage are required to sell these plans at their standard rates only during the first six months that the recipient is Medigap eligible. After that, these companies might charge prohibitive premiums or deny coverage entirely.

So while you could switch from a Medicare Advantage Plan to original Medicare during open enrollment, you might not be able to add a Medigap plan to supplement that original Medicare at a decent price. And while you could switch from original Medicare and a Medigap plan to a Medicare Advantage plan during open enrollment, you might not be able to reenroll in that Medigap plan at a reasonable price during a future open enrollment if you change your mind.

Medigap plans are regulated by states, however, and there might be rules in your state that mean you do still have access to some or all Medigap options at a reasonable price after your initial six-month eligibility even if you have preexisting health conditions. Search online for your state's State Health Insurance Assistance Program for details.

MISTAKE: **Choosing your Medigap plan based on its issuer.** Medigap plans are offered by many different insurance companies in most states, but any plan, regardless of issuer, will carry one of 10 "letter codes"—A, B, C, D, F, G, K, L, M or N. Every plan with a particular letter code is required to offer exactly the same coverage as every other plan available in that state with the same letter code. Any plan with a code of F or C will cover your entire Medicare Part B and Part A deductibles, for example, along with a preset list of other expenses. (In certain cases, plans with a certain letter code might be offered with either a low or high deductible. Plan options and rules are different in Massachusetts, Minnesota and Wisconsin.)

Because all Medigap plans with a given letter code in a given state provide the same coverage, it usually is not worth paying extra to obtain one from an insurance company you know and trust...or from an insurer that suggests in its marketing materials that its plans are somehow special. If you choose to pay for a Medigap plan in addition to original Medicare, just pick the Medigap letter code that makes the most sense for you and then buy it from the insurer that offers you the lowest price.

MISTAKE: **Expecting too much from your Medicare Advantage dental, vision and hear-**

ing coverage. Companies that sell Medicare Advantage plans often heavily promote the fact that their plans include dental, vision and hearing coverage—all things that original Medicare does not cover except in very limited circumstances. But the dental, vision and hearing coverage included in Medicare Advantage plans usually is quite limited, and plan participants still end up paying most of these costs out of pocket.

If dental, vision and hearing costs are a big part of the reason that you are considering a Medicare Advantage plan, take the time to carefully read the section of the contract that lays out the details of this coverage before signing up. What types of services are covered? What are the annual coverage maximums? Do not assume that the coverage fits your needs because the marketing materials imply this is so.

If you have major upcoming dental costs, for example, a stand-alone dental insurance plan might be the better choice. AARP offers dental insurance, for instance...and some retirees can obtain dental insurance through a former employer's retiree benefits package.

MEDICARE HOSPITAL TRAP

Not every patient in a hospital has been *admitted* to the hospital. Hospitals, under pressure to reduce their readmission rates, recently have been holding an increasing percentage of patients "for observation" rather than formally admitting them—including patients who are in the hospital for days.

That lack of a formal hospital admission can have devastating financial consequences for Medicare patients who require rehabilitation in a nursing home following their hospital stays. Original Medicare will pay for up to 20 days of rehabilitation at a skilled nursing facility—*if* the nursing home stay occurs immediately after the patient was admitted to a hospital for a minimum of three consecutive midnights. Patients given observation status do not qualify under this rule and might have to pay thousands of dollars out of pocket as a result. A federal law that took effect this year requires hospitals to notify patients that they have been given observation status—previously, patients often did not learn about this until they received their bills, if at all. If you or a loved one is given observation status and a nursing home stay could follow, ask the doctor whether he/she can change this status decision...contest the decision with the hospital's ombudsman...and if that fails, follow the appeal instructions on the Medicare "summary notice" that arrives in your mail every three months, assuming that you receive medical treatment.

Health Insurance Alert If You Work Past Age 65

Aaron Tidball, manager of Medicare operations at Allsup Inc., a nationwide service based in Belleville, Illinois, that helps guide people with Social Security disability and Medicare. AllsupInc.com

---

Two-thirds of baby boomers plan to work past age 65—the age at which they become eligible for Medicare—according to a study by the Transamerica Center for Retirement Studies. One of the challenges they might face is determining whether they can and should remain on an employer's health insurance plan or make the switch to Medicare. And it often is a very tricky choice that even human resources departments may not fully understand. *What you need to know if you plan to work (or already are working) past age 65...*

• **The number of workers that your employer employs dramatically affects your health-care options.** If there are *20 or more* employees, the employer is required to offer you the same coverage after you turn 65 that it offers its younger employees. This means you generally can remain on this group plan—and it is considered "primary coverage"—unless the employer's prescription drug coverage is not considered "creditable." For more information, put "CMS: creditable coverage" into a search engine and go to the CMS.gov site listed.

If your employer has *fewer than 20 employees,* you almost certainly should sign up for Medicare. That's because Medicare generally is considered to be your primary health coverage...and your employer-based insurance, should you choose to continue to be covered, becomes "secondary" coverage (unless your employer opts to provide primary coverage to employees age 65 and over, though this is rare). That means the employer-based coverage will pay only the portion of your eligible health-care bills that Medicare does not cover. In this case, if you failed to sign up for Medicare, you would have to pay the lion's share of your medical bills out of pocket.

For details and exceptions to these rules, including how they apply to disabled employees, check publication 02179 at Medicare.gov.

Caution: It sometimes is difficult to know whether a company has 20 or more employees under Medicare rules. A seemingly small company might legally be part of a larger organization...while a seemingly large company might actually have many part-time or contract workers who do not count toward the 20-employee threshold. Ask your company's human resources department.

•Medicare could be the better option even if you can choose your employer's plan as primary coverage. In decades past, employer health insurance plans almost always were more attractive than Medicare. But many employer plans have become less appealing in recent years—deductibles, co-pays and premiums have grown larger, while in-network medical-provider options have shrunk. So an increasing percentage of employees age 65 or older now would be better off switching to Medicare.

To figure out if Medicare is the better choice for you, start by going to Medicare.gov and putting "Which insurance pays first?" in the search box.

If your employer's coverage has a four-figure deductible and a 20%-or-higher copay after that, for example, there's a good chance that Medicare would be better.

Helpful: Although ordinarily you must enroll with Medicare within a few months before or after you turn 65 to avoid late-enrollment penalties, if you stick with your large employer's plan as primary coverage, you don't have to sign up for Medicare at that point. The penalties do not apply as long as you sign up within eight months after the date your employer coverage ceases or your employment ends, whichever comes earlier.

•If you are at a small company and do sign up for Medicare, it sometimes makes sense to also keep your employer plan despite the extra cost. This isn't common because the combined premiums of Medicare Part B (which covers medical services and supplies), Medicare Part D (which covers prescription drugs) and employer health coverage get pricey. But dual coverage could be best if you have a serious medical condition whose costs would be well-covered by the employer plan but not by Medicare. Ask your health-care providers if they can help to determine whether you would face significantly different out-of-pocket costs or coverage gaps for your current needs if you don't keep your employer coverage in addition to Medicare.

•Your spouse and dependents can't stay on your employer's health plan if you leave it for Medicare. It might be worth continuing your employer coverage even if Medicare makes more sense for you as an individual, especially if your employer's plan is the best way for your family members to obtain affordable high-quality health insurance.

However, there might be a way you could keep family members on your large-company employer plan even when you switch to Medicare for your own coverage. This involves COBRA coverage, which might be available to extend your family coverage, typically for up to 18 months, after you switch to Medicare. Ask your employer's human resources department for details.

THE HSA MEDICARE MISTAKE

Medicare often is discussed as if it is a single service, but it actually includes several components that eligible Americans could opt to sign up for at different times. Among these components is Medicare Part A, which covers hospital costs. There generally are no premiums for Medicare Part A, so people often are advised that they might as well go ahead and sign up for this "free" part of Medicare as soon as they become eligible even if they intend to remain on an employer's coverage.

For many employees, that can be a *costly mistake*. That's because more and more employer plans now include high deductibles and a Health Savings Account (HSA), a type of tax-advantaged savings account that can be used to pay medical bills.

If you sign up for Part A and continue to make HSA contributions, you will be subject to tax penalties. So if you opt to remain in an employer plan that includes an HSA, do not sign up for Part A until you leave this plan. (Rules differ for a spouse covered under your plan. For details, type into a search engine, "AARP: Can I have a health savings account as well as Medicare?" and go to the AARP website.)

Caution: Do not file for *Social Security retirement benefits* if you wish to continue contributing to an HSA. Starting Social Security anytime after age 65 automatically begins your Part A coverage up to six months retroactive to your Social Security signup date. If you made HSA contributions during that six-month period, you likely will face tax penalties.

LIFE INSURANCE WARNING...

Beware These Life Insurance Policies

Beware life insurance policies that claim to also provide long-term-care coverage. "Chronic care riders" allow you to tap death benefits early to pay for long-term-care costs, but the riders tend to be fairly restrictive. They might cover fewer types of care than a typical long-term-care policy would, for example. And life insurance companies can increase the amount charged for these riders without even informing policyholders, reducing the cash value of the policy and/or the death benefit.

Tony Steuer, CLU, founder of the Insurance Literacy Institute, a consumer-advocacy organization, Alameda, California, and author of *Questions and Answers on Life Insurance*. InsuranceLiteracy.org

Collect on a Lost Life Insurance Policy

Jim Miller, an advocate for older Americans, writes "Savvy Senior," a weekly information column syndicated in more than 400 newspapers. He is based in Norman, Oklahoma. SavvySenior.org

Every year, hundreds of millions of dollars in life insurance proceeds go unclaimed because the beneficiaries simply don't know that the policies exist. If you suspect that your deceased parent, spouse or other relative may have had a policy naming you as a beneficiary but you are not sure how to find it, here are some strategies and resources that can help you search, assuming that you have access to these sources of information...

Personal records: If the person died recently, start by checking his/her will and estate papers and then searching for a policy in drawers, files and a safe-deposit box if one exists. Also look for records of premium payments or bills from an insurer. Ask the deceased person's former insurance agent, financial planner, employer and/or accountant whether there were any life insurance policies. And review the deceased's recent income tax returns looking for interest income or interest expense for a life insurance policy—some insurance policies include investment accounts.

If you suspect that an insurer underwrote a policy, contact the insurer's claims office and ask—in most cases, the insurer will tell you without requiring proof of your relationship to the deceased.

Policy-locator service: The National Association of Insurance Commissioners (NAIC), an insurance regulatory support organization, recently created a national policy-locator service. If you request a free search at Locator.NAIC.org, the NAIC asks its 463 member insurance companies to search records for any life insurance policies in the name of the deceased. If any are found, the insurer will contact you within 90 days and request information about your affiliation with the deceased before giving you pertinent information about the policy.

Unclaimed property: If your deceased relative died more than two years ago, his insurance benefit may have already been turned over to the unclaimed property office in the state where the policy was purchased. The National Association of Unclaimed Property Administrators website (Unclaimed.org) has links to all state programs that will allow you to do a free search for such benefits online.

Claiming benefits: Once you have found a policy, contact the insurance company to ask what information it needs to process your claim.

Easy Way to Calculate Life Insurance Needs

Take your salary and multiply it by 20—if your salary is $50,000, that means you need $1 million in insurance. Buy a 20-year term policy for that amount. Term insurance is the least expensive kind and is pure insurance—not an investment or savings account. In most cases, it is the best type to have to protect your loved ones against an economic loss, which is the purpose of life insurance.

The New York Times, NYTimes.com.

Misconceptions About Car Insurance

Car color does not affect rates—but 44% of Americans think it does, and 53% of millennials have this mistaken belief. *Auto insurance covers you even if an accident is your fault,* but only 56% of people surveyed know that. And 20% believe that insurance does not cover repairs, even for drivers who are not at fault. *Car insurance does not replace items stolen from a vehicle,* but 34% of those surveyed think it does—actually, homeowner's or renter's insurance covers stolen items. *Car insurance also does not pay for a vehicle's mechanical problems,* but 14% of people think it does.

Self-defense: Read your insurance policy carefully to know what is and is not covered.

Survey conducted for insurance-comparison website InsuranceQuotes.com by Princeton Survey Research Associates and reported by InsuranceQuotes.com.

Auto Insurance Alert

Below are some nondriving reasons for losing car insurance...

- **Health issues affecting driving,** such as epilepsy, unstable diabetes, chronic depression or substance abuse, may lead insurers in some states to drop customers.
- **Submitting more than one claim a year,** even if all the claims are legitimate, may lead insurers to fail to renew your policy.
- **The auto insurer shuts down in your area**—to guard against this possibility, check out a company's financial ratings at either AMBest.com or JDPower.com, and buy insurance only from licensed companies and agents.

Roundup of experts on car insurance, reported at Credit.com.

TAKE NOTE...

Premium Rises Even If It's *Not* Your Fault!

Your auto insurance premium is likely to rise after an accident even if you were *not* at fault. After a driver had just one accident in which another driver was at fault, Allstate, Farmers, Geico and Progressive raised annual premiums by an average of $176 (10%). Among the five major auto insurers studied in 10 big US cities, only State Farm did not penalize innocent drivers. In California and Oklahoma, consumer laws prohibit such premium hikes.

Douglas Heller, an insurance consultant for Consumer Federation of America, conducted a study of auto-insurance premiums. ConsumerFed.org

Do You Qualify for This Discount?

Car insurance rates often are reduced by 10% for those age 55 or older. However, you may have to take a driving class to qualify, depending on the insurance company.

Fidelity.com

7 Surprising Things That Could Get Your Homeowner's Insurance Canceled

Laura Adams, senior insurance analyst at insurance Quotes.com. She is host of the free weekly *Money Girl* podcast. QuickandDirtyTips.com/money-girl

You might not be surprised if your homeowner's insurance premium is increased after you file a costly claim. But did you know that the insurer might go a step further and cancel your coverage or refuse to renew it? And it isn't just claims that can torpedo a policy. Insurers sometimes terminate a policy or raise premiums to prohibitively high levels for much more surprising reasons—ranging from a drop in your credit score to your purchase of a trampoline to a broken gutter.

Having a policy terminated can be more than a minor inconvenience. When you seek to replace your policy elsewhere, other insurers might quote very steep premiums or decline to offer coverage at all. That's because when an insurer terminates a policy, the insurer typically notes that it has done so in a database that other insurers check before approving applicants. That policy termination can scare off other issuers.

Here, seven surprising reasons your homeowner's insurance could be terminated or your premiums pushed up...

THINGS SEEMINGLY UNRELATED TO YOUR HOME (OR TO YOU)

• **Credit score.** A drop in your credit score could result in nonrenewal of your policy or a dramatic increase in your premiums. How dramatic? In 37 states, people with poor credit pay more than twice as much as people with excellent credit, on average, according to a 2014 study. Only three states—California, Massachusetts and Maryland—prohibit homeowner's insurance issuers from considering credit scores. (Credit scores also seem to have little effect on homeowner's insurance in Florida.) Insurers have determined that people who are responsible with credit also tend to be responsible with home maintenance and make fewer claims.

If your insurer tells you that your credit score is among the reasons your policy is not being renewed or your rates are rising, examine your credit report for any inaccurate information that might be unfairly pulling down your score. (You can obtain a free copy of your report each year at the website Annual CreditReport.com.) If you find inaccuracies, inform your insurer of this and ask whether it would reconsider its decision if you get the problem sorted out. If not, resolve the credit problem as quickly as possible and then ask to be "re-rated" by the insurer.

Helpful: If there is no easy way to improve your score, apply for homeowner's coverage through small and midsize regional homeowner's insurance issuers, which are less likely to check scores. An insurance-shopping website, insurance broker or your state department of insurance could help you locate these smaller issuers.

• **Driving infractions.** Believe it or not, speeding tickets can affect your homeowner's insurance. Insurers have concluded that irresponsible drivers tend to be irresponsible home owners, too.

There are no hard-and-fast rules here, but if you get more than two moving violations that put points on your driving record in a year—or even one serious citation such as for a DUI—you could have trouble maintaining your homeowner's insurance at a reasonable rate. It's worth investigating whether your state offers any way to quickly remove some of the bad-driving "points" that will appear on your record, such as by taking a driver-safety course. It's these points—not the violations themselves—that can catch the notice of homeowner's insurance providers.

• **Insurance claims by your home's previous owners.** If the home's previous owners filed multiple claims, that could increase the risk that your policy will not be renewed if you make even one or two claims. This is particularly likely if the claims are similar and point to a serious underlying problem with the home, such as wiring issues that have led to multiple fires.

What to do: If you have owned your home for less than seven years, request the property's Comprehensive Loss Underwriting Exchange (or CLUE) report. You can obtain this report for free as often as once per year at PersonalReports.LexisNexis.com (select "Personal Property Report" under "FACT Act Disclosure Reports"). If you discover multiple claims by the prior owners, you should consider that an additional reason to pay for covered repairs of modest size out of pocket rather than file claims. (By law, CLUE reports can include claims only up to seven years old—less in some states—so if you have owned your home longer than that, there's no reason to check for former owners' claims.)

Helpful: Before purchasing a home, insist that the seller provide you with the property's CLUE report. This report could point to underlying problems.

THINGS THAT MIGHT SEEM INCONSEQUENTIAL

• **Small claims.** It isn't just big claims that scare off home insurers. Repeated small claims can lead to termination, too. Insurers sometimes consider policyholders who file repeated small claims to be nuisances who are not worth the trouble.

What to do: Increase your deductible to at least $1,000 and preferably $2,000 or $2,500 to remove the temptation to make small claims. Use the money this saves you in premiums to pay for minor home repairs.

• **Asking questions.** Call your insurer to discuss the *possibility* that making a claim could lead to an entry in your CLUE report. Having a number of CLUE entries that your insurer deems excessive can cause nonrenewal.

Do not contact your insurer to discuss a potential claim unless it is extremely likely that you actually will make a claim. If you feel you must call your insurer to discuss the possibility of making a claim, speak in hypothetical terms and make it very clear that you are not currently making a claim.

Example: "I'm not filing a claim, but in theory, if someone had the following happen, would it be covered?" There is anecdotal evidence that phrasing things this way reduces the odds that the call will be logged into your CLUE file, though it still is possible.

• **Home-maintenance issues that are visible from the road.** Your insurer might be watching you. Insurers sometimes conduct unannounced drive-by inspections of properties. If your property is deemed to have maintenance issues, you might receive a letter threatening cancellation or nonrenewal if repairs are not made within 60 or 90 days.

Inspectors often focus on things such as missing shingles or broken gutters that can lead to greater home damage and insurance claims, but even basic upkeep issues such as an unmowed lawn could trigger unwanted insurer attention. To insurers, such things can be signs that the home is not being well-maintained in other, more important ways.

Warning: It is especially important for landlords to keep the portion of property that is visible from the road well-maintained—drive-by inspections of rental properties are particularly common.

• **Trampolines, tree houses, swimming pools and dog breeds that are considered dangerous.** Many home owners do not realize that their policies require them to inform the insurer if they obtain one of these potential liability risks. Some policies prohibit these things altogether or have detailed rules that must be followed if they are obtained—perhaps a fence is required around a pool, for example. Read your homeowner's

GOOD TO KNOW...

Is Your Home Covered for Catastrophic Loss?

To be sure your home is completely insured in case of a catastrophic loss that could run into hundreds of thousands of dollars...

• **Update your insurance profile annually,** including home improvements, and ask your agent to be sure that the amount of insurance you carry will cover "full replacement" if your home is destroyed.

• **Cover all your possessions**—take inventory and estimate their replacement cost using the UPHelp Home Inventory app from United Policyholders.

• **Increase liability coverage** to be sure that you are protected if you, a family member or a pet causes injury—a typical policy provides $300,000, which you can increase to $500,000 for $25 to $50 a year or to $1 million with an umbrella policy costing $150 to $300 annually.

Kiplinger's Personal Finance, Kiplinger.com.

policy carefully before obtaining any of these things.

Similar: Many homeowner's policies restrict or prohibit renting out the home, such as through Airbnb. Violating this rule could result in policy cancellation or nonrenewal.

WHAT TO DO IF YOUR POLICY IS TERMINATED

Homeowner's insurance policies can be terminated through either cancellation or nonrenewal. Cancellation means that the policy is ended during a contract period. Nonrenewal means that the insurer declines to continue covering the property when the policy term expires.

Issuers generally must provide at least 30 or 60 days' notice. Start shopping for a new policy as soon as you learn that your current one is ending—other issuers might be wary once the termination is on your record, so it might not be easy for you to find coverage at an appealing rate.

If all the quotes you receive are significantly higher than what you previously paid, also contact your state's insurance department to see if it has a high-risk insurance pool for home owners. (To find it, go to NAIC.org, select "Map" and then click on your state.)

This coverage could be expensive and/or limited, but it might be your best option if private issuers do not want your business.

9

Tax and Estate Planning Talk

Can You Trust Your Trust? To Protect Your Family Avoid These Big Traps...

Whether you are well off or otherwise, a well-designed trust can make your financial planning much more successful. Trusts can ensure that your assets will go to your intended beneficiaries rather than giving unnecessarily to creditors, former spouses, estate taxes, long-term-care bills or other threats.

Unfortunately, many trust documents contain language that limits their ability to protect assets—and no one notices the problem until it is too late. If you don't have a trust, there's a good chance that you should have one. *And if you do have a trust, make sure that it does not include certain terrible mistakes...*

***MISTAKE:* Ignoring trusts because of the high federal estate-tax exemption.** Keeping assets safe from estate taxes has long been one of the major reasons to create a trust. But with the federal estate-tax exemption at $5.49 million (and twice that for couples) for 2017, very few families have to worry about this threat.

What some people still don't realize is that federal estate taxes were never the only reason to create a trust. Trusts also can safeguard assets until heirs are old enough to manage money responsibly. They can protect assets from state estate taxes—some states still have relatively low estate-tax exemptions, as low as $1 million in some cases, although several states are raising their low exemption levels.

Note: Rates, prices and offers throughout this chapter and book are subject to change.

Gideon Rothschild, Esq., chair of trusts, estates and asset-protection practices with the New York City–based law firm Moses & Singer LLP. Rothschild is immediate past chair of the American Bar Association's real property trust & estate law section and a vice-chair of the Society of Trust & Estate Practitioners (STEP)-US Region. MosesSinger.com/attorneys/gideon-rothschild

And failing to use a trust to protect assets from various potential costs can end up being a very expensive mistake.

Example: A New York man left a $1 million estate to his wife. She later required a lengthy stay in a nursing home, which ate up virtually all of those assets. Had the man instead left his money to an "irrevocable" trust that named the wife as beneficiary, Medicaid would have paid most of her nursing home bills, keeping the money in the family.

BETTER: **Speak with an estate-planning attorney about the possibility of setting up a trust** to protect potentially vulnerable assets…not just if you have enough assets to trigger federal estate taxes.

MISTAKE: **The trust terminates when beneficiaries reach a predetermined age or at some other specified date.** It is very common for trusts to terminate when beneficiaries reach a particular birthday—often 18, 21, 25 or 30—with all remaining assets distributed to beneficiaries then. That's because when people set up trusts, their primary goal often is to ensure that assets remain safe until young heirs are old enough to handle money maturely. But a trust set up this way does nothing to protect the assets from other threats and could dump a large sum of money into a beneficiary's lap at an inopportune moment, such as when a spouse is about to file for divorce or when a lawsuit or bankruptcy looms.

BETTER: **Ask your estate-planning attorney to *not* include a termination date in your trust.** Instead, grant the trust's beneficiaries broad powers to replace the trustee when those beneficiaries reach an age when they are likely to be responsible—perhaps 25 or 30. That way, beneficiaries continue to receive the asset protection provided by the trust but also have some ability to manage and utilize the assets as they see fit, including selecting a new trustee whose thinking is in line with their own if necessary.

MISTAKE: **Using the word "shall" in trustee directions.** Trusts often contain language dictating that the trustee "shall" distribute assets to beneficiaries in particular amounts at particular times. Trouble is, the word "shall" ties the trustee's hands—it means that he/she must distribute the assets as directed even if it is obvious that doing so would be foolish, perhaps because the beneficiary expects to soon declare bankruptcy and the money would just end up in the hands of creditors. (If a trustee tried to not make a distribution under these circumstances, creditors could take the trustee to court and likely force the distribution.)

BETTER: **Change trust language to say that the trustee "may" distribute assets and/or income in a specific amount** and/or after the beneficiary reaches a certain age. This lets the trustee know that your intention is that he make this distribution, but it also gives him the option of not doing so if it doesn't make sense for some unforeseen reason. If a creditor tried to force such a distribution in court, he almost certainly would fail—courts respect the authority of trustees to not make distributions when the word "may" is used. Using the word "may" does give the trustee great power over the trust assets, but if you also give beneficiaries the power to change trustees, that power is unlikely to be abused.

MISTAKE: **Choosing a family member or friend as trustee.** This is extremely common because most people do not want to pay a professional trustee and because most people have at least one family member or close friend whom they trust to handle this task responsibly. But even if the family member or friend selected truly is honest (which is far from certain—plenty of seemingly reputable family and friend trustees have been caught stealing trust assets), disagreements between trustees and beneficiaries often create family discord or end long-standing friendships. And because these amateur trustees often have little or no experience in this role, they sometimes make costly mistakes, some of which may result in crippling IRS penalties.

BETTER: **Choose a professional trustee.** Not only will this trustee be much better equipped than an amateur to handle the responsibilities of the role, but also your beneficiaries will be able to sue for breach of fiduciary duty if he fails to do so. (Beneficiaries could sue a family member trustee, but such a lawsuit likely would devastate the family.) To keep the costs of this professional trustee in check, use the trustee services offered by a trust company that also will manage the trust's investments (see below for details).

TYPICAL COSTS OF A TRUST

Adding trust provisions to a simple will is likely to cost $1,000 to $3,000. If you use a professional trustee, you also will have to pay ongoing fees. If you use the trust services of the bank and trust company that also manages the trust's investments, the annual fee for trustee services might be 0.20% or 0.25% of the assets under management (in addition to an annual fee of perhaps 1% for asset management). These fees will vary depending on a number of factors including the investment company selected and size of the trust's investment portfolio.

TAKE NOTE...

Do You Have a Will?

Only 42% of US adults have a will or other estate-planning document, such as a living trust. The percentage is lower among people with children under age 18—only 36%.

Analysis by Caring.com based on a survey of 1,003 US adults by Princeton Survey Research Associates International.

If You've Agreed to Be an Executor or Trustee, Don't Make These Costly Mistakes

Douglas D. Wilson, CFP, CTFA, who counsels executors and trustees through his Honolulu-based firm, Trustee Consulting, LLC. He is a former senior vice president of First Hawaiian Bank's Trust and Investments Division and is author of *The Everything Executor and Trustee Book* and *Executor & Trustee Survival Guide.*

Family members and friends who agree to serve as trustees or estate executors often find themselves in over their heads. The rules governing trusts and estates are complex and difficult for novices to understand. If something goes wrong, it might not just be the beneficiaries who pay the price. Trustees and executors have a legal responsibility to act in the best interests of the trust or estate beneficiaries and can be sued if they fail to do so—even if their missteps were accidental. *Five common trustee and executor mistakes to avoid...*

MISTAKE: **Comingling estate and trust accounts with personal accounts.** This is especially common when the executor or trustee is the surviving spouse. This spouse might, for example, pay the trust or estate bills out of the couple's existing checking account rather than set up a new account. But comingling estate/trust assets with personal assets creates a tax-reporting nightmare. An accountant will have to be hired to separate the accounts—a job so difficult that some accountants turn down this sort of work. I know of one executor whose comingling accounts resulted in an accountant's bill of almost $6,000.

MISTAKE: **Purchasing items from the estate/trust.** Let's say that you're the executor of an estate and you need a car. As it happens, the estate needs to sell the deceased's car. Buying the car seems like a win-win solution—but doing that could open the door to a lawsuit from one of the estate's beneficiaries. As an executor or a trustee, you are legally responsible for obtaining the best possible prices and terms for any assets sold. If you sell something to yourself—even at a fair price—it leaves you open to accusations that you might have been able to sell the item for more.

What to do: Obtain written permission from all of the beneficiaries before purchasing an item from the estate or trust, and include the purchase price in this document. If it isn't possible to obtain written permission from the beneficiaries, hire a professional who has experience selling items of this sort, ask him/her to offer the item for sale to the public, then purchase it the same way anyone else could. And do not purchase the item until you confirm that the estate will have enough funds to pay off its creditors. Otherwise one of those creditors might argue in court that you could have obtained more for the item.

MISTAKE: **Failing to communicate with beneficiaries.** Beneficiaries who are not kept up to date on what's going on with an estate or a trust sometimes start to suspect that someone might be keeping their money from them. Their next step might be to hire an attorney.

What to do: Let beneficiaries know as soon as possible that they are named as beneficiaries. Warn them that it might be a while before they receive assets. (Distribution of assets is unlikely to occur for at least several months with even a simple estate or trust and could take several years if there is complex litigation against the estate or trust.) Then send them regular updates as things progress. Also provide beneficiaries with periodic summaries of the estate/trust's income and expenses. Not only do beneficiaries grow suspicious if they do not receive this information, many states have laws requiring that these accountings be provided at least annually.

MISTAKE: **Failing to secure valuables.** Heirs have been known to start grabbing items as soon as someone passes away. They might be doing this in good faith—perhaps Mom told your sister that she could have her jewelry. But by law, when someone dies, what that person said about the distribution of his/her possessions does not matter. What matters is what is in the will or trust. The executor or trustee is responsible for protecting the deceased's possessions until they can be distributed according to the terms of these documents.

What to do: If no one is living in the deceased's house, change the door locks as soon as possible, since you don't know how many keys may be floating around. As executor or trustee, you have a legal right to have the locks changed. If you don't have a key, you can grant permission to a locksmith to break in, if necessary, to change the locks. Move portable valuables to a secure location, such as a storage locker, a safe in your home or a bank safe-deposit box. (Do this even if you are confident that the beneficiaries will not take items—a burglar who sees the deceased's name in the obituaries might target the house.) Move vehicles to a secured location, such as a private garage, as well. If some of the deceased's possessions already have gone missing, let heirs know that you have to keep track of these things until the estate is settled. If no one admits to taking the missing items, tell them you will contact the police. This shows that you are trying to fulfill your legal responsibilities as executor or trustee, reducing the odds that you could be successfully sued.

Example: A painting worth thousands of dollars disappeared from a deceased person's home. The beneficiary who took it gave it back—but only after the executor threatened police involvement.

MISTAKE: **Distributing property before all estate/trust obligations are satisfied.** Beneficiaries might pressure you to give them their inheritance right away. But if creditors make claims against the estate or trust after you have distributed some or all of its assets, you could be personally liable for paying off those creditors.

Example: An executor who also was one of the descendants of the deceased was pressured by his siblings to divide up his parent's estate quickly. Only after the money was distributed did this executor learn that his parents had taken out a loan of more than $50,000 that now had to be repaid by the estate. Two of his siblings refused to give back their shares of the inheritance, leaving the executor to pay most of the $50,000 out of his own pocket... and ruining the siblings' relationships.

Similar: Paying an estate's or a trust's bills promptly sometimes is a mistake, too. If it later is determined that the estate owes federal taxes, that tax bill likely would take legal precedence over other obligations. If there isn't enough left to pay the taxes, an executor who already paid other estate bills could become personally liable for the remaining tax bill.

What to do: It is OK to make partial distributions before all claims against the estate or trust are in as long as you are confident that there will be sufficient assets remaining to cover all obligations. Otherwise, wait until you are sure all claims and bills have been received and paid before making distributions. Confirm that any tax payments made by the estate have been accepted, not just submitted. Be aware that in most states, creditors must make claims against estates within a limited window following the death—often three months. The executor might be responsible for placing notices of the death in local newspapers to start this clock ticking, however. Consult an estate-planning attorney familiar with the laws in the deceased's state if you are not certain.

WHEN TO SAY "NO" TO BEING A TRUSTEE OR EXECUTOR

Serving as an executor or trustee usually is within the average person's abilities, but it could become a massive burden if...

- **There is litigation pending against the trust or estate.**
- **The trust or estate contains many complex business interests.**
- **There are litigious, bickering or otherwise unpleasant beneficiaries.**

Even if you informally agreed beforehand to take on the role, after the person dies, ask the deceased's attorney, family members and/or business associates for details about the estate or trust *before* formally agreeing to start acting as executor or trustee. You can decline simply by refusing to sign documents accepting the position. If you decline, do not take on any of the responsibilities of the role even temporarily until a replacement can be found—doing this could cause a court to rule that you officially accepted the position, and once you have done that, it can be difficult to back out.

Are Heirs Responsible for the Deceased's Debt?

Edward Mendlowitz, CPA and partner at the accounting firm WithumSmith+Brown, New Brunswick, New Jersey, and author of *Getting Your Affairs in Order.*

A recent client was concerned that he was responsible for paying off thousands of dollars in debt that his father left behind after his death.

Heirs rarely are directly liable for unpaid bills after a person dies—but the estate usually must pay the bills, which reduces the amount that heirs inherit. Certain assets do not go through probate, including retirement accounts and life insurance payouts, so creditors usually cannot claim them. The estate is responsible for credit card debt, car loans, home-equity lines of credit and mortgages. Federal student loans are discharged at a student's death, and some private student loan lenders offer a death discharge, including Sallie Mae, Wells Fargo and Discover.

Mortgage payoffs can be complicated. The estate may pay off a mortgage so that heirs can keep the house...a surviving relative may become owner of the house and assume the mortgage...or heirs may sell the home—or walk away if it is worth less than the mortgage balance.

If the estate does not have enough money to repay debts, creditors typically erase what is owed. But if there are cosigners on loans or credit cards, creditors will go after them—and some unscrupulous lenders demand payment from heirs even when they are not obligated to repay.

Self-defense when creating a will: Specify what should happen to any high-value items—such as a home on which there is an outstanding mortgage.

Benefits of a Trusteed IRA

Prevent heirs from mismanaging money—and save on fees—with a "trusteed IRA." Like a traditional trust, a trusteed IRA allows you to dictate terms of withdrawals.

Bonus: A trusteed IRA, which is set up by an IRS-approved provider such as Merrill Lynch or USAA Federal Savings Bank, lets you avoid thousands of dollars in trust attorney costs.

The provider, which then serves as trustee, charges an annual maintenance fee, typically 1% of assets.

Ed Slott, CPA, president of Ed Slott and Company, an IRA advisory firm in Rockville Centre, New York. IRAHelp.com

Make Sure Your Power of Attorney Actually Works

Martin M. Shenkman, CPA, JD, an estate- and tax-planning attorney based in New York City and Fort Lee, New Jersey. He is also coauthor of *Powers of Attorney: The Essential Guide to Protecting Your Family's Wealth.* ShenkmanLaw.com

A power of attorney (POA) can be a tremendously valuable tool when a person needs to designate someone to act on his/her behalf in financial, legal and other matters. But banks, brokerages and other financial institutions sometimes refuse to accept a POA—instead sending the designated "agent" away and complicating such tasks as withdrawing money from accounts or buying and selling investments in an account. Those institutions may want to try to make sure that the document, which typically is invoked when the account holder is incapacitated, is valid and that the person named as agent is not engaged in "financial abuse"—that is, trying to cheat the account holder.

Here's how to reduce the odds that a designated agent will encounter problems and how an agent can convince financial institutions to let him take control...

CREATING THE POA

If a POA is being created for you or someone you are helping, such as a parent, be sure to follow these guidelines...

- **Consolidate financial matters at as few financial institutions as possible.** Fewer financial institutions means fewer future hassles for the agent.
- **Get preapproval.** Many institutions will review and accept a POA in advance.
- **Complete POA forms provided by the financial institutions,** if available, rather than a general POA. Institutions are more likely to honor their own forms.
- **Set up a durable immediate POA, not a springing POA.** The latter type will "spring" into effect only when the person creating the POA becomes incapacitated. Proving incapacitation creates an additional hurdle for the agent. The durable immediate POA takes effect as soon as the document is signed and remains in effect if the person becomes incapacitated.
- **Have two witnesses and a notary present when the POA is signed.** In some states, this is required, and even when it isn't, it can help confirm the legitimacy of the document.

IF YOU ARE THE AGENT

When a financial institution balks...

- **Remain calm and courteous with the institution.** Flying off the handle will only increase the concern that you cannot be trusted to look after the client's interests.
- **Ask the institution, "What can I do to help with this process?"** For example, it might allay the institution's concerns if all the heirs come in together and agree that you should be allowed to manage the account.
- **Ask an attorney whether the institution is legally mandated to accept the POA.** In many states, institutions must accept POAs as long as that state's "statutory" POA form was used. Institutions generally back down when this is called to their attention.
- **Ask a court to name you as the financial guardian for the account holder.** This allows you to manage the account even if the institution won't accept the POA. It is time-consuming and expensive, however, so it should be considered a last resort.

GOOD TO KNOW...

Little-Known Tax-Deductible Donations

Unwanted paint can be given to GlobalPaints.org...*building materials* can be donated to Habitat for Humanity's ReStores...and *old linens* can be used for pet bedding—you can give them to tax-exempt animal-rescue groups and animal shelters.

Also worth looking into: Some utility companies now offer free pickup of older, energy-inefficient appliances, and they even may pay about $50 for them.

AARP Bulletin, AARP.org/bulletin.

Check Out a Charity Before Donating

Check out a charity's tax-exempt status before donating to it and claiming a deduction. Go to IRS.gov and enter Publication 78 in the search bar. Click on "Exempt Organizations Select Check Search Tool"...then click on the blue "Exempt Organizations Select Check Tool" link...then select "Are eligible to receive tax-deductible charitable contributions." Fill in the blanks with information about the charity that you are investigating, scroll down, and when you find it, click on the group's "deductibility status" link on the far right.

Roundup of experts on charity tax deductions, reported at MarketWatch.com.

Beware These Tax Scams

Major tax scams to watch out for this filing season...

- **Phony help-desk calls or e-mails** that seem to come from legitimate firms such as TurboTax but are oddly written and ask users to click links—never reply or click unless you are sure that a notice is legitimate.
- **Fraudulent e-mails asking for W-2 forms** are going to some corporations.
- **Identity thieves file quickly and create returns** that generate refunds so that legitimate returns from victims are rejected—use IRS Form 14039 if you find that a fraudulent return has been filed.
- **Criminals send e-mails to tax professionals** claiming to be potential clients whose documents can be obtained by clicking on a link provided. If the tax professional clicks on the link, malware is downloaded to his/her computer.
- **Crooked tax professionals** file returns designed to get illegitimate refunds that the thieves keep or share with clients.

Roundup of experts on tax fraud, reported in *USA Today.*

Don't Get Fooled by "Free" Online Tax Prep

Clark Howard, host of *The Clark Howard Show,* a radio program about saving money, and author of *Clark Howard's Living Large for the Long Haul.* Clark.com

The major tax-preparation software companies promote "free" online versions of their tax-prep software. But these free versions are extremely limited. If you require a Schedule A to itemize deductions...a Schedule C to report investment income...or almost any other form beyond a 1040EZ or 1040A, you likely will have to pay $35 or more to upgrade...and perhaps $30 or so to file a state tax return.

Many taxpayers learn that they need an upgrade only after spending hours entering financial information.

What to do: Consider using the free online tax-prep software CreditKarma.com/tax—it is free even if you use a variety of forms beyond 1040 forms. CreditKarma's software is not as comprehensive as some tax software, but it's sufficient for most taxpayers.

Or see if you are eligible for the free online tax-prep software that is offered by TurboTax and H&R Block, among others, through the IRS "Free File" web page (search "free file" at IRS.gov). It tends to be fairly comprehensive and often includes state returns. But it's mainly for taxpayers of modest income—most of the offerings require adjusted gross income below $64,000.

GOOD TO KNOW...

Common Tax-Filing Mistakes

Input mistakes—double-check to make sure that you're entering your figures correctly. *Missing out*—look out for credits and special deductions and a larger standard deduction if you are age 65 or older. *Misspelled or different names*—be sure yours matches whatever the Social Security Administration has on record. *Direct-deposit errors*—be sure the routing and account numbers are correct. *Additional income*—be sure to record it from forms such as 1099-MISC, 1099-INT and 1099-DIV. *Social Security number omissions*—be careful to write it wherever it is called for. *Charitable contributions*—follow all donation tax rules carefully. *Signature omission*—the return must be signed before mailing or signed electronically if it is filed online.

Kay Bell, contributing tax editor, Bankrate.com.

The US Is Becoming a Tax Haven

The US has resisted new global financial-disclosure standards, so wealthy foreigners are taking money from places such as Switzerland, Bermuda and the Cayman Islands and putting it in the US. Well-to-do foreigners still must comply with their home countries' tax laws, but they may be concerned about extortion and believe their assets are safer in the US.

Roundup of experts on offshore tax havens, reported at Bloomberg.com.

How Long to Keep Financial Paperwork

Tax documents typically can be discarded three years after a return is filed but should be held longer in certain situations. *Example:* Seven years if you file a claim for a loss from worthless securities. *Investment documents* can be checked against online records and discarded if they match. But for taxable accounts with holdings from before brokerages were required to track cost basis, you must provide the cost data yourself after a sale. That means keeping cost-basis information until you sell the investment—and then for three to seven years more with your tax documents. *Bank and credit card statements:* Review and shred—if you need them in the future, get them electronically. *Home-related documents:* Keep as long as you own the home to have details of exactly what you paid and any improvements you made that affect your cost basis at sale.

Roundup of experts on document storage, reported at Morningstar.com.

10

Investment Insight

Don't Let a Financial Adviser Rip You Off

Do you ever suspect that financial advisers put a greater priority on making profits and earning commissions for themselves than looking out for you and your nest egg—whether they are suggesting a stock, a fund, an annuity or something else?

An Obama-era federal rule sought to require advisers who work with tax-advantaged retirement savings to put client interests first. President Donald Trump has told the Department of Labor to review and possibly revise or scrap that "fiduciary rule," suggesting that the rule may hurt investors by limiting their access to certain investment products and advice.

If you have a financial adviser or are considering hiring one, it's important for you to understand how the adviser gets paid and what conflicts of interest he/she may have. We asked financial adviser Mark Cortazzo to explain how you can be sure that you're getting financial advice that is given in your interest—regardless of the fate of the fiduciary rule.

Some questions Cortazzo suggests you ask to help you understand how your current or prospective financial adviser gets paid and how that might influence the advice you get...

THE KEY QUESTIONS TO ASK

- **Is your advice to me subject to a fiduciary standard?** With the government's fiduciary rule under review as of August 2017, this is a good question to start the discussion. You may get a simple "yes," as in the case of a registered investment adviser (RIA), who already

Note: Rates, prices and offers throughout this chapter and book are subject to change.

Mark Cortazzo, CFP, CIMA, founder and senior partner of Macro Consulting Group LLC in Parsippany, New Jersey, which oversees $380 million in client assets. Cortazzo has been named one of the 250 best financial advisers in America by *Worth* and one of America's top financial advisers by both *Barron's* and *Fortune.* MacroConsultingGroup.com is subject to a fiduciary standard and typically charges clients a fee that's a percentage of the clients' assets rather than commissions on specific products.

Or you may get a more complicated answer if you're talking to a broker, wealth manager or insurance agent. The term "fiduciary" just means that there's a commitment to put the client's interests first. Even if your adviser is not subject to a legal requirement, the firm may have rules in place meant to approximate such a standard. Make sure that the firm's rules are explained clearly and in writing.

Some advisers might answer you by saying, "Part of the time." For example, an adviser could act as a fiduciary when recommending mutual funds but not when selling you an insurance product such as an annuity. Be more skeptical of anything offered under such an exception, and don't hesitate to go elsewhere to buy or get advice on that product.

Helpful: A designation of CFP, or certified financial planner, from the CFP Board of Standards, an industry group, requires that the adviser meet a fiduciary standard, but there is no guarantee of full compliance. Also, you can ask your investment adviser to notify you, in writing, of any instance in which he will not be acting as a fiduciary.

- **Have you changed your standards or practices at all since the fiduciary rule was announced?** Some investment firms have said that they would go ahead with changes to how their advisers function no matter what happens with the federal rule. For instance, Merrill Lynch has said it will stop offering most new commission-based IRAs through advisers. Instead, it will allow customers to choose whether to work with human advisers by paying fees based on the amount of assets in the account...or to use commission-based self-directed brokerage accounts...or to use fee-based automated robo-adviser accounts.

Some advisers will tell you that there is no need for a change. If that's because the individual or firm has been subject to a fiduciary requirement all along, fine. If the adviser starts talking about the flexibility to offer you more products or get you a better deal—or if he seems most interested in talking about the importance of his own compensation—be wary. Consider going elsewhere.

- **Will you earn more by putting my money into this fund rather than something similar from another company?** The answer with the least potential for a conflict of interest is that the adviser collects an advisory fee based on your account value rather than commissions or transaction-based fees of any kind, because that isn't going to create an incentive to sell a particular product. An adviser whose compensation will vary depending on what funds or investments you buy faces a conflict. You should make certain that you understand all the costs and how they compare with competing products and services. Of course, if you highly value a particular adviser's advice, you might choose to accept higher costs than you would be charged elsewhere.

You can arm yourself for this discussion with this simple step: Read your adviser's business card. If the name on a fund or other financial product that you are offered is the same as any name on the card—the name of the firm in large type or an affiliate in the fine-print disclosures—then you should ask a lot more questions.

Helpful: Even if your adviser has answered this question to your satisfaction, consider the next question.

- **Are you more loyal to your clients or to your employer?** The answer may not always be completely honest, but it's worth raising the issue of whether your adviser is pushing the "house brand" of investments—and whether that's appropriate. Even if the adviser has no direct financial incentive, he still might recommend the company's own products because selling more of them might earn favor from the boss.

Helpful: Ask whether selling more company products is a factor in deciding promotions, and if the answer is yes, consider whether the honesty the person is showing outweighs the conflict of interest.

- **Do you go on "due-diligence" trips?** Due-diligence trips offer advisers a chance to meet investment managers and learn about their funds and other products. And that can be a good thing. For instance, last year I went on a two-day due-diligence trip during which

I spent six to eight hours a day listening to speakers, including three Nobel Prize laureates, and I didn't play any golf or tennis or go swimming. But if these trips involve less time learning about the investments and more time dining, drinking and golfing, that's not a good thing. If an adviser seems nervous and evasive in describing the agendas and details of his past three trips, be wary.

• **Is the product I am investing in the lowest-cost share class?** Mutual funds and exchange-traded funds (ETFs) often have different classes with identical management but different expense ratios. Everyone wants low costs, which boost investment returns, but there sometimes are trade-offs worth considering. For example, an investor with a small amount of money might choose a share class that's slightly more expensive but has no transaction fees when it's bought or sold. If this investor is rebalancing his portfolio (and therefore selling/buying shares) multiple times a year, this could be cost-effective.

Helpful: At some large brokerages, you may find that a more expensive share class lowers your advisory fee, but make sure that the cost trade-offs have been explained clearly and completely.

ONE LAST QUESTION...

The Trick Question

There's one more question to ask your current or prospective financial adviser, and it really is a trick question because it is designed to keep an adviser from tricking you about how big the annual fee is...*Why is your advisory fee a quarterly rate?* An advisory fee should always be quoted and discussed as a percentage of assets per year. If your adviser is talking about a quarterly fee, that's a red flag that he is probably trying to hide things. I know of a firm that quoted its fee as 0.375% per quarter. That's 1.5% annually, which in my opinion is on the high side.

Helpful: Always do the math so that you can compare annual fees.

Mark Cortazzo, CFP, CIMA, founder and senior partner of Macro Consulting Group LLC in Parsippany, New Jersey.

How to Judge a Financial Newsletter

Mark Hulbert, columnist for MarketWatch and *The New York Times*, and founder of *The Hulbert Financial Digest*.

After 36 years of objectively comparing the performance of investment newsletters, *The Hulbert Financial Digest* ceased publication in 2016. *Bottom Line Personal* found Hulbert's newsletter rankings to be so helpful over the years that we decided to ask its founder and editor, Mark Hulbert, to tell us how our readers can continue to assess the performance of newsletter advice...

My first suggestion is, once you have chosen an investment newsletter, sign up for a trial subscription, if available, and "paper-trade" the recommendations over that trial period—that is, carry out the recommended transactions on paper rather than actually investing. Pay close attention not only to whether your overall numbers match those quoted by the adviser but also such details as whether the execution prices you would be able to obtain in actual trading are close to what the newsletter reports.

If paper trading an adviser's portfolio is too cumbersome, there are some rules of thumb that can be helpful...

• **Determine whether the adviser maintains a specific model portfolio.** If it includes numbers of shares or portfolio percentages assigned to each holding, all the better. Other things being equal, if you have doubt about a newsletter's trustworthiness, you should give more credence to the performance numbers from an adviser who does provide this information, since advice this precise makes it difficult to fudge the numbers.

I say this because I have found that outright lying about performance by newsletters is relatively rare. Far more common is spinning the numbers in a way that *implies* something that is false. It's a good sign when a newsletter's portfolio isn't hypothetical but real world—and when the adviser offers to share brokerage statements with customers.

EASY TO DO...

Check Your Broker's Record!

Financial-adviser misconduct is more common than investors think. Seven percent of advisers have misconduct records. And 44% of those fired for misconduct get back into the industry within a year.

Self-defense: Check a broker's record at BrokerCheck.Finra.org.

Research from University of Minnesota, Minneapolis, and University of Chicago, published in *Social Science Research Network*.

•**Be skeptical of performance claims** that are based on the average return of a list of recommended positions. That's because the order in which those recommendations were made makes a big difference. It's theoretically possible that you could lose a lot of money by following stocks whose average return is quite impressive. For that reason, a newsletter should report its own performance based on the results that would have been experienced by a subscriber following its recommendations *at the times that subscribers received the recommendations.*

When the newsletter makes performance claims, does it report the precise period over which the performance was produced and the assumptions used to calculate that performance? The more vague the parameters, the less weight you should give them.

• **Short-term performance is mostly noise.** That means, when choosing a newsletter, you should pay barely any attention to recent performance and focus instead on returns produced over many years. My rule of thumb is 15 years, although there is no magical threshold for how long is enough.

• **If a performance claim seems too good to be true, it probably is.** I'm amazed by some investors' gullibility. Those who are incredibly shrewd elsewhere in their lives can become surprisingly naive in the face of newsletters claiming sky-high returns.

Warren Buffett's Book List

Lawrence A. Cunningham, JD, a professor at The George Washington University and editor of *The Essays of Warren Buffett: Lessons for Corporate America*, reported by Karen Larson, editor, *Bottom Line Personal.*

Years ago, a college student asked Warren Buffett how to prepare for a career on Wall Street. The legendary investor reportedly held up a stack of publications and reports and said, "Read 500 pages like this every day. That's how knowledge works. It builds up, like compound interest." Yes, that's right—500 pages a day.

Buffett, the chairman of the investment holding company Berkshire Hathaway, considers reading to be a core part of his job, according to Lawrence A. Cunningham, JD, a professor at The George Washington University and editor of *The Essays of Warren Buffett: Lessons for Corporate America.* "Reading is how he knows as much as or more than those he's speaking with."

Buffett doesn't have a book club like Oprah, but Cunningham notes that there are ways to determine some of the books he really likes—for starters, Buffett personally approves every title sold at the bookstore kiosk at Berkshire Hathaway's annual shareholder meeting. *Here are five general interest books and two about Buffett himself...*

- *No Two Alike: Human Nature and Human Individuality* by Judith Rich Harris
- *Influence: The Psychology of Persuasion* by Robert B. Cialdini, PhD
- *Outliers: The Story of Success* by Malcolm Gladwell
- *The Intelligent Investor* by Benjamin Graham
- *Where Are the Customers' Yachts? Or a Good Hard Look at Wall Street* by Fred Schwed, Jr.
- *Warren Buffett's Ground Rules* by Jeremy C. Miller
- *The Warren Buffett Way* by Robert G. Hagstrom.

Avoid These Common ETF Missteps

Neena Mishra, CFA, ETF research director at Zacks Investment Research, Chicago. Zacks.com

Investments in exchange-traded funds have topped $4 trillion as of August 2017, more than double the $1.1 trillion at the end of 2011. ETFs have benefited from a shift away from actively managed mutual funds toward funds that passively track various investment indexes. However, in buying ETFs, which trade much like stocks on exchanges, many investors make false assumptions that cut into their returns. *How to avoid costly misconceptions...*

- **Don't assume that all ETFs carry very low fees.** Highly specialized ETFs can be as expensive as or more expensive than actively managed funds. And even various similar ETFs can charge very different fees.

An example: iShares US Technology ETF (IYW) and Technology Select Sector SPDR ETF (XLK) both track large-cap tech stocks. But, in August 2017, IYW had an annual expense ratio of 0.44%, more than three times the 0.14% for XLK.

- **Don't assume that an ETF's assets are spread broadly across its portfolio's stocks.** Even if an ETF portfolio includes many different names, its weightings might not provide much diversification.

For instance, although the popular Energy Select Sector SPDR ETF (XLE) tracks all 36 energy companies in the Standard & Poor's 500 stock index, its top three holdings—Exxon Mobil, Chevron and Schlumberger—account for 47% of its total assets. Such high concentration typically leads to much greater volatility.

- **Do not ignore extra costs for trading ETFs.** Just as with a stock, you typically must pay a brokerage commission ranging from $7.99 to $19.99 each time you buy or sell ETF shares. *Smart:* Trading in many in-house ETFs at Vanguard and Charles Schwab is commission-free for investors who open a brokerage account. And at Fidelity, account holders can trade 70 iShares ETFs commission-free.

The Lump-Sum Investing Mistake

Michael E. Kitces, CFP, partner and director of wealth management for Pinnacle Advisory Group, which oversees more than $1.8 billion in client assets, Columbia, Maryland (PinnacleAdvisory.com). He also is publisher of the financial-planning industry blog "Nerd's Eye View." Kitces.com

Dollar-cost averaging is a popular strategy to avoid plopping a big lump sum into the stock market only to see the market (or your particular stocks) take a dive. But it's usually not the best strategy. With dollar-cost averaging, if you receive an inheritance, a work bonus, proceeds from the sale of a house or other big infusion of cash, you take your time investing the money, spreading out purchases over regular intervals. What research actually shows is that long-term investors usually would be better off investing every dollar they intend to invest as soon as possible.

Why people tend to think dollar-cost averaging a lump sum is a good thing: If you spread out the investments, you will automatically buy relatively few shares of a stock or a fund when prices are high (because the same dollar investment buys fewer shares at high prices), and you automatically will buy relatively more shares when prices are low. And everyone knows that it's better to buy low than to buy high.

Problem with the strategy: Historically, going back decades, the stock market has gone up far more often on an annual basis—about three-quarters of the time—than it has fallen. So, other things being equal, investing evenly over many months or years actually means that you are likely to buy shares at higher and higher prices, reducing your eventual overall return. So even though you won't always be better off investing a lump sum immediately, the odds are in your favor of being better off if you do.

How to reduce the risk of lump-sum investing: Even though the odds are in your favor, it may not be best to invest an entire lump sum in stocks, which many investors do when they come into a windfall. Instead, you should apply the same allocations that you use in your overall long-term portfolio plan. For example, if your overall plan is to have 60% of your portfolio in stocks and 40% in bonds, you can split a lump-sum investment in the same manner.

Tiptoe Investing

Jonathan D. Pond, president of a Newton, Massachusetts, investment advisory firm. He has hosted 23 public television specials on personal finance advice. JonathanPond.com

Sometimes it pays to be wishy-washy if you're an investor. That goes against what investors typically think. They mistakenly believe that every financial decision has to be all-or-nothing. *Examples:* "Do I load up on a bargain-priced stock or wait for it to fall further?"..."Do I convert my traditional IRA into a Roth IRA or just leave it alone?"

But such binary thinking can be detrimental. There's a better way—one practiced by many successful professional investors. When they are faced with a difficult decision, those investors often take a small step, see how it works out, then reevaluate what the next step should be. Even Warren Buffett often tiptoes into a new holding at first, then waits until he sees a strategic advantage before he buys more.

I had a client earlier this year with $600,000 in cash to invest. He was struggling with whether to seize a risky opportunity and put the money into the cheapest part of the market—energy stocks—or stay away because it could see a lot more pain. I suggested he invest $100,000 in energy and watch the sector for the next six months. If share prices dropped, he could buy at an even lower price. If they rose, he would miss out on some gains but perhaps have a clearer idea of whether the sector was really turning around.

Another client, a woman in her early 70s, had a $750,000 traditional IRA. She talked every year about converting it to a tax-free Roth IRA to leave to her grandchildren, but the idea of paying a huge tax bill upon converting the traditional IRA seemed overwhelming. I finally convinced her to convert just $5,000 this year. Next year, if she's comfortable, we may convert $10,000 and continue to increase the amount every year. Small moves can eventually have big payoffs, especially since the Roth could continue to grow tax-free when the grandchildren inherit it.

Don't Pick a Fund Before Checking This Number (Few Investors Know About It)

Tom Roseen, head of research services for Thomson Reuters Lipper, which supplies fund analysis, ratings and research to financial institutions and wealth managers. He is based in Denver. LipperAlpha.Financial.ThomsonReuters.com

You may be choosing funds for your portfolio the wrong way. Many investors overlook one of the most useful measures of a fund's performance. The measure, called by the technical term *Sharpe ratio*, takes into account not just the raw returns that a fund has delivered but also how risky, or volatile, the fund has been in delivering those returns.

Overlooking this measure can be a big mistake. Many investors think that they can handle a lot of volatility. But when steep or frequent losses occur, they feel anxious and nervous and even might bail out of the fund when its share price is down, then miss out on the rebound when the price rises again. That is no fun and leads to terrible overall results.

Another reason to consider a fund's volatility even if you can stomach risk emotionally: When you need to generate cash by selling fund shares, the more volatile your fund is, the more likely you are to have to sell shares when the price is way down.

We asked fund analyst Tom Roseen how our readers can best use Sharpe ratios to make better fund choices...

HOW IT WORKS

By looking at Sharpe ratios, you get a much better picture of *risk-adjusted performance* rather than just raw returns. As with raw returns, higher is better with Sharpe ratios. The lower a fund's Sharpe ratio, the less impressive its returns will look to an investor who cares a lot about volatility.

The Sharpe ratio has been used by professional investors since the 1960s, when a Stanford University professor named William Sharpe—who went on to win a Nobel Prize for his economic theories—created an ingenious formula. It captured the relationship between volatility and returns in a single number.

Sharpe took a fund's returns over a given period and subtracted from that the returns you would have gotten if you instead put your money into a virtually risk-free investment—short-term US Treasuries—over the same period. He then divided that numerical result by a measure (standard deviation) of how volatile the fund had been over that period.

Because this is a ratio rather than a percentage, it looks very different from the performance figures you may be used to. The higher a fund's returns and the lower its volatility, the larger its Sharpe ratio. It's best to check the Sharpe ratio covering at least the past five years, a period that typically is varied enough between up and down markets to judge how a fund really behaves.

Over the past five years, Sharpe ratios have ranged from negative 3.0 to positive 2.0. A Sharpe ratio of 0.75 or higher is considered good, and 1.0 or higher indicates excellent returns for the amount of volatility the fund has exhibited.

A fund might rank very differently based on its Sharpe ratio than it does based on raw returns.

For example: Eventide Gilead, a mid-cap growth-stock fund, ranks in the top 2% of its category based on annualized returns of 16.9% over the five years through August 2017. But risk-adjusted performance reveals something very different. The fund's Sharpe ratio of 0.58 is below average for mid-cap growth-stock funds. That's because the fund has delivered a white-knuckle ride for shareholders. It experienced 50% more volatility than the Standard & Poor's 500 stock index.

You can find the Sharpe ratios for funds either at the websites of the fund companies or at investment research websites such as Google.com/finance and Morningstar.com…or at Funds.US.Reuters.com/US/overview.asp.

GOOD TO KNOW…

Get Free Management from a Robo-Adviser

Wealthfront.com is an investment company that will set up and oversee a $1,000 diversified portfolio of five to 10 ETFs for you based on an online questionnaire that you fill out to assess your investment goals and risk tolerance. The portfolio is "managed" by software—what the industry calls a "robo-adviser"—not by a human. But the software is quite sophisticated and should be able to keep your portfolio risk right about where you want it. There's no fee for accounts of up to $10,000 other than the underlying expense ratios of the ETFs.

Pam Krueger, CEO of WealthRamp.com, an online service that matches investors with registered financial advisers. She is a former stockbroker and was executive producer of *MoneyTrack,* which aired on PBS stations. PamKrueger.com

SMART WAYS TO USE IT

The way you use the Sharpe ratio can vary depending on your goal…

- **You can compare Sharpe ratios for various funds with similar raw returns.** *Example:* You are searching for a foreign stock fund to round out your portfolio and care a lot about reducing volatility, not just maximizing performance. You see that FMI International has a five-year Sharpe ratio of 1.58, better than the Sharpe ratio of Oberweis International Opportunities (1.46). Although the Oberweis fund's five-year annualized return of 18.4% is much higher than the 11.1% return of the FMI fund, the FMI fund was 40% less volatile. And since the FMI fund's returns rank in the top 4% of funds in its category—still impressive—it may be the better choice for you.

Caution: Keep in mind that various other factors also can be important in predicting a fund's performance—including the fund expenses, whether the current manager has created its long-term record and whether the fund has had a consistent investment style.

fees up to 0.65%. In comparison, actively managed stock fund fees average 0.7% and bond funds, 0.54%.

A Customized Portfolio

Charles Rotblut, CFA, vice president, American Association of Individual Investors, Chicago. AAII.com

When you invest in most mutual funds in a taxable account, you depend on an expert to manage the fund portfolio—leaving you with no control and with tax consequences that you share with thousands of investors. When, instead, you create your own portfolio at a brokerage, you get control and greater ability to save on taxes, but success depends on your own expertise. Neither way is ideal. Now brokerages are offering an increasingly popular alternative that features advantages of both approaches, and they are making it available to investors with as little as $25,000, compared with previous minimums as high as $1 million.

The alternative? A "separately managed account" (SMA). With SMAs, you choose the kind of portfolio you want, including what kinds of sectors, stocks and bonds you favor. Based on those preferences, an SMA specialist chooses investments—typically a few dozen. The SMA team then manages the portfolio, deciding when to buy and sell investments and trying to minimize your tax bite by balancing gains and losses.

Keep in mind that fees tend to be higher than for mutual funds, and because they are customized, SMAs don't have track records.

Examples of SMAs: Fidelity has four basic SMAs with a range of options. The lowest minimum is $50,000, and annual fees range from 0.2% to 1.1% depending on the strategy and the size of your investment. Both TD Ameritrade and E*Trade require a minimum of $25,000. Charles Schwab offers 110 strategies, ranging from foreign small-caps to "socially responsible" stocks, with a minimum for stock accounts of $100,000 and annual fees up to 1.35%...for bond accounts, $250,000 with

Misleading Fund Returns

Christine Benz, director of personal finance, Morningstar Inc., Chicago, which tracks 530,000 investment offerings. Morningstar.com

Investors are notoriously bad at choosing when to buy and sell mutual fund shares. And certain funds make it especially difficult. The volatile nature of these funds makes it more likely that you will buy shares after the fund has had an exciting run-up and is about to retreat…and sell shares when the fund has been in the doldrums but is set to rebound.

Example: As of August 2017, the Guinness Atkinson Global Innovators Fund had annualized returns of 8.6% over the past 10 years, ranking in the top 4% of its category. But many investors in the volatile fund didn't do nearly as well. The typical investor saw annualized returns of just 5.6% over that period.

Fund shareholders in general over the past decade have averaged 1.13 percentage points less in annualized returns than fund performance figures indicate.

There's a way you can identify which funds are most or least likely to foster such inopportune behavior. Look at "investor returns." This measure reflects how the typical investor in a fund has fared based on returns adjusted for the fund's asset inflows and outflows.

Example: Over the past 10 years, FPA Crescent—a fund that is nearly 40% less volatile than the overall stock market—had inves-

JUST FOR FUN...

Follow the Money

Register a dollar bill in the online database at WheresGeorge.com...write the website's URL on it...and then track its travels across the globe. This is not considered defacing the bill.

tor returns averaging 7.4%, which is greater than its overall annualized returns of 6.9%.

You can find investor returns at Morningstar.com. In general, a gap of more than one percentage point warrants further investigation into a fund's volatility.

To smooth out the ride, if you decide to invest in a very volatile fund, consider automatically buying a certain fixed dollar amount of shares each month regardless of how the stock market is doing.

---

8 Ways to Keep Financial Information Safer on Your Phone

Eva Velasquez, president and CEO of the Identity Theft Resource Center in San Diego. The nonprofit provides information about how to make online activities safer, and it offers a toll-free hotline, 888-400-5530, for victims of identity theft and those whose financial information has been compromised. Velasquez previously worked in the San Diego district attorney's office investigating white-collar crime and consumer fraud and for the Better Business Bureau. IDTheftCenter.org

---

More and more of your financial life happens right on your smartphone—and not just buying stuff on Amazon and elsewhere. Banking and brokerage apps let you check accounts...move money...pay bills...manage investments. Payment apps let you pay with your phone at stores. And then there is the financial information that could be mined from your e-mails, texts, downloaded documents and contact list. *Is it all secure?* It probably isn't.

TAKE RESPONSIBILITY

I work with victims of identity theft, and I can tell you that people often don't know how their information was compromised. It could have been a computer virus...a data breach at a company you did business with... or even someone who snooped directly on your phone transmissions. No computer—and your smartphone is a computer—will ever be impenetrable. *But there are many things you can do to make yourself safer...*

• **Create better passwords.** The front-line protection for your digital life is the collection of passwords that you use across the Internet. Make your passwords stronger. You want a longer string of characters, with symbols, numerals and upper- and lower-case letters—not the usual passwords made from the name of a pet or your child's birth date. And then you must vary your passwords—don't use the same one for multiple sites. That way if a password is compromised, it's less useful to hackers and thieves.

Of course, if you are good about varying your passwords, you will soon face a sizable challenge in remembering all of them. Keeping a list on your laptop or your phone or a yellow sticky on your computer monitor is not OK! I use a system that's going to sound complicated as I explain it—but isn't hard once you get the hang of it. Start with a phrase you'll remember but that isn't terribly common—"The dude abides," for example, from the movie *The Big Lebowski*. Capitalize each word, and substitute a symbol such as the % sign for the spaces. This is your core password phrase—in this example, The%Dude%Abides. Then you can vary your core password according to a rule that you set, such as using the first two letters of the website as a prefix and the season and year as a suffix, so you can change it multiple times a year. By this system, your password for Chase Bank could be chThe%Dude%AbidesSP2017. No one's going to break that password, and if you keep the rules of your system consistent, it's really not hard at all to keep track of it.

That said, a password manager—a phone app to store all your passwords safely—can be a good alternative. If you really can't master my memory system or the technology of a password manager app, and you resort to pen and paper, keep your password list in a locked drawer, not in an easily accessible place such as your wallet or purse.

• **Avoid public Wi-Fi.** Don't use public Wi-Fi without also using your own *virtual private network* (explained below). You should be particularly wary when public Wi-Fi doesn't require a password, but even networks that require a hotel room number or other credential are likely to have very weak security. Accessing the Internet through your cell phone service is a much safer option.

• **Avoid public charging stations.** I'm talking about the charging stations, usually plastered with advertising, that are proliferating at airports and convention sites and that provide the USB or Apple Lightning connector to plug into your phone. That's not just a charging cable—it also can be a two-way street for data. Security experts have demonstrated that public charging stations might be used to collect passwords and other information from users' phones. If you plug your own charging cable into a wall-type power outlet, you're almost certainly safe. Or buy a rechargeable external battery pack, and use that to charge your phone when you are on the go.

• **Use a virtual private network (VPN).** Many people will first encounter a VPN on devices issued by their employers for their work, but this is an option for individual consumers now, too. A VPN is a way of creating a safer network that still operates over a public Wi-Fi connection. With encryption and some other technical tricks, the VPN makes it much harder for a snoop to intercept data as it moves across the Internet. To get a VPN on your phone, you must sign up for a service, pay a small monthly fee and download an app. A VPN is especially important if you use your smartphone on an airplane, where cellphone service is unavailable and public Wi-Fi is the only option. You can find VPN services on Google Play for Android phones and in the App Store for Apple devices.

• **Update your software.** Keep your phone's operating system and individual apps up-to-date. One of the things that happens in software updates is that security flaws get fixed!

• **Choose two-factor authentication.** This is a way of authenticating your identity when you log into sensitive apps, such as for banking or brokerage accounts. It adds an extra step in which, typically, a code is texted to your phone or e-mailed and must be used in addition to your password as you log in. This adds an extra layer of security because a hacker would need to access both your password and your phone to obtain the code. Not every financial institution offers two-factor authentication, but when it's available, go for it.

• **Sign up for account activity notifications.** A growing number of banks and other financial companies have systems to notify you by text, e-mail or a phone call about activity on your account. This helps you keep track of routine things, such as automated bill payments, and allows the bank to flag suspicious activity, such as a big online purchase or a withdrawal from an ATM in an unusual city. You have to sign up for some of these notifications. Then you also have to pay attention. The point of getting messages about routine transactions is that someday one of them might be something not routine, something unauthorized, perhaps the start of a fraud. And one more thing—make sure that you keep your contact information up-to-date at all the financial companies that might legitimately need to reach you.

• **Make yourself phishing-proof.** You have no doubt heard of phishing scams—e-mails or texts that pretend to be from legitimate companies but that try to get you to follow dangerous links and reveal private information. And you can try to identify and selectively ignore them. But there's an even better way to avoid ever being the victim of phishing. Even when a communication from a company doesn't seem suspicious, my best advice is, don't click—go to the source. You already know how to reach your bank or brokerage or insurance company. If you get an e-mail or text that purports to be a warning about a problem with your account or any other matter, contact the purported sender the way you normally would. That is, go to the app or website you always use for that financial institution, or call the phone number on your credit card or statement.

Phishing scams are ever more sophisticated. I used to tell people they might spot one with visual clues such as a funky logo or bad spelling or grammar. But such tips aren't that useful anymore and can provide a false sense of security. Many texts and e-mails do a good job of looking like real communications from companies you do business with.

11

Savvy Shopping

Save More Money Every Time You Shop Online

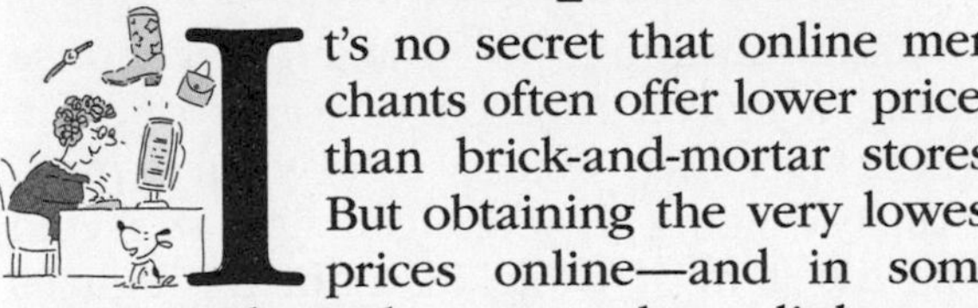

It's no secret that online merchants often offer lower prices than brick-and-mortar stores. But obtaining the very lowest prices online—and in some cases, at physical stores—takes a little extra ingenuity and some assistance, which you can get from the following helpful websites and strategies...

DISCOUNT AND COUPON SITES

These sites provide discount coupons...rebates...and/or discount codes—codes that you can use at shopping websites to obtain special deals.

• **RetailMeNot.com,** one of the best-known sites for discounts, is worth checking before you buy almost anything online, ranging from electronics to clothes to pizza. It lists tens of thousands of discount codes at any given time, plus rebates, printable coupons and various other savings opportunities, and it even indicates how likely it is that a certain discount offer will actually work on a given day. Just enter the name of the business you might buy from and/or the product you want to buy in RetailMeNot's search box to see if any relevant offers are available.

Recent examples: Save up to 20% at BarnesandNoble.com...25% off at PapaJohns.com.

• **EBates.com** enables consumers to earn cash back when they buy from any of more than 2,000 shopping sites. EBates does this by sharing the "referral fees" it gets for sending visitors from its site to the shopping sites. Before buying anything online, check whether EBates has a link to the site where you intend to buy. If so, you could earn anywhere from 1% to 40% back

Note: Prices, rates and offers throughout this chapter and book are subject to change.

David Pogue, technology critic for Yahoo Finance. He spent 13 years as the personal technology columnist for *The New York Times* and is author of *Pogue's Basics: Money—Essential Tips and Shortcuts (That No One Bothers to Tell You).* DavidPogue.com on your purchase simply by navigating to that shopping site through the EBates link. In addition to retail sites, EBates offers cash back for purchases made on many travel sites, including sites for hotel chains, car-rental firms and even some airlines. Every three months, EBates will mail you a check or deposit the cash you have earned into your PayPal account—your choice. (The payment will be deferred if you have earned less than $5.01.)

Recent examples of EBates cash back: 10% at 1-800-Flowers…6% at Macy's…4% at Thrifty Car Rental…3.5% at Red Roof Inns.

• **Coupons.com.** Not only does this site provide discount codes and rebates for online shopping, it also is the best site for obtaining hundreds of coupons to print out and use in physical stores just like coupons clipped from newspapers. You must supply your phone number to use the site, but the number is used only for verification, not for marketing calls. Other coupon websites worth trying include RedPlum.com and SmartSource.com.

Recent examples: Save $2 on a 24-can case of Pepsi…save $1 on Hefty trash bags.

AMAZON SAVINGS TRICKS

More than 300 million customers shop at Amazon.com, including more than 60 million who belong to Amazon Prime, which provides benefits ranging from free two-day shipping to streaming video content and unlimited photo storage. *Yet many customers are unaware of the best ways to save the most at the site…*

• **Share a Prime membership.** Amazon's rules allow any two adults to share a single $99 annual membership and get nearly all Prime benefits.

One catch: The two of you also must share access to the same credit/debit cards for use on the site, so share only with someone you trust.

• **Share a digital library.** If you and a friend or family member each has a separate Prime membership, you can link the two accounts and share any Kindle e-books, audiobooks and apps that you have purchased. As with shared Prime membership, you also must share access to credit/debit cards.

• **Complain your way to extra months of Prime membership.** If you are a Prime member and an item that you ordered doesn't reach you by its expected delivery date or the wrong item is shipped or you have any other problem with an Amazon purchase, politely complain about this to an Amazon.com customer service rep. There's a good chance that the rep will extend your Prime membership for an additional month or two to keep you happy. (To reach customer service, call 888-280-4331.)

• **"Clip" Amazon coupons.** Most Amazon users don't realize that there are digital coupons available on the site. These are comparable to those found in newspapers or on Coupons.com, but they can be redeemed at Amazon.com. At Amazon.com, click "Today's Deals," followed by "Coupons." Click the "Clip Coupon" button for any coupons you might want to use. The savings will be applied when you put the appropriate product in your Amazon shopping cart and make your purchase.

Recent examples: $10 off an Oral-B Pro 1000 rechargeable electric toothbrush…$2 off 18 rolls of Charmin Sensitive Toilet Paper.

• **Sign up for the Amazon Prime Rewards Visa Signature credit card or Prime Store Card.** Prime members receive 5% back when they use either of these cards to make Amazon.com purchases. The cards have no annual fee beyond the usual Prime membership fee.

• **Take advantage of Amazon Warehouse Deals.** When an Amazon customer opens a product but then returns it or when a product's packaging is damaged, Amazon.com sells the item at a big discount through its "warehouse." Savings range from 25% to 75% off the usual price. To reach Amazon's warehouse, click "Today's Deals" on Amazon.com, then select "Open Box & Used."

Similar: Amazon Outlet offers clearance, overstock and slightly imperfect new items at discounts that range from 20% to 80%. Click "Today's Deals," followed by "Outlet."

• **Use CamelCamelCamel.com to decide when to buy on Amazon.com.** Third-party website CamelCamelCamel lets you view the price history of any item Amazon stocks so that you can make your purchase when the fluctuating price is relatively low. Or choose a target price for an item, and have CamelCamelCamel send you an e-mail if and when the price drops to that level or below.

ADDITIONAL ONLINE SAVINGS

Two other online money savers…

• **Buy "refurbished" computers through manufacturers' websites.** Most people assume that "refurbished" computers are lemons that have already broken once and are likely to do so again. In reality, many items sold as refurbished on computer manufacturer websites have never been used (or were barely used) and have never experienced any problems. In some cases, an item might have been returned by an earlier buyer because the incorrect item was shipped, for example. In other cases, an item might have arrived with dented packaging.

Even if there was once a problem with a refurbished computer, these computers have been repaired and inspected. They almost always come with warranties when purchased directly from manufacturers, so if there is a problem, you probably can get it corrected at no cost (except perhaps shipping charges). Savings of 15% are common on sites including Apple.com, Dell.com and HP.com, and larger savings are possible. Look for terms such as "refurbished" or "outlet" in these sites' menus.

One recent example: A refurbished $1,200 MacBook Air was available for $950 on Apple.com.

• **Find fine-art photos for free—and have them framed for cheap.** Art photography prints sold in galleries can cost hundreds of dollars or more, and the options are limited. Instead, choose among the hundreds of millions of photos posted on Flickr.com that can be legally printed and used for free. Just enter topics or types of photos of interest—anything from cityscapes to sea horses to rusty tractors—and select "All creative commons" from the "Any license" menu to view those that can be legally used without paying royalties.

When you find a photo that you would like to hang on your wall or give as a gift, click on it, download it to your device using the download button at the lower right of the photo, then upload the file to MPix.com, a site that will print the photo, mat it and put it in an attractive frame for a very reasonable price.

5 Ways to Spend Less Online

SnagShout.com gives discounts on products from Amazon.com in return for reviews, which do not have to be positive—after you get a deal, you cannot get another until your review is posted. *AliExpress.com* lets you buy products directly from Chinese manufacturers—everything from watches and clothing to selfie sticks and toys. *Wish* and its sub-brand, *Geek,* are similar to AliExpress—Geek is exclusively for gadgets and technology. *Hollar.com* prices everything at $2 to $5, with occasional items for $1 and free shipping when you spend more than $25—its offerings include health and beauty items, school supplies and kitchen goods. *Online liquidators* resell returned, refurbished and overstock clothing, electronics, home goods and more at discounts of up to 70%—try *Blinq.com.*

Clark.com

FREEBIES…

Free Apps for Better Buying

SnipSnap lets you scan retailer and restaurant coupons and save them to your phone. For supermarket coupons and deals, try *MyGrocery Deals.* See weekly ads from nearby retailers with *Retale.* Use *Brad's Deals* to find deals on kids' shoes, electronics, school supplies, ink and toner and more. *Target Cartwheel* lets you choose the Target offers you want, save them on the app and scan your personalized bar code at checkout. With *Walmart Savings Catcher,* you scan a Walmart receipt within seven days of purchase and the app checks for lower advertised prices—and credits the difference to you on an e-gift card. *Ibotta* works with more than 300 chain retailers, pharmacies, convenience stores and more—scan bar codes of purchases, and photograph your receipts, submit everything to Ibotta, and it searches for qualifying rebates that it collects for you to withdraw later through PayPal or Venmo.

Bankrate.com

Growing Craigslist Scams

Below are three common Craigslist scams to watch out for...

Phony moving companies: Scammers entice victims with a low price, then steal their possessions.

Hijacked rental or home-purchase listings: Scammers find legitimate sales listings and create ads saying that the home is available for rent. They get victims to send them personal information and rental deposits, then make off with the money and steal people's identities.

Ticket counterfeiting: Some scammers get victims to pay for tickets that are unusable. Fake tickets often are offered for much less than market value.

Komando.com

Get Rewards for Your Opinion

Sites that offer rewards for your opinion or habits...

PointClub gives you points for taking surveys. You exchange points for gift cards. The average survey earns 200 to 2,000 points, and 1,000 points is equal to one dollar. You must sign up and enter personal information to be matched to specific surveys. *Harris Poll Online* offers survey takers a sweepstakes entry and offers reward points that can be exchanged for prizes. *VIP Voice* wants feedback on products and services you use. In return, it gives chances to win prizes such as vacations and electronics. *Nielsen Digital Voice* looks only for permission to follow what you do online—you do not answer surveys. Participants are entered into a monthly $10,000 sweepstakes drawing.

MoneyTalksNews.com

Best Deals at Walmart

Simple Furniture, Walmart's house brand, is good-quality and sold at hard-to-beat prices. *TVs* are deeply discounted if you opt for off-brands such as Vizio, Sceptre and Element. *Lego sets* cost less than at toy retailers—especially expensive sets such as Minecraft and Ghostbusters. *Sewing and craft supplies* are far less expensive than at craft and fabric stores. *Brand-name laundry detergent* can cost 10.8 cents per ounce at Walmart, compared with 12.9 cents per ounce on average elsewhere. *Photo prints* cost nine cents apiece for a four-by-six-inch photo, compared with 12 cents or more at other stores. *Beauty products* such as makeup and nail polish are well-priced. *Example:* CoverGirl LashBlast Super Size Mascara was recently $5.94 at Walmart but $7.49 at Walgreens. *Kitchen appliances* cost less than at stores such as Bed Bath & Beyond.

Roundup of experts on comparison shopping, reported at GoBankingRates.com.

Top Bargains at Dollar Stores

Toiletries, including such brands as VO5, Suave, Pantene, Colgate, Crest, Dial and others...*household tools* such as hammers and wrenches...*cleaning supplies,* including brand names such as Lysol, Palmolive and Comet... *pregnancy tests...party supplies,* including plates, napkins and plastic utensils...*reading glasses* ($1 versus $16 for reading glasses at Walgreens)...*storage containers* and organizing products of many types and in multiple sizes...*hair accessories* such as combs, brushes, scrunchies and more...*greeting cards... wrapping paper* and gift bags...*books*—both fiction and nonfiction, usually hardcovers that have been out for a year or two.

Roundup of experts on dollar-store shopping, reported at WiseBread.com.

Best Places to Buy Eyeglasses

In a recent analysis, the highest-rated seller of eyeglasses based on quality of frames and lenses, selection, care taken in fitting, employee knowledge, follow-up service and price was Costco Optical, with an average price of $184. Independent shops rated second, but the average price was high—$414 ($230 more than Costco). Third was the chain and web retailer Warby Parker, average price $141... fourth, a private doctor's office, $396...fifth, ZenniOptical.com, $69.

Consumer Reports, ConsumerReports.org.

For a Better Deal on a Diamond Ring...

Look for stones just below benchmarks for weight, color and clarity. *Example:* A 0.95-carat stone costs much less than a one-carat stone of the same quality. *Focus on cut rather than size*—diamonds with more sparkle, caused by the way they are cut, look larger. *Negotiate price*—local jewelers have plenty of room to reduce prices...national chains have less, but because their salespeople work on commission, they will be motivated to make a deal if they can. *Visit multiple stores,* from large chains to local shops, to compare offerings. *If using credit to buy a ring,* try to get store financing with 0% interest instead of using higher-cost credit card debt.

Josh Holland, spokesperson, BlueNile.com, online diamond seller, quoted in *USA Today.*

Save on Shoes

To save money when buying shoes...

Check Groupon.com—it sells some merchandise, including shoes, at closeout prices. *Subscribe to DealNews.com* for daily e-mail alerts on shoe deals from major retailers and websites. *Go to the clearance section* at Overstock.com for the biggest markdowns. *Shop at Costco or Sam's Club*—both often stock shoes and sell them at wholesale prices. *Visit online consignment stores* for discounts up to 90%. *Check eBay for sales* from official retailers. *Buy higher-quality* shoes so that you do not have to replace them as often. *Use the free Shoes-Daily Deals & Coupons app* for Android devices for alerts on the best daily deal from multiple retailers.

GoBankingRates.com

The Real Deals at Retailers

Sale and clearance price codes guide you to the "real" deals at retailers—those that are not just the result of a markup followed by a sale.

Gap: Sale prices end in 9, even lower clearance prices in 7.

JC Penney: Clearance items end in 96 or 97.

Lands' End: Reduced prices, whether sale or clearance, end in 97 or 99.

PetSmart: Clearance prices end in 7.

REI: Sale prices end in 9, clearance prices in 3.

Cheapism.com

GOOD TO KNOW...

Outdoor Gear Marketplace

Buy or sell outdoor apparel, fishing equipment, life jackets (for adults, children and dogs), mountain/road bikes and more at GearTrade.com. Both new and preowned items are offered.

Hair Products Linked to Hair Loss

Tina Sigurdson, assistant general counsel for the Environmental Working Group (EWG), a nonprofit environmental health research and advocacy organization. EWG maintains a database called Skin Deep, which offers health and safety ratings for thousands of personal-care products. Ewg.org/skindeep

More than 21,000 consumers have made complaints about WEN Cleansing Conditioners, a line of hair-care products heavily advertised on television. Many of the complaints cite significant problems such as hair loss and serious skin irritation. But despite this flood of complaints…an alert issued by the Food and Drug Administration (FDA)…and at least one class-action lawsuit, the products remain on the market. It's not clear which ingredients in the WEN conditioners may be causing the problems—which contributes to the FDA's inability to address the issue more strongly.

Hair-care and other personal-care products including cosmetics, toothpaste, mouthwash, baby wipes, baby powder, shaving cream and body wash are virtually unregulated by the government. The FDA has no authority to recall these items, and manufacturers are not required to confirm that the products are safe to use. Legislation that would increase FDA oversight of personal-care products is being considered by the Senate. But any changes are unlikely to take effect for many months.

What to do: Never assume that a product is safe because its packaging or advertising features words such as "Natural," "Healthy" or "Gentle." The use of these words is unregulated when it comes to personal-care products, so they often mean little or nothing.

Example: The makers of WEN Cleansing Conditioners have used the word "Natural" in their marketing materials even though these products contain synthetic chemicals—including at least one known to cause allergic reactions.

The Pink Tax Rip-Off

Clark Howard, host of *The Clark Howard Show,* a syndicated radio program about saving money, Clark.com, reported by Karen Larson, editor, *Bottom Line Personal.*

A recent report by New York City's Department of Consumer Affairs found that products designed for women cost 7% more on average than virtually identical products marketed to men. This pricing gap is greatest with personal-care products—women's deodorant, shampoo and conditioner tend to cost around 50% more than men's.

One solution: Skip the women's versions, when possible, and purchase men's products instead.

We asked consumer expert Clark Howard, host of *The Clark Howard Show,* a syndicated radio program, and author of *Clark Howard's Living Large for the Long Haul,* to share some other examples of how women and men can both save…

• **Clothes and shoes tend to be much cheaper in the children's section.** And if you're a man or woman of less-than-average stature, there's a good chance that the largest children's sizes will fit you just fine. Walmart stocks especially large kid's clothing.

• **Battery prices can vary depending on where you pick them up in a big-box store.** Batteries often are stocked near the toy department…in the electronics department…and by the cash registers. It is difficult to predict where they will be cheapest, but batteries shelved in checkout aisles often are priciest.

• **Prescription medications can be 50% cheaper per dose if you buy higher-dosage pills.** If you or your child is prescribed a low-dosage pill, ask your doctor if he can prescribe a higher dosage that can be split, then use a pill splitter to cut each pill in half. (*Caution:* Not all types of pills can be split safely.) With over-the-counter medications, dollar stores and deep discounters generally charge less than pharmacies.

Best Food Deals at Costco

Organic eggs—two dozen for about $1 more than what other stores charge for one dozen. *Almond butter*—about 37 cents per ounce, compared with 56 cents per ounce at Target. *Organic frozen fruit*—three pounds cost $1 less than nonorganic fruit elsewhere. *KIND bars*—buying a pack of 18 means each bar costs about 25 cents less than at Walmart. *Local honey*—about 24 cents per ounce, 50% savings over typical prices elsewhere. *Cabot Vintage Extra Sharp Cheddar*—about $10 for two pounds, half or less than half the price charged at other stores. *BarkThins*—$8 for a 17-ounce bag of these snacking chocolates, compared with $17.99 at Target. *Pumpkin pie*—a 12-inch Costco pie costs about $5 around Thanksgiving, much less than elsewhere. *Extra-virgin olive oil*—at $15 for two liters, it costs much less than at other stores.

Roundup of comparison shopping experts, reported at GoBankingRates.com plus additional research by *Bottom Line Personal.*

TAKE NOTE...

Deli Smarts

When buying sliced meat or cheese, ask if the slicing machines are cleaned every four hours. The Food and Drug Administration (FDA) recommends the four-hour cleaning frequency—but in a recent study of 298 delis in six states, only half adhered to it. Deli meats can be a source of foodborne illness from *Listeria* bacteria, and slicing machines can be a cause of bacterial cross-contamination if not cleaned frequently. Chain-owned delis and ones with more customers and more slicers were the most likely to clean the machines according to FDA recommendations. If a deli does not disassemble, clean and sanitize its slicer every four hours, go elsewhere.

Study in *Morbidity and Mortality Weekly Report*, Centers for Disease Control and Prevention, Atlanta, reported in *University of California, Berkeley Wellness Letter.*

Discount Coupons for Fresh Produce

SavingStar.com/coupons is free to join and gives cash back for items purchased from major grocery store chains...*Earthbound Farm* (EarthboundFarm.com) offers recipes and coupons when you sign up for the Organic Bound guide...*FreshExpress.com* offers coupons if you sign up for the company's newsletter...Target occasionally offers produce coupons, especially through its mobile *Cartwheel* app, Cartwheel. Target.com (*a recent example:* 25% off all produce)...*Organic Girl* (ILoveOrganicGirl.com) offers coupons and promotions when you join its e-mail list.

MoneyTalksNews.com

Better Steak Buying

Get a steak that is at least 1.25 inches thick and up to 1.75 inches—anything thinner can easily get overdone and may be less tender. Look for meat that is bright red or slightly gray if it has been dry-aged. Do not buy any steak with a film on it. Also, if you buy in bulk, ask the butcher to wrap your extra steaks in freezer paper, which has a special plastic lining to keep moisture out. Then put your wrapped steaks in a zip-top plastic bag, squeeze out all the air and freeze immediately.

Roundup of experts on steak selection, reported at GoBankingRates.com.

What Does "Dark Chocolate" Really Mean?

Which chocolates can be labeled "dark" has not yet been determined. The Food and Drug Administration (FDA) has not established rules for which ingredients must be present before a chocolate can be classified as dark. But the Cleveland Clinic says dark chocolate should contain at least 35% cocoa. Some varieties have up to 85% cocoa. The darker, the healthier. They have the largest amount of flavonoids, which are antioxidants and anti-inflammatories.

Less healthful: Milk chocolate because it contains less cocoa—and more fat and sugar.

Roundup of experts on nutrition in chocolate, reported at MoneyTalksNews.com.

The Extra-Virgin Olive Oil Hoax

Larry Olmsted, author of *Real Food, Fake Food: Why You Don't Know What You're Eating & What You Can Do About It.* Based in Hartland, Vermont, he also writes the "Great American Bites" column for *USA Today.* RealFoodFakeFood.com

The "extra-virgin olive oil" in your kitchen is probably not extra-virgin at all. To qualify as extra-virgin, olive oil is supposed to be subjected to minimal processing and be made exclusively from fresh, high-quality olives. But a highly publicized research report from the Olive Center at University of California, Davis, found that 69% of the olive oil sold as "extra-virgin" in the US does not meet those standards. The flavor of these fakes typically falls well short of the real thing. Also, a diluted or heavily processed olive oil might not provide the same cancer- and heart disease–fighting benefits of a true extra-virgin olive oil.

Producers get away with selling fake extra-virgin olive oil because the US government does little to enforce olive oil standards...and because most Americans have never tasted a true high-quality, extra-virgin olive oil, which makes it difficult to spot fakes.

What to do: Buy from trustworthy brands, such as California Olive Ranch (about $12 for a 500-ml bottle, CaliforniaOliveRanch.com)... Cobram Estate (from $12.99 for a 375-ml bottle, CobramEstate.com)...Whole Foods' 365 Everyday Value brand (from $5.99 for a 500-ml bottle)...and Oro Bailén (often $20 or more for a 500-ml bottle, OroBailen.com).

Or purchase from an importer or a distributor of high-quality olive oils, such as Oliviers & Co. (OliviersandCo.com) and Zingerman's (Zingermans.com). Alternately, you could join the Fresh-Pressed Olive Oil Club and receive three bottles of stellar olive oil four times a year ($99 per quarter for three 250-ml bottles, FreshPressedOliveOil.com).

Other good bets include any US-produced olive oil that has the "COOC" seal of the California Olive Oil Council on its label...or any Italian olive oil that says "100% Qualità Italiana." Extra-virgin olive oil produced in Australia is a reasonable choice, too—Australia enforces the world's strictest extra-virgin olive oil standards.

Note: To read research results from the University of California, Davis, go to OliveCenter.UCDavis.edu and click on "Research" and then "Reports."

13 Secrets Restaurants Don't Want You to Know

Darron Cardosa, who has more than 25 years of experience waiting tables in the New York City area. He is author of *The Bitchy Waiter: Tales, Tips & Trials from a Life in Food Service.* TheBitchyWaiter.com

Eating out means trusting strangers to prepare and handle your food. Usually that trust is well-placed—but at times, the hectic pace and financial pressures facing restaurants result in corners being cut in ways that could jeopardize your enjoyment of the meal...or even jeopardize your health. *Here, a veteran waiter shares what restaurants don't want you to know...*

FOOD QUALITY AND SAFETY

- **Seafood stew, soup and pasta "specials" often feature fish that's too old to serve any other way.** Restaurants do not like to throw away expensive ingredients. When seafood is no longer fresh enough to serve on its own, it might be chopped up and served in a stew, soup or pasta dish, where sauces and other bold flavors can be used to hide its age. This can happen with meat and poultry, too, but it's most common with seafood, which has an especially short shelf life.

Tip from the waiter: It's generally OK to order a seafood stew, soup or pasta dish if it is on the regular menu. But when these are listed as specials, the odds are high that the restaurant is trying to sell past-its-prime seafood.

• **Restaurant menus rarely are cleaned.** Responsible restaurants take cleanliness very seriously. Almost everything in the kitchen and dining room is cleaned regularly—except the menus. At most restaurants, menus are rarely, if ever, wiped down, even though they are handled by many people and occasionally dropped on the floor.

Tip from the waiter: Wash your hands after you've ordered and handed your menu back to the waiter.

• **Complimentary bread or chips might have been served to other tables before yours.** A Mexican restaurant in Michigan recently received negative press when it was caught taking chips and salsa that were not consumed at one table and serving them to a second table. That restaurant is far from alone—it is not uncommon for uneaten slices of complimentary bread to find their way onto multiple tables rather than get thrown away. And even restaurants that hold themselves to a very high standard usually send out the butter packages that accompany bread to table after table until they are used.

Tip from the waiter: It might be worth skipping complimentary premeal items such as bread and chips unless the restaurant has an open area where you can watch these items being prepared specifically for you.

• **The week following an extended power failure might be the wrong time to eat out.** Cash-strapped restaurants often cannot afford to throw away everything that was in their fridges and freezers after power outages, so ingredients may no longer be as fresh as they should be.

Tip from the waiter: If you want to eat out following a long power failure, choose a restaurant in a neighboring area that did not lose its power.

• **You might not want to eat your leftovers if you saw how they were put into to-go containers.** This task might be delegated to a busboy who has little training in hygienic food handling...or it might be done by a harried server who uses the same spoon to transfer multiple customers' partially eaten meals.

Tip from the waiter: Ask your server to bring to-go containers to your table, and then transfer your leftovers yourself.

• **Your dessert might not be fresh even if the menu says desserts are "made fresh in house every day."** Typically this means that one or two of the dessert options are made fresh each day, while others remain from earlier days.

Tip from the waiter: Before choosing a dessert, ask your server which desserts were made that day. Be leery of any dessert that features "chocolate crumble" or "chocolate crunchies" sprinkled on top. That chocolate topping might have been made by breaking apart stale chocolate cake, cookies or brownies that didn't sell in their original form.

BILLING AND SERVICE

• **Billing mistakes are common—and rarely spotted.** Servers are responsible for multiple tables at the same time—and billing mistakes are inevitable. But patrons rarely catch the mistakes, in part because roughly half of all restaurant customers do not bother to check their bills at all.

Tip from the waiter: If you do not want to take the time to check your bill closely, at least do a quick count to confirm that there are not more drinks, appetizers or entrées listed than you ordered. If at lunch, also make sure that you were charged lunch prices and not dinner prices for entrées, a particularly common billing error.

• **The last tables seated often receive less-than-stellar service—but you can be treated better.** If you walk into a restaurant shortly before its closing time, there's a good chance that both your server and the kitchen staff will be more focused on getting you out the door than on providing an enjoyable meal.

Tip from the waiter: Say something that sends a message to your server that you understand time is an issue, such as, "Don't worry, we won't order dessert"...and/or, "What can the kitchen prepare quickly?" This shows respect for the restaurant employees' priorities, greatly increasing the odds that they will show you respect in the form of a quality dining experience.

• **Chefs are sick of the gluten-free trend.** Restaurant employees usually are sympathetic when customers must make special requests because of allergies or other serious health concerns—but they hate it when they have to adjust dishes for customers who seem to be jumping on dietary fads. Gluten-free is the most prominent dietary fad at the moment, so servers and chefs might label you an annoyance if you ask to have a dish modified for a gluten-free diet—which could lead to a subpar dining experience.

Tip from the waiter: If you truly cannot consume gluten for health reasons—for example, you have celiac disease—preface your order with words to the effect of, "I know you have to deal with a lot of gluten-free requests these days, but I really am gluten-intolerant."

BEVERAGES

• **Wine sold by the glass could come from a bottle that has been open for days.** It even could come from a bottle that was originally ordered by another patron but rejected because that customer didn't like it.

Tip from the waiter: Order wine by the bottle, not by the glass, when possible. If you want only a single glass, boost the odds that it was opened recently by choosing something that's likely to be ordered often, such as the "house wine."

• **Your regular coffee actually might be decaf if closing time is near.** The regular coffeepot often is one of the first things emptied and cleaned by the restaurant staff at the end of the day. If you order a regular coffee after this has occurred, there's a good chance that you'll be given decaf with no mention of the substitution. (The reverse—receiving regular after ordering decaf—is much less common in well-run restaurants because the staff would not want to risk giving caffeine to a customer who, for example, has a heart condition.)

Tip from the waiter: If you really need a cup of regular coffee after a restaurant meal that concludes late in the evening—for example, if you're feeling drowsy and need to drive home—explain that to your waiter. He may be able to have a cup of regular coffee made for you. Or order cappuccino, which is typically made in an espresso machine one cup at a time.

• **Your water might not be as pure as you are told.** Some restaurants serve only filtered water...and some patrons pay extra for bottled water. But if there is ice in the water, that ice is almost certainly made from unfiltered tap water. Restaurant ice makers rarely have filters.

Tip from the waiter: If water purity is important to you, skip the ice.

• **Drink garnishes sometimes are germy or old.** That lemon or lime slice in your drink might have been cut hours earlier and then left to sit in an open, unrefrigerated container where numerous restaurant employees pick out pieces with their bare hands. Restaurants may have policies requiring the use of tongs for grabbing these garnishes, but rushed servers and bartenders frequently skip that.

MONEYSAVER...

Save Money at Popular Chain Restaurants

Restaurant substitutions that save you money or give you more for what you spend...

At McDonald's, instead of a Big Mac, order a McDouble with no ketchup—but with lettuce, onion, pickles and secret sauce. It is essentially the same sandwich as a Big Mac except for the extra bread in the middle, but average cost is only $1.39 rather than $3.99. *At Chipotle,* order a half order of two kinds of meat instead of a single meat, and both bean types instead of pinto or black beans alone—this typically ends up being larger. *At Starbucks,* ask for half ice in your iced coffee to get more coffee, and skip its bottled water. The free ice water it offers is triple-filtered.

WiseBread.com

Tip from the waiter: Tell your server to "hold the lemon" when you order a drink.

Menu Deceptions

Don't waste money at restaurants by buying these menu items—their descriptions typically are deceptive.

Kobe beef: Real Kobe beef is sold at only nine US restaurants (and they each prominently display a certification plaque) and costs more than $20 per ounce.

Red snapper: 38% of restaurants—and 74% of sushi places—mislabel seafood, with red snapper the most likely fish to be mislabeled. In one study, only seven of 120 fish labeled as red snapper were what they claimed to be.

Truffle oil: European white truffles cost $3,600 per pound. The vast majority of truffle oil is made from oils and chemical compounds intended to taste like truffles.

Larry Olmsted, author of *Real Food/Fake Food,* writing at Eater.com.

Restaurants Often Keep Their Beef Grades a Secret

In a study of 17 national restaurant chains, 80% did not disclose the grade of beef for some or all of their steaks. The only chains that disclosed the grade of beef for all their steaks were Applebee's, Sizzler and TGI Friday's. Only Applebee's integrated the grade disclosure into every steak's description.

Self-defense: If a steak's grade is not disclosed on the menu, ask the chef or manager for it—the highest grade is prime, followed by choice or select. Higher grades of meat are more tender, flavorful and juicy. However, tasty steaks can be made from any grade of beef—check online reviews for recommendations of what to order at specific restaurants.

ConsumerWorld.org

Where to Buy/Sell Gift Cards

Buy gift cards at a discount or sell unwanted ones (including e-cards) to people who can use them through websites set up as gift-card clearinghouses. *Raise* (Raise.com) enables users to list cards and to have money from selling them deposited directly into their bank accounts. *Cardpool* (Cardpool.com) is similar but pays via an Amazon eGift Card or by sending users checks. *Zeek* (Zeek.me), based in London, advertises discounts of up to 25% and says 90% of cards listed at its site sell within 24 hours. Zeek has mostly British retailers but also features some from the US.

Experts on gift cards, reported at MarketWatch.com.

Little-Known Cell Phone Insurance Facts

If you want cell phone insurance, you usually can buy it for a lower price directly from a third party, such as Asurion or SquareTrade, rather than from your carrier.

Example: A two-year insurance plan from Sprint costs $312, compared with $149 from SquareTrade—a savings of $163.

If you make a claim, you may not get the same phone as a replacement—it could be a different color or type and might not be new.

USA Today, USAToday.com.

Smartphones That Offer the Best Battery Life

The following smartphones have the best battery life…

Motorola Droid Turbo…Motorola Droid Turbo 2…Samsung Galaxy Note 4…Samsung Galaxy S5…Samsung Galaxy S6.

These smartphones each boast 24 or more hours of talk time, except for the Samsung Galaxy S5, which gets about 20 hours of talk time. A bonus feature of the Samsung Galaxy Note 4 and Samsung Galaxy S5 is that they have removable batteries, so you can carry a spare battery if you expect to need extra power.

To get longer battery life from all smartphones: Set the screen brightness to Auto…lower the baseline brightness…set the screen to sleep after 15 to 30 seconds without activity…turn on airplane mode when you are in an area with no signal…reduce the frequency of updates for e-mail, social-network feeds and other apps to once per hour.

ConsumerReports.org

GOOD TO KNOW…

Better Way to Charge Your Smartphone

Avoid repeatedly charging your smartphone overnight when the battery is near empty. Although your phone automatically shuts off the current once the lithium-ion battery is fully charged to prevent overheating, each charge cycle from 0% or near-0% to 100% reduces battery life span.

Better: Charge your battery in small bursts whenever you get a chance. Optimally, you want to keep levels between 50% and 80%.

Shane Broesky, CEO of Färbe Technik, a global manufacturer of portable electronics and phone accessories, Kelowna, British Columbia.

Buy a Computer with Money from a 529 Plan

To use money from a 529 college-savings plan to purchase a computer, the computer must be for a student enrolled at an eligible college, and he/she must be the primary user. Software and Internet access can be paid for through 529 plans as well. But the plans may not be used for equipment for high school students and probably not for students who are in a gap year between high school and college.

Detroit Free Press, Freep.com.

Sports Channels Drive Up Cable Bills

Sports channels are the main reason for high cable bills. More than $18 of an average $103/month cable bill goes to sports networks, such as ESPN and FoxSports. In areas where there are extra charges for seeing local sports teams, the monthly cost of sports is $20 to $25. Cable bills rose 39% from 2011 to 2015, eight times the rate of inflation, and the huge costs of sports programming are expected to drive bills even higher in coming years.

If you don't watch sports: Consider switching to a cable bundle that excludes sports channels or to on-demand streaming from sources such as Hulu, Netflix or Amazon Prime.

Time.com

Save Money on a Gym Membership

Roundup of experts on gym memberships, reported at Cosmopolitan.com.

There are numerous ways that you can save money on your gym membership cost. *See below…*

- **Compare gym prices close to home and work.**

- **Request the best possible rate**—check whether the gym is running any online promotions, and ask whether further discounts will be offered later in the month. Even if there are no discounts provided, you can request one if you are a student, teacher or civil servant...or can explain why you are on a tight budget and would appreciate some help.
- **Find out if there are off-peak rates** available if you use the gym at less crowded times.
- **Sign up for free trials** at all gyms you are considering.
- **If you intend to use only specific equipment**—just the treadmills, for example—ask if you can get a lower price.
- **If you have the money, offer to pay for a full year up-front** in return for a discount.
- **Consider joining with other people**—many gyms offer group discounts.
- **Find out if your employer or insurance plan has negotiated discounted rates** at specific gyms.

How to Prevent Common Garage Sale Swindles

Theft of cash—don't use a cash box...instead use a fanny pack or an apron with pockets so that money stays close to you. *Counterfeit money*—buy a counterfeit-detection pen for $5, or don't accept large-denomination bills. *Distraction scams* in which large groups of people show up at once or shoppers bring a child and ask for help putting purchases in a car. To avoid this, have friends or family members help with your sale. *Big-item scams* in which shoppers put small items in larger ones—inspect items that have pockets or drawers before selling them. *In-your-home scams*—shoppers ask to go inside to try on an item or use the bathroom, then steal the item or check out your home to break in later. Keep your house locked and off limits.

NJ.com

Moving Company Traps and Hidden Costs

Estimates for moving made over the phone are likely to be inaccurate and may even be scams—have movers visit your home, and get estimates from at least three companies. *Additional fees* can raise costs—for instance, packing and unpacking, temporary warehousing and specific-date delivery. *Movers that insist on a deposit* probably are scammers—up-front payments may disappear. *Cardboard boxes*—save by getting them for free from liquor stores and other retailers or look for giveaways on Craigslist. *Moving permits* may be required to park the moving van. Check the website of the city you're moving to. *Full-value coverage* can be costly, but it requires movers to pay replacement value for lost or damaged goods. *Hidden costs of renting a truck* to move on your own—these can include gas, charges per mile driven, damage coverage and supplies such as furniture pads.

Experts on moving, reported at GoBankingRates.com.

10 Least-Expensive Purebred Dogs

The 10 least-expensive pure-bred dog breeds to own, based on purchase cost, grooming expense and potential minimum health-care costs—Harrier, $300 to buy, $27 for grooming, $1,500 for health care...rat terrier, $350, $25 and $1,500...black-and-tan coonhound, $350, $27 and $1,500...plot hound, $275, $31 and $3,000...Parson Russell (Jack Russell) terrier, $400, $25 and $2,800...American foxhound, $475, $27 and $1,500...miniature pinscher, $500, $25 and $2,500...Treeing Walker coonhound, $500, $31 and $1,500...English setter, $350, $40 and $3,900...pug, $350, $27 and $9,600.

More information: GoBankingRates.com, and search for "Least Expensive Dog Breeds."

GoBankingRates.com

Save on Pet Meds

Don't pay extra for pet medicines from your vet—the markups can be more than 100%. If your pet is taking a medication that also is prescribed to humans, as is often the case, you might be able to have the prescription filled inexpensively at a chain drugstore, supermarket pharmacy or big-box retailer. To locate free or discounted programs for vaccines, spaying and neutering, microchip implants and pet supplies, go to HumaneSociety.org and type "afford" in the search box.

Consumer Reports, ConsumerReports.org.

To Cancel Recurring Charges...

You can easily cancel unwanted recurring charges with free apps from start-ups such as Trim and Truebill. They summarize your regular subscriptions and recurring payments and give you an update each month. You get an alert if a recurring cost rises or falls or a new one appears. To get rid of a charge you no longer want, let the service know through the app. The service will get in touch with the company and process a cancellation.

More information: AskTrim.com...Truebill.com.

Kiplinger's Personal Finance, Kiplinger.com.

TAKE NOTE...

For Better Customer Service When Calling Fails...

Here's a shrewd way to get helpful customer service when phoning doesn't work...

Check online forums where a company's employees and customers address issues such as how to change a service contract or get a charge removed. (To find a forum, look under "Help" on the company website or enter the company's name into a search engine with the words "forum" and "customer.") Some forums allow you to send a question to an employee.

Example: One Comcast customer recently saved $2,000 by scaling down a service plan at Comcast/Xfinity (Forums.Xfinity.com).

Edgar Dworsky, founder of the consumer websites ConsumerWorld.org and MousePrint.org

Help an Elderly Parent Stop Unwanted Mail

Help an elderly parent or other relative stop unsolicited mail. You can opt out of most of it at DMAChoice.org, a website run by the Direct Marketing Association. However, if the relative has donated to a charity or purchased something from a company, you must contact the charity/company directly. If that is impractical, have your relative's mail diverted to you so that you can sort through it, throw out everything unwanted and give your relative only important letters and bills.

WCPO.com, an ABC affiliate in Cincinnati.

12

Richer Retirement

Surprise! Retirement Costs Less Than You Think

It's easy to wildly miscalculate how much money you'll need in retirement—even if you are already retired. And that can have major consequences.

Underestimate what you will need, and you might retire too soon...and/or run out of money in your retirement years.

Overestimate, and you might keep working longer than is necessary...and/or unnecessarily deprive yourself of trips, restaurant meals and other enjoyable endeavors.

We recently consulted with retirement-planning professor Michael Finke, PhD, CFP, to learn how we all can do a much better job with calculating our own personalized retirement-spending needs...

FORGET THE 80% RULE

Many financial advisers suggest that in retirement, you will need to replace 80% of the gross income you earned in your final years of work. That means, for example, that if your work earned you $100,000 a year before taxes, you'd need annual income of $80,000 in retirement to avoid cutting back on your lifestyle.

But after looking at thousands of retirees' spending patterns, my research suggests that retirees are able to maintain the same lifestyle as in their working years with even less than 80%. In fact, they actually spend an average of 60% of their last working year's gross income in the first few years of retirement, although that percentage varies widely depending on

Note: Rates, prices and offers throughout this chapter and book are subject to change.

Michael Finke, PhD, CFP, professor and director of retirement planning and living in the personal financial-planning department at Texas Tech University, Lubbock. *Investment Advisor* magazine has named Finke one of the 25 most influential people in the investment-advising industry. TTU.edu income, ranging from 40% for people with very high incomes to 100% for those with very low incomes.

What's more, traditional guidelines assume that overall retirement expenses remain fixed every year or even rise due to increasing medical expenses. They don't necessarily do that. Typically the percentage of preretirement income that is spent each year in retirement starts to decline steadily by about one percentage point each year. In fact, by the time most retirees hit their mid-70s, increasing physical limitations cause average spending to start falling by two percentage points a year. My research found that by age 85, overall expenses tend to be nearly one-third less than when people first retired.

Note: Medical expenses can ruin the above scenario. For relatively healthy people, medical expenses do rise, but they are naturally offset by lower spending in the rest of the budget. For most retirees, average annual health-care expenses aren't more than their health insurance costs before retirement. A small percentage of Americans, however, will pay exorbitant costs for extended nursing-home care.

FOCUS ON YOUR SPENDING

The best way to estimate your future retirement spending is not to look at your income, but at how much you actually *spend* in the year or two before you retire. This sounds straightforward, but my research has shown that many people actually have a poor idea of how much they spend and what they spend it on. *A detailed spending analysis isn't that hard to do…*

STEP 1: **Add up your essential spending.** This includes "must-haves" that you have to pay monthly or on a regular basis, such as groceries, insurance premiums, housing, transportation, property taxes and utilities. Also include essential expenses that may not occur on a regular schedule, such as clothing…medical deductibles and co-pays…and home- and car-repair bills.

STEP 2: **Total your discretionary spending.** These include nonessential expenses ranging from cable-TV bills and gym memberships to restaurant meals, gifts and vacations.

Helpful: Technology can make it easier to monitor all expenses. For example, I try to make all my purchases with a single credit card that provides a tally of annual spending by category at the end of each year. You also can use a free online service such as Mint.com to track and aggregate your credit card and bank transactions automatically.

STEP 3: **Adjust estimates of future expenses that are likely to decrease or disappear in retirement.** These may include business clothing…mortgage payments if your house is paid off…educational costs for children…changes in lifestyle such as downsizing to just one automobile or moving to a state with no income tax. Talk to your accountant to check whether you will be in a lower tax bracket when you stop working. If you elect to start taking Social Security benefits, no more than 85% of those benefits are taxable. You also get a higher standard deduction on your tax return starting at age 65.

STEP 4: **Adjust estimates of costs likely to rise in retirement.** These include additional travel and entertainment costs in your initial years of retirement and health-care expenses.

HEALTH-CARE COSTS

On average, a 65-year-old woman is likely to live until 87 and spend $130,000 on health care. That figure includes premiums, co-pays, deductibles and out-of-pocket expenses that Medicare doesn't cover. A 65-year-old man is likely to live to 85 and spend $115,000 on health care. But medical costs are unpredictable. The best way I have found to work around this unpredictability is to start with what you currently spend on health care annually. Or if that figure has fluctuated greatly, take the average you have spent over the past five years. If you already have complex medical problems, consider reviewing your future health-care expenses with a financial planner. *Common mistakes I see individuals make…*

MISTAKE: **Overestimating how much will be covered by Medicare.** You might assume that when you turn 65, your health-care costs are covered. But Medicare pays for only 62% of recipients' total health-care costs, on average. Out-of-pocket expenses include Medicare co-payments and deductibles, premiums on supplemental policies such as drug coverage and items not covered, such as dentures, hearing aids and eyeglasses. Also, if you plan to retire early, you will have to pay for private health-care insurance until you reach age 65 and become eligible for Medicare.

***MISTAKE:* Underestimating health-care inflation.** Medical costs are rising more quickly than the cost of most other consumer goods. Plan on 4.5% annual inflation.

***MISTAKE:* Not factoring in the possibility of long-term care,** which Medicare generally does not pay for. The average stay in a nursing home is three years at a median annual cost today of $92,378 for a private room. It's important to see how the costs might affect your retirement spending and whether you should consider long-term-care insurance.

The Classic 4% Rule Can Ruin Your Retirement

Michael Finke, PhD, CFP, professor and director of retirement planning and living at Texas Tech University, Lubbock. TTU.edu

There's a simple old rule to help make sure you don't run out of money in your retirement years—withdraw 4% of your investment portfolio in the first year of retirement, then increase the dollar amount each year by the previous year's rate of inflation. Based on market history, that gives you a 96% likelihood that the money will last 30 years. The problem is that the 4% rule is no longer dependable. That's because, after having experienced long bull markets, bond and stock returns are likely to be lower than historical averages over the next several years.

In late 1994, when the 4% rule was popularized, the yield on a 10-year Treasury bill—a key benchmark for interest rates—was nearly 8%, compared with less than 2% in August 2017. If yields remain near their current low levels for the next 30 years, the likely failure

TAKE NOTE...

Retirement-Planning Calculators

Online retirement-planning calculators ask you a variety of financial, lifestyle and health questions, then estimate how much you might need to save, spend and invest to afford the lifestyle you want and not run out of money. *My favorite calculators...*

•**AARP Health Care Costs Calculator** estimates your health-care costs based on a database of $136 billion in actual retiree insurance health-care claims. The calculator shows how your potential costs in retirement might change depending on specific factors such as what age you retire and 82 specific medical conditions. Graphs show how your total health-care costs might vary year by year, plus how much Medicare is likely to cover and what you may need to pay out-of-pocket. AARP.org/hccc

•**AARP Long Term Care Calculator** allows you to compare types of care services in your area and their costs, including nursing homes, assisted-living facilities and home health aides. AARP.org (click the magnifying glass, then type in "Long Term Care Calculator")

•**BlackRock Retirement Expense Worksheet** lets you list and track dozens of essential and discretionary expenses on an interactive PDF. BlackRock.com (search for "Retirement Expense Worksheet")

•**T. Rowe Price Retirement Income Calculator** helps preretirees figure out how to meet retirement spending needs...and if you already are retired, it helps you determine whether your current level of spending is sustainable. It also helps you choose suitable investments. I like its extensive use of visually rich and easy-to-understand graphics and pie charts. www3.TRowePrice.com/ric/ricweb/public/ric.do

Walter Updegrave, founder, RealDealRetirement.com, which provides retirement-planning advice. For nearly three decades, he worked as an editor at *Money* magazine and wrote the popular "Ask the Expert" column.

rate of a portfolio following the 4% rule would be 57%, not 4%.

And even if five years from now yields are back up to historical averages, the likely failure rate still would be a worrisome 18%. A relatively weak stock market also will hurt returns.

Two alternative strategies...

Based on a 50% stocks/50% bonds portfolio, you withdraw 4% the first year, but in subsequent years, don't increase the withdrawal amount if the portfolio has lost money in the previous year. This may require that you cut back on your discretionary spending after any losing years.

Or, instead, to determine how much to withdraw from all your assets every year during retirement, use the same formula that the IRS uses to determine the required minimum distributions (or RMDs) that you must make from your IRAs starting at age 70½. Each year, you calculate the maximum amount you can withdraw to make your money last the rest of your life based on your current life expectancy at that age and your portfolio's current value. You can find the formula to do this, including life-expectancy tables, at IRS.gov/publications/p590b.

How to Never Run Out of Money...and Still Enjoy Life

Jeff Yeager, author of four popular books on frugal living including, *How to Retire the Cheapskate Way*. He is also AARP's official "Savings Expert."

Comedian Henny Youngman used to tell a story about meeting with his advisers to discuss his finances and retirement prospects. What Youngman said he told his advisers is, "I've got all the money I'll ever need...if I die by four o'clock."

But the prospect of running out of money in retirement is no laughing matter. For my book *How to Retire the Cheapskate Way*, I asked more than 100 happily retired frugal folks how they planned for and manage their finances in retirement to avoid running short. *Here are their winning strategies...*

• **Test-drive your retirement budget.** Many people wait until they are on the cusp of retirement—or even fully retired—before they crunch the numbers and put in place a realistic household budget based on the actual income they will have to work with in retirement. As a result, their lifestyles often change abruptly as the effect of less income takes hold. Then their newly minted budgets are quickly shelved as they return to their previous spending patterns—a move that can quickly drain their resources.

In contrast, the successfully retired people I spoke with often "test-drove" their retirement budgets in the years leading up to retirement, experiencing what it would be like to live on their projected retirement incomes. This allowed them to more gradually adjust their spending. Sometimes, as a result of the test-drive, they even decided that they needed to postpone retirement, and when they did finally retire, their lifestyles changed very little, making it much easier for them to stick to their budgets.

• **Fix your expenses to fit your fixed income.** Speaking of retirement budgets, the safest model to avoid running out of money during retirement is pretty straightforward. If you can limit your *fixed expenses*—the true necessities of life, including food, housing and health care—so that your guaranteed or fixed income (such as Social Security and any pensions or annuity income) will at least cover those expenses, you should be OK even in the worst-case scenario. Assuming that you have other, variable income (such as income from an investment account or from working part-time), then that can be allocated for your variable expenses—the "wants" as opposed to the "needs" in your life—or put back into savings. You might ask, *Aren't regular withdrawals from an IRA and other investments also fixed income?* If the assets are invested in a no-risk or very low-risk portfolio and the withdrawal rate is ultraconservative based on your potential life span, then perhaps it's safe to consider that income "fixed." But otherwise, plan for the absolute worst-case scenario and assume that those funds might not always be available. For people who have lots of money (even millions) in higher-risk investments and think that those investments afford them the ability to splurge on housing, food and other fixed expenses—be careful! You are safe only as long as you move enough money into low-risk investments to cover these splurges. (Obviously if there's any chance that your combined fixed income and variable income may not cover even your fixed expenses, you have a problem and should consider postponing retirement and/or downsizing your spending to fit within your income.)

• **Don't count on Social Security alone—** but don't count it out, either. It's important to know that Social Security was never intended to be the sole source of income for a comfortable retirement. In fact, the system was designed to replace only 30% to 40% of most recipients' preretirement income. With the average monthly Social Security retirement benefit at $1,370 in 2017, you'll be living only a little above the official US poverty threshold if that's your sole source of income. This is why it's important to have a pension, 401(k), IRA or other supplemental income before retiring. That said, at the other end of the spectrum, a lot of people planning for retirement—particularly younger individuals—discount Social Security entirely, buying into the common myth that our Social Security system is nearing extinction. While the issues are complicated and Social Security does face a number of financial challenges, they are not as serious or insurmountable as many people seem to believe. Benefits may be reduced and/or the qualifying ages to receive benefits may be extended by lawmakers, but I'm among the many who strongly believe that if you're old enough to be reading this article today, you still can count on a not insignificant level of Social Security support by the time you retire.

Check out the Social Security Administration's user-friendly website (SSA.gov) for the latest news on the program and to calculate exactly what your benefits will be under different retirement scenarios. While you should never plan to retire on Social Security alone, you should plan to have it and work to reduce expenses so that you can stretch it to at least cover routine monthly bills.

• **Retire your debt before you retire yourself.** This is a tough concept for many would-be retirees to accept, and some financial advisers beg to differ, at least with regard to paying off home mortgage debt. But my happily retired "cheapskates" take a hard-line approach on the issue of debt, insisting that you should retire all of your debt—including your home mortgage—before you stop working. Once you're debt-free, you can use the money you would otherwise spend on interest for other things in retirement and you've also safeguarded your other assets against creditors (since you have no creditors). In fact, most frugal retirees I interviewed were successful in fully paying off their debts before they retired even if it meant postponing retirement or selling off other assets in order to do so.

• **Medicare is wonderful, but never underestimate health-care costs.** Under current policies, most Americans turning 65 today qualify for Medicare health-care coverage, and that really is an extremely valuable benefit you've earned and need to understand (visit Medicare.gov). So breathe a sigh of relief once you've qualified for Medicare—but don't for a minute think that your health-care-cost worries are over. In fact, Fidelity Benefits Consulting estimates that a couple retiring these days will spend an average of $260,000 of their own money on premiums, deductibles and other out-of-pocket health-care costs in retirement. Talk about a retirement nest egg buster! Buying an appropriate Medicare supplement insurance policy ("Medigap"), which covers some of the costs not covered by Medicare, is worth it to hedge your bets. There are up to 10 different types of Medigap plans (depending on your state). When choosing, you should factor in your projected health, lifestyle, risk tolerance, ability to pay and other factors. For help with all that, search for "Choosing a Medigap Policy" at Medicare.gov. And if you can afford it, consider long-term-care insurance, which can cover nursing home costs.

• **Stay active...and keep earning.** Staying active in retirement not only increases quality of life, but it can help keep you healthy and reduce your medical costs. And it also can supplement your retirement income if, like an increasing number of Americans, you choose to work part-time during retirement. A Gallup poll found that about 60% of Americans say they intend to work part-time during at least a portion of their retirement years, and most of them are choosing to do so primarily to stay active, not just to supplement their income. A common scenario for many of my frugal retirees who are under full retirement age is to work at least enough to generate the $16,920 they are allowed to earn annually under current law without reducing the Social Security benefits they are drawing at the same time (once they reach full retirement age, there's no reduction in benefits regardless of their earnings from a job or self-employment).

That's smart. Beyond that annual earning threshold, you still will continue to receive Social Security benefits at a reduced rate. So if you truly enjoy your part-time work, go ahead and earn more—that's smart, too!

• **Practice income procrastination.** As a cheapskate, I've always been a proponent of "spending procrastination"—putting off buying something today when you can just as well buy it tomorrow instead. In my opinion, that's good advice for anyone of any age, but in retirement, "income procrastination" also is an important concept worth considering. The idea is to delay as long as possible drawing on the funding sources you have available to you in retirement (such as Social Security, an IRA or a 401(k) account, reverse mortgage, etc.), both to ensure that you don't outlive your resources and to allow those resources to continue to increase in value as long as possible. For example, if you postpone drawing Social Security retirement benefits until age 70, under current policies your monthly benefit check will be 32% more than it would be if you started collecting at 66. Of course, most retirement accounts do have required minimum distributions (RMDs) starting at age 70½—but while you have to withdraw a certain amount of money from these accounts starting at that age, you don't have to spend that money right away! According to the Society of Actuaries, more than half of preretirees underestimate how long they are going to live. Hopefully you'll be one of the lucky ones who outlives your own prediction—and spends wisely in the meantime.

Retirement Income for Life—A New Way to Get It

Michael Finke, PhD, CFP, professor and director of retirement planning and living at Texas Tech University, Lubbock. TTU.edu

---

Do you think you'll live past 85? If so, there's a surprisingly attractive type of investment you can make now that starts paying off big once you reach that age—and never stops as long as you live. And thanks to a new twist, you can easily dip into your retirement accounts to fund it.

Don't be scared off by its name. It's called a *Qualified Longevity Annuity Contract*, or QLAC for short. And don't be frightened by the fact that it's an annuity—even though there are many types of annuities that have bad reputations and should be shunned. Unlike many of those annuities, which can be very complex and charge high annual fees, QLACs are easy to understand and have no annual fees. And your payout amount is fixed and guaranteed, unlike with some annuities that are linked to the performance of stocks.

For many people, a QLAC is the best way to guarantee that they won't run out of money if they live past age 85. And it has big tax advantages (see below).

How a QLAC typically works: You hand over a lump sum of money, which can come from a taxable account or a retirement account such as a traditional IRA or 401(k), to an insurance company that provides the annuity. You don't get anything back at first. But once you turn 85, the insurer starts paying you a guaranteed fixed monthly amount. This amount will depend on your age when you purchased the annuity, how much money you paid, your gender (women will receive a lower monthly amount than men because they tend to live longer) and how high interest rates were when you bought the QLAC.

The payments typically are a lot bigger than what you could earn from a long-term bond portfolio you might invest in on your own.

THE NEW DIFFERENCE

In the past, there was a serious drawback to longevity annuities for people who had most of their money tucked away in retirement accounts. That was because upon turning age 70½, all investors in traditional IRAs, 401(k)s and some other accounts are required to begin taking required minimum distributions (RMDs) from those accounts—but if a big chunk of the money in those accounts was tied up in a longevity annuity, these people might not be able to withdraw enough to meet the RMD requirement. The result would be substantial penalties.

New solution: In 2014, the IRS approved a twist on the longevity annuity and called it a QLAC, which too many investors still are not taking advantage of. With this type of longevity annuity, you don't have to start meeting RMD requirements from the portion of the account devoted to the QLAC until age 85, when you will start receiving payouts from the annuity. Even better, the payouts themselves are deemed to fulfill the RMD requirements for the invested amount. (Some investors buy QLACs that start paying out at a younger age, but that is uncommon because it diminishes the size of the payouts and the advantage of delaying RMDs.) Only a limited amount of money can be used to buy QLACs—a total up to 25% of the value of all your retirement accounts or up to $125,000, whichever is less.

KEY ADVANTAGES

Because you are not taking RMDs for all those years between age 70½ and 85, you are not paying taxes on those RMDs. You also benefit from what insurance companies call "mortality pooling," which means that the monthly payout amount that the QLAC offers reflects, in part, the money that the insurer won't have to pay out to QLAC holders who die before age 85.

Example of how much a QLAC might pay out: A 65-year-old man who buys a $125,000 QLAC today can expect to receive about $60,000 in income each year starting at age 85 and then as long as he lives. In comparison, if he invested in a portfolio of 20-year AAA-rated corporate bonds at age 65 and wanted to re-create the same payouts from age 85 to 100, he would have to start out with a $304,000 investment, not $125,000 (thus costing $179,000 more), assuming a 4% interest rate. Since women live longer, a 65-year-old woman who pays $125,000 for a QLAC today would get $50,000 of annual income.

WHO SHOULD *NOT* BUY A QLAC

QLACs probably won't work for you if one or more of the following applies...

- **Because of your health and/or family history,** you don't expect to live much past age 85. (Go to the life-expectancy calculator at SSA.gov to determine how long you are likely to live.) If you die before age 85, your heirs get nothing from a QLAC unless you bought a "return-of-premium" death benefit guarantee (see below under strategies).
- **Your assets total enough that you are sure you will have sufficient money to live on no matter how long you live.** In that case, buying a QLAC would not make sense because you don't need the guaranteed income.
- **Your assets total so little that you are likely to exhaust them before the age of 85.** In that case, buying a QLAC would not make sense because you need the money to live on.

Important: Even if you will have plenty of income from such sources as pensions and Social Security, be sure not to invest so much in a QLAC that you are not able to also maintain a sufficient emergency cash fund.

STRATEGIES FOR BUYING A QLAC

Ways to get the most out of a QLAC...

- **Buy only from a major, highly rated insurance company.** Check quotes for QLACs from various insurers at ImmediateAnnuities.com. Check that insurers' credit ratings are A+ or better at AMBest.com or StandardandPoors.com. However, if an insurer runs into financial problems and is unable to meet its QLAC payouts, each state has an insurance guarantee fund that takes over the obligation but is subject to coverage limitations. *Example:* Florida pays out a maximum of $300,000.

• **Calculate how much a QLAC will cost and end up paying out based on a purchase at different ages.** You can do this calculation at ImmediateAnnuities.com for various annuity providers. The younger you are, the cheaper it is to get a QLAC that offers a certain level of income starting at age 85. *Example:* If a 65-year-old man wants guaranteed income of about $35,000 a year, he must pay about $70,000 for a QLAC now. A 70-year-old man would have to pay $82,750 to obtain the same income.

Because it is likely that long-term rates will rise, it may make sense to spread QLAC purchases over several years, perhaps buying one per year over four years. That's because higher rates when you buy a QLAC mean higher payouts.

• **Consider adding riders to your QLAC,** but keep in mind that riders will reduce your eventual payouts. *Common riders...*

Cost-of-living-adjustment (COLA) rider: This adjusts payouts starting in the second year. The rider generally pays for itself within five to eight years after payouts begin, depending on how high inflation is.

Return-of-premium rider: With this, your spouse and other heirs receive the initial amount you invested in the QLAC if you die before you get any payouts. For couples, I often suggest that both spouses get a QLAC, if they can afford to, likely making this rider unnecessary. Costs vary widely.

DID YOU KNOW THAT...

More Senior Couples Are Opting to Live Together

More US seniors are living together instead of getting married.

Reasons: Retaining Social Security benefits from an earlier marriage...being sure children and grandchildren remain your sole heirs...not wanting to be tied down later in life.

US Census Bureau statistics, reported at Money.com.

What You Don't Know About IRAs Could Hurt You

Bob Carlson, editor of the monthly newsletter *Retirement Watch*. He is a managing member of Carlson Wealth Advisors, LLC, Centreville, Virginia, and chairman of the board of trustees of the Fairfax County (Virginia) Employees' Retirement System. RetirementWatch.com

Do you know all you need to know about your IRA? You probably don't. That's because getting the most out of these tremendously popular retirement accounts—and avoiding traps that can cost you money—doesn't just depend on which investments you choose and how much you contribute. It also requires that you follow some little-known rules that affect whether you can withdraw assets without penalty...how protected your money will be from creditors...and how much in taxes you eventually will pay.

We asked retirement-investing expert Bob Carlson to describe the most surprising things most individuals don't know about IRAs and how you can use that information to your best advantage...

AVOIDING WITHDRAWAL PENALTIES

You may know that most advisers recommend not tapping money in a traditional IRA before age 59½, in part because you might incur a 10% penalty on the withdrawn amount. But it is possible to avoid the penalty in certain circumstances. *Examples...*

• **You agree to withdraw all the funds in your IRA in "substantially equal periodic payments," known as SEPP payments.** You must spread out the withdrawals over at least five years or until you turn 59½, whichever time period is longer. For more information, search for "SEPP payments" at IRS.gov.

• **You use withdrawn IRA assets to pay unreimbursed medical expenses for yourself and/or your family that are in excess of 10% of your adjusted gross income (AGI).** In that case, there is no penalty.

• **You become permanently disabled—meaning that you are unable to perform any substantially gainful employment.** In that case, you can use the withdrawals for any purpose without penalty, but your withdrawals will be taxed as income.

SEPARATING IRAs

You generally can split up a traditional IRA into separate IRAs without tax consequences. This goes against conventional wisdom, which says that if you have several IRAs of the same type (such as IRAs rolled over from 401(k)s ...or inherited IRAs), you should combine them into a single IRA to make it easier to manage investments and to calculate required minimum distributions (RMDs) starting when you turn 70½. But in some cases, having *more* IRAs is preferable. *Examples...*

- **If you have several beneficiaries, you may want to split a large IRA into separate ones for each beneficiary.** This would make it easier to choose and pass on particular investments for each beneficiary based on such factors as the beneficiary's age, income and financial needs. For instance, you might want to leave one child a rental property and another one dividend-paying stocks.

- **To use some of your IRA assets for an investment that requires a specialized IRA custodian, it may make sense to create a separate IRA for that investment.** *Example:* Legal tender gold coins, mortgages or a small business may require a specialized custodian.

CONTRIBUTING FOR A NONWORKING SPOUSE

You can contribute to an IRA for your spouse —even if he/she has no income. For 2017, you are allowed to put up to $5,500 into your own IRA as long as you had at least that much earned income for the year ($6,500 if you are age 50 or over)...and you also can contribute to an account in your spouse's name regardless of whether the spouse's income was enough to normally qualify. What matters is that your combined earned income must be at least as much as your combined contributions to the two accounts and that neither contribution can be more than the individual limits stated above. (Roth IRA contributions are allowed only if your income is below a certain level.)

401(K) CONTRIBUTIONS VS. IRA CONTRIBUTIONS

You are allowed to contribute to *both* your 401(k) plan at work *and* an IRA in the same year. If your employer matches part of your 401(k) contributions, it typically makes sense to first contribute enough to get your full employer match. Contributions to a traditional 401(k) are not taxed until you withdraw money from the 401(k).

Caution: When you are covered by an employer plan such as a 401(k), the tax deduction you can take on your contributions to a traditional IRA depend on your modified adjusted gross income (MAGI).

Example: For married couples filing jointly, if they both have retirement plans at work, they can take a full deduction on IRA contributions up to the allowable amounts if their MAGI in 2017 is $99,000 or less...a partial deduction if their MAGI is more than $99,000 but less than $119,000...and no deduction if their MAGI is $119,000 or more. If only one spouse has a retirement plan at work, the ability to claim a deduction is phased out between $186,000 and $196,000 for 2017.

PROTECTING ASSETS

There may be limits on how much you can protect your IRA assets from creditors if you declare bankruptcy or get sued. This is different from the rules for some other retirement accounts, such as most 401(k)s, which may receive near-ironclad protection from creditors under federal law if you face bankruptcy or a personal-injury or other lawsuit. (You are not protected from federal tax liens or spousal/child support payments, among other exceptions.) *Examples...*

Inherited IRAs receive no federal bankruptcy protection unless you inherited the account from your spouse. For traditional and Roth IRAs, the amount shielded from bankruptcy creditors is capped at a total of $1,283,025 in 2017 for all of your IRAs combined. Rollover IRAs from employer 401(k) plans, Simplified Employee Pension (SEP) plans and SIMPLE IRAs do get federal protection from creditors in a bankruptcy, but like all IRAs, state laws define the protection you get from other creditors such as an individual who wins a civil lawsuit against you.

Say you injure someone in a car accident... the injured person's claims exceed your insurance coverage...and he/she sues you. Most states provide some protection for your IRA assets, but how much varies drastically.

Examples: In California, you can exempt only as much as a judge deems "reasonably necessary" to support your dependents. In Ohio, traditional and Roth IRAs are protected, but SEP plans and SIMPLE IRAs are not. For rules in your state, consult an estate-planning attorney.

Self-defense: When you have a very large amount of assets in your IRAs, you may want to consider a personal umbrella liability policy and/or malpractice insurance if, say, you are a surgeon or in some other occupation at high risk from creditors. Or if you plan to leave your IRA to a child who has financial problems and could wind up seeking bankruptcy protection, you may want to name a trust as beneficiary of the IRA instead and let the trust distribute the money to the child.

FUNDING AN HSA

You can fund a Health Savings Account (HSA) with your IRA without facing a penalty or paying taxes. Transfer money directly from your IRA to your HSA using a Qualified HSA Funding Distribution (QHFD). You may take only one QHFD in your lifetime, and the transferred money can be used only for qualified medical expenses. For more information, including limits on the amount transferred, see Form 8889, *Health Savings Accounts* (HSAs), at IRS.gov. This transaction is not taxable or subject to the 10% penalty.

MAKING REQUIRED MINIMUM DISTRIBUTIONS (RMDs)

- **You don't have to liquidate an investment in your IRA in order to take an RMD.** You can do this by making an "in-kind" distribution rather than a cash withdrawal. Have your IRA custodian transfer IRA investments with a value at least equal to the RMD amount into a taxable account.

Example: You can transfer shares of a mutual fund or stock or, if you own real estate, you can transfer all or part of the property.

Advantages: You get to keep investments that you want to hold long-term or that you might have trouble selling in a timely and profitable fashion, such as real estate.

- **You may be able to avoid RMDs by using a "reverse rollover" to a 401(k) at your current employer.** You might know that you can roll an employer retirement account such as a 401(k) into a traditional IRA. But some employers allow you to do the opposite—roll assets from an IRA into a 401(k). This strategy is attractive for individuals who have reached age 70½ but still are working and don't need additional income. The IRS does not require you to begin taking RMDs from your 401(k) accounts until April 1 of the year following the end of your employment.

How to Fund Roth IRAs for Your Grandkids

Ed Slott, CPA, president of Ed Slott and Company, LLC, an IRA advisory firm in Rockville Centre, New York. He is author of *The Retirement Savings Time Bomb...and How to Defuse It.* IRAHelp.com

You might know that a Roth IRA is a way to grow your nest egg without any future tax payments on withdrawals. But it also can be a smart way to contribute to your grandchildren's financial future.

There are better and worse ways to use a Roth IRA for a grandchild, though. *Here's what grandparents need to know...*

- **Name grandchildren as beneficiaries of one or more of your own Roth IRAs on a form provided by the financial firm.** If there is more than one grandchild, you need to list the percentage of the Roth that each will receive. If the grandchildren are minors, you also need to designate a custodian who will oversee the accounts after your death until they reach adulthood, typically age 18 but sometimes 21, depending on the state.

Advantage over a traditional IRA: Although the IRS will require your grandchildren to take annual withdrawals (known as required minimum distributions, or RMDs) from the Roth starting in the tax year they inherit it, the Roth withdrawals are tax-free. RMDs usually are minimal at first, ranging from 1.2% to 2% a year up to age 33, for instance, based on how many more years your grandchildren would be expected to live.

Caution: Don't leave a Roth to a grandchild in your will instead of on the beneficiary form. If you make this mistake, your estate or your spouse could automatically be designated as the beneficiary, depending on the rules at the financial firm. For that to be changed after your death, a probate court would have to review the case. And although the grandchild would probably be granted your Roth, he/she would have "nondesignated" beneficiary status. That means that under IRS rules, instead of stretching out the withdrawals, the grandchild might have to withdraw all assets within five years after the end of the year in which you died—potentially losing thousands in tax-free investment gains.

Safeguard: If you worry that an adult grandchild might withdraw and spend the money frivolously, have an estate attorney establish a trust for the child with your specific instructions. Designate the trust as the beneficiary of your Roth IRA.

- **Contribute to your grandchild's existing Roth IRA**—or create a new one in the grandchild's name if he has earned income. If the child is a minor, you or a parent might act as custodian of the child's account, overseeing the account and any investment decisions. You also should name a backup custodian.

Advantage over leaving your own Roth to the grandchild: The child never has to take RMDs.

Disadvantage: You can contribute to a grandchild's Roth only up to the amount of his earned income that year—and not at all if there is no earned income, so this is probably not a good option if you want to use the Roth to help fund your grandchild's college expenses.

Note: There are annual limits on total contributions to one or more IRAs for any individual IRA owner, whether they're your own IRAs or your grandchild's. For 2017, that's $5,500, plus an extra $1,000 if the IRA owner is age 50 or older.

Financial Help for Seniors: Cash and Discounts!

Jim Miller, an advocate for older Americans, writes "Savvy Senior," a weekly column syndicated in more than 400 newspapers nationwide. Based in Norman, Oklahoma, he also offers a free senior e-news service at SavvySenior.org.

Retirement is not "golden" for all seniors. More than 25 million Americans age 60 and older are living with limited assets and incomes below $30,000 per year. And even with a higher income than that, it can be difficult to make ends meet.

There are numerous financial-assistance programs, both public and private, that can help struggling seniors, as well as give relief to family members who help provide financial support for their loved ones. And because of a comprehensive resource called BenefitsCheckUp.org, a free service of the National Council on Aging, locating these benefits and applying for them have never been easier.

The website is a confidential tool designed for people age 55 and older and their families. It includes information on more than 2,000 programs. Many are available to anyone in need who qualifies, while others are available only to older adults and can help them retain their independence.

To use the site, you enter basic information about the person in need—date of birth, zip code—and check boxes for what the person needs assistance with. The site generates a report instantly, listing links to the programs and services that the person may qualify for.

Some assistance programs can be applied for online...some have downloadable application forms to be printed and mailed, faxed or e-mailed in...and some ask that you contact the program's administrative office directly.

It's also possible to get help in person at a Benefits Enrollment Center. There currently are 59 centers around the country. Visit NCOA.org/centerforbenefits/becs to locate a nearby center.

TYPES OF BENEFITS

Here are some benefits that a senior may be eligible for...

• **Food assistance.** Programs such as the Supplemental Nutrition Assistance Program (or SNAP)—previously known as "food stamps"—can help pay for groceries. The average monthly SNAP benefit currently is around $126 per person. Other programs that may be available include The Emergency Food Assistance Program (TEFAP)...Commodity Supplemental Food Program (CSFP)...and the Senior Farmers' Market Nutrition Program (SFMNP).

• **Health care.** Medicaid and Medicare can help or completely pay for out-of-pocket health-care costs. And there are special Medicaid waiver programs that provide in-home care and assistance.

• **Prescription drugs.** There are hundreds of programs offered through drug companies, government agencies and charitable organizations that help reduce or eliminate prescription drug costs, including the federal low-income subsidy known as "Extra Help" that pays premiums, deductibles and prescription copayments for Medicare Part D prescription drug plan beneficiaries.

• **Utility assistance.** There's the Low Income Home Energy Assistance Program (LIHEAP), as well as local utility companies and charitable organizations that provide assistance in lowering home heating and cooling costs.

• **Supplemental Security Income (SSI).** Administered by the Social Security Administration, SSI provides monthly payments to very-low-income seniors, age 65 and older, as well as to people of any age who are blind or who have disabilities. SSI pays up to $735 per month for a single person and up to $1,103 for couples.

In addition to these programs, there are numerous other benefits that are available such as HUD housing (affordable housing for low-income families, the elderly and people with disabilities)...tax relief...veterans' benefits...respite care (short-term care that gives regular caregivers a break)...and free legal assistance.

WHEN YOU NO LONGER DRIVE

What would happen if you or someone close to you could no longer drive? *Here's a rundown of transportation solutions...*

• **Family and friends.** Include all possible candidates you might call on to get rides, and determine their availability and contact information.

• **Volunteer-driver programs.** These types of programs—usually sponsored by nonprofit organizations that serve seniors and people with disabilities—typically offer flexible transportation to and from doctor appointments, shopping and other activities. Many charge a nominal fee or suggest donations, though some are free.

Examples: The Senior Corps Retired & Senior Volunteer Program (NationalService.gov/programs/senior-corps/rsvp), which offers volunteer-driver services in communities around the country, provides free transportation primarily to and from medical appointments. iTN America (iTNAmerica.org) includes transportation programs in about 20 areas across the US and has more in development. It charges riders age 60 and older and visually impaired adults of any age annual membership dues of around $50, plus a $4 pick-up fee and a mileage fee of around $1.50 per mile.

• **iTN America programs** (see above) offer a car trade-in program that lets you convert your car into a fund to pay for future rides...and a car-donation program that provides a tax deduction if you itemize on your tax returns.

• **Paratransit services,** also called "dial-a-ride" or "elderly and disabled transportation services," often are government-funded programs that charge a small fee, typically ranging from $0.50 to $10 per ride. Some services may be free for people who can't afford to pay. To locate a paratransit service in your area, contact your Area Agency on Aging (call 800-677-1116 or visit ElderCare.gov).

• **Ride-sharing services.** The two biggest ride-sharing services are Uber and Lyft, which operate in major cities across the US. You request a ride from a driver who uses his/her vehicle to transport you. Ride requests with Uber are made using the Uber smartphone app or at the Uber mobile website...with Lyft, you use its smartphone app only. Costs are comparable to taxi fares.

• **Private transportation services.** Some hospitals, health clinics, senior centers, adult day centers, malls and other businesses offer free transportation for program participants or customers. And some nonmedical home-care agencies offer fee-based transportation services.

Two excellent resources for finding local transportation options include your local Area Agency on Aging (see above)...and a nonprofit service called Rides in Sight (855-607-4337, RidesinSight.org).

Moving Gets More Stressful as We Age: How to Make It Much Less Painful

Jennifer Pickett, associate executive director of the National Association of Senior Move Managers, an Illinois-based organization with nearly 1,000 members nationwide. She has 10 years of experience in senior move management and nearly a quarter century of experience working with senior housing. NASMM.org

---

Moving can be tremendously stressful. Possessions must be boxed up or discarded...a house must be scrubbed down and displayed to strangers...and dozens of details must be dealt with. But as unpleasant as any move tends to be, it can be worse when the people who are moving are older, whether that is you or someone you help to move.

For older people, a move is most likely to involve downsizing—and that means parting with lots of possessions. The move may be from a home with memories of raising a family, which triggers powerful emotions. And it frequently evokes a strong sense of loss.

When young people move, they tend to be heading to an exciting new place, taking a promising new job or otherwise opening a new chapter in their lives. When older people move, they may feel that their story is winding down.

Only later do they discover that these feelings of loss are not necessarily justified. Even for moves by people over 70, which often are into retirement communities or grown children's homes, there may be greater opportunities for social interaction, which open the door to an interesting new chapter of life.

To reduce the stress and make the move a success, it is important to be aware that there are psychological minefields to navigate and tough decisions to be made. Here are eight things that senior move managers—professionals who specialize in handling moves involving older people—have learned about making it work...

• **Take as much time as possible.** People generally try to get moves over with as quickly as possible. That's particularly true when grown children try to help an aging parent move—those grown children want to finish the task so that they can get back to their own lives.

But rushing is the wrong way to handle moves that involve downsizing and/or moving away from a home where a family was raised. People making these moves are not just letting go of a house or an attic full of stuff...they feel as if they are letting go of part of themselves.

Example: That old pie tin is not just a pie tin, but a memory of baking pies for children who are now grown...or a memory of a spouse who baked pies but is now deceased.

What to do: Make sure that there is time to reflect on what items mean before deciding their fate—and that the people who are moving can share the stories with someone, ideally descendants. This will greatly slow the process, but sharing these stories might inspire descendants to take certain objects home with them, keeping the items alive in the family. And if not, this at least keeps the objects' stories alive, which can substantially reduce the pain of parting with them.

Alternative: Take photographs of meaningful possessions so that they can be viewed at any time—possibly even as part of a collage of the photos hung on a wall of the new home—so the possessions won't feel completely gone.

• **Use scale drawings or apps to get a handle on space limitations.** People who downsize often arrive at their new, smaller homes with too much furniture and too many other bulky items that just won't fit. They then have to figure out what to do with these things on the fly, adding to the stress of moving day and adding to the dissatisfaction afterward.

Instead, measure the dimensions of the new living space and plot this to scale on a piece of graph paper. Then measure the furniture and other large items, and cut pieces of colored paper in the same scale to represent them. Arrange these colored paper pieces on the graph paper to determine what will actually fit well in the new home.

Alternative: Interior decoration web tools, such as RoomStyler.com/3d planner or Home.By.Me (both free)...or smartphone apps such as MagicPlan (basic version is free, available for iOS and Android)...and Floor Plan Creator (free, available for Android) can help do this without all the paper cutting.

• **Use auction websites to sell excess possessions.** Holding a garage sale is a hassle. Hiring a conventional estate-liquidation service is invasive if people are still living in the home—they'll have strangers tromping through the home for days. Instead, list possessions that won't come with you through an online estate auction company such as MaxSold (MaxSold.com) or Everything But the House (EBTH.com). These sites auction off furniture, antiques, art and more online and coordinate details including payments and pickups with a minimum of fuss. They tend to generate more cash than the traditional sales options, too.

• **Donate to a nonprofit the possessions that don't sell.** Lots of furniture will not find buyers these days, including some pieces that were considered desirable antiques a decade or two ago. There's a furniture glut on the market as the baby boomer generation downsizes, and it's exacerbated by the fact that today's young adults have shown little interest in antiques.

Exception: "Midcentury Modern" furniture made in a style evocative of the mid-1930s to the mid-1960s is very much in demand.

But relegating once-treasured items to the dump only adds to the pain of parting with them. Instead, donate them to a nonprofit such as Habitat for Humanity's ReStore or a local thrift shop that will find them a new home with a family that needs them. This imbues downsizing with a sense of meaning. The dining room table where your family celebrated so many of its important moments is not reaching its end. Instead, it is going to a new family that will enjoy it just as yours did.

• **Skip the storage unit.** In a downsizing, renting a storage unit is just an expensive and complicated way to delay making decisions that will have to be made eventually anyway. A storage unit makes sense only if there is a specific end date for the rental in the not-too-distant future—for example, if a descendant wants a living room set but cannot pick it up until a month after the move.

• **Ditch the throw rugs.** Throw rugs seem like the perfect possessions to bring along when people downsize—they don't take up any space and they provide a visual link to the prior residence. But throw rugs are a common cause of trips and slips, which are a big health risk as people age. Take advantage of the move to get rid of them.

• **Create continuity where you can.** Take photos of the interior of closets and drawers... and the arrangement of pictures on walls before you pack them up for the move. When you unpack in the new home, use these photos to re-create these parts of the home as closely as possible. These little areas of familiarity can make the new home feel more comfortable and the move less jarring.

• **Ask about moving rules before making the move.** Condominiums and senior-living communities often have strict guidelines about how and when residents can move in. For example, you might not be allowed to transport large boxes or furniture on the elevator during certain hours...park a moving van right next to the building...or leave furniture in a shared hallway while you make room inside the living space. It always pays to learn these rules before moving day so that you can plan accordingly and have an easier day.

Home Renovations to Age in Place

Roundup of experts on home design, reported at USNews.com.

These home renovations look good and help you age in place. Some changes can be made at any time—they will benefit people of any age while allowing seniors to remain more easily in their own homes.

- **Lighting improvements** include redesign for more natural light, more lamps, recessed lighting and task lighting in the kitchen.
- **Bathroom grab bars** now look like towel bars and other accent pieces.
- **Kitchen drawers and pull-out shelves** are better than cabinets for access to items.
- **Easier-to-use appliances** range from a raised dishwasher or wall oven to appliances with larger, easier-to-see controls.
- **Adding a bench in the shower** provides a place to sit.
- **Wider doorways** can make a home look more open.
- **Replacing doorknobs with levers**—they are easier to use and make it possible to open doors with knees or elbows if you're carrying packages.

How to Erase Years from Your Face: Simple Changes Do a Lot

Sanam Hafeez, PsyD, founder and clinical director of Comprehensive Consultation Psychological Services, with offices in New York City, Forest Hills and Uniondale, New York. ComprehendtheMind.com

---

Compare the faces of two people in your life. Person One is happy, relaxed and pleased with life. Person Two is overworked, stressed and harried. Guess which face appears younger and more attractive?

Stress can add years to your looks. When you're stressed, your body churns out *cortisol*, the hormone that primes you for action. Some cortisol is helpful (and motivating), but too much triggers inflammation, which affects every organ in your body, including the skin.

Experts have coined a term for the link between emotions and the skin—*psychodermatology*. This new field is based on research that shows that chronic stress and other psychological issues can trigger or exacerbate skin changes. But you can reverse those changes using emotional strategies and other lifestyle changes.

Example: Critically ill children who were given relaxing massages showed improvements in itching, redness and other skin conditions, according to researchers at the Touch Research Institute at University of Miami.

You can spend a fortune on antiaging products and cosmetic procedures, but unless you manage stress at the same time, you'll still look older than you should.

WHAT STRESS DOES TO SKIN

Stress can cause blotches, itching, redness and acne. The cortisol-driven rise in inflammation damages tissues and capillaries that are readily apparent in the mirror. *Stress also causes...*

- **Dryness.** The constant bombardment of cortisol in women with chronic stress can mean a drop in estrogen that has been called *minimenopause*. Estrogen is largely responsible for the differences in appearance between young women and older ones. Women who are frequently stressed tend to develop dryness and a loss of skin elasticity.

While women need estrogen more than men and are more impacted on a monthly basis by its regulation, hormonal imbalance also happens in men with the excess secretion of the stress hormone *androgen*, as well as *glucocorticoids*. This can cause a loss of estrogen leading to dryness in both men and women and an overproduction of sebum (an oily secretion of the sebaceous glands), which can trigger acne and razor bumps.

• **Wrinkles.** There's a reason that forehead furrows, between-the-eye creases and other wrinkles are known as "frown lines," "worry lines" or even "battle lines." Repeated expressions can etch themselves permanently in your face.

• **Circles under the eyes.** They make you look tired and can age your appearance even more than wrinkles. Some people are genetically prone to under-eye circles. They also can be caused by sun exposure, a lack of sleep or allergic skin conditions, along with stress.

What happens: Stress increases blood flow, and the tiny capillaries under the eyes become engorged. Those dark circles really are blood vessels that are visible through the skin.

• **Under-eye bags.** Like circles under the eyes, these puffy areas are partly due to genetics. But they're also common in people whose stress keeps them up at night. A lack of sleep causes fluids to accumulate under the eyes and makes your face appear puffy and tired.

WHAT TO DO

• **Take "mini-vacations."** Almost everyone can benefit from frequent "mini-vacations" that provide a break from stress. These can be as simple as a lunchtime walk...admiring a piece of art...or listening to a favorite song.

• **Eat an estrogen-enhancing diet** including fresh fruits and vegetables, salmon and whole grains. These antioxidant-rich foods fight inflammation. Fruits and vegetables also are naturally rich in *phytoestrogens*, plant compounds that mimic the effects of estrogen in the body. Estrogen "plumps" the skin and gives women and men a healthy glow.

• **Avoid excess sugar in all forms,** including refined carbohydrates, alcohol and highly processed foods, such as cake and cookies. These cause the body to produce *advanced glycation end-products*, toxins that trigger inflammation in the skin. The sugars in carbohydrates attach to certain proteins and can break down skin collagen, causing a loss of elasticity and the plumpness we associate with young skin.

• **Drink more water.** People who stay hydrated tend to have plumper, younger-looking skin. Also, water can flush excess salt from the body, which reduces under-eye puffiness. If you don't care for regular water, try coconut water. It is a natural source of electrolytes that help to keep you hydrated.

• **Relax your face.** You are probably not aware of your facial expressions, but you can learn to relax your face. When you're feeling stressed, remind yourself not to squint or frown. Be mindful of your expressions. Eventually, *not frowning* will become a habit. If you find yourself frowning, make it a habit to smooth your hand over your forehead and think happy, tranquil thoughts until your face naturally relaxes to a resting state.

• **Get a good night's sleep.** Even if you find that you can't log a full eight hours, at least make sure that the sleep you get is quality sleep. Relax for an hour before going to bed. Turn off the TV and computers. This puts your mind into the "sleep mode" so that it starts to shut down or cool off in preparation for bedtime. Pull the blinds or curtains so that your room is dark. If you can't fall asleep in 15 or 20 minutes, get up and do something relaxing, such as gazing out the window or holding a yoga pose. You want to stay within yourself instead of engaging with electronics or the outside world until you're tired enough to try again. If you find yourself becoming anxious about all the things you have to do, make a list of what needs to be done. You'll feel like you accomplished something and are in control of your tasks. And you won't be worried about forgetting them the next day.

BETTER WAY...

Computer Use Benefits Seniors

Seniors who used computers at least once a week had a 42% decreased risk for onset of mild cognitive impairment (MCI) over a four-year period. Other activities that reduced risk for MCI included magazine reading, 30%...participating in social activities, 23%...doing crafts, 16%...and playing games such as cards, 14%.

Janina Krell-Roesch, PhD, Translational Neuroscience and Aging Program, Mayo Clinic, Scottsdale, Arizona.

•**Sleep with your head slightly elevated**—a thick pillow will do it. The increased pull of gravity will help fluids drain away from your eyes.

•**Exercise.** Exercise relieves stress. You'll almost instantly see a difference when you attend a yoga class or go for a power walk. Your face will look smoother and younger.

Do-It-Yourself Face-Lift That Takes Off Years!

Victoria J. Mogilner, CA, certified acupuncturist and acupressurist and owner of Total Rejuvenation Center, Scottsdale, Arizona. A specialist in facial rejuvenation, she is author of *Ancient Secrets of Facial Rejuvenation: A Holistic, Nonsurgical Approach to Youth & Well-Being.* VictoriaMogilner.com

---

Do you look older than you feel? You don't have to have cosmetic surgery to take years off your look. Facial acupressure, the ancient practice derived from Traditional Chinese medicine, involves lightly pressing certain points on the face. It can tighten the skin, create a youthful glow and promote the production of collagen, all without having to go under the knife.

HOW DOES IT WORK?

Traditional Chinese medicine focuses on restoring balance throughout the body and promoting the flow of energy, called *qi* (pronounced *chee*). Qi is circulated along a network of channels called meridians. There are 12 meridians in the body, each relating to a vital organ, such as the stomach, large intestine, gallbladder and bladder. When the meridians become clogged because of poor diet, stress, dehydration or other factors, skin can age prematurely. When you put pressure on points on your face and open these pathways, circulation is improved, bringing blood and energy to the skin and other organs.

Digestion also is improved, ensuring the absorption of nutrients that are beneficial to the skin. And the lymphatic system, which drains damaging toxins and waste from the body, is stimulated. Improving the movement of qi and opening meridians result in a more youthful appearance. This may sound strange to you, but the techniques really do work, and they are very safe. If you do the exercises for 15 minutes a day, you will start to notice a difference within a week to 10 days.

GETTING STARTED

Acupressure face-lifts aren't difficult to do. *Just remember these guidelines...*

•**Set aside about five minutes for your "pre-facial warm-up" and at least 10 minutes a day for the face-lift.** To begin, choose one or two points (described on the next page) to treat each day. As you become more experienced, you can spend more time and treat more points.

•**Don't worry about finding the exact point**—as long as you are in the general area, you will affect each point along the pathway. As you continue, you will become more sensitive to the energy flow and your fingers will instinctively go to the correct points.

• **Touch and press each point with steady, gentle pressure** on both sides of your face. Release after one minute.

Important: Don't pull your skin, which is extremely delicate on the face. Just press with the pads of your fingers.

THE ACUPRESSURE FACE-LIFT

A successful acupressure face-lift isn't just "physical"—to reduce stress and help restore the flow of qi, there is a mental component, too...

Pre-facial warm-up: Sit away from distractions, where you feel safe, tranquil and nurtured. Begin to breathe steadily through your nose. Picture every part of your body, every pore, every cell receiving nourishment. Sit quietly, and relax your mind. As you breathe out, let go of stress. As you breathe in, repeat to yourself, *I let go of old thoughts. I work on myself to replenish myself at the cellular level.* Or you can make up your own affirmation. Do this for five minutes. Continue to be aware of your breath while doing the following exercises. While you focus on each affirmation, take a deep breath to the count of five, hold it for a count of five, breathe out to the count of five, and let your mind focus on your breath.

YANG BRIGHTNESS

The gallbladder meridian is a yang, or active, meridian and is the partner of the liver. The liver controls the eyes.

Benefits: Stimulating the gallbladder meridian from the forehead improves circulation and stimulates production of collagen, tightening skin and reducing forehead wrinkles. It also brightens eyes and improves mental clarity.

How to do it: Place your middle three fingers right above the middle of the eyebrow at the highest point in the indentation of your forehead. Gently touch the skin as you say your affirmation.

Suggested affirmation: I release the negativity of the past and bring health and wellness into every pore of my being.

PUPIL BONE

This point also works on the gallbladder meridian. The name refers to the acupressure point on the face—and the fact that it influences the eyes.

Benefits: Increases blood flow to the eyes, restoring youthfulness to the skin around the eyes, particularly lessening crow's-feet—those stubborn wrinkles located on the outer corner of the eye. This meridian also relates to decision-making, and by stimulating it, you can choose to create a more positive state of mind and physical health.

How to do it: Place the middle three fingers in the hollows next to the eyes, and close your eyes. Do both eyes at once.

Suggested affirmation: As I move forward, I make the decision to release negative thought patterns and have a positive state of mind and inner well-being.

RECEIVING CURES

This point, on the stomach meridian, promotes digestion.

Benefits: Stimulates the stomach pathway so that nutrients are better absorbed, resulting in healthier-looking skin. This point also increases circulation and aids in the removal of toxins, which reduces the swelling and puffiness under the eyes.

How to do it: Place your middle three fingers in the indentations under the eyes. Close your eyes.

Suggested affirmation: I receive all that life offers to nourish me. I connect with my inner self.

WELCOME FRAGRANCE

On the large intestine meridian, this point is located next to the sinuses, aiding deep breathing.

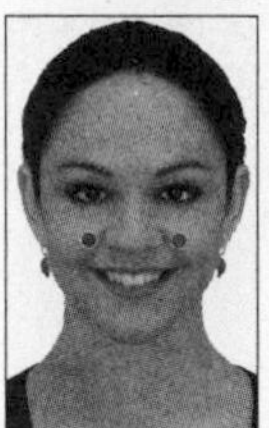

Benefits: Stimulates circulation and collagen production in the area under the nose, helping to eradicate fine lines and tighten skin in this area. Improves sense of smell and eases sinus congestion.

How to do it: Place your middle three fingers next to your nose so that your ring fingers line up with the bottom of the nose. Gently touch the point.

Suggested affirmation: I release my difficulties and problems regarding my spiritual essence, and I come home to my soul for guidance and protection.

LOWER HINGE

This point, along the stomach meridian, is located on the lower part of the jaw, acting like a hinge that helps the jaw relax.

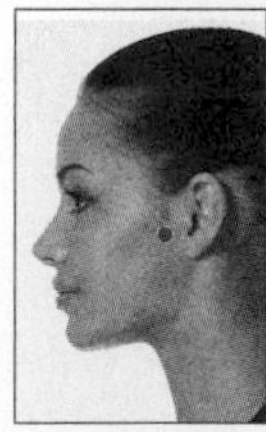

Benefits: Relaxes the cheek muscles and stimulates the production of collagen, smoothing the skin. Also relieves pain from teeth grinding and jaw tightness. Improves hearing and helps you to filter out negative self-talk.

How to do it: The jaw hinge is located about two inches from the tip of your earlobe. You can find it by opening and closing your mouth. Press gently upward as you breathe. Feel your jaw relax as you let go of stress.

Suggested affirmation: I deserve to receive the best that life has to offer.

13

Travel Time

Cheapskate Travelers Travel Well for Less

When you're known as "The Ultimate Cheapskate," people often think that you must lead a deprived, stay-at-home life, spending every waking hour clipping coupons and pinching pennies. But that's not the kind of life my wife and I lead, nor is it the lifestyle of the very special "cheapskates" I've surveyed and written about in my books. In fact, the black belts of smart spending say that they think and worry less about money than most of their peers and that they are happier because of it. And when it comes to their leisure time, they love to travel and are nearly twice as likely as the average American to have traveled abroad. How can they afford it?

Here are some of my secrets and those of my fellow cheapskates...

• **Start planning your trip at Kayak.com/explore.** Because airfare often is the single largest travel expense, check out the "Explore" tool on the Kayak website (Kayak.com/explore) before you even decide where to go. Enter the month or season when you want to travel, the airport you want to use and the amount your budget will allow for airline tickets. The Kayak Explore tool will show you everywhere in the world you can fly during the specified period for the dollar amount you've indicated or less. Date restrictions and other conditions may apply, and you'll need to act quickly if you see a deal that interests you because airfares change constantly.

Case in point: My wife and I ended up spending three wonderful weeks in Russia last year when Kayak Explore revealed that

Note: Prices, rates and offers throughout this chapter and book are subject to change.

Jeff Yeager, author of four popular books on frugal living including, *How to Retire the Cheapskate Way.* He is also AARP's official "Savings Expert."

for just $550 per person, we could fly round-trip from Washington, DC, to St. Petersburg during the time we had available to travel. We had always wanted to visit Russia, but it shot to the top of our list when we saw that bargain-basement airfare.

There also is a tool for learning average travel costs per day in nearly 150 countries at BudgetYourTrip.com. This tool lets you specify whether you'll be traveling on a tight, midrange or luxury budget and then breaks down expenses for accommodations, food, local transportation, entertainment, etc.

• **Maximize your credit card travel rewards points.** There are many good rewards credit cards for travelers, and finding the right card for you will depend on your spending habits and financial eligibility. For starters, compare cards using the annual lists of the top cards for travel rewards at NerdWallet.com and CreditCards.com. Based on our particular circumstances, my wife and I almost exclusively use the Chase Sapphire Preferred Visa card, which is consistently ranked as one of the top travel rewards cards, even though it carries a hefty $95 annual fee (waived the first year). We use it for just about everything that can be charged—including groceries and direct bill pays—accruing rewards points quickly but, of course, paying off the full balance every month to avoid interest. Perks of that particular card include a large sign-up bonus (currently 50,000 bonus points if you charge a total of $4,000 in the first three months, which are redeemable for $625 in travel)...no foreign transaction fees when using it abroad (which easily can save you more than the $95 annual fee on even a short foreign trip)...and the flexibility to redeem points for any type of travel service, not just services on certain airlines or from certain hotels. When you book travel using points from this card on the Chase Ultimate Rewards website, you get 25% more value with your points than if you redeemed them directly with the airline or other travel providers.

Another tip: If you sign up for a credit card that requires you to charge a minimum amount within a certain period in order to receive sign-up bonus points, consider reaching that amount by simply buying gift cards for stores where you know you'll eventually shop anyway.

• **Make it a working vacation (sort of).** Particularly if you have a long block of time for travel, doing a little part-time work along the way can be an interesting diversion and help stretch your travel budget. Websites such as WorkAway.info and BackDoorJobs.com list a wide range of part-time job opportunities for travelers ranging from helping young business professionals in Spain practice their English skills to tending livestock on a working farm in Australia to helping out at a hostel in Thailand. Some come with a paycheck, while others (like most of the gigs available through WorkAway.info) provide only complimentary room and board. Before signing up for one of these work gigs, speak with other travelers who have worked for the same outfit to make sure that you know what you're getting into. Some of the websites are like Facebook and allow you to connect with fellow travelers/workers directly, and in other cases, you can ask the potential employer to provide references from previous workers.

And check out TrustedHouseSitters.com, a clearinghouse for temporary pet-sitting and house-sitting opportunities around the world. In exchange for looking after someone's house and possibly their pet, you get a place to stay.

• **Forget hotels.** If you haven't used Airbnb or one of its competitor sites, it's time! Savvy budget-conscious travelers are increasingly opting to stay in private rooms, apartments or entire homes rented directly from the owners via websites such as Airbnb.com, Booking.com and Wimdu.com. In our travels, we've found that staying in privately owned accommodations offers a lot of advantages, including access to cooking facilities (in most instances), more space to stretch out than in a typical hotel room and a chance to truly feel like you're "living" someplace rather than just visiting. Using the robust map feature on most of these websites, you can scroll over available properties to find rentals in your price range in the areas where you would like to stay—and the savings can be considerable. A few years ago, my wife and I rented a gorgeously appointed three-room, luxury apartment in Budapest on Booking.com—directly across the street from one of the city's finest hotels—for almost 80% less than the least expensive room would have cost at that hotel.

• **Save money at home while you travel.** How much will a trip *really* cost you? The answer to that question involves not just the direct costs of the trip but also how much money you'd probably spend anyhow if you stayed home and how much you might be able to save while you're away. For example, since we prepare most of our own meals when we travel (lots of picnics in pretty places!), we find that our food costs increase very little, compared with when we're at home, so that's pretty much a wash. We also tend to travel during the times of year when our home heating or cooling costs are the highest so that we can set our programmable thermostats for maximum savings while we're away. Of course, we're not filling up the cars with gas every week as we do when we're at home, which typically saves us about $200 a month when we're traveling. For longer trips of a month or more, we usually have the water service shut off while we're away (a net savings of $120 off the minimum monthly water bill after factoring in the shut-off/turn-on fees), as well as cancel the cable service, since we have a contract with no cancellation fees. Using all of these measures, we can easily save $500 to $800 per month while we're traveling, and that savings comes right off the bottom line of what the trip actually costs. Who said it costs a fortune to travel the world?

GOOD TO KNOW...

Cheapest Day to Fly...

The cheapest day to fly is Sunday. Business travelers will pay higher fares to book flights to get home by the end of the workweek. Fares are 13% higher, on average, on Fridays than on Sundays. And there usually is a greater inventory of available cheap seats at the start of the week.

The Wall Street Journal, WSJ.com.

Websites That Cut the Cost of Vacation Travel

Seth Kugel, travel writer, writing in *The New York Times*.

Start by listing some possible destinations and compare them by typical costs. At Numbeo.com/travel-prices, you can determine the costs of restaurant meals, beverages and transportation, including taxis and gasoline prices. The site Fareness.com will help you compare the costs of getting to the destinations at various times of the year. Use Travel Hacker at Kayak.com to determine the best dates for booking flights. Depending on your destination, also check prices on airlines such as Southwest and Air Panama, which are not included at sites such as Kayak.com. If you decide not to book right away, set an airfare and/or hotel rate alert at AirfareWatchdog.com—the site will let you know when prices are especially low. Before booking to a foreign country, search for a list of national and local holidays so that you do not arrive at a pricey time or when businesses are closed. Go to JoinHoney.com, and install its browser extension that alerts you to discount codes while you are making purchases at several prominent travel websites.

Airline Refund? Good Luck

Christopher Elliott, founder of the traveler consumer rights website Elliott.org and author of *How to Be the World's Smartest Traveler*, reported by Karen Larson, editor, *Bottom Line Personal*.

An airline recently offered my husband and me a low-cost upgrade to first class when we checked in for a flight from Rome to New York. After we bought the first-class upgrade, the airline rep said that I could get a refund for a $90 upgrade that I'd previously purchased for an extra-legroom seat in economy class. But after weeks of trying, I still hadn't gotten that money back.

Airline customers often struggle to recover refund money they are due, notes Christopher Elliott, founder of the traveler consumer rights website Elliott.org and author of *How to Be the World's Smartest Traveler.*

One especially egregious example: If you buy a first-class ticket but get bumped to economy class, the airline likely won't refund the difference between the amount you paid for the first-class ticket and the amount you would have paid for an economy-class seat when you booked...but instead, the difference between what you paid and the walk-up price of an economy-class seat. Walk-up prices—charged at the airport on flight day—tend to be extremely high, meaning that your refund is likely to be unfairly low.

What to do: If you cannot get a refund that you deserve from an airline's customer service department, send an e-mail to the airline's VP of customer service. Briefly and calmly explain the situation, and request a refund. If that doesn't work, e-mail the CEO. E-mail addresses for these airline execs can be found on Elliott.org, under the "Company Contacts" tab.

If all else fails, contact the issuer of the credit card you used to buy the tickets to dispute the charge. That's how I finally got my $90 back.

3 Best Airlines

The three best US-based airlines are Alaska Airlines, United and Virgin America, according to a recent survey. The survery considered factors such as airfare, route networks, bag/change fees, cabin comfort, customer satisfaction, frequent-flier program quality, on-time arrivals and lost luggage.

The worst-rated airlines: Discount carriers Spirit Airlines and Frontier, which scored well only for low fares.

Julian Kheel, an analyst with ThePointsGuy.com, which did a survey of 10 major airlines.

5 Ways to Get Through Airport Security *Faster*

George Hobica, founder of AirfareWatchdog.com, which reports on airfare bargains. He previously was a travel writer for *Travel + Leisure, National Geographic Traveler* and other magazines.

The *average* wait time at Los Angeles International Airport security checkpoints is 40 minutes, according to the airport-delay monitoring app *MiFlight.* Waits longer than three hours have occurred at Chicago's O'Hare...at Miami International Airport...and at New York City's John F. Kennedy International Airport. It's not unheard of for travelers to spend more time getting though airport security at US airports than they do in the air. It even has become common to miss flights because of extensive security delays.

Enrolling in the "PreCheck" expedited security program administered by the Transportation Security Administration (TSA) was supposed to allow travelers to sidestep these delays—but the PreCheck program has had problems of its own.

Travelers who sign up for PreCheck and fly on participating airlines get to use special security lines where several time-consuming steps are not required—they do not have to remove their shoes and belts...or take their electronic devices out of their luggage, for example.

In theory, that should make PreCheck security lines a big time-saver. In practice, PreCheck has experienced a huge surge in popularity in the past year, and a growing glut of PreCheck travelers means that its lines sometimes take longer than standard airport-security lines.

What's more, these days it can take upward of one month just to get the in-person interview that is required by the PreCheck application process. Travelers must pay an $85 five-year membership fee and pass a security vetting process to participate in PreCheck (TSA.gov/precheck).

Fortunately, PreCheck is not the only way to get though airport security faster. *Potentially better options include...*

- **Global Entry,** a government program that lets preapproved travelers speed through customs and immigration checkpoints in more than 59 US and international airports. And if you are a Global Entry member, you also qualify to use PreCheck security lines. To take advantage of PreCheck if you are a Global Entry member, enter your Global Entry membership number (which is in the upper-left corner on the back of your Global Entry "Trusted Traveler" card) into the "Known Traveler Number" field when you book flights on participating airlines—or enter it on your frequent-flier profile with the airline.

As noted above, those PreCheck lines are not always as quick as they should be, but Global Entry membership truly does reduce delays at customs and immigration. And it outdoes PreCheck in another way—the Global Entry interview-and-approval process often is weeks quicker than the PreCheck process, though this does vary by location. (Go to CBP.gov, then select "Global Entry" from the "Travel" menu.)

Cost: Global Entry has a $100 application fee. That's only $15 more than the application fee for PreCheck alone, so Global Entry is the better deal. After approval, renewal is not required for five years, so the annual cost is just $20.

You even can avoid this expense by charging Global Entry's application fee to a credit card that provides a statement credit to cover it. Predictably, these tend to be cards that have high annual fees, however, including The Platinum Card from American Express ($450 annual fee, AmericanExpress.com)...and Citi Prestige and Citi AAdvantage Executive World Elite MasterCard (both with a $450 annual fee, Citi.com).

• **Clear,** a private security-screening alternative to the government-run PreCheck and Global Entry programs. Clear features high-tech, automated biometric authentication—that is, fingerprint or retinal scanners—and usually is much faster than all other airport security options. Often there is virtually no Clear line at all...except when those high-tech biometric scanners go down, which does happen on occasion (ClearMe.com).

Clear currently is available in 21 airports—Atlanta...Austin...Baltimore...Dallas/Ft. Worth ...Denver...Detroit...Houston's George Bush and William Hobby airports...Las Vegas... Miami...Minneapolis...New York's JFK, LaGuardia and Westchester County airports... Orlando...San Antonio...San Francisco...San Jose...Seattle...Washington's Dulles and Ronald Reagan National airports. The company that runs Clear expects to offer the service in Los Angeles soon, and Clear is available in a number of major league sports stadiums, where it enables you to avoid the sometimes lengthy security checkpoint lines.

Because of the cost, most people will find that it's worth enrolling in Clear only if they frequently use at least one of the currently served airports or, perhaps, if they have season tickets with a team that plays in a stadium that offers Clear.

Cost: $179 per year, or $79 to $99 per year for Delta SkyMiles members. Family members 18 and over can be added for $50 each. Family members under 18 can use Clear for free when traveling with a Clear member.

Other possible ways to avoid long security lines...

• **Paying airlines for expedited security occasionally is possible.** JetBlue and United offer passengers the option of paying a modest fee for onetime access to a special security line in some airports. (Travelers who have elite status in an airline's frequent-flier program and/or who are flying business or first class often qualify for access to a special security line without paying an added fee.)

This option typically is offered at the airport check-in kiosk or desk when available.

Strategy: Check the length of security lines before checking in to a JetBlue or United flight. Pay the extra fee if the lines look longer than is acceptable to you.

Cost: JetBlue's Even More Speed starts at $10...United's Premier Access starts at $15. (Some other airlines offer VIP airport services that include significantly expedited security, such as the American Airlines Five Star Service program. But these programs tend to cost hundreds of dollars per flight and often are available to only first-class passengers.)

• **Investigate alternative security checkpoints.** Most of the larger airports have multiple security checkpoints—and one might have significantly shorter lines than another.

Ask an airport or Transportation Security Administration employee whether there is another security checkpoint where the lines tend to be shorter. It might be a long walk to get to the other checkpoint, but even so, this can be a time-saver.

Helpful: Apps including GateGuru (free, iOS, Android and Windows. GateGuru.com) and *MiFlight* (free, iOS, GoMiFlight.com) can help you locate alternate security checkpoints and sometimes provide user-generated wait-time estimates.

For a More Comfortable Airline Seat...

Choose airlines that generally offer more legroom, such as JetBlue, with 32 to 34 inches in most planes—compared with 30 to 32 inches for most domestic airlines and only 28 inches on Spirit. *Know which planes have the most space*—Airbus planes generally are roomier than Boeing's, but for specific flights, go to SeatGuru.com to check. Avoid regional jets, which generally have tighter seating. *Ask the gate agent if the bulkhead seat is available*—you may be allowed to move into it for free. *Consider paying for a roomier seat* if your flight will last more than four hours.

Roundup of experts on airline seating, reported at MarketWatch.com.

Fake Uber Drivers Lurk at Airports

Detective Sergeant Kevin Coffey, who recently retired from the Los Angeles Police Department after 35 years of service. He founded the LAPD's Airport Crimes Investigations Detail and currently is a travel-risk consultant and trainer. CorporateTravelSafety.com

Summon an Uber or a Lyft car from the airport, and you could get taken for a ride in more ways than one if you're not careful. Scammers posing as drivers for these ride-share services sometimes trick airport travelers into their vehicles. Victims might be charged exorbitant rates for the resulting rides...or they could be at physical risk.

In one version of this scam, a driver pulls up to an airport terminal and asks, "Who booked an Uber?" until he finds someone who has. This scammer has an excuse ready if the passenger notices that the car is not the one he/she was told to expect—he might say that the original car broke down, for example. During the trip, the driver asks for the passenger's credit card and has an explanation prepared if the passenger protests that his payment info is on file—he could claim that the processing system is temporarily down.

In a variation, a scammer standing in or near the terminal claims to be an Uber or a Lyft dispatcher. He directs victims to accomplices posing as ride-share drivers.

These scams could happen anywhere, but they seem to be most common at airports because so many people call for rides there.

What to do: When you request a ride from Uber or Lyft and are matched with a driver, your smartphone app provides details including the driver's name and photo...the make and model of vehicle...and the license-plate number. Confirm that both car and driver match the information provided before getting in. Also ask ride-share drivers, "Who are you here to pick up?" and don't get into the car if the driver cannot supply your name (or

BETTER WAYS...

No More Lost Luggage

To protect against lost luggage...

Arrive extra-early at the airport with a well-labeled bag and watch the gate agent tag it. Be sure to make the bag distinctive with decorations that set it apart from similar luggage. And choose airlines with good reputations for luggage handling, such as JetBlue, Virgin America and Delta instead of regional airlines such as Skywest and ExpressJet, which tend to lose more luggage.

Roundup of experts on air travel, reported in *USA Today.*

the name of the person whose ride-share account was used to request thc ride).

Never trust anyone who claims to be an on-site Uber or Lyft "dispatcher"—these services never use on-site dispatchers. And never give your credit card or any other payment to an Uber or a Lyft driver—there is no legitimate reason for them to request this.

Foreign Rental Cars Can Be Death Traps—Taxis, Too

David Ward, secretary general of the Global New Car Assessment Programme, a registered charity based in London that supports the development of crash-test programs in emerging markets. GlobalNCAP.org

---

The car you rent in a foreign country might fall far short of modern safety standards. In many countries, cars are not required to have basic safety equipment such as air bags…nor must they pass crash tests. Rental companies tend not to adopt vehicle safety standards any stricter than local laws.

Vehicle safety is especially important when driving abroad. The risk of crashing increases dramatically when people drive unfamiliar cars on unfamiliar roads in countries with unfamiliar driving laws and customs.

Rental cars meet modern safety standards in the US, Canada, Western Europe, Japan, Australia and in a few other smaller countries. But this is a problem virtually everywhere else in the world.

Renting from a major car-rental agency and/or choosing a make and model that also is driven in the US is no guarantee of safety—some models are built to vastly different safety standards for different countries. The Chevrolet Aveo, for example, has been sold in both Mexico and the US, but the standard Mexican version does not have air bags.

Taxi passengers are at risk, too.

Example: The Nissan Tsuru, the most common car in the Mexican taxi fleet, dramatically failed a recent crash test, earning a zero-star safety rating.

What to do: When you rent a vehicle, choose a midsize or larger SUV or a full-sized sedan. These higher-end cars are more likely to have modern safety equipment…and even if they don't, their larger frames will provide more protection than a small car in a crash.

If possible, contact the rental agency before your trip and ask for a car that has air bags.

If you need a taxi, ask your hotel's concierge to call a taxi company that has safe, modern vehicles. This is no guarantee, but it may help. Before climbing into any taxi, check to make sure that it has seat belts in the backseat. If it doesn't, get out and try another cab.

Reduce Rental-Car Fees

To reduce car-rental charges, which can inflate your bill by 50% or more…

Use apps and kiosks to sign in instead of going to the rental counter, where employees are trained in the hard sell of unwanted extras. And refuse rental-company insurance—be sure that you are covered by your own auto insurer or through your credit card, or use a rental app such as *Carla*, which compares 900 companies and includes insurance costs in car pricing.

Roundup of experts on car rentals, reported in *USA Today.*

Little-Known Ways to Save at Hotels

Book 30 days in advance…and if that is not possible, good rates often are offered seven to 10 days in advance of a stay. If you can wait until the last minute, try booking on the day you want to stay—only 60% of rooms are occupied on most nights, so hotels may cut rates drastically at the last minute. Also, you can book a room and get any price drops refunded to you by booking through Tingo.com.

More ideas: Stay on a Sunday, the day with the lowest room rates...visit tourist locations midweek, not on weekends...go to major business areas on weekends, after business travelers have left...book during shoulder season, between high-cost high season and off-peak times when weather tends to be poor...stay in the suburbs rather than in major cities...and check on local events before booking—rates may rise when big events occur.

Experts on travel, reported at GoBankingRates.com.

Sell Your Nonrefundable Hotel Reservation

You can sell your nonrefundable hotel reservation—or you can purchase someone else's. Two services—RoomerTravel.com and Cancelon.com—allow you to list your reservation for resale. The online sites handle the actual transaction, contact the hotel or booking agency to transfer the name on your reservation and guarantee that you'll be paid.

Caveats: To get a buyer, you may have to offer a price much lower than what you paid. And the fee for sellers is 15% of the selling price at RoomerTravel and 10% at Cancelon.

Pauline Frommer, editorial director of the Frommer Guides and cohost of *The Travel Show* radio program, New York City. Frommers.com

How to Handle Poor Hotel Service

Speak up—complain as soon as a problem occurs instead of waiting until checkout or after you return home. This gives the hotel a chance to make amends while you still are there. *Be friendly and smile* even when you have been inconvenienced—hotel staff are more likely to help someone who makes the request pleasantly. And say thank you for their assistance. *Fill out the guest comment card* to let the hotel staff know what happened. *If you travel for business*, inform your corporate travel manager about the issue. *Stop giving the hotel your business* if a problem is not addressed to your satisfaction.

Roundup of experts on hotel stays, reported in *USA Today*.

Better Hotel Stay If You Have Allergies

If you have allergies, ask a hotel about its fragrance use *before* booking a room. Many hotels pump fragrances into common areas and even individual rooms. If you are concerned, choose a different hotel.

Peter Greenberg, travel editor for CBS News, Studio City, California, and author of *The Best Places for Everything*.

To Run a Successful Airbnb Rental...

Be *honest about the pluses and minuses* of your home so that guests do not expect more than you offer, become disappointed and give you bad reviews. *Solve problems* quickly when they arise, whether that means calling a plumber about a broken fixture or having a spare remote control in case one is lost. *Hire top-notch professional cleaners* so that your home meets the highest possible cleanliness standards at all times. *Document everything valuable* in your home by taking photos of countertops, appliances, furniture and electronic equipment—if anything is damaged, Airbnb will need before-and-after photos to prove that guests caused the damage.

Brian X. Chen, Airbnb "Superhost," writing in *The New York Times*. A Superhost has hosted many guests and consistently received five-star reviews—only about 7% of Airbnb hosts are Superhosts.

Self-Defense Before Buying a Time-Share

Roundup of experts on time-shares, reported at MarketWatch.com.

K*now that the price usually is negotiable*—salespeople often use hard-sell tactics and offer gifts, but if you want a time-share, withstand the pressure and figure out what price you are willing to pay. If one operator of a time-share will not accept your offer, another one may. *Consider buying from an existing owner*—time-shares are notoriously hard to resell, so you may get a very good deal. *Know whether you actually get a property deed*—as you would with a normal real estate purchase—or just a right to use the property, which typically is more restrictive. *If you are buying a time-share in an unfinished building,* deposit your money in escrow until the property is completed. This way you can get your money back if the developer goes out of business. *Know your state's right of rescission*—the time within which you can change your mind and get your money back, typically about a week. *Find out how to trade for time at a different resort* before you make a purchase. *Understand that time-shares are a way of simplifying the planning of future vacations*—they are not typically real estate investments.

Red Flags When Renting a Vacation Home

T*he price is too low*—if it is 20% below the rate for other units in the area, the offer may be a scam. *It looks too perfect in the ad*—it may be photographed to look like it is the only house on the beach, for example. Use the Street View option on Google Maps to see what the area looks like. *The ad uses words such as "cozy," "secure" and "rustic"*—these imply that the property may be cramped, in a bad neighborhood and lacking amenities, respectively.

Self-defense: Consider renting through a property-management company that handles everything.

Roundup of experts on vacation rentals, reported in *USA Today.*

You'll Love These Places! 7 Overlooked Destinations

Patricia Schultz, a New York City–based travel journalist. She is author of *The New York Times* number-one best seller *1,000 Places to See Before You Die* as well as the recently updated *1,000 Places to See in the United States & Canada Before You Die.* 1000Places.com

Tired of overcrowded, overhyped vacation destinations? We asked travel writer Patricia Schultz, author of the recently updated *1,000 Places to See in the United States & Canada Before You Die*, to name some of her favorite destinations and activities in the US (or within a short drive of the US border) that most people overlook…

- **Explore a slice of Spanish history without leaving the US—St. Augustine, Florida.** The oldest continuously inhabited European settlement in the continental US isn't Jamestown, Virginia, or Plymouth, Massachusetts—it's St. Augustine, a coastal city 105 miles northeast of Orlando that was settled by the Spanish in 1565. While much of Florida's coast is overrun by cookie-cutter motels and strip malls these days, St. Augustine's historic district still has a distinctly Old World Spanish charm, with many buildings dating back to the 16th through 19th centuries. The Castillo de San Marcos is the only 17th-century fort still standing in the US, for example…and the romantic Casa Monica Hotel is completely unlike any other hotel in Florida—it's a 19th-century Moorish Revival–style castle.

The best time to visit St. Augustine is between late November and early January when the weather is not sticky hot and the historic district is lit by three million holiday lights. Rooms in the Casa Monica Hotel start at $170 to $259 per night, depending on the season. CasaMonica.com

• **Take a cruise the old-fashioned way—The Maine Windjammers, Rockland and Camden, Maine.** A cruise on a historic 19th- or early 20th-century sailing ship is a wonderful way to see the craggy coast and islands of Maine. These three-to-six-day cruises typically include stops in fishing towns that are anything but touristy...and in quiet coves for lobster bakes. They are trips that transport passengers not just down the coast but also back in time to when ships were made of wood and propelled by wind.

These ships are not luxurious by modern cruising standards. Their cabins tend to be small and simple, and bathrooms often are shared. But the lack of luxury is easily made up for by the memorable and unusual experience. Details about specific ships' accommodations, amenities, rates and schedules are available online. Find links through the website of the Maine Windjammer Association (SailMaineCoast.com). Prices for three-night cruises start at $610 per person, all inclusive. Ships operate late May through mid-October.

• **Visit one of the prettiest little towns almost in America—Niagara-on-the-Lake, Ontario.** Niagara Falls is among the best-known tourist destinations in the US, but few visitors seek out this little waterfront town just to the north, across the Canadian border. They're missing out on one of the most picturesque communities in North America...and on an opportunity to take advantage of a favorable exchange rate in a location just 10 miles from a US border crossing—one US dollar recently was worth $1.34 Canadian.

Stroll or bike along the Niagara Parks Garden Trail, which follows the edge of the Niagara River...catch a play during the highly regarded Shaw Festival, which celebrates the work of George Bernard Shaw and his contemporaries from April through November each year...shop in the town's eclectic boutiques...or go wine tasting at the region's numerous surprisingly fine wineries—Canada might not be the first nation that comes to mind when you think of wine, but this part of Ontario produces an excellent award-winning dessert wine known as Icewine. Top wineries include Peller Estates...Inniskillin Wines...Château des Charmes...and Vineland Estates Winery. Tickets for the Shaw Festival can be purchased at ShawFest.com with prices starting at $24.77 US at recent exchange rates. Keep in mind that US travelers must have valid passports to visit Canada. NiagaraontheLake.com

• **Escape to a simpler time and place—The Shaker Village of Pleasant Hill, Kentucky.** The Shakers, a religious sect that believed in gender equality, communal living and pacifism, flourished in the US in the mid-19th century (only a handful exist today). The Shaker Village of Pleasant Hill, located in a pastoral part of central Kentucky, closed in 1910, but 34 of its original buildings have been painstakingly restored. Guided tours are available, and costumed historical reenactors demonstrate traditional Shaker skills such as weaving and woodworking. The Village's property includes 40 miles of nature trails through 3,000 acres of beautiful rolling hills. The Trustees' Table is an excellent restaurant that serves tra-

MONEYSAVER...

See These Cities Before Prices Rise

Demand for travel to some cities is increasing, which means that the cost to visit them is likely to go up in the near future. Ho Chi Minh City, Vietnam, had the highest percentage growth in bookings.

Other cities with big increases in year-over-year bookings: Shanghai, China...Dublin, Ireland...Edinburgh, Scotland...Kyoto, Japan...Lisbon, Portugal...Seville, Spain...Singapore...Stockholm, Sweden...Kuala Lumpur, Malaysia...Copenhagen, Denmark...Bangkok, Thailand...Milan, Italy...Athens, Greece...Taipei, Taiwan.

For a less expensive trip: Consider visiting during each location's off-season—winter in Stockholm and Copenhagen, for example, and summer in Kyoto.

Analysis by Booking.com, reported at GoBankingRates.com.

ditional Kentucky and Shaker dishes—try the country ham and tart lemon pie. You can stay in the village overnight at the Inn at Pleasant Hill (rooms recently were available for $126). If you're looking for an action-packed getaway, look elsewhere—but if you're looking for a peaceful place in Kentucky's rolling bluegrass country to take a break from the modern world, it's hard to do better. The village is located 25 miles southwest of Lexington. ShakerVillageKY.org

• **Explore a world where canoes outnumber cars—Boundary Waters Canoe Area, Ely, Minnesota.** This wilderness preserve located along the northern border of Minnesota is the largest in the US east of the Rockies, with more than one million protected acres. Together with the even larger Quetico Provincial Park just across the border in Canada, there are more than 1,000 lakes scattered across this vast pine forest.

There are few cars and motorboats allowed, creating a world that feels untouched by time. Most visitors bring or rent canoes—there are more than 1,200 miles of canoe routes—and then paddle and portage (carry the canoe short distances overland) for days or weeks, camping onshore and dining on the fish they catch. A permit system ensures that the woods are never very crowded.

Ely is 100 miles northwest of Duluth. Overnight visitors must pay a "user fee" of $16 per person per trip. For more information about permits, visit the US Forest Services' website (FS.Fed.us, select "Destinations" from the "Visit Us" pull-down menu, enter "Minnesota," then select the "Boundary Waters Canoe Area Wilderness"). If you wish to hire a guide or rent canoes and equipment, contact Williams & Hall Outfitters (WilliamsandHall.com). If you're looking for a good hotel nearby, the log cabins of the Burntside Lodge are an excellent choice (from $171 off-season, from $219 peak summer season, Burntside.com).

• **Watch the world take flight at the Albuquerque International Balloon Fiesta, New Mexico.** It isn't accurate to call this well-attended fiesta an "overlooked" event, but it is underappreciated and not well-known outside the region. It is an astounding, unforgettable experience to stand on the fiesta field early in the morning as the sun rises and more than 500 colorful hot-air balloons inflate to the size of houses around you and take flight.

Arrive early—gates open at 4:30 am for the morning session (3:30 pm for the evening session), and cars are lining up by 4 am. (There are nine morning and five evening sessions in all.) In 2018, the fiesta will be held from October 6 to 14. Prices for 2018 were unavailable at press time, but in 2017, general admission tickets cost $10 per "session" and parking cost $15 per car. Admission was free for children age 12 and under. For more information, go to BalloonFiesta.com.

• **Go wine tasting without being overrun by tourists—Walla Walla Wine Region, Washington.** More than 100 wineries have sprung up in and around Walla Walla, a small city in southeastern Washington State approximately 150 miles south of Spokane by car. There are wineries in almost every state these days, but the Walla Walla region vineyards produce highly regarded wines. Walla Walla's wineries and inns are much less overrun with tourists and are more affordable than California wine regions such as Napa and Sonoma, making this an excellent place for a relaxing, enjoyable wine-tasting trip.

Some wineries to visit include Abeja, which is on a restored early 20th-century farmstead, and Seven Hills Winery, which is next door to Whitehouse-Crawford Restaurant, one of Walla Walla's best eateries. Go to WallaWallaWine.com for more information.

---

7 Cruise Mistakes That Can Cost You Big

Dori Saltzman, senior editor with the travel website Cruise Critic, which offers cruise reviews and information. CruiseCritic.com

The simplicity of cruise vacations is part of their appeal. You choose a ship going where you want to go…and it is easy to imagine that the planning virtually is complete. Unlike with most journeys, there is no need to choose hotels, reserve rental cars or even find restaurants.

But novice cruisers still can stumble into mistakes that make their voyages less enjoyable—or more expensive—than they should have been. Experienced cruisers sometimes make mistakes, too, particularly when they book trips on cruise lines that they have not sailed with previously.

Seven cruise-planning mistakes...

MISTAKE: **Booking with the wrong cruise line.** Different cruise lines provide very different cruise experiences—even when they stop at the same ports. Perhaps most notably, some cruise lines strive to supply a high-energy environment for passengers...while others offer a more relaxing experience. Choose the wrong cruise line, and you could feel out of place. If you have not previously cruised on a particular line, speak to experienced cruisers about it...use search engines to find online reviews of it...and/or book through an experienced travel agent who can help you select an appropriate cruise line.

Examples: Carnival Cruise Line's party atmosphere attracts people who want to be social, let down their hair and be silly...Disney Cruise Lines attracts primarily families. On the other hand, Crystal, Oceania, Seabourn and Silversea offer a relaxed atmosphere and higher pricing that tends to draw cruisers age 45 and older.

Helpful: Any cruise that is three weeks or longer is likely to be dominated by retirees. Few younger people can spare that much time.

MISTAKE: **Picking the wrong cabin.** Do not select a cabin based only on its size, cost and the presence of a porthole or balcony. Also, pay careful attention to the cabin's location on the ship. Avoid cabins adjacent to elevator shafts, theaters, nightclubs, casinos or crew entrances, especially if you are a light sleeper. And don't just look for potentially noisy neighbors such as those on a map of the cabin's deck—also check the decks immediately above and below to make sure that the cabin is not under or over something that is likely to be loud. (Avoid cabins under pool decks, too—chairs scraping on these decks are a common source of annoyance for the occupants of cabins directly underneath.) Crew-only spaces such as staff storage rooms might not be labeled at all on ship maps, so be wary of rooms next to map "white spaces." Ideally a cabin should be surrounded by other cabins.

If you are prone to motion sickness, avoid cabins that are high on the ship and/or near the front or rear of the ship—that's where the nausea-inducing feeling of movement tends to be greatest. Cabins low and near midship will be much better for you.

MISTAKE: **Failing to notice the downside of a special price.** Always read the fine print before snagging a cruise line special offer—special fares sometimes come with unexpected restrictions.

Examples: A special low fare might be nonrefundable...a special low-deposit requirement might mean that the deposit is nonrefundable...if the cruise line is running a special promotion, such as "$100 in free onboard credit upon booking," this might not be included with certain discounted fares.

MISTAKE: **Packing items that are not allowed.** Many cruise lines impose severe restrictions on outside alcohol, such as allowing passengers to bring only one or two bottles of outside wine onboard and no outside beer or liquor. A few don't allow any outside alcohol at all.

The portable surge protectors that many travelers use to protect their laptops and other electronics usually are not allowed on cruise ships. Shipboard electrical systems work somewhat differently from electrical systems on land (in part because there is no easy way to "ground" an electrical system at sea). One consequence of this is that surge protectors can create a fire risk. Non-surge-protecting power strips and plug adaptors generally are permitted.

Electrical devices that heat up, such as travel irons and coffeepots, are almost always banned for safety reasons—though curling irons usually are allowed and most cabins come equipped with hair dryers. Read the packing rules on the cruise line's website for details. Cruise line employees do search bags, so don't assume that you can sneak things aboard. Confiscated items generally can be reclaimed after the cruise.

Helpful: Some ships have self-service launderettes where passengers can use irons and ironing boards—Carnival has these fleetwide, for example.

MISTAKE: **Failing to prebook reservations for shore excursions and/or onboard spa treatments and specialty restaurants.** These sometimes fill up, so it's worth investigating these options and booking as soon as the cruise line allows—often that's when you make your final cruise payment, long before the ship sets sail.

It typically is possible to cancel these reservations later without penalty, so there likely is little downside to making these early reservations. This can vary, however, so it is worth reading the fine print to learn cancellation rules.

MISTAKE: **Cutting your arrival too close.** If your flight is scheduled to arrive in the departure port city the same day that the cruise begins, any delay could cause you to miss your ship. A much safer plan is to fly in the day before your ship departs—particularly during winter, when weather-related flight delays are common. Flying in a day early means that you must pay for lodging the night before, but a night in a port city is not a bad thing—it just means that your vacation is one day longer. Some people think that if their airfare is part of the cruise package and the plane is late, the ship automatically will be held in port until their arrival. That's not so, but the cruise line typically will make arrangements to get you to the ship at the next port—always check the fine print before purchasing airfare from a cruise line.

Alternative: If you cannot fly in a day early, purchase travel insurance that will cover your losses if you miss your ship's departure.

MISTAKE: **Waiting for last-minute deals.** In decades past, the best way to get big cruise discounts was to wait until a few weeks before departure dates and snap up remaining cabins for a fraction of their original price. But cruise lines have become much more aggressive about offering appealing deals earlier, so fewer cabins remain as departure dates near...and the cabins that do remain often are unappealing. If you are willing to be extremely patient and flexible, you still can find some attractive last-minute cruise deals from time to time. But for most travelers, the downside of waiting outweighs the upside. To find attractive prices, start to monitor prices on cruises of interest starting up to a year before the departure date. Buy when you see a special offer significantly below the usual rate. Locking in a cruise sooner also gives you time to shop for a good deal on airfare into and out of port cities.

TAKE NOTE...

Tipping Protocol While Traveling in the US

Tipping rental car shuttle bus driver, $1 or $2... skycap, $2 to $3 per bag... airport wheelchair attendant, at least $5, depending on the assistance provided...hotel maid, $2 to $5 per night...bellhop, $1 to $2 per bag...taxi or Uber driver, 15% to 20%, but varies depending on length of trip...half-day or full-day tour guide, $5 to $25...bus tour guide, $5 to $10.

Roundup of experts on tipping and travel, reported in *USA Today*.

Is There a Doctor On Board? What Happens During an In-Flight Medical Emergency

Christian Martin-Gill, MD, MPH, an assistant professor of emergency medicine at the University of Pittsburgh Medical Center (UPMC). Dr. Martin-Gill also serves as a medical command physician for the UPMC Medical Communications Center, providing in-flight medical consultations for commercial airlines. He is a board-certified emergency medicine and emergency medical services physician.

It's a terrifying thought—what happens if you're in an airplane and suffer a health crisis at 36,000 feet? Who will help...and will you be in capable hands? Perhaps even more important, is there anything you can do to prevent a midair emergency from happening in the first place?

Here's what you need to know...

GET THE FACTS

Even though it's frightening to contemplate needing emergency medical care while on a plane, the reality is that these situations are statistically quite rare.

Here are the facts: While about 2.75 billion people fly worldwide on commercial aircraft annually, just 16 passengers for every one million (or about 44,000) require medical care while on a flight, and only 0.3% (about 132) of those passengers end up dying as a result of the health problem.

To better understand the nature of midair medical problems, a seminal study published in 2013 in *The New England Journal of Medicine* analyzed in-flight emergency calls that occurred over a nearly three-year span from five domestic and international airlines.

What were the passengers' primary health complaints? Most common was feeling lightheaded or faint (37%)...respiratory symptoms, such as an asthma attack (12%)...and nausea or vomiting (9.5%). Lower down the list were cardiac symptoms (7.7%)...seizures (5.8%)... and abdominal pain (4%).

Temporary problems: Since only about one-third of airline passengers who become ill mid-flight get transported to a hospital upon landing—and just 9% of them end up being admitted—that leaves two-thirds who walk away once they reach the next airport.

Most often, the medical problems that passengers experience while on a plane are minor. Dehydration is a common complaint, likely due to a combination of dry cabin air and passengers not eating or drinking on a regular schedule. For most ill passengers, symptoms resolve quickly—often within 30 minutes.

WHO STEPS UP?

There's no question that it can be alarming to hear the captain's voice announce over the loudspeaker: "If there's a physician or medical personnel on board, please identify yourself to a flight attendant." But that announcement occurs only after cabin personnel and/or a medical volunteer has already performed an initial assessment of the ill passenger. In most cases, a ground-based medical communications center has also been contacted for immediate input on the situation.

What most people don't realize is that flight attendants—who are better known for handing out drinks and snacks—must have basic emergency medical skills, such as annual training in cardiopulmonary resuscitation (CPR). They must also receive training on using the plane's medical kit (which includes oxygen...medication, such as nitroglycerin...IV fluids...and resuscitation equipment). These requirements, which also include having an automated emergency defibrillator (AED) on board, apply to US-based airlines, while other countries have different requirements.

Safety in numbers: Nearly half the time, there is a physician passenger on board who steps up to provide input on the patient's medical status. In roughly one-quarter of in-flight emergencies, a nurse or other health-care professional, such as a paramedic, comes forward.

Even if there's no doctor or other health-care professional on board, a sick passenger can get the benefit of professional medical guidance because the pilot in command has the ability to communicate with ground-based medical support (while the copilot flies the plane) to ask real-time questions to guide those offering medical assistance.

TO DIVERT OR NOT TO DIVERT

Movie portrayals of in-flight emergencies often depict a hasty landing at a nearby airport so the passenger can be whisked away for emergency medical treatment. But in reality, that outcome occurs less than 7% of the time—and only for serious problems such as chest pain, significant respiratory distress or stroke symptoms.

To divert or not? Diverting a flight for a medical emergency is a huge inconvenience for the other passengers, and sometimes the intended airport is not that far away. Flight and ground medical personnel must consider not only the seriousness of the passenger's medical situation but also the likelihood that he/she will benefit from an earlier landing to receive emergency medical assistance. In many cases, there's no realistic option for diverting—for example, if the plane is over an ocean. While these factors are being weighed, the ill passenger continues to receive medical attention on board the plane.

HOW TO AVOID AN EMERGENCY

Many in-flight emergencies aren't necessarily a surprise to the sick passengers. People with chronic health conditions, such as diabetes or lung or cardiac problems, are generally aware if they're not feeling quite right—and know how to counteract routine symptoms—*before* boarding an airplane. In this regard, travelers have some control *and responsibility* to lower their risks of a midair medical crisis.

Plan ahead: If you are newly diagnosed or have a preexisting medical condition, such as chronic lung disease or heart disease, or have had a recent medical procedure, discuss upcoming air travel (regardless of the duration of the flight) with your doctor to determine if special equipment or care is needed.

For example, people with diabetes need to measure their blood sugar (glucose) levels regularly, so they should bring their glucometer and medications on board with them—and not stow them in checked bags. Anyone needing supplemental oxygen can coordinate the use of an airline-approved portable oxygen concentrator with the airline at least a few days in advance.

Also: If you're feeling ill just before flying, alert a gate attendant or other airline personnel for guidance on continuing with travel plans.

The most sensible tip for all? Make sure you're hydrated and rested (exhaustion can contribute to feeling ill) before you board a plane. And after passing through the security gate, it never hurts to grab a bottle of water!

How to Avoid Jet Lag

Murray Grossan, MD, otolaryngologist, Tower Ear, Nose & Throat, Los Angeles.

A patient recently asked me how he could avoid jet lag after flying to Italy for a vacation.

My answer: You can minimize the impact of flying east (across time zones) by taking measures to reset your body's sleep-wake cycle. The trick is to get more exposure to light earlier in the day and darkness earlier in the evening.

How: A few days before you leave, start to go to bed a bit earlier every night and get up earlier every day so that you're going to bed at 8 pm and getting up at 4 am, for example. (Reverse this when flying west.) Also, be sure to shut off your smartphone or laptop a few hours before bed, since blue light from these devices can disrupt the sleep cycle. A small dose (1 mg) of melatonin before bedtime can be useful as well.

What works for me: A nightly routine (brushing teeth, washing face, etc.) that signals my body that it's time for sleep—and I even do this on the plane. I bring a pillow or small blanket from home when I travel, which also helps trigger sleep. If I still have trouble dozing off, I count slowly…and usually don't get past 20 before I'm asleep.

Surprising Brain Booster: *Travel!*

Paul Nussbaum, PhD, a clinical neuropsychologist and president of the Brain Health Center, Wexford, Pennsylvania, BrainHealthCtr.com, reported by Rebecca Shannonhouse, editor, *Bottom Line Health*.

Some people love to travel. But if you're someone who needs a good reason to pack your bags, here's one to consider: Your brain will love it if you hit the road!

Here is why: The brain's ability to grow, known as plasticity, never ceases. When you take in new sights and information—walking unfamiliar streets, admiring the scenery and listening to (and speaking) unfamiliar languages—the brain forms new neurons and connections. It literally gets bigger and more vibrant, explains Paul Nussbaum, PhD, a clinical neuropsychologist and president of the Brain Health Center in Wexford, Pennsylvania.

You may also get a boost in creativity. Research that looked at fashion executives found that those who had lived abroad created products that were consistently more creative than those produced by their stay-at-home peers.

Of course, not everyone has the time (or the cash or inclination) for exotic vacations. That's OK. Your brain will also be happy with a stimulating "staycation."

The trick: Do anything that isn't routine. Go on weekend road trips. Visit that museum you've always been meaning to see. Introduce yourself to someone whom you've been tempted to talk to but never did.

But if you can travel, go ahead and book those tickets. Even when the trip is over, you'll hopefully have photos to remind you of your adventures and memories to share with others. Remembering stimulates the same neurochemistry as the experience itself. Your brain wants to be stimulated, and reliving your travels is yet another great way to do it.

11 Clever Gadgets for Travelers

Gary Kaye, founder/chief content officer of Tech50+, a website that covers consumer electronics–related topics. Based in Oxford, Connecticut, he has reported on technology for more than 30 years at NBC News, ABC News, CNN, Fox Business Network and other organizations. Tech50Plus.com

There are hundreds of gadgets on the market meant to make travel safer, easier and more enjoyable.* *Here's a look at 11 that you might want to invite along on your next trip...*

HEALTH AND SAFETY

• **Portable humidifier.** Boneco Travel Ultrasonic Humidifier 7146 reduces the odds of parched throats and nasal cavities when visiting arid climates or staying in overly air-conditioned hotel rooms. (It sometimes is sold under Air-O-Swiss.) Dried-out sinuses also make us more vulnerable to vacation-ruining viruses. This humidifier's designers came up with a clever way to make it travel-size—they didn't include a water tank. Instead, you simply attach it to a disposable plastic drinking water bottle. A standard 16.9-ounce bottle should get you through the night. The humidifier comes with exchangeable plugs so that it can be used in both North America and Europe without an additional converter.

Price: $59.99.

Weight: 11.2 ounces.

Site: Boneco.us

• **Travel carbon monoxide detector.** American Red Cross Blackout Buddy—CO from Etón. Almost all hotels have fire alarms, but in most parts of the US and the world, they are not required to have carbon monoxide detectors—and that can be deadly. A 2012 study found that at least 170 US hotel guests had been treated for carbon monoxide poisoning during the previous three years, and eight had died. This lightweight Etón carbon monoxide sensor also features a night-light and a flashlight, so if its alarm sounds in the middle of the night, you can grab it and get out fast without fumbling around for a light switch in an unfamiliar hotel room.

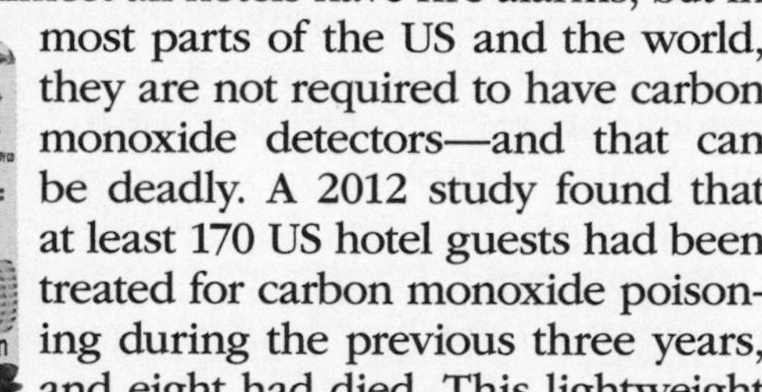

Price: $50.

Weight: 2 lbs.

Site: EtonCorp.com

• **An ultra-portable sleep apnea machine.** Transcend miniCPAP machine provides the continuous positive airway pressure that people who have sleep apnea often require to sleep safely through the night. Unlike most CPAP machines, this one is small enough and light enough to take almost anywhere—just 6.1″ x 3.5″ x 2.8″. It's quiet, too—29 decibels...compatible with any CPAP mask...and approved by the FAA for use on commercial aircraft.

Price: $499. It may be covered by insurance—check with your insurer.

Weight: 15 ounces.

Site: MyTranscend.com

*Prices listed are manufacturer's suggested retail and are subject to change.

Helpful: An optional multinight rechargeable battery ($250) and solar charger ($299.99) also are available. With these, the Transcend miniCPAP can be used on camping trips and in other places with no electrical outlets.

• **A lightweight blood pressure monitor.** iHealth Wireless Wrist Blood Pressure Monitor offers the accuracy of a full-sized digital blood pressure cuff from a significantly smaller, lighter unit. Unlike most digital blood pressure cuffs, it does not include a display unit—it wirelessly pairs to an iOS or Android smartphone via Bluetooth. Its app does not just report blood pressure readings, it can track them over time and share this information with a doctor, caregiver and/or loved one from anywhere in the world as long as there is a cellular or Wi-Fi connection.

Price: $79.95.

Weight: 3.7 ounces.

Site: iHealthLabs.com

• **Tiny water purifier.** SteriPEN UV Ultra Water Purifier is a small, battery-powered device that uses ultraviolet light to quickly kill almost all of the bacteria, viruses and protozoa responsible for water-borne illnesses—it can sterilize 32 ounces of water in just 90 seconds. That's a potential vacation saver when you visit a country where the drinking water is not as well-treated as it is in most parts of the US…or on a camping trip where you drink water that is not treated at all. It can sterilize up to 50 liters of water on a single battery charge (it recharges via a USB cable) and up to 8,000 liters of water during the unit's life.

Price: $99.95.

Weight: 4.9 ounces.

Site: SteriPen.com

PORTABLE POWER PRODUCTS

• **Go-anywhere phone and camera charger.** Kodiak Plus from Outdoor Tech is a lightweight, durable battery that can be used to recharge a phone, digital camera, tablet or anything else that charges via a USB port—up to two devices at a time—even if you don't have access to an electrical outlet. It is waterproof and shockproof and small enough to fit in a pocket—it's just 4.67″ x 3.1″x 0.92″—yet it can charge the typical smartphone up to four times before it must be recharged itself.

Price: $79.95.

Weight: 10.3 ounces.

Site: OutdoorTechnology.com

• **Downsized laptop charger.** Zolt Laptop Charger Plus is a small, light, more versatile replacement for your laptop's power supply—and a way to eliminate the tangle of charging cords that accompany us on our travels these days. Not only can it charge most common laptops, it also can charge electronic devices that recharge by connecting to a USB port, including phones, tablets, digital cameras and portable speakers. In fact, Zolt can charge up to two of these devices at the same time that it's charging a laptop.

Price: About $60.

Weight: 3.5 ounces.

Site: Amazon.com

• **Global plug adapter and USB charger.** Ventev Global ChargingHub 300 is ultra-versatile. There are many plug adapters on the market, but this adapter offers so many different prong configurations that it works virtually everywhere—150 countries in all. It also has a pair of USB charging ports to power up things such as phones and digital cameras.

Price: $34.99.

Weight: 8 ounces.

Site: MobileAccessories.Ventev.com

OTHER CLEVER GADGETS

• **Incredibly bright pocket-size flashlight.** Olight S1 Baton flashlight is tiny enough to take anywhere—just 2.4 inches long—yet its beam can shine usefully up to 110 meters, roughly the length of a football field. Expect 50 minutes of use per battery at the maximum 500-lumen setting…six hours at 80 lumens…or 40 hours at eight lumens. (The 80-lumen setting provides enough light to read by, while the eight-lumen setting is sufficient to walk down a dark road.) One catch—it uses two somewhat unusual CR123A batteries. A 12-

pack can be purchased online for less than $20—but they could be tough to find if you run out in the middle of a vacation.

Price: $49.95.

Weight: 1.5 ounces.

Site: OLightWorld.com

• **Luggage you can track with a smartphone app.** Bluesmart Carry-On is a rolling suitcase that has a built-in tracker. If it is forgotten in a cab, lost by an airline, snatched by thieves in a hotel or otherwise misplaced anywhere in the world, you can find out its exact location using the Bluesmart app, available for iOS and Android phones. This durable, hard-sided bag also features a charging dock with two USB ports—you can use your luggage to charge your phone, tablet or digital camera while on the road. It has a scale built into its handle so that you can easily confirm that your bag does not exceed airline luggage weight limits. In addition, at 22″ x 14″ x 9″, it is small enough to meet virtually all carry-on bag dimensional restrictions.

Price: $314.

Weight: 9.4 pounds.

Site: Bluesmart.com

• **Portable international Wi-Fi hotspot.** Skyroam Hotspot makes it easy and affordable to obtain secure Wi-Fi access in 80 countries around the world. With it, you can obtain unlimited data for up to five digital devices for a very reasonable flat fee of $10 a day, avoiding the risk of big international roaming charges and eliminating the need to install local SIM cards in your digital devices.

One catch—while Skyroam provides "unlimited" data, its connection speed slows considerably after 350MB of data are used each day. So while Skyroam is a wonderful way to send and receive e-mails and texts and to access the Internet, it is not appropriate for streaming video or for sending large photo files.

Price: $124.99.

Weight: 2.4 ounces.

Site: Skyroam.com

TRAVEL TIP...

Better Packing

To prevent wrinkled clothing when traveling...*Roll clothes instead of folding them.* Rolling saves space as well as prevents wrinkles. *Consider using a wrinkle-release spray* such as Downy Wrinkle Releaser—these sprays coat clothes with a thin silicone layer that relaxes the fibers so that they smooth out easily without ironing. *Pack just the right amount of clothing*—both under-packed and overstuffed bags lead to wrinkling. It can help to *group similar items together* and pack them in the order in which you expect to use them. This prevents rummaging in the bag, which can be another cause of wrinkles.

Roundup of experts on travel packing, reported in *USA Today.*

14

Focus on Fun

Get the TV and Movies You Really Want…for a Great Price!

Netflix and Amazon Prime Video are the big names, but they are far from the only options if you want to stream movies and TV shows to your television, computer or other digital devices.

There are plenty of lesser known services that offer various combinations of old and new programming—and many do it for less than the $100 per year charged by Netflix and Amazon. You could combine a few of them to serve as a less expensive substitute for cable or satellite TV—or pick one or two as a supplement to cable or satellite. Many offer free trials, so there's no harm in trying them.

Eight attractive streaming services you may not know about…

• **Acorn TV** concentrates on British television shows and offers programs from Australia, New Zealand, Canada and Ireland as well. It has a particularly strong catalog of British mystery shows including popular series such as *Foyle's War*, *Midsomer Murders* and *Agatha Christie's Poirot*. There are plenty of lesser known shows worth watching, too, such as the award-winning Canadian police drama 19-2…the Australian period drama *A Place to Call Home*…and the Acorn original British mystery series *Agatha Raisin*. All programs are free of ads.

Details: $4.99 per month or $49.99 per year. A seven-day free trial is available. Acorn.tv

• **CuriosityStream** is the streaming service for people who especially like intellectually stimulating television. There's a two-part

Note: Prices, rates and offers throughout this chapter and book are subject to change.

Ryan Downey, executive director, The Streaming Advisor, a website providing news, reviews and guidance related to online video content. TheStreamingAdvisor.com series titled *The Secrets of Quantum Physics*... a David Attenborough documentary about bioluminescence called *Light on Earth*...a three-part series called *Deep Time History* about how civilization has been influenced by events that occurred long before humans ever walked on Earth...and hundreds of other thought-provoking shows. All programming is free of ads.

Details: $2.99 per month. A seven-day free trial is available. CuriosityStream.com

• **FilmStruck** could be the streaming site for you if you strongly prefer art-house movies and classics over recent Hollywood blockbusters. It offers hundreds of films of the type that win awards at festivals—there recently were several films related to the breakup of Yugoslavia, for example. There also are plenty of older films along the lines of those you might see on the cable channel Turner Classic Movies—FilmStruck was created in part by Turner Classic. For an additional monthly fee, FilmStruck provides access to the films of "The Criterion Collection," which features more than 1,000 "cinematic masterpieces" such as *The Lady Vanishes*, *Belle de Jour* and *Seven Samurai*. All the content is commercial free.

Details: $6.99 per month...or $10.99 per month or $99 per year with Criterion Channel access. A 14-day free trial is available. FilmStruck.com

• **HBO Now** offers access to the HBO network's original programming as well as the dozens of movies that HBO is playing in any given month—without having to subscribe to a premium package of cable- or satellite-TV service or even subscribe to cable or satellite at all. (If you do subscribe to the HBO network through a cable or satellite company, you likely can stream much of this programming at no additional charge through a video-on-demand service called HBO Go.) HBO Now provides more than just HBO's current programs, such as *Game of Thrones* and *Westworld*—subscribers also gain access to HBO's complete archive, including programs that it originally ran years earlier. You could watch the entire runs of the critically acclaimed series *The Sopranos* and *The Wire*, for example.

Details: $14.99 per month. A one-month free trial is available. HBONow.com

• **History Vault** offers access to many of the documentaries and shows that have run on the History Channel over the years. Its emphasis is on the history-related content that the History Channel used to specialize in before it turned into yet another cable channel airing reality shows such as *Pawn Stars*. On History Vault, you will find documentaries that cover everything from Incan mummies to the space shuttle and from the Vikings to Vietnam.

Details: $4.99 per month or $49.99 per year. A seven-day free trial is available. HistoryVault.com

• **Hulu** is probably the best-known streaming service after Netflix and Amazon Prime Video, and it certainly provides an impressive amount of content. The service offers access to most of the shows currently airing on ABC, CBS, Fox and NBC (but not CW), with new episodes generally available the day after the first broadcast. Hulu also offers programming from dozens of cable networks (ranging from Comedy Central, Disney and MTV to CNN, Discovery and ESPN) as well as classic older series—Hulu offers every episode of *Seinfeld*, for example. And it has a small number of original shows that are not available on cable or satellite or other streaming services, such as 11.22.63, an action series featuring James Franco...and *Casual*, a Golden Globe–nominated comedy. Hulu's movie selection is less impressive but not without some highlights—for example, recently more than a dozen James Bond flicks were available.

Details: $7.99 per month with commercials or $11.99 per month for a version with commercials during only a few programs. A seven-day free trial is available. Hulu.com

Smart: If you want to add CW to the lineup, its streaming service is available for free, with programs such as *Supergirl* and *Jane the Virgin* available one day after they originally air.

• **NewsOn** lets you stream local news broadcasts from stations across the US either live or up to 48 hours after they originally air. Broadcasts from more than 175 local TV stations in more than 110 US markets are available. You could use NewsOn to watch your own local news from anywhere in the world (assuming that you have Internet access)...or to watch the local news of a different part of the country—maybe you like to keep up with what's happening where you used to live or where your adult child recently moved, for example. These newscasts include commercial breaks just as they would if you were watching them over the air.

Details: Free. WatchNewsOn.com

• **Showtime streaming service** is the Showtime equivalent of HBO Now, described above. (If you subscribe to the Showtime network through a cable or satellite provider, you likely can stream its current and past movie and TV programming to other devices at no additional charge through a similar video-on-demand service called Showtime Anytime.) Current Showtime hits range from the spy thriller *Homeland* and the comedy-drama *Shameless* to the Wall Street drama *Billions* and the dramas *Masters of Sex* and *The Affair*. There are no ads on this service.

Details: $10.99 per month. A 30-day free trial is available. Showtime.com

FREEBIES...

Free Reading and Entertainment!

Apple, Amazon, Google Play and other e-book sellers make some free e-book titles available—and with e-books typically about $10, this can save you $240 a year if you read two books a month. Many libraries offer Kindle and other formats of e-books for reading or listening on a phone, tablet, e-reader or computer. Availability is limited to the number of electronic copies the library owns, and e-books vanish from borrower's devices after one to two weeks. If your library does not offer this, you can use your library card with services such as *Hoopla* and *OverDrive* to borrow e-books and audiobooks for various devices, usually for two to three weeks.

More entertainment for free: The *Freegal* app enables library card holders to download five songs a week...the Google Play store offers free music from well-known artists...the *Hoopla* app lets you download videos to mobile devices for offline viewing for 72 hours.

Roundup of experts on free entertainment content, reported at Time.com/Money.

How to Get Your Artwork Sold: Forget Galleries

Barney Davey, founder of ArtMarketingNews.com and author of six books about the business of being an artist, including *Straight Advice: How to Market Art Online Now.* He is a former marketing executive with *Décor* magazine and founder of Bold Star Communications, a Phoenix-based art-marketing and communications firm.

If you're an artist, you would probably love a reliable way to sell your work. Galleries used to be the best way for artists to get their work seen by art buyers, but in the past decade, many galleries have gone out of business. Those that remain often struggle to attract buyers.

Solution: Take advantage of today's increasingly diverse ways to sell your work without using galleries at all.

This is more feasible than you might imagine because artists have one big advantage over writers, filmmakers and other self-employed creative professionals. While a writer or filmmaker needs tens of thousands of people to read his books or watch her movies to make a significant income, full-time professional artists often produce just 30 to 35 original works a year. They can establish a career if 50 to 100 art collectors buy their pieces regularly or if they can get a licensing deal.

Here are six ways that artists can get their art seen by potential buyers in this "post-gallery" era...

FIND ART BUYERS ONLINE

• **Join online groups.** If you paint equine art, for example, join Facebook and Google Plus groups for horse owners, rodeo fans and other horse-related hobbies. If you produce drawings of cars, join online groups of classic-car collectors. Become known and respected in these online groups by posting useful information, answering questions and/or writing articles. Mention that you're an artist who produces work in this area only after you have become part of the group—it is much easier to sell to people who already feel that they know you.

Once you are established, you can post appropriate pictures of your work from time to time...ask for opinions...and provide a link to your social-media page or website where people can view and purchase your works if they wish to. You also can create special offers for group members.

• **Advertise on Facebook.** Advertising this way can be surprisingly affordable. For less than $100, you can promote a Facebook page featuring your artwork to hundreds or thousands of potential fans, though ad rates can vary based on numerous factors. One effective strategy is to target Facebook users who already have expressed an affinity for art comparable to your own.

Example: If your art's style is sometimes likened to that of Vincent van Gogh, you could have Facebook send your ad to people who have expressed an interest in the art of van Gogh on their Facebook pages. For more information, go to Facebook.com/business.

• **Post on SaatchiArt.com.** There are hundreds of "virtual gallery" websites where artists can post and sell their work, but Saatchi Art is the most effective. While other sites often are little more than a place to post pictures and make occasional sales, Saatchi Art allows artists to promote themselves as well as their work. Artists can create profile pages and then link those profiles to their own social-media pages. This helps artists forge deep connections with buyers, inspiring repeat customers and loyal fan bases—the real key to success.

Unlike many other virtual galleries, Saatchi Art does not charge posting fees—artists pay only a reasonable 30% commission when their works sell. Nor does it bar artists from marketing works through other venues as well. Follow the excellent tips on SaatchiArt.com/promoting to improve your sales on the site.

CONNECT WITH BUYERS IN PERSON

• **Rent booths at art shows and fairs.** Renting booths at art gatherings is an old-fashioned technique but still can be an effective way to sell art and network with potential collectors. Choose your shows wisely. In many areas, there are dozens of these events every year, and some inevitably are not worth the time and booth fees.

Visit several shows in your area before taking a booth. Arrive at a quiet time—early or late in the day often is best—when there are few other shoppers and the artists selling their work have time to chat. Ask these artists about their opinions of the show you are attending and other ones in the area. Pay close attention to responses from artists whose work is close to your own in terms of price and style. You also can solicit opinions about local art shows and fairs through the websites and social-media sites of local art associations.

Helpful: When you take a booth at a show, focus not just on selling the art you have on display but also on building a list of potential collectors. When people ask if you have a business card or catalog, say that you don't but that you would be happy to put these people on your e-mail mailing list—and have a pad and pen so that they can write down their e-mail addresses. E-mail lists provide an effective ongoing reminder about an artist's work. Send out periodic updates about your latest pieces.

• **Arrange home shows.** If a well-to-do art fan starts collecting your work, casually ask whether he/she would be willing to host a home show for you. The host invites his art-fan friends to his house...and the artist displays his art there, chats about his work and provides wine and cheese. It's a win-win—the collector looks like a patron of the arts to his friends, while the artist networks with potential buyers.

• **Display your art in local businesses—but not restaurants.** Having your art hung on the walls of a high-end boutique, spa or antiques store can get it seen by the sort of people who tend to buy art.

Having your art hung on the walls of restaurants or cafés is less likely to be useful. In my experience, even when diners do notice restaurant art, they almost never purchase these works. Approach restaurants about displaying your art only if you have a lot of art to show and no better place to show it.

LICENSE YOUR ART

Licensing art means granting a company the right to reproduce it on products such as notebooks, wallpaper, shower curtains and dishes. Licensers generally look for art that is highly decorative—that is, visually appealing to a broad audience. That could be anything from colorful patterns to cute cats to seashore scenes.

Example: The Florida painter Paul Brent (PaulBrent.com) has made millions of dollars licensing mainly tropical coastal scenes.

Before you can get involved with licensing, you need to know the basics of the business. An Internet search for terms such as "how to license artwork" is a good starting point.

Also helpful: Maria Brophy provides a wealth of licensing information for artists at MariaBrophy.com/category/art-licensing. After your initial research, start reviewing the websites of the exhibitors at Surtex, the premier show for licensing artwork held annually in New York City, to get a feel for what kinds of art are licensed.

Collector Alert: What's Hot Now… and What's Fizzled

Terry Kovel, author of more than 100 books about collecting including *Kovels' Antiques & Collectibles Price Guide 2017.* Based in Cleveland, her nationally syndicated column appears in more than 150 newspapers. Kovels.com

---

Is your Norman Rockwell print still valuable? What about that set of fine china you paid a fortune for years ago? Or those figurines you've been collecting? Collectibles go in and out of style—and the collectibles market has experienced some dramatic shifts recently. *Here what's hot now in the world of collecting—and what's not…*

ON THE RISE

Prices have increased in the following categories. If you own any of these items—or see an opportunity to snap them up at a garage sale—this could be a good time to sell them at a profit…

- **Vinyl records.** Old record albums seemed likely to fade into history in this age of digital music. Instead they have resurged in value. Prices vary, but many albums from the 1980s and earlier in near-mint or mint condition can bring $10 to $30 these days, and rare desirable albums sometimes sell for thousands.

Example: A rare original issue of the David Bowie album *The Man Who Sold the World* recently sold for slightly more than $10,000 on eBay. A near-mint copy of the more common Bowie album *Space Oddity* might bring $25 to $30.

- **Old stuff made of iron.** Almost anything old, interesting and made of iron is popular. That includes iron doorstops…garden statues…pots and pans…ornate fencing and railings…and distinctive household devices.

Example: A cast-iron doorstop from 1927 in the shape of a lighthouse recently sold for $715.51 on eBay.

- **Norman Rockwell prints.** These were little more than flea market fodder a decade ago, but the art world has reevaluated Rockwell, who died in 1978, and decided that he should be considered a serious artist after all. That has dramatically increased the value of original Rockwell paintings—a Rockwell painting titled *Saying Grace* sold for $46 million in 2013—and increased the value of Rockwell prints, too, even as much of the rest of the print market has declined. Original Rockwell prints come from three publishers—Abrams, Circle Fine Art and Eleanor Ettinger, Inc.—and have an original pencil signature by Norman Rockwell on the right side of the lower margin.

Example: Original prints of the Rockwell painting *After the Prom* can bring $4,000 to $5,000 on eBay.

• **Midcentury modern housewares and furniture.** Furniture and housewares from the 1940s through the 1960s made in the then-futuristic "midcentury modern" style is hot now.

Examples: An Eames 670 lounge chair and an ottoman in a red leather from 1956 recently sold for $7,500 on eBay...a Finn Juhl Design teak salad bowl recently sold for $3,827.99.

• **Distinctive antique typewriters.** Rare typewriters made before the 1920s with unusual shapes are very much in demand these days, perhaps as a backlash against soulless computer keyboards.

Example: An 1881 Hammond 1 Typewriter with ebony keys and a curved keyboard sold for $1,600.

• **Hermès handbags.** Used Hermès handbags can sell for thousands of dollars even if they are not exceptionally old and rare. Bags that feature high-end flourishes such as diamonds, gold or platinum hardware sometimes fetch five or even six figures.

Example: Heritage Auctions sold a Hermès Himalayan Nilo Crocodile Birkin bag with diamonds and gold hardware for $185,000. A basic Hermès Rouge Garance Evelyn bag sold for $2,000 on eBay.

• **Vintage political collectibles.** Campaign buttons, posters and items with images of political candidates from the 1920s or earlier are selling well.

Example: A Calvin Coolidge and Charles Dawes 1924 campaign button with an attached eagle pin recently sold for more than $5,600 on eBay.

• **Oil- and gas-related antiques and advertising items.** "Petroliana"—that is, gas station–related collectibles—including vintage enameled gas station signs, pre-1960 oil cans and the glass globes that once sat atop early gas pumps are in great demand.

Example: An enameled Gulf Supreme Motor Oil sign from the 1930s sold for $2,925 on eBay.

• **Taxidermy.** Stuffed, mounted animals and animal heads used to attract little interest at estate sales, but lately they have been climbing in value. Exotic animals are especially desirable, but some states have laws controlling their sale—a local taxidermist might be able to provide details.

Examples: A mounted bison head in good condition can bring $1,000 to $2,000 on eBay. A more common six- or eight-point whitetail deer head often will fetch $60 to $150.

ON THE OUTS

The market has dried up for the following collectibles. That doesn't mean you shouldn't buy these things—in fact, this is a great time to find great deals. But it does mean that you should buy these items only if you love them, not as investments. *After collectibles fall out of favor, they might rebound, but there is no guarantee that they will...*

• **Figurines.** Knickknack-size items are increasingly seen as clutter to avoid. Figurine values have fallen farthest due to this trend, but other undersized collectibles ranging from antique bottle openers to decorative thimbles have seen their values slide, too.

Examples: The Royal Doulton Bunnykins figurines once sold for perhaps $100 apiece. Today you can find them at $25 for a lot of six. (The most desirable ones can bring more.) Most examples of the Hummel figurine "Stormy Weather" sell for between $40 and $60 on eBay, a fraction of what they sold for two decades ago.

• **Antique wood furniture.** The typical piece of antique wood furniture has lost around two-thirds of its value in the past decade or so. Many 19th-century tables, chairs and desks now can be had for $200 to $400—right around what you might pay for a piece of pressed-wood furniture at Ikea. (Exceptionally well-made or attractive pieces of antique furniture still can have considerable value despite this decline in interest.)

Example: A maple drop-front Chippendale-style desk made in New Hampshire in 1780 would have sold for $3,000 in an antiques shop in the late 1990s...but just $300 to $500 today.

• **Modern toys in less-than-mint condition.** Toys from the 1970s and 1980s were a hot collector category, but they have cooled dramatically and now have significant value only if they are extremely rare and/or are in such great condition that they look like they were never played with (or, better yet, still are in their original boxes).

Example: A typical Hot Wheels car from the 1970s in good but not perfect condition might have sold for $5 a few years ago...but now is worth the 25 cents it might fetch at a garage sale.

- **Fine china.** Many older people who own fine china are downsizing, and the younger generations have shown little interest in purchasing this collectible. That has created a supply/demand imbalance that has devastated prices.

Example: A vintage Limoges set of 12 berry bowls sells for $150, a fraction of what it brought a decade or two ago.

Helpful: This could be a good time to buy a set of china that you've always wanted or add to a set you already have.

- **Lithographs and other prints.** Norman Rockwell aside, the print market has fallen sharply in the past decade as tastes have shifted away from the historic and Americana scenes that many prints depict. (Prints of birds and fish are among the exceptions—they have held their value well.)

Example: A Currier & Ives large print that might have sold for $1,000 a decade ago now might bring $500.

- **Bakelite jewelry.** In this century's early years, jewelry from the 1930s and 1940s made of Bakelite, a type of plastic, commanded prices in the hundreds of dollars, occasionally more. Values have collapsed—the market has become flooded by so-called "fakelite," a modern version of Bakelite that is extremely difficult to distinguish from the real thing.

Example: Now a Bakelite bracelet that might have sold for $500 a decade ago could bring just $100 at auction.

6 Tricks to Improve Your Golf Score

Joel Zuckerman, author of eight books on golf and the only two-time winner of the Book of the Year Award as bestowed by the International Network of Golf. VagabondGolfer.com

There's a reason why golf is such a difficult game to master. Part of it is the fact that swinging a slender club and making solid contact with a small ball requires a degree of coordination that can be elusive. In addition, players need to familiarize themselves with nearly 150 different scenarios that they might encounter in any 18-hole round. This is because there are many different clubs in the bag, from driver to putter, and you will encounter many different playing surfaces. With all these variables, finding consistency with any club on all surfaces is daunting.

Fortunately, there are a number of uncomplicated techniques that can help you meet these challenges. *These course-management suggestions will shave strokes from your scorecard the very next time you play—no practice needed...*

- **Drive the ball from the proper side of the tee box.** A straight tee shot is rare. Most golfers curve the ball from the tee box, the vast majority hitting a fade or slice—for example, curving from left-to-right for a right-handed player. To increase the odds of hitting the fairway, golfers who fade the ball should set up on the extreme right-hand portion of the teeing ground. This means that you'll rotate a bit to keep the fairway in view and give yourself more room for the ball to curve back to the middle of the fairway. For those with a tendency to draw or hook the tee shot—for example, curve the ball from right to left—the opposite applies. They should set up on the left side of the tee box, giving themselves a better chance to curve the shot back toward the middle.

- **Don't go from bad to worse.** Inevitably a golfer will find himself/herself out of position. The ball will come to rest among trees, in thick rough, amid bushes, etc. We watch the world's best players extricate themselves from "jail" on TV every weekend, pulling off seemingly impossible hero shots, and we often feel compelled to try the same thing. Don't! If the ultimate goal is to save shots on the scorecard, then keep both ego and adrenaline in check, and play out laterally to the safety of the fairway. Hopefully it will cost you only that single shot, and with a fine approach or a long putt made, perhaps you'll escape with par. The hero shot often is the zero shot, and by going out of the frying pan and into the fire (trying to thread the needle between tall pines or rip it toward the green from beneath a bush), one most often will worsen the situation.

Remember this mantra: "If you try and thread it, you'll soon regret it."

• **Play to uneven lies.** Golf courses are three-dimensional and often will present a player with uneven, as opposed to perfectly flat, lies. Just remember these four tendencies to keep the ball traveling in the intended direction. These directives are for right-handed golfers. *For points one and two, lefties should do the opposite...*

1. If the ball is above your feet, when struck it generally will travel to the left, with a hook.

2. If the ball is below your feet, it will likely do the opposite, traveling toward the right, with a fade or slice.

3. If the ball comes to rest on a straight uphill lie, the ball will tend to fly higher and shorter than from a flat lie.

4. If the ball is directly downhill, the shot will tend to come out lower and straighter, more of a line drive than a normal arcing trajectory.

Bear all of these tendencies in mind and adjust accordingly for a more accurate shot.

• **Use less loft for long bunker shots.** The long bunker shot (20 to 50 yards) is considered one of golf's most difficult shots. However, few amateur players are aware of the fact that they can increase their odds of success simply by choosing a club with less loft. There's no need to swing harder or manipulate the club in an unfamiliar way to try to cover the additional distance.

Example: In a typical greenside bunker, with the flagstick 10 yards away, most golfers use a sand wedge or lob wedge, typically with 56 or 60 degrees of loft. If the shot is two or three times that distance, simply choose a pitching wedge, even a nine iron (generally speaking, the former has about 50 degrees of loft, the latter about 47). You make the same swing, displacing the sand in the same manner used with a sand wedge, and the reduction in loft will make the ball fly a little lower and travel farther.

• **The shorter the shot, the more you should grip down on the club.** When faced with delicate shots near the green, choke down on the club, placing your hands closer to the bare shaft and farther from the top of the grip. A shorter club is easier to control and allows you to swing the club more vertically and stand closer to the ball. All of these techniques are designed to keep a player more upright, swinging the club closer to the body, which automatically increases accuracy. Stand farther from the ball and hold the club nearer the top when you need speed to generate power to hit longer. Since length and power are moot points with greenside shots, golfers need to do the opposite.

• **Around the green, keep the ball on or near the ground.** Far too many golfers automatically reach for the pitching wedge or sand wedge for short shots. The problem with using lofted clubs exclusively is that there is little room for error. Sometimes the shot will be "chunked," which means that the player hits the ground instead of the ball, and it barely moves forward. Other times the ball gets "bladed," or hit thin, and the result is a ball that rockets well past the target, over the green and often into serious trouble. The solution is to use less lofted clubs and strike the ball so that it bounces and rolls toward the

GOOD TO KNOW...

For a database of more than 16,000 US golf courses including fees, par values, locations, directions and links to websites, go to PublicCourses.com.

target, as opposed to flying through the air. This type of ground shot often is used in the UK, and by using the seven iron, eight iron or a hybrid club, employing a putting-type motion, mistakes can be mitigated. If there's water or sand between the ball and the green, this technique cannot be used and the golfer must loft the shot over the trouble. However, if there are no impediments between the ball and target, keeping the ball on or near the ground is a much safer play. Major mistakes are minimized with this technique, and over time, the result can be as good as using the more difficult-to-control wedges.

---

6 Amazing Courses Every Golfer Should Play

Joel Zuckerman, author of eight books on golf and the only two-time winner of the Book of the Year Award as bestowed by the International Network of Golf. VagabondGolfer.com

---

There are more than 16,000 golf courses in the US, but just a handful would be considered "bucket list" destinations for the game's aficionados. These six courses may be a bit pricey, but playing them will stir the soul and remain an indelible memory for those fortunate enough to visit. It shouldn't be difficult to get on the courses, but advance reservations are always helpful. Plan ahead for the spring or summer, or get discount rates this winter (only Whistling Straits is closed in the winter).

PEBBLE BEACH
MONTEREY, CALIFORNIA

Located on California's Monterey Peninsula about two hours south of San Francisco, Pebble Beach tops most any golfer's bucket list for several compelling reasons. The first is the scintillating beauty of the golf course. The crashing surf of the Pacific just steps from the emerald fairways is as breathtaking a site as most golfers will ever behold. Second, the strategy and skill the golf course requires test all who confront it.

Example: The eighth hole is a par four that no less of an authority than Jack Nicklaus says offers the greatest approach shot in golf. An ocean inlet, found at the base of a practically vertical cliff, bisects the fairway. The tee shot requires careful placement, as a too-bold stroke will tumble your ball into the sea. The third factor is that Pebble drips history. Nicklaus won a US Open here. So did Tom Watson and Tiger Woods, among other luminaries. To stroll the fairways of Pebble Beach is to walk in the shadows of the giants.

Details: Pebble Beach green fees run about $500 per person. PebbleBeach.com

THE OCEAN COURSE
KIAWAH ISLAND, SOUTH CAROLINA

The Ocean Course at South Carolina's Kiawah Island was created in the early 1990s by mastermind golf course architect Peter Dye. It doesn't yet have the history of Pebble Beach, but it is a "must-play" by any standard. It's an exhilarating, windswept walk among the dunes featuring bottomless bunkers, perched greens, dense foliage, waving fescue grasses, sea views from every hole and an unrelenting series of challenges. Golfers walking off the final hole who aren't bushed by the challenges they confronted on this seaside gem will be few and far between. The course is fairly narrow, always in close proximity to the beach, and stretches almost three miles in length. The course has some notable history despite its relative youth. The 1991 Ryder Cup was played there, the outcome in doubt until the final putt. It remains the most memorably famous international match since these biennial competitions commenced in the 1920s. The Ocean Course also hosted the 2012 PGA Championship, won by Rory McIlroy, and will host the PGA Championship again in 2021.

Details: Green fees run about $375 per person...December through February, about $100 less. KiawahResort.com

WHISTLING STRAITS
SHEBOYGAN, WISCONSIN

Whistling Straits in Sheboygan, Wisconsin, about one hour from Milwaukee, is another wonderful creation by Pete Dye. And the backstory is astonishing. The site was a World War II army base, an ecological ruin filled with concrete bunkers and fuel storage tanks. But it also featured seventy-foot bluffs rising above the shoreline of Lake Michigan, which compelled resort owner Herb Kohler (the plumbing-supply magnate) to envision a one-of-a-kind golf course there. By the time Pete Dye was done scalloping the landscape, the wondrous creation of fescue grasses and bunkers surrounding tilting fairways looked as if it were sitting on top of the Irish Sea. Kohler even imported a flock of blackface sheep to roam the course along the lakeshore unencumbered, adding a uniquely appealing touch.

The wind whips, and temperatures can drop a dozen degrees in an hour's time when a front moves through. This is wild and woolly golf, although occasionally serene and perfect on a midsummer's day, and one of the nation's most coveted tee times. The Straits hosted the 2004, 2010 and 2015 PGA championships and will host the 2020 Ryder Cup.

Details: Green fees start at $410 per person. AmericanClubResort.com

BANDON DUNES AND PACIFIC DUNES
BANDON, OREGON

Bandon Dunes, on the central Oregon coast about four hours south of the international airport in Portland, is one of golf's unlikeliest success stories. Golf-loving entrepreneur Mike Keiser searched the nation for a seaside locale with springy, firm turf similar to that of the traditional courses he admired in the UK. When he discovered the desired topography, he wasn't concerned that the property was so far from a population center—he felt the course would be worth the drive. To make things tougher, he decreed that there would be no golf carts available—all visitors would walk. The first course was a success and spurred the development of another course, then a third and a fourth. The original course debuted in 1999 and was designed by a young Scotsman named David McLay Kidd. The architect produced an elegant figure-eight routing that proceeds from the clubhouse to the sea and back on each nine. The course features broad fairways, deep sod-walled bunkers and sizable greens. Several holes on each nine are in close proximity to the cliffs abutting the roiling sea, which is pockmarked with the elaborate rock formations jutting from the water and pounded ceaselessly by the surf that makes this stretch of coastline so memorable.

Iconoclastic architect Tom Doak came on the scene soon after. Pacific Dunes, which debuted in 2001, is located north of the first course and is even more dramatic. It has seven holes perched precariously 100 feet above Whiskey Run Beach, where a lucky golfer might see migrating whales beyond the surf line. Pacific Dunes offers quirkier, riskier golf than the original, with less dirt moved and more humps and hummocks in the fairways. Tee shots and approaches are more exacting here than on Bandon Dunes, and the routing is decidedly nontraditional, with four par 3s and three par 5s coming on the inward nine. In less than two decades, the Bandon Dunes complex has been elevated to "must play" status by golf cognoscenti the world over.

Details: Green fees can be as high as $275 per resort guest in midsummer high season, but replay rates (playing a second round in the same day) are about half off. BandonDunesGolf.com

PINEHURST #2
PINEHURST, NORTH CAROLINA

Pinehurst #2 is one of nine courses available at this bastion of tradition and gentility in the North Carolina sand hills. It is far and away the marquee venue and the most compelling reason visitors have been making the trek to the area for more than a century. This is a Donald Ross design, and of the hundreds of courses that the Scottish master created, none are held in higher regard than #2. The course, created in 1907, is a Plain Jane in comparison with other courses that are, say, perched above the sea. Instead the genius of the design of Pinehurst #2 is in the subtlety of the green complexes. Approaches that are seemingly targeting the flag end up rolling back off the front edge, while boldly stroked shots will easily filter past the pin, over the putting surface and down into the swale behind. It's maddening, but that's why it's a masterpiece. In 2010, the design firm of Bill Coore & Ben Crenshaw (the latter a two-time Masters champion) began to restore the natural and strategic characteristics that were the essence of Ross's original design and that had changed over time. The result is a golf course where very few trees encroach and there is virtually no water in play. Pinehurst #2 has hosted more than a dozen important championships. The US Open has been played there on several occasions, as has the Ryder Cup, PGA Championship and others.

Details: Green fees are about $480 per person, reduced to $370 in November and December. Pinehurst.com

---

If You Like These Popular Wine Brands... You'll Love These Even More

Jeff Siegel, the Wine Curmudgeon, is a wine writer, wine critic and wine judge who specializes in inexpensive wine. He is author of *The Wine Curmudgeon's Guide to Cheap Wine* and oversees the award-winning Wine Curmudgeon website (WineCurmudgeon.com). He also is an adjunct instructor at El Centro College in Dallas.

When people enjoy a brand of wine, they often drink it to the exclusion of everything else. That's one reason why Kendall-Jackson's $12 chardonnay has been the best-selling wine in the US for about 25 years. We buy it, we like it, and it's easier to keep buying it than to try something else.

But wine can be so much more than drinking the same thing year after year. Given the thousands of wines most of us have never had, there's almost certainly something else in the same price range that we would enjoy—and enjoy more.

Here are six very popular brands of wines... along with suggestions for other brands that could become your new favorites...

- **If you like Barefoot Merlot ($7), try The Velvet Devil Merlot ($15).** Barefoot is the best-selling wine brand in the US, mostly because it offers simple, soft wines at a fair price. The merlot is an excellent example, with the chocolate-cherry flavor that so many casual wine drinkers enjoy. The Velvet Devil from Washington State used to be a more traditional merlot, with the acidity and tannins (the astringent taste in the back of your mouth) typical of the varietal, but it has evolved into a more sophisticated version of the Barefoot. It's not quite as chocolaty, but there is lots and lots of rich red cherry fruit sure to please anyone looking for a smooth red wine.

- **If you like Kendall-Jackson Chardonnay ($12), try Argento Chardonnay ($10).** Kendall-Jackson's chardonnay is famous for its fruity, almost sweet character (using a production technique that wine geeks call *stuck fermentation*), as well as a dash of vanilla. This is not easy for other producers to do, but Argentina's Argento pulls it off nicely. Look for white stone fruit flavors and the same hint of sweetness as in Kendall-Jackson. In all, the Argento offers a balance between the fruit and sweetness that many other chardonnays can't manage.

- **If you like Yellow Tail Shiraz ($8), try Henry's Drive Pillar Box Red ($10).** Expensive Australian shiraz is deep, dark and spicy, with almost overwhelming black fruit. Yellow Tail, long one of the best-selling imported wines in the US, translates this style using an affordable, much less sophisticated approach. It's almost juicy, in the way that fruit juice is juicy, and again with little acidity and tannins to get in the way. The Pillar Box Red, also from Australia, is a red blend made with shiraz that is not as simple as Yellow Tail, and it tastes more like the expensive shirazes. It's an opportunity to see what something more complex tastes like without spending too much money or taking a chance that the wine will be too far over the top to be enjoyable.

- **If you like Ecco Domani Pinot Grigio ($10), try Alois Lageder Pinot Grigio ($14).** Ecco Domani is one of a half dozen or so

EASY TO DO...

Revive Flat Champagne

When a sparkling wine has started to lose its fizz but isn't entirely flat, drop a single raisin into the bottle a few minutes before pouring to revive the fizz.

RealSimple.com

immensely popular Italian pinot grigios (including Costco's Kirkland Signature and the Cavit and Mezzacorona brands), best known for their crisp, almost fruitless style, with something like a tonic water minerality and a short, clean finish that is one reason pinot grigio drinkers enjoy the wine so much. These wines are refreshing and lend themselves to ice cubes in summer. The Lageder, also Italian, offers something that many pinot grigio drinkers have never tried—more fruit, a flowery aroma and a richer style.

• **If you like Beringer White Zinfandel ($6), try Charles & Charles Rosé ($10).** The surge in rosé's popularity over the past several years may make a lot of white zinfandel drinkers who have never tried a dry rosé wonder what they're missing. Classic rosés are dry, while white zinfandel is sweet, and rosés usually are more crisp and feature tart berry flavors (cranberry, in particular) as opposed to white zinfandel's ripe strawberry fruit. The Charles & Charles rosé, from Washington State, is a dry rosé but with the strawberry fruit, which isn't as tart as many rosés—in other words, a white zinfandel-friendly introduction to rosé.

• **If you like La Marca Prosecco ($14), try Jaume Serra Cristalino Brut Cava ($10).** The La Marca, an Italian sparkling wine, has lemon fruit, lively bubbles and a hint of sweetness. It's quite well-made for the price and, given the millions of cases produced every year, quite popular. The Cristalino, a sparkling wine from Spain, doesn't have the hint of sweetness, and there is more apple fruit than lemon. But it's even better made, and the tight, crisp bubbles usually come only in more expensive wine. It's an ideal wine to try if you're ready to experiment with something other than Prosecco.

WINEGLASSES AND GADGETS FOR ABOUT $10

Here are useful wine accessories that cost about $10 each...

• **Tritan Forte wineglasses.** These affordable all-purpose glasses from Schott Zwiesel—good for white and red wines—are crystal, a step up from the glass restaurant kind, and they're more difficult to break than more expensive glasses.

• **Rialto Waiter's corkscrew.** This offers a double-hinged lever and a Teflon-coated screw (technically called a worm). It will open any bottle with a cork, and learning to use it isn't as difficult as it seems. That's because, after a half-dozen times or so, you'll figure out how to screw the worm into the cork, work the levers to pull the cork out and impress others with your ability to do so.

• **Rabbit wine preserver.** Those of us who don't finish a bottle of wine in one sitting will notice that the wine goes off after a day or two in the same way that a cut apple will turn brown. This is called oxidation, when oxygen gets to the wine and changes its flavor. The Rabbit preserver, which pumps the air out of an open wine bottle and comes with seals to replace the cork or screw cap, is simple to use and helps the wine last a few days longer.

BETTER WAY...

Wine Portion Control

To keep from drinking more than you should for your health, pour five ounces of wine (one standard drink) into a measuring cup, then transfer it into each type of wineglass you have, noting the level reached. Some glasses look nearly empty when holding a full drink!

Bottom Line Research

Dating Again? 8 Signs You've Found the Right Person

Sandy Weiner, dating coach, speaker and author who focuses on helping women over 40 date with dignity. Based in Stamford, Connecticut, she is host of the online radio show *Last First Date Radio* (BlogTalkRadio.com/lastfirstdate) and coauthor of *The Secrets to Setting Healthy Boundaries in Dating.* LastFirstDate.com

Dating advice often focuses on finding red flags—signs that a potential partner is not really Mr. or Ms. Right. We're advised to avoid anyone who treats waiters poorly...or who leaves his/her phone on the table at dinner, for example. These red flags have merit, but they create an undue focus on the negative.

The secret to finding a great partner is not just about weeding out anyone who has anything wrong with him or her, but rather selecting someone who has lots of great qualities—someone with the traits and temperament to participate in a happy, healthy relationship.

Here are eight of the most important "green flags" to look for in a partner. Some of these may be evident very early in a relationship... some after you've been dating for a while. All are crucial to a satisfying relationship.

1. He/she can express and take responsibility for his own feelings. It's a big green flag if a partner can say, "I'm feeling sad" or "I'm feeling angry," rather than sulk, rage or give you the silent treatment. Such a person is open about his feelings, which is a lot better than bottling them up inside until they explode.

It's even more promising if a partner not only identifies his feelings but also does not hold you responsible for them—even when your actions contributed to them. We are always responsible for our own feelings, regardless of who or what might have triggered them.

Example: You make an ill-considered joke at your partner's expense. It's a good sign if rather than saying, "You made me upset," she says, "I'm feeling upset" or "That joke upset me, but I understand that you probably weren't trying to upset me. I'm a bit touchy about jokes like that because I was teased in school. Would you be willing to not tell jokes like that anymore?"

Similar: It's also a great sign if a partner realizes when he is too emotional to have a productive conversation and says something such as, "I'm too angry to talk right now. I need time to calm down. Can we talk in about a half hour?" then returns to the topic later with less emotion.

2. He/she responds with both empathy and honesty when you mention a behavior that doesn't work for you. What characteristics and behaviors are especially important to you in a partner? If your partner says or does something that's not in alignment with your needs, calmly explain that this matters to you and listen to the response. It's a green flag if that response is not defensive. Your partner calmly discusses your needs while staying true to his. It's a bad sign if your partner makes excuses...denies falling short in this area...belittles your priorities...and/or makes no real effort to improve.

Example: You value punctuality, but your partner often is late. Explain that you need a partner who understands that your time has value and who does not regularly leave you sitting around waiting. It's a great sign if this person acknowledges having a punctuality problem and makes an honest effort to improve, perhaps by starting to get ready for dates 10 minutes earlier—even if he never becomes as punctual as you would like.

3. He/she is responsible with money. This is important even if you never tie your financial lives together by getting married. People who are financially responsible tend to be responsible with other aspects of their lives as well—including their relationships. A partner who lives within his means is much more likely to live up to his promises and make you feel safe and comfortable than one who has revolving credit card debt and likes to gamble.

Similar: It's also a great sign if a partner eats right and exercises. These, too, point to overall responsibility.

4. He/she continues to evolve and learn new things. It is a green flag if your partner continues to seek out new hobbies...enjoys traveling to new places and trying new restaurants...and is interested in a wide range of subjects. A partner who enjoys growing and trying new things is much more likely to continue to be interesting as time passes. When you first meet someone, that person might seem interesting simply because he's new to you. But if this person is set in his ways, there's a good chance that the relationship will eventually stagnate...or that he won't be willing to modify his life to include things that you like.

5. He/she has strong friendships. People who have multiple close friends tend to be people who have the emotional health and interpersonal skills needed to sustain a romantic relationship. They're also less likely to expect their romantic partners to fulfill every interpersonal need, something that is not feasible or healthy.

Similar: Consider it a good sign if your partner wants to introduce you to her friends. It shows that she's proud to be with you and that she is taking your relationship seriously. (*Note:* It is advisable for single parents who are dating to delay introducing romantic partners to their children until they are in a serious long-term relationship. This is particularly important if those kids are still young.)

6. He/she asks for your input on decisions. Obviously a partner should include you in decisions that involve you. But consider it a green flag if a partner also asks for your opinion on matters that do not directly involve you—a career decision, perhaps, or the selection of a new car. This shows that the partner respects you...and that his general attitude is one of collaboration.

7. He/she accepts a share of the blame for past relationship failures. Most couples eventually get around to talking about what went wrong with their prior relationships. It's a green flag if your partner admits that he was at least partially to blame. This shows a willingness to take responsibility as well as general maturity. It also hints at an ability to improve—people who are willing to admit their mistakes tend to be people who learn from those mistakes and do better in the future.

8. You feel just as good about your relationship when you're apart as when you are together. Some people have sufficient charm or physical appeal to make their partners feel good when they're with them, but that tends to fade fast when they depart. With a good partner, there's usually a deep-down sense of security that the relationship is right—even when the partner isn't around.

Take a Break from Social Media

Removing yourself from social media can give you a lot more time to do other things. And it can eliminate the fear of missing out that drives many people to spend huge amounts of time at social-media sites. To get rid of entire profiles, use sites such as AccountKiller.com, Deseat.me and JustDelete.me—the sites give step-by-step instructions. Deleting Facebook, Twitter, LinkedIn and GooglePlus accounts will eliminate most of your online presence. But dating sites, blogs, Flickr, eBay, Amazon, Craigslist, PayPal and support forums may retain data even if you rarely use them. Also, sites may retain your data in an inactive version of your account—and you cannot stop others from posting about you.

Remember: Some social-media profiles may make sense to keep, such as a LinkedIn account if you are looking for a job.

Roundup of experts on social-media-site use, reported in *The New York Times*.

15

Auto Adviser

How to Survive 6 Deadly Driving Emergencies

One moment you are driving down the road, the very next moment your brakes fail...your throttle sticks...or one of your tires blows out. Respond wisely and quickly to automotive emergencies such as these, and there's an excellent chance that you and your car will escape unharmed.

Unfortunately, drivers' initial panicked responses often make these situations worse. Even drivers who remain calm sometimes do the wrong thing—the conventional wisdom on how to handle certain driving emergencies is dangerously flawed.

Here are simple and effective strategies for dealing with six worst-case driving scenarios...

TIRE BLOWOUT

A tire comes apart as you drive down the highway. Suddenly it feels as if you are driving on a rumble strip. Many drivers' first reaction is to slam on the brakes, but doing that is likely to put the car into a spin, making a bad situation much worse.

Response: Hold the steering wheel firmly so that you stay in your lane—the car might try to pull to the side of the blowout—and slowly lift your foot off the accelerator. Keep your steering slow and steady. Then ease your vehicle to the shoulder and coast to a stop. Don't brake until your speed is below 50 miles per hour.

Exception: If you experience a blowout with a heavily loaded vehicle while going quickly around a sweeping curve, there might be no way to avoid spinning out. If you already are

Note: Prices, rates and offers throughout this chapter and book are subject to change.

Ben Collins, author of *How to Drive: Real-World Instructions from Hollywood's Top Driver.* He is a professional race-car driver and stunt driver based in Bristol, England. He has won Screen Actor's Guild awards for his stunt driving on the James Bond movie *Skyfall* and the movie *Fast & Furious 6.* BenCollins.com in a spin, slamming on the brakes could be your best option.

Warning: Keep in mind that run-flat tires are not designed to run flat forever. If they are not repaired or replaced soon after going flat, they, too, can blow out. If your car is equipped with run-flats, your vehicle owner's manual should provide details about how far and fast your run-flats can be safely driven after a flat.

STUCK ACCELERATOR

You take your foot off the accelerator, but your car continues to go faster and faster. This could be the result of an electronics issue, though more often the problem is a rusted accelerator pedal hinge or a dislodged floor mat pressing down on the pedal. Whatever the cause, it is one of the most terrifying experiences a driver can have, causing many drivers to freeze up.

Response: Get the car out of gear. If it has a manual transmission, this is easy—simply depress the clutch pedal. If it has an automatic transmission, you will have to shift into neutral. It might take some force to get the shift lever out of gear while the vehicle is moving. The engine will make an ugly over-revving sound when it is taken out of gear, but this can be done and it typically won't hurt the motor.

If you're the passenger in a car with a stuck throttle and the driver freezes up, you can reach over and shift the car into neutral yourself.

Meanwhile, brake hard. Brakes alone often are not sufficient to stop a car when its accelerator is stuck, but they can bleed off much of the vehicle's speed and bring you to a stop once you get the car out of gear.

If the cause of the stuck throttle is not something you can easily diagnose and correct—you can fix an out-of-place floor mat, for example—have the car towed to a mechanic before driving it again.

Warning: Do not turn off the ignition in response to a stuck throttle unless all else fails. This ends the acceleration, but it also turns off the power steering and power-assist braking, rendering the speeding car virtually uncontrollable.

BRAKE FAILURE

You press down the brake pedal, but your car won't stop—and you're rapidly approaching an intersection...stopped traffic...or some other danger.

Response: Pump the brake pedal several times quickly. This should build up hydraulic pressure in the brake line and/or dislodge something that is jammed underneath the pedal.

If that doesn't work, downshift into increasingly lower-numbered gears if your car has a manual transmission...or shift into "low" if your car has an automatic transmission. The engine will make noises of protest when you downshift, but the damage caused should be minimal.

Meanwhile, gently engage the hand brake (or parking brake) until it is fully engaged, and alert other drivers by using your hazard lights or honking your horn.

Have the vehicle towed to a mechanic unless the problem is easy to identify and correct, such as a bottle lodged under the brake pedal.

If your brakes fail as you descend a steep mountain road, however, brake overheating is probably to blame. Once again, downshift through the gears as described above, and engage the hand brake until it is fully engaged. The hand brake is attached to the car's rear brakes, which likely are still working well—it is the front brakes that tend to overheat. Do not engage a hand brake abruptly, however, or you could put the car into a slide or spin.

After you come to a stop, let your brakes cool for at least 20 minutes before driving.

STEERING FAILURE

Your power steering fails, and suddenly your steering wheel feels extremely heavy. Modern cars are tremendously difficult to turn without power steering.

Response: Use all your strength to maneuver the car to the shoulder or any other safe spot, then park and call for a tow truck. You can brake to reduce speed, but often the steering will get even heavier as the car slows. If you don't have the strength to steer the car, put on your hazard lights and stop the vehicle.

Better yet, prevent this emergency before it occurs. Power steering usually does not fail all at once—if your car's steering seems to be becoming heavier, take it to a mechanic as soon as you possibly can.

BLOCKED WINDSHIELD

You are driving down the highway when suddenly your hood flies open and completely blocks your view...or a rock hits your windshield causing it to spiderweb so badly that you cannot see through it.

Response: If you're on an open stretch of road with no cars following closely, hold the wheel straight and brake hard. But if you're on a busy road, slamming on the brakes could cause an accident. Here the best option is to hold the wheel straight, lift your foot off the accelerator, lower your window and stick your head out far enough so that you can see the road ahead. That should provide sufficient visibility to steer the car to a spot where you can park and correct the problem or call for a tow.

SINKING CAR

You crash off of a road or bridge into deep water. The conventional wisdom is to wait until the car is nearly full of water before trying to open your car door and escape—we're told that water pressure will pin the doors shut until then—but following that advice could kill you.

Response: Disconnect your seat belt as soon as your car hits the water, unlock the electronic car-door locks and *immediately* try to force the door open. Urge any passengers to do the same. Cars sometimes float on top of the water for a moment or two before beginning to sink, so it might be possible to push the doors open before external water pressure builds.

If you can't quickly get your door open to escape, immediately lower your windows and escape that way (if there are passengers in the car, lower their windows, too, if you can do so from the controls on your driver's door). Electric window controls often fail when cars go into deep water, but they don't necessarily do so immediately.

If you can't open the doors or windows, try to break a window. If there is something heavy within reach, such as a steering wheel lock, use that. If not, remove one of the car's headrests (if the car has removable headrests), jam one of its metal posts into the seam where the window emerges from the door, and then pry upward until the glass shatters. (You may want to keep in your car an emergency escape tool that cuts seat belts and breaks windows, such as LifeHammer. This is available online and at stores that sell auto supplies.)

Only if all of these options fail should you follow the conventional wisdom of trying to open the car door once the car is nearly full of water, equalizing internal and external water pressure. This should be considered the last-ditch option because if it fails, there are no more backup plans—you'll be out of air.

SURPRISING FINDING...

Hands-Free Danger

In a recent study, *both* handheld and hands-free cell phones caused a 40% increase in reaction time during a simulation of a pedestrian entering a crosswalk from the driver's peripheral vision compared with drivers not using a phone.

Explanation: The cognitive power needed to hold a conversation can decrease the ability to process some visual information.

Takeaway: Do not assume that hands-free calls are safe—be sure to stay off the phone altogether when driving.

Md. Mazharul (Shimul) Haque, PhD, senior lecturer, Queensland University of Technology, Brisbane, Australia.

Dusk and Dawn Driving Can Be Deadly: How to Stay Safe

William Van Tassel, PhD, manager of driver-training operations at the AAA's national office in Heathrow, Florida. He holds a doctorate in safety education. AAA.com

Dusk and dawn are dangerous times to be behind the wheel. The road surface, pedestrians and other vehicles often are shrouded in shadow at these hours, but the sky still can be fairly bright. That contrast creates a problem—the light sky prevents drivers' eyes from adjusting to the dark road. Meanwhile, the setting or rising sun sometimes is directly in our eyes...other drivers might not yet have turned on their headlights...and we might be feeling drowsy.

Here are smart ways to stay safe when driving at dusk or dawn...

SEE AND BE SEEN

•**Turn your headlights on *before* it gets dark.** Don't wait until night falls to use your headlights. Turn them on when the sun is low in the sky. Not only will your headlights provide additional illumination for you, they will make it easier for other drivers to see your car (and your taillights will be on so others can see you better from behind). And if drivers around you on the road notice that you have your headlights on as night approaches, it might remind them to turn theirs on, too, making it easier for you to see them.

•**Polish your headlights.** Even the best headlight bulbs will not perform well if the front of the headlight is dirty, cloudy or otherwise blocked. Regularly wiping away dirt and road grime is a good start, but also use a headlight-restoration kit every year or two. These polishing kits, available in auto-parts stores and online for $15 to $25, can dramatically improve headlight performance by reducing the hazing, scratching and discoloration that can develop on the outside of headlights.

•**Clean your windshield inside and out.** Dirt, dust and road grime on a windshield can refract light, creating glare. That glare might be only a minor annoyance during the day, but it can greatly reduce your ability to see the road at dawn and dusk when your eyes are struggling to cope with the lighting conditions. Use standard glass cleaner to thoroughly clean the windshield inside and out.

•**Get polarized lenses if you wear prescription eyeglasses.** These lenses have an embedded chemical film that is likely to add at least $50 or more to the cost of your glasses, but it's worth that price if you use the glasses for driving—polarized lenses dramatically reduce the glare in your eyes, especially in low-light situations and/or when the sun is low in the sky.

•**Wear sunglasses judiciously.** If the sun is directly in your eyes, certainly put on sunglasses. Otherwise leave them off at dawn and dusk—they reduce the already limited light reaching your eyes at these hours. Besides, drivers sometimes forget that they are wearing sunglasses as dusk fades into night.

Helpful: Some drivers find that yellow-tinted glasses, which generally block less light than gray or green sunglasses, offer a nice compromise between wearing sunglasses and not wearing sunglasses at dusk and dawn.

•**Turn down your dash lights.** Bright dash lights may make it easier to read gauges, but having these bright lights in your field of vision will further detract from your eyes' ability to see a darkened dusk, dawn or nighttime roadway. Set the dash lights as low as you can and still read the dash.

•**Turn your head frequently to monitor surrounding traffic.** During the day, you can track the cars around you on multilane roads out of the corners of your eyes. After night falls, other vehicles' headlight beams reveal where these cars are. But at dawn and dusk, nearby cars can be a challenge to track—their headlights might not be obvious, and you might not be able to spot these cars out of the corners of your eyes—peripheral vision declines dramatically in low-light situations. Look side to side periodically to keep track of other vehicles on multilane roads.

Also, in neighborhoods, make a special effort to scan for pedestrians at dawn and dusk. People on foot can be very hard to spot at these low-light hours, and because there still is light in the sky, pedestrians might not realize that drivers cannot see them and step into their path.

DRIVING STRATEGIES

•**Monitor your speed very closely.** During the day, many experienced drivers have a general sense of how fast they are traveling even without checking their speedometers. But this ability to estimate speed is rooted in their peripheral vision—their brains are noting the speed at which things are whizzing by in the corners of their eyes. As noted above, peripheral vision declines greatly in low light. Drivers should either check the speedometer regularly when sunlight is limited or, better yet, use cruise control or a GPS device that makes a warning sound when they exceed the speed limit.

• **Choose routes that are not directly into the sun.** If you are traveling northwest at dusk, for example, you could choose a northbound road when the sun is right on the horizon, then switch to a westbound road after it sets so that you never have to contend with sunlight directly in your eyes. If you cannot avoid traveling east at dawn or west at dusk, choose a road that has tall trees and buildings alongside. These can block the sun as long as your route is not dead at the sun. If neither of these options is available, strongly consider pulling over until the sun is no longer right in your eyes. This is when the dangers of dusk and dawn driving are greatest.

• **Watch for signs of driver drowsiness in the vehicles around you.** Drowsy driving doesn't just happen late at night. Our brains start to release *melatonin*, a light-sensitive hormone that causes sleepiness, at dusk. If a car near you on the road seems to be having trouble staying in its lane or maintaining its speed, its driver might be drowsy. (He/she also might be drunk or distracted—the symptoms can be similar.) Put some distance between your vehicle and this one. Depending on the situation, you could drop back and follow at a distance…accelerate and pass…or pick a lane that is not adjacent to this vehicle on a multilane highway.

Monitor yourself for any signs of drowsiness as well. If you are having trouble staying in your lane, maintaining your speed or keeping your attention on the road, stop driving for the night or at least take a break for a cup of coffee.

• **Minimize distractions.** Dusk and dawn driving require all of your attention. Pull over before doing anything that takes your focus away from the road—this isn't the time to try to pick something up off the floor of the car or refer to a map. (Distractions are dangerous for drivers during the day, too, but the risks increase as sunlight decreases.) If conditions are especially challenging—say, you are driving toward the setting sun on unfamiliar roads—turn off the radio, too, so your focus is 100% on driving.

• **Increase your following distance.** The less light there is in the sky, the longer it takes drivers to identify and react to potential dangers. One smart response is to drop farther back from the car ahead of you. The usual rule of thumb is to follow at least two to three seconds behind, but in low-light situations four seconds or more is prudent. (To judge this distance, start counting "one Mississippi…two Mississippi…" when the car ahead passes a road sign and stop counting when you pass it.)

SAFETY ALERT…

Driving Habits Most Likely to Cause Crashes

Tailgating: Drivers who slam on the brakes more than eight times per 500 miles are 73% more likely to have an accident in a year than ones who keep their distance from other cars. *Speeding:* People with one speeding ticket are 27% more likely to have an accident than drivers with clean records. *Driving on residential streets* is 12 times riskier than highway driving, and multiple short trips are riskier than a single long trip.

Roundup of insurance-company data obtained by using devices installed in cars to monitor driver behavior, reported in *The Wall Street Journal*.

Young Adults Are Unsafe Drivers!

In a survey of drivers ages 19 to 24, 88% acknowledged engaging in risky behavior in the previous month—such as texting while driving, speeding or running red lights.

Young adults were far more likely than other age groups to admit to unsafe driving: 59.3% said that they had typed or sent a text or e-mail while driving, compared with 31.4% of other drivers...and nearly half said that they had run a red light even if they could have stopped safely, compared with 36% of other drivers.

Study by AAA Foundation for Traffic Safety.

Car Window Caution

Car windows will not protect against UV rays. Windshields generally block 96% of cancer-causing UVA rays. But the side windows block only 71%, on average. This could increase drivers' risk for left-eye cataracts and cancer on the left side of the face.

Self-defense: Wear sunscreen whenever you drive...and consider buying special window-tint products that block 99% of UVA rays.

Study of ultraviolet protection provided by glass in 29 cars by researchers at Boxer Wachler Vision Institute, Beverly Hills, California, published in *JAMA Ophthalmology*.

You Can Help Prevent Traffic Jams

Behaviors that seem counterintuitive can be used to prevent traffic jams or avoid making them worse. Drive at a steady speed, and keep a space of several car lengths in front of your vehicle so that you are less likely to hit the brakes and cause drivers behind you to hit theirs—slowing everyone down. Also, let aggressive drivers get in front of you and avoid rubbernecking. When entering a congested area where lanes merge, maintain a wide gap behind other cars so that other drivers can merge into your lane without stopping.

William Beaty, a civil engineer based in Seattle, whose traffic-jam-avoidance maneuvers have been studied by researchers in Chicago and Japan, quoted in *The Wall Street Journal*.

How to Beat the Traffic on Memorial Day

The Friday before Memorial Day has had less traffic than the Thursday before the holiday, according to a five-year study of the Washington, DC, area.

Reason: So many people try to leave early to beat the expected Friday rush that Friday has become less crowded.

Study by AAA, reported in *USA Today*.

Best Times to Buy a New Car

In the market for a new car? *Here are the best times to buy...*

End of the year, especially right before New Year's Day, if you want the previous year's model—although choices likely will be limited. *Labor Day*, when dealer lots still have many old models just as new ones are coming in. *After a major model redesign* if you like the old model and the redesign is more for appearance than functionality. *End of the day at the end of the month*—salespeople need to meet quotas and even may sell a few cars at a loss if it boosts total sales so that they get a special bonus. *Black Friday*—some dealers offer special discounts because many people are in the mood to make purchases on the day after Thanksgiving.

Experts on car sales, reported at Kiplinger.com.

Most Popular "American-Made" Cars

The most popular "American-made" car is the Toyota Camry, according to a recent survey. To be in contention, vehicles must have at least 75% domestic content.

All five of the most-American-made vehicles have Japanese nameplates: Honda Accord is second, followed by Toyota Sienna, Honda Odyssey and Honda Pilot.

Annual survey by Cars.com.

Save $1,000s on a Used Car: Big Bargains on Demos, Fleet Cars and Rental Cars

Ron Montoya, senior consumer advice editor for the company Edmunds.com, a leading provider of automotive information. Montoya is based in Santa Monica, California.

Not every used vehicle has been owned by an individual. Some are "demos," which dealerships have used for test-drives and other purposes..."program" vehicles, which have been used by the maker in various settings such as trade shows..."fleet" vehicles, which have been owned by municipalities or corporations and used by employees...or rental vehicles. These sometimes are priced hundreds or even thousands of dollars below vehicles of a similar model, age and mileage. But are they great bargains...or no better than a standard used car? *Here's what you need to know...*

DEMO AND PROGRAM VEHICLES

Demos usually are from the current model year. They have been driven by employees of the auto dealership...have been taken on test-drives...and/or have been loaned to customers while their own vehicles were being worked on by the dealer's service department.

Program vehicles might have been put on display at trade shows, driven by one of the automaker's employees or test-driven by journalists writing reviews. Unlike the other vehicles covered in this article, demos and program vehicles usually are classified as new cars, not used cars. Autos are legally considered new until someone takes out a title on them, something that dealerships and manufacturers rarely do with demos and program vehicles.

Buying a demo or program vehicle likely will shorten your warranty coverage compared with buying a truly new car. Ask the salesperson to tell you the "in-service" date. This will serve as the vehicle's warranty start date—which is likely many months earlier than the date you purchase the auto, reducing your warranty coverage. The miles already on the odometer will cut into your warranty, too. Demo/program vehicle warranties do not reset when the car is purchased.

But demos and program vehicles still can be smart buys. They tend to have extremely low mileage (potentially a few thousand miles or less)...may include attractive options packages...and, for the most part, have been driven responsibly and were well-maintained. When dealership employees drive demos, for example, they tend to baby them because they know that any damage or serious wear would detract from their value. Salespeople often are in vehicles during customer test-drives, which tends to discourage irresponsible test-driving.

If you can locate a manufacturer-certified used car of similar age and mileage, it might sell for a lower price than a comparable demo/program car—but it might not be possible to find the used car that you want with just a few thousand miles on the odometer. Privately owned cars rarely are resold that soon.

What to do: If you consider buying a demo or program car, confirm that you really are getting a good deal. Sometimes a salesperson will present a demo or program vehicle as though the price is a steal when the price actually is very similar to what a buyer could have negotiated on a 100%-new vehicle. Use a car-shopping website such as Edmunds.com (where I am employed) to compare the price you are being offered to what other buyers actually are paying for the new vehicle. (Remember to include the value of any options packages.) Also, use this or another car-shopping site to research the fair purchase price of this make and model as a low-mileage used car, and make a counteroffer based on this figure. A demo or program car might legally be new, but it is reasonable to argue that it really is more like a low-mileage used car despite its legal status. The dealership is unlikely to come down to this used price because it probably can find a buyer willing to pay more, but because of the mileage, it should be willing to offer you a significantly better deal than you would get on a similar 100% new vehicle.

Ask what the dealership charges for an extended warranty on the vehicle as well, and then use this in your negotiation. If one year of the demo's warranty already is used up, for example, and it would cost you an average of $300 per year to extend the warranty, point this out and ask to have the price reduced to compensate. If you are asked to sign any disclosures about the vehicle, read this paperwork carefully—occasionally dealerships disclose precisely how a demo or program vehicle was used because its use was atypical or extreme. You probably don't want to buy a program car, for example, that was used to teach people how to drive aggressively on a track.

Where to find them: Ask in person whether a dealership has a demo or program version of the car you are shopping for.

FORMER RENTAL CARS

Car-rental companies will often sell vehicles when they are one to four years old and have 25,000 to 50,000 miles on their odometers. Most—though not all—rental cars are base or midlevel models with few options. Are they a smart buy? Only if you are comfortable with the fact that your car has been driven by hundreds of different people, at least some of whom probably treated it poorly.

On the plus side, major rental companies generally maintain their cars well, and they often sell them for hundreds less than you likely would pay for similar individual-owned cars at a used-car lot. These days, many rental-car companies also make used-car buying simple—you can view the cars for sale in your area on their websites along with their no-haggle prices. If your priority is a low-pressure, no-haggle used-car buying experience, this could be the way to go. Some rental agencies provide limited warranty protection in addition to any remaining manufacturer warranty. Enterprise and Hertz, for example, provide 12-month, 12,000-mile limited powertrain warranties.

What to do: Check whether the rental company will let you rent the car for a few days before you commit to buying it. This usually is allowed, and it's a great way to weed out problem vehicles. (Besides driving the car to see how it performs and feels, take the car to an independent mechanic for a once-over during this extended test-drive.) Most major rental firms will waive the resulting rental charges if you decide to buy the car.

Where to find them: Check on the major rental firms' websites.

FLEET VEHICLES

Governments and companies sometimes sell cars that they owned for employee use.

Are they a smart buy? Potentially—if the price is attractive and you choose carefully. Overall, fleet vehicles tend to be in no worse shape than similar used cars that were in private hands. They even might be a bit better because they usually are professionally maintained on a regular schedule.

Fleet cars are more likely than rental cars to have been driven responsibly. The employees who drive fleet vehicles know that getting a ticket or getting into an accident in their employer's car could have negative career ramifications. There are exceptions, however—former police cars and taxi cabs often are driven very hard, for example. Some delivery vehicles have endured hard miles as well.

What to do: Before buying a fleet vehicle, ferret out details about how it was driven and who drove it. If it is a nice sedan that was used to ferry around clients, it probably was driven conservatively...but if it's a pickup truck that was used to carry heavy loads or pull a trailer, it has had a tougher life than the average privately owned used pickup.

Request a copy of the vehicle's service records—most companies keep meticulous fleet records. Check these to confirm that maintenance was handled on a regular basis and that the vehicle had no major accidents or recurring problems.

Where to find them: Former fleet vehicles are sold in the same places that other used vehicles are sold—on used-car lots, through classified ads or Craigslist.com, etc. But when

GOOD TO KNOW...

Best Tire Brands

Here are the best tire brands for performance, including braking, comfort, handling, hydroplaning, noise, traction and other elements...

The highest-rated overall: Michelin, with a score of 71.5 out of a possible 100. Its all-season, all-terrain and summer tires all scored well for grip, handling and tread life, and all have tread-wear warranties.

Other top-rated brands: Pirelli, 69.5...Continental, 69...Nokian, 67.5...Goodyear, 67.5.

Lowest-rated brands studied: GT Radial, 56.5...Firestone, 58.5...Sumitomo, 59.5...Uniroyal, 59.5...Falken, 60.

For the full list: ConsumerReports.org/tires/best-tire-brands.

ConsumerReports.org

a fleet vehicle is sold on a used-car lot, it might not be possible to obtain that vehicle's service history...and you might not learn that it was in a fleet unless you obtain a vehicle history report from a service such as CarFax. Some fleet vehicles are sold at auctions—but these auctions are best avoided if you are not an auto expert (or cannot bring an expert with you). Bidders often are not even allowed to test-drive vehicles before bidding on them.

Better Way to Buy a Used Car

Roundup of experts on used-car buying, reported at Bankrate.com.

First, create a target list of cars to consider, including make, model and year. Then choose the newest version of cars you can afford—car quality improves every year, and newer models usually have more and better equipment. Research recalls—if the car you want is affected, be sure that it has been fixed or will be.

Buy from friends or family if at all possible—people you know will be honest with you about a car they are selling, and you may have a good idea of their history with it. Go to auto dealerships if you cannot buy from someone you know—dealers usually keep the good trade-ins they get and get rid of ones with problems.

It's best to take a lengthy test-drive, or preferably two, to get a good sense of a car's condition and performance. And get a dealership warranty and a vehicle history report—history reports cost around $50 and often are free at dealerships. Also get an independent inspection—the cost of about $100 is well worth it to learn of possible problems.

Beware These Used Cars

Tom McParland, who operates New Jersey–based Automatch Consulting, reported by Karen Larson, editor, *Bottom Line Personal.*

A friend is looking for a used car, but with all the storms lately, he's wary of getting stuck with a flood-damaged vehicle. He's right to be concerned—flooded vehicles often later experience massive problems with their electronics and other systems.

The titles of flood-damaged vehicles often are branded "salvage" or "flood." But that doesn't always happen...and unscrupulous sellers have tricks for obtaining new "clean" titles when it does.

Car buyers in storm-ravaged regions are not the only ones at risk. "Cars damaged during a hurricane will be sold in places far away where buyers are not as on guard about flood damage," warns Tom McParland, who operates New Jersey–based Automatch Consulting. *What to do...*

- **Look under the spare tire for mud, water or rust.** Unethical resellers of flood-damaged vehicles typically try to remove evidence of the immersion, but McParland says they often don't bother to take the spare out of the trunk and clean underneath.

- **Check for discolored or replaced carpeting.** Slide the front seats all the way forward and back. It could suggest flood damage if the carpeting under the seats is discolored.

Related red flags include brand-new carpeting in an older car…or sections of carpeting that have been replaced.

• **Get the vehicle history report.** Go to Carfax.com ($39.99) or AutoCheck.com ($24.99). Proceed with extreme caution if the vehicle came from an area with flooding. If shopping on a used-car lot, ask the salesperson to provide at no charge one of these reports—be suspicious if he/she resists.

For a Multiday Test-Drive…

Multiday used-car test-drives are available from some rental-car companies on cars that they are ready to sell, but the price for this service can vary widely. Rent2Buy from Hertz ($66/day over three days, but the cost is refunded if you buy the car) and Ultimate Test Drive from Avis/Budget (you are charged the daily rental rate for three days, but the cost is refunded if you buy the car) let you browse the fleets online, pick the vehicle you may want to buy, then take it for up to three days. You can have your mechanic inspect it during the extended test-drive.

Alternative: Enterprise Car Sales does not offer a multiday tryout but will buy back a car at the price you paid within seven days if you do not like it.

Prices change constantly, and warranty coverage varies. Shop all the rental fleets, and compare their cars with those at AutoTrader.com and CarMax.com.

Kiplinger's Personal Finance, Kiplinger.com.

How to Make Money from Your Car

Make money from your car without becoming a driver for Uber or Lyft…

Sell advertising to a firm that leases ad space on cars—check Wrapify and Carvertise. *Run errands and make deliveries* with firms such as TaskRabbit, Postmates, Amazon Flex and Munchery—all available in limited areas. *Help people move large items* if you have a van or other big vehicle—check GoShare or BuddyTruk. *Lease your car to airport passengers through FlightCar or Turo*—the firms arrange for you to park at the airport or meet renters after they arrive.

Forbes.com

Get Gas Delivered to You

You can fill up your car's gas tank without ever leaving your home or office. New apps, such as *Filld, WeFuel, Booster Fuels, Purple* and *Yoshi*, offer the convenience of getting gas delivered to your location and pumped into your tank. Currently, the apps are available only in San Francisco, Los Angeles and a few other cities, but more are coming soon. Per-gallon rates are comparable to those charged by nearby stations, but users pay a delivery fee.

USA Today, USAToday.com.

Keep Your Gas Tank at Least One-Quarter Full

The fuel gauge in cars is not always accurate, and you could run out of gas sooner than you think. Also, gas helps cool the electric fuel-pump motor—when the tank level gets low, the pump sucks in air and can overheat, costing hundreds of dollars to fix.

Self-defense: Fill up before starting a long trip or heading to work…don't rely on the vehicle to show how many miles you have left—range numbers often are not accurate.

ConsumerReports.org

16

Happy Home

How to Save Your Marriage After an Affair

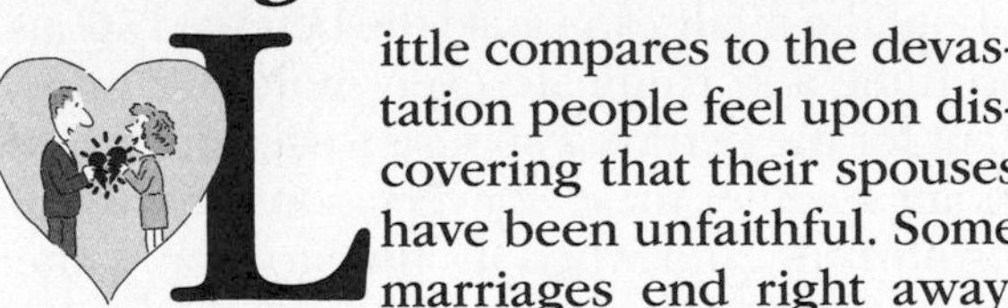

Little compares to the devastation people feel upon discovering that their spouses have been unfaithful. Some marriages end right away. But many others hit agonizing impasses as couples struggle to get past the intense anger, sadness and mistrust.

These hurtful interactions wreak emotional havoc on *both* spouses, and typically neither one has a clue how to help the marriage recover. As a result, many couples who do in fact love each other decide to call it quits.

The good news is that it's possible to move beyond the pain, put the past in the past, rebuild trust and reconnect with your spouse both emotionally and physically. In fact, many couples who have done the hard work of repairing their marriages after affairs report that their relationships are stronger than ever.

The first weeks and months after the affair is out in the open often are the "make-or-break" stage for the marriage. *Here's what the unfaithful spouse and the betrayed spouse need to do…*

UNFAITHFUL SPOUSE'S TASKS

The unfaithful partner needs to rebuild his/her spouse's trust…

• **End the affair.** It's not realistic to expect a marriage to improve while an affair is ongoing. Yet sometimes, when an affair has filled a void in the unfaithful spouse's life, the unfaithful spouse feels unsettled about ending it. This is natural and not to be interpreted as a sign that ending the affair is the wrong choice. It is normal to grieve the loss of the illicit relationship even if repairing the marriage is decidedly the desired outcome.

Michele Weiner-Davis, LCSW, founder of The Divorce Busting Center in Boulder, Colorado, that helps on-the-brink couples save their marriages. She is the best-selling author of eight books, including *Healing from Infidelity*, *The Sex-Starved Marriage* and *Divorce Busting*. DivorceBusting.com

• **Answer questions.** Most betrayed spouses have many questions about what happened and the meaning the affair had to the unfaithful spouse. As difficult as it might be, it is imperative to answer these questions openly and honestly. Withholding information—even very painful information—that eventually leaks out over time retraumatizes the betrayed spouse and can cause irreparable damage. As counterintuitive as it might seem, honesty is the best policy, particularly in the early stages of recovery when the marriage is fragile and trust is being rebuilt.

• **Be transparent.** During the crisis period, it is necessary for the unfaithful spouse to be willing to be totally transparent and allow the betrayed spouse to have access to personal information including e-mail, cell-phone records, Facebook accounts, credit card bills and so on. Demonstrating a willingness to be an "open book," though often uncomfortable, goes a long way to rebuilding trust. This level of personal accountability is temporary—it's not intended to become a way of life. Once trust is rebuilt, most betrayed spouses tire of the constant vigilance and wish to focus on other, more positive aspects of life.

• **Apologize.** Betrayed spouses really need to know that their partners are remorseful about the hurt they caused. Apologies must be heartfelt and include explanations of why the unfaithful spouse feels contrite.

Example: It will help to say, "I am very sorry that I had an affair. You've trusted me throughout our marriage, and I betrayed your trust. I understand why you are so devastated."

Apologies that are defensive typically don't work as well. For instance, "I'm sorry you're feeling hurt. But our marriage hasn't been going so well, and I needed some emotional support." Keep in mind that a single apology is never enough, because a betrayed spouse's pain comes in waves. Express your regrets often about having hurt your spouse.

BETRAYED SPOUSE'S TASKS

After an affair, if you want your marriage to survive, you can't leave the ball only in the unfaithful spouse's court…

• **Express emotions—but constructively.** The betrayed spouse often will be overwhelmed by intense feelings of hurt, anger, sadness and utter confusion. Express those feelings when they arise, but express them in helpful rather than combative ways. Rather than resorting to name calling, use "I-messages" to talk about how you feel.

Example: It's reasonable to say, "I don't know if I can ever trust you again because you hurt me so much. I feel like I'm dying inside." But it simply won't help your marriage to say, "You're the worst person in the world. You're a liar and have no integrity."

• **Ask questions—but know when to stop.** It is very common for a betrayed spouse to have questions about the affair partner, the length of the affair, the places and times they met, what took place during those times and what the relationship meant to the unfaithful spouse.

Sometimes asking questions can be very helpful—the answers often confirm long-standing suspicions, and that enables the betrayed spouse to regain trust in his/her own instincts. Plus, there usually is an overwhelming need to try to make sense of what happened and to connect the dots. Asking pertinent questions often satisfies this need.

However, knowing more and more details about the affair can cause the betrayed spouse to fume and ruminate even more. It's important for the betrayed spouse to decide at some point whether these conversations are healing or hurtful…and when it's time to stop gathering information.

In the early stages of recovery from an affair, many couples have marathon discussions about the infidelity, but eventually they must strike a balance between talking about the affair and focusing on other aspects of their lives—otherwise, the relationship will become too problem-saturated, and it simply won't feel good to either partner. Intentionally engaging in neutral or even positive interactions will improve the relationship exponentially. That's because what you focus on expands quickly.

If you ask your unfaithful spouse a question and the honest response is hurtful to you, it's important not to lash out angrily. It may take courage to share hurtful information, and it's important for the betrayed spouse to encourage honesty. Therefore, even though your mind may be roiling, state your feelings as calmly as possible by using I-messages and acknowledge the unfaithful partner's willingness to come clean.

• **Keep track of what helps you.** Although it may seem as if the hurt is ever-present following the discovery of an affair, the truth is, there are times when sadness and anger dissipate. It's helpful to ask yourself, *What's different about the times during the day when I feel just a little bit better?* and keep a running list of what works.

Example: Many people say that it helps to exercise, be with friends, meditate, do yoga, pray, spend time with kids if you have them, keep a journal and so on. After taking an emotional hit, knowing how to help yourself feel more at peace can be extremely empowering.

• **Examine what might need to change in the marriage.** Although it usually doesn't occur during the initial crisis period, it will be important for the betrayed spouse eventually to take a close look at the factors that might have contributed to the affair. Though some people stray even though they're perfectly happy in their marriages, others feel that there has been an emotional or a physical void. Addressing these issues leads to deeper empathy and intimacy on all levels.

TAKE NOTE...

Better Way to Discuss Hurt Feelings with Your Partner

Check with him/her to be sure it is a good time to talk so that he won't tune you out. *Talk about one thing at a time*, not a series of concerns. *Don't accuse*—use an "I" statement, such as "I felt X when you did Y." After making the statement, check in again—ask your partner how he feels about what you have said. *Develop a mutual resolution*—not an apology or a general promise to be more sensitive, but something specific that you both agree to do the next time a similar issue comes up.

BetterAfter50.com

A Healthier Way to Argue...

Claudia Haase, PhD, assistant professor of human development and social policy at Northwestern University and one of the authors of the study, reported by Karen Larson, editor, *Bottom Line Personal.*

It's no secret that arguing can cause stress. Nor will it come as a shock that stress can be bad for your health. But a recent study published in *Emotion* introduced an interesting new twist to this story—it turns out that *how* you argue could determine what sort of health problems you are likely to have.

The researchers tracked 156 married couples for more than 20 years and found compelling evidence that spouses who fly off the handle during arguments are prone to cardiovascular problems such as high blood pressure and chest pain...while spouses who shut down and bottle up their feelings tend to develop muscular problems such as back or neck pain. These findings apply to both men and women, but they are significantly more pronounced among men.

The good news is that it might be possible to reduce the odds of these future health problems by modifying your arguing style, says Claudia Haase, PhD, assistant professor of human development and social policy at Northwestern University and one of the authors of the study. Hotheads could go for a walk when they feel a blowup coming and then return to resume the discussion when they've cooled down. If they continue to get excessively worked up, they could seek anger-management counseling.

People who shut down must understand that not voicing their feelings is not good for their relationships or their health. If they truly cannot bring themselves to tell others what they feel, it might be worth going into therapy, either individual or couples counseling.

"I Hate You": A 7-Step Plan for Getting Along with Adult Siblings

Cathy Jo Cress, MSW, a social worker specializing in issues involving families and aging. She is cofounder of CHN Consultants, an aging-services consulting firm based in Santa Cruz, California, and coauthor of *Mom Loves You Best: Forgiving and Forging Sibling Relationships.* CathyCress.com

It seems like siblings should be very close friends. After all, they probably understand each other in a deeper, more meaningful way than almost anyone else alive.

But many sibling relationships are very badly strained. According to one survey, 35% of adults have either an apathetic or an outright hostile relationship with a brother or sister.

Damaged adult sibling relationships can be difficult to fix, but it can be done. *Here's how...*

1. Uncover your "I hate you" story. When adult siblings have very troubled relationships—not just short-term spats—the problem typically has roots in childhood. What anecdotes come to mind when you consider your childhood interactions with your sibling? Is there a story that you have relived and repeated over the years that casts you as the victim and your sibling as a scoundrel? This story might emphasize that your sibling bullied you...belittled you...or received preferential treatment from your parents. (Or, conversely, does your sibling tell such a story about you?) Or your "I hate you" story might have developed when you were both adults.

Write about this story during a relaxed, private moment. Write what happened and how it made you feel. As you write, consciously let go of any tension the story stirs up inside you. Take deep breaths...unclench your teeth and fists, and relax the muscles of your face...and touch your tongue to the roof of your mouth just behind your front teeth—this tends to make people feel calm.

2. Bring the story into present day. There is no way to change what happened between you and your sibling in the past, but you can change how those past events make you feel in the present. Discuss these feelings with someone you trust—that's better than allowing the feelings to continue to simmer silently inside you. Try to choose someone outside the family so that he/she doesn't get caught in the middle.

Also, do something that makes you feel calm whenever thoughts of or interactions with this sibling make you stressed or angry. This should begin to erode your mind's association between this sibling and the unpleasant feelings.

Potential calming activities include exercising...playing calming music...deep breathing ...petting your pet...meditating...or writing in a journal.

3. Acknowledge your family's hierarchical structure and unspoken inequalities. In many families the kids are not treated exactly the same.

Examples: Older siblings often are given additional responsibilities, while younger siblings are told they must do as the older ones say. And parents may become less strict with younger siblings. In past decades, boys often faced different expectations and received a larger share of the resources than girls. Write down the inequalities and hierarchies that prevailed in your family when you were growing up. (If these do not come quickly to mind, think about how household rules and responsibilities varied based on gender and birth order...and/or consult with siblings with whom you get along well.) Now consider what you have written—could these childhood hierarchies and inequalities be affecting the way you and your sibling interact with each other to this day?

4. Consider what made your sibling hurt you (or vice versa). Could the discord between you actually have been caused not by either of you, but by a family situation completely out of both of your control?

Example: Ted hated his elder brother, John, because John mistreated Ted when he babysat him after school as children. Ted's hatred festered well into adulthood—until he considered *why* John had mistreated him. His elder brother had been deeply unhappy because he did not want to be stuck home babysitting every afternoon. Once Ted realized this, he stopped seeing his brother as a monster and instead saw that they both were victims of the family's financial struggles—their parents had to work and couldn't afford a sitter.

5. Reflect upon how your sibling still wounds you (or vice versa). Does the sister who said mean things to you in childhood still say mean things today? Does the brother who ignored your opinions as a child still ignore what you say today? Make a list of the sibling's traits that have bothered you since childhood.

Now think about how you have grown and changed since childhood. You are not the same person you were when you were a child, so you do not have to let your sibling's words and actions wound you the way they once did.

Example: Your sister has always diminished your accomplishments, and this contributed to your feeling like a failure. Reflect on all that you have achieved in your life—you no longer are that child who needs to feel insecure about her worth. Remind yourself of this when your sister says something mean. Also list the ways in which your sibling has changed since childhood. It is easy to define people by their enduring traits, but everyone changes over time—which means that your sibling is capable of changing the behaviors that wound you.

6. Share what you have learned with your sibling. Invite your sibling to meet with you. Practice relaxation techniques before you get together. Then begin by expressing the positive feelings you still have for this sibling and explaining why you think fixing the relationship is worth the trouble. Then explain that you have put a lot of thought into what's gone wrong between you and why you think the pattern can be overcome. Do this in a way that avoids placing blame.

Example: "You're my brother, and I love you. I want us to have a closer relationship, for our sake, for our kids' sakes, and so we can work together to take care of Mom if she ever needs our help. I've been putting a lot of thought into why we don't get along. I was younger, so Mom put you in charge. I think that made me resentful about having to do what you said...and maybe it made you resentful about having to take so much responsibility. But the situation wasn't your fault or mine, and we don't have to let it stand in the way of us getting along as adults."

Alternative: If your sibling harbors a deep well of anger toward you and tells you so, instead acknowledge your past mistakes and the legitimacy of the sibling's anger, then say that you would like to try to fix things if your sibling is ever interested in doing so. Understand that your sibling might not yet be ready.

7. Start building a new relationship. Add a new ending to your "I hate you" story so that it now includes how the two of you are overcoming your problems and becoming friends. Remind yourself of this ending whenever the old "I hate you" story comes to mind.

Discuss with your sibling that there inevitably will be setbacks along the way, but pledge to overcome these rather than allow the relationship to disintegrate.

Make a ritual of celebrating the rebirth of the relationship. Note the date when you agreed to patch things up, and call, write or get together to commemorate this date in future years.

Don't consider your efforts a failure if your sibling doesn't agree to rebuild the relationship. The main benefit of forgiveness is the peace that surrounds you when you move out of the past into the present...have used self-help to heal yourself...and turned off the endless spigot of your "I hate you" story. Forgiveness is about transforming yourself.

Beyond Ancestry.com: 8 Great Ways to Trace Your Family Tree

George G. Morgan, author of *How to Do Everything: Genealogy, Fourth Edition*. He is president of Aha! Seminars, Inc., a Tampa Bay–based service that offers genealogy training to librarians and amateur genealogists. He has been doing genealogical research for more than a half century. AhaSeminars.com

Researching your family history could connect you with relatives you never knew you had. It could uncover a famous or an interesting ancestor or a personal connection with an historical event. It could help you understand who you are or where you came from.

But you may not need to pay for a genealogical resource such as Ancestry.com. You may be able to do your family tree on your own. *Here's how...*

1. Look for important family tree clues hidden in your home. Look through boxes in your attic or basement for old family Bibles, address books, photos and letters, deeds, tax bills, wills, insurance policies and other documents. Generations of births, marriages and deaths sometimes are recorded in Bibles. A parent or grandparent's old address book might yield former family members' names and addresses. Old photos could have names on the back identifying family members you didn't know you had. Now-departed relatives' wills, trusts and insurance policies might list additional family members among the heirs or beneficiaries.

Helpful: When you ask family members what they recall about your ancestors, also ask them if they have any of these items in their homes...or if they know of relatives who do.

2. Don't overlook old-fashioned libraries. Local public and academic libraries still play a key role in genealogy. Once you identify towns where your relatives have lived, contact those towns' libraries to see if they have local histories, family histories, old diaries or other books or documents in their collections that might mention your family. If they do, visit the library...ask the librarians if they can scan and e-mail (or copy and mail) relevant pages...and/or see if you can use the interlibrary loan system to borrow books from these libraries through your town's library. (A librarian at your local library should be able to provide details about interlibrary loan.)

Helpful: The website WorldCat.org offers a searchable catalog of more than two billion items available at libraries around the world.

3. Try free family history research sites. Ancestry.com is the most popular genealogy site not because it is the best but because it advertises very heavily. Before you ante up their subscription fee ($99 to $199 for a six-month membership), consider trying FamilySearch.org, a free genealogy website provided by the Church of Jesus Christ of Latter-day Saints. It contains a large number of digital genealogical records from around the globe plus thousands of instructional articles and videos about conducting genealogical research (sign-up is required).

If your heritage traces to England, Ireland, Canada or Australia, go to FindMyPast.com, which is comparable to Ancestry.com but much stronger with records from those countries ($9.95 per month or $34.95 for 12 months).

Or consider MyHeritage.com, which is much like Ancestry.com but costs less—$9.95 a month.

4. Explore newspaper search sites. Old newspapers are a great place to find obituaries and many other articles that mention ancestors. And you no longer have to spend long hours scanning reels of microfilm to accomplish this. Several websites now provide searchable digital access to thousands of newspapers, including local newspapers. Newspapers.com ($7.95 per month to $74.90 for six months, depending on the plan) and GenealogyBank.com ($19.95 per month after a $9.95 30-day trial or $69.95 for one year) are the most comprehensive of these. Chronicling America.LOC.gov, a 100% free site offered by the Library of Congress, is excellent, too.

Also: Fold3.com is another often-overlooked online resource. It offers US military personnel records going all the way back to the Revolutionary War ($7.95 per month after a seven-day free trial, though some information can be accessed for free). I found military records from my fourth-great-grandfather on this site, including a request by his wife to continue his pension after his 1834 death.

5. Try DNA testing. Send a swab of your saliva to any of several companies, and they will provide you with a report that details where your ancestors were from. You might discover that one of your great-great-grandparents was Native American, for example.

But ethnic heritage is not the only thing DNA testing can tell you. You could learn of a long-lost relative—these sites will let you know if your DNA shows a family connection to someone else who has used its services (as long as this other person has given permission). These services are great ways to double-check genealogical research as well—if you and someone you suspect is related to you submit saliva samples, the testing can confirm the family connection.

There are three major DNA testing companies in the US, all offering the same basic service. Ancestry.com is the most popular (DNA. Ancestry.com, $99)...followed by 23andMe. com ($199)...and then FamilyTreeDNA.com ($89 for the basic DNA test, though more extensive tests are available for higher prices). This is one time when popularity is important—because Ancestry.com is most popular, it has the largest database of DNA profiles, increasing the odds of locating relatives.

Also: Enter the DNA results you receive from any of these services into GEDMatch. com (basic information is free). If someone you are related to has done the same, you can learn of each other even if you used different genetic-testing services.

6. Look for any misspellings of ancestors' names. The further back in history you go, the greater the odds that your ancestors were flexible with the spelling of their names. Brainstorm about potential variations of ancestors' names, and enter those into Internet databases and search tools, too.

Example: One of my ancestors suddenly changed the spelling of his name from Whitfield to Whitefield.

7. Don't let a foreign language stand in your way. If your family tree search leads to records that are in a foreign language that you cannot read, enter the text into Google Translate (Translate.Google.com). If this Google resource will not translate a particular document—it cannot handle certain formats—contact the languages department of a local university and ask if a student might be available to help.

8. Don't give up. Every family tree search reaches an apparent dead end where the direct line seems to disappear into the fog of history. Before you give up, try tracing your seemingly untraceable ancestors' *siblings.* This sometimes leads to clues about where to look for the missing ancestor. This "side step" technique is very useful when an ancestor has a very common name, such as John Smith, but a sibling has a less common name such as Obadiah Smith.

Don't Call Me Nana

Pamela Redmond Satran, author, *How Not to Act Old* and cofounder of the baby-name website, Nameberry.com, reported by Karen Larson, editor, *Bottom Line Personal.*

A friend of mine is about to have her name changed...by an infant. She recently became a grandmother, so she soon will be called Nana or Grammy or something similar. But what if she's not ready to be called Grammy?

A grandparent nickname might seem like a silly thing to fret about, but these names are more than what our children's children call us. "They define how we see ourselves," says Pamela Redmond Satran, author of *How Not to Act Old* and cofounder of the baby-name website Nameberry.com.

Redmond Satran balked at being called Nanny when she recently became a grandmother. That's what she called her grandmother, whom she remembered as an old lady. She wasn't ready to see herself that way, so the family settled on Gaga, which was easy for her grandchild to say.

It turns out that unconventional grandparent names are popular. Former President George W. Bush is Jefe. Actress Goldie Hawn is GoGo. Singer Naomi Judd is Mawmaw. These names are more fun than conventional names, which in comparison seem old-fashioned and, well, old.

But if you want to have a say in your grandparent nickname, say so early on. If you fail to push a particular name by the time your oldest grandchild starts speaking, he/she might choose one for you.

Some grandparents have names such as Bubbles, G-Dawg, Muddy, Muffer, MaxiMa, Jeepers, Punky, Paddles and Peppers. If a young grandchild tries to hang one of those on you and you don't like it, find a private moment and tell him that he's looking at years of itchy sweaters for his birthday if he doesn't do a quick rethink. That ought to set things straight.

Early Antibiotic Use May Raise Allergy Risk

Babies treated with antibiotics before age two had a 15%-to-41% higher risk for eczema and a 14%-to-56% increased risk for hay fever later in life. Risk was higher when babies got two courses of antibiotics in early life than when they received one.

While the study does not prove cause and effect, it is possible that antibiotics disrupt microorganisms in the gut, leading to reduced immune response.

Analysis of studies published between 1966 and 2015 by researchers at Utrecht University, the Netherlands, presented at a recent meeting of the European Respiratory Society.

GOOD TO KNOW...

3 Crucial Questions for Babysitters

These questions will help you "profile" a sitter's mental state and protect your children from abuse. *What bothered you about the last family you worked for?* A long list, given with a know-it-all and/or angry attitude, is a red flag. *Did you ever make suggestions to the parents?* Listen for negative comments, such as a statement that no one ever listened. *How would you solve a problem such as the kids fighting?* Beware of answers focusing on confrontation or excessive discipline.

Dale Yeager, forensic profiler and criminal behavior analyst and CEO of the security-consulting firm Seraph. DaleYeagerDotCom.Wordpress.com

Most Common Cause of Infant Poisoning

The pain reliever provided in Tylenol (*acetaminophen*) is the medicine most often involved in overdoses in babies less than six months old, according to a recent study. Other common poisonings involved gastrointestinal medicines, cough-and-cold products, antibiotics and *ibuprofen*. Nearly half the medication errors—47%—involved incorrect dosage...43% involved giving a medicine too frequently or mistakenly giving the wrong medication.

Review of more than 270,000 calls to poison control centers, led by researchers at Banner-University Medical Center, Phoenix, published in *Pediatrics*.

Whole Milk and Young Kids

Whole milk may be better for young children than low-fat milk. Healthy children, ages one to six, who drank a cup of whole milk daily had a vitamin D level comparable to that of children who drank nearly three cups of 1% milk. And the whole-milk drinkers had lower body mass.

Possible reason: Vitamin D is better absorbed with fat—and full-fat milk may make a child feel fuller and less inclined to seek out calorie-dense foods that can cause weight gain.

Study of 2,745 children led by researchers at University of Toronto, published in *American Journal of Clinical Nutrition*.

Screen Time for Kids OK?

Data analyzed from the 2013 Youth Risk Behavior Survey indicated virtually no association between screen time—such as watching TV, playing video games and other screen activity—and delinquency, risky behavior, sexual activity, substance abuse, reduced grades or mental health problems.

Christopher Ferguson, PhD, professor of psychology, Stetson University, DeLand, Florida, and leader of a study of children, average age 16, that was published in *Psychiatric Quarterly.*

Traits That Put Teens at Risk for Addiction

The four traits that put teenagers at risk for addiction are sensation-seeking, impulsiveness, anxiety sensitivity and hopelessness...

Sensation seekers are drawn to intense experiences such as those produced by drugs. The other traits are linked to mental-health issues. *Impulsiveness* is common in people who have ADHD—a diagnosis that makes addiction three times more likely. *Anxiety sensitivity,* being overly aware of physical signs of anxiety and frightened by them, is tied to panic disorder. *Hopelessness* is tied to depression. Early trials of a new antidrug program suggest that personality testing can identify 90% of the highest-risk children.

Patricia Conrad, PhD, professor of psychiatry, University of Montreal, Canada, quoted in *The New York Times.*

How to Get Your Grown Kids to Call You More

Jane Isay, author of *Walking on Eggshells: Navigating the Delicate Relationship Between Adult Children and Parents* and *Unconditional Love: A GPS for Grandparents.*

To start with, do not assume that your grown kids don't want to communicate with you. Instead, look at things going on in their lives that may make it hard for them to stay in touch. The basic one is likely to be that they are very busy. Most of us raised our kids to have independent, full lives, and being busy is one outcome of that. Sometimes the lack of a phone call simply means, "I'm busy," not "I don't love you or care about you."

Next, if a child lives across the country, think about the time difference. That could be an obstacle. When it is convenient for you to talk, it may not be a good time for him/her and vice versa. Try picking a regular time for the call—one that works for both of you.

Also, do not focus too much on the idea of a phone call. Some young people would rather communicate by text. You might even try video calls if that suits them. The important thing is to find out how they like to communicate—then try reaching out to them that way. It may not be the heart-to-heart phone conversation you want, but it may be the best way to stay in touch.

Two additional points to keep in mind: First, do your best not to make your kids feel guilty. Guilt will make them less likely to respond. Second, even if it seems very hard to communicate with them on a regular basis, keep trying—you might try sending them texts or e-mails from time to time. Even if they do not respond to them, they still will be aware that you are staying in touch.

How to Arrange Your Own Funeral

Joshua Slocum, executive director of the Funeral Consumers Alliance, a nonprofit consumer-rights organization based in South Burlington, Vermont. Funerals.org

Most people don't want to think about their own death, much less plan their own funeral. But thinking through your funeral wishes now, regardless of your age or health—and sharing your desires and guidelines with your loved ones—helps ensure that the arrangements will be handled as you would have wanted. It also will reduce stress on your family when you die...and might even head off disputes among loved ones who have strong opinions. And it easily could save your family thousands of dollars.

That doesn't mean you have to pin down every detail. But giving your family an idea of what is most important to you about your funeral—and why—could save them a lot of steps. Remember that this process has as much to do with defining who you think you are and how you want to be remembered as it does helping your loved ones deal with the process.

Here's how to create a plan that can put your mind at ease now and help your family and friends later…

• **Identify one family member or friend to take the lead.** Choose someone you believe will understand and appreciate your wishes about your funeral but who is flexible…who will make sensible decisions in emotional situations…and who will communicate well with other loved ones. Name a backup, too, in case this person is not available. In most states, you can complete a form to officially name someone your "designated agent for body disposition." (At the website Funerals.org, enter the words "designated agent" into the search box and then select "Who has the legal right to make decisions about your funeral?" to obtain the appropriate form if one is available for your state.) Give your agent a printed copy of your detailed funeral plans, and give copies to other trusted loved ones, just to be safe. Don't forget to include where your will is and whether you want any of your organs donated.

• **In choosing burial, cremation, body donation or another option, consider costs as well as your wishes and those of your loved ones.** In general, costs could range from nothing for donating your body to a medical school…to $1,000 for a simple cremation…to a few thousand or many thousands for burial.

If you already have a family plot, crypt or mausoleum, it might be an obvious choice. Otherwise, it's worth comparing costs among various cemeteries. While it is thoughtful to choose one that is convenient for loved ones to visit—or pleasing to pick one with a beautiful setting for visitors—keep in mind that people tend not to visit cemeteries as often as they did in earlier decades. These days, they are more likely to remember the deceased by sharing stories and looking at photos and videos. It may make sense to choose a cemetery that costs thousands of dollars less than the most convenient or attractive one so that you can leave the family a smaller bill or larger inheritance. Besides, people move around, so your survivors might not live nearby for long. That's one reason it's often unwise to prepay a cemetery before you need it.

• **Comparison-shop funeral homes.** Different funeral homes in the same area often charge vastly different prices, so you should comparison-shop—call at least four in your area. When you find one that seems reasonable, get details in writing so that your family can refer to them when it comes time to lock in the arrangements. Keep in mind that you don't have to accept all the options that a funeral home suggests. For instance, embalming, which could cost around $500 or more, typically is appropriate only when there will be a public viewing. Embalming is rarely required by law—some states require it when the body cannot be buried, cremated or refrigerated for more than a few days, for example. And although a limousine for a funeral procession is traditional, it can be sacrificed to save on costs. By specifying these choices, you lessen the chance that a high-cost provider will prey on family members who are too rushed or emotional to shop around following your death.

If my nonprofit, the Funeral Consumers Alliance, has a chapter in your area, you can get a price comparison of local funeral homes. At Funerals.org, click the "local fca" tab. Keep in mind that your place of worship may have special arrangements with particular funeral homes and/or cemeteries.

Warning: Don't prepay a funeral home. Heirs often forget that funeral bills already have been paid…or unforeseen circumstances alter funeral plans.

• **Consider providing input into how your funeral service will be conducted.** Your religious beliefs and/or family traditions (or lack of them) may determine some or many of these decisions, including where to hold a funeral service…whether a certain cleric will preside… whether to also include a graveside service… what sort of prayers will be recited…and what kind of "event" to suggest before or after the funeral, such as a wake or the Jewish tradition of visits after the funeral, called *shiva*. But there are many options that may depend more on your personal beliefs or desires or family considerations.

DID YOU KNOW THAT...

Happiness Increases with Age

Even though aging is tied to declines in physical health and cognition, older people report experiencing more satisfaction, happiness and well-being than younger ones, on average...and less anxiety, stress and depression.

Study of 1,546 people ages 21 to 99 led by researchers at University of California, San Diego, published in *The Journal of Clinical Psychiatry*.

For instance, should mourners be able to view your body at your funeral? Some people think it isn't a funeral if there is no body to see...while others prefer to be remembered as they were alive and/or consider viewing dead bodies morbid. A compromise is to have your body present but your casket closed.

You even might want to specify what clothing you want to be wearing, especially if there will be a viewing. You might prefer something formal to show you at your best...or something that you have found to be very comfortable or that evokes your personality, especially if it's a quirky one.

You might want to mention some things about your life or personality—certain memories—that you would like the cleric or your friends or family to speak about...and that you might want mentioned in an obituary or a funeral notice.

You also might want to suggest that certain people be included among those who serve as pallbearers and/or who deliver eulogies. Keep in mind that when the time comes, some of them may not want to speak because they are too emotional or uncomfortable doing so.

- **Consider picking some favorite or meaningful songs, poems, verses and/or readings...**and possibly what kinds of flowers you prefer at the service (or naming a charity in lieu of flowers). You even can suggest which loved ones should be asked to read which passages, but consider leaving this flexible instead so that your family and friends can participate in ways that are most meaningful to them.

- **Check whether you are eligible for veterans' burial benefits.** These may include a headstone or marker...a Presidential Memorial Certificate...and, if desired, burial in a national cemetery with military honors, all at no charge, plus, if certain eligibility requirements are met, a burial expense allowance of as much as $2,000. Call the Department of Veterans Affairs at 800-827-1000 for more information.

WHAT ABOUT YOUR CASKET?

The following recommendations apply if you plan your own funeral—but will help your loved ones choose a casket even if you don't...

Choose a casket based on price and appearance, not on materials or construction quality. Family members often feel guilty about choosing less than the best, agonizing over what type of wood or metal to choose and whether the handles are brass or something less impressive. But a casket made of inexpensive materials can approximate the look of a higher-end one, and any casket is capable of holding the body until it is in the ground, which is its only job. By exploring and discussing this in advance, you can make things less stressful (and less expensive) for your family.

Also, don't go overboard in choosing a type of burial vault. This vault typically is made of concrete and helps prevent the grave from sinking. Any vault can do that, so there's no need to pay extra for a high-end option. Laws don't even require a vault—though most cemeteries do. And despite what a cemetery or funeral home might tell you, no burial vault will protect a body from groundwater for long.

How to Share a Bed with Your Pet

Pat Miller, a certified dog trainer and owner of Peaceable Paws, LLC, a dog and puppy training center in Fairplay, Maryland. She has more than 35 years of experience in dog training and recently was named one of the 45 people who have changed the dog world by *Dog Fancy* magazine. Miller is author of *The Power of Positive Dog Training*. PeaceablePaws.com

Many of your friends and neighbors are sleeping with someone other than their spouse. According to a recent survey by the American Pet Products Association, the majority of pet cats and nearly half of all pet dogs sleep in their owners' beds.

"Co-sleeping" with pets usually causes few problems. But when pet owners are light sleepers…pets are restless at night…and/or pets act aggressively toward their bed partners, it can lead to a loss of sleep or other issues. Some pet owners who are chronically tired might not even realize that unsettled sleep as a result of having their pets in bed is what's causing their fatigue.

To make these sleep arrangements work well…

• **Give your pet plenty of exercise in the evenings.** A tired pet is less likely to be restless at night. This advice applies to cats as well as dogs—you can teach a cat to play fetch or use treats or toys to encourage him/her to run, jump or climb.

Caution: Do not give cats access to cat toys or treats containing catnip in the evening. Catnip can make it more difficult for cats to settle down.

• **Let your pet have a toy in bed.** Some pets find it comforting to have a favorite toy in bed with them just as some young children find it easier to sleep with a favorite stuffed animal. This should be a soft toy that does not contain any bells or squeakers. The pet-toy-in-bed strategy does not work with all dogs and cats, however—remove the toy from the bedroom if nighttime access to it makes the pet more playful and active.

• **Teach your pet to stay on one particular part of the bed.** Some dogs and many cats disrupt their human bedmates' sleep by getting too close to their faces and/or positioning themselves between human partners. To train a dog or cat to stay on a specific part of the bed, such as near the foot of the bed, lie on the bed at times other than bedtime and invite the pet to join you. When the pet ventures onto the part of the bed where you would like him to sleep, click a clicker, available in pet stores (or say a positive word such as "yes"), and immediately give the pet a treat.

Alternative: If after a few weeks of this training, the pet still is not staying on his part of the bed, cut out a square of cloth large enough for the pet to curl up on. Place this piece of cloth on top of the bed's blankets in the spot where you want the pet to sleep. Use the clicker/treat training technique described above to train the pet to associate positioning himself on this cloth with praise and food.

• **Ignore your pets when they try to get your attention in bed.** Pets who sleep on beds sometimes wake their owners on purpose because they are bored, lonely or hungry. If your pet does this, do not speak to the pet, make eye contact with him or even pick up the animal to move him away—doing any of these things gives the animal the attention he craves, increasing the odds that this problematic behavior will be reinforced and continue.

Instead, ignore the pet when he wakes you intentionally. In fact, pay the pet as little attention as possible whenever you are in bed, at least after the bedroom lights are turned off.

Helpful: If your pet climbs on top of you while you are lying in bed, use the "earthquake technique" to dislodge him rather than picking him up or pushing him—roll from side to side until the animal figures out that this is not a comfortable place to relax.

If your pet gets right in your face while you lie in bed, turn so your face is right at the edge of the bed facing outward so the pet cannot position himself directly in front of you. You also can hide your head under the covers if you prefer.

Ignore a pet's nighttime attention-seeking behavior consistently for a few weeks, and there's a very good chance that he will stop bothering you.

• **Temporarily remove your pet from the bed if he acts aggressively toward an approaching bedmate.** Pets sometimes growl or exhibit other signs of aggression when certain family members (or other pets) approach the bed. A pet might accept the presence of one spouse in the bed but growl at the other, for example.

To overcome this, do not allow the pet into the bed until *after* this person (or pet) already is in bed. In my experience, dogs and cats that show this sort of aggression generally do so only toward people who are *approaching* the bed. If these people are already in the bed, the pets usually accept their presence.

Meanwhile, use the clicker/treat training technique described above to teach your pet to get off the bed when told "off." That way, if the pet does get on the bed before this person approaches, your pet can be instructed to temporarily vacate.

Warning: It is much more difficult, though not impossible, to modify the behavior of a pet that acts aggressively toward a person or pet who already is in the bed. The best solution with these pets often is to require them to sleep somewhere other than the bed.

• **Get the pet a baby bassinet if all else fails.** If you want your pet to be close to you at night but letting him sleep in your bed proves too disruptive, purchase a baby bassinet that's about the height of your bed and large enough for the animal, position this next to your bed, then use the clicker/treat training technique to encourage the pet to sleep in the bassinet. This form of co-sleeping provides most of the closeness and companionship of allowing the pet into the bed with significantly less potential for sleep disruption.

DOG DANGER...

Common Sugar Substitute Deadly to Dogs

The sugar substitute *xylitol* can be deadly to dogs. The no-calorie sweetener is widely used in sugar-free candies, chocolate bars, cough syrups, mouthwashes, chewable vitamins, even nut butters such as peanut butter—which some people use to give their dogs medicine. Symptoms include vomiting, lethargy and walking as if unstable or drunk. Read product labels carefully, and contact your veterinarian immediately if your dog shows any symptoms that could indicate xylitol poisoning.

Carmela Stamper, DVM, FDA Center for Veterinary Medicine, Silver Spring, Maryland, quoted at WebMD.com.

The Benefits of Sleeping with Your Pet

Bradley Smith, PhD, senior lecturer in psychology at Central Queensland University, North Rockhampton, Queensland, Australia. He specializes in the relationship between humans and animals, and he has published several articles in academic journals about co-sleeping with pets. He is author of *The Dingo Debate: Origins, Behaviour and Conservation.* HowlingDingo.com.au

Allowing a pet to sleep in one's bed might seem like a strange and overly indulgent modern trend, but it actually is surprisingly common and anything but new. Many indigenous societies have traditionally co-slept with their animals—Aboriginal Australians slept with dogs and dingoes, for example, for warmth and protection.

The decision is one that often divides owners. The two main arguments against co-sleeping are that the animal's presence in the bed will cost its owner sleep...and that humans will catch diseases from the close proximity to dog and cat bedmates.

Co-sleeping with pets does indeed cause some reduction to sleep quality and quantity, but our research suggests this sleep loss is not severe. On average, it seems to be no worse than allowing a pet into the bedroom at night but not onto the bed. And while a 2011 report raised the possibility that humans could contract certain diseases from pets that sleep on their beds, this risk actually is minimal as long as pets are kept clean and healthy and receive regular veterinary care (including vaccinations and flea and tick control).

Meanwhile, the potential advantages of co-sleeping with a pet include...

• **Safety.** Some people report feeling more secure and protected when they sleep with their pet—they know that the animal would provide a warning if anyone approached the bedroom during the night.

• **Companionship.** Pets can be a source of comfort and companionship for their owners. The fact that many owners co-sleep with their pets is a reflection of how important the pets are in their lives. Owners who are unable to be with their pets during the day might attempt to maximize contact and interaction by co-sleeping with them during the night.

• **Pet contentment.** Some pets become loud and disruptive when kept out of the bed at night. Allowing these pets into the bed could eliminate these problems and help everyone in the household sleep easier.

How to Prevent a Dog Fight

Watch dogs for raised hackles, stiff tail or posture, deeper-than-usual growling or barking, snarling that shows a lot of teeth and snapping. If you notice stress in your dog or other dogs in a group, call your dog to you and give an obedience reward. Know your dog's triggers—for instance, becoming aggressive around food, in which case do not let other dogs nearby when food is involved.

If a dog fight happens anyway: Many are over within seconds. If dogs separate on their own, approach yours calmly, attach your leash and leave the area. If the fight continues, throw water in the dogs' faces—use a hose if possible. If necessary, find something to put between the dogs, such as a board, large branch, blanket or an umbrella that you open quickly to startle them. Check your dog for injuries after the fight.

Caution: To avoid getting injured, never reach for your dog's collar or head while it is fighting.

PetMD.com

You Can Train Your Cat

Sarah Ellis, PhD, feline behavior specialist at International Cat Care, an international charity based in England that provides education and training for veterinarians, breeders, cat boarders, rescue workers and cat owners. She is a visiting fellow in the School of Life Sciences at University of Lincoln in England and coauthor of *The Trainable Cat: A Practical Guide to Making Life Happier for You and Your Cat.* ICatCare.org

Most cat owners would say that their cats have minds of their own and that, unlike dogs, cats cannot be trained. Not true! By following these steps, you can train your cat—even a mature cat—and solve these common cat problems. The training may take a few hours, a day or a few weeks depending on how often you practice and your cat's temperament.

CAT-TRAINING ESSENTIALS

• **Rewards.** The key to successful cat training is a reward that your cat really values. A food treat—animal protein, in particular, because cats are carnivores—likely will be the most motivating reward.

Examples: Tiny pieces of cooked meat or fish, a very small portion of the cat's normal diet or store-bought cat treats such as semi-moist or air-dried meat snacks. Always give tiny portions so that your cat doesn't gain weight.

For affectionate cats, stroking can be an effective reward in addition to food. Cats prefer brief strokes, and those that concentrate on the top of the head and under the chin typically produce the most positive response.

• **Comfortable blanket.** You can create a link in the cat's mind between a blanket and relaxation. The blanket can then be used in new places or situations (see below) to elicit relaxation and promote successful training.

Choose a blanket, and place it in front of you on the floor. Reward positive behavior that your cat exhibits toward the blanket, such as sniffing the blanket or a quick step onto it. Because these types of behaviors happen so fast, you can use a verbal marker, such as the word "good," at the precise time the behavior happens, then follow up with the food reward or stroking reward shortly afterward. Eventually, withhold the word "good" and the reward for an extra second each time to build up the amount of time your cat spends on the blanket.

Once your cat is comfortable on the blanket, the next step is to teach the cat to relax there. Any signs of relaxation, such as moving from standing to sitting or lying down, should be rewarded. Keep your voice quiet and calm when saying "good," and intersperse food rewards with chin scratches and gentle stroking of the head.

GETTING YOUR CAT INTO THE CARRIER

Cats typically aren't fond of carriers because they don't like feeling trapped. And many times carriers are associated with negative experiences such as harrowing visits to the vet or a boarding facility. But you can change your cat's response to the carrier to a much more positive one, reducing stress for the cat and for you when you need to use the carrier.

• **Choosing a carrier.** When buying a carrier, make sure that the entry door allows your cat to walk in rather than be lifted in and that the door can be completely removed in the initial training. The lid should be removable, too, so that in the initial training stages the carrier appears less enclosed. (A removable lid also may allow a veterinarian to examine your cat while the animal remains "safe" in the base of the carrier.)

• **Do not hide the carrier.** Most pet owners make the mistake of keeping their carriers tucked away in closets when not in use, but that's a mistake. Your carrier should be left out at all times so that your cat is familiar with it.

• **Familiarize your cat with the carrier well before you have to use it.** Start by removing the lid and the door of the carrier so that you have just the base. If your cat seems very wary of the carrier, begin carrier training by rewarding your cat when he stays in the same room as the base of the carrier. You can take the "relaxation blanket" and slowly move it closer and closer to the carrier, rewarding your cat each time he relaxes on the blanket. Eventually, place the blanket in the carrier. This should be enough to get the cat into the carrier.

Once your cat is comfortable in the base of the carrier—he has slept in it or lays down to groom in it—you can gradually slide the door into place. Start by sliding the door in partway, and reward your cat for staying relaxed. Continue to use the marker word "good" to condition your cat to know a food reward is coming—and continue to reward anytime he does not attempt to leave the carrier. Use the same steps when putting the lid back on.

• **Keep the carrier stable.** Cats find being carried in the air unsettling. Always use two hands to keep the carrier steady, and begin to train your cat to be comfortable in a moving carrier by holding the carrier off the floor for only a few seconds. Progress to walking a few steps at a time, and then farther, always continuing to reward your cat.

THE VET APPOINTMENT

A trip to the vet is terrifying for many cats, so removing as many stressors as possible and preparing your cat ahead of time are key.

• **Choose a cat-friendly clinic.** These veterinary practices treat only cats and/or offer cat-only waiting areas. You can find these practices at CatVets.com/cfp.

• **Take a practice visit to the vet.** Ask the clinic staff if you can visit with your cat during a quiet time to promote a positive association. Simply sit in the waiting room for a short time for the first visit. You even can ask the staff if they will feed your cat some treats, though it may be that your cat will accept treats only from you initially. Once the positive association grows, the cat may then feel comfortable taking treats from the staff.

• **Allow your cat to walk out of the carrier.** At a real visit to the vet, when you are in the examination room, open the door and ignore the cat. Give him time to look around the room from inside the carrier and take the first step out. Many vets make the mistake of pulling cats out of carriers, which is stressful for the cats. Tell your vet ahead of time that you'd like to allow your cat to come out on his own and/or ask whether the examination can take place in the carrier with the lid removed.

• **Practice handling at home.** During a basic veterinary examination, the vet will lift a cat's tail, look in his ears, mouth and eyes, and listen to his heart. To make these routines less stressful, practice them at home with rewards.

For example, while stroking your cat's head, subtly lift his lip. Then reward him. Do the same with widening your cat's eye with your forefinger and looking in his ears. To approximate a stethoscope, familiarize your cat with a spoon. Show it to the cat while giving rewards. Then eventually hold the handle of the spoon in your hand, and press the round part on the cat's chest. Incorporate all these types of touches in your daily routine, and the vet visit will be much less stressful. Also, unless your cat is having gastrointestinal issues or requires an anesthetic, bring treats to the vet to reward your cat during exams.

ACCEPTING MEDICATION

Many times, oral medications prescribed for cats are never actually taken because cats spit them out or refuse to have their mouths opened at all.

• ***Before* medication is needed, practice with pill pockets or pill putty.** These products, found in pet-supply stores, conceal pills and are tasty to cats. Try a few different brands as treats (with no medicine) to see which brand your cat likes best. Then when you need to give a pill, your cat won't suspect anything and will probably gobble the treat along with the pill without hesitation.

• **Placing a pill in the mouth.** If your cat is not fond of any pill pockets or pill putty or uncovers and rejects pills, you will have to train him to take pills from you. Have the cat sit on the relaxation blanket to help the process. Start by training him to be comfortable with your hand placed over the top of his head, rewarding him along the way. Then progress to placing the forefinger and thumb of your other hand gently on your cat's lower jaw. Give plentiful rewards during this process—and if the cat flinches at all, take time to let him relax again before continuing. The goal is to get the cat to lower his bottom jaw when the jaw is touched. You will need to use a little pressure to open the mouth, but the key is to make sure that the cat is comfortable with this and doesn't find it distressing. As soon as your cat's jaw opens, provide a reward. Once your cat is accustomed to your assisting in opening his mouth—and this can take a number of training sessions!—and you have to give a pill, make the cat open his mouth and then, holding the pill between your thumb and index finger, place it as far back in the cat's mouth as possible.

GOOD TO KNOW...

Protect Your Pets

Get travel tips...poison prevention...reviews of carriers, crates and other equipment...recalls... more at CenterforPetSafety.org.

17 Household Help

6 Common Home-Maintenance Goofs...and How to Avoid Them

Replacing your air conditioner filter...lubricating a lock...cleaning dust off a refrigerator coil—*what could possibly go wrong?* More than you would expect! Make a mistake with a seemingly simple home-maintenance task, and you could create a big home repair bill. *Here's what home owners need to know before tackling six common—and commonly mismanaged—maintenance chores...*

MISTAKE: **Backward furnace and air conditioner filters.** Most home owners know that furnaces and air conditioners have filters that should be replaced every few months when they are in use. (Certain filters can be cleaned rather than replaced.) But some home owners do not realize that these filters are designed to work in only one direction, and even home owners who do realize this often get the direction wrong. Install them backward, and not only will they do a poor job filtering airborne particulates—they will inhibit airflow, making the system less energy-efficient and potentially burning out components.

Look for the arrow on the side of the replacement filter. This arrow should point in the direction of airflow—which almost always means it should point *toward* the furnace or air conditioner, not away from it, because air going through the filter should be flowing into the unit, not out of it.

Most home owners also neglect to vacuum out the filter compartment when they replace these air filters. This is an important step that is easy to do with a vacuum or shop-vac wand.

Note: Prices, rates and offers throughout this chapter and book are subject to change.

Danny Lipford, who has been a remodeling contractor for 37 years. He is based in Mobile, Alabama, and is host of *Today's Homeowner with Danny Lipford*, a nationally syndicated TV program. TodaysHomeowner.com

Similar: Even home owners who change their furnace and air conditioner filters usually ignore the air filters in their oven range hoods. These should be popped out and cleaned at least a few times a year. Most can simply be washed in the dishwasher. Failing to do so can reduce a range hood exhaust fan's ability to remove smoke and cooking smells from the kitchen by as much as 50%.

***MISTAKE:* Cleaning central-air drain lines without checking for clogs.** You might already know that in order to inhibit mold and mildew growth, once or twice a year it's smart to pour one cup of bleach down an air conditioner system's condensate drain line—the plastic pipe through which condensation produced by the evaporator coil drips off. But if you're like most home owners, you probably don't bother to check this line for clogs. Clogs caused by mold, algae or insect nests could cause water to back up in the line, potentially leading to musty odors in the home and even water damage, particularly if the air conditioner evaporator is located in the attic.

Before pouring bleach into the condensate drain line (there typically is an access opening in the drain line near the internal component of the A/C system), ask someone to watch the other end of the line where water from the line drips outside the home or down a basement drain. If you're not certain where to find the end of your condensate drain line, follow the PVC tubing leading away from the A/C unit inside your house. If you pour water in and your helper does not see water flow out, you'll need to clear away clogs before treating the line with bleach. The easiest way to clear clogs is to use duct tape to create a seal between the end of a shop-vac hose and the external end of the condensate line (or purchase a shop-vac hose adaptor), then turn on the shop vac to suck out the obstruction. You'll save $150 or more by avoiding a maintenance call. (The bleach method does not apply to systems that pump condensation upward. Check with the pump maker if you suspect a clog.)

***MISTAKE:* Wrong lock lubricant.** Home owners typically spray lubricant into keyholes when door locks start sticking. Unfortunately, they usually use the wrong lubricant—the most common household lubricant in the US is the multipurpose WD-40, which is poorly suited to this job. A multipurpose lube might provide some short-term improvement in a lock's function, but soon it will start gumming up the intricate mechanism, leaving the lock worse than ever.

Graphite is a far better lubricant for sticking locks. Graphite lubricants are available in home centers and hardware stores, but you don't even need to buy these. Just rub a #2 pencil liberally all over the surfaces of the key that will enter the sticking lock, then insert this key into the lock several times, turning it each time. (Wipe any remaining graphite off the key afterward so that it doesn't make your purse or pocket messy.)

Similar: Home owners tend to use a multipurpose lube on garage door hinges, wheels and chains—if they bother to lubricate their garage doors at all. This is the wrong lube here, too, because it tends to drip all over the garage and cars below. Lithium grease lubricant, available at home centers and hardware stores, is a better choice because it is more likely to cling without dripping.

***MISTAKE:* Damaging floors when cleaning refrigerator coils.** Most home owners know that they're supposed to remove dust and pet hair from their refrigerator condenser coils a few times a year. Doing this helps refrigerators work efficiently, reducing energy bills and extending the life of fridge motors. But cleaning these coils has become more difficult. Traditionally, a refrigerator's coils could easily be accessed by removing a kick plate on the front of the fridge. But the coils of refrigerators made in the past decade or two often can be accessed only from behind the fridge—and home owners sometimes damage their kitchen floors when they try to slide the fridge away from the wall to access the coils. To avoid this, slip a thick piece of cardboard or a carpet remnant under the fridge before sliding it.

***MISTAKE:* Using chemicals to clear up a clogged sink, tub, toilet or shower drain.** Not only are drain-cleaning chemicals often ineffective, they sometimes damage pipes and septic systems. The best way to clear drain clogs is almost always with a plunger.

Buy a small plunger—this will be easier to fit over sink drains. When plunging a bathroom sink, cover the overflow drain hole with your hand so that the plunger can create suction. Try moving the plunger up and down in a series of small, quick movements—that's a good way to form a seal and dislodge drain debris.

Similar: To avoid garbage disposal clogs, run cold water when you use the disposal, not hot. Hot water tends to soften food debris, increasing the odds that it will stick. Cold water tends to solidify food debris, making it easier for the disposal to chop it up and send it down the drain.

***MISTAKE:* Cleaning out gutters but neglecting to clear the roof.** Removing dead leaves and other debris from gutters is an essential autumn home-maintenance chore. Fail to do this, and leaves might clog your gutters and downspouts in the winter, leading to ice dams and, potentially, water damage. But while most home owners do clear leaves from their gutters (or hire someone to do this for them) once tree branches are bare each year, some neglect to also clear leaves and debris off their roofs. This roof debris eventually gets swept into their gutters by rain or wind and ends up causing the clogs they worked so hard to avoid. When you clean your gutters, clear off your roof, too.

How to Fix Your Broken Garage Door Opener

When your automatic garage door doesn't open, you can check the system yourself before calling for garage door service. Be sure the wall station that operates the opener is in its unlocked position, and check the circuit breaker. Try using the opener in your car—if the door opens, there is a problem in the wall station. If there is sound when you press the wall-station button but no door movement, someone may have pulled the red cord—pull it the opposite way to reengage it. If the door starts to open, then stops, a spring may be broken—look above the door and examine the coils. If the door starts closing and then reverses, a photoelectric safety sensor may be blocked or out of alignment.

Roundup of various experts on garage doors, quoted at DailyCommercial.com.

Kitchen Spruce-Ups You'll Love

Kelly Morisseau, certified master kitchen and bath designer and lead designer for the San Francisco–area remodeling firm MSK Design Build. She has more than 25 years of experience in kitchen and bath design and is founder of the *Kitchen Sync* blog and author of the book *Kelly's Kitchen Savvy: Solutions for Partial Kitchen Remodels.* KellyMorisseau.com/blog

A full kitchen renovation is likely to cost more than $20,000, according to the site HomeAdvisor.com—and potentially much more if you select high-end appliances and materials. But there are ways to make a drab, dated or worn-out kitchen look significantly better for a whole lot less money. Of course, a new coat of paint and new cabinet hardware can get you started—but there are other low-cost ways to spruce up your kitchen that can have surprisingly dramatic results. *Here are seven great kitchen spruce-ups, ranging from $35.99 to $1,000...*

- **Replace underpowered bulbs and "flush mount" ceiling lights.** Insufficient lighting is a big reason why many older kitchens look dated and dingy. Hiring an electrician to install additional fixtures can cost thousands, but for a few hundred dollars you could replace the "flush mount" overhead lighting fixtures often found in older kitchens with "semi flush" fixtures. Unlike flush-mount fixtures, which position bulbs at or very near ceiling level, semi-flush fixtures extend down perhaps a foot from the ceiling. They're generally more attractive and almost always do a better job of distributing light throughout the room.

Example: Feiss Boulevard Indoor Semi-Flush Mount light in oil-rubbed bronze can be found for around $140 (Feiss.com).

• **Install laminate countertops and backsplashes that look like high-end stone.** Laminates lack the prestige of high-end quartz or stone countertops, but today the best of these man-made products really do resemble stone countertops for a fraction of the price.

Example: Formica 180fx laminate effectively mimics marble, granite and travertine, yet it can be found for $100 to $200 per 48-inch-x-96-inch sheet.

If you have a small kitchen, you might be able to have new laminate countertops installed for about $1,000. Granite would likely cost at least twice that. If new countertops aren't in your budget, you still could use these laminates as an eye-catching backsplash.

Additional backsplash alternatives: If you have a traditional-style kitchen, consider installing a painted bead-board backsplash—bead board costs around $20 per 48-inch-x-8-inch panel. Tile is a fine choice for traditional or modern kitchens—choose large-scale 18-x-18-inch tiles, which are in style and easy to install. Larger tiles mean fewer tiles and less grout work. You'll find plenty of tile options for less than $3 a square foot.

• **Replace the countertop microwave.** If your budget is tight, you almost certainly can't replace a kitchen full of older appliances. But for $200 or less, you can replace an old or a low-end microwave with a new one that looks modern and stylish. Microwaves generally are positioned prominently on countertops or hung at eye level, so updating this one seemingly minor appliance can make a kitchen feel more modern. Today's microwaves tend to be smaller than the microwaves of decades past, too, so updating a countertop microwave could free up counter space, making a small kitchen seem a bit less cramped.

• **Update the *inside* of your cabinets** with roll-outs, stacked shelving and cutlery holders. Painting kitchen cabinets is an inexpensive and oft-mentioned way to pep up their appearance...but a coat of paint won't make old cabinets any more functional on the inside, and that's important, too. Today's cabinets often feature roll-out racks, rotating trays and other amenities that help home owners get the most out of kitchen storage space. Efficient cabinets don't just make kitchens more convenient—they make them more attractive, too, because clutter will more likely be stowed out of sight.

Fortunately, you do not need to install new cabinets to accomplish this. There is a wide range of aftermarket kitchen roll-out racks and other organization products on the market that can transform old, basic cabinets into modern, functional storage spaces. The Container Store has perhaps the best selection, but you also can find kitchen-cabinet organizing items at places ranging from Amazon.com to a home-improvement center or a hardware store.

Example: The Container Store's Chrome Pull-Out Cabinet Drawers recently were available for $35.99 to $59.00 apiece (ContainerStore.com).

• **Add a rolling or freestanding island.** Installing a permanent kitchen island costs thousands, but attractive rolling and freestanding islands are available at home centers for $500 or less. These islands can provide additional counter space and serve as an attractive addition to the kitchen. (They're not right for every kitchen, however. If there isn't enough room to position the island at least 36 inches from the main kitchen counters, it will make the kitchen feel cramped.)

If you decide on a rolling island, make sure its wheels lock and—if you have vinyl or softwood kitchen floors—the island should be relatively lightweight so that it won't damage your flooring.

• **Install or expand moldings.** Crown moldings, which run along the top edge of walls... decorative baseboards, which run along the bottom edge...and decorative door and window casings can make a plain kitchen seem much more upscale. Add these moldings if your kitchen lacks them.

Example: Replace standard two-inch-high baseboards with decorative five-inch baseboards. A small kitchen could have new

DID YOU KNOW...

Home Remodeling Usually Doesn't Increase Home Value

A recent study found that only two remodeling projects raised home value by as much as they cost—midrange kitchen remodeling...and replacing windows with midrange wooden ones.

What some other projects return: Turning the attic into a bedroom, 83% of the cost... installing a steel entry door, 77%...replacing vinyl siding, 73%...master suite addition, 51% to 58%...bathroom addition, 46%...sunroom, 45%...home office, 45%.

Remodeling Magazine, Remodeling.hw.net/magazine.

baseboards, crown molding and window casings fitted for less than $500, and potentially much less if you have basic woodworking skills and can tackle this as a do-it-yourself project.

• **Hang colorful window coverings.** Brightly colored kitchen curtains or shades will instantly make a dull kitchen seem more stylish and interesting. In fact, this is among the cheapest, easiest ways to significantly update the look of a kitchen, particularly a kitchen that currently features mostly whites and neutral tones.

Caution: If a kitchen window is near a sink, make sure that the curtain or shade is made from stain-resistant material.

The 8 Best Homemade Cleaners: Much Safer Than Store-Bought

Mandy O'Brien, Wisconsin-based biologist and coauthor of *Homemade Cleaners: Quick-and-Easy, Toxic-Free Recipes*. LivingPeacefullywithChildrencom.

There's no way to know all the chemicals you are bringing into your home when you use commercial cleaning products. Thanks to loopholes in ingredient-disclosure laws, cleaning-product makers are not required to supply a complete list. But independent testing shows that many cleaners contain harsh or even toxic chemicals that have been linked to cancer, asthma, and skin and lung irritation. That includes some cleaners labeled with reassuring words such as "green," "nontoxic" and "biodegradable."

Example: The product Simple Green Concentrated All-Purpose Cleaner says "nontoxic" and "biodegradable" on its label, but testing by the Environmental Working Group, an organization of independent scientists, found that it contains a solvent known to damage red blood cells.

If you make your own cleaning products, you can better control what comes into your home. *The following eight do-it-yourself cleaners are safe, effective, inexpensive and easy to make...*

• **Two-step disinfectant that kills germs better than chlorine bleach...**

1. Combine white distilled vinegar and water in a spray bottle in a 1:1 ratio. Spray this on surfaces as you would bleach.

2. Thoroughly wipe away the vinegar with a cloth or sponge.

3. In a separate bottle, add hydrogen peroxide and spray on the surface. Wipe off.

A researcher at Virginia Polytechnic Institute found that this system kills germs better than chlorine-based bleach. It's safer, too. Chlorine-based bleach (and commercial cleaners that contain it) can cause skin irritation and respiratory problems including asthma attacks, among other health concerns. Hydrogen peroxide is a type of bleach but is safer.

Important: Do not skip the wipe-down step. When vinegar and hydrogen peroxide combine, they produce *peracetic acid*, which has respiratory health risks similar to those of chlorine bleach.

• **Sweet-smelling sink scrub...**

1. Mix one cup of baking soda...one tablespoon of ground cinnamon...and five drops of sweet orange essential oil in an airtight container. (Essential oils are available online and in pharmacies, health-food stores and at

big-box retailers such as Target and Walmart. Prices vary but start at about $3 per ounce.)

2. Sprinkle a small amount of this mixture on a wet sink, and scrub with a cloth.

3. Rinse.

Baking soda is a wonderful mild abrasive—it removes grease, grime and soap scum without scratching surfaces.

• **Safe liquid hand soap...**

1. Combine three tablespoons of liquid castile soap with one cup of water. (Liquid castile soap can be purchased online and in pharmacies, health-food stores and at big-box retailers such as Target and Walmart, typically for 50 cents to $1 an ounce.)

2. Add up to 10 drops of your favorite essential oil. (This step is optional. Essential oil makes the soap slightly more antibacterial, but mainly it adds scent.)

3. Stir until the soap dissolves.

4. Pour the mixture into a liquid soap dispenser.

Traditional detergent soaps contain harsh chemicals that are derived from petroleum. Castile soaps are instead made from plant oils and are extremely safe to use in our homes and on our skin.

Helpful: Unlike some natural hand soaps, this one foams. Foaming does not improve soap's cleaning power, but it could save you money—when soap doesn't foam, people tend to use more than necessary.

• **Floor cleaner with that familiar lemony scent...**

1. Fill a bucket with hot water.

2. Mix in two tablespoons (or two large squirts) of liquid castile soap and 20 drops of lemon essential oil.

3. Allow your mop to soak in this mixture until it's saturated, then mop as normal.

This simple mixture cleans hard-surface floors including wood, tile and linoleum without harsh chemicals. It leaves behind a lemon smell that those of us raised in the era of Lemon Pledge associate with cleanliness.

Tip: If you're bored with lemon-scented cleaners, feel free to substitute another essential oil, such as lime, orange or grapefruit.

• **Glass cleaner that won't streak...**

1. Combine one-half cup of white distilled vinegar with three-quarters cup of water in a spray bottle, and shake until mixed.

2. Spray on windows and mirrors.

3. Dry with a lint-free cloth or crumpled newspaper. (Newspaper is slightly more abrasive than paper towels, so it does a better job of removing dirt and debris...and newspaper does not leave behind bits of lint.)

Commercial glass cleaners often contain detergents that can leave streaks of residue. This simple vinegar-based detergent-free cleaner will not streak. (You might see streaks the first time or two you use it—that's the lingering residue from a previously used commercial cleaner.)

Tip: If you dislike the smell of vinegar, soak lemon peels, lime peels and/or orange peels in one-half cup of vinegar for at least one week. Strain out the peels, then use the now citrus-scented vinegar in place of the standard vinegar in the recipe above.

• **Effective, all-natural dish soap...**

This soap is meant for washing dishes by hand...

1. Add one-quarter cup of tightly packed, grated bar soap (castile soap is available in bar form) to one-and-a-quarter cups of boiling water, and stir until dissolved.

2. Add one tablespoon of washing soda (washing soda can cause skin irritation, so be careful handling it) and one-quarter cup of liquid castile soap, stir again, then remove the mixture from the heat. (Washing soda can

EASY TO DO...

Hammer Any Nail Easily

To get a nail started in a wall, especially in a hard-to-reach spot, stick some modeling clay on the wall and let the clay hold the nail for you. Once you've hammered in the nail far enough so that it's steady, peel away the clay.

Joan Wilen and Lydia Wilen, writers and researchers who have spent decades collecting household tips and "cures from the cupboard." They are authors of *Bottom Line's Treasury of Home Remedies & Natural Cures*. BottomLineInc.com be found in the laundry aisle of many supermarkets.)

3. Allow the mixture to cool, then add 20 to 30 drops of the essential oil of your choice.

4. Store in a glass jar or a soap dispenser.

• **Effective natural dishwasher soap...** To make a natural dishwasher soap, combine one cup of borax...one cup of washing soda...one-half cup of kosher salt...and one-half cup of citric acid. Store in an airtight container. Use one tablespoon per dishwasher load.

• **Safe air freshener...**

1. Mix one cup of baking soda with 20 to 30 drops of your favorite essential oil. (Citrus oils, such as grapefruit, lemon, lime or orange, are good options.)

2. Sprinkle the mixture on surfaces that require deodorization, such as carpets or upholstery. Leave on for 20 minutes or more, then vacuum up. Or place an open container of the mixture near the source of the odor.

Some commercial air fresheners actually spread neurotoxins throughout the home. Rather than remove or cover the odor, many work by deadening your sense of smell.

Best Way to Clean Spots on a Microfiber Couch

To get spots out of a microfiber couch, try rubbing them gently with artists' gum, a powerful eraser found at art-supply stores. If you spill something on microfiber, immediately apply cornmeal or baking soda to the spill and leave it on for 15 minutes, then vacuum—and repeat if necessary. To clean very dirty microfiber, check the item's tag. If it has a W on it, you can use water and soap for cleaning. If it has an S, water could stain the fabric—solvent is required. In that case, spray rubbing alcohol over soiled areas, then rub with a rough sponge or old toothbrush—the stains should come right off. If the fabric seems hard or discolored when it dries, stroke it with a toothbrush or soft scrub brush until it feels velvety again.

QuickandDirtyTips.com

10 Ways to Clean with Baking Soda

Teapots and coffeepots come clean with one-quarter cup of baking soda in one quart of water—for tough stains, also add a little detergent and let soak overnight. *Fruits and vegetables* clean up safely with a little baking soda on a clean sponge. *For oil and grease stains,* sprinkle on some baking soda and scrub with a brush. *Car parts* come clean with one-quarter cup of baking soda in one quart of water—or make a paste for stubborn spots, such as tar or tree sap. *Tubs, sinks and tile* can be cleaned with baking soda and water. *For hands with onion or garlic smell,* rub on a baking-soda-and-water mixture. *To keep sneakers fresh,* shake some baking soda into them when not in use and shake them out before wearing them. *Washing machines* that have odors can be easily cleaned by running them empty with one-half cup of baking soda.

SavingFreak.com

How to Machine-Wash Hard-to-Wash Items

Backpacks can be washed by placing them in a laundry bag after opening pockets, then using a gentle cold-water cycle with a little detergent. *Baseball caps* should be pretreated with stain remover and washed on a short cycle with cold water. *Gym bags* can be cleaned on a gentle cold-water cycle. *Legos and other small toys* can be washed in a mesh laundry bag on a cool, delicate cycle. Oven mitts can go in with dish towels and washcloths. *Pillows* can be washed two at a time on a gentle, warm-water cycle, followed by a cold-water rinse and spin. *Reusable canvas grocery bags* can be washed using a regular hot-water cycle. *Sneakers,* with laces and inner soles removed, can be washed in a pillowcase using a delicate, cold-water cycle, with one tablespoon of white vinegar added for deodorizing.

Reader's Digest, RD.com.

When Moving to a New Home...

Change the locks—it is impossible to know how many people have copies of the previous locks' keys. *Replace all filters*—the aeration filters in bathroom/kitchen faucets...the air filter above the stove...and the filter in the heating/air-conditioning unit. *Clean the house completely*—when it is empty, you can clean more efficiently. *Buff and seal wood floors* before placing furniture on them. *Get a list of contacts and service people from the prior owner*—and if you have a good relationship, ask if you can get in touch with the previous owner in case some unforeseen problem arises.

Experts on moving, reported at Bankrate.com.

Best Place for the Wireless Router

The best place for your home wireless router typically is as close as you can get to the center of your home. Routers broadcast signals roughly in the shape of a globe, so if you're outside that globe, you won't get a signal.

CNET.com

Get More Food from Your Food! Delicious Ways to Use Every Bit

Sherri Brooks Vinton, author of the best-selling *Put 'em Up!* series on home food preservation and *Eat It Up! 150 Recipes to Use Every Bit and Enjoy Every Bite of the Food You Buy.* SherriBrooksVinton.com

Americans now discard a whopping 31 million tons of edible food each year. Sometimes we throw out food simply because we don't know of an appetizing way to use it—this includes "scraps" such as potato peels, apple peels and broccoli stems. But Sherri Brooks Vinton knows just what to do with such perfectly fine food—and it isn't throwing it away. She is the author of *Eat It Up! 150 Recipes to Use Every Bit and Enjoy Every Bite of the Food You Buy. Here are some of her delicious recipes...*

POTATO PEEL "CROUTONS"

When a recipe calls for peeled potatoes, you can use the peels from any variety—fingerlings, russets, Yukon golds—to make these tasty, crunchy croutons that can liven up a salad or top a cooked casserole.

When possible, buy organic or locally grown potatoes that are sprayed only minimally with chemicals. Scrub all potatoes well to remove any dirt. Cut away small blemishes or eyes. You might want to hand-peel potatoes with a knife so that you can cut down deeper and wider than with a vegetable peeler to ensure

TAKE NOTE...

For Longer-Lasting Flowers...

To make fresh-cut flowers last longer, combine a few drops of bleach or a clear liquor, such as vodka or gin, with a crushed vitamin C tablet and a few drops of clear soda or superfine sugar. The bleach or liquor fights bacterial growth...the soda or sugar provides nourishment...and the vitamin C lowers the pH so that the water can move up the stems faster, preventing wilting.

Consumer Reports, ConsumerReports.org.

substantial strips of peel. Otherwise the peels can be too papery to use.

2 cups potato peels from well-scrubbed potatoes
6 garlic cloves, with peel on
2 Tablespoons olive oil
Pinch of dried thyme
Salt and freshly ground black pepper
1 ounce Parmigiano-Reggiano cheese, grated (about ¼ cup)

Preheat the oven to 275°F.

Toss the potato peels and garlic cloves with the oil, thyme and salt and pepper to taste. Arrange the peels and garlic in a single layer on a rimmed cookie sheet. Roast until the peels are crisp, about 20 minutes, tossing occasionally to ensure even cooking. Remove from the oven, pick out the garlic cloves,* and toss the potato peels with the cheese. They can be stored in an airtight container for up to one week. Makes two cups.

APPLE TEA

When a recipe—or a finicky eater—calls for peeled apples, save the peels and make your own fruit-flavored tea. You can do this with pears and other fruits as well. Peels can keep in an airtight container in the refrigerator for up to two days.

Note: Many grocery stores wax their fruit to prolong its shelf life and make it shine. When possible, buy apples directly from a farmer or a market that doesn't sell waxed fruit.

If you have waxed apples: Fill a large bowl with warm water, and add a few drops of fragrance-free dish soap or one tablespoon each of lemon juice and baking soda. Roll the apples around in the water for two minutes, then gently scrub them with a soft-bristled brush.

5 teaspoons black tea leaves, or 2 tea bags
1-2 cups of apple peels (from 2 to 4 apples)
Granulated sugar or other sweetener, if desired

Bring one quart of water to a boil, and turn off the heat. Add the tea leaves, encased in a tea ball, or the tea bags, and steep for five minutes. Remove the tea ball or bags, and add the peels. Return the tea to a simmer, then turn off the heat. Allow the peels to steep until the tea has cooled completely. Strain the tea, and compost or discard the peels. Serve over ice or reheat. Sweeten, if desired. Keeps, refrigerated, for up to five days. Makes one quart.

*Don't throw out that roasted garlic! Squeeze the pulp out of the papery skin, and blend it into dressings or dips or spread it on toast points.

BROCCOLI SLAW

Many people believe that broccoli stalks are tough and fibrous, but once trimmed, the stalks actually are tender and sweet.

To prepare the stalks: Use a vegetable peeler to remove the tough outer layer. Trim off the bottom, then you can shred with a box grater or cut into matchsticks.

If you need to store stalks before using them, leave them untrimmed, wrapped in a damp paper towel or stored in an airtight container for two to three days in the refrigerator.

Any extra vegetables—radishes, cabbage or peppers, for example—that you may have on hand can be prepped the same way and added to the slaw.

2 Tablespoons soy sauce
1 Tablespoon rice vinegar or white wine vinegar
Pinch of granulated sugar
1 teaspoon sesame oil
2 Tablespoons neutral oil, such as canola
Red pepper flakes (optional)
Broccoli stalks from 1 bunch of broccoli, peeled, trimmed and shredded or cut into matchsticks
2 carrots, shredded or cut into matchsticks
2 Tablespoons minced fresh cilantro (optional)
2 Tablespoons sesame seeds

In a large bowl, whisk the soy sauce, vinegar and sugar until the sugar is dissolved. Whisk in the oils and red pepper flakes, if using. Add the broccoli and carrots, and toss to combine. Garnish with the cilantro, if using, and sesame seeds. Can be made up to two hours ahead. Makes two to four side-dish servings.

ASPARAGUS SOUP

This is the perfect recipe for using up asparagus ends—it gives you the flavor, but straining the soup leaves the tough texture of the ends behind. You can store asparagus ends in an airtight container in the freezer before using them.

1 shallot, diced, or 1 leek, white and light green parts diced (you can save the dark green stalks for vegetable stock, see below)
2 Tablespoons unsalted butter
1 pound starchy potatoes, such as russets, peeled and chopped (save skins for Potato Peel Croutons above)
2 cups asparagus ends
1 quart vegetable stock (see below)
¼ cup heavy cream (optional)
Salt and freshly ground black pepper
A few minced chives, croutons or a little sour cream, for garnish (optional)

Sauté the shallot or leek in the butter in a medium-sized saucepan over medium heat until translucent, three to five minutes. Add the potatoes, asparagus ends and stock, and bring to a simmer. Cook until the potatoes are falling apart, about 25 minutes. Remove from the heat. Use an immersion blender to purée the soup. Or you can ladle the soup into a regular blender to purée.

Pour the blended soup through a fine-mesh strainer into a medium-sized heat-proof bowl, taking care to press as much of the thick asparagus pulp through the strainer as possible, leaving only the stringy, fibrous material behind. Return the strained soup to the pot, and heat at a gentle simmer. If using the cream, add it and continue to simmer for two to three minutes. Adjust the seasoning with salt and pepper. Ladle into bowls and garnish, if you like, with chives, croutons and/or sour cream.

The soup (without the cream) can be cooled and refrigerated for two to three days or frozen for up to three months. Reheat and add the cream, if using, before serving.

VEGETABLE STOCK MADE FROM SCRAPS

A great way to use leftover vegetable stems and peels is to make a vegetable stock.

What to do: Keep a clean, half-gallon paper carton (such as a milk carton) in the freezer, and add veggie scraps—such as the ends, peels and trimmings from potatoes, carrots, celery, garlic, leeks, shallots, parsley, scallions, mushrooms and tomatoes.

Important: Don't use strong-flavored vegetables, including peppers or chilies, or cruciferous vegetables, such as broccoli, cabbage, cauliflower and brussels sprouts, because their taste will dominate the broth.

When you are ready to make the stock, peel away the paper carton to retrieve the frozen contents. Place in a medium-sized saucepan, and cover with cold water by two inches. Add one bay leaf and salt and pepper to taste. Slowly bring to a simmer over medium heat.

Lower the heat on the stove, and gently simmer for one hour. (Avoid the temptation to simmer for an extended period of time. Vegetables that simmer for more than two hours taste bitter.)

Remove from the heat, and strain through a colander into a heat-proof bowl. Compost or discard the spent vegetables. Set the stock aside to cool to room temperature, and allow any grit to settle. Carefully pour off the broth, leaving any sediment behind.

Store in the refrigerator for up to five days, or freeze for up to six months.

Have a Healthier Thanksgiving!

Jamison Starbuck, ND, naturopathic physician in family practice and producer of *Dr. Starbuck's Health Tips for Kids*, a weekly program on Montana Public Radio, MTPR.org, both in Missoula. She is also a past president of the American Association of Naturopathic Physicians and a contributing editor to *The Alternative Advisor: The Complete Guide to Natural Therapies and Alternative Treatments.* DrJamisonStarbuck.com

---

This year, why not make Thanksgiving not only delicious but also a health-boosting experience that's truer to the origins of the holiday? For most of us, our traditional Thanksgiving meal has shifted away from the natural foods enjoyed by the 17th-century celebrants. But it's not that difficult to get back to preparing delicious food that is fresh from the harvest…and packed with nutrition. *Here's my advice on how you can get started…*

• **Make your own cranberry sauce.** It is easy, economical and much healthier to make your own cranberry sauce instead of buying the canned, highly sweetened version. All you need is a bag of fresh cranberries, an orange and a little sugar. The recipe is on the package of fresh cranberries found in grocery stores all over America. I suggest using about half the amount of sugar that is called for (or a similarly reduced amount of a sweetener you may prefer, such as stevia, honey, date sugar or even maple syrup, though it may alter the consistency of the sauce). Use an organic orange so you can add the whole fruit, including the peel (chopped), which will soften and add a marmalade-like quality to your cranberry sauce. Preparing cranberries this way preserves more of the antioxidants and heart-healthy nutrients that naturally occur in the fruit.

• **Try hummus as an appetizer.** Instead of cheese, crackers, salami and dairy-based dips and chips, try hummus (combine mashed chickpeas, tahini, olive oil, lemon juice and garlic) and raw veggies. This combo is a great source of healthy fats and protein, with fewer calories than the appetizers we often choose. Raw veggies also contain lots of fiber, which will fill you up a bit, so you won't eat too much before the turkey arrives. They also help with digestion and elimination of this big holiday meal. If carrots and celery are old hat, try jicama, cauliflower or daikon (white winter) radishes.

• **Bake potatoes whole.** Instead of mashing potatoes and mixing them with lots of butter and milk, try baking them instead. I like whole baked sweet potatoes—they are a great source of vitamins A, C, B-5 and B-6, potassium, manganese and copper. You can enjoy your baked potatoes plain with the stuffing (instead of white-bread croutons, try whole-wheat croutons, corn bread, chestnuts, mushrooms and celery), turkey and gravy, which will provide the fat we all enjoy—plus, we all need some fat to stay healthy!

• **Choose veggies harvested later in autumn.** Opt for broccoli, kale, brussels sprouts and thick-skinned squash such as acorn or butternut. If possible, buy these vegetables in late autumn from local growers. These steps help ensure that the veggies haven't been stored and/or shipped across country.

Also: Don't slather your veggies with butter—use lemon juice, a small amount of olive oil and your favorite fresh herbs instead.

• **Serve peppermint or ginger tea at the end of the meal.*** It's natural to overindulge in such scrumptious foods. These teas reduce gas and bloating to tame indigestion naturally.

With these simple approaches, your Thanksgiving will be much healthier—and even more enjoyable!

*People with gastroesophageal reflux disease should avoid peppermint, since it can worsen heartburn and indigestion.

EASY TO DO...

Reheating Trick

Arrange leftovers in a circle around the edge of the plate before microwaving. This helps ensure the microwave heats the leftovers evenly.

TheKitchn.com

Vegetarian Dishes Even Veggie Haters Will Love

Linda Gassenheimer, an award-winning author of numerous cookbooks including *Delicious One-Pot Dishes* and *Quick & Easy Chicken*. She also created the recipes for *Beat Diabetes Now!* (available at BottomLineStore.com). Gassenheimer writes the syndicated newspaper column "Dinner in Minutes." DinnerinMinutes.com

You know that you should add more vegetables to your diet, maybe even have a vegetarian dinner once a week. But what can you do if you aren't a vegetable lover?

These recipes will solve that problem! The vegetables are in the background, picking up the wonderful flavors of the spices and sauces...

GARLIC BLACK BEAN CHILI

The broccoli is cut into small pieces that absorb the flavor of the spicy sauce.

2 teaspoons olive oil
1 cup thinly sliced red onion
2 crushed garlic cloves
1 16-ounce can low-sodium black beans, drained and rinsed
1 medium tomato, cut into 1-inch pieces (about 1 cup)
1 cup frozen corn kernels
1 cup broccoli florets, cut into 1-inch pieces
1½ Tablespoons chili powder
1 teaspoon ground cumin
1 Tablespoon tomato paste
1 cup vegetable broth
Salt and freshly ground black pepper
¼ cup shredded Monterey jack cheese, for garnish

Heat the oil in a large frying pan over medium-high heat. Add the onion and garlic, and sauté three minutes. Add the black beans, tomato, corn, broccoli, chili powder and cumin. In a bowl, mix the tomato paste into the broth, then stir into the chili. Simmer, covered, 15 minutes. Add salt and pepper to taste. Add more chili powder or cumin as desired. Serve the chili over rice, and sprinkle with cheese. Serves two.

MEDITERRANEAN LINGUINE WITH FENNEL ORANGE SALAD

Raisins, pine nuts, olives and grated Pecorino cheese flavor the pasta and kale. The fennel orange salad works well with the main dish.

¼ pound baby kale, large center ribs removed
2 teaspoons olive oil
1 cup thinly sliced yellow onion
1 crushed garlic clove
2 cups canned whole tomatoes, including their liquid
Salt and freshly ground black pepper
¼ cup raisins
2 Tablespoons pine nuts
8 pitted green olives
¼ pound whole-wheat linguine
3 sprigs fresh basil
2 Tablespoons grated Pecorino cheese

Place a large pot with three to four quarts of water on to boil.

Stack the kale leaves, and roll them into a cigar shape. Cut the roll into quarter-inch slices, making thin strands—about four cups total. Heat the oil in a large skillet over medium heat. Add the onion, garlic and kale, and sauté five minutes. Add the tomatoes, cutting them in quarters in the pan with a spoon. Add salt and pepper to taste. Add the raisins, pine nuts and olives. Cover and simmer five minutes.

Meanwhile, add the pasta to boiling water and return to a boil. Cook eight minutes or according to package instructions. Drain and divide the pasta between two plates. Pour the sauce over the pasta. Tear the basil into small pieces, and sprinkle cheese on top. Serves two.

FENNEL ORANGE SALAD

1 medium fennel bulb
1 medium orange
1 Tablespoon orange juice (from the orange)
½ Tablespoon olive oil
Salt, to taste

Remove the stalks and stem from the fennel. Cut the remaining bulb in quarters, and slice thin. You'll net about two cups. Peel the orange, and cut it into one-to-two-inch cubes over a bowl, capturing the juice to make one tablespoon. Add the olive oil, and mix well. Add salt to taste. Then add the fennel, and toss again. Serves two.

WILD MUSHROOM AND CAULIFLOWER MASHED "POTATOES"

Veggie haters will think they are having mashed potatoes!

½ head cauliflower (4 cups florets and stems)
1 Tablespoon canola oil
2 cups thinly sliced shiitake mushrooms
4 crushed garlic cloves
2 Tablespoons milk
¼ cup sour cream
2 scallions, sliced (about ¼ cup)
Salt and freshly ground black pepper

Separate the cauliflower into florets, and chop the core. Place in a steamer basket over boiling water. Cover and steam 15 minutes or until the cauliflower is tender.

Meanwhile, heat the canola oil in a medium-sized skillet over medium-high heat, and sauté the mushrooms three minutes. Add the garlic, and continue to sauté one minute more. When the cauliflower is ready, remove to a colander and press out any excess water. Add to a food processor, and coarsely chop. Spoon into a bowl, and stir in the mushrooms and garlic. Add the milk, sour cream, scallions and salt and pepper to taste. Mix well. Serves two.

RICOTTA AND ROASTED VEGGIE SOUFFLÉ

Roasting the vegetables brings out their natural sweetness. The vegetables are thinly sliced, which helps them roast faster and melt into the dish.

1 cup thinly sliced zucchini
1 cup thinly sliced carrots
1½ cups thinly sliced button mushrooms
½ cup thinly sliced onion
1 Tablespoon olive oil
¼ cup chopped fresh basil
½ cup plain bread crumbs
1 Tablespoon red pepper flakes
Salt and freshly ground black pepper
1 cup ricotta cheese
1 large egg

Preheat the oven to 450°F. Cover a large baking tray with foil. Spread the zucchini, carrots, mushrooms and onion on the tray. Drizzle olive oil over the vegetables. Mix evenly to coat the veggies. Then place them in the oven for 10 minutes. Watch to make sure the vegetables do not brown.

Meanwhile, in a small bowl, mix the basil with the bread crumbs, and add salt and pepper to taste. Set aside. Remove the vegetables from the oven, and spoon them into a small lasagna dish about seven-by-10 inches or a 10-inch pie plate. Sprinkle with red pepper flakes and a little salt and pepper to taste.

Mix the ricotta cheese and egg together, and spread the mixture over the vegetables. Sprinkle the bread crumb mixture evenly over the top. Bake in the preheated oven for 15 minutes. Serves two.

FIVE-SPICE STIR-FRY

This colorful dish has a tasty Asian sauce that masks the vegetables. If there's a vegetable in the recipe that your veggie hater really despises, you can substitute a more palatable one (most people like *some* veggies). You can substitute most vegetables including green beans, corn kernels, peas, bok choy, even cucumbers.

¼ cup vegetable broth
1 Tablespoon rice wine vinegar
1 teaspoon Chinese five-spice powder
3 crushed garlic cloves
1 Tablespoon low-sodium soy sauce
2 Tablespoons slivered almonds
1 teaspoon canola oil
½ cup thinly sliced yellow onion
½ cup thinly sliced red bell pepper
½ cup thinly sliced celery
½ cup thinly sliced carrots
½ teaspoon cornstarch
½ Tablespoon water

Mix the vegetable broth, vinegar, Chinese five-spice powder, garlic and soy sauce together. Set aside.

Heat a wok or large skillet over high heat. Add the almonds, and toss until golden, about 30 seconds. Remove to a plate, and set aside.

Add the oil to the wok, and heat until it is smoking. Add the onion, red bell pepper, celery and carrots, and stir-fry three minutes. Remove to a bowl. Add the sauce to the wok, and boil one minute. In a bowl, whisk the cornstarch with one-half tablespoon of water. Add that to the wok. Boil about 30 seconds to thicken the sauce. Remove from heat, and return the vegetables to the wok, tossing with sauce to coat the vegetables.

Divide the stir-fry between dinner plates, and sprinkle almonds on top. Serve with rice, if desired. Serves two.

FUN RECIPE...

Make Crispy Chips in Your Microwave

Thinly slice a raw baking potato, and toss the slices lightly with oil. Coat a microwavable plate with cooking spray. Lay the slices in one layer on the plate. Microwave for four minutes (experiment with timing—you don't want the slices too brown), then turn the chips and microwave for two minutes more. They will crisp up as they sit for a minute or two.

Food.com

Shhh...They'll Never Know They're Eating Vegetables

Missy Chase Lapine, *New York Times* best-selling author of a series of healthy cookbooks, which includes *The Sneaky Chef* and *Sneaky Blends*. For more information, go to TheSneakyChef.com.

We may try to get the recommended number of servings of fruits and vegetables each day, but most of us fall short. According to the Centers for Disease Control and Prevention, 91% of Americans do not eat enough veggies and 87% aren't getting enough fruit. An easy way to rectify this—and cut calories and fat at the same time—is to add my "sneaky" vegetable and fruit blends to your food (see how to make the blends on the next page). Don't worry—your food still will be delicious, maybe even more so!

These blends can replace one-third to one-half the calories and fat in recipes, so you can lose weight (or stay trim) and continue to eat foods you love. Also, the blends are high in fiber, which helps you feel satisfied longer. A study by Pennsylvania State University researchers found that adults who were given meals made with vegetable purées ate 350 fewer calories a day and reported feeling as full as those who ate the same meals without the vegetables.

Here are recipes for two delicious American favorites made much healthier with my sneaky blends...

SINGLE-SERVE MAC AND CHEESE

This dish may seem decadent, but it has only 302 calories per serving and it is rich in fiber with six grams per serving.

¾ cup cooked whole-grain rotini pasta
⅓ cup Carrot–Sweet Potato Blend (recipe on next page)
1 egg white
⅛ teaspoon mustard powder
½ ounce goat cheese, crumbled (if you don't like goat cheese, you can double up on the Cheddar and Parmesan)
1 Tablespoon low-fat milk
1 heaping Tablespoon grated sharp Cheddar cheese
½ cup chopped cauliflower florets
Pinch of sea salt and freshly ground black pepper
1 Tablespoon freshly grated Parmesan cheese

Preheat the oven to 400°F. In a large bowl, mix together all of the ingredients except the Parmesan. Pour into an ovenproof bowl, sprinkle the Parmesan over the top, and bake for 20 minutes or until the top is browned and bubbly. Makes one serving.

NOT YOUR GRANDMA'S (TURKEY) MEAT LOAF

Instead of the refined, nutrient-devoid white bread crumbs in your grandmother's meat loaf, this recipe uses oats and flaxseed, which offers a hearty dose of fiber, antioxidants and omega-3s. And the Black Bean–Blueberry–Baby Kale Blend gives the meat loaf moisture, adds another hit of nutrition and allows you to use half as much meat as needed for most recipes. There are 227 calories and four grams of fiber in a one-and-a-half-inch-thick slice.

½ cup Black Bean–Blueberry–Baby Kale Blend (see recipe on next page)
¼ teaspoon sea salt
Freshly ground black pepper
¼ teaspoon onion powder
1 large egg
1 teaspoon Worcestershire sauce
2 Tablespoons ground flaxseed
½ cup oats, finely ground
1 Tablespoon tomato paste
½ teaspoon dried oregano
1 pound lean ground turkey breast
Nonstick cooking spray
3 Tablespoons ketchup (optional)

Preheat the oven to 350°F. In a large bowl, combine the first 10 ingredients and mix well using the back of a fork. Mix in the turkey. Transfer to a standard-sized loaf pan that has been misted with cooking spray, and top with the ketchup, if using. Bake for 35 to 45 minutes or until the meat reaches an internal temperature of 160°F. Makes six servings.

THE SNEAKY CHEF VEGETABLE AND FRUIT BLENDS

These blends keep for three days in the refrigerator and three months in the freezer. I like to freeze them in half-cup quantities so that I thaw only what I need.

CARROT–SWEET POTATO BLEND

This blend has a creamy texture and deliciously sweet flavor. Carrots are high in beta-carotene and other carotenoids—antioxidants that promote eye health and are protective against many cancers. Sweet potatoes also are loaded with beta-carotene, plus fiber, B vitamins and potassium. Unlike white potatoes, which cause a sugar spike and subsequent crash, which increases hunger, sweet potatoes stabilize blood sugar levels. Orange vegetables also are protective against heart disease.

In addition to the Mac and Cheese (see above), here are a variety of ways you can use this blend to boost nutrition and replace calories and fat in foods you eat every day…

• **Stir into soups or any red sauces,** such as marinara, to add creaminess (without the cream).

• **Use to replace half the fat and sugar in baked goods** such as muffins and in breakfast favorites such as pancakes and waffles.

• **Mix into salad dressings, brown gravies and condiments,** such as ketchup and mustard.

• **Mix into nut butters and store-bought hummus.**

• **Use in prepared baked beans.**

For this recipe, don't drive yourself crazy dicing the veggies—a rough chop is fine. Just try to make them about the same size so that they cook evenly. Or use frozen diced sweet potatoes, available in many markets. Pick up some frozen carrots, too. Then you can skip the steaming and simply flash-thaw them by pouring hot water over both veggies, and go directly to the blending step. You will need about four cups of frozen chopped sweet potatoes and three cups of frozen chopped carrots.

2 large sweet potatoes or yams, peeled and roughly chopped
6 large carrots, peeled and roughly chopped
Filtered water

Place a steamer basket into a large pot, pour in a few inches of tap water (make sure that the water is below the bottom of the basket) and set it over high heat. Add the sweet potatoes and carrots and steam, covered, for 15 to 20 minutes, until fork-tender. In a blender or food processor, blend the veggies with two to three tablespoons of filtered water until smooth, adding more water as necessary. Makes about four-and-a-half cups.

BLACK BEAN–BLUEBERRY–BABY KALE BLEND

This blend combines three nutrition powerhouses. High in fiber and protein, black beans are particularly satisfying and have been shown to reduce the risk for diabetes, heart disease and colon cancer. Blueberries are one of the fruits highest in antioxidants. Kale is high in fiber, calcium, iron, vitamin C and many other antioxidants. It has heart-protective and anticancer properties.

In addition to using this blend in the Turkey Meat Loaf recipe (see above), use it to…

• **Replace half the fat and sugar in chocolaty baked goods,** such as brownies and chocolate cake.

• **Mix into meat dishes,** such as tacos and burgers.

• **Add to a smoothie or a breakfast shake.**

If you prefer dried beans, feel free to sub them in (they will need to be soaked overnight and cooked). And if you don't love kale, swap in fresh baby spinach or your favorite dark leafy green.

4 cups baby kale
2 cups frozen blueberries, ideally wild (Frozen berries tend to be cheaper and are available year-round. Wild blueberries have more antioxidants.)
2 15-ounce cans (BPA-free) black beans, drained and rinsed
Filtered water

Place the kale into a high-powered blender or food processor, and pulse a few times. Rinse the blueberries in cold water to thaw them. Add the berries and the beans to the blender, along with one to two tablespoons of filtered water, and purée until smooth. Makes four cups.

Great Uses for Lemons

F***or fish:*** Put lemon slices under fish when poaching to keep the fish off the bottom of the pan so that it cooks evenly.

For pasta: Add two teaspoons of lemon juice to four quarts of water when cooking pasta to prevent stickiness.

Salad dressing: Make vinaigrette with lemon rather than vinegar for dressing milder greens—use one part lemon juice to three parts oil.

For soups: Add lemon juice to soups made with chicken, fish or vegetables to enhance the taste.

For side dishes: Season side dishes such as rice, grains, potatoes and vegetables with lemon juice and zest.

Soups and pan sauces: If you don't have or don't want to use wine, use one-half cup of chicken broth and one teaspoon of lemon juice to replace every one-half cup of wine.

Cook's Illustrated, CooksIllustrated.com.

How to Keep Produce Fresh Longer

A***pples:*** Store in a plastic bag in the fruit crisper drawer, away from vegetables, because the ethylene gas that apples emit will make vegetables go bad sooner. Also, eat the largest apples first—they ripen fastest.

Beets: Cut off greens, then store the beets in a perforated plastic bag in the vegetable crisper.

Cabbage: Wrap in plastic and refrigerate.

Garlic: Store in a dark kitchen cabinet.

Onions: Keep them in a dry, cool area…or in mesh bags in a dark cabinet.

Potatoes: Keep them in a dry, cool area, and store away from onions and apples, which both emit gases that will make the potatoes go bad faster. (Refrigerating potatoes encourages starches to convert into sugars, which can give them an unpleasant taste.)

Rutabagas: Store these in the refrigerator, wrapped in plastic, on a low shelf.

RodalesOrganicLife.com

Keep These Foods at Room Temperature

W*hole melons* retain antioxidants much better when not refrigerated—but refrigerate sliced melons to prevent bacterial growth. *Basil* turns black if stored below 40°F—keep it on the counter in a glass containing enough water to submerge the stems. *Potatoes* develop a gritty texture if stored in the refrigerator—keep them in a paper bag in a cool pantry. The pantry also is the place for *onions*—store them in a paper bag with holes punched for air circulation. But keep them away from potatoes, which spoil quickly when stored near onions. *Tomatoes* taste better when stored on the counter—refrigeration dulls their flavor.

Sheryl Barringer, PhD, professor and chair of the department of food science and technology, The Ohio State University, Columbus, quoted in *Reader's Digest*.

Clever Uses for Cooking Spray

C*oat measuring cups* before putting honey or syrup in them—the contents will slide right out. *Remove soap scum* on glass shower doors—just spray the inside and wipe with an absorbent cloth. *Wipe dead bugs off a car grille* and bumper—spray the area, and rub gently with a clean cloth. *Stop a door from squeaking*—spray the hinges. *Stop food from sticking to a knife* when chopping—spray the knife before using it. *Keep candleholders wax-free*—spray them before placing the candles inside.

Prevent stains on plastic containers—spray them before putting tomato sauce or similar foods in them. *Stop ice from forming in a freezer* by spraying along walls and shelves. *Prevent cheese from sticking* to a grater by spraying before use. *Remove a stuck ring* by spraying your finger. *Stop snow from sticking to a shovel* by spraying the blade before use.

TheKrazyCouponLady.com

Surprising Uses for Duct Tape

Hem pants or a skirt quickly—fold the hem inward to the length you want, and put duct tape all around the edges. *Trap bugs*—lay tape, sticky side up, along basement-floor edges, and hang strips or loops from the basement ceiling to catch flying pests. *Remove lint*—wrap tape, sticky side out, around an old paint roller, or for smaller jobs, just wrap it around your hand. *Remove sticky residue* from glass—put duct tape on the area, rub a few times and peel the tape away.

BobVila.com

Clever Uses for 2 Common Items

Used tea bags can be placed on tired eyes to reduce swelling...and they can be used to clean mirrors and windows. Used tea bags also absorb odors in the refrigerator—just put them in a mug, and leave the mug on a shelf.

Hair clips can be great cord and cable organizers—you even can use clips that coordinate with wire colors. Hair clips also are good for keeping large bags of chips closed and for keeping pairs of socks together—strong, water-resistant ones also can be used to keep socks together in the washing machine.

WiseBread.com

Kitchen Gadgets That Make Great Gifts

Linda Gassenheimer, an award-winning author of numerous cookbooks including *Delicious One-Pot Dishes* and *Quick & Easy Chicken*. She also created the recipes for *Beat Diabetes Now!* (available at BottomLineStore.com). Gassenheimer writes the syndicated newspaper column "Dinner in Minutes." DinnerinMinutes.com

Kitchen gadgets make great gifts. *Here are six cleverly useful ones for $20 or less...*

- **11-inch Kuhn Rikon Kochblume Spill Stopper.** How many times has your pot of rice or pasta boiled over? This colorful lid solves that problem. It sits on top of a saucepan (six to 10 inches in diameter) and prevents pasta, soups and other dishes from spilling over. It also works as a microwave splatter guard. $20.
- **Kuhn Rikon Silicone Toaster Oven Sheet.** This silicone mat keeps food from spilling on your toaster oven racks and coils. It sits on the rack, and the food goes right on the sheet. My husband was worried his cheese toast wouldn't come out crispy, but it did! No oils or cooking sprays needed. $15.
- **Taylor Plan & Prep Four-Event Timer with Whiteboard.** You can monitor four cooking times at once—and each of the four timers has a different alarm tone. The small attached dry erase whiteboard allows you to make a note of which timer is for which dish. It can stand on the counter or hang with a magnet and uses two AA batteries. $15.
- **Ronco Meat Tenderizer.** This nice gadget makes steaks and other meat tender and flavorful. The 72 stainless steel blades penetrate the meat, creating channels for rubs and marinades to infuse into the cuts. It reduces marinating times—depending on the type of meat and marinade, it can cut marinating time in half. $13.
- **Kuhn Rikon Mise en Place Cooking Set.** This colorful set of three measuring containers makes it easy to measure liquids and solids. Each measuring cup can be laid flat on a cutting board so that you can quickly and easily fill the cup with whatever you are prep-

ping. Each one measures from one-quarter to two cups. $10.

•**Joseph Joseph M-Cuisine Rice Cooker.** Make perfect rice and grains in your microwave oven with this rice cooker. It comes with a two-liter cooking pot and lid made of BPA-free polypropylene, a colander, a measuring cup and a rice paddle that also locks the lid closed and becomes a carrying handle. $15.

How Heloise Attacks Stubborn Odors—Naturally

Heloise, internationally syndicated newspaper columnist and contributing editor to *Good Housekeeping* magazine. Based in San Antonio, she is author of the syndicated "Hints from Heloise" column that runs in more than 500 newspapers around the world. She has written more than 15 books about household cleaning and organization, including *Handy Household Hints from Heloise.* Heloise.com

---

Musty spare rooms...lingering cooking smells...dogs overdue for baths. Even well-maintained homes develop unpleasant odors from time to time. Living in a foul-smelling home could leave you in a foul mood—what people smell affects how they feel far more than they tend to realize.

Here are natural ways to solve 11 common home odor problems...

KITCHEN SMELLS

• **Stinky dishwasher.** Mold or mildew usually is the culprit when dishwashers develop unpleasant odors. Pour several cups of standard household vinegar into the bottom of the dishwasher, and let it sit for an hour. Then run the dishwasher through a full cycle. You don't need to add soap. The vinegar should kill any mold and mildew.

Alternative: If you know your dishwasher is going to sit unused for a few days or longer—when you go on vacation, for example—sprinkle a few tablespoons of baking soda inside. This reduces the odds that it will smell musty when it is next used.

• **Malodorous microwave.** Unpleasant smells can linger in a microwave. Cut up two or three oranges (or another citrus fruit), and put the pieces in one to two cups of water in a large microwave-safe bowl. Microwave this fruit/water combo until the water boils, then stop the microwave but leave the microwave door shut with the steaming mixture inside for at least another 15 minutes. When you do eventually remove the bowl, leave the microwave door open for a few minutes.

Tip: Select a bowl that has a wide opening for this—the greater the surface area of water, the more effective this odor-removal strategy will be.

• **Smelly kitchen sink drain/garbage disposal.** Pour one-half cup of baking soda down the drain, followed by one cup of vinegar that you've warmed up slightly in the microwave (warming the vinegar makes it more effective)—foam might rise up out of the drain. Wait 15 to 20 minutes, then put the stopper in the drain and fill the sink with cold water. When the sink is nearly full, remove the stopper. (Do not let the sink get so full that it overflows when you reach in.) The rush of water down the drain will flush away both the baking soda residue and any bits of food that were rotting in the drain.

If you have a double kitchen sink, it works best if you do this in both sinks at the same time.

If it's a bathroom sink drain that's smelly, pour one-half cup of hydrogen peroxide down the drain. Use the highest concentration hydrogen peroxide you can find—it's available at grocery stores and drugstores (it won't damage pipes). Hydrogen peroxide is especially effective at clearing away the hair- and skin-oil–based residue often responsible for unpleasant bathroom drain smells.

If you want, before pouring in the peroxide, you can lift out the stopper and remove any hair and gunk that may have gotten caught on the underside of the stopper.

• **Foul-smelling trash cans.** Anytime you throw out something that's especially smelly, put a few drops of lemon essential oil or vanilla extract on a paper towel or paper napkin and place this in the trash on top of the smelly garbage.

Also: Sprinkle a little baking soda into the bottom of the can each time you change trash bags. Occasionally wash out trash cans with hot, soapy water.

• **Lingering cooking odors or smoking odors.** Dampen a dish towel or hand towel with vinegar, then wring it out over a sink until it is no longer dripping. Walk around the affected rooms waiving this towel around like a flag for a few minutes. This will not remove all of the odor, but it often can reduce it by more than half.

Act fast—the longer you wait, the more odor-causing molecules will settle onto surfaces and into carpets and fabrics where more extensive cleaning might be required to remove them.

• **Rank refrigerator.** Save the squeezed-out remains of a lemon, lime, orange or grapefruit after you use the juice in a recipe or drink. Place these fruit remnants in a small bowl, pour a few tablespoons of salt on top of them, then put the bowl in the fridge. The bad odor soon should be replaced by a fresh citrus smell.

Alternative: People often place a box of baking soda in the fridge to absorb odors, and baking soda can indeed be effective here. But if you choose this solution, pour the baking soda into a bowl (or some other container with a wide opening) rather than leave it in the box. The more baking soda surface area exposed to the air, the greater its odor-absorbing capacity.

BETTER WAY...

Simple Way to Make Your Whole Home Smell Fresh

Place a few drops of lemon extract or lemon essential oil on the filter of the home's forced-air heating/cooling system. Each time the heat or air-conditioning comes on, it will circulate the clean, pleasant smell of lemon throughout the home. A single application typically lasts for a few days, though this varies depending on how often the system runs. Do not apply more than a few drops of essential oil or extract, or the smell could be overbearing.

Alternative: Slowly simmer pieces of cut citrus fruit on the stove in a large pot of water. If you don't have any citrus, cinnamon or rose petals smell nice here as well. This is a better option in winter than in summer, however, because the simmering pot will heat and humidify the home.

Heloise, internationally syndicated newspaper columnist and contributing editor to *Good Housekeeping* magazine. Based in San Antonio, she is author of the syndicated "Hints from Heloise" column that runs in more than 500 newspapers around the world.

OUTSIDE THE KITCHEN

• **Dogs in need of baths.** If your dog isn't smelling his/her best but you don't have time to give the pet a bath right away, sprinkle a little baking soda onto the dog's fur and massage it in by rubbing against the direction of the fur—that helps work the baking soda all the way down to the dog's skin.

After a few minutes, brush out the baking soda—brush against the direction of the fur first, then brush as you normally would. This is the best way to remove the baking soda that has worked deep into the coat, particularly with shaggy dogs.

• **Cat litter boxes.** Sprinkle a little baking soda into the litter box before you put in fresh litter.

Warning: Cats can be finicky about their litter boxes—any change in smell can cause them to relieve themselves elsewhere in the house instead. If your cat does this when you add baking soda, change the litter again immediately and do not add baking soda. It isn't worth battling with a cat over this—you won't win. The only safe way to control litter box odor with a very finicky cat is to change its litter box more often.

• **Bedrooms.** Place a few drops of lavender essential oil on your pillows, then put the pillows in the dryer for five to 10 minutes on the fluff or low-heat setting. This will leave the pillows smelling clean and fresh, and most people find the scent of lavender very relaxing—that's why baby oils often are lavender scented.

• **Musty closets and spare rooms.** Fill a shallow bowl with fresh ground coffee, and place it in this underused space. Coffee grounds not only have a pleasing aroma, they do a wonderful job of absorbing musty smells in confined spaces.

• **Sick rooms/hospital rooms.** Each day, place two to three drops of orange (or lemon) essential oil on a tissue. Wave the tissue around in the air of the sick room or hospital room for a few minutes, then discard it in a trash can in the room.

People tend to associate orange and lemon scents with cleanliness and health, so this actually can help sick people feel a bit better. It certainly supplies a more uplifting odor than the typical medicinal hospital room smell.

Example: When I did this in a friend's nursing home room, everyone who came in commented on the wonderful smell. The doctors even stayed longer than usual.

GOOD TO KNOW...

Is It OK to Cut Away Mold and Eat the Food?

Mold spreads deep beneath the surface rather quickly in soft foods such as breads and strawberries but does not penetrate as deeply in hard foods. You can safely eat firm vegetables and fruits, such as apples and carrots, or hard cheeses if you can cut away at least one inch around the mold and discard it. Any other foods, such as sliced bread, soft fruits and vegetables and meat, that are moldy should be thrown out. Some molds make toxins that can cause severe illness.

Stephanie Smith, PhD, food safety specialists, Washington State University, Pullman.

Nasty Germs Are Lurking in Your Home: 7 Hot Spots Most People Miss

Lisa Yakas, MS, a microbiologist and senior certification project manager, food equipment, for NSF International (formerly National Sanitation Foundation), based in Ann Arbor, Michigan. The nonprofit group has a professional staff of engineers, microbiologists, toxicologists and other health experts who provide testing, certification and technical services, along with human health-risk assessments. NSF.org

A clean house feels so great! But germs are wily and can thrive even in sparkling "clean" homes—particularly in areas that people don't realize are microbial hot spots. Research shows that about 12% of foodborne diseases in the US actually start in the home.

Shocking statistics: Coliform bacteria (a family of organisms that includes *Salmonella* and *E. coli)* were present in 81% of tested households...nearly one-third of the homes tested positive for yeast and molds...and more than 5% harbored *Staph*, a bacterium that can cause serious—sometimes antibiotic-resistant—diseases and infections, including abscesses, pneumonia and food poisoning, according to the NSF International Household Germ Study. These germs can make anyone sick—especially people who are immunocompromised, young children and the elderly.

WHERE GERMS HIDE OUT

Most people know that doorknobs are often teeming with germs, and the kitchen sink, even a shiny one, can harbor more bacteria than the average toilet seat.

Smart ideas: Use disinfectant wipes to clean high-touch areas, such as doorknobs and kitchen door handles. The kitchen sink should be washed and disinfected on the sides and bottom once or twice each week with a disinfecting cleanser.

Even worse: The kitchen sponge. It can harbor more than 321 *million* germs, so put wet sponges in the microwave for two minutes once a day, and replace them often—every two weeks or so.

But in every home, there are other areas that people simply don't think to disinfect. *Where you're vulnerable...**

*Use dishwashing liquid whenever soapy water is mentioned.

• **Toothbrush holders.** You probably know to store toothbrushes upright to air-dry between uses—it helps prevent the growth of microorganisms that could cause oral or systemic infection. This is good advice, but it doesn't address the holders themselves.

What most people ignore is the significant amount of "drippage" from multihole toothbrush holders. This provides a perfect germ environment. We found that 64% were contaminated with yeast or molds...27% had coliform bacteria...and 14% tested positive for Staph.

What to do: Clean the holders at least once a week with warm, soapy water. (If you can't reach inside, fill the holder with soapy water and give a vigorous shake...rinse...and repeat until the water runs clean.) If the holder is dishwasher-safe, run it through a hot cycle. *Also:* There are no regulations that brand-new toothbrushes must be sterile, so give yours an overnight soak in antimicrobial mouth rinse before the first use.

• **Can openers.** How often do you clean yours? Once a week? Never? Can openers are actually among the most germ-laden objects in the entire house. E. coli and/or Salmonella were found on can openers in 36% of the households we studied.

What to do: Wash the can opener every time you use it. If it's dishwasher safe, place it in the dishwasher after every use. If you are handwashing it, wash the can opener in hot, soapy water and rinse thoroughly before air-drying. Be sure all food residue is removed from the area around cutting blades. Use an old toothbrush to scrub hard-to-reach crannies.

• **Refrigerator door seals.** Research we conducted has found that refrigerator door seals (along with refrigerator vegetable compartments) often are contaminated with *Listeria*, a bacterium that can cause serious illness such as sepsis or meningitis.

What to do: Run a damp, soapy cloth across the surface of the door seal and through the inner channel once a week. Pay particular attention to areas where crumbs or drippings are most likely to accumulate.

• **Blenders.** They're among the "dirtiest" items in the kitchen. Many people, inspired by the smoothie craze, use their blenders daily. To save time, they just give the blender a quick rinse. *Not good enough.*

The rubber gasket at the base of the pitcher is often contaminated with mold, yeast, E. coli and/or Salmonella. Washing the pitcher will clean only the outer edge of the gasket and won't touch the "sealed" part that can come in contact with the food.

What to do: You have to disassemble the blender to get it really clean. After every use, remove the screw-on bottom, the gasket and the top components. Clean each item separately in warm, soapy water, then let everything dry completely before putting it back together.

• **Pet bowls.** Not surprisingly, the food/water bowls used by your dogs and/or cats are often contaminated with Staph, E. coli and other germs.

What you may not realize: When you pick up your pet's bowl, bacteria from the rim/sides can be transferred to your hands—and from there to counters, kitchen knives, cutting boards, etc.

What to do: Pet bowls should be washed daily either in a sanitizing dishwasher (with the family's dishes if you like)...or scrubbed by hand in hot, soapy water, then rinsed. Once a week, soak pet bowls in a bleach rinse (one tablespoon of bleach per one gallon of water) for 10 minutes. Rinse well and allow to dry.

• **Remote controls.** In general, objects with hard, smooth, cool surfaces—remote controls, cell phones, computer keyboards, etc.—tend to harbor fewer germs than other objects/places in the home. But "fewer" doesn't mean "none." For example, in tests, 55% of remote controls were found to be contaminated with yeasts/molds, and 5% had coliform bacteria. Nearly one-quarter of cell phones had yeast and mold, and 5% had Staph or coliform bacteria.

What to do: Use a disinfectant wipe (or an alcohol cleaning pad) to wipe the surfaces and keys at least weekly. Be sure to check the manufacturer's cleaning instructions first.

• **Dirty laundry.** It's not surprising that germs love dirty laundry. Clothes that you've worn have skin cells, bodily secretions and plenty of moisture—all the things that germs need to survive. And the fecal material that's *always* present on used underwear is a common cause of infections.

What to do: Use the "hot" setting when washing underwear. The water should be 140°F to 150°F. If you're buying a new washer/dryer, look for one that's NSF certified. To earn certification, the machine must be able to reduce microbe populations by 99.9%.

Lawn Rescue! Fixes for Common Problems

Matt Blashaw, a licensed contractor and real estate agent who remodels homes and yards in Orange County, California. He is host of the HGTV program *Vacation House for Free* and previously was host of HGTV's landscape and lawn-improvement show *Yard Crashers*. HGTV.com

It isn't easy to grow a great lawn, and it's painful when the lawn ends up looking bad despite your best efforts. *Here are potential causes of—and solutions for—the things that might be wrong with your lawn...*

BARE AND THINNING AREAS

You might think that the simplest remedy to fill bare and thinning areas in your lawn is to loosen up the soil with a rake and then sprinkle grass seed. The problem with this simple solution is that there's a good chance the new grass will fail as well. These sections of your lawn are struggling for a reason. Before you reseed, it's worth trying to figure out why the problem exists. *Ask yourself...*

- **Is the bare patch in a heavily shaded area, such as under a tree?** If so, one option is to reseed this area using a shade-tolerant grass, such as fine fescue. (Consult a local garden shop for guidance on which shade-tolerant grasses grow best in your part of the country.) But these grasses still generally need at least four hours of sunlight per day to thrive...and even if the grass you choose does thrive, it might look noticeably different from the grass of your surrounding lawn. An alternative is to stop trying to grow grass in the shady area and instead install a mulch bed and/or shade-tolerant plants or ground cover.

Examples: Shade-tolerant shrubs include gray dogwood, laurel and viburnum. Shade-tolerant ground covers include lily of the valley, sweet woodruff and periwinkle.

- **Is the bare patch in an area that is often walked on?** If you reseed this area, use stakes and string to keep pedestrians off it for at least a month to give the young grass a chance to grow. But if you don't want to face the same situation again in future years, rather than growing more grass, construct a path or patio using paving stones, concrete, gravel or other materials so that the grass doesn't have to compete with people's feet.

- **Is something lurking under your lawn?** Probe down a few inches under the bare area. If there's a large rock or the remains of a stump right under the surface, this might be creating a thin soil layer, inhibiting healthy grass growth. Remove the obstruction if possible... fill the hole with soil...cover it with a layer of topsoil, available in garden stores... then reseed.

- **Is there thick thatch where the lawn is failing?** Thatch—the layer of old, dead blades of grass and other organic material immediately above the soil—should not be a problem as long as the thatch layer is no more than one-half-inch thick or so. But if the thatch is much thicker than that, it might be preventing enough rainwater from penetrating into the soil and preventing air from circulating around the bases of grass blades. Clear away thick thatch using a thatch rake and/or a gas-powered core aerator, then reseed. (Core aerators make holes in the soil beneath the lawn, which encourages growth of the microbes that help decompose the thatch layer.)

Helpful: Core aerators are available for rent at many home centers and rental centers, generally for $50 to $100 a day. Aerating helps with other lawn problems as well—see below.

BROWN PATCHES

In the growing season, brown grass is not healthy grass. It might be possible to save the brown sections of lawn, but first you must figure out what is causing the problem...

• **Do you have a dog?** The salts and nitrogen in dog urine can damage or kill grass in the spots where Fido often does his business. The most effective solution is to have the dog urinate elsewhere—ideally in a section of your property that is not covered by lawn or that is out of sight. If that isn't possible, use garden fencing to stop the dog from urinating on the sections of lawn that are brown to give the damaged grass a chance to recover—or better yet, take the dog for a walk.

Meanwhile, water these brown patches heavily (and if the dog still is urinating on other sections of the lawn, water these sections heavily, too, as soon as possible after the dog has peed on them). If the brown grass does not recover, remove a two-inch-thick layer of the topsoil and add new soil before reseeding.

Helpful: Certain grasses, including St. Augustine and Bermuda grass, stand up relatively well to dog urine but are not appropriate for cooler climates.

• **Do you see insects or insect damage?** Take a very close look at the blades in the brown area, as well as the still-green grass immediately adjacent to the brown area. Do you see insects and/or holes suggesting that insects have been eating this grass? Also, carefully peel back the sod—the layer of topsoil containing grass roots—near the edge of one of the brown areas to check for grubs. Grubs are small, soft, whitish larvae, often curled into small "c" shapes, that feed on the roots of your grass. Put a few samples of the damaged grass and/or the pests you find in a sandwich bag, and bring them to a garden shop or home center to ask if these insects might be causing the problem. If so, ask which insecticide is best. (There also are all-in-one insecticides that kill most common lawn-damaging bugs.)

Act quickly, before the infestation spreads any further. Be sure to purchase a "curative" insecticide meant to deal with an existing insect problem, not a "preventive" one designed mainly to avoid future problems. Follow the directions precisely.

• **Have you fertilized the lawn within the past few days?** If so, you might have used too much in the brown areas, causing "fertilizer burn." Water the brown sections heavily and repeatedly during the week immediately following fertilization to dilute the fertilizer, and wash as much of it as possible out of the topsoil and away from the roots of your grass. If this fails to save the damaged grass, continue watering to flush away as much fertilizer as possible from the topsoil down into lower layers of soil below your lawn where it will have much less effect on grass roots. Alternatively, you could replace the topsoil in these areas—then reseed.

Helpful: Fertilizer burn sometimes appears in long brown lines. This occurs when the person applying the fertilizer with a spreader makes passes that are too close together, resulting in double-fertilized strips.

SWAMPY AREAS

Large, long-lasting puddles in a lawn do not just make it more difficult to enjoy the lawn—that standing water could lead to lawn-killing grass diseases or encourage mosquito growth as well. *Potential causes and solutions...*

• **Do you have a sprinkler system?** If so, keep an eye on the swampy area as the sprinkler operates. Perhaps one of the sprinkler heads has stopped working properly and now is depositing an excessive amount of water in this spot.

• **Is the swampy area very close to your house, driveway or road?** The excess moisture might be the result of rainwater running off the roof or off a paved area into this part of the lawn. If so, divert water away from the lawn by improving or extending the home's gutter system and/or adding French drains, buried drainage pipes or drainage ditches along the affected edge of the lawn.

• **Is there highly compacted soil and/or a thick thatch layer in the swampy area?** If the soil is highly compacted, water might not be able to drain down through it properly. And a thatch layer thicker than one-half inch or so can act as a sponge, holding water in the area. Using a core aerator should dramatically improve drainage if either of these is the problem.

• **Is the swampy area in a low spot in the lawn?** Use a shovel to carefully remove the sod, and set it aside. Add topsoil...walk over this soil to compact it somewhat...then add additional topsoil to raise this section of lawn to roughly the level of the rest of the yard... then replace the sod you set aside earlier. (Or if the grass in this area was dead, reseed.)

Additional options: If the do-it-yourself solutions above fail to solve the swampiness problem, you could hire a landscaper to install a drainage system beneath the lawn—but that is a major project that could cost thousands of dollars. If you don't want to spend that much, you could replace the lawn in the swampy area with a mulch bed that is raised perhaps one inch above the level of the lawn so that the swampy area is hidden underneath. Add plants that love wet soil, such as certain river irises...ferns...sedge...hydrangea...or dogwood. This is a beautiful-looking alternative.

Kill Garden Weeds Without Harsh Chemicals

Teri Dunn Chace, author of more than 35 gardening titles, including *How to Eradicate Invasive Plants.* She lives in upstate New York. TeriChaceWriter.com

Yes, weeds in your garden are tough to deal with, but you don't need to use toxic commercial weed killers in flower beds, vegetable gardens or other gardens to get rid of them. *Here, an expert gardener's weed-beating strategies...*

- **Start early.** You can save yourself a lot of trouble if you intervene promptly. In early spring, yank weeds out by the roots (right after a rain, when the ground is soft and damp). Or drag a sharp hoe across them, which dislodges them, roots and all.

- **Kill top growth.** For larger weeds that are deeply rooted, try an aboveground attack. If you persist, the root systems will struggle and eventually die. *There are several ways you can do this...*

  - Cut. Use a weed whacker or lawn mower set low to scalp them.

  - Smother. Lay cardboard, one-half inch of old newspapers, a plastic or heavy cloth tarp or a combination of these, over a weed patch. Anchor with rocks or bricks. For a badly infested or very weedy area, leave the covering in place for an entire growing season. It won't look beautiful, but neither would the weeds, and it's only temporary. To inhibit an invasion among desired plants, lay down at least one inch of bagged bark mulch or straw.

  - Scald. It is possible to kill weeds by dousing them with boiling water. This works best for spot-treating small patches. Use a tea kettle filled with just-boiled water. Use oven mitts, and pour with care so that you don't splash the water on your legs or shoes.

- **Use homemade weed killer.** In a large, clean plastic jug, mix one gallon of white vinegar, one cup of table salt and one tablespoon of liquid dish-washing soap. Shake well. Vinegar and salt dry out plant cell membranes, causing death by dehydration—soap helps the mixture adhere to the plants. Fill a spray bottle with the mixture, and direct it at all aboveground growth on a sunny day—sunlight boosts the vinegar's effectiveness. Repeated applications often are necessary. Protect nearby valued plants by covering them with an old towel or with an empty carton.

- **If the above options fail,** use one or more of the following products, available at garden stores or online. Follow the label directions on your product, and be prepared to repeat treatments on larger plants and stubborn targets.

  - Citrus oils. Organic herbicides, such as Avenger, have citrus oil as their active ingredient—this strips leaves of their protective waxy covering, drying them out past the point of no return. These work best on broadleaf weeds including dandelion, pigweed and bindweed.

  - Garden torches. You can zap pesky weeds with a propane-fueled flame tool called the Mini Dragon. This works brilliantly on nonflammable surfaces such as stone terraces, walkways and sidewalks where weeds have encroached or reared up between cracks and in rock gardens. For safety, follow the instructions that come with this product to the letter.

18 Wise Ways

How to Get More Done: Secrets from Scientists, CEOs and Four-Star Generals

Charles Duhigg felt that he was always wasting time. In a world where he was able to communicate with anyone at any hour and learn any fact within seconds, technology should have enabled him to do everything faster and better. But it often just made him busier and less focused, not more productive. As a Pulitzer Prize–winning newspaper reporter, Duhigg realized that he was in a unique position to find out why. He had access not only to leading cognitive scientists studying productivity but also to some of the country's most accomplished and productive individuals ranging from Fortune 500 CEOs to four-star generals.

What Duhigg discovered after years of investigation was that highly productive people don't necessarily work longer hours or make more sacrifices than everyone else. Instead, they use certain strategies to decide how to prioritize their time and energy, avoid procrastination, make better decisions and motivate themselves. That's especially valuable nowadays because more than one-third of all working Americans are freelancers or in transitory positions. Succeeding in the so-called New Economy requires the ability to take care of things that are important to your success with less stress, struggle and waste.

Below are five practical strategies Duhigg learned that anyone can use to become much more productive…

Charles Duhigg, a reporter at *The New York Times*. In 2013, he was part of a team that won the Pulitzer Prize for Explanatory Reporting. He is author of two best sellers, including *Smarter Faster Better: The Secrets of Being Productive in Life and Business.* CharlesDuhigg.com

MAKE SMALL CHOICES

When highly productive people are faced with tasks that seem either too intimidating or too mundane, rather than put off the tasks as most people do, they pinpoint some aspect of the tasks in which they can make an immediate choice—and then they make that choice. Exercising even a little bit of influence over an activity helps break up your "internal logjam." And once you gain even a little momentum, it's much easier to keep going.

Example: For years, geriatric researchers have been trying to figure out why some seniors thrive inside nursing homes. At one facility in Santa Fe, the residents who fared best practiced an odd ritual in the dining hall. As soon as they were served their meals, this group of seniors started trading various food items. This small act of control—or even defiance—may sound inconsequential, but it invigorated and empowered the residents for other parts of their day.

Before I started using this strategy of making many small choices, I used to let hundreds of e-mails pile up in my in-box. Now I hit *reply* to a dozen e-mails at a time. In each of the reply windows that opens, I quickly write an initial sentence in which I assert some preference.

Example: If someone has asked to meet with me, I might write, "Sure, I'll do it, but I'm only going to spend 15 minutes." Immediately afterward, I go back to each e-mail to decide whether each of my choices is a good one. Getting out that initial sentence makes me feel more in control and makes it a lot easier to fill out the rest of each e-mail and plow through my in-box.

IDENTIFY A LARGER PURPOSE

When you run into a setback or challenge, you might lose enthusiasm for what you're doing. At times like that, highly productive people step back and ask themselves, *Why is this task important to me?*

By interpreting what they're doing as being part of a larger constellation of projects, goals and/or values that are emotionally rewarding, they can tap into hidden reserves of motivation. Alternatively, if they can't answer the question of why the task is important, it's a sign that they should find a way to avoid or minimize it in the future.

Example: In the 1990s, US Marine Commandant Gen. Charles C. Krulak, a two-time Purple Heart recipient, began an experiment in which all recruits in basic training challenged one another to explain what motivated them most in the midst of the grueling 13-week course of training. A group of recruits might shout to one of their own, "It's your birthday today. Why are you here cleaning a mess hall?" And the recruit might shout back, "To serve my country and build a better life for my family!"

In the years after Krulak began encouraging this technique and implemented several other changes, performance scores of new recruits and the number who completed boot camp both increased by more than 20%.

SMARTER "TO-DO" LISTS

To-do lists were an essential organizational tool for me, but they actually were hurting my productivity.

The problem: My lists were filled with easily achievable tasks (for example, buy groceries, weed the garden) that felt satisfying to check off but didn't make for any real progress in my life. The to-do lists of highly productive people are different. For starters, they tend to include steps necessary to accomplish one or more large, ambitious tasks such as writing a novel, running a marathon or losing 40 pounds.

On a trip to Japan in 1993, legendary General Electric CEO Jack Welch was so impressed by the country's super-fast bullet trains that he required every division at GE to start setting a "stretch goal"—the kind of audacious goal that had resulted in the bullet trains.

Even if you're not going to match the bullet train accomplishment, you should put at least one personal stretch goal at the top of your to-do list every day. Making the time for that goal forces you to think about what your deepest priorities are, not just about what chores need to be done.

Important: Welch realized that writing down grand aspirations didn't assure they could be achieved. That's why he always ran

EASY TO DO...

Motivation Trick

Instead of saying "I should," say "I could," as in "I could write a blog." The word "should" is burdensome, connoting that you must do it, while "could" is empowering, carrying the message that you have the right and the capacity to decide what you'll do. Try it!

Linda Sapadin, PhD, a clinical psychologist in private practice in Valley Stream, New York, and author of *How to Beat Procrastination in the Digital Age*. PsychWisdom.com

his stretch goals through a five-point analysis aimed at turning the goal into a concrete and realistic plan. The so-called SMART system that he used was created by a pair of psychologists in the 1970s. *The acronym stands for...*

Specific—write down exactly what you want to achieve.

Measurable—how will you assess how you are doing as you go along?

Achievable—how can you break this goal into a series of smaller actions that will move you in the right direction each day?

Realistic—what could go wrong as you carry out these small actions? How can you avoid and/or bounce back from the potential pitfalls?

Timeline—how long will working toward the goal take each day, week or month? What has to change in your life so that you can find the time to do it?

AVOID INFORMATION BLINDNESS

It makes sense that the more information and choices you have, the more effective your decision-making and the greater your productivity should be. But in the last decade, the amount of information at our fingertips has soared while the ability to learn and benefit from this information hasn't kept pace. The result is that we often feel overwhelmed by information and therefore stop moving ahead on a particular matter as we should. *When you feel overwhelmed by information...*

• **Break data into binary choices.** Human beings are much more likely to engage and make effective decisions when they evaluate just two or three options at a time.

Example: When someone hands you a huge wine list at a restaurant, don't peruse the whole thing. Instead, make a decision efficiently by winnowing your options in quick stages. First, *Do I want red or white?* Next, *Expensive, moderate or cheap?* Then, *A $30 bottle of Chardonnay or a $35 Sauvignon Blanc?*

• **Grapple with the information in front of you**—don't just look at the information.

Example: I was trying to lose weight. I got a bathroom scale that wirelessly transmitted my weight each morning to an app on my phone that recorded it. The technology made the procedure so effortless that I soon stopped paying attention.

I did not lose weight until I began transcribing my daily weight manually and plotting the measurements on graph paper. Having to write the number down every day had much more of an impact on my efforts. The more we interact with information, the more we tend to absorb it.

MAKE YOUR BED

What I am about to tell you, I do mean quite literally—make your bed. Only about 40% of people make their beds every day. But extensive research suggests that this very simple action, which will take you just a few minutes, has a high correlation with increased productivity.

It may be that inherently highly productive people are more apt to make their beds because they are so productive. But I think it works in the other direction as well—making one's bed helps start a chain reaction each day that spurs better motivation and decision-making. It creates an immediate and visual sense of accomplishment and momentum at the start of the day that enhances your ability to achieve other goals. And it's too easy not to try.

How the World Is Making You Anxious...and What You Can Do to Feel Happier

Robert L. Leahy, PhD, director of the American Institute for Cognitive Therapy and a clinical professor of psychology at Weill Cornell Medical College, New York City. He is past president of the Association for Behavioral and Cognitive Therapies and author of *The Worry Cure: Seven Steps to Stop Worry from Stopping You.*

Could the worries of a troubled world be taking a toll on your life? It's one thing to be anxious about personal and family matters—*Will my medical test come back positive? How will I pay my bills? Will my troubled son ever find his way?* We all know that living with such anxieties can hurt our health and happiness.

Recently, however, many of us have been feeling extreme stress over far less personal problems—disturbing national and global developments that repeatedly draw our attention. And this stress, while perhaps rooted in events far from home, still can hit home in severely damaging ways—it can hurt our sleep and our health...and even shorten our lives.

Examples: Global terrorism increasingly feels like an omnipresent danger. US politics has devolved in a way that triggers extreme emotions, including anger, fear and even hatred. Financial markets worldwide have become much more volatile, sparking fears of economic upheaval. Confrontations involving police have fueled racial tensions. Refugee crises around the world show us horrific suffering. The threat of nuclear proliferation and attack seem reignited as Iran and North Korea beat their chests. The Zika virus and, before it, the Ebola virus rise up as health threats. And never-ending cyber attacks threaten our privacy and security.

But are the dangers any more extreme than in the past, and must they disrupt our daily lives? Here's why global and national problems can cause anxiety disproportionate to their true risk—and how to stop these anxieties from standing in the way of living a calm and happy life...

UNDERSTANDING GLOBAL ANXIETY

The human mind is very good at providing warnings about risks. Unfortunately, it can stumble when it comes to evaluating and prioritizing those risks. *For example, we tend to overestimate risks when...*

- **We hear about them frequently.** The more often someone hears about a threat, the more likely that person is to conclude that the threat must be substantial. This translates into out-of-proportion anxieties about global and national threats that are discussed endlessly in the media.
- **The images can be hard to forget.** Troubling events often are accompanied by shocking photographs and/or video—including such recent images as shootings, beheadings and dead bodies—that can trigger deep emotional responses.
- **We don't know what we can do to stop the threat.** Worried about your family's finances? There's probably something you can do to mitigate the risks and ease your fears, such as economizing, adjusting your investment portfolio and/or earning additional income. But there is little you can do to reduce global dangers or to head off a recession or a market meltdown.
- **The threats are relatively new.** The longer a threat is around, the more comfortable people grow with it. Heart disease and cancer have always been around, so people tend not to consider them pressing dangers—even though they kill far more Americans than terrorism does.
- **We perceive malicious intent.** People tend to overestimate risks related to forces that seem to want to cause them harm. That's another reason we might worry more about ISIS or North Korea than about a car accident—there is no "bad guy" trying to crash our car.

CONTROLLING GLOBAL ANXIETY

An important step in overcoming anxiety is to realize which problems actually are responsible for your worries. It can be especially difficult to pinpoint the source of anxiety when global problems are to blame because these problems are far removed from daily life.

What to do: Consciously monitor your emotions throughout the day. When you experience moments of anxiety, anger or sadness, jot down what you are doing, reading, discussing or thinking. Within a few days, you should see trends appearing.

If you discover that national or global problems cause you anxiety...

• **Carefully weigh the odds that what you fear actually will turn into reality.** If your anxieties revolve around terrorism, for example, your specific worry likely is that you or someone you love will be killed in an attack. If your anxieties revolve around an economic meltdown, your specific worry might be that you will lose your job and not be able to find a new one or that your retirement savings will disappear. As a next step, estimate the chance that this event actually will occur on a scale of 0% to 100%.

To do this, consider what evidence you really have that the risk is great—and keep in mind that people experiencing anxiety often inflate risks. If you fear not being able to find work, for example, consider that three of every four Americans in the labor force remained employed even at the deepest depths of the Great Depression. You may be surprised to find that the risk of your feared event occurring is not quite as high as you had automatically assumed.

Next, think of a person you know and respect who is not especially concerned about this particular national or global worry, and imagine how *that* person would estimate your risk on the same 0% to 100% scale. Now list some reasons why your worry will not come true. Ordinarily you might struggle to list reasons why something you fear will not come true—but this should become a bit easier after you take a moment to see things from the perspective of someone who sees little risk. Refer to this list when you experience anxiety on the subject in the future—it could help calm your fears.

• **Determine what productive action, if any, you can take.** You might not be able to stop a global threat, but there may be something you can do to stand in opposition to it...or to minimize the damage that it will do to you should it occur. Taking this step should ease your anxiety by helping you regain some sense of control. Make a list of potential productive actions, and refer to this list whenever your anxieties arise.

Example: If terrorism frightens you, you could attend a rally for a cause that terrorists would despise—perhaps something related to religious freedom or equal rights.

• **Schedule daily time to confront this concern.** Believe it or not, if you cannot stop yourself from worrying about an issue, you still can minimize the impact that the issue has on your life by scheduling a specific time to worry—it actually works. To do this, select a 20-minute window each day during which you are "allowed" to worry about the troubling topic. If you catch yourself experiencing anxiety about it at other times, reassure yourself that you will sort through these thoughts during the designated worry time, and then turn your attention back to something else. But don't just sit around worrying during these 20 minutes. Use at least some of this time to review the other steps described here.

• **Reduce your exposure to negative news,** negative political commentary and negative social-media interactions. If something chronically discussed on the TV news, on the radio or in newspapers causes you anxiety, reduce your time spent engaging with these media outlets and do something more calming instead.

• **Consider the evidence that the US and the world actually are *improving*.** If you think that the US and the world are headed in the wrong direction, you're not alone—polls suggest that the majority of Americans would agree. *But despite all the bad news we encounter, evidence suggests quite the opposite...*

• *Violent crimes* are in the news every day—but what the news rarely mentions is that the violent-crime rate in the US actually is very low by historical standards. For example, the per-capita homicide rate has fallen by more than 50% in the past 25 years.

• *Horrible diseases* such as Zika and Ebola are frequently in the news, too—but Americans are living longer, healthier lives.

• *Authoritarian regimes* such as North Korea and ISIS are in the news, as is the bloody conflict in Syria—but the world is, overall, more democratic than ever...and by historical standards, global war deaths per capita have been very low for the past quarter century.

How to Stop Fear from Stopping You

Linda Sapadin, PhD, a clinical psychologist in private practice in Valley Stream, New York. She specializes in helping people overcome self-defeating patterns and is author of *Master Your Fears: How to Triumph Over Your Worries and Get On with Your Life*. PsychWisdom.com

There's no need to be afraid of fear. It is there to protect us. Fear can warn us of lurking dangers...and spur us to take action to improve our lives. Unfortunately, many people respond to fear in counterproductive ways. But it is possible to overcome problematic "fear styles." *Here's how...*

PROBLEM FEAR STYLES

People who struggle to cope with fear are likely to recognize themselves in one or more of these fear styles. Knowing which of these styles applies to you can help you to take steps toward a more helpful, less debilitating fear response...

FEAR STYLE: **Safety first.** When faced with something frightening, your immediate reaction is to retreat toward something that seems safe. The thoughts running through your head might include, *I can't* or *It's too difficult for me*. Because of this knee-jerk retreat-to-safety fear response, your life never seems to progress or improve.

Example: An exciting new job opportunity presents itself. Rather than give this option careful thought, you immediately think, *I can't do that*, and you stick with the safe, comfortable job that you have had for years.

What to do: When you're thinking, *I can't do it,* think instead, *I can do it...I can calm myself down, reflect on my choices and decide what to do.* Make this your mantra. You may never be someone who dives into the deep end of the pool, but you are perfectly capable of walking slowly into the shallow end, then cautiously inching your way down to the deep end where you belong.

FEAR STYLE: **What if?** Whenever you feel fear, a flood of "What if?" questions fill your mind. *What if this goes wrong? What if they hate me? What if I fail?* You don't even bother to answer most or all of these questions—the questions themselves are enough to deter you from moving forward.

Example: Whenever you think about investing in stocks, you think, *What if the stock market crashes?* Then your savings remain in CDs and bank accounts, earning little or no interest.

What to do: Answer your "What if" questions. It's leaving these questions unanswered that revs up your fears. Supply realistic, rational answers, and the fear will start to fade. If the first answer leads to additional "What ifs?" you should continue providing answers.

Example: If your fear is, *What if I get lost?* you might first answer, *I'll use my phone's GPS*. If that is met by the fear, *What if the phone's battery dies?* then answer, *I'll bring a map, too.*

FEAR STYLE: **Disastrous danger.** This is similar to "What if?" but rather than think of unanswered questions, you imagine (or even visualize) catastrophic outcomes whenever you are doing something that frightens you. Some of these outcomes are implausible, but they seem real to you.

Example: When you think about taking a trip on an airplane, you picture the plane crashing. So you travel only when absolutely necessary.

What to do: Remind yourself that the chances of a disaster happening are similar to the chances of winning a mega-jackpot lottery. When was the last time you won the lottery? Also search for a relaxation technique that works for you, such as deep breathing, yoga or meditation.

FEAR STYLE: **Wishy-washy.** You are so afraid of choosing the wrong response in frightening situations that you struggle to make any decision at all. When forced to make a decision, you inevitably second-guess it, torturing yourself by thinking, *Maybe I should have chosen the other road.*

Example: You are not certain which roofer to call to repair a dislodged shingle, so you don't call any of them. What was a small problem eventually leads to major water damage.

What to do: Take a few moments to picture yourself standing at a fork in the road. You can choose the left fork...you can choose the right fork...or you can choose to continue standing at the crossroads forever. This mental image can help you to see that not choosing essentially is making a choice—the choice to stay right where you are. Remind yourself that while you might not be certain where the two roads lead, choosing to move forward is almost always better than staying right where you are because you're too frightened to make a choice.

FEAR STYLE: **Pop a pill.** When you feel even a little anxious, your first response is to take prescription anxiety medication, consume alcohol or use illegal drugs. (Having one drink or taking prescription anxiety medication in prescribed dosages generally is not a problem. The problem is when numbing the mind becomes the standard response to fears and challenges.)

What to do: Tell yourself, *I can do this without a pill (or a drink).* Then take a deep breath, and think of a positive image—something that makes you feel calm and secure. Sign up for an adult-education course in relaxation or stress relief. If none of this allows you to face your fears without drugs or alcohol, it might be time to seek professional counseling or join a 12-step program.

MORE STEPS FOR FACING FEAR

These additional steps can help overcome any unproductive fear style...

1. Talk to yourself calmly. When you are afraid, fear takes control of what you *say*, what you *think* and what you *do*. If you can reclaim control of any one of these three things, it will become much easier to reclaim the other two.

Talk tends to be the easiest to reclaim. When you think negative phrases such as, *I can't do it* or *Oh my gosh, this is going to be horrible*, immediately respond with comforting, positive phrases such as, *It's not as bad as I think it is. It never is...I'll get through it. I always do...I can handle this...*or *It will be OK.* Some people even find it helpful to speak aggressively to fear itself, telling it to *Get out of my life! I've got stuff to do!*

Backup plan: If you cannot talk to yourself calmly, engage in an activity that tends to make you calm. That might be sitting in a comfortable spot with a magazine and a cup of tea...doing yoga...watching a movie...walking outside...or chatting with someone who has a calm demeanor.

2. Reflect on what you could do to improve your situation. Do not worry about actually doing any of these things yet. And don't worry if you can't think of anything that will make everything completely fine. Just jot down ideas and options that might make things seem at least a little more hopeful or secure than they seem right now.

Example: If you're worried about whether you have sufficient retirement savings, you might list ways that you could trim expenses... bring in some income during retirement...or tap the equity in your home.

Next, review this list and focus on the idea that you would like to pursue. This might be the idea that seems like it would help the most or the idea that seems most within your abilities to achieve. Don't get bogged down in worrying about which is the absolute best option—just pick one that you believe holds some promise. Moving forward with even the second- or third-best solution is preferable to not moving forward at all. If nothing else, settling on a path forward will help you regain a sense of control over your situation, a crucial step in overcoming fear.

Helpful: If you are someone who struggles with what to do to move forward in the face of fear, reassure yourself that the option you choose does not need to be a final decision.

If you later discover that what you decided isn't working as well as you expected, you can change course. If you still can't move forward, explain your options to a trusted friend and ask for help making the decision.

3. Take the action you selected in step two. It is useful to think of "take action" as a completely separate step from "reflect on an action," discussed above. Some people who struggle to respond productively to fear have no trouble thinking up appropriate responses, but they don't put those plans into action. If you follow the steps here, by the time you get to the "take action" stage, you're halfway home, creating a sense of momentum that can push you forward.

Example: If you decided to bring in some income to quell retirement savings fears, you might take action by reaching out to contacts at your former employer or in your former field to see if any of them could hire you on a part-time freelance basis.

MORE ON HANDLING FEAR...

When Fear Sneaks Back In...

Fear almost certainly will stop in for a visit during this process. Bleak thoughts will sneak into your mind...dark words will slip out of your mouth. This is perfectly normal and need not create a major problem—as long as you dismiss the fear before it takes up residence in your mind. When fear sneaks back in, dismiss it by thinking, *That's just my fear talking not my reality.*

Backup plan: If you cannot quickly dismiss fear with the phrase above, repeat step one in the article above—talk to yourself calmly. Also, spend some time each day doing things that you know you do well—even if those things are completely unrelated to the situation currently causing you fear. Doing things that you know you do well increases your appreciation for who you are and what you have to offer the world. The sense of confidence that this fosters in one part of your life can gradually increase your overall confidence level, improving your ability to face fears wherever and whenever they intrude on your life.

How to Stop Your Worst Memories from Tormenting You

Ronald A. Ruden, MD, PhD, an internist on the clinical staff at NYU Langone Medical Center and Lenox Hill Hospital. He sees patients at his private practice in New York City. He created Havening Techniques to eliminate the consequences that arise from stressful or traumatic events. Havening Techniques now provides training and certification in more than a dozen countries (see the website for locations and trainers). He is author of *Havening Techniques: A Primer* and *When the Past Is Always Present: Emotional Traumatization, Causes and Cures.* Havening.org

What can you do if you suffer from phobias, panic attacks, traumatic memories or other emotional disturbances? Like millions of Americans, you might choose to see a psychiatrist or other therapist. You could engage in some form of talk therapy to gain a fuller understanding of your emotions. You might take an antidepressant or other medication. Both talk therapy and medication (often used together) are helpful, but they may not eliminate the root causes of your distress.

New approach: Havening. It's a technique ("havening" means to put into a safe place) that uses touch to change how electrical signals are transmitted in the brain. After a successful havening session, the traumatic memory is viewed as distant and detached from the emotions, such as fear and anger, that are generated during the event—that is, it no longer causes distress. The havening technique still is considered experimental and is not scientifically proven, but it is inexpensive, safe, rapid and gentle, and there is growing anecdotal experience suggesting that it works.

EMOTIONS LINGER

To understand the theory behind the havening technique, it helps to understand what happens when we experience a traumatic event. Let's say, for example, that you get mugged in an alley—if you're lucky, you'll put it behind you over time. But for some people, the event may be encoded in the brain as a trauma. When you perceive a threat, your brain activates neurons in the amygdala, the region of the brain associated with threat detection and other emotions. If certain criteria are met, cell receptors in the amygdala are *potentiated*. In other words, they increase in number and remain permanently primed for activation by related stimuli.

Because the encoded receptors are always present, the *emotions* associated with traumatic memories can be reactivated over and over again. Individuals might experience nightmares, worry every time they walk past an alley or even stop leaving the house altogether. This leads to a worsening of emotional distress.

Experts used to think that traumatic events caused lifelong distress because the memories—and associated emotions—could never be erased. But the brain is essentially an electrochemical system. The theory behind havening is that if you change the brain's circuitry, you can eliminate the response to signals that have been causing emotional pain—even if the memory originally associated with that pain is not gone.

HAVENING TOUCH

The goal of havening therapy is to delink the emotions from the encoded traumatic event. The therapy is designed to generate brain waves that remove the potentiated receptors so that the individual won't experience again those fears or other emotional disturbances associated with the event.

During a typical havening session, a patient is asked to recall the painful memory. This activates the potentiated receptors. He/she then is exposed to "havening touch"—gentle, soothing stroking of the arms, face and hands. At the same time, the patient distracts himself from the memory by counting or singing a song.

How it works: Touching triggers the production of low-frequency *delta waves* in the brain. Delta waves open calcium channels in the amygdala. The influx of calcium sets off an enzymatic reaction that causes "trauma" receptors to disappear. A patient might still remember the details of the traumatic event, but he will no longer feel disturbed by the memories.

DOES SCIENCE SUPPORT IT?

Only one peer-reviewed, published scientific study has examined the effects of havening. Two others are completed and awaiting publication. The published study, which appeared in *Health Science Journal*, looked at workers in the UK who self-reported that they suffered occupational impairments because of depression and/or anxiety due to a traumatic event. After a havening session, participants showed improvements in tests that measured depression, anxiety and work and social adjustment.

Important caveats: The study was small (27 participants) and didn't include a control group...and the participants weren't randomly selected. In addition, the workers were all health-care professionals, so they might have been more open to—and affected by—psychotherapy than other adults.

WHAT TO DO

In the US, there are only about 40 havening practitioners who have participated in courses and trainer events and have been certified by a Havening Techniques trainer. These practitioners are mainly in New York City and on Long Island and in Chicago and Los Angeles...and there's one in the Louisville, Kentucky, area. Worldwide there are about 140 certified practitioners. The average cost for a havening session is about $200 to $400. But because there are only a small number of havening professionals, some people choose to practice the therapy on their own. In our experience, self-havening often is as effective as practitioner-guided sessions.

What happens in a session...

- **Activate the emotion.** You'll be asked (or you'll ask yourself) to recall the distressing event and all of the details. It might be a street crime...a memory of childhood abuse...even a cruel thing you yourself once did...or another memory that causes you repeated distress. You'll rate the distress that the memory causes on a scale of 0 to 10.

- **Apply havening touch.** The practitioner (or you or a loved one) will offer comforting touch that involves stroking the arms from shoulder to elbow, stroking the forehead and rubbing palms.

• **Distraction.** Simultaneously, with your eyes closed, you will distract yourself by imagining that you're climbing a staircase with 20 steps. Count the steps aloud. With each step, you'll imagine that your distress is diminishing.

After the twentieth step, with eyes still closed, you'll hum two rounds of "Row, Row, Row Your Boat" or another neutral song. You'll open your eyes, look to the right and left, and inhale and exhale deeply. If your distress level is still high, you should repeat the touch/distraction components (using different visualizations and tunes) until the level of distress is zero or remains fixed after two rounds.

The distraction is important because your mind can't process two thoughts at the same time. The idea is that distracting yourself from the memory displaces the recalled event and prevents it from continually activating the amygdala. At the same time, the touch part of the therapy produces the brain waves that delink the memory from your emotions.

A single session can last for minutes to hours, but a typical session lasts 60 minutes. In my experience, many people will notice permanent improvement after a single session.

Why Bad Moods Are Good for You

Susan David, PhD, psychologist on the faculty of Harvard Medical School, Boston, and cofounder and codirector of the Institute of Coaching at McLean Hospital in Belmont, Massachusetts. She is author of *Emotional Agility: Get Unstuck, Embrace Change and Thrive in Work and Life*. If you want to assess how effective you are with your moods and emotions, a free quiz is offered at SusanDavid.com/learn.

Many people embrace happiness but try to push aside sadness and anger. Our culture encourages this—books about how to be happy frequently find their way onto best-seller lists, and "the pursuit of happiness" is written into our Declaration of Independence. Sadness and anger are viewed as problems to overcome on the road to happiness.

But these so-called "negative" emotions can be useful. *Here are some of the powerful benefits of bad moods and how to use them to your advantage...*

• **Bad moods make us more careful and less gullible.** When people are happy, they tend to have an "everything will be all right" mentality—which can get them into trouble when everything is not all right. When people are unhappy, on the other hand, their minds are on a higher state of alert, carefully analyzing what they see and hear. That's a useful mind-set to have when digging through potentially important details or dealing with slick salespeople.

What to do: If you soon will need to be detail-oriented or skeptical—for example, if you're on your way to negotiate a major purchase—you can intentionally put yourself in a negative mood. Recall an unhappy but not devastating memory, such as a time when your career hit a rough patch. Or listen to a piece of music that always makes you feel melancholy—Samuel Barber's "Adagio for Strings" may be a good choice.

• **Bad moods make us more convincing.** People who are in negative moods are better able to formulate arguments that sway other people to their points of view, according to a study published in *Journal of Personality and Social Psychology*. This is probably because people are more detail-oriented and attentive when they are in bad moods, as noted above, and thus more likely to provide convincing evidence and respond effectively when doubts are voiced. When people feel happy, they are prone to overlooking such details out of potentially misplaced optimism that everyone is sure to see things their way.

What to do: Do not just give yourself a pep talk before you make a presentation (or write

TAKE NOTE...

Happiness Is a Snap

Regularly snapping selfies of yourself smiling and sharing the photos with friends can help make you a happier person, a recent study finds.

Study conducted at University of California, Irvine, published in *Psychology of Well-Being*.

a letter or a report) that is intended to bring people around to your way of thinking. Think about the challenges that your position could face. Who might disagree? Why might they disagree? Focusing on the challenges that lie ahead tends to temper overly positive moods.

• **Bad moods boost memory.** Ever wondered how a spouse who cannot remember where he put his keys can remember every detail of all 393 arguments you have had in the past 10 years? It's because human memory is sharpest at times of unhappiness. A study published in *Journal of Experimental Social Psychology* found that people's memories were stronger on gloomy-weather days than on sunny ones, for example. This finding likely stems from the fact that memory was most crucial for the survival of our early ancestors during their unhappiest moments. If an early human was about to be attacked by a predator, for example, his life might have depended on being able to remember which defensive tactics worked best against that predator in prior attacks...and if his watering hole dried up, his survival might have depended on remembering where else water could be found.

What to do: If you are struggling to remember something, allow yourself to experience sadness or anger, perhaps by recalling a sad memory or listening to a sad song. If you still cannot remember, do something relaxing and mind-clearing such as taking a warm shower or a quiet walk in nature. The period of transition immediately following a sad mood is another common time for "aha" breakthroughs.

• **Bad moods encourage perseverance.** When people are in good moods, they see little reason to push themselves hard—why bother when everything already seems great? Unhappy people often are more likely to put in extra effort because they see problems all around them and are motivated to do what it takes to make things better.

What to do: If you catch yourself about to throw in the towel on a tough task when you're feeling happy, use the sad-memory or music strategy mentioned above to reset your mood, and then give it another go.

• **Bad moods make us more polite and empathic.** When people feel happy, they can become so caught up in their own positive moods that they may fail to fully notice the needs, deeds and moods of the people around them, leading to an apparent lack of empathy and politeness. A happy person might fail to ask his friend, "What's wrong?" because he missed the slight quiver in his friend's voice. People who are feeling unhappy (but not deeply depressed) are more likely to notice details such as these.

What to do: When in a good mood, make a conscious effort to evaluate your initial interpretations of other people's words and actions.

• **Bad moods can help us come to terms with both our priorities and problems.** Bad moods can be like beacons shining a light on core beliefs and key concerns that we might not yet have fully acknowledged.

What to do: When you find yourself naturally feeling sad or angry, take the time to explore why you feel this way and what you could do about it. For example, perhaps you feel deeply hurt because you did not receive as much recognition as you expected for a good idea. Does the person who didn't give you your due chronically fail to do so? If so, it might be time to confront this person or bring your good ideas to someone else. Or maybe the problem is not with this person but that you feel generally undervalued. Perhaps volunteering in your free time or serving as a mentor would help.

EASY TO DO...

Overwhelmed? Try This...

Use a quick "5-4-3-2-1" trick to work your way through your five senses: Name five things you can see right now...then four things you can hear...three things you can touch...two things you can smell...and one thing you can taste, such as the taste in your own mouth. This interrupts your spinning thoughts, and you should emerge calmer.

Ellen Hendriksen, PhD, clinical psychologist and host of the "Savvy Psychologist" podcast.

Do You Have a Short Fuse? How to Stop Feeling So Angry...

Bernard Golden, PhD, a psychologist and founder of Anger Management Education, a clinical practice in Chicago. In addition to treating anger issues, he specializes in anxiety, depression and motivation. He is the author of *Overcoming Destructive Anger*. AngerManagementEducation.com

Here are a few questions worth asking yourself...

Do you often snap at people and later regret it...or continue to stew after a disagreement has passed?

Do friends or loved ones ever call you a hothead?

Does the intensity of your anger sometimes escalate from 0 to 10 in a matter of seconds?

If any of these situations ring true, then you may be experiencing destructive anger.

And it's hurting you!

HEALTHY OR HARMFUL?

Like all emotions, anger can express itself in good or bad ways. *Healthy anger* motivates us to make important changes in our lives...challenges us to overcome unfairness and social injustices...and is a signal to look inward to identify our core desires, needs and values.

Destructive anger is another story. Whether you quietly simmer with rage or erupt at even slight provocations, destructive anger has been shown to increase one's risk for health problems such as high blood pressure, heart attack, stroke, digestive ailments and depression.

The unfortunate truth: Far too many people assume that they can simply turn off their anger like a spigot. But it doesn't work that way.

THE TOOL THAT WORKS

If you want to reduce your anger, the first step is to realize that out-of-proportion or out-of-control anger stems from a chain of internal experiences and is almost always not just a reaction to whatever has set you off.

For example, you might experience intense anger when someone cuts in front of you in the checkout line, but this triggering event may evoke past anger as well.

To better understand your anger, it helps to complete an anger log, identifying the interplay of your thoughts, feelings and body sensations that occurred before and during your episodes of anger. By doing this, you'll start to see patterns and can interrupt the cycle.

Ideally, you will complete a log entry every time you get angry—but you should wait at least an hour or two so you're calm enough to recognize all of the important elements.

Key aspects to write down...

- **Motivating forces.** People experience anger when they're feeling threatened or when a need—for safety, for respect or to feel important, for example—isn't being met.

Let's say that you shouted an obscenity while arguing with your spouse. Maybe he/she had scolded you for something you did—but did it really warrant that level of verbal retaliation? You might realize that the motivation *behind* the anger was your (unmet) need for love and connection and respect.

- **Expectations.** We get angry when things run counter to our expectations. In the example above, one expectation might be, "We're a couple, so we should care about each other's feelings." But your conflict is putting that basic expectation into doubt.

- **Triggering event.** Sometimes it's obvious what makes you angry—the car that cuts in front of you...a negative job review...or a curt reply from a store clerk. But sometimes it is less clear—for example, the triggering event could be something that you *anticipate* will happen. You might, for example, become angry because you anticipate not getting a job for which you interviewed.

- **Body reactions.** Anger evolves in the body. Identifying a pounding heart, sweating palms and other such reactions will help you become more alert to anger in its initial stage.

GIVE IT TIME

You may be surprised by the range of feelings that accompany a "simple" episode of anger.

Example: A client sought my help because of conflicts with her teenage daughter. When she first completed her anger log, she wrote that the motivating factor was "to be respected." Her main expectation was that "she should listen to me."

But the more my client thought about it, the more she realized that the real motivating factor was her desire for closeness and a meaningful relationship with her daughter. She also had the expectation that "our closeness will never change."

Emotional discoveries don't happen all at once. Keeping a log will help you understand the *trajectory* of your anger—and become much more skillful at altering its course. You'll know you're making progress when there's a decrease in the intensity, duration and/or frequency of anger episodes.

For additional help: Consult The National Anger Management Association, NAMAss.org, for a referral to a therapist.

BETTER WAY...

5 Steps to a Better Apology

Express regret—list the hurtful effects of what you did. *Accept responsibility*—take on the fault of the specific mistake or mistakes. *Make restitution*—ask the person you wronged how you can make amends—do not specify what you will do, since it may not be what the person wants. *Repent*—say that you will work to resolve the issue or change your behavior and will not let the problem recur. *Request forgiveness*—ask for it directly.

Lisa B. Marshall, professional consultant and author of *Smart Talk* and *Ace Your Interview*, writing at QuickandDirtyTips.com.

How to Deal with Critical People

Mark Goulston, MD, founder and CEO of the Goulston Group, a consulting company in Santa Monica, California, that helps business owners think outside the box. A psychiatrist and an FBI and police hostage negotiation trainer, he has written numerous books including *Just Listen: Discover the Secret to Getting Through to Absolutely Anyone* and *Talking to Crazy: How to Deal with the Irrational and Impossible People in Your Life*. His website is GoulstonGroup.com.

Being criticized can bring out the worst in us. It's easy to become defensive...get drawn into an argument about who is right...and/or seethe quietly.

If you have a chronically critical person (or several) in your life, your first goal should be to stop repeated fights about the criticism and reach the point where you can have an actual discussion.

To do that, I recommend a counterintuitive response to criticism called *assertive humility*—taking responsibility instead of becoming defensive or counterattacking. This approach gives you a surprising amount of power and dignity in the face of criticism. Rather than criticizing the critic or trying to disprove his criticism, you offer an unsolicited apology.

How this works: When you are criticized, pause for a moment so that you do not react impulsively. Then say, "What you just said made me realize that I owe you an apology." The other person will be completely dumbfounded—it is likely that he/she has never received a spontaneous apology before.

Continue with, "I want to apologize for never making the effort to find out how you came to look at this issue the way you do. I was too busy reacting or trying to prove my point of view. That was disrespectful and counterproductive. If you are willing—and you don't have to be—I'd like to fix that right now by having you tell me how you came to think about this the way you do. I will do my best to listen and understand your point of view."

Adapt the language above using words that you would naturally use in conversation. It is important to keep your tone matter-of-fact and to have a genuine desire to understand. If you come across as phony or patronizing, the technique will backfire.

Turning a critical statement toward you into an apology from you is effective because the other person is expecting a defensive reaction from you. This disarms the person, and at that point, you have a much better chance of actually discussing the issue rather than just fighting.

Example: A husband feels that his wife has been criticizing him about everything. She says that he's not eating right, not exercising enough and has been moody and sullen. The husband offers an apology and an invitation for discussion, as described above. The wife is likely to feel stunned and might even look like a deer caught in headlights. She might respond by speaking constructively about her issues with her husband's behavior. But even if she doesn't, this gives her husband an opening to try to engage her in constructive conversation—possibly for the first time in a long time.

If apologizing seems like too big a leap for you, remind yourself that this is a technique—and ask yourself how much dealing with the critical person in the usual way is costing you in stress, anxiety and exhaustion. Being defensive or arguing with a chronic critic won't work because you won't win. Why not try an approach that has a better chance of working?

Is There an Almost-Psychopath in Your Life? How to Recognize the Signs...

Ronald Schouten, MD, JD, director of the Law & Psychiatry Service at Massachusetts General Hospital and associate professor of psychiatry at Harvard Medical School, both in Boston. He is coauthor of *Almost a Psychopath*.

When most of us think of psychopaths, we imagine cold-blooded killers or con men who rob the elderly of their life savings without a qualm—deviant individuals we assume we have little chance of encountering. (True psychopaths make up only about 1% of the US population.) But did you ever suspect that there might be an *almost-psychopath* in your life?

What research is now showing: People known as almost-psychopaths are much more common—it's estimated that they make up 5% to 15% of the population.

The traits that define psychopaths and almost-psychopaths have many possible causes, including genetics and/or dysfunctional family relationships. The symptoms can also signal an underlying illness, such as depression or bipolar disorder, or certain medical conditions, such as a brain tumor or thyroid disease.

Almost-psychopaths (whose problematic behaviors don't quite meet the standard definition of a diagnosable disorder) may not wreak the havoc and harm of a true psychopath, but they can cause serious damage. And it's essential to recognize them and know how to deal with them.

TELLING BEHAVIORS

Almost-psychopaths have many of the qualities of a true psychopath but to a *lesser degree*. For example, they have a strong sense of self-importance, but it's not as pronounced as it is in the psychopath. Their capacity for empathy is severely stunted but not invariably defunct—they retain a glimmer of compassion for those with whom they have relationships or who can serve their needs. The stirrings of a conscience may be there, but it's weak. They also are superficially charming, lie, con and manipulate and are expert at rationalizing their misdeeds and crafting excuses for their behavior.

However, almost-psychopaths often lack the fearless sense of invulnerability that powers true psychopaths. They feel they *should* be above the law but generally realize that they're not and fear getting caught. This limits their capacity to hurt but also makes them harder to spot and adept at weaving a web of lies to cover their transgressions.

Unlike psychopaths, almost-psychopaths are capable of living more easily among the general population. Psychopaths may frequently be in prison for crimes, have a string of failed marriages and be estranged from their children while an almost-psychopath may, for example, be a grandiose coworker who routinely bends the rules at work or someone who serially cheats on his/her spouse.

THE RELATIONSHIP TRAP

Their easy charm and adept lies can get you involved with—and sometimes married to—

an almost-psychopath. The sense that something is seriously wrong often develops slowly and uncertainly.

What helps: Keep a private and careful record of behaviors that concern you (such as betrayals, deceptions, examples of callous actions toward you or others, or any other behaviors described below) in order to determine if there's a problem. This record can also be helpful to a psychotherapist should you consult one later.

Relationships with almost-psychopaths are frequently filled with conflict. These individuals truly believe that their wants are more important than anyone else's. There is typically a constant demand to accommodate the almost-psychopath's needs and desires. Additionally, there often are chronic infidelities, excessive bragging, abruptly canceled plans and extravagant expenses.

Almost-psychopaths also are very good at shifting blame, turning the tables and generating self-doubt and even guilt in those who question their honesty. How could you even think such things? There are numerous excuses and promises to change, given with a look of extreme innocence. Deceit and manipulation keep you perpetually off balance.

Unlike the true psychopaths, almost-psychopaths can sometimes change their ways—if they acknowledge their behaviors and want to change.

What to do if you think you are living with an almost-psychopath:

- **Acknowledge the problem** and realize that there may be hope for improvement.
- **Reach out to trusted friends or family members.** Your gut instincts are probably on target, but it helps to get another person's input and support.
- **Talk to the almost-psychopath in a calm manner** (if you feel comfortable doing so) about his behaviors. He may not be aware of them or may have grown up in a household where the behaviors were common.
- **Track progress and have additional conversations.** Once the lines of communication are open, further conversations are often easier.
- **Seek professional help if there are ongoing concerns.** Sometimes your best chance for improving the relationship is psychotherapy for your partner and/or couples therapy for both of you.

Also advisable: A visit to a primary care physician, who can rule out medical conditions that may be contributing to the situation and/or provide a referral to a psychiatrist or therapist. If your partner won't go to therapy, seek individual therapy to help you determine how to move ahead.

Warning: The threat of physical harm and/or psychological aggression is very real in a close relationship with an almost-psychopath. If a discussion leads to threats or outright violence, take steps to protect yourself—leave the situation and/or seek help from friends and, if necessary, law enforcement.

TAKE NOTE...

10 Key Signs of an Almost-Psychopath

1. He/she is superficially charming and glib.
2. There is a lack of empathy.
3. When he's confronted with a difficult moral choice, he more often than not arrives at a decision to act in his own self-interest.
4. He repeatedly lies, even when unnecessary and for minor reasons.
5. He is cunning and manipulative.
6. When criticized for something, it is always someone else's fault.
7. When he causes harm to others, there is a lack of true remorse.
8. There is difficulty in maintaining relationships.
9. He finds it easy to ignore responsibilities.
10. People and situations exist solely for the purpose of gratifying his needs and wants.

How to Be a Much Better Listener

Roger Flax, PhD, who has been a corporate communications and leadership coach and consultant for more than 45 years. He is the creator of Horizon Talent Developer, a nationally known self-awareness/leadership-perception exercise. HorizonTalentDeveloper.com

We're taught to read and talk as children, but rarely are we taught how to listen. As a result, almost everyone has bad listening habits—habits that can damage our careers and relationships.

Not being a good listener might mean that you miss out on potentially valuable information...that you fail to develop a truly deep understanding of your friends and acquaintances...or that you simply annoy the heck out of conversation partners.

Most people don't think that they're bad listeners—but they are. Are you? The first and most important step in overcoming bad listening habits is to become more aware of them.

Here's a look at nine common bad listening habits, plus strategies for becoming a great listener...

PROBLEM: DISTRACTION

Many bad listening habits involve a lack of focus on what's being said...

***BAD HABIT:* Jumping to conclusions.** The speaker still is providing information, but your mind has raced ahead to where you think he/she is headed. Unfortunately, you sometimes jump to the wrong conclusions...and even when you jump to the correct ones, jumping ahead still means that you miss key details.

Example: Your boss tells you that your presentations are weak. As you're being told of the specific weak areas, your mind immediately jumps to the conclusion that you're losing your job. As a result, you don't hear how you could make your presentations stronger.

***BAD HABIT:* Ducking potentially dull topics.** The first words out of a speaker's mouth (or the topic printed on an agenda) hint that a talk will be dry or even pointless, so you mentally check out. But even if the speaker or the topic is indeed less than thrilling, there still might be an important detail or two provided. In fact, if everyone else present tunes out this dull talk, you might be able to pick up something that no one else knows by listening closely, providing you with a strategic advantage.

Example: The speaker at a conference titles his talk "Achieving Quality" and starts by spouting jargon. Eventually he gets to specific strategies and case histories that are truly useful—but only for those few in the audience who are still paying attention.

***BAD HABIT:* Closed-mindedness.** Someone utters a word or phrase that tends to be spoken by people with whom you disagree. For some, that phrase might be "global warming"...for others, "gun rights." You immediately think, *Here we go again*, and tune him out.

***BAD HABIT:* Letting offensive or emotional content distract.** Someone says something that you consider insulting. You become so upset that you hear little else during the minutes that follow.

Example: Someone refers to you as a "senior"—even though you're only 60 years old.

What to do: Use the Purpose/Detail/Action (PDA) strategy to overcome distraction-related bad listening habits. When you notice your mind drifting, assign yourself the following three tasks to regain focus.

First, try to determine the speaker's purpose—what is he trying to tell you? Listeners' minds tend to drift when speakers are not skilled at conveying their purpose. Setting your mind to work ferreting out this purpose can turn listening to a poor speaker into a mental challenge that locks in your attention.

Once you have a sense of the speaker's purpose, seek out detail. Is this speaker providing factual evidence that proves his point to your satisfaction or just unfounded opinions? If you do not hear evidence, politely ask the speaker to provide it.

Finally, consider what action the speaker wants you to take—it's OK to ask if this isn't clear. Do you think this action is appropriate? And if not, what action, if any, do you believe would be more appropriate?

PROBLEM: INWARD FOCUS

Sometimes the problem isn't just that we aren't paying enough attention to the speaker—it's that we're paying too much attention to ourselves...

***BAD HABIT:* Planning what you are going to say while someone else is still speaking.** It might seem prudent to plan out your words before you speak during a conversation—but if you start planning your words while someone else is still talking, you will miss much of what he is saying.

What's more, your response might not be as appropriate as you imagine if you have missed key nuances of the conversation.

***BAD HABIT:* Ascribing your thoughts to other people.** A speaker says something that is related to something you already know or believe. Rather than hear his actual words, you hear a confirmation of your existing thoughts.

Example: A friend recommends the Sherlock Holmes TV show on PBS. You already enjoy the Sherlock Holmes TV show that runs on CBS, so you say you already watch it...and fail to realize there is a second show based on the same fictional detective that you might enjoy as well.

What to do: To avoid focusing on yourself, make a conscious effort to keep conversations focused on the other person. This might feel unnatural at first—most people steer conversations toward themselves and what's in it for them without even realizing that they are doing so. We tell our family what happened during our day...we tell our colleagues our opinions about a project. But we will learn much more—and people will enjoy interacting with us much more—if we do exactly the opposite.

Example: You ask a friend what he is planning to do this weekend, and he says that he is going camping with his family. Before you were trying to become a better listener, you would have responded by supplying your weekend plans, shifting the conversation from him to you.

Instead, ask follow-up questions about his camping trip—where he will camp...how often he camps...or for his recommendations about camping equipment. This transforms the conversation from soon-forgotten small talk into a relationship-building, informative exchange.

PROBLEM: PERFUNCTORY LISTENING

Sometimes we truly do listen—we just don't listen deeply enough, in the right way or with sufficient compassion and patience...

***BAD HABIT:* Ignoring body language and/or tone of voice.** The words that are spoken to you might not be the entire message. They might not even be the most important part of the message.

Example: You ask a friend how she has been, and she says, "Fine." You miss the slight tremor in her voice that suggests that everything is not really fine.

***BAD HABIT:* Rushing speakers.** When someone says something that you think you already know, you hurry them along with "yes, yes, yes..." or "I get it, I get it..." You think this is saving everyone time, but mainly it just annoys people, and you may prevent the speaker from giving important details.

What to do: To prevent perfunctory listening, when the words that someone is speaking fail to hold your complete attention, consider it a perfect opportunity to practice listening between the lines. Study the speaker's tone of voice, posture and expression to try to glean an overall sense of what this person is thinking and feeling. Most people are surprised to discover how quickly their ability to identify nonverbal messages improves. And even if you are not especially skilled at this, making the effort will help you pay closer attention.

One useful listen-between-the-lines strategy is to try to determine whether a speaker truly believes what he is saying. Monitor the number of "ums" and "uhs" and the overall smoothness of speech. People tend to stammer and insert "um" and "uh" at greater than their usual rate when they are lying, uncertain or indecisive. This is a great way for bosses to check whether their employees truly believe their upbeat reports...or whether they are just afraid to be the bearers of bad news.

When Your Loved One Is Depressed...and Won't Get Help...

Susan J. Noonan, MD, MPH, a physician who has personally suffered from depression and currently counsels patients at McLean Hospital in Belmont, Massachusetts, about depression and recovery. She is also a volunteer consultant at Massachusetts General Hospital in Boston and the author of *When Someone You Know Has Depression*. SusanNoonanMD.com

It's gratifying (if a little tiring) to care for a loved one who's recovering from surgery or suffering from a physical illness like the flu. Whether you cook up a pot of chicken soup or help out around the house, your efforts are bound to be appreciated.

But that's rarely the case when a loved one is depressed. Your efforts to help are more likely to be met with silence or withdrawal.

Most people who are depressed don't like to talk about it—assuming they even realize that they *are* depressed. And it's easy to get frustrated when they won't take the smallest steps to help themselves, especially if they've also stopped pulling their weight with household and family obligations. So what's your best course of action?

YOU *CAN* HELP

Depression—as well as other mood disorders (such as bipolar disorder)—can literally change the way the mind works. That's why the sufferer may find it nearly impossible to even imagine feeling better. So the nudge to get help often has to come from outside.

It's crucial to do your part because about 80% of those with depression *will* improve substantially when treated with therapy and/or medication. What you can do...

***STEP 1:* Talk about any changes that you've observed.** You're likely aware of many classic signs of depression such as a loss of interest in things that used to be enjoyable...changes in appearance or hygiene...sleeping more or less (or in fragments)...eating more or less than usual...and feelings of hopelessness and/or withdrawal from friends and family. But signs of depression can also be less obvious to you (or the person who's suffering).

Examples: Having more bad days at work...and/or drinking more than usual.

If you observe any such changes, you might say something like, "I've noticed that things are different with you lately. You seem to be sleeping a lot more and have not been getting cleaned up in the morning. Do you think it might be depression?"

Your comments might be well received, but don't count on it. Even people who know they are depressed don't like to admit it. Denial is part of the process. You don't have to push the issue right away...but do bring it up again (every four days or so) if the person doesn't start to show more interest in his/her physical and mental well-being.

The gender difference: Women are more likely to see signs of depression in themselves. A man's depression might be marked by less recognizable red flags such as anger, irritability and/or the use of drugs or alcohol. He'll probably be less likely than a woman to seek professional help, so don't hesitate to reach out if you notice behavior or personality changes. Let him know that you're concerned.

***STEP 2:* Encourage treatment...but don't push.** The first time you suggest to a loved one that he might want to see a mental health professional, you're likely to get a response such as "I'm fine"...or "Just leave me alone."

At first, just raise the *possibility* of treatment and give your full—and nonjudgmental—support. You may even offer to help find someone to talk to. When a person is depressed, just picking up the phone to call a doctor or other health-care professional can feel overwhelming. Your loved one's efforts to get help should include a visit to his primary care physician, who can rule out any medical conditions and make a referral to a therapist, if necessary.

Important: People who begin treatment for depression need a lot of encouragement. Treatment can be effective, but it typically takes at least a few months to notice improvement with therapy and/or medication.

***STEP 3:* Keep the conversation going.** Most people with depression know (or eventually learn) that they're "off" but need to feel safe before opening up about it.

To encourage the free expression of feelings, I recommend what's known as *active listening*. When your loved one does open up, remind yourself to be fully present...let him speak without interruption ...and ask "open" questions (such as, "How do you feel about that?") to keep the person talking.

Another good technique is *reflection*. When talking with your loved one, you identify the emotions that you're hearing the person express. If someone says, "Life is no good," you can "reflect" the emotions by saying something like, "I hear that life feels no good to you right now and everything seems hopeless." With this approach, you acknowledge the person's feelings and show that you're listening closely.

Caution: It's tempting to give assurances by saying something like, "Everything will be fine." To someone who's depressed, this type of response can feel like a brush-off.

STEP 4: **Challenge your loved one's thinking.** Depression causes people to view the world through a negative—and distorted—lens. They may truly believe that "I have no friends." When you hear something like this, offer them a more realistic (and fact-based) substitute.

You could say: "What do you mean you have no friends? Didn't you tell me you're getting along with people in your book group?" The idea isn't to argue but to point out the inaccuracy of what's being said.

Also helpful: Encourage your loved one to write two columns on a piece of paper. One column will say "Evidence For"...the other will say "Evidence Against." Seeing evidence that refutes reflexively negative thoughts in writing can help people shift their thinking.

STEP 5: **Recognize that action precedes motivation.** If you do not have depression, you probably do things when you want to do them. But someone who's depressed never feels motivated and might need to commit to an activity—joining a social group, going out to dinner, etc.—despite a lack of enthusiasm.

Example: If a loved one is too depressed to take the long walks you know he used to enjoy, you might say something like, "It's a nice day and I'm going for a short walk. Would you like to come with me?"

Once outside, your loved one may realize how good it feels to get some exercise. Your goal is not to apply pressure...but to encourage an activity until the person feels motivated to do it again.

For more on supporting a loved one with depression, contact the National Alliance on Mental Illness (NAMI.org). If you're concerned that your loved one could be suicidal, call the National Suicide Prevention Lifeline at 800-273-8255.

A Novel Therapy for Depression

Christopher Martell, PhD, clinic director of the Psychological Services Center at the University of Massachusetts, Amherst, author of two textbooks on behavioral activation (BA) for therapists and coauthor (with Michael Addis, PhD) of the client workbook on BA, *Overcoming Depression One Step at a Time: The New Behavioral Activation Approach to Getting Your Life Back*.

If you think of therapy for depression as all talk and no action, here's a pleasant surprise—a simple, short-term and inexpensive new form of therapy helps people with depression feel better and improve their states of mind by "doing." Doing what? *You'll see...*

FROM THE OUTSIDE IN

Behavioral activation (BA), as the approach is called, helps people reengage with others and with activities that they enjoy—or used to enjoy—rather than focusing on their inner thoughts and feelings.

When people are depressed, they naturally withdraw socially and from activities they used to enjoy—and get pulled in by their negative moods. This sets up a bad cycle.

That's where BA comes in—breaking this negative cycle. It targets inertia, encouraging people to treat their depression through their behavior.

Let's say you enjoy, or used to enjoy, quilting. (In fact, it could be any activity you like, either alone or with others—cooking with friends, hiking, playing piano, being in a book club, drawing, etc.) With BA therapy, you would be encouraged to pursue that pastime in a small, incremental way—perhaps, say, by searching online for local quilting clubs to join. The next step might involve choosing a particular club and making inquiries about when it meets and whether it's open to new members. When internal barriers arise—if you can't mobilize your efforts because you feel so down and tired, for example—you and the therapist would try to identify what's really standing in your way and what you can do to get around those obstacles.

HOW WELL DOES BA WORK?

BA therapy has developed in its current form only within the past 20 years, so it is not as thoroughly researched as other forms of therapy. *But there's a growing body of supportive evidence...*

• **It works as well as cognitive behavioral therapy (CBT),** according to a recent study published in *The Lancet.* When 440 adults who met a primary diagnosis of depression but who were not yet getting any treatment received at least eight weekly sessions of CBT—a well-established approach that focuses on changing thought patterns and behaviors—or BA, the therapies were found to be equally effective.

• **It works in older people.** A recent study from the Weill Cornell Institute of Geriatric Psychiatry in White Plains, New York, published in *The American Journal of Geriatric Psychiatry,* looked at 48 adults over age 60 with mild-to-moderate depression. After the patients were treated with nine weekly sessions of BA, they were engaged, participating in many more personally rewarding activities—and they experienced a sharp decline in their depressive symptoms.

THE EXERCISE CONNECTION

There's another potential benefit offered by BA. If this therapy could help people with depression become more physically active, the effects could be profound.

Here's why: According to a recent study published in *Psychosomatic Medicine,* 30 minutes of brisk exercise three times a week is not only as effective in treating depression as major antidepressants but also much more effective in preventing the return of depression. Six months after treatment ended, only 8% in the exercise-only group had their depression return, compared with 38% in the drug-only group.

SHOULD YOU TRY IT?

Even though BA isn't successful for everyone, when it works, it can work very quickly. The exact mechanism of action isn't clear, but reengaging in activity can increase positive feelings—and the negative thinking that's associated with depression can change as you change your behavior.

While each patient and each therapist is individual, a typical course of BA consists of weekly 50-minute sessions for up to 24 weeks. It is a nondrug approach but can also work for individuals who are being treated with psychiatric medications, such as antidepressants.

To find a BA therapist, the best place to start is with a therapist trained in CBT (most therapists trained in CBT can do BA). To find a CBT therapist, click on "Find Help," then on "Find a CBT Therapist" at ABCT.org, the site of the Association for Behavioral and Cognitive Therapies. Like other psychotherapies, BA is generally covered by insurance.

And the great news is that the key to this therapy is doing what you *enjoy!*

BETTER WAY...

A Depression-Fighting Regimen

Depressed adults who completed 30 minutes of meditation followed by a half-hour of moderate-intensity exercise twice a week (on a treadmill, stationary bike or elliptical machine) lowered depressive symptoms by an average of 40% after two months—regardless of whether they were taking an antidepressant. Researchers theorize that the combination of meditation and exercise may result in brain changes that reduce negative feelings.

Brandon Alderman, PhD, assistant professor of exercise science, Rutgers, The State University of New Jersey, New Brunswick.

19

Business Bulletin

The Real Secret to Success—It's Not IQ or Talent...It's Grit!

As a math teacher for high school, many years prior to becoming a psychologist, Angela Duckworth observed that her most successful students were the ones who tried the hardest—and not necessarily the ones who had a natural aptitude for the subject. Dr. Duckworth wanted to know why this was so and what role effort plays in a person's success. After years of study, she determined that perseverance and passion for long-term goals—in a word, grit—is a better indicator of success and happiness than IQ or talent.

In her book *Grit: The Power of Passion and Perseverance*, Dr. Duckworth explains why grit is so important—and how you can develop it. *Here are some of her key findings...*

WHAT IS GRIT?

Grit is about holding steadfast to a goal even when there are bumps in the road and progress toward that goal is slow. While talent and luck matter to success, in the long run, grit may matter more. Dr. Duckworth developed a scale while studying cadets at the United States Military Academy at West Point to predict which men and women would make it through the intensive summer training program for new cadets called "Beast Barracks." Those who scored highest for grit were the least likely to drop out. This score was a more reliable predictor than intelligence, leadership experience or athletic ability.

Note: Prices, rates and offers throughout this chapter and book are subject to change.

Angela Duckworth, PhD, professor of psychology at University of Pennsylvania in Philadelphia and adviser to the White House, the World Bank, Fortune 500 CEOs and NBA and NFL teams. She is founder and scientific director of the Character Lab, a nonprofit that advances the science and practice of character development. She is author of *Grit: The Power of Passion and Perseverance*. AngelaDuckworth.com

In the box below, there are three questions from the Grit Scale developed for the West Point study and used in other studies. Your answers to those questions can help you determine how gritty you are.

Good news: You can grow grit "from the inside out." You can do this by developing a habit of daily practice...connecting your activity to a purpose beyond yourself...and learning not to give up when all seems lost.

PRACTICE

To help develop grit, practice the *Hard Thing Rule*, which has three parts...

Part one: Select at least one hard thing that requires daily and deliberate practice. It could be yoga. It could be playing the piano. It could be writing a book.

Part two: You cannot quit, especially on a bad day. You must choose an amount of time—for example, a season or a semester—and stay committed during that time.

Part three: Only you are allowed to pick your hard thing. Nobody picks it for you because it would make no sense to do a hard thing that you're not interested in.

Parents who would like to encourage grit in their children can have them follow the Hard Thing Rule, too.

PURPOSE

The "grittiest" people tend to have developed their passions from personal interests, but also from one particular kind of broader purpose—the intention to contribute to the well-being of others. It could be their children, their clients, their students or our country or society.

For some, purpose comes first. However, most people become attracted to things they enjoy or that are needed to pay the bills and later realize how these interests can benefit others.

It is never too early or too late to begin cultivating a purpose. *Three recommendations for developing a purpose...*

1. Reflect on how what you're already doing can make a positive contribution to society. Developmental psychologists David Yeager, MEd, and Dave Paunesku, PhD, asked high school students how the world could become a better place—and told them to draw connections to what they were learning in school. Compared with a placebo control exercise, reflecting on purpose significantly energized students, leading them to double the amount they studied for an upcoming exam... to choose to work harder on tough math problems instead of watching a fun video... and to get better grades in math and science.

2. Think about how, in small but meaningful ways, you can enhance your connection to your core values. Amy Wrzesniewski, PhD, professor of organizational behavior at Yale School of Management, calls this "job crafting." Job crafting is redefining and reimagining a job to make it more personally meaningful. She tested the idea in various workplaces.

Example: She studied a cleaning crew at a university hospital. Some of the workers didn't find the work especially satisfying and were there mainly for the money. Others found their work meaningful. When they described their jobs, they mentioned activities that weren't in their job descriptions, such as spending time with patients and walking visitors back to their cars. They had molded their jobs to become more meaningful.

3. Find inspiration in a purposeful role model. Stanford University developmental psychologist Bill Damon, PhD, who has studied purpose for more than 40 years, suggests we ask ourselves, *Can I think of someone whose life inspires me to be a better person? Who? Why?* It could be a family member, a historical figure or a political figure, as long as it's someone who demonstrates that it is possible to accomplish something on behalf of others.

OPTIMISM

Grit depends on the expectation that our own efforts can improve our future. *Here's how to develop this optimistic outlook...*

• **Adopt a growth mind-set.** The brain is like a muscle that gets stronger with use—neurons in our brain retain the potential to grow new connections and strengthen existing connections. Intelligence and talent can improve with effort. People who feel that intelligence is

TAKE NOTE...

How Gritty Are You?

Below are three statements. Choose the answer that seems most like you. There are no right or wrong answers, so answer each question honestly.

1. ***New ideas and projects sometimes distract me from previous ones.***
   - Very much like me
   - Mostly like me
   - Somewhat like me
   - Not much like me
   - Not like me at all
2. ***Setbacks don't discourage me. I don't give up easily.***
   - Very much like me
   - Mostly like me
   - Somewhat like me
   - Not much like me
   - Not like me at all
3. ***I often set a goal but later choose to pursue a different one.***
   - Very much like me
   - Mostly like me
   - Somewhat like me
   - Not much like me
   - Not like me at all

People with high levels of grit typically answer "Not like me at all" for questions 1 and 3, and "Very much like me" for question 2.

To take the entire 10-question Grit Scale questionnaire and get your grit score, visit the website AngelaDuckworth.com.

fixed tend to have pessimistic views of adversity. They avoid challenges or just give up.

A growth mind-set leads to optimistic views of adversity, leading you to seek out new challenges and become stronger. Gritty people explain setbacks optimistically. They believe that everything that happens can be learned from—and that one should move on from setbacks.

• **Practice some optimistic self-talk.** Studies have shown that cognitive behavioral therapy, which helps you identify, understand and change inaccurate or negative thinking, can help you respond more effectively and become more positive. You can try this on your own by being aware of negative self-talk and instead making a conscious effort to interpret events as an optimist would interpret them.

If this doesn't work and you find that you still are a pessimist, seek out the help of a cognitive behavioral therapist. Gritty people know to ask for help when they need it.

Now Anyone Can Own a Piece of a Start-Up

Matthew R. Nutting, JD, an attorney at Coleman & Horowitt, LLP, where he advises start-ups and investors on business law, Fresno, California. He was a director of the National Crowdfunding Association and coauthor, with David Freedman, of *Equity Crowdfunding for Investors*. CH-Law.com

You can be a "shark"—the kind of shark that invests in promising small businesses that have not begun offering shares to the public on a stock exchange. And you can be that kind of shark even if you have just a few hundred or a few thousand dollars to invest.

How? Through a new fund-raising option. It allows businesses to raise $1 million per 12-month period from anyone—rather than just from wealthy investors. The option, known as "equity crowdfunding," became available May 16, 2016, under the 2012 federal Jumpstart Our Business Startups (JOBS) Act.

Previously, federal securities law allowed such investments only from "accredited" investors who had to meet certain wealth criteria. Now equity crowdfunding gives you ownership shares in the business, unlike ordinary crowdfunding through sites such as Kickstarter that typically gives you early access to a new product or another reward in exchange for supporting a venture—but no ownership stake.

Examples of businesses that have recently used equity crowdfunding: A Boston University professor's firm is developing an artificial pancreas to help children suffering from diabetes. A Brazilian fashion designer sells high-tech clothing that protects people from mosquitoes carrying the Zika virus. A racehorse owner distributes winnings of horses in his elite stable to shareholders. A design engineer's firm is developing a high-tech bathroom scale that scans your body in 3D so that you can track changes not just in your weight but also in your muscle tone and appearance.

About $10 million has been committed to equity crowdfunding by investors so far in the short period since it became available, and 100 to 150 investment offerings currently are available. But that number is expected to grow into the thousands over the next few years.

GOOD TO KNOW...

Basics Before Quitting Your Job...

Be sure that you are not establishing a job-hopping pattern by leaving every year or two—employers do not want to hire job hoppers...*have an emergency fund* to cover six months of living expenses in case your search takes a while...*network with friends* and former coworkers so that you have some leads before you quit...*consider trying to resolve any fixable problems* at your current job before you quit and face the stresses of a job hunt...and *decide whether searching for a new job will further your career goals* or you would do better to stay in your current job and add something to it—for instance, by going back to school.

If You're Fired...

Use career self-defense if you are fired from your job...

Minimize employment gaps—if you cannot find a job right away, volunteer or do freelance work to show future employers that you stayed active in your field. *Choose references carefully*—even if your immediate supervisor is a poor choice, you may be able to get a reference from another manager or a team leader. *If possible, avoid saying "fired"*—use "laid off" or "downsized" or another term. *Be sure to exit your company gracefully* even if you are leaving under negative circumstances—the way you depart may be reported to future interviewers and can affect potential job offers.

Roundup of experts at WiseBread.com.

Of course, this type of investing can be highly risky and isn't for everyone. The Securities and Exchange Commission (SEC) spent several years coming up with safeguards meant to protect small investors from fraud and/or their own naïveté, but the requirements are not as rigorous as those regulating publicly traded companies. Also, keep in mind that in general, about half of all start-ups fail within the first five years.

Here's how small investors can navigate this new world of speculative investments...

HOW IT WORKS

In equity crowdfunding, you buy shares from business start-ups through crowdfunding websites known as portals. Running a portal typically requires a broker-dealer license, and the brokers must meet extensive SEC regulations on crowdfunding. The portals review the credentials of the start-ups.

There currently are about 25 active portals, which include FlashFunders.com...NextSeed.com...Republic.co...SeedInvest.com...StartEngine.com...and WeFunder.com. And dozens more are on the way. You can register with portals for free to gain access to information about "Regulation CF" (crowdfunding) offerings. It is too soon to say whether any particular portals are better than others, but it makes sense to start looking at opportunities at WeFunder.com, which recently had the largest number of offerings, about 30.

Each offering provides an extensive overview of the business, known as a "pitch deck," which includes financial statements and a term sheet with details of the investment offering. The business specifies a target amount that it hopes to raise within a defined period of time...the share price...and the minimum investment that it will accept, which typically ranges from $20 to $2,000.

Example: Beta Bionics, the first to raise $1 million, attracted investments averaging $1,300 from 775 investors. The company created the iLet, a wearable medical device that helps manage blood sugar levels for type 1 diabetics by automatically pumping insulin into the body when needed.

Any crowdfunding money you invest is held in escrow until the date an offering closes. If the company fails to raise its target amount, your money is returned. If it successfully raises the target amount, you typically are sent digital documents detailing your share ownership rather than a stock certificate.

INVESTMENT LIMITS

There are legal limits on how much an investor can put into equity crowdfunding within any 12-month period. Anyone can invest $2,000, including assets from IRAs. Whether you can invest more than that within 12 months depends on an SEC formula that accounts for your income and net worth.

If either your income or net worth (excluding the value of your primary residence) is less than $100,000, you can invest up to 5% of the lower of those two amounts. If both your income and net worth are above $100,000, you can invest up to 10% of the lower amount. But no one can invest more than $100,000 in a 12-month period.

HOW YOU MAKE MONEY

Unlike ordinary publicly traded stocks, equity crowdfunding stocks are highly illiquid. SEC rules generally do not allow you to sell your shares for one year after purchase unless you are selling to an accredited investor, a family member or in the event of your death or divorce. And there is no large, convenient secondary market, such as a stock exchange, to trade crowdfunding shares, so you may have to find a willing buyer on your own.

There are three other ways to profit...

- **A company you invested in is acquired,** and you get part of the proceeds from the sale or stock in the acquiring company.
- **The company generates enough free cash flow** to pay you dividends.
- **The company launches an initial public offering (IPO)** of its stock that helps boost the value of your own shares.

THE BEST STRATEGIES

These guidelines can help you be a successful crowdfunding investor...

- **Invest for the long term.** Don't expect there to be a good opportunity to sell your shares for at least three to 10 years. It often takes that long for a company to become established enough to attract a takeover offer or declare an IPO.
- **Spread your bets.** Venture-capital professionals routinely invest in a number of different start-ups because they know that few end up taking off. One or two successes can make up for multiple losers.
- **Be sure to get answers to some key financial questions.**

Examples: What problem does the product or service solve? How does the company differentiate its product or service from competitors in terms of quality, convenience, ease of use, patents, etc.? What are the company's expenses and profit margins? The answers should be found in the company's pitch deck.

THREE TYPES OF OFFERINGS

So far, most equity crowdfunding offerings fall into one of three categories that appeal to different types of investors...

- **Start-ups that have regional appeal or that serve a narrow audience.** These companies may not have the potential for huge profits, but they offer less tangible benefits to a small investor, perhaps contributing to the investor's community or to a cause that the investor cares about.

Example: StartMart Cleveland operates a 35,000-square-foot coworking space that is raising funds to expand and become an integral part of the revitalization of Cleveland's downtown area.

In addition, some of the Kickstarter type of investment money that has been going to socially motivated causes, where profit is not necessarily the primary goal, may now go to equity crowdfunding of such ventures if they are commercially viable businesses.

Example: Green technology that offers environmental benefits.

- **Collective ownership.** These companies invest in expensive assets that you might not be able to invest in on your own, such as commercial real estate or collectibles. They are likely to pay dividends.

Example: The LRF Thoroughbred Fund is managed by one of the largest Thoroughbred racing clubs, Little Red Feather Racing. Its horses have won 192 races in 1,063 starts and grossed $10.7 million in purses over the past 15 years. Investors receive a share of the purse winnings.

• **Innovative products and services.** These start-ups have the most potential for small investors because they could sell nationally and/or attract the attention of a large company and get a buyout offer.

Examples of equity crowdfunding companies with innovative products...

• *ShapeScale.* Its bathroom scale helps users optimize their fitness routines and determine which exercises and diets are working. The scale takes a 360-degree scan of the body and creates a 3D rendering that can be accessed via a smartphone app.

• *Maternova.* It designs apparel made of material infused with an odorless repellent that is safe for pregnant women but that repels more than 40 different insects including ticks that carry Lyme disease and the Asian tiger mosquito that spreads the Zika virus.

Job Hunting Over 50? Don't Fall for These Myths

Nancy Collamer, a coach and speaker based in Old Greenwich, Connecticut. Collamer is author of *Second-Act Careers: 50+ Ways to Profit from Your Passions During Semi-Retirement* and founder of the website MyLifestyleCareer.com.

Conventional wisdom says that it's hard to find a good job after age 50. Employers are said to consider older workers overpaid, unenergetic and out of touch. In truth, it's this bleak assessment that's out of touch—these days, many 50-plus job hunters are discovering that their age is not as big an issue as they had feared. Don't let these myths about finding work hold you back...

***MYTH:* No one is going to offer me a good job at my age.**

Reality: It's easier than ever for people age 50 and older to find meaningful work that pays well.

Why? The combination of an aging US population—the 50-plus group now represents more than one-third of the total US workforce—and a relatively strong economy means that there are not enough qualified young job applicants to replace retiring baby boomers in many sectors and regions, leaving employers with little choice but to hire older applicants. Plus, fewer and fewer US jobs involve manual labor, while even more are in the information sector where jobs require using a computer and the Internet. Younger workers might have an advantage when it comes to manual labor, but older workers are more desirable in the information sector—they've spent decades acquiring useful knowledge.

Exception: Older job seekers in blue-collar fields could find it very difficult to land good jobs these days. Their best option often is to seek retraining.

***MYTH:* Employers are going to assume that I'm out of touch with current technology and trends.**

Reality: This stereotype finally is beginning to fade. The US economy has been extremely fast-moving and technology-focused for several decades now, so many 50-plus employees have extensive experience coping with rapid change and advanced technology—and a growing number of employers realize this. Still, it's prudent for older job hunters to take extra steps to prove that they have kept up to date.

Read up on the latest trends and technology in your sector so that you can discuss them intelligently during your interviews—depending on your field, that might mean reading trade publications, scientific journals and/or taking a course or seminar on a cutting-edge topic related to your field.

Example: A man in his 60s took a computer-coding class before applying for jobs. He was not applying for jobs as a coder—one class was not nearly enough to make him hirable in that field—but having the class on his résumé sent a strong message that he wasn't out of touch with technology and wasn't afraid to learn new things.

Warning: The terminology on your résumé and/or cover letter could make you look out of touch even if your skills are up to date. Visit job boards to see whether the job titles and buzzwords used in your field have changed, and then update the language on your résumé and cover letters if necessary.

For example, if you served as the head of the "personnel department" at a former employer, you might update this to head of "human resources" or even to head of "talent management," a new and trendy term for this department. These changes are unlikely to be viewed as dishonest as long as you do not inflate your job title when you update terms.

***MYTH:* I shouldn't include a photo on my LinkedIn page because it will reveal that I'm not young.**

Reality: People who do not include photos of themselves on their pages at LinkedIn—the world's largest professional networking platform—are severely hurting their chances to even get in the door for job interviews. According to LinkedIn's data, profiles with photos receive 14 times more views than profiles that lack them. Being able to see a photo of an applicant gives employers and human resource professionals a chance to feel a connection with the applicant and fosters a sense of trust.

Ageism does exist, however, so hire a professional photographer who specializes in portraits to take your LinkedIn picture—expect to pay at least $100. Skilled use of lighting and discreet photo editing will help you look your best, no matter what your age. Dress professionally and smile warmly in the photo—an approachable, upbeat facial expression in a LinkedIn photo is among the very best ways to make employers want to work with you.

***MYTH:* The only way to get a job at my age is part-time or freelance work.**

Reality: Older job applicants usually can find well-paying full-time positions these days if that's what they want. In fact, more than 60% of workers age 65 and older now work full time, up from less than 45% in 1995.

But older job hunters should not necessarily ignore freelance, part-time and temporary opportunities—these can be great ways to get a foot in the door.

Example: A woman in her late 50s knew that a small marketing firm was reluctant to hire her for budgetary reasons. So she offered to tackle a single project on a contract basis. That project eventually led to her being offered a full-time job.

***MYTH:* Employers would rather hire someone young and cheap than an experienced employee at a higher salary.**

Reality: What employers want most of all from a new hire is value. If the salary you intend to ask for is likely to be more than an employer hopes to pay, identify specific ways in which you could help the company generate more revenue than a lower-paid, less experienced applicant could...and/or ways in which you could help the company save more money than such an applicant. Do your homework about the employer and its sector so that you can provide specific bottom-line–focused ideas during the interview, along with examples of times when you delivered value in similar ways for your prior employers.

Example: A 61-year-old man knew that he would be competing with younger, lower-paid job hunters when he applied for a marketing position at a university's law school. During his interview, he provided examples of ways in which the law school could rebrand itself to stand out from other law schools and attract more students. He also showed how he had

BETTER WAY...

Avoid the 10 Worst Résumé Buzzwords

A LinkedIn study analyzed 400 million members' profiles to identify language that has become so overused that it's likely to alienate potential employers. The top 10 clichéd words are specialized...leadership...passionate...strategic...experienced...focused...expert...certified...creative...excellent. Wherever possible, replace these words with action verbs and/or specific measurements that describe how you added value in previous jobs.

Blair Decembrele, a senior manager at LinkedIn.com.

successfully helped prior employers rebrand themselves. The law school stretched its budget to hire him.

***MYTH:* I'm too old to start my own business.**

Reality: Age 50 and up is in many ways the best time to launch a business. In 2015, 26% of entrepreneurs who launched businesses were between ages 55 and 64, up from 14.3% in 1996. Why? Older entrepreneurs typically have more savings to help get their businesses off the ground...more time to devote to the business (their kids usually are grown and out of the house)...more success convincing potential clients to trust them...and more and better contacts—many of their peers have risen into decision-making roles at their companies and have the authority to send business to these 50+ entrepreneurs.

***MYTH:* No one will hire me after I've been retired for a few years.**

Reality: It's much easier than it used to be—and much more common—for retirees to climb back into the working world. In fact, according to one recent report, around 40% of people who retire later return to work. There's a reason employers have become more willing to consider applicants whose résumés include retirement work gaps—they don't have much choice these days. There's a shortage of experienced employees in many sectors right now because of the relatively robust economy and the ongoing retirement of the baby boomer generation. Besides, atypical work histories have become the norm. These days, even applicants who have not previously retired often have gaps where they worked for themselves...worked part-time for others...or took breaks to raise a family.

It is true that if you have been out of the workforce for a while, employers are especially likely to have concerns that your skills and knowledge could be out of date.

But as noted above, those concerns can be overcome by adding something to your résumé that shows that you have kept in touch with the sector. Take courses or attend seminars related to your field, or seek a temporary position or short-term consulting assignment in the field before applying for full-time jobs.

Often-Forgotten Job-Hunting Expenses

When looking for a job, expect to spend $150 or more for a professional writer to polish the writing and presentation of your résumé. *Other expenses...*

Professional head shots: Get rid of any photo of you online that does not look suitable for work, and pay a photographer to take a top-quality photo for your LinkedIn profile and other sites where potential employers may look.

New clothing: So that you look as professional as possible.

Transportation costs: Consider what it will cost to get to interviews by car, train or even plane.

Domestic help may be necessary if you have children.

WiseBread.com

Fake Jobs at Real Companies

Steven J. Weisman, JD, senior lecturer at Bentley University in Waltham, Massachusetts, and founder of the scam-information website Scamicide.com.

Scammers are pretending that they work for well-known companies and then are stealing job seekers' identities and their savings.

What happens: The scammer spreads the word about a job opening at a real company—often a well-respected company. The scammer might do this by sending e-mails to potential applicants...posting ads on job-search websites...and/or reaching out to potential applicants through social-network websites such as LinkedIn. In each case, a "job opening" is described, along with contact information.

Although the employer cited in the job listing is legitimate, the e-mail or phone number provided actually connects would-be applicants with a scammer who does not work for that company. The scammer is co-opting the respected company's name because doing this confers an aura of legitimacy.

During the ensuing "job interview," which could be lengthy and realistic, applicants are asked to provide their Social Security numbers so that the "employer" can run a background check. Later on, applicants often are told that they got the job and are asked for bank account information—purportedly so that the company can set up direct deposit of paychecks. These are things that real employers often request, which makes the scam difficult to sniff out. In reality, of course, the scammer will use the information to steal applicants' identities and loot their bank accounts.

What to do: Rather than call the phone number provided in a job listing, look up the employer's main switchboard phone number online. Get in touch with the company's human resources department, and confirm that the job is being offered and that it is being offered through the avenue you are using. Certainly do this if you are asked to provide sensitive personal information before you meet with a representative of that employer inside the employer's facilities.

Good Answers to Tough Interview Questions

Would you rather be respected or feared? In a team environment, being respected is better...in a business that's struggling, fear may be more useful. *Why are you here today?* Emphasize the benefits you would bring to the company, not the ones you would get by being hired. *What is your biggest dream?* Show that you are ambitious and willing to work hard to make your dream a reality. *What is your favorite property in Monopoly, and why?* Any property is fine—this is a chance to show how you evaluate risks and rewards. *Tell me about a time you failed.* Be honest—and focus on how the experience made you better qualified for the job you want. *What did you want to be when you were seven years old?* Talk about your childhood dreams and how you fulfilled or hope to fulfill them or why they changed.

Roundup of questions asked by CEOs during interviews, reported at Finance.Yahoo.com.

Best Way to Follow Up After a Job Interview

Send a thank-you note the same day if you had a morning interview or first thing the next day if you interviewed in the afternoon. If the interviewer mentioned a specific date or time frame for a decision and you have not heard by then, check in. If you get positive feedback at each contact but no time frame, stay in touch but do not pester the hiring manager. If weeks or months go by without a decision, contact the firm occasionally but vary your messages—send links to interesting articles, a note on projects you recently completed, charitable work you are doing and so on. If you do not get the job, send a final e-mail thanking the interviewer for his/her time and asking for any feedback—and for the chance to explore other opportunities in the future.

BusinessInsider.com

Salary Gender Gap Still Exists

The highest male-female gender salary gap is in computer programming. Female computer scientists are paid an average of 28% less than their male counterparts. Other professions where the gap is above 25% include chef, dentist and optician.

Study of 505,000 salary reports in 25 industries by salary website Glassdoor, reported at Bloomberg.com.

TAKE NOTE...

Companies with Unusual Job Perks

Employees of Airbnb get a quarterly travel credit of $500 to use at any Airbnb listing. Google offers an unusual death benefit—if someone dies while employed there, the surviving spouse or domestic partner receives 50% of the employee's salary for 10 years. Netflix gives new parents as much time off as they need during the first year after the birth or adoption of a child. Zillow gives each employee a Fitbit activity tracker to encourage more healthful living. The maker of the Clif Bar makes personal trainers, massage therapists, a chiropractor and an acupuncturist available to employees.

Experts on job perks, reported at GoBankingRates.com.

Ways to Earn Some Extra Money

B*e a tutor* in a second language, math, science or writing—$15 to $60 per hour. *Model* for artists—an average session lasts three hours at $12 to $13 per hour. *Join a street team to promote products*—$20 to $25 per hour. *Walk dogs*—$15 to $30 per hour. *Become a driver* for Uber or Lyft—earnings can be $19 to $35 per hour. *Do substitute teaching*—salary averages $90 to $120 per day (qualifications for substitute teaching vary by state).

Kiplinger.com

Top-Paying Jobs for High School Graduates

M*anagers in transportation, storage and distribution* have a median annual wage of $86,630. *Elevator installers and repairers* have a median wage of $80,870. *Detectives and criminal investigators* have a median wage of $77,210. *First-line supervisors* of nonretail sales workers have a median wage of $72,300. *Transportation inspectors* have a median wage of $70,820. *Postmasters* and mail superintendents have a median wage of $70,640. *Media and communication equipment workers* have a median wage of $70,590.

Bureau of Labor Statistics data from 247WallSt.com.

Higher Salaries for Liberal Arts Graduates

By midcareer—about 15 years after graduation—graduates of some liberal arts colleges are earning an average of $80,000 a year. That's $6,000 more than college graduates in general.

Top liberal-arts schools for an earnings boost: Harvey Mudd College, starting average salary $79,700, midcareer average $130,000... Colgate University, starting salary $55,800 and $121,000 midcareer...Williams College, $53,100 and $120,000...Claremont McKenna College, $58,800 and $112,000...Washington and Lee University, $53,900 and $115,000...Virginia Military Institute, $56,400 and $111,000...Bucknell University, $57,900 and $109,000...and Lafayette College, $57,800 and $106,000.

Data from PayScale, reported at Time.com/Money.

More Companies *Require* Vacation Time

Mandatory vacation policies *require* employees to take a certain number of days off per year—and in some cases, companies insist that people stop checking e-mail or staying in touch with work through other means. A growing number of companies are starting to require vacations, which helps employees who are reluctant to leave the office find time to recharge. The policies are most common at tech firms and young companies that are fast-growing.

Some firms actually pay people to vacation: Software company FullContact requires at least three weeks off and gives a $7,500 stipend...digital-note firm Evernote also offers stipends.

Roundup of experts on required-vacation policies, reported at Kiplinger.com.

Unused Vacations Hurt the Economy

Unused vacations cost the economy $223 billion in 2015. That is the estimated loss to businesses in 2015 because workers used only 16.2 vacation days, on average—compared with an average of 20.3 days from 1976 to 2000. This resulted in less spending on restaurants, hotels, travel and home improvement.

Study by travel-industry initiative Project: Time Off, quoted in *The Wall Street Journal.*

Best Ways to End/Start an E-mail

Barbara Pachter, business communication consultant and author of *The Essentials of Business Etiquette,* reported by Karen Larson, editor, *Bottom Line Personal.*

A colleague recently confided in me that he didn't know how to end his e-mails. Should he sign off with "Sincerely" as he was taught to do when writing a formal letter? Or just use "Best," though that seemed vague to him? "'Best' makes me think 'Best what?'" he said. "Best regards? Best wishes?"

And really, does it matter?

It matters, says Barbara Pachter, a business communication consultant and author of *The Essentials of Business Etiquette.* When we communicate via e-mail, people cannot hear our tone of voice, so they search for clues about what we think of them. If we strike the wrong note with a sign-off—or a salutation—we could give the wrong impression.

When e-mail first appeared, most people didn't bother to use salutations or sign-offs, says Pachter. So e-mails came off as abrupt and were off-putting.

Formality is the safest choice the first time you send an e-mail to someone you don't know well. Start with "Dear Mr. Smith" or "Dear Justin" and end with "Best regards." ("Sincerely" is a bit too formal.)

When e-mailing an existing acquaintance, it's fine to open with an informal salutation, such as "Hi"...and/or use the recipient's first name. You can use a sign-off such as "Best" or "Regards." ("Best" and "Regards" on their own seem less formal than "Best regards.") Or use a short sign-off message such as "Thanks for your help."

If an e-mail is work-related, avoid a salutation or sign-off that could be viewed as unprofessional, such as "Happy Monday!" or "Go Packers!" Best regards!

The Truth About Standing Desks

Shani Soloff, PT, ThePosturePeople.net and author of *A Standing Desk: Is It Right for You? A Guide to Improve Your Work Wellness,* reported by Karen Larson, editor, *Bottom Line Personal.*

Excessive sitting has been linked with increased rates of type 2 diabetes, heart disease, cancer and dementia. So, when Bottom Line Inc. recently moved into new offices and offered employees the option of standing desks—desks that can be used at regular height or raised so that you can use them while on your feet—many of us leapt at the offer. But after just a few months of standing, several of my colleagues are complaining of ankle and foot pain...and I tried the high position of my desk and didn't like it.

This comes as no surprise to ergonomics consultant Shani Soloff, PT, author of *A Standing Desk: Is It Right for You? A Guide to Improve Your Work Wellness.* She has seen many office workers try and fail to switch to standing desks over the years.

Some office workers make the change hoping to overcome back or neck pain stemming from sitting hunched over a desk all day. But based on what Soloff has seen, people who have poor posture while seated at a desk tend to have poor posture standing at a desk. A standing desk might not even help us avoid the health risks of sitting—a recent study found that more standing at work leads to more sitting at home.

Soloff's advice before buying a standing desk: Create an ad hoc standing desk by placing a sturdy box on a countertop or traditional desk. Use this for a few weeks to make sure it works for you. Stand on an antifatigue mat, available online or in office-supply stores, to improve your odds of success.

If a traditional desk is the better choice, just get up and walk around for one to five minutes every hour.

GOOD TO KNOW...

More Opportunities to Work from Home

Part-time work-from-home job positions continue to rise. Top companies seeking people who want to work part-time from home include K12, Active Network, Edmentum, Kaplan, Connections Education, Chamberlain College of Nursing, LifeBook, University of Maryland, VocoVision and Yelp. Jobs range from online adjunct professorships to project management and customer service representatives. You can find a list of current opportunities at FlexJobs.com/blog (search for "top 20 companies").

Survey of remote jobs at more than 40,000 companies by FlexJobs.com.

Working from Home Benefits Employees

Working from home makes workers feel more engaged with their jobs. Workers who spent three or four out of five days a week working from home reported the most engagement with their jobs. The workers least engaged in their jobs were those spending all their time at home or all of it in the office. Workers were particularly dissatisfied with open-office plans when they did have to come in. Those who could shut a door were 1.3 times as likely to be engaged in their jobs as those who could not, and those who said they could have privacy when they needed it were 1.7 times more engaged in their jobs.

Gallup "State of the American Workplace" study, based on survey of more than 7,000 US workers, reported in *The Washington Post*.

Dangers of a Long Commute

American commuters average 50 hours in traffic a year. The nation as a whole spends eight billion hours in traffic.

One result: Higher exposure to pollutants. Pollution levels inside cars at red lights or in traffic jams are up to 40% higher than when traffic is moving.

Imrix 2015 Traffic Scorecard and study by researchers at University of Surrey, UK, published in *Environmental Science: Processes & Impacts*.

20 Safety Solutions

Get Out Alive! Strategies to Survive 3 Deadly Emergencies

When emergencies occur, you don't always have the time or opportunity to call 911 and wait for someone to come to your rescue. It pays to plan before an emergency occurs so that you know just what to do when one does. Here, Clint Emerson, a retired Navy SEAL who spent 20 years conducting special-ops missions, shares his strategies for surviving three terrifying emergencies...

EMERGENCY: CARJACKING

Before there's a problem: If you are in a high-crime area, leave at least one car length's space between your vehicle and the vehicle in front of yours when you come to a stop at a red light or stop sign. This greatly improves the odds that you will have sufficient room to speed away in an emergency. While stopped in traffic, keep your car doors locked, windows up and transmission in drive (or in first gear if the car has a standard transmission). Monitor your side and rearview mirrors, and glance out the side windows. Drivers who focus only on the traffic light or who become distracted by their phones or radios at stops are more likely to be targeted by carjackers.

Also, pay close attention to your surroundings when in parking garages and when pulling up to drive-through ATMs—these are both common carjacking locations. If you see anyone lurking, drive away and find a different parking place or ATM. After using an ATM, don't stop to count your cash or put it in your wallet—drive away quickly.

Clint Emerson, a retired Navy SEAL who spent 20 years conducting special-ops missions. He is also author of *100 Deadly Skills: Survival Edition* and founding partner of Escape the Wolf, a crisis-management and risk-mitigation company based in Frisco, Texas. EscapetheWolf.com

During an emergency: The best response depends on how the carjacking occurs…

• **If you are walking in a parking area when someone demands your keys,** locate an exit for an escape on foot and then toss the keys as far as you can in the direction opposite this exit to allow yourself time to run. What you hope will happen is that while you are making your escape, the criminal will go in the other direction to pick up your car keys and then simply will take your car. If there is no nearby exit, toss the keys and take cover behind a solid obstacle such as a concrete pillar. The carjacker will get your car, but removing yourself as a factor as best you can decreases the odds that you will be kidnapped or harmed.

• **If you are stopped at a stop sign or red light when you see someone approaching with a weapon,** drive away even if this means going up on a sidewalk or running a red light (assuming that you can do so without causing an accident or running over a pedestrian).

• **If a carjacker gets into the passenger seat of your car while you are stopped,** immediately jump out and run. If he shows a gun and orders you to drive, offer to surrender the vehicle. If this offer is rejected, speed up, then slam on the brakes and quickly get out and run, ideally toward nearby people or into a building.

• **If a carjacker sticks a gun or a knife through your driver's side window** while you are stopped, offer to surrender the car. If the carjacker refuses and orders you to slide over to the passenger seat, raise your arms slowly as if in surrender and then suddenly use your raised arms to push the carjacker's arm forward into your dashboard while simultaneously flooring the gas. The carjacker will not expect this, and his attention will immediately shift from stealing your car to not being hurt by your car.

**EMERGENCY:
HOME INVASION**

Before there's a problem: Identify escape routes from your home. These should not just lead out of your house but also off your property. The ideal route exits your home only a short distance from a tree line or a neighbor's home that can shield you from view. Your escape route should conclude at a "rally point"—a predetermined place where family members can gather safely.

Keep your car keys, cell phone and flashlight near your bedside at night. These can come in handy (see below).

During an emergency: Resist the urge to turn on a light if you think someone has broken into your home at night. Light might make you feel safer, but turning on a light actually shows the home invader which room you are in. It also robs you of a tactical advantage—you know your home's layout better than the home invader does, so you can navigate it in the dark better than he can.

Grab your cell phone, car keys and flashlight…gather other household members…and head for your escape route. Sometimes it is not possible for everyone to move together as a family, so everyone, including children, should know that escape is the priority. What you don't want is your family waiting around while Mom or Dad confronts the intruder. If your car keys have a fob with a panic button, press this—the sound of your car alarm might scare off the home invader. Even if it doesn't, the alarm may provide a distraction that buys you time to escape while also alerting your neighbors. If you have a home-security system with a panic button, press this, too. (You should have either a wall keypad or remote alarm button located in your bedroom.)

Dial 911 as you proceed along your escape route or when you reach a safe spot—do not halt your escape to make this call. Do not hide inside your home unless you see no way to escape and/or there is a secure safe room in the home. Running is better than hiding because people who hide usually are found.

Warning about guns: If you are proficient with a gun, use it. But if it sits in your nightstand and you never use it, you should run rather than pull your gun—the last thing you want is to shoot a round through a few walls and injure or kill a family member or have the gun used against you.

EMERGENCY: OFFICE FIRE

Before there's a problem: Learn the location of the primary and secondary fire escape routes from your office.

In your desk in a backpack or some other easily carried "bolt bag," keep a flashlight, a bottle of water, a dust mask (douse the mask with the water to make a short-term smoke filter), a whistle (to alert others of your location) and chemical lights (sometimes called glow sticks).

During an emergency: Grab your bolt bag and your phone, and head for the closest emergency exit. If fire blocks your escape, try the secondary exit. Encourage other people to join you—bigger groups have more eyes, ears and brains to help them locate a way out. Use the glow sticks to mark your escape route to help other people follow you out...or help emergency services personnel find you if you cannot escape.

TAKE NOTE...

Make Your Home Look Lived-In While You're Away

To reduce the chance of burglary, you'll want to make your home looked lived-in while you're away. *What to do...*

- **Ask a neighbor to park a car in your driveway.**
- **In addition to having the post office hold all mail and packages for you,** have a neighbor check in case FedEx, UPS or another delivery service drops anything off.
- **Have a trusted neighbor take your trash and recycling bins out** on collection days and bring them back afterward.
- **If it could snow while you are gone,** hire someone to shovel your walk.
- **Consider buying gadgets that can turn lamps in your house on and off**—BeOn bulbs can learn your lighting habits and replicate them when you're away.
- **Consider FakeTV.com,** which sells a programmable device that looks, from outside your home, like a TV being watched but uses much less energy than actually leaving a TV on.

BobVila.com

FLASHLIGHTS CAN BE TACTICAL TOOLS

A flashlight can do more than light your way during an emergency. *You also can...*

- **Shine a flashlight into a neighbor's window or at passing cars to signal for help.**
- **Disorient a home invader by shining a flashlight in his/her eyes in a dark room.** Then quickly turn the flashlight back off and run—the light burst should temporarily rob him of his ability to see in low light.
- **Use a flashlight as a club.** This requires a big metal flashlight loaded with heavy D-cell batteries. It can be an effective weapon or can be used to break a window.

"Someone's Shooting!" How to Survive

David Austin, program manager for Civilian Response to Active Shooter Events, a component of the Advanced Law Enforcement Rapid Response Training (ALERRT) Center, an active-shooter response training curriculum developed by Texas State University. The ALERRT curriculum has been adopted by at least nine states and is considered the national standard by the FBI. Austin also is a Hays County deputy sheriff. AvoidDenyDefend.org.

In 2007, a gunman murdered 32 people on the Virginia Tech campus. It was the deadliest mass shooting in US history. But while dozens were killed in that tragedy, other potential victims survived, in some cases because they made smart decisions. A number of students escaped by jumping out windows...and in one classroom, everyone lived even though the gunman tried to enter—the students successfully barricaded the door.

If you manage to make smart, fast decisions during a mass shooting, your own life might not be the only one you save. People often follow crowds during emergencies, so some of those around you could follow you to safety.

The odds are low that you will ever be caught up in a mass shooting—but these terrible events have been occurring with alarming frequency. A 2013 FBI report found that there were more than 11 per year, on average, in the US during the first 14 years of this century, and the rate continues to rise. That FBI report also suggests that nowhere in the US is truly safe—there were mass shootings in 40 of the 50 states and the District of Columbia during the 14 years studied, with 486 people killed and 557 people wounded. And mass shootings have occurred since the report.

Smart: It's worth knowing what to do in a mass shooting even if you never are in one—knowing what to do in an emergency can reduce anxieties about that danger.

TRY TO GET AWAY

How to improve your odds of survival...

• **Identify secondary exits before trouble happens.** Your first response in an "active shooter" situation should be to try to run away. But in many public spaces, there is only one main entrance, and that's often where the shooter enters and begins firing.

When you are in a public location, such as a workplace, shopping mall, supermarket, restaurant, movie theater or anywhere where large groups of people gather, take a moment to scan for exits other than the main exit. Is there a fire exit? An unmarked door leading to a loading dock? A ground-level window that opens...or on the second floor, a window that opens and is above a soft, grassy landing spot...or on a higher floor, a window that opens onto a fire escape? Do not wait until there is an emergency to identify this alternate exit. It is difficult to think clearly during emergencies, so people who do not have a plan in place before the emergency begins tend to either freeze up or follow a panicked crowd.

Helpful: Restaurants almost always have secondary exits through their kitchens.

• **React immediately when you hear a sound that might be gunfire.** Most people's initial reaction to the sound of gunfire is to dismiss it as fireworks or a car backfiring...or to remain stationary while wondering, *What was that?* This delay can significantly reduce the odds of survival.

Instead, immediately start to move away from the gunfire and/or toward a secondary exit that you have identified when you hear something that might be gunfire.

If you can't think of a good explanation for why this would be something other than gunfire by the time you reach an exit—if you realize it's Fourth of July weekend, for example, so someone probably is setting off fireworks—strongly consider continuing out the exit and putting some distance between yourself and the sound. Perhaps it will turn out that it wasn't gunfire after all, but it is better to lose a few minutes because you retreated unnecessarily than lose your life because you didn't.

• **If the shooter is within sight, your best bet still probably is to run.** Most people's first reaction when they actually see a gunman is to *hide*. People in offices tend to duck under their desks, for example. Situations vary, but hiding generally is a poor choice—it makes you a sitting duck. Moving from the danger zone usually is preferable—avoiding the shooter. *Warning*: Playing dead tends not to be a great option, either. Mass shooters have been known to target victims who are lying still to confirm they are dead.

• **Dial 9-1-1 *after* you clear the area.** This is not a time to call the police and then sit back and wait for them to arrive. The average police response time to these types of attacks in the US is around three minutes—which is tremendously fast but often not fast enough if you are in the same building as a mass shooter.

IF YOU CANNOT GET AWAY

Running might not be a viable option if the shooter is between you and the only exit, or if you are with family or friends who are not very mobile and who need your help. *If so, the most effective plan B usually is to deny the shooter access to your area...*

• **Lock or block a door.** Get into a storeroom...closet...bathroom...office...or some other space that has a door that shuts. If this door locks from the inside, lock yourself (and other potential victims) in. Then use desks, chairs, file cabinets or any other available heavy items to barricade the door, assuming that it opens in. Turn off the lights in the room, close the blinds, turn off your cell-phone ringer/buzzer to avoid signaling the shooter that you are in the room, and remain silent. Quietly instruct everyone else in the room to turn off their cell phones and remain silent as well.

Barricades can be effective even when they fall far short of being impenetrable. History tells us that mass shooters usually give up or move on when confronted by impediments that would take more than a few seconds to overcome. They know that the police are likely to arrive soon, so they generally seek out targets they can shoot very easily and quickly.

Alternatives: If the door does not lock and you do not have the time, strength or heavy items necessary to produce a barricade, you could use your body to hold the door shut. But do not brace your back or shoulder against the door—shooters sometimes fire through doors to kill people who attempt this. Instead, lie on the ground and use your feet to hold the door shut. If the killer shoots blindly through the door, there's a good chance he will assume that you are standing and aim too high.

If the door opens *out* and does not lock, loop a belt around the doorknob, then hold the other end of the belt while remaining as low to the ground as possible and to the side of the door.

- **Do not unlock the door or dismantle your barricade for "the police."** The shooter might be claiming to be the police to draw you out. *Example*: In 2011, a Norwegian mass shooter lured victims out of hiding by claiming to be a policeman. The death toll was close to 100.

The real police almost certainly will not seek to free people safely barricaded in rooms until after the shooter has been captured or killed... and if the shooter has indeed been stopped, the police can take the time to dismantle your barricade themselves. The best practice is for you to dial 9-1-1, explain where you are and ask for confirmation that the person outside the room truly is with the police.

- **If neither running nor denying access is possible, you have the right to defend yourself.** Unarmed people stop gunmen more often than you might imagine, though obviously this should be considered an extremely risky last resort. A 2013 FBI report of 160 recent active shooter incidents found that 21 were stopped by unarmed potential victims.

If a potential weapon is close at hand, grab it—fire extinguisher, scissors, staplers and letter openers are good choices, and metal trash cans will pack a punch, too.

Attack from the side or behind, if possible. If you are in a different room from the shooter, one option is to position yourself to the side of the doorway so that you are not in the shooter's initial field of vision if he enters the room. That can buy you enough time to attack the shooter before he can turn his gun on you. (If the door opens in, position yourself on the hinged side of the door so that you will be hidden by the door itself if it is opened.)

If you can grab the barrel of the shooter's gun and point it away from yourself, you will greatly reduce his advantage.

If there are other people in the area, yell that you have a grip on the gun and need help—others might join the fight upon hearing this, allowing you to overtake the would-be killer with superior numbers.

Helpful: Take a class in defensive tactics or martial arts.

Don't Let Home Wi-Fi Spy on You

Robert Siciliano, security analyst and CEO at the firm IDTheftSecurity.com, Boston, and author of *99 Things You Wish You Knew Before...Your Identity Was Stolen.* RobertSiciliano.com

---

Your home Wi-Fi network might have helped contribute to a massive cyber-attack last year.

What happened: In October 2016, hackers released a virus that infected millions of home Wi-Fi routers, which beam Internet signals to wirelessly connected computers, printers, phones, video-streaming devices, home-security systems, thermostats, refrigerators and many other devices.

The routers and devices have their own internal software that comes with password protection. But the default passwords set at the factory tend to be simple and easily cracked (such as "12345"). Many consumers don't know about this or never bother to change the default password. The infected devices across the country were commandeered to produce spam messages that eventually blocked access for several hours to popular websites including Airbnb, Amazon, Netflix, PayPal and Twitter.

The potential for personalized attacks in your own home are unnerving. What if a cyberthief opened your Wi-Fi–enabled door locks or garage door, disabled your security system or turned off your home heat? Relying on antivirus software on your computer won't necessarily protect you because your router and devices don't depend on the computer to connect to the Internet.

Steps that you need to take…

• **Change the default password set by the factory on your home router and all of your Wi-Fi–connected devices.** Each device should be given its own unique password, at least eight characters that mix numbers, upper- and lower-case letters, and symbols. To change passwords, see the instructions in the software or app that you used to install your devices, or search for instructions on the manufacturers' websites.

• **Set your router and other devices to automatically update their internal software.** Manufacturers commonly issue software patches to improve product performance, add new features or address security weakness. But you won't get these patches unless you elected to receive them when you set up your devices. You typically can re-select this option at the same time that you change your password.

BEWARE…

Cameras in Coat Hooks!

Cameras in coat hooks may be spying on you. Hidden cameras were found in some hooks mounted in women's bathrooms and changing rooms at three locations in the Florida Keys. The cameras were identical to ones sold online as home-security devices. Officials asked business owners to check restrooms and dressing rooms for the cameras—their batteries last only two to six hours, so someone would have to have fairly frequent access to them to use them. If you spot one of these cameras, alert store personnel and the police.

MiamiHerald.com

Your Smoke Alarm Might Not Be Working

Susan McKelvey, communications manager, National Fire Protection Association (NFPA), a nonprofit organization based in Quincy, Massachusetts, that has been working to eliminate fire deaths since 1896. NFPA.org

Your smoke alarms and carbon monoxide detectors might not be working properly—even if you never let their batteries run out or they are hardwired into your home's electrical system. That's because sensors in these alarms can fail over time.

To stay safe, replace a smoke alarm 10 years after its date of *manufacture*—an anniversary that can come sooner than 10 years after you installed the device depending on how old the smoke alarm was when you installed it.

For carbon monoxide detectors, check the manufacturer's website for replacement details if this is not spelled out on the device and you no longer have its instructions.

Dates of manufacture typically are printed on the backs of smoke alarms and carbon monoxide detectors, so you might have to remove them from walls or ceilings to check them.

More than 20% of residential fire deaths occur in homes where there were smoke alarms but those alarms were not working properly, either because of expired batteries or nonfunctional alarms.

Replace an alarm *before* the 10-year mark if it continuously "chirps" or displays a flashing red light or if its alarm does not sound when you press the "test" button (when battery replacement is not the issue).

Smoke alarms can cost less than $10 apiece, and carbon monoxide detectors can cost less than $25, so there is little financial reason to continue using an older unit. Make sure that the new alarms you install have been approved by a recognized independent testing lab such as Underwriters Laboratories (look for the "UL" logo on the packaging).

Index

D

E

J

K

L

M